*Childhood in
Contemporary Cultures*

Childhood in Contemporary Cultures

Edited by

MARGARET MEAD

and MARTHA WOLFENSTEIN

THE UNIVERSITY OF CHICAGO PRESS

CHICAGO AND LONDON

ISBN: 0-226-51506-0 (clothbound); 0-226-51507-9 (paperbound)

THE UNIVERSITY OF CHICAGO PRESS, CHICAGO 60637
The University of Chicago Press, Ltd., London

TO NATHAN LEITES

Acknowledgments

THIS book grew out of the Columbia University Research in Contemporary Cultures, inaugurated by Ruth Benedict in 1947; it also includes research done under the American Museum of Natural History Studies in Contemporary Culture. Both these projects were conducted under grants from the Human Resources Division of the Office of Naval Research. According to the terms of the contract, all the articles stemming from these two projects may be reproduced in whole or in part for any purpose of the United States government. We have also drawn on the materials of the American Museum of Natural History Studies in Soviet Culture, conducted under a contract with the RAND Corporation. Various aspects of the work of these projects have been reported in *The Study of Culture at a Distance*,[1] as well as in a number of other publications on particular cultures. Comparative studies of child rearing, which formed part of the project, have been reserved for the present volume. We have also included some subsequent researches which developed from the project; some earlier, closely related studies; and concurrent work of other investigators.

We wish to acknowledge our thanks for permission to reprint to: *American Journal of Orthopsychiatry*, for "Sex Differences in the Play Configurations of Preadolescents," by Erik Erikson and for "Patterns of Social and Cognitive Outlook in Children and Parents," by Else Frenkel-Brunswik, both of which articles appear in this volume in revised form; *Harvard Educational Review*, for "The Place of Book-Learning in Traditional Jewish Culture," by Mark Zborowski; International Universities Press, New York, for Martha Wolfenstein's "Some Variants in Moral Training of Children," which appeared in *The Psychoanalytic Study of the Child*, Volume V (1950); *Journal of Social Issues*, for "Fun Morality," by Martha Wolfenstein; McGraw-Hill Book Company, New York, and RAND Corporation, for selections from Margaret Mead's *Soviet Attitudes toward Authority*; the New York Academy of Sciences, for passages from "Themes in Japanese Culture," by Geoffrey Gorer, which appeared in the *Transactions*, Series 2; *Psychiatry*, for "Continuities and Discontinuities in Cultural Conditioning," by Ruth Benedict; Yale University Press, New Haven, Connecticut, for David Riesman's "Tootle: A Modern Cautionary Tale," a chapter adapted from his book *The Lonely Crowd*.

1. Margaret Mead and Rhoda Métraux. *The Study of Culture at a Distance* (Chicago: University of Chicago Press, 1953).

For permission to use some of the illustrations in this volume, we wish to express our thanks to the following: *Current Digest of the Soviet Press,* New York, for the cartoon reprinted from *Krokodil* and used in chapter 11 of this volume; John Day and Company, New York, for illustrations from Colin McPhee's *Club of Small Men* and *House in Bali;* London Film Productions, Inc., and the Motion Picture Association of America, Inc., for illustrations used in chapter 17 of this volume; the New York Academy of Sciences for Plate 67, No. 7, Plate 10, No. 3, and Plate 61, No. 4, taken from *Balinese Character* by Gregory Bateson and Margaret Mead and used in chapter 4 of this volume; the Yiddish Scientific Institute (Yivo), New York, for the illustrations used by Mark Zborowski in chapter 8.

For editorial assistance in the preparation of the manuscript, we have to thank Mrs. Leila Lee and Mrs. Constance Sutton.

M. M.
M. W.

New York
October 31, 1954

Table of Contents

List of Illustrations

PART I

Cultural Approaches to the Study of Childhood

CHAPTER 1

Theoretical Setting—1954

————————MARGARET MEAD

CHILDREN are newcomers as a subject of literature, newcomers in the study of human physiology and anatomy, newcomers in the social sciences. Although each historical period of which we have any record has had its own version of childhood—in paintings of the Christ Child and St. John, in portraits of little princes and princesses, in charming compositions of languid ladies and their lovely children—childhood was still something that one took for granted, a figure of speech, a mythological subject rather than a subject of articulate scrutiny. As in all areas in which disciplined observation replaces traditional points of view, the study of real children has met with many kinds of opposition. Members of different Western cultures have reacted—in terms of their own cultural predispositions—against robbing childhood of its innocence, denigrating adults by suggesting that their characters are formed in childhood, frightening mothers by insisting that irreparable damage can be done in childhood, stirring up adult emotions to an uncomfortable degree by activating memories of their childhood, giving the maladjusted adult an alibi for avoiding moral responsibility by permitting him to blame his present shortcomings on his childhood, denying the full assimilation of adult immigrants or adult revolutionaries, or—in the words of a psychiatrist from modern India—paying attention to the past rather than to the future in countries which are attempting to escape from the thralldom of their traditions.

In the present social ferment, when we live in a world in which peoples jostle one another in the news, in the corridors of the United Nations, as students in universities all over the world—some of whom are just escaping from the Stone Age, some battling with elaborate and sophisticated oriental and Near Eastern traditions far older than the West's, some attempting to recapture lost homogeneities, some clinging fanatically to new, just attained, cultural styles—it is inevitable that the whole problem of how childhood is to be conceptualized, how studied, how utilized in cultural change, should become a focus of controversy.

Although the chief impetus to the study of children came from psychology, on the one hand, and from medicine—through Freud—on the other, even in these fields there have been and still are many unresolved hostilities. Psychologists have concentrated on "child psychology"[1]—the accumulation of specific bodies of information based on tests and on controlled and severely limited experimental situations, and students have been inducted into the field by reading books about experiments and test results, not by the study of live children. Too often the only live children seriously observed were the one or two children of the psychologist, who provided him with anecdotal material which frequently overweighted his judgments. Thus it became necessary to introduce a new field called "child development," in which live children could be studied in nurseries and play groups; but even here, over and over again, the demands for standard examinations, standard test situations, home visits and parental interviews, have come to replace the study of children, even in the limited natural setting of the nursery school. In turn, these segments of certain aspects of the child— its growth curve, its somatype, its test performance, its school performance—have been laboriously put together again, using elaborate statistical devices, to reconstruct that which had been dissected. In psychoanalysis it took some time for child analysis—the study of real children in analytic situations—to replace constructs of childhood derived from the associations of adult patients; and the conceptions of childhood which recur in psychoanalytic theory are still more often based on such reconstructions of infantile omnipotence or infantile diffused identity than upon the careful detailed observations made by modern students of infants and children.

In anthropological work the same history was repeated. First came vivid naturalistic accounts of primitive childhood by a few amateur observers, notably Kidd and Grinnell;[2] then the development of a technique of formally including childhood within the account of any primitive culture, under the heading of "the life-cycle" or "the development of the individual"; then a theoretical *tour de force*, such as Malinowski's construct of the way in which Trobriand matriliny and denial of paternity might have influenced the character structure of the Trobrianders[3] and Piaget's use of Lévy-Bruhl's concept of primitive mentality as childish;[4] and, finally, the serious study of primitive children themselves.[5]

The interest in children in culture, as part of the culture and personality field, and in the "socialization process," as studied today by psychologists and sociologists, is an outgrowth of work in these three fields: psychology, particularly psychoanalysis, child-development research, and cultural anthropology. Although there are distinguished male workers in the field, notably John Dollard, Erik Erikson, Arnold Gesell, Geoffrey Gorer, Jean Piaget, and René Spitz, it is probably not an accident that all of them have worked closely with women teachers or collaborators. This volume of primary studies owes a great deal to their theoretical formulations, and the contributors to this volume have worked in collaborative two-sex teams in doing their research.

The last thirty years, when serious work on children was beginning, have also been a period when women played an increasingly serious professional role in medicine, psychology, psychoanalysis, and anthropology. Women's traditional preoccupation with young children made the study of children a natural choice, and there is also reason to believe that the study of children may be easier—in the present generation of research workers—for women than for men. Although we are now entering a new era in which fathers take a great deal of care of young children, the present working generation grew up in a period when child care was women's work. For men who are studying infants and young children, if they are not comfortable in a temporary identification with a woman's role, the alternative route to understanding is remembering their own childhood feelings and experiences. Like all intense retrospective work, this is psychologically expensive. Women investigators need not take this arduous route but, instead, can identify easily with the remembered roles of mother, grandmother, nurse, and primary teacher, as they spend hours working with, or thinking about, young children.

In this volume we do not propose to present an exhaustive study of ways of studying children within a cultural context but rather to give the student and interested reader some idea of the kinds of research which may fruitfully be explored from the standpoint both of method and of results. We have included several kinds of studies on the same culture, so that the student can see what it looks like to study French films, French children's drawings, and French children in a park, or German child-care literature, German juvenile fiction, and story completion by German children.

It has long been the experience of workers in the cultural field that a great deal is lost to science if the research worker does not approach each new piece of work with a fresh mind, ready to learn new things as well as to recheck earlier insights, repeat former check lists, and try the same tests over again. What is needed is a general sense of problem, of what it means to look at something from the cultural point of view, of what kind of observations are used, what kind of material can be analyzed and how. Mere repetition of work on one culture or a different culture is a stale and tasteless operation. The initial exploration of cultural material must be free, resourceful, and disciplined, but untrammeled. Once the basic regularities have been outlined, cross-cultural tests, check lists, projective techniques, as validation, may be used with some confidence that something new will be added to our knowledge of human behavior. But the mere mechanical repeating of any approach such as a thematic analysis of films, on different films in the same culture or of the same themes in another culture, constricts rather than expands the field.

This means the use of a closed system of reference—to the extent that all research on human beings must include the species-specific characteristics of human beings—and an open system in which we may expect to find entirely new patterns of behavior, depending on different historical circumstances and utilizing hitherto unguessed potentialities of human nature. Concentration on oedipal themes is more rewarding in some cultures than in others, but limiting analysis to oedipal themes would do serious violence in those cultures where the first two to three years of life provide the ground plan for later periods of development. Furthermore, the verification of a pattern by the use of a larger number of cases, a wider choice of materials, or by materials drawn from a longer period of time, while useful and necessary parts of scientific work, do not call for the special skill of initial pattern recognition on which the studies in this book are mainly based.

So in looking at the various sources of material on childhood, child-training literature, children in fiction and drama, observations on children, interviews with children and adults, games and toys and children's books, it is important to look not just for "oedipal fantasies," "rejecting mothers," "castration fears," "initiatory rites," "inner directedness," or "mesomorphic emphases," but to look instead at the living material and to place it within the entire context of our knowledge of cultures and of our knowledge of human growth and development. The work in this book was done by examining such areas, bearing in mind that the parent-child relationship was always a fruitful source of inquiry, that the role of the body, the attitude of the parent toward the child's body and of the child toward its own body, would always appear somehow in the material and that children in each society develop some kind of character which enables them to function within that society.

In the study of personality in culture we start with a recognition of the biologically given, of what all human beings have in common. In every human society, human infants are born helpless and relatively undeveloped, dependent upon adult nurture and adult transmission of the great body of culture—beliefs, practices, skills—which make it possible for any human group, and for this human group in particular, to function as human beings. Humanity as we know it is not merely a matter of our human physique, of our prehensile thumbs, upright posture, and highly developed brains, but of our capacity to accumulate and build upon the inventions and experience of previous generations. A child who does not participate in this great body of tradition, whether because of defect, neglect, injury, a disease, never becomes fully human.

As every child must learn to accept food, to trust those who care for him, to make his wants known, to walk and talk and assume control of his own body and actions, to identify with own sex and age and develop appropriate behavior toward individuals of the opposite sex and other ages, we may expect that in the course of this long maturation and learning there will be a great deal in common between childhood among the unclothed, nomadic Australian aborigines and childhood on Park Avenue, or in rural Alabama, in Paris or Bali, Devon or Provence. Whether children are breast-fed, bottle-fed, cup-fed, or spoon-fed, they must eat with their mouths, learn to suck or drink, chew their food, swallow, and discriminate between that which is and that which is not food. They may learn to walk by being hand-led, by being given a walking rail, put in a harness, kept in a play pen, but they all learn to walk within relatively close age limits. Whether they learn to swim, climb, roller skate, or dance will depend on their own culture; minor sequences like standing, then squatting, or squatting, then standing, may be altered by culture. Whether their movements will be rigidly stylized and resistant to new learning or flexibly adjustable to new requirements will again depend on their culture. But walk they must and do, walk in a world where adults are taller, much taller than they, pygmies among giants, ignorant among the knowledgeable, wordless among the articulate, with incomprehensible urgencies and desires and fears among adults who appear to have such matters reduced to a system—a system which must be mastered. And to the adults, children everywhere represent something weak and helpless, in need of protection, supervision, training, models, skills, beliefs, "character." Children cling and grab and scream, children are periodically inaccessible to any appeal, children in their lack of control represent the impulses which the adults in their childhood laboriously learned to discipline and control. The double threat of fearing to behave like a child and of yearning to behave like a child runs through all adult lives, just as the fear and hope of some day becoming an adult inform the play and fantasies of children.

Because of these recurrent biological similarities—of growth, of parent-child relationships, of needs and fears, and resonances—it is possible to compare childhood in one society with childhood in another. The common elements, the uniformities, are the basis of the comparisons. In some primitive tribes infants born with teeth will be killed as unnatural; Russian children were terrified by the image of the witch baby born with iron teeth,[6] but most babies continue to be born without teeth and to cut their teeth within narrow chronological limits.

Furthermore, men everywhere have to solve certain problems if they are to live in societies—problems of food supply, shelter, and protection from sun, rain, and cold; of sexual jealousy and permanence of mating for the care of children; of social order, protection against enemies, disease, and catastrophe; of a relationship to the world around them and to the conceived universe which gives them spiritual balance, patterns their fantasies, stylizes their aspirations, and releases their capacity to invent, create, and change. The solution to these problems provides a second set of uniformities. Children will have to learn to live in houses, to use tools, to observe social rules, to respect the person and property of others, to see the stars—as the lights of heaven, the frozen residue of celestial mischief, miraculous embodiments of the animals which they must hunt to live, or as future husbands for young girls who wish hard enough. Houses have to have entrances and vents for smoke; clothing has to be put on and taken off; with growing complexity, people have special places to sit, to sleep, to eat. Furthermore, culture grows by borrowing; people incorporate traits of their neighbors, learn their myths, sing their songs, or copy their clothes. People of areas which are in touch with one another—contiguous in space or because of political or religious ties—share the same solutions, and such institutions as currency or law courts, libraries, hospitals, schools, purification offerings or confession, armies and navies and embassies, become characteristic, and characteristic in their particular forms, over large sections of the world.

If the naïve reader encounters a statement on child-rearing practice in modern society, nine-tenths or more of it will seem very familiar. The reader who is not trained in noting small details as significant and who is unaccustomed to thinking in patterns will say, "Why practically everything those people do to their children is just like what we do— babies are breast- or bottle-fed, trained to be clean, learn to talk, go to school, join the church, pass examinations, etc." Often the next step is to seize on the one or two things which do sound a little peculiar— such as the use of wet nurses or swaddling or being constantly carried on the back—and to treat these unfamiliar details as if they had unique importance in producing any differences in adult character which may be admitted.

But, while striking differences in behavior may give rapid clues to important differences in the whole pattern, it is important to realize that it is not any single item of child-rearing practice or of culturally patterned child behavior—not the presence or absence of feeding bottles or slates, skates or hoops or balls, prayers or homilies or bribes— which is significant in isolation.[7] It is the way in which all these thousands of items, most of which are shared with other cultures, some of which are shared with all other cultures, are patterned or fitted together to make a whole. Within these patterns children grow up, young people learn to be parents, people age and die in terms of the complex learning which has been provided for them and which they have evoked from others, from birth until death.

When we look at behavior culturally, it means that we look at it comparatively. If there were only one human culture, it would be much harder to identify what behavior was cultural, what idiosyncratic but learned, and what instinctive. If human beings spoke only one language and we had no records of former versions of that language, the task of identifying which aspects of the language were biologically given, which one alternative among many, which purely fortuitous, which so redundant that they made no contribution, would be very difficult indeed. So when the anthropologist says, "Children take their father's surname," the culturally naïve will answer, "Of course, who else's name would they take?" But the culturally sophisticated, whether their sophistication comes from reading, travel, or study, from the knowledge of other periods of history or from a knowledge of other cultures, will realize that in many societies there are no surnames, while in others children take their mother's surname or take the surnames of both parents, and that taking the father's surname is a particular type of cultural behavior, neither natural to the human race nor a predictable occurrence even for a given part of the world. Every single statement that an anthropologist makes is a comparative statement. "These people cook their food in pots" implies a comparison with other peoples who cook in bamboo, in earth ovens, or with food wrapped in leaves, on skewers, or in wooden boxes. "The baby is weaned at a year" compares this people to others who wean at six months, nine months, two years, at walking, when the mother is pregnant again, or who attempt never to wean the youngest child at all. The context of comparison may change—sometimes, for example, American behavior will be discussed as part of modern Euro-American culture, or as part of the Christian world, or as an inheritor of the Judeo-Christian tradition, or as Protestant in emphasis, or as part of the free world. But, however the context may shift, it is always a comparative context.

Furthermore, anthropological statements refer to identified materials or observations in which class, locality, occupation, age, sex, and religion have been taken into account when the background observations were made. In the statement "The American flag has forty-eight stars and thirteen stripes," there is explicit recognition that there is no need to qualify this statement by remarks about class, race, or religion. But if a statement has to be made about saluting the flag, then qualifications would have to be introduced about the date at which the salute came in, situations in which the salute has become compulsory, about religious groups like Jehovah's Witnesses who refuse to salute the flag. In the absence of such specific knowledge, an anthropologist could still describe a group of children standing at attention, hands to hearts, facing a banner with specified designs upon it. Provided that place and date were specified, this remains valid cultural information. So in the description of the behavior of children in 1953 in a Paris park, the place, time, and observer are specified, and this material is related to other observations on the French, but statements are not made about the behavior of French children in parks—in general—which would apply to Dijon and Grenoble.

In relating observations about groups of French children in Paris parks to general statements about French culture, we are doing the same thing that we would do if we were to identify the dialect of a particular region or class with the French language and then discuss the ways in which it was distinctive. After deciding what larger unit we wish to refer to—in this case the culture of France, but instead we might have included the culture of France and the French colonies—then smaller observations are considered in terms of the regularities which have been identified for the whole. The term *cultural regularities* includes the way in which the versions of the culture found in different classes, regions, or occupations are systematically related to one another. So a member of the French bourgeoisie who is also a Protestant will manifest behavior which is French, which has certain peculiarities in common with the behavior of French Protestants, which has other peculiarities in common with the French bourgeois, and still others in common with his province, and others in common with his generation, etc. Any single item of his behavior—that he saves money, drinks wine with his dinner, has a house with a garden gate—will be shared outside France as well as inside, and the circumstance that he walks upright, uses tools, and speaks an organized language will be shared with the entire human race. But when we are making a cultural analysis, we are interested in identifying those characteristics—including, if not specifying, the possibilities of variation by class, region, religion, period, etc.—which can be attributed to sharing in the tradition of the larger group, whether that group be nation, tribe, province, or some even larger unit with a common tradition, such as the culture of an area like Southeast Asia.

The regularities of behavior of all those who share a common culture may be attributed to the uniformities in their biological endowments, that all are human beings with bodies and brains which have much in common. The peculiarities of any culture, as compared with any other culture, and the peculiarities of the versions of the culture which one class or region displays are to be referred to different historical conditions, including the whole ecological situation—so that lake dwellers, plains dwellers, and mountain dwellers will have different versions of a common tradition—and to the differences between human beings, whether these differences are regarded as hereditary, congenital, or as resulting from an individual life-history. So at any given period in history, French or American or German culture is an expression of what the predecessors—whether the biological and cultural or cultural only—of the present population have developed, including the particular stamp that has been given by outstanding individuals or members of a particular class.

The regularizing features, which make it possible to abstract from the behavior of all Frenchmen or all Americans certain systematic statements, are their shared humanity and their shared tradition. Each individual who must live out a series of roles—as husband, father, church member, employer or employee, member of a political party, member of an audience, taxpayer, member of the armed forces, sometimes spectator, sometimes actor in the social scene—relates these various aspects of the culture, these various roles, within his own personality. They may be related directly, as when the father role and the employer role and the citizen role are felt to call for the same kind of behavior; or they may be related tangentially or contrapuntally; that is, a man may treat his children differently from his employees, he may perform quite differently for spectators of his own class as compared to those of another class, but he is the same person performing the different roles, and they become in time systematically related to one another within the framework of the historical culture within which he acts.

In changing societies like our own, especially in societies like the United States in which immigration has been such an important factor, these various relationships between roles, between classes, between age groups, will not be so perfectly related, and the regularities will be of a different order. So we may say that it is a regularity of American culture that children expect to behave differently from their parents and will treat their children differently from the way they were treated. Even in those cases where a young mother does treat her baby as her mother treated her, she is conscious of doing so, in contrast to her friends, to people in books, who are behaving differently from their parents. In a homogeneous, very slowly changing culture, a young mother will repeat, without being conscious of any other course, the "right" way of doing things—of feeding or lulling or scolding a child—and will regard her successes and failures as being as good as, better than, or worse than her mother's. But in a culture like America, the occasional mother who does repeat her mother's practices systematically relates this repetition to an expected nonrepeating pattern.

Similarly, in the United States, where adult immigrants have consciously learned to adjust to American culture after knowing what it means to speak a language and relate themselves in habits and manners to other people, people are regularly conscious of the degree to which they conform to the behavior of the people with whom they associate. They may choose to conform, they may choose to deviate, but they cannot choose to be unconscious of the problem. So children whose parents have no servants will feel different and inferior among children whose parents have servants, and children whose parents have servants, when no other associated household does, also will feel different and potentially inferior. Here again, this contrast between American culture and other cultures is not absolute. The Balinese girl who reaches puberty later than the girls who are her age mates is shy and embarrassed; Balinese parents will worry about a little son who delays longer than his age mates "daring the rice fields" alone with an ox or water buffalo. But whereas the Balinese refer to a common chronological age and an expected speed of maturation, people in the United States include also an expected attentiveness to the standards of the group around one.

Some students are helped in identifying the cultural factor in behavior—which may be found in the play of children in a park, the scenes on a film, the response to a political situation—as "American" or "French" by the idea of "style," that intangible configuration of widely shared items which makes it possible to distinguish one "style" from another or the literature or art of one period from another. Other principles of organizing observation—as when a nursery-school teacher says, "He's behaving like a three-year-old," "I'd expect that from a Park Avenue child but not from a Washington Square child," "He's pushing that scooter like a girl"—are all abstractions of something that has been observed to be common to a group. Learning to see the regularities of behavior that are "American" or "English" requires the same kind of disciplined familiarity that makes it possible to make statements about the expected play behavior of children of a given age or sex or class, all of which involves having compared the behavior of different ages, both sexes, and different classes, so that the differences come into focus, and one no longer thinks that the way a three-year-old Park Avenue girl plays with a scooter is either "simply human" or "simply individual, because each individual is different from each other individual."

Students and commentators on human behavior in the twentieth century vary between the extremes of a high sensitivity to style—style appropriate to age, sex, constitution, class, culture, period, and experience—and a low sensitivity to style, in which differences in detail are never perceived as anything but variations of one over-all pattern. These possibly innate temperamental preferences for working with or without a sense of style and pattern have been accentuated by the traditions of different professions. Social and experimental psychologists and sociologists tend to work with such units as attitudes and traits, where the more-or-less of one trait is correlated with the more-or-less of another ("more people with incomes between three and four thousand tend to own their own homes if they are in a white-collar group than . . ."), in which the integration provided either by identified human beings or by identified groups of human beings is lost. Clinical psychologists, psychoanalysts, and cultural anthropologists, who work with a large number of observations on a small number of individuals,[8] the validity of whose work comes from the number and kinds of *items* of behavior sampled rather than from the number of *individuals* sampled, have been trained to work with pattern.[9]

The studies in this volume are all studies of pattern, of the stylistic interrelationships of different aspects of childhood, of the way in which, in a given culture, the image of the child, the way the child is rewarded and punished, children's toys, the literature written for children, the literature written about children, the selective memories of adults about their childhood, the games the children play, their fears and fantasies, hopes and daydreams, and behavior on projective tests are all systematically related to one another.

The relationships may be of many sorts. Children may learn to play peacefully with each other, never engaging in physical conflict, but when they draw or play with toys, they may construct violent scenes, as is the case in Bali. Or they may lead a life of active struggle and belligerency, but when they draw or play, they may construct frozen lifeless tableaux. Adults may learn to forget or to remember only the painful or only the pleasant incidents of their childhood. The adult on the verge of death may be permitted a return to childhood, as is the Japanese *kamikaze* flier who is given toys to play with. The American condemned criminal may be permitted to order an enormous meal, or he may be required to show the most mature form of self-control and stoicism, like the American Indian, who was required to sing as he burned at the stake, or the Soviet party member, who "confesses" at a public trial. In institutions where there are Negro and white American child delinquents, the girls may equate sex and race, so that strong attachments between girls are formed on a cross-race basis, while the boys, more preoccupied with rivalry and less with complementary behavior, may make no such equation. Children of the quietest German religious sects of Pennsylvania may be regaled with stories of torture and sadism, which secular American parents, among whom men have been trained as commandos and saboteurs, feel are far too horrible for children, and so give their children only bowdlerized tales about hard-working little engines or Red Riding Hood without the wolf. The use of mythological, threatening male figures to terrify French middle- and upper-class children may be missing among the working class,[10] where fathers themselves are often drunken, abusive, and cruel.

But these are not contradictions. As long as they appear to be contradictions, the student of culture feels that his analysis still lacks the completeness that is necessary. In the same way the clinician, laboriously listening day after day to the productions of a disturbed patient, knows that his understanding of his patient is incomplete as long as the patient produces unpredictable material which he cannot relate to other productions of the same patient or to his reported behavior outside the consulting room. Either he does not know enough yet, or some of the reports of the outside behavior are erroneous, or his theoretical scheme of analysis is inadequate to cover the case and must be expanded and extended. Possibly the patient is in a fugue state; possibly the patient is that very rare thing, a double personality; possibly—as a handwriting analyst found after working and working over specimens of handwriting of what appeared to be a double personality—the patient is a member of one race, passing as the member of another.

The cultural student, like the psychoanalytically trained clinician or the student of the art and literature of a period, works with the expectation of there being a pattern; failures to identify it are attributed to the type of information or to one's own individual inadequacies, but not to the material. Furthermore, an adequate knowledge of the pattern—of the culture, the period, or the particular individual who is being intensively studied—should make it possible to explain all past events by relating them to this knowledge and to predict the style, but *not the detail*, of future events. Prediction as a test of adequacy of a theory—in studies of human behavior, as in geology—must be retrospective. When we examine the life-histories of delinquents, we find that a very large proportion come from broken homes; but, when we compare a large sample of children from broken and unbroken homes, we can predict neither *which* children nor *how many* of the children from broken homes will become delinquent. Once the sequence of events has occurred—though the events themselves were subject to a large number of historical accidents outside the realm of our present scientific equipment—we should be able to relate them to our understanding of the other behavior of the members of a culture, or a period, or the previous behavior of an individual.

This book is concerned with studies of particular aspects of childhood, of child-rearing practice, of children's behavior, which always are referred to the culture. These are studies of French children, American children, Balinese children; of French, German, and Russian child-rearing literature; of responses of Czech and Eastern European Jewish mothers in America to interviews about how they are rearing their children; of the image of the child in films in American, French, and English films.

The interpretive structure, a body of systematic statements about the culture, has been based on qualitative analyses—intensive analyses of large numbers of observations on limited numbers of persons, documents, or events, in which the exact temporal, spatial, and social position of each person, document, or event was carefully specified.[11] Where really good statistical studies of the incidence of types of behavior exist, these qualitatively derived statements have been checked against them. Statements about American cultural character have been cross-checked against the impressive samples in *The American Soldier*.[12] Any careful, large quantitative study which produced results challenging any of these qualitative formulations would be treated in the same way as any other piece of cultural behavior; if it is reliably reported, then our schema must be revised.

The statement "Frenchmen speak French" is an acceptable generalization on the basis of which other work can be done; but "Most Frenchmen speak French" is an imperfect quantitative statement which requires quantification to make it meaningful. Or the statement "In Eastern European Jewish culture, an individual who was ill or poor or ignorant was permitted to exhibit this state to invoke and identify the magnanimity of the well, the rich, or the learned who was giving him help" may be used to explain the observation that Eastern European Jewish patients "make a fuss" in American hospitals; but it is not possible to predict that any given Eastern European Jewish patient will make a fuss. Such statements as "many Eastern European Jews" do this or that, while seeming more accurate, are actually much less so. We can say, "Demonstrating that one is really ill and needs help is a value in Eastern European Jewish culture" and that "keeping a stiff upper lip" is a value of Anglo-American culture and that "exhibiting the ability to keep a stiff upper lip" is a value in Polish culture. The use of terms like *many, some, more, less, rather,* or *somewhat* simply obscures the issue and makes it more difficult to see what is being hypothesized.

This book, then, presents a series of studies of parts, but each study has been related to a larger cultural whole. Readers may follow out such part studies in various ways. From "The Place of Book-Learning in Traditional Jewish Culture" the reader may turn to *Life Is with People: The Jewish Little Town in Eastern Europe*,[13] a volume dealing with the culture of Eastern European Jews, and then to the voluminous literature on the history of the Jews. The context of Soviet ideals of child rearing will be found in *Soviet Attitudes toward Authority*[14] and in the many studies of the emerging Soviet culture. The way in which such part studies as those aspects of German culture written about in

"A Portrait of the Family in German Juvenile Literature" and "Parents and Children: An Analysis of Contemporary German Child-Care and Youth-Guidance Literature" are fitted together to make a whole is explicitly demonstrated in *Themes in French Culture*.[15] If it is clearly recognized how such parts can be related to cultural wholes, then each small study—of a play group in a park, of the responses of California children to questionnaires, interviews, and tests on social attitudes on race, of a set of children who came to a guidance clinic—becomes immediately more meaningful. It is by the accumulated interlocking of such partial studies that the details of whole studies can be ultimately filled in. So, for example, the responses of Iowa Mennonite and ordinary Iowa Protestant children to a Bavelas test on "What is a good thing for a child to eat, and who would praise him for it?"—the Mennonites answering "parent," and the others answering "mother"—became intelligible by referring the differences to the German tradition of parental unity and the American tradition of maternal disciplinary responsibility, and referring both to the current—1942—American emphasis on praising children for "eating the right food." What children eat, what they wear, how they play; what adults think of children, of their own childhood, of their children's future adulthood; the image of the child created by the insurance advertisement, "Make him safe," and that of the child on the automobile advertisement, "Mother's little darling says Nash"; the mothers who say they want their children to be free, spontaneous, natural, and happy, and neat, clean, and obedient are all intricate and elaborately related parts of one whole.

The same American mothers who expect these contrasting behaviors from their children provide the opportunities for freedom, carelessness, and spontaneity and for control and neatness within the same house, with differential rules for living-room, playroom, bathroom, front and back hall. The time rhythm of the culture is arranged with provision for work, recreation, sleep, for free and prescribed periods—for periods when it is appropriate to grow a three-day beard or to wear dirty blue jeans out in the woods and periods when starch and absolute freshness of skin and clothes are essential. When we relate such a description of the whole culture back to the statements of the mothers who want their children to be both "spontaneous" and "obedient," "natural" and "clean," we find that it is *only* the *composite* of the seemingly contradictory parental ideals which is an adequate patterned representation of what parental ideals would "predictably" be in the middle-class culture of the United States in the mid-twentieth century.

About half the work on childhood in this volume is work on understanding adults through the childhood experience that they can be demonstrated to have had, as when the books read by a generation of German children were analyzed to throw light on the writers who prepared them, the parents who selected them, and the adults, part of whose childhood experience they formed. Similarly, the studies of the child-rearing literature throw light on the explicit and changing ideals of the adult culture and only to a very limited degree on the practice to which living children are subjected. David Riesman discusses "Tootle" as a comment on American culture; the story of *Monkey* is analyzed partly as a comment on Chinese adult culture. This use of material on child-rearing practices, ideals, and materials or on adult memories as a way of understanding the cultural character of adults can be theoretically related to what we know of developmental sequences, of cultural consistency, of the maintenance of personality through time. But the circumstance that these particular materials have been analyzed in this way does not preclude many other ways of analyzing them. These are essential varieties of research on children and childhood, which can be used to learn more about children, more about human beings, more about a given culture, more about the former, present, or future cultural character of a particular historical group.

The studies in this book fall into three main groups on the basis of the materials used: observations of living children; analysis of materials made by, for, or about children—which is based mainly on the materials (that is, we neither observe the children who make the drawings nor the writer who writes the children's story nor the children who read the story, but draw our inferences from these objects); and various kinds of interviews of different degrees of stylization and intent—from the purely research interviews with immigrant parents in the American scene reported in "The Place of Book-Learning in Traditional Jewish Culture" to the clinically oriented interviews in "Two Types of Jewish Mothers." This division is, of course, partly artificial, as when Mark Zborowski combines recent *interviews* with Eastern European Jews in New York City by fellow-research workers with his original observations as a member of an Eastern European Jewish little town; or as when Erik Erikson *observes* a child responding to a standard block-building situation and later analyzes the construction itself as an *artifact*, using in his interpretations *interviews* with the same child on other occasions and by other members of the research team.

In all anthropological studies of living cultures, all three methods are combined. So we have placed the three studies of Bali together at the beginning—parts of the study of a whole culture by three research workers who co-operated in the field and in the subsequent analysis of the material. But when we have placed in separate parts studies on the same culture, such as Rhoda Métraux's "Parents and Children: An Analysis of Contemporary German Child-Care and Youth-Guidance Literature," "A Portrait of the Family in German Juvenile Fiction," and "The Consequences of Wrongdoing: An Analysis of Story Completions by German Children," or two studies by different authors on the same culture, such as "The Place of Book-Learning in Traditional Jewish Culture" by Mark Zborowski and "Two Types of Jewish Mothers" by Martha Wolfenstein, we have separated them for two reasons—to stress the emphasis on one method rather than another and to stress that these are partial studies, where the culture, exceedingly complex and shared by millions of people with a long recorded history, is not known and has not been studied as a whole in the way in which Bali was studied.

A number of diagnostic and stimulating accounts of American culture have been published, but as yet there is no organized published body of materials which provides an adequate total cultural frame of reference. Furthermore, not only does a picture of a complex modern culture have to be built up by large teams of workers with different skills and areas of knowledge, observing, analyzing, and interviewing in many different contexts, but also such detailed partial studies of particular aspects or problems when undertaken as class projects and thesis subjects are a practical way in which students may begin to do research.

The new field of personality and culture, within which these studies lie, was built by co-operative effort among research workers trained in one of the co-operative disciplines—anthropology, psychiatry, psychology, child development, etc. Today, however, a new type of research worker is developing within these various, once isolated, disciplines, who combines his work on human materials so that the chapters by Martha Wolfenstein report work in the field of free observation, fantasies about children, interviews on moral training, analysis of child-training literature, and clinical work. Here human beings are seen in both their idiosyncratic and their cultural aspects, neither one obscuring or dominating the other.

The three studies on Bali together present an intermediate picture between the traditional work on primitive peoples and our present-day attempt to study complex Western cultures. They also represent one of the first attempts to have a group of research workers interested in different problems work together in the field.

Cultural studies in modern complex societies date only from World War II. To emphasize both the roots and the recency of this approach, we have included an article written by Ruth Benedict in 1938, which should be read carefully with the date in mind, and Geoffrey Gorer's original statement of the premises on which he based his pioneer study of Japanese character. One measure of the potentialities of an approach is a study of the pace of the development.

NOTES

1. Carmichael, 1954. Lists of references appear at the ends of chapters.
2. Kidd, 1906; Grinnell, 1923.
3. Malinowski, 1927.
4. Piaget, 1926.
5. A comparison of what it was possible to say in this field in 1931 and in 1949 (Mead, 1931; Mead, 1954*a*) highlights this position in anthropology. Child-development monographs were started in 1935, and the *Psychoanalytic Study of the Child* is in its ninth volume in the fall of 1954. Serious studies of children's growth are less than forty years old.
6. Ransome, 1938.
7. Mead, 1954*c*.
8. Mead, 1954*b*.
9. Mead, 1947; Hutchinson, 1950; Ford, 1954.
10. Meadow, 1954.
11. Mead and Métraux, 1953.
12. Stouffer, 1949.
13. Zborowski and Herzog, 1952.
14. Mead, 1951.
15. Métraux and Mead, 1954.

LIST OF REFERENCES

CARMICHAEL, LEONARD (ed.). 1954. *Manual of Child Psychology*. 2d ed. New York: John Wiley & Sons.

FORD, JAMES A. 1954. "On the Concept of Types," *American Anthropologist*, LVI, No. 1, 42–57.

GRINNELL, GEORGE B. 1923. *The Cheyenne Indians*. New Haven: Yale University Press.

HUTCHINSON, G. E. 1950. Review of MARGARET MEAD, *Male and Female*, in "Marginalia," *American Scientist*, XXXVIII, No. 2, 282–89.

KIDD, DUDLEY. 1906. *Savage Childhood: A Study of Kafir Children*. London: Macmillan & Co., Ltd.

MALINOWSKI, BRONISLAW. 1927. *Sex and Repression in Savage Society*. New York: Harcourt, Brace & Co.

MEAD, MARGARET. 1931. "The Primitive Child." In *Handbook of Child Psychology*, ed. CARL MURCHISON. Worcester, Mass.: Clark University Press.

———. 1947. "The Concept of Culture and the Psychosomatic Approach," *Psychiatry*, X, No. 1, 57–76.

———. 1951. *Soviet Attitudes toward Authority*. New York: McGraw-Hill Book Co.

———. 1954*a*. "Research on Primitive Children." In *Manual of Child Psychology*, ed. LEONARD CARMICHAEL. 2d ed. New York: John Wiley & Sons.

———. 1954*b*. "Some Theoretical Considerations on the Problem of Mother-Child Separation," *American Journal of Orthopsychiatry*, XXIV, No. 3, 471–83.

———. 1954*c*. "The Swaddling Hypothesis: Its Reception," *American Anthropologist*, LVI, No. 3, 395–409.

MEAD, MARGARET, and MÉTRAUX, RHODA (eds.). 1953. *The Study of Culture at a Distance*. Chicago: University of Chicago Press.

MEADOW, LLOYD. 1954. "A Study of Dyadic Relationships in the French Family." Unpublished paper read before the sixty-second annual meeting of the American Psychological Association, New York, September 5.

MÉTRAUX, RHODA, and MEAD, MARGARET. 1954. *Themes in French Culture: A Preface to a Study of French Community.* ("Hoover Institute Studies.") Stanford, Calif.: Stanford University Press.

PIAGET, JEAN. 1926. *Language and Thought of the Child.* New York: Harcourt, Brace & Co.

Psychoanalytic Study of the Child. 9 vols. New York: International Universities Press, 1945–54.

RANSOME, ARTHUR. 1938. *Old Peter's Russian Tales.* New York: Thomas Nelson & Sons.

STOUFFER, S. A., et al. 1949. *The American Soldier.* Vol. I: *Adjustment during Army Life;* Vol. II: *Combat and Its Aftermath.* Princeton, N.J.: Princeton University Press.

ZBOROWSKI, MARK, and HERZOG, ELIZABETH. 1952. *Life Is with People: The Jewish Little Town in Eastern Europe.* New York: International Universities Press.

CHAPTER 2

Continuities and Discontinuities in Cultural Conditioning

—RUTH BENEDICT

This paper was published originally in Psychiatry, I, *No. 2 (1938), 161–67. It was a specific attempt on Ruth Benedict's part to apply to our own society considerations based on the observations of field anthropologists, to which her interest had been originally drawn by the extreme discontinuities of Manus culture. It is illustrative of the traditional cross-cultural illumination of a problem in our own society.—M.M.*

A LL cultures must deal in one way or another with the cycle of growth from infancy to adulthood. Nature has posed the situation dramatically: on the one hand, the newborn baby, physiologically vulnerable, unable to fend for itself or to participate of its own initiative in the life of the group, and, on the other, the adult man or woman. Every man who rounds out his human potentialities must have been a son first and a father later, and the two roles are physiologically in great contrast; he must first have been dependent upon others for his very existence, and later he must provide such security for others. This discontinuity in the life-cycle is a fact of nature and is inescapable. Facts of nature, however, in any discussion of human problems, are ordinarily read off not at their bare minimal but surrounded by all the local accretions of behavior to which the student of human affairs has become accustomed in his own culture. For that reason it is illuminating to examine comparative material from other societies in order to get a wider perspective on our own special accretions. The anthropologist's role is not to question the facts of nature but to insist upon the interposition of a middle term between "nature" and "human behavior"; his role is to analyze that term, to document local man-made doctorings of nature, and to insist that these doctorings should not be read off in any one culture as nature itself. Although it is a fact of nature that the child becomes a man, the way in which this transition is effected varies from one society to another, and no one of these particular cultural bridges should be regarded as the "natural" path to maturity.

From a comparative point of view our culture goes to great extremes in emphasizing contrasts between the child and the adult. The child is sexless, the adult estimates his virility by his sexual activities; the child must be protected from the ugly facts of life, the adult must meet them without psychic catastrophe; the child must obey, the adult must command this obedience. These are all dogmas of our culture, dogmas which, in spite of the facts of nature, other cultures commonly do not share. In spite of the physiological contrasts between child and adult, these are cultural accretions.

It will make the point clearer if we consider one habit in our own culture in regard to which there is not this discontinuity of conditioning. With the greatest clarity of purpose and economy of training, we achieve our goal of conditioning everyone to eat three meals a day. The baby's training in regular food periods begins at birth, and no crying of the child and no inconvenience to the mother is allowed to interfere. We gauge the child's physiological makeup and at first allow it food oftener than adults, but, because our goal is firmly set and our training consistent, before the child is two years old it has achieved the adult schedule. From the point of view of other cultures this is as startling as the fact of three-year-old babies perfectly at home in deep water is to us. Modesty is another sphere in which our child training is consistent and economical; we waste no time in clothing the baby, and, in contrast to many societies where the child runs naked till it is ceremonially given its skirt or its pubic sheath at adolescence, the child's training fits it precisely for adult conventions.

In neither of these aspects of behavior is there need for an individual in our culture to embark before puberty, at puberty, or at some later date upon a course of action which all his previous training has tabooed. He is spared the unsureness inevitable in such a transition.

The illustrations I have chosen may appear trivial, but in larger and more important aspects of behavior our methods are obviously different. Because of the great variety of child training in different families in our society, I might illustrate continuity of conditioning from individual life-histories in our culture, but even these, from a comparative point of view, stop far short of consistency, and I shall therefore confine myself to describing arrangements in other cultures in which training which with us is idiosyncratic is accepted and traditional and does not therefore involve the same possibility of conflict. I shall choose childhood rather than infant and nursing situations, not because the latter do not vary strikingly in different cultures but because they are nevertheless more circumscribed by the baby's physiological needs than is its later training. Childhood situations provide an excellent field in which to illustrate the range of cultural adjustments which are possible within a universally given, but not so drastic, set of physiological facts.

The major *discontinuity* in the life-cycle is, of course, that the child who is at one point a son must later be a father. These roles in our society are strongly differentiated; a good son is tractable and does not assume adult responsibilities; a good father provides for his children and should not allow his authority to be flouted. In addition, the child must be sexless so far as his family is concerned, whereas the father's sexual role is primarily in the family. The individual in one role must revise his behavior from almost all points of view when he assumes the second role.

I shall select for discussion three such contrasts that occur in our culture between the individual's role as child and as father: (1) responsible-nonresponsible status role, (2) dominance-submission, (3) contrasted sexual role. It is largely upon our cultural commitments to these three contrasts that the discontinuity in the life-cycle of an individual in our culture depends.

RESPONSIBLE-NONRESPONSIBLE STATUS ROLE

The techniques adopted by societies which achieve continuity during the life-cycle in this sphere in no way differ from those we employ in our uniform conditioning to three meals a day. They are merely applied to other areas of life. We think of the child as wanting to play and the adult as having to work, but in many societies the mother takes the baby daily in her shawl or carrying net to the garden or to gather roots, and adult labor is seen even in infancy from the pleasant security of its position in close contact with its mother. When the child can run about, it accompanies its parents, still doing tasks which are essential and yet suited to its powers, and its dichotomy between work and play is not different from that its parents recognize, namely, the distinction between the busy day and the free evening. The tasks it is asked to perform are graded to its powers, and its elders wait quietly by, not offering to do the task in the child's place. Everyone who is familiar with such societies has been struck by the contrast with our child training. Dr. Ruth Underhill tells me of sitting with a group of Papago elders in Arizona when the man of the house turned to his little three-year-old granddaughter and asked her to close the door. The door was heavy and hard to shut. The child tried, but it did not move. Several times the grandfather repeated, "Yes, close the door." No one jumped to the child's assistance. No one took the responsibility away from her. On the other hand, there was no impatience, for, after all, the child was small. They sat gravely waiting till the child succeeded and her grandfather gravely thanked her. It was assumed that the task would not be asked of her unless she could perform it, and, having been asked, the responsibility was hers alone just as if she were a grown woman.

The essential point of such child training is that the child is from infancy continuously conditioned to responsible social participation, while at the same time the tasks that are expected of it are adapted to its capacity. The contrast with our society is very great. A child does not make any labor contribution to our industrial society except as it competes with an adult; its work is not measured against its own strength and skill but against high-geared industrial requirements. Even when we praise a child's achievement in the home, we are outraged if such praise is interpreted as being of the same order as praise of adults. The child is praised because the parent feels well disposed, regardless of whether the task is well done by adult standards, and the child acquires no sensible standard by which to measure its achievement. The gravity of a Cheyenne Indian family ceremoniously making a feast out of the little boy's first snowbird is at the furthest remove from our behavior. At birth the little boy was presented with a toy bow, and, from the time he could run about, serviceable bows suited to his stature were specially made for him by the man of the family. Animals and birds were taught him in a graded series beginning with those most easily taken; and as he brought in his first of each species, his family duly made a feast of it, accepting his contribution as gravely as the buffalo his father brought. When he finally killed a buffalo, it was only the final step of his childhood conditioning, not a new adult role with which his childhood experience had been at variance.

The Canadian Ojibwa show clearly what results can be achieved. This tribe gains its livelihood by winter trapping, and the small family of father, mother, and children live during the long winter alone on their great frozen hunting grounds. The boy accompanies his father and brings in his catch to his sister, as his father does to his mother; the girl prepares the meat and skins for him, just as his mother does for her husband. By the time the boy is twelve, he may have set his own line of traps on a hunting territory of his own and returned to his parents' house only once in several months—still bringing the meat and skins to his sister. The young child is taught consistently that it has only itself to rely upon in life, and this is as true in the dealings it will have with the supernatural as in the business of getting a livelihood. This attitude he will accept as a successful adult just as he accepted it as a child.[1]

DOMINANCE-SUBMISSION

Dominance-submission is the most striking of those categories of behavior where like does not respond to like but where one type of behavior stimulates the opposite response. It is one of the most prominent ways in which behavior is patterned in our culture. When it obtains between classes, it may be nourished by continuous experience;

the difficulty in its use between children and adults lies in the fact that an individual conditioned to one set of behavior in childhood must adopt the opposite as an adult. Its opposite is a pattern of approximately identical reciprocal behavior, and societies which rely upon continuous conditioning characteristically invoke this pattern. In some prmitive cultures the very terminology of address between father and son and, more commonly, between grandfather and grandson or uncle and nephew reflects this attitude. In such kinship terminologies one reciprocal expresses each of these relationships, so that son and father, for instance, exchange the same term with one another, just as we exchange the same term with a cousin. The child later will exchange it with his son. "Father-son," therefore, is a continuous relationship he enjoys throughout life. The same continuity, backed up by verbal reciprocity, occurs far oftener in the grandfather-grandson relationship or that of mother's brother–sister's son. When these are "joking" relationships, as they often are, travelers report wonderingly upon the liberties and pretensions of tiny toddlers in their dealings with these family elders. In place of our dogma of respect to elders, such societies employ in these cases a reciprocity as nearly identical as may be. The teasing and practical joking the grandfather visits upon his grandchild, the grandchild returns in like coin; he would be led to believe that he failed in propriety if he did not give like for like. If the sister's son has right of access without leave to his mother's brother's possessions, the mother's brother has such rights also to the child's possessions. They share reciprocal privileges and obligations which in our society can develop only between age mates.

From the point of view of our present discussion, such kinship conventions allow the child to put into practice from infancy the same forms of behavior which it will rely upon as an adult; behavior is not polarized into a general requirement of submission for the child and dominance for the adult.

It is clear from the techniques described above by which the child is conditioned to a responsible status role that these depend chiefly upon arousing in the child the desire to share responsibility in adult life. To achieve this, little stress is laid upon obedience but much stress upon approval and praise. Punishment is very commonly regarded as quite outside the realm of possibility, and natives in many parts of the world have drawn the conclusion from our usual disciplinary methods that white parents do not love their children. If the child is not required to be submissive, however, many occasions for punishment melt away; a variety of situations which call for it do not occur. Many American Indian tribes are especially explicit in rejecting the ideal of a child's submissive or obedient behavior. Prince Maximilian von Wied, who visited the Crow Indians over a hundred years ago, describes a father's boasting about his young son's intractability even when it was the father himself who was flouted: "He will be a man," his father said. He would have been baffled at the idea that his child should show behavior which would obviously make him appear a poor creature in the eyes of his fellows if he used it as an adult. Dr. George Devereux tells me of a special case of such an attitude among the Mohave at the present time. The child's mother was white and protested to its father that he must take action when the child disobeyed and struck him. "But why?" the father said. "He is little. He cannot possibly injure me." He did not know of any dichotomy according to which an adult expects obedience and a child must accord it. If his child had been docile, he would simply have judged that it would become a docile adult—an eventuality of which he would not have approved.

Child training which brings about the same result is common also in other areas of life than that of reciprocal kinship obligations between child and adult. There is a tendency in our culture to regard every situation as having in it the seeds of a dominance-submission relationship. Even where dominance-submission is patently irrelevant, we read in the dichotomy. On the other hand, some cultures, even when the situation calls for leadership, do not see it in terms of dominance-submission. To do justice to this attitude, it would be necessary to describe their political, and especially their economic, arrangements, because the persistence of such an attitude must certainly be supported by economic mechanisms that are congruent with it. But it must also be supported by—or what comes to the same thing, express itself in—child training and familial situations.

CONTRASTED SEXUAL ROLE

Continuity of conditioning in training the child to assume responsibility and to behave no more submissively than adults is quite possible in terms of the child's physiological endowment if his participation is suited to his strength. Because of the late development of the child's reproductive organs, continuity of conditioning in sex experience presents a difficult problem. So far as their belief that the child is anything but a sexless being is concerned, they are probably more nearly right than we are with an opposite dogma. But the great break is presented by the universally sterile unions before puberty and the presumably fertile ones after maturation. This physiological fact no amount of cultural manipulation can minimize or alter, and societies therefore which stress continuous conditioning most strongly sometimes do not expect children to be interested in sex experience until they have matured physically. This is striking among Amercan Indian tribes like the Dakota; adults observe great privacy in sex acts and in no way stimulate children's sexual activity. There need be no discontinuity, in the sense in which I have used the term, in such a program if the child is taught nothing it does not have to unlearn later. In such cultures adults view children's experimentation as in no way wicked or dangerous but merely as innocuous play which can have no serious consequences. In some societies such play is minimal, and the children manifest little interest in it. But the same attitude may be taken by adults in societies where such play is encouraged and forms a major activity among small children. This is true among most of the Melanesian cultures of southeast New Guinea; adults go as far as to laugh off sexual affairs within the prohibited class if the children are not mature, saying that since they cannot marry, there can be no harm done.

It is this physiological fact of the difference between children's sterile unions and adults' presumably fertile sex relations which must be kept in mind in order to understand the different mores which almost always govern sex expression in children and in adults in the same culture. A great many cultures with preadolescent sexual license require marital fidelity, and a great many which value premarital virginity in either male or female arrange their marital life with great license. Continuity in sex experience is complicated by factors which it was unnecessary to consider in the problems previously discussed. The essential problem is not whether or not the child's sexuality is consistently exploited—for even where such exploitation is favored, in the majority of cases the child must seriously modify his behavior at puberty or at marriage. Continuity in sex expression means rather that the child is taught nothing it must unlearn later. If the cultural emphasis is upon sexual pleasure, the child who is continuously conditioned will be encouraged to experiment freely and pleasurably, as among the Marquesans;[2] if emphasis is upon reproduction, as among the Zuni of New Mexico, childish sex proclivities will not be exploited, for the only important use which sex is thought to serve in his culture is not yet possible to him. The important contrast with our child training is that, although a Zuni child is impressed with the wickedness of premature sex experimentation, he does not run the risk, as in our culture, of associating this wickedness with sex itself rather than with sex at his age. The adult in our culture has often failed to unlearn the wickedness or the dangerousness of sex, a lesson which was impressed upon him strongly in his most formative years.

DISCONTINUITY IN CONDITIONING

Even from this very summary statement of continuous conditioning, the economy of such mores is evident. In spite of the obvious advantages, however, there are difficulties in its way. Many primitive societies expect as different behavior from an individual as child and as adult as we do, and such discontinuity involves a presumption of strain.

Many societies of this type, however, minimize strain by the techniques they employ, and some techniques are more successful than others in insuring the individual's functioning without conflict. It is from this point of view that age-grade societies reveal their fundamental significance. Age-graded cultures characteristically demand different behavior of the individual at different times of his life, and persons of a like age grade are grouped into a society whose activities are all oriented toward the behavior desired at that age. Individuals "graduate" publicly and with honor from one of these groups to another. Where age-society members are enjoined to loyalty and mutual support and are drawn not only from the local group but from the whole tribe, as among the Arapaho, or even from other tribes, as among the Wagawaga of southeast New Guinea, such an institution has many advantages in eliminating conflicts among local groups and fostering intratribal peace. This seems to be also a factor in the tribal military solidarity of the similarly organized Masai of East Africa. The point that is of chief interest for our present discussion, however, is that by this means an individual who at any time takes on a new set of duties and virtues is supported not only by a solid phalanx of age mates but by the traditional prestige of the organized "secret" society into which he has now graduated. Fortified in this way, individuals in such cultures often swing between remarkable extremes of opposite behavior without apparent psychic threat. For example, the great majority exhibit prideful and nonconflicted behavior at each stage in the life-cycle, even when a prime of life devoted to passionate and aggressive head hunting must be followed by a later life dedicated to ritual and to mild and peaceable civic virtues.[3]

Our chief interest here, however, is in discontinuity which primarily affects the child. In many primitive societies such discontinuity has been fostered not because of economic or polititical necessity or because such discontinuity provides for a socially valuable division of labor but because of some conceptual dogma. The most striking of these are the Australian and Papuan cultures, where the ceremony of the "Making of Man" flourishes. In such societies it is believed that men and women have opposite and conflicting powers. And male children, who are of undefined status, must be initiated into the male role. In central Australia the boy child is of the woman's side, and women are taboo in the final adult stages of tribal ritual. The elaborate and protracted initiation ceremonies of the Arunta therefore snatch the boy from the mother, dramatize his gradual repudiation of her. In a final ceremony he is reborn as a man out of the men's ceremonial "baby pouch." The men's ceremonies are ritual statements of a masculine solidarity, carried out by fondling one another's *churingas*, the material symbol of each man's life, and by letting out over one another blood drawn from their veins. After this warm bond among men has been established through the ceremonies, the boy joins the men in the men's house and participates in tribal rites.[4] The enjoined discontinuity has been tribally bridged.

West of the Fly River in southern New Guinea there is a striking development of this "Making of Men" cult which involves a childhood period of passive homosexuality. Among the Keraki,[5] it is thought that no boy can grow to full stature without playing this role for some years. Men slightly older take the active role, and the older man is a jealous partner. The life-cycle of the Keraki includes, therefore, in succession, passive homosexuality, active homosexuality, and heterosexuality. The Keraki believe that pregnancy will result from postpubertal passive homosexuality and see evidences of such practices in any fat man, whom, even as an old man, they may kill or drive out of the tribe because of their fear. The ceremony that is of interest in connection with the present discussion takes place at the end of the period of passive homosexuality. This ceremony consists in burning out the possibility of pregnancy from the boy by pouring lye down his throat, after which he has no further protection if he gives way to the practice. There is no technique for ending active homosexuality, but this is not explicitly taboo for older men; heterosexuality and children, however, are highly valued. Unlike the neighboring Marimd-amin, who share their homosexual practices, Keraki husband and wife share the same house and work together in the gardens.

I have chosen illustrations of discontinuous conditioning where it is not too much to say that the cultural institutions furnish adequate support to the individual as he progresses from role to role or interdicts the previous behavior in a summary fashion. The contrast with arrangements in our culture is very striking, and against this background of social arrangements in other cultures the adolescent period of *Sturm und Drang* with which we are so familiar becomes intelligible in terms of our discontinuous cultural institutions and dogmas rather than in terms of physiological necessity. It is even more pertinent to consider these comparative facts in relation to maladjusted persons in our culture who are said to be fixated at one or another preadult level. It is clear that if we were to look at our social arrangements as an outsider, we should infer directly from our family institutions and habits of child training that many individuals would not "put off childish things"; we should have to say that our adult activity demands traits that are interdicted in children and that, far from redoubling efforts to help children bridge this gap, adults in our culture put all the blame on the child when he fails to manifest spontaneously the new behavior or, overstepping the mark, manifests it with untoward belligerence. It is not surprising that in such a society many individuals fear to use behavior which has up to that time been under a ban and trust instead, though at great psychic cost, to attitudes that have been exercised with approval during their formative years. In so far as we invoke a physiological scheme to account for these neurotic adjustments, we are led to overlook the possibility of developing social institutions which would lessen the social cost we now pay; instead we elaborate a set of dogmas which prove inapplicable under other social conditions.

NOTES

1. Landes, 1938, Part I, "Youth."
2. Ralph Linton, class notes on the Marquesas.
3. Henry Elkin, manuscript on the Arapaho.
4. Spencer and Gillen, 1927; Róheim, 1932, particularly chap. iii.
5. Williams, 1936.

LIST OF REFERENCES

LANDES, RUTH. 1938. *The Ojibwa Woman.* ("Columbia University Contributions to Anthropology," Vol. XXXI.) New York: Columbia University Press.

RÓHEIM, GÉZA. 1932. "Psycho-analysis of Primitive Cultural Types," *International Journal of Psycho-analysis*, XIII, 1–224.

SPENCER, W. B., and GILLEN, F. J. 1927. *The Arunta.* 2 vols. London: Macmillan & Co., Ltd.

WILLIAMS, FRANCIS E. 1936. *Papuans of the Trans-Fly.* Oxford: Clarendon Press.

CHAPTER 3

Theoretical Approach—1941[1]

————————————————————GEOFFREY GORER

The study of child-rearing practices as a method of analyzing cultures at a distance was inaugurated originally by Geoffrey Gorer's research on Japanese character. At that time he stated the twelve postulates which formed the basis of his approach and which have been elaborated subsequently, both theoretically and methodologically, in The American People *(1948),* "Some Aspects of the Psychology of the People of Great Russia" *(1949),* "The Concept of National Character" *(1950), and* "National Character: Theory and Practice" *(1953). They are reproduced here to provide historical perspective in a rapidly developing science.—M. M.*

THE following postulates are derived from the disciplines of social anthropology, psychoanalysis, and stimulus-response psychology and represent a first attempt to construct a unified theory of social science. These formulations are inevitably tentative. There are twelve of them.

1. Human behavior is understandable: with sufficient evidence it is possible to explain any observed behavior, however incongruous isolated items may appear.

2. Human behavior is predominantly learned. Although the human infant may be born with some instincts and is born with some basic drives whose satisfaction is necessary to its survival, it is the treatment which the infant undergoes from the other members of the society into which it is born and its experiences of its environment which are of preponderating importance in molding adult behavior. (In this context I may as well state that I have assumed consistently that the genetic peculiarities of the Japanese do not involve any inherent psychological differences from other groups of human beings.)

3. In all societies the behavior of the component individuals of similar age, sex, and status shows a relative uniformity in similar situations. This is equally true in unformulated and unverbalized situations.

4. All societies have an ideal adult character (or characters, depending on sex and status) which is of major importance for the parents in selecting which items of their children's behavior to reward and which to punish.

5. Habits are established by differential reward and punishment, chiefly meted out by other members of the society.

6. The habits established early in the life of the individual influence all subsequent learning, and therefore the experiences of early childhood are of predominant importance.

7. The chief learning in early childhood consists of the modifications of the innate drives of hunger, optimum-temperature seeking, pain-avoidance, sex and excretion, and of the (probably learned) drives of fear and anger (anxiety and aggression) which are demanded by the adult members of the society; consequently, a knowledge of the types of modifications imposed, the means by which they are imposed, and the times at which they are imposed is of major importance in understanding adult behavior.

8. Since everywhere it is predominantly the parents who reward and punish their children, the attitudes of the child to his father and mother and, to a lesser degree, toward his siblings will become the prototypes of his attitudes toward all subsequently met people.

9. Except in situations of the greatest physiological stress, adult behavior is motivated by learned (derived, secondary) drives or wishes superimposed upon the primary biological drives.

10. Many of these wishes are unverbalized or unconscious, since the rewards and punishments which established the habits of which these wishes are the motives were undergone in early childhood, or because the verbalization of these wishes was very heavily punished. As a derivative from this hypothesis, people frequently cannot verbalize their motives, which have to be deduced from the observation of what satisfactions are actually obtained in a given situation.

11. When these wishes, acquired through early training, are shared by a majority of the population, some social institutions will eventually be evolved to gratify them; and existing social institutions and those that are borrowed from other societies will be modified to congruence with these wishes, in so far as this is possible without impeding the gratification of the primary biological drives.

12. In a homogeneous culture the patterns of superordination and subordination, of deference and arrogance, will show a certain consistency in all spheres from the family to the religious and political organizations; and consequently the patterns of behavior demanded in all these institutions will mutually reinforce each other.

NOTES

1. Originally issued in mimeographed form in 1941 by the Institute of Human Relations, Yale University, and later reprinted as part of an article published in the *Transactions of the New York Academy of Sciences* (Gorer, 1943).

LIST OF REFERENCES

GORER, GEOFFREY. 1943. "Themes in Japanese Culture," *Transactions of the New York Academy of Sciences,* Ser. II, V, 106–24.

———. 1948. *The American People.* New York: W. W. Norton & Co.

———. 1949. "Some Aspects of the Psychology of the People of Great Russia," *American Slavic and East European Review,* VIII, No. 3, 155–66.

———. 1950. "The Concept of National Character," *Science News,* No. 18, pp. 105–22. Harmondsworth, Middlesex: Penguin Books.

———. 1953. "National Character: Theory and Practice." In *The Study of Culture at a Distance,* ed. MARGARET MEAD and RHODA MÉTRAUX, pp. 57–82. Chicago: University of Chicago Press.

Observational Studies

Observational Studies

Introduction

PARTIAL and specialized studies of modern culture are modeled, more or less explicitly, upon studies of whole living societies in which the anthropologist observes the life of a people, witnesses birth and death, participates in ceremonials, visits individual households, and establishes relationships with many members of the community within which he is working. In the course of such observation and participation—participation in which his role as interested observer from another culture is conspicuously defined—he also uses the verbal accounts and explanations which can be given by individuals who are willing to talk, to translate, to interpret, and to explain. One not only attends ceremonies but also obtains accounts of other ceremonies, writes down from dictation myths about the ceremony, and discusses with informants, within interview situations, the traditional interpretation and rationale of details of the ceremony. Furthermore, in a living culture there are always artifacts, cultural products of one sort or another—houses, carvings, costumes, masks and offerings, pictorial representations of religious and magical ideas, charms constructed of fur and feathers or leaves and flowers, and the play constructions of children. When a whole culture is being studied, the observed style of architecture, the ways in which a house form differs from the house forms in adjacent or related cultures, the ways in which people use a house, who sits where and when, the meaning of the screen across a Balinese courtyard gate (to outwit devils who do not know how to go around corners) are all materials for the anthropologist. By observation of living behavior, by questioning and listening to verbal statements, and by analysis of physical objects, he arrives at a rounded presentation of the cultural whole.

Any one of these three methods, such as observing people with whom one cannot talk in situations in which no object of their own manufacture or tradition is present—as when one might watch a group of Asiatic workmen in dungarees in an American-designed barracks—is at best partial and, for scientific use, depends for interpretation upon previous experiences in the observation of whole culture or work with materials on other aspects of the culture which have been collected by others. Which of the three methods will be most emphasized in any piece of research depends upon the conditions of observation. In the study of a culture at a distance, as of present Soviet culture, one seldom has good opportunities to observe whole communities. In the study of a culture which has vanished, like America of the early nineteenth century, both interviews with living informants and observations of living children, parents, and teachers are out of the question, and one depends entirely on documents and pictorial representations (plus experience in contemporary cultures and knowledge of human childhood) to make interpretations. In the study of accessible living cultures, observation is resorted to most frequently in studying essentially nonverbal activities, like dancing, ritual gestures, drawings, or play, and may be thought of as appropriate to any activity in which a battery of stills and movie cameras or a sound-recording machine can be used, without the intervention of speech in any form, to obtain a record which can be analyzed subsequently. While the interests of the student will often dictate how much observation is used, sometimes the subject matter determines the choice, such as observation in the case of young infants, dancing, verbal records, making a collection of myths, etc.

There are also important differences between cultures. Some peoples rely more upon nonverbal cues in their communication with one another, devote proportionally more time to nonverbal activities, teach and learn without verbal explanations. The Balinese are such a culture, and the following three chapters on Bali serve to illustrate the use of all three methods in a complex, living culture, where nonverbal artistic behavior is of great importance. All of us who worked together in Bali spoke the language, questioned as well as observed, analyzed the products as well as watched the producer, but the observation was particularly crucial in each study.

Martha Wolfenstein's study of children in a French park is a composite of observations made in a study in 1947, while on a short visit to Paris, before the organization of the multidisciplinary group who developed the study of French culture at a distance. Her early observations—made without benefit of interviews or knowledge of the children observed—were part of her contribution to building the later working hypotheses about French culture. In the chapter in this volume, prepared in 1953, she has incorporated, interpretatively, both materials gained from other types of studies on French culture—interviews, analyses of literature and films, analysis of an exhibition of French children's paintings held in New York in 1948—and a second observational experience in Paris in the summer of 1953. She has presented only the formal observational context. The children are unidentified individually; they had never been seen before and were never seen again. The entire material provided is a scene in which only the nationality and the location—Paris, 1947—is known. A perfect film and a perfect sound recording, identified in the same way, could have been analyzed similarly across an ocean or across a century, provided that the words used were capable of translation.

Mark Zborowski's chapter on the education of Eastern European Jewish children provides an example of another type of observation. The culture of the *shtetl*, the little town of Eastern European Jewry, has vanished from its original habitat under the totalitarian destructiveness of Nazi and Communist. But this destruction is so recent that the actual life of the *shtetl* is still vivid in the memory of those who grew up there. Mark Zborowski writes, as an anthropologist, of the scene of his own childhood and early youth, combining the vivid images of sights and sounds, smell and taste, of this warmly remembered, vanished way of life with the materials gathered from interviews done by other members of the group who worked on the Eastern European Jewish cultures—interviews made by American Jewish interviewers who had never seen a *shtetl*, with men and women who had been reared in this society which has vanished so recently that we still have many beautiful photographs and contemporary paintings.

Until the development of modern still cameras, moving-picture cameras, and the recorder—and it is worth noting that the Balinese bibliography includes listings of both films and music—observations had either to be reduced to words on the spot or else treated as relatively unanalyzed wholes in single still photographs—interesting illustrations, evocative rather than scientific. But with our modern methods of recording,[1] sets of visual or auditory observations can be reproduced over and over again. We can discard the dubious practice of equating interobserver reliability with what actually occurs and at the same time develop ways of studying the patterning of observable material without the present dependence on very specialized, culturally sophisticated observers.

M. M.

NOTES

1. For discussions of methods see, *inter alia,* Bateson and Mead, 1942; and Mead and Macgregor, 1951.

LIST OF REFERENCES

BATESON, GREGORY, and MEAD, MARGARET. *Balinese Character: A Photographic Analysis.* ("Special Publications of the New York Academy of Sciences," Vol. II.) New York: The Academy.

MEAD, MARGARET, and MACGREGOR, FRANCES C. 1951. *Growth and Culture: A Photographic Study of Balinese Children.* New York: G. P. Putnam's Sons.

CHAPTER 4

Children and Ritual in Bali

————————————————————————MARGARET MEAD

Based on field work done in Bali, in 1936–39, by Gregory Bateson, Jane Belo, Colin McPhee, Katherine Mershon, and myself. Bali is now part of modern Indonesia, and many parts of this description would no longer hold. I am using a historical present for the description of old, i.e., pre–World War II Bali. Cf. Mead, 1939b.

IN BALI, children are called "small human beings," and the conception of the nature and place of the child is different from that of the West. The whole of life is seen as a circular stage on which human beings, born small, as they grow taller, heavier, and more skilled, play predetermined roles, unchanging in their main outlines, endlessly various and subject to improvisation in detail.

The world of the dead is one part of the circle, from which human souls return, born again into the same family every fourth generation, to stay too briefly—dying before they have shared rice—or for a long time, or even for too long, for it is inappropriate for great-grandparents to be alive at the same time as their great-grandchildren. Such lingerers have to pay a penny to their great-grandchildren, chance-met on the street. The newborn child and the aged great-grandparent are both too close to the other world for easy entrance into the temple. The baby cannot enter until after a special feast at three and a half or seven months, and the very aged enter through a special side gate.

The newborn are treated as celestial creatures entering a more humdrum existence and, at the moment of birth, are addressed with high-sounding honorific phrases reserved for gods, the souls of ancestors, princes, and people of a higher caste. Human beings do not increase in stature and importance, as is so often the case in societies where men have only one life to live; rather, they round a half-circle in which middle age, being farthest from the other world, is the most secular. There is little acceptance of any task being difficult or inappropriate for a child, except that an infant at birth is, of course, expected to do nothing for itself. Words are put into the mouth of the infant, spoken on its behalf by an adult; the hands of the seven-month-old baby are cupped to receive holy water, folded in prayer, opened to waft the incense offered to it as a god, and when the ceremony is over the child

sits, dreamily repeating the gestures which its hands have momen-
tarily experienced.[1]

The Balinese may comment with amusement but without surprise
if the leading metallophone player in a noted orchestra is so small that
he has to have a stool in order to reach the keys; the same mild amusement may be expressed if someone takes up a different art after his
hands have a tremor of age to confuse their precision. But in a continuum within which the distinction between the most gifted and the
least gifted is muted by the fact that everyone participates, the distinction between child and adult—as performer, as actor, as musician
—is lost except in those cases where the distinction is ritual, as where
a special dance form requires a little girl who has not reached puberty.

This treatment of human history as an unending series of rebirths
is matched in the treatment of the calendar. The Balinese have a
whole series of weeks, of three, four, five, six, up to ten days, which
turn on each other, like wheels of different sizes, and there are important occasions when two or three weeks recurrently coincide. These
have special names and may be an occasion for festival—like Gal-
oengan, a New Year's feast associated with the souls of the dead, and
a postfestival season of special theatricals. But, although there is a
way of noting the year in a continuous irreversible sequence, it is seldom used. A man who has labored long to recopy a sacred text on
pages of lontar palm will simply note, when his task of intricate elaboration of a beautiful archaic script is over, that this was finished on
the such-and-such, a recurrent combination of days—as we might say,
·on Friday the thirteenth of September. The principal calendrical unit,
the ceremonial year, is two hundred and ten days long. The lunar
calendar simply marks the pattern of planting and harvest.

Children, then, are smaller and more fragile than adults, as well as
closer to the other world. Their essential personality characteristics—
gaiety or seriousness, gentleness or harshness—are recognized early,
and those around each child combine to set its formal character in an
expected mold. The baby of six months with silver bracelets welded
on its tiny wrists, waves and bangs its arms; if someone is hurt in the
process, there comes the exclamation, "Isama is harsh." It takes only a
few such acts to stereotype the judgment which will be echoed and
re-echoed through its life, setting and defining its ways, but quite forgotten after death as other events—day of birth, experience in other in-
carnations—combine to give new personality. So, while the people take
ritual pains over a corpse—that the individual may be born again
fleeter of foot or more beautiful of face—they cannot describe the
character or the looks of someone who died two years ago. Personality
characteristics are accidents, held gently constant through any given
incarnation, that dissolve at death. But the baby who is identified as

"gay and mischievous" has a way of life plotted out for it, which again is independent of age. Old men who have been "gay" all their lives still know who sleeps with whom in the fields at night in the brief, wordless first encounters which for the Balinese represent the height of passion; and men and women, labeled "serious," may bear many children, but people will comment instead on their industriousness in the rice fields or their faithfulness at the temple.

The child is made conscious of its sex very early. People pat the little girl's vulva, repeating an adjective for feminine beauty, and applaud the little boy's phallus with the word for "handsome male." The child is fitted into words appropriate to its caste, gestures appropriate to each ceremony, and before the child can walk, it is taught to dance with its hands. Before he can stand, the little boy, who has sat on his father's knees while his father played the *gamelan*, begins to play himself. Peeking over a house wall, one may see diminutive girls of three, sitting all alone, practicing hand gestures. The child learns to walk around a single walking rail,[2] learning that it is safe as long as it holds to this central support, in danger of falling when it loosens its hold and strays out into the unknown. When it learns to walk, its ventures away from support and parents are controlled by the mother or child nurse mimicking terror and calling it back with threats that are random in content—"Tiger!" "Policeman!" "Snake!" "Feces!"—but constant in theatrical affect, until the child learns that undefined outer space may at any moment be filled with unknown terrors.[3]

In the village, in familiar territory, the child learns the directions—*kadja*, the center of the island, where the high mountain of the gods stands; *kelod*, toward the sea, the point of least sanctity; and *kangin*, to the right, *kaoeh*, to the left, when one faces *kadja*. Every act is likely to be expressed in these terms as babies are bidden to come a little *kadja* or to brush a speck off the *kelod* side of their face, and little boys of different caste play together happily but learn that the boy of higher caste must get into bed first or sit on the *kadja* side of the food tray.

Children learn the vertical hierarchies of life—that the head, even of a casteless peasant child, is something sacred, that a flower which has fallen to the ground from an offering carried on the head may not be replaced in the offering, that those of highest caste or sanctity must be given the highest seats. As they learn to speak, they learn that the words addressed to them by their elders and superiors are never the words in which they may answer, although sometimes the lesson is imperfectly learned, and a low-caste boy will marvel at the fact that "they say Brahman parents are very polite to their children, that they say *tiang* to them," not knowing that the children must reply with an exaggeratedly more polite term, *titiang*, in which the pronoun "I" is made more self-deprecating by a stylized stutter.

From birth until long after they can walk, children live most of their waking hours in human arms, carried in a sling or on the hip, even sleeping suspended about the neck of an adult or a child nurse.[4] They learn a plastic adaptation, to take cognizance of the other's movement in limp relaxation, neither resisting nor wholly following the pounding of the rice or the game the child nurse is playing. When there is teaching to be done, the teacher uses this flaccid adaptivity and, holding the hands and body of the learner with vigorous, precise intent, twists and turns them into place or pattern.[5] Verbal directions are meager; children learn from the feel of other people's bodies and from watching, although this watching itself has a kinesthetic quality. An artist who attempts to draw a group of men will draw himself over and over again, feeling the image.

The children are everywhere. Very little babies cannot enter the temple, but the toddler is present in the midst of the most solemn ceremonial, attached to parent or grandparent, watching the blessing of the trance dancer, the throw of coins of the diviner, the killing of the fowl as exorcism. Women attending a theatrical performance carry their babies in their arms, and the front row of every performance is given over to the very small children, who watch and doze and are hastily rescued when the play threatens to break the bounds of the audience square and to involve the crowd in the plot. At the shadow play the children sit in front, and the puppet master increases the number of battles in the plot in proportion to the number of children. As the women kneel in the temple, placing the petals of a flower between their praying fingers, a flower is placed in the hands of the child who is with them. For the temple feast, small children, who at other times may run about stark naked, will appear elaborately dressed, boys in headdress and kris.

They look like dolls, and they are treated like playthings, playthings which are more exciting than fighting cocks—over which the men spend many fascinated hours—or the kites and crickets which amuse little boys. Everyone joins in the mild titillating teasing of little babies, flipping their fingers, their toes, their genitals, threatening them, playfully disregarding the sanctity of their heads, and, when the children respond by heightened excitement and mounting tension, the teaser turns away, breaks the thread of interplay, allows no climax.[6] Children learn not to respond, to resist provocation, to skirt the group of elders who would touch or snatch, to refuse the gambit when their mothers borrow babies to make them jealous. They develop an unresponsiveness to the provocative intent of others at the same time that they remain plastic to music and pattern. It is a childhood training which, if followed here, would seem dangerously certain to bring out schizoid trends in the growing child's character.

But there is one great difference between Bali and the changing Western world as we know it. In the Western world children are traumatized in childhood in ways which are new and strange, for which no ritual healing, no artistic form, exists in the culture. Those who are very gifted may become prophets, or artists, or revolutionaries, using their hurt, their made deviancy, or their innate deviancy exaggerated by adult treatment as the basis for a new religion or a new art form. Those who are not so gifted or who are less fortunate in finding a medium for their gifts go mad or dwindle away, using little even of what they have. We are beginning to recognize how damaging a trauma can be—administered by a parent who is ignorant of the world the child lives in and lived out by the child in a still different world later. The present emphasis in America is on the application of psychiatric techniques—in childhood itself—to undo the damage, take out the false stitches, relearn the abandoned stance. Our conception of life is a sequential, changing, and climactic one. So a trauma in childhood is seen as producing mental damage or intolerable yearning, which must then be solved in later life—and solved alone by the traumatized individuals.[7]

Old Bali is a striking example of a quite different solution, in which the child each day meets rituals accurately matched to the intensities and the insatiabilities which are being developed by the interplay between itself and others. Little children are not permitted to quarrel, they are not allowed to struggle over toys, or to pull and claw at each other—there are always elders there to separate them, gently, impersonally, and inexorably, and so completely that, in over two years of living in Balinese villages, I never saw two children or adolescents fight. When conflict arises, the elder child is continually told to give in to the younger; the younger, responding to the invitation of the older, is jealous of every favor and demanding of anything the elder has.

But day after day, as the child is prevented from fighting, he sees magnificent battles on the stage, and the children are part of the crowd that streams down to the river bank to duck some character in the play. He sees the elder brother—who must always be deferred to in real life—insulted, tricked, defeated, in the theater. When his mother teases him in the eerie, disassociated manner of a witch, the child can also watch the witch in the play—the masked witch wearing the accentuated symbols of both sexes, with long protruding tongue, pendulous breasts, covered with repulsive hair—watch her recurrent battle with the dragon, who in his warmer and puppy-like behavior resembles his father. He can see the followers of the dragon attack the witch and fall down in a trance, as if killed, only to be brought back

to life again by the magic healing power of the dragon.[8] These followers of the dragon, like the younger brother, go further than he will
ever dare to go in showing hostility to his mother, in open resentment
of her laughter. He sees his possible destructive wish lived out before
his eyes, but in the end no one is slain, no one is destroyed, no one is
hurt. The trancers, who have fallen into convulsions when they attack
the witch, are revived by holy water and prayers, the play ends, the
masks are taken off, the actors lay aside their golden garments for
stained workday clothes; the young men who lay twitching in convulsions half an hour ago go off singing gaily for a bath. Over and over
again, as babies in their mothers' arms, as toddlers being lifted out of
the path of a pair of dancing warriors, as members of the solemn row
of children who line the audience square, they see it happen—the play
begins, mounts to intensity, ends in ritual safety. And in the villages,
when theatrical troupes under the protection of the dragon mask,
patron of the theater and enemy of death, parade about a village in
which they have just arrived, people buy a little of the dragon's hair
as bracelets for their children to protect them from evil dreams.[9]

In this absence of change, the experience of the parent is repeated
in that of the child, and the child, a full participant in ritual and art,
is presented with the last elaborations almost with its first breath. The
people themselves treat time as a circular process rather than a progressive one, with the future ever behind one, unrolling beneath one's
feet, an already exposed but undeveloped film. Here we find a perfect
expression of the historical nature of culture, in which any separation
between cause and effect, any attempt to turn either childhood experience or adult ritual into the cause, one of the other, is seen to be a
hopeless endeavor. The two recur together, at every stage; the teased
baby of the witchlike human mother watches the witch on the stage,
and the teasing mother, even as she teases her baby, also sees the
witch, attacked, apparently destroying, but in the end doing no harm.
The effect on child and mother must both be reckoned in a round of
simultaneous events, repeating and repeating until the child in arms
again becomes a parent.

And yet, in spite of their conception of life as a circle, we may, if we
wish, break the circle—as they are unwilling to do—and, for purposes
of a type of scientific analysis born of our Western conceptions of
time, space, and causality, ask the question: What happens as babies
born to Balinese parents, equipped at birth with the same potentialities
as other human babies, learn to be Balinese? How do they make the
ritual of Balinese life part of themselves and so become as able to
dance the intricate dances, carve or play or weave or go into trance, as
did their parents or their grandparents? How do they learn to be Balinese and so perpetuate Balinese culture? This is no question which

treats Balinese culture as a mere projection from childhood experience. The themes enacted in the Balinese theater have a long history.[10] On the shadow-play screen there appear the heroes and heroines of the *Ramayana,* the great Indian epic. The witch Rangda is also the Javanese Tjalonarang, and she is also Derga, the destroyer. The dragon is found around the world—in Japan, in the streets of New York for Chinese New Year, where he blesses the local merchants whose restaurants may contain a juke box or a cigarette-vending machine. It is only in the particular details of the plots that one can find the distinctive mark of Balinese culture—in the refusal to let the witch die, in the permission to show a violence on the stage which is not permitted in real life, and in the way in which artist, actor, and priest participate in everyday life.

But children in Bali, like human children everywhere, are born helpless, dependent, and cultureless and must be bathed and fed and protected, taught to balance and to walk, to touch and to refrain from touching, to relate themselves to other people, to talk, to work, to become sure members of their own sex, and finally to marry and produce and rear children. We cannot find that which is distinctively Balinese in the mere presence of the witch and the dragon, who recur in many forms throughout the world. It is necessary to look at fine details of difference. For example, the Balinese witch has got hold of a dragon's fiery tongue—and the Balinese dragon has no tongue at all. This can be seen as a part of the way in which the witch combines all the gross, overaccentuated aspects of secondary sex characters. In the Balinese ideal physical type, both men and women are slender; male breasts are more pronounced than among us; women's breasts are high and small; hips of both sexes are closer in dimensions. Men are almost beardless, and the muscles of their arms are not developed. The witch's hairy legs and long pendulous breasts accentuate the frightening aspects of highly developed sex differences, and we find, counterpointing her, protecting the people from the illness and death she brings, and presiding with her over the theater, the dragon, a mythical creature, wearing lovely fluffy, feather-like "hair" or crow feathers sent especially by the gods. Only as the Balinese witch is contrasted with her historical predecessors and as the Balinese dragon is seen in a world perspective of other dragons, is it possible to say what is distinctively Balinese. In the same way, by placing Balinese childhood experience in a context of our knowledge of child development, we can see in what particular ways Balinese children, while repeating universal human experiences, also have special ones.

The Balinese infant has preserved a kind of neonatal flexibility, which in the children who have been studied in Western culture tends to disappear very early, so that both the way a baby relaxes in its mother's arms and the way the mother holds it are sharply contrasting to our patterns.[11] The disallowance of infancy, as adults speak in behalf of the child or press its compliant learning hands into ritual gestures, is again distinctive; and the way in which the child is constantly discouraged from walking, taught to use its right hand rather than the left, which is exposed by the carrying posture, left free to drink from its mother's breast when it chooses, as it is carried high above her high breast, but fed in a helpless prone position as a mound of prechewed food is piled on its mouth—all these details go to build the kind of Balinese personality which will be receptive to rituals danced and acted by others who have been treated in the same way. The constant provocative teasing and threatening which never reaches any but a theatrical climax, the denial of all violence and expressed hostility toward siblings, the serial experience of being the pampered baby, the displaced knee baby, and the child nurse, who, as guardian of the baby, stays to see the usurper dethroned in turn, all these form a background for the plots of ritual and theater to which the child is exposed.[12]

But there is something more here than the correspondence between childhood experience and dramatic plot, something different from the sort of cultural situation discussed by Róheim when a terrifying infantile experience—of a male child sleeping beneath the mother —is abreacted by initiation rites in adolescence.[13] In Bali the absence of sequence even in the life-span of the individual and the absence of discontinuity between ritual role and everyday role seem crucial. The artist, the dancer, the priest, is also a husbandman who tills his rice fields. Occasionally an artist becomes so famous that he lets his fingernails grow as he does no other work, and, say the Balinese, he begins to grow fat and careless and lazy, and his artistic skills decrease. The priest may stand robed in white during a ceremony, officiating at the long ritual of inviting the gods down to earth, dressing them, feeding them, bathing them, presenting them with dance and theater, and then sending them back again for another two hundred and ten days in heaven.[14] But the day after the ceremony he is a simple citizen of the village, only owing the land which he cultivates to his work on feast days as guardian of the temple.

Nor is there any gap between professional and amateur. There are virtually no amateurs in Bali, no folk dancing in which people do traditional things without responsibility to an artistic canon.[15] There are enormous differences in skill and grace and beauty of performance, but prince and peasant, very gifted and slightly gifted, all do what they do seriously and become, in turn, critical spectators, laughing with untender laughter at the technical failures of others. Between the audience that gathers to watch the play and the players there is always the bond of professional interest, as the audience criticizes the way the actor or actress who plays the princess postures or sings, rather than identifying with her fate—however lost she may be in some dense theatrical forest.

Nor is there any gap between rehearsal and performance. From the moment an orchestra begins to practice an old piece of music, there is a ring of spectators, aspiring players, substitute players, small boys, and old men, all equally engrossed in the ever fresh creation of a new way of playing an old piece of music.[16] Where in Java the shadow-play screen divided men from women, the women seeing only the faint shadow on the screen, the men the brightly painted figures, in Bali people can sit on either side, in front to watch the finished play, behind—and this is where little boys prefer to sit—to watch the individual designs on the figures and the deft hands of the puppet master. When a village club decides to learn a new play—a play in which the main serious parts are traditional and the parts of clowns, servants, and incidental characters are all improvised, never set, even in consecutive performances—half the village attends the rehearsals, enjoys the discussions of costume, the sharp words of the visiting virtuoso come to teach a dance step, the discovery of some new talent among the actors. In the rectangular piece of ground which becomes a four-sided stage as the audience gathers around it, isolated pairs of curtains borrowed from a theater with a quite different style of handling surprise may be set up near each end. The actors, their crowns a little askew, sit in almost full view dozing behind these curtains or among the audience, and then, as they make their appearance, part the curtain for a prolonged stylized "entrance," from which they later return to their full visibility offstage.[17] People advance from the audience to pin up a dancer's fallen scarf, and dramatic scenes of chase and conquest will be pursued into the midst of the audience.

Thus in Bali the ritual world of art and theater and temple is not a world of fantasy, an endless recurrent daydream, or a new set of daydreams woven from the desperations of the gifted of each generation. It is rather a real world of skill and application—a world in which members of a dance club scheme to get money for the gold of a new headdress or to buy new instruments for the orchestra; where long hours are spent in the basic work of learning to dance; where disciplined hands and wrists and eyes that click to one side in perfect time to the music, are all the result of continuous, although relaxed, rather dreamy, work. And the temple feasts, where many of these activities combine to make a great spectacle, are called appropriately "the work of the Gods."

Children have not only the precocious postural participation in prayer and offering, dance and music, but also a whole series of parallel participations. A little boy will be given bamboo clappers with which to imitate the clapping of the dragon's tongueless jaws and, covered by his mother's cloth shawl—the same shawl with which the witch will dance in the play and which she will carry in her arms as if it were a baby—goes about clapping in imitation of the dragon. In the nonceremonial seasons, when life is a little less crowded, secular dance clubs go about with a tinkly orchestra, which has a hurdy-gurdy quality, and a little girl dancer, who dances with the young men of the village and, in between, dances as the witch, combining the beautiful ballet of the witch's disciples with being the witch herself and placing her foot firmly on the neck of a doll, enacting her role of bringing death.[18]

Children stay in a deep resistant sleep during a childbirth in their houses, a sleep from which it is necessary to shake them awake, lest they see the witches which may come to kill the child. But the same children participate with delight in the play in which the witch child, after stealing a doll, born of a man and dressed as a woman, is chased up a tree or into a near-by stream. Children make puppets of banana leaf and parody the puppet master, especially the puppet master who performs with puppets in the daytime, whose screen has shrunk to a single line of thread. They draw in the sand with twigs while master artists work at little shallow wooden tables. And children may form clubs of their own, make their own dragon and witch, and progress about the village, collecting pennies for further finery for the masks.[19]

If one follows these activities carefully, notes the expressions on the children's faces at different kinds of ceremonies, follows the same child on different occasions, and watches the play in which the children think they are reproducing the full theatricals, one begins to get clues to the dynamic mechanisms by which the children, born human like all other human children, become such very different people from other people—as Balinese. The mother who teases her child—who borrows a baby to provoke its jealousy, although preventing any expression of jealousy of a real sibling; who borrows a baby to set on its head, although at the same time protecting its head from real insult—has learned that all this is a safe game. When she watches the witch dance and watches the men and women who have gone into trance and are slow in coming out, she watches with the same relaxed enjoyment or ready criticism for some ritual or technical defect with which she watches the trance dance in which children dance as goddesses. But the child, teased into a violent temper, screaming and clawing to get the borrowed baby away from his mother's breast, has not yet learned that all this is safe. In his intensity and grief, in his fervent acceptance of his mother's theatrical amends for a real hurt, he still shows a capacity for hurt which will not be manifest later. Even as he withdraws from the recurrently disappointing sequences which have no climax, he learns to trust the arts, and he learns to avoid hurting responsiveness to human stimulation.[20]

The faces of the children who watch the trance dance in which little girls replace dancing wooden puppets—and as child dancers are indulged by their parents and wilful in their demands—are as relaxed as their parents' faces. But during the witch dance the children's faces are strained and anxious.[21] When the witch dances or when some woman worshiper in the temple is possessed by the witch, the fingers are flexed backward in a gesture of fear, spoken of as *kapar*—the gesture made by a baby falling or a man falling from a tree—for the witch is both frightening and afraid, the picture of Fear itself.[22] But when children play the witch, especially when they play her without benefit of costume or music or any of the elements which accompany the finished ritual, their hands are bent like claws, and they threaten an attack in witchlike gestures which can be found in many parts of the world. When the young men, who, as followers of the dragon, fall down before the witch's magic, thrust their daggers against their breasts, they thrust them in response to an intolerable itching feeling in their breasts—a possible reciprocal to the mother's breast during the period when they were so teased, provoked, and given only theatrical climaxes.

When Balinese children are frightened of strangers or strange situations, their elders shout at them, "Don't show fear!" and they learn not to run but to stand stock still, often with their hands pressed over their eyes.[23] In situations of danger or uncertainty—during childbirth in a tiny one-room house, after an accident for which one may be blamed—children and older people also fall into a deep sleep from which it is hard to rouse them.

The Balinese move easily in a group. A whole village may make a pilgrimage of two or three days to make offerings at the seaside or in the high mountains. A troupe of Balinese went to the Paris Exposition in 1931, and a troupe visited New York in 1952. But one Balinese, isolated from those he knows and taken to a strange place, wilts and sickens; people say it is because he is *paling*—disoriented—the word used for trance, insanity, for being drunk, confused, or lost. And the Balinese are mortally afraid of drunkenness, where the clues to the directions, the calendar, the caste system, the framework of life—which gives safety as the walking rail gave it to the little child who learned how dangerous it was to venture away from it—are lost or blurred.

Following the children as they grow up reveals that, even within the simultaneity of ritual satisfaction and individual fear, the capacity to enjoy such rituals, to dance the lovely dances and fill the air with music, has been—in the case of the Balinese—developed at certain

PLATE I. *Children and Ritual in Bali. I*

FIG. 1.—A group of children watching the two-man *barong* mask which is circling the village.
Bajoeng Gede, May 18, 1937. 8-Z-35

FIG. 2.—I Pantos wearing a toy mask made of coconut shell.
Bajoeng Gede, May 21, 1937. 9-D-32

FIG. 3.—I Karsa playing at being the *barong* by putting a mat over his head.
Bajoeng Gede, May 25, 1937. 9-J-31

PLATE II. *Children and Ritual in Bali. II*

Fig. 1.—At the beginning of the Tjalonarang play, conflict between *barong* (dragon) and *ran* (witch), the witch appears as still mortal, already wearing part of her costume of h legs, pendulous breasts, and long fingern Pagoetan, December 16, 1937. 20-F-16

Fig. 2.—Instructed by the witch, *sisiers*, her girl apprentic dance. The parts are played either preadolescent girls boys.
Pagoetan, December 16, 19 20-E-21

Fig. 3.—Witch and apprentices appear in their supern ral masked form.
Pagoetan, December 1937. 20-H-28

PLATE III. *Children and Ritual in Bali.* IV

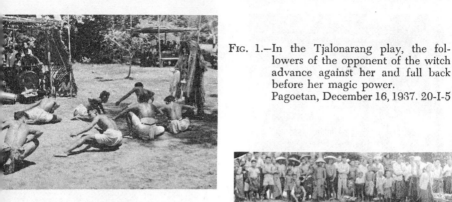

FIG. 1.—In the Tjalonarang play, the followers of the opponent of the witch advance against her and fall back before her magic power.
Pagoetan, December 16, 1937. 20-I-5

FIG. 2.—After attacking the witch, who does not resist them, they fall down in deep trance and are then arranged in rows to be revived by the dragon.
Pagoetan, December 16, 1937. 20-I-21

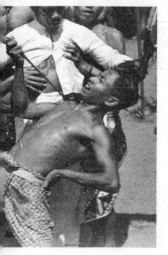

FIG. 3.—Revived into a somnambulistic state, the trancers turn their krisses against their own breasts. Here a priest, himself in trance, attempts to calm such a trancer.
Denjalan, May 26, 1936. 1-K-1

FIG. 4.—After the kris dance, the trancers are restored to their everyday selves with incense and holy water.
Denjalan, November 23, 1936. 3-I-8

PLATE IV. *Children and Ritual in Bali.* IV

FIG. 1.—I Renoe, a girl trance dancer, in trance, waiting to have her headdress put on.
Bajoeng Gede, May 26, 1937. 9-O-1

FIG. 2.—I Renoe, at an earlier performance of the same ceremony, as her headdress is arranged by two members of the club.
Bajoeng Gede, July 13, 1936. 2-A-15

FIG. 3.—I Misi, I Renoe's dancing partner, in trance, dancing supported on the shoulders of a male member of the club.
Bajoeng Gede, May 26, 1937. 9-O-32

FIG. 4.—I Renoe, the trance dancer, as an ordinary little girl caring for a neighbor's baby.
Bajoeng Gede, June 6, 1937. 11-K-25

PLATE V. *Children and Ritual in Bali.* V

FIG. 1.—12-A-9

FIG. 2.—12-A-10

FIG. 3.—12-A-11

ee scenes from a dance in which a *djoget,* an itinerant little girl dancer, dances for
village men and boys. Here she is caricaturing, within a coquettish dance, the be-
or of the witch in playing out a teasing game with a doll which she will finally
" with a witchlike gesture.

get from Malat in Bajoeng Gede, June 27, 1937

PLATE VI. *Children and Ritual in Bali. VI*

FIG. 1.—Children watching the performance of part of a cremation ritua
Batoean, September 27, 1937. 16-C-13

FIG. 2.—Two children participating in
the ceremonial sweeping of the
courtyard during the cremation
ritual.
Batoean, October 5, 1937.
16-N-26

FIG. 3.—Little girls playing at pr
in the midst of a dram
re-enactment of the crema
ceremonies.
Batoean, October 7, 1937
16-V-21

costs. The culture contains—or did contain until the recent upheavals about which we know little—ritual solutions for the instabilities it created, and the people, on their little island, were safe. But it was the safety of a tightrope dancer, beautiful and precarious.

NOTES

1. *Karba's First Years* (film); Bateson and Mead, 1942, Pl. 100, Figs. 1 and 2. References are listed alphabetically in the Balinese bibliography which appears on pp. 95–98.
2. Bateson and Mead, 1942, Pl. 17, Figs. 1 and 2; Mead and Macgregor, 1951, Pl. XXVI, Fig. 7, and Pl. LII, Fig. 3.
3. *Karba's First Years* (film); Bateson and Mead, 1942, pp. 30–32 and Pl. 46.
4. Bateson and Mead, 1942, Pl. 79; Mead and Macgregor, 1951, Pl. XVII.
5. *Karba's First Years* (film); Bateson and Mead, 1942, Pl. 16.
6. *Karba's First Years* (film); Bateson and Mead, 1942, p. 32, and Pls. 47–49.
7. Mead, 1940*a*.
8. *Trance and Dance in Bali* (film); Bateson and Mead, 1942, pp. 34–35, and Pls. 55–58.
9. Mead, 1939*c*.
10. Belo, 1949; McPhee, 1936.
11. Mead and Macgregor, 1951, Pls. XXXIX–XLI.
12. Mead, 1947.
13. G. Róheim, 1934. *The Riddle of the Sphinx* (London: Hogarth Press and Institute of Psychoanalysis). (Not listed in Balinese bibliography.)
14. Belo, 1953.
15. Mead, 1941–42; McPhee, 1948.
16. McPhee, 1946.
17. Mead, 1939*c*.
18. Bateson and Mead, 1942, Pls. 60–62.
19. McPhee, 1947.
20. Bateson and Mead, 1942.
21. *Trance and Dance in Bali* (film).
22. *Ibid.*; Bateson and Mead, 1942, Pl. 62.
23. Bateson and Mead, 1942, Pl. 67.

CHAPTER 5

Balinese Children's Drawing

———JANE BELO

This paper was originally prepared for the Cultural Congress organized by the Java Instituut, the first conference to bring together in Bali scholars from other specialized areas of Indonesia. The congress was held in October, 1937. The paper was published in Djawa, *publication of the Java Instituut, Nos. 5 and 6 (1937) and has been re-edited for a Western audience.*

Balinese art has a style and a character of its own. The artists are numerous and prolific, distinguished by the patience and efficiency of their craftsmanship and by their extreme faithfulness to an artistic tradition. Unlike Western artists, they seem to try to produce works conforming as nearly as possible to the patterns used by their fellow-artists. Any individuality in the artist is not stressed, as it is with us, but rather the contrary. If any works which show an unusual vision, a touch of originality, are produced, it would seem that they have come about through the agency of an artist's particular gifts, not by intention, but, as it were, in spite of his effort to make them like everyone else's. In all the aspects of the plastic arts in Bali, in painting, in sculpture, in the design of the puppets of the shadow play and the carving of masks, the similarity to a traditional form is strikingly apparent.

From the past there remain a sufficient number of objects to show that, although the classical styles changed from century to century, each period was characterized by a set of conventions to which the artist adhered, much as they did in Europe during Gothic times—and not since then—without showing any desire to make each his statement in terms which he might call his own. And even today, when various "modern" movements are growing up in the Balinese arts, the tendency of the great mass of the artists seems to be toward perfecting themselves in the technique of the new conventions rather than in any effort to create a personal idiom. Although the motivation for the artistic production of these modern schools appears radically at variance with that of the classic periods, the same tendency toward uniformity rather than toward differentiation is to be remarked. The talented Balinese of modern times seems as willing to turn his abilities into those of a craftsman, who copies and recopies the accepted motifs in the accepted manner, as were his grandfather and his great-grandfather who dwelt under the rule of the rajahs.

Where there exists this readiness to follow a set of conventions, the artist is provided with a short cut in the learning of his trade. Very possibly the great number of Balinese artists and the quantity of their output are due to the simplification of their problem by the very rigidity of the artistic tradition. It would seem that less talented individuals can make more presentable pictures, and more of them, under such a scheme. We are not here concerned with the ultimate aesthetic value of the product but with the fact that the arts thrive in Bali. And whatever their starting point, whatever the influences acting upon them, they turn out to be characteristically Balinese.

Because the artist in Bali functions under conditions which are foreign to the Western world, it should be of interest to investigate the beginnings of the effect on him of his cultural tradition. The Balinese child is already subject to the conditions of his culture; he is learning the meaning of the symbols, learning to adopt a special attitude toward the arts. He will grow up into a Balinese adult, who practices the arts or who is audience for them—in Bali the arts are everybody's business, not the affair of a restricted few. Through the medium of children's drawings, I would inquire into the manner of transmission of the tradition. How does the child absorb its influences? How does he learn to wish to draw things, not as he himself would like to draw them, but as his society is accustomed to seeing them drawn?

Some years ago I was asked to collect a number of drawings by Balinese children of from four to ten years, to be shown in an international exhibition of children's drawings. In those days, before the movement for free drawing in the schools had been instituted, the school children were directed to draw tables, cupboards, and lamps. I was therefore forced to seek out children who had never had paper or pencil in their hands. Nevertheless, the drawings which these children produced, when they were exhibited in New York in 1934, attracted a great deal of attention from artists and educators. There were numerous notices in the press, stating that the work of the Balinese children, with that of the Mexican children, outdistanced in interest the work from the various European and American countries represented. The qualities in these drawings which made them stand out from the work of other children were the strict stylization of the forms, the dramatic portrayal of demons, witches, and mythological beasts with gaping mouths and glaring eyes, the decisiveness of the line, and the free and spontaneous recklessness of composition, combining uproarious action with a balanced, if rudimentary, sense of design.

In comparing the work of Balinese children with that of Western children whom I have observed (working under free conditions, outside the old-fashioned schools), my impression was that the drawings of these children did not differ up to about four years of age, but that very soon after this the tendencies characteristic of the culture began to show themselves. Very little children, the world over, like to draw. When they are undirected, they take the pencil in their hands and let it run over the page, describing mysterious shapes meaningful only to the child himself. At the same time they may tell themselves stories, whose content is not to be recognized from the representations on the page, yet which will often be found to be reducible to common terms. To the child, the lack of representational value of his drawing seems to matter not at all; the pleasure is in the drawing and the telling of the tale. As the child's skill develops, the forms which he draws assume a likeness to the subjects of his story, but the affective basis for the symbolism strongly persists and remains the most significant part of the drawing to him. Later, among children whom I have observed, the child began to be conscious of his drawing as a thing-in-itself, a symbolic rendering of a certain content, which should be interpretable by others as well as himself. At this time, if his advancement in skill had not kept pace with his development of social consciousness, the richness of his fantasy was cramped by his inability to render it. Still later, certain children found their results so unsatisfying that they stopped drawing altogether. Then they had lost the joy of creating with which they began.

I should suppose that, in any culture in which the arts are practiced and which therefore possesses a standard for a modicum of skill, it would be at this time in the development of the child or in the development of any artist that the traditional conventions come most forcibly to his aid. They would provide a key to his problem of representation. The ready-made symbolism, already significant to his audience, can be a mold into which he pours his fantasy. It is probable that this assistance helps over an obstacle a great many potential artists who would have dropped out of the race, had they been required (as they are in Western culture) to find a symbolic language of their own. Does a culture possessing such a tradition produce for this reason a more uniform art and a greater number of artists than one which demands individualism? To throw light upon this question, I instituted an experiment dealing with the drawings of Balinese children, in order to ascertain at what point and in what way the effects of the artistic tradition begin to make themselves felt.

The subjects of this experiment were a group of children, twenty in all, ranging in age from three to ten years. They lived in the undistinguished village of Sajan (District Gianjar), Bandjar Koetoeh, which possessed neither a professional puppet master nor a professional painter. Not one of the little boys who drew—and, true to Balinese custom, they were all boys—had a father or an elder brother whose business it was to paint or to carve or to cut out in leather the wajang puppets. They were therefore not in a position to observe directly the practice of Balinese techniques or to serve an apprenticeship from an early age, as do the children in the households of master-craftsmen. They were not more closely in touch with the Balinese cultural background than the children of the average village, unrenowned for elaborate temple-carving or for wall decorations. But they shared with the rest of Bali the all-pervading artistry of Balinese life, which underlies and makes coherent all the varied manifestations of the arts. The same stories which are depicted in color or in relief are acted out in the plays; they recur in formal dancing and, most important of all, in the representations of the shadow play, from which a preponderance of the conventions are derived. When there are temple festivals or private rituals celebrated with a dramatic performance or when at New Year season the streets are gay with roaming dragons and bands of wandering players, the children attend en masse. And especially at shadow-play performances, the children constitute the most devoted and enthusiastic section of the audience. Certainly for the children of the village in question, the shadow play was the chief medium through which they were initiated into their heritage, a knowledge of the legends and the distinctive characterizations of the major roles.

The shadow play is the form of visual entertainment which the children see most often, a form of storytelling which has a special intensity for them. It takes place at night. In the darkness of the village, a screen of white cloth is set up, and behind this screen an oil-burning lamp is lighted, which illuminates the oblong of space upon which the pictured performance will take place, and yet which flickers, flares up in a passing breeze, and sends out eddies of light which lend to the picture a magical quality of life. Upon this focused rectangle of light the figures who are to enact the play appear as shadows, cut in sharp silhouette as they are held by the performer between the light and the screen, or wavering and flowing in outline and in movement as he passes them to and fro in such a manner as to indicate action upon the stage which the screen defines. The figures which cast the shadows are small in scale, a foot to eighteen inches or so in height, and cut out of stiff leather to a sharp and highly stylized outline. Perforations in the leather allow the delineation of the features, the details of the dress, and especially of the elaborate headdress, which, with the character of the features, serves to identify the figure. Quite a number of the figures recur in different series of plays: various heroes of the Hindu mythology, some well-known demons, monkey princes, and other fearsome forms and, with these, some well-beloved stock characters who belong to and speak the language of the people, translating for the audience the sense of the more abstruse passages and lending an earthy commentary to all that transpires. All these characters become in time familiar to the playgoer, and the children quite early learn to distinguish the finely drawn and delicately noble heroes from the large-mouthed, threatening demon figures and the more robust, crude-featured outlines of the comics.

The shadow play is called *wajang koelit* throughout Indonesia, *wajang* meaning "shadow," and *koelit* meaning "leather," referring to the material of which the puppets are made. The word *wajang* in Bali may refer to the performance itself or to the figures. An individual figure drawn in the characteristic style of the *wajang* is spoken of as a *wajang* and is distinguished from figures drawn with a more realistic intention, which are spoken of as representing "men" (*djelema*). Historically, the shadow play had a ceremonial significance and served to portray the stories from the Hindu literature, recounting the epic episodes believed to have actually occurred in the past and in this manner ritually bringing to life the ancestral personages of the Hinduistic genealogical line. Thus though the connection of present-day men with the events of this early past was remote, it was nonetheless of a piece with their history and their religion. And perhaps the word "shade" as it is used in English to refer to the departed spirits, and especially to the spirits of departed heroes, comes nearest to a translation of the word *wajang* in Indonesia, with its manifold connotations. The shadow puppet and the shadow play are the medium through which the invisible world is made tenuously visible; the *shade* itself, without the interposition of the dramatic medium impossible to visualize, becomes formalized in the mind's eye as a characteristic shape.

To the children this conventionalization of the forms of the heroes, the demonic figures, and the favorite clowns offers an acceptable patterning for their developing fantasy. It is a parallel influence to that which picture-books have had upon our children in the past and that television is having upon them at the present time. The Balinese children show evidence in their drawings of the influence of shadow play in three major directions. The wajang characters themselves are the subjects of the drawings, selected as more lively in the imagination and more technically precise in pattern than ordinary "men." The scene of the drawings is very often an action picture, as if there were an attempt to fix upon the page a scene of battle or the climax of a dangerous situation, taken from the more animated passages of the shadow-play performances.

In the mass of the children's drawings it is possible to point out a great number which portray a "typical wajang scene," that is, a scene in which the two sides in a contest are set in opposition to each other. Although the child's drawing freezes the moment of action, it is a scene of animated combat or of the opposition of the forces of good and evil in a moment of confrontation which is selected for representation. The action itself is rendered by means of certain conventions derived from the structure of the wajang puppets, the elongated arms (which are movable in the puppets) appearing at full stretch, caught in the hurling of a weapon or in a threatening gesture. The feet of the puppets are immovable, placed one before the other and in profile, and in this feature also the children's drawings reproduce the puppets, rendering considerably less movement of the feet than of the arms. The puppeteer's custom of bringing the puppets in from the side of the screen and across the scene, either at the base or halfway up the screen, to represent walking or flying, also finds its counterpart in the children's rendering, and the figures in motion may appear in the child's drawing anywhere on the page, from the base line to the upper corners. Because of this carrying-over from the dramatic into the plastic medium, a certain turbulence is to be remarked as a characteristic of the children's composition; there is balance, often a marked symmetry, a tendency to fill the page, and beyond this a tendency to compress into the picture the action of a heroic scene, at times the sequence in a saga leading up to and including the moment of climax. It is as if it were not possible to put in the picture all the action of the moment portrayed without including a bit of what went before. There is no sense of the static in these pictures, and, in so far as the composition itself is concerned, it is from the influence of the wajang play that this attribute of the drawings is derived.

I estimated that the children saw an average of eight to ten wajang performances a year. Attendance begins when the child is still a baby in arms, and I knew many a three-year-old who could stay awake throughout most of the night watching the play. From this, most magical of storytelling means, the children learned to recognize Ardjoena, Bhima, Toealen, Merdah, Sangoet, Delem, Hanoman, Rawana, and so on, and to associate with each his characteristic headdress, profile, shape of eye, and stretch of mouth. As the familiar characters appear and reappear upon the screen, the sharp lines of the silhouette fix themselves in the child's mind, the more easily remembered because of the rigid conventional forms to which each puppet must be cut. The motion of the puppets is limited and also stylized. Their only movable parts are the jointed arms, which may be extended or bent at the elbow, and the lower jaw of the most talkative characters. Often, to create an illusion of action, the puppet master passes the puppets rapidly across the screen or slaps them back and forth against each other, for a fight, in good old Punch and Judy style. The children evidently become accustomed to this manner of representing action in a simplified way and to the sudden appearance of mythical serpents, giant birds, gods, or nymphs flying in the sky and the hurtling to and fro of the strange-shaped weapons.

If one is familiar with the shadow play, one can trace many of the compositional elements in the children's drawings to scenes and arrangements occurring in the wajang: the position of the arms, the setting of two figures in opposition to each other, the appearance of others hovering in the air, the filling of space with weapons in flight. The special attention given to the headdress is due to wajang influence, since it is chiefly by the headdress that a great many specific characters are identified, while others are recognized as belonging to a certain category, "holy men," "demon," "warriors," etc. From wajang, too, comes the children's disregard for feet, which they often leave out of the picture, just as in wajang they are off the screen—strikingly out of accordance with the usual precise *mise en page* of these children's drawings. If the course of the play were consistently as violent as in the battle scenes, no one would have much chance to concentrate upon the conventional forms. But they include many long and rather static passages in which nothing much happens. Through these the child sits patiently, at times dropping off to sleep without leaving his place in the audience. Possibly the long hours of attendance, sometimes lasting throughout the night, serve to impress upon the child the outline and the detail associated with each character, the names of heroes, demons, and evil spirits, and the roles attributed to them. We will see later how the little children begin to give wajang names to the figures in their drawings even before they are able to attempt, in line, the depiction of their favorites. And this mythological infiltration into their fantasy occurs at a stage when Balinese children, like other children anywhere, are still drawing, in vague amorphous shapes, puppy dogs with little ones inside, snakes, "men," or birds with droppings.

The world beyond reality, the world of the supernatural and of creatures of the fancy, seems to be present with intensity to the Balinese child. A world of unreality exists for him, and the conventionalized figures of the shadow play offer a visible model for these creatures of the invisible world. Supernaturals, heroes, witches, and animal forms, handed down to the child by his culture, become easily mixed with those which his own fancy may spontaneously call up, and the culturally stylized patterns offer him a symbolic language for expression. The mythological characters are loved, feared, and thought about, I believe, with the same sort of feeling as our children have for Cinderella or for Peter Rabbit. But, because they have a very definite, unalterable, concrete shape, because they may actually be seen, time after time, against the magic screen and be heard to speak, they take on a conviction of reality with which no story-book character is imbued. Perhaps the nearest rival of Bhima and Merdah in the Western world would be Mickey Mouse, who also lives upon a screen and every detail of whose fascinating anatomy is delightfully familiar. If

Mickey Mouse meant to the adults what the wajang characters mean to the Balinese, if he were a figure believed to have existed in the past which their ancestors knew, who conversed in those not-so-remote times with the gods they honor to this day, if he appeared again and again in the paintings and bas-reliefs which decorate the temples, if, in short, he were a character as closely integrated with the life of an entire people as the wajang characters are with the life of the Balinese, then he might be expected to take hold on and to dominate with steadily increasing persistence the artistic trend of the child's development, as do the wajangs.

And in Bali there is not one "Mickey Mouse" but a score or more of figures familiar to the children—some brave, some fierce, some jolly, and some beautiful to behold. There are heroes and demons, horrifying enemies who burst out at one in dangerous places, and brothers who come to the rescue when one is in a difficult situation. Thus the wajang provides the Balinese child with a whole gallery of puppets for the play of his own fantasy. Later I will show with what freedom the young child adapts these characters to his ends; for if he introduces them fully formed into his picture, he does not by any means remain faithful to the plots and situations which classic purity would require. It is, however, not unusual for adults in Bali to take great liberties with their classics, to revise and extend the well-known tales, and a lively and not very erudite puppet master or a group of actors often play out an unorthodox story with the stock characters. The child shares this tendency with his elders. But little by little, as his knowledge increases, he makes his characters more true to their traditional prototypes and to the roles assigned to them in legend.

The vivid unrealities of the Balinese child's world are taken not only from wajang. There are also hordes of evil spirits, the witches, malevolent spirits of trees and rivers, the frightful beasts which infest lonely places and whose pleasure it is, everyone knows, to devour the defenceless *djelema* ("person," "human being," in contradistinction to *wajangs*, "gods, demons, and spirits"). The life of the little boys keeps them a great deal of the time outside the safe limits of the village. They drive the cattle out into the fields, cut grass for them in lonely places, lead them for their bath, perhaps, to some deep and gloomy ravine, where the water flows mysteriously out from the ground and in under the choking, tangled foliage, to disappear in a dark cave. These are the sites which Balinese fancy has peopled with a host of grotesque and fearsome spirits of whom even the adults stand in dread. Grown men whisper to one another that a tiger is not a mere tiger but a sorcerer who has taken that form, the better to eat up his prey. Young mothers carry charms to protect themselves and their newborn infants from the evil spirits which might attack them when they go to the river to bathe. The adults are genuinely afraid for themselves. But they also cheerfully use fear of these bugaboos to frighten their children into caution, to keep them in order. Fear of the supernatural can be so intensely felt by the Balinese that he is rendered speechless and turns greenly pale. But when the danger is not imminent, he likes to play with it, to summon up a Grand Guignol situation, to laugh and shudder at once, like a child saying "Boo!" to himself on a dark stair. The Balinese, as a people, love to make fun with fright. They love to relate, to re-enact and dramatize, some terrifying episode from their own experience or from some legendary or factitious source. That is why the little boy's fancy will dwell with persistence upon strange creatures, and why the big-mouthed, long-toothed monsters, in demonic or in animal form, devouring or anxious to devour, recur again and again as the subjects of his drawings.

It is possible that the whole feeling of the Balinese toward these exponents of the powers of evil is condensed and crystallized in the masked figures of the *barong* and the *rangda*—the former commonly representing a gaping-mouthed lion, tiger, or wild boar, the latter a witch, whose wild hair reaches to the ground and from whose tusked jaws dangles a long red tongue. They are dancing figures which may play alone or may take part in a drama. They exist in thousands of Balinese villages, honored often as demigods, and performances by them may be interpreted as an exorcism of the powers of evil. Here again we find a concrete and stylized form given to what we would term "unreality," turning it into visible reality. So that when *barongs* and *rangdas* appear in the drawings of the children, we must consider that they may be, not representations of the reality of a performance, but a repetition of the symbol for all that is mysterious and magical and frightening in the dream world of the child. Indeed, in some cases it is impossible to distinguish a child's rendering of a *rangda* from that of a *tonja*, an animistic spirit, not a "character" of the plays. The child has never seen a *tonja*, but he has heard much of them. Therefore, when he draws one, he may give to it the formalized shape of the *rangda*, as an equivalent. (It may be noted that adult Balinese do likewise in their drawings.) Apparently, the child responds in the same way to the performance of *rangdas* and *barongs* as he does to the *wajang*, taking over from them a stylized pattern for the representation of some underlying emotion for which they also stand. In other words, when he witnesses a performance, he may be said to be verifying with his own eyes the existence, the living aspect, of that in which he already believes.

My observations of the drawings of children were undertaken with the idea of clarifying the way in which their style develops, the way in which they adapt the ready-made symbolic patterns of their culture for the expression of their own fantasies.

CONTROLLED OBSERVATION

It was necessary for the children to draw at my house, so that they might be observed and also to prevent cheating in the form of assistance from their elders. My observations covered a period of three months. One hundred and seventy-three drawings were made by a total of twenty children. For purposes of convenience I have divided them into groups according to approximate age as in the accompanying table.

	Group A	Group B	Group C	Group D
Age (years)	9–10	7–8	5–6	3–4
No. of children	7	5	4	4

They were all boys. (The girls of this village persistently refused to draw.) The children in Group C had just lost their first teeth, those in Group D were a year or so younger. They did not draw separately according to these groups, for they came to draw when they pleased, with greater or less regularity. One child made fifty-four drawings, another twenty-five, others no more than two or three. As a rule, the more talented turned up more frequently; but there were also two bigger boys who drew with no more skill than a six-year-old but who were most devoted in attendance. Two of the children had been to school, but, as they had no particular talent, the school influence had not spread over from them to the other members of the group. Rather the contrary was the case.

No pressure was put upon the children to draw, other than the attraction of the pennies which they received for their pains. The work was done on a commission basis. I provided the materials— pencil, pen, or brush, occasionally colors. The paper given them was of big size, 60 × 80 cm., and they were allowed to subdivide it if they wished. The subjects were not suggested to them. They drew what they pleased, and when they were done, they told me the "story," often more remarkable than the drawing. The artist then received a penny or two and departed to cut grass for his cow. Rarely did he ask to see again one of his former works.

The children took an interest in one another's drawings at the time of making them, admired the more proficient, but often admitted that they liked their own the best. We pinned up on the wall, from time to time, examples of the work of all ages, done in various media. New boys, who were strangers to the house, often came to see what was going on. They stared for a few moments at the children's drawings on the wall, then asked for paper and popped themselves down with utter confidence to make drawings of their own. I did not observe any instance of the direct taking-over by the new boy of subject matter from the drawings on the wall. Subjects already treated by one boy might recur days later in the drawings of another, but in quite a different style so that it was not clear how much of their influence on each other was carried over through time. On the wall hung two works by adult Balinese, the one a modern drawing of two warriors, the other a painting of mythological beasts in classical style. Neither was directly copied by the children in any of the four groups. I will describe later how one of the children seemed to learn an anatomical point from the old painting, indirectly, through the intermediacy of another child.

Contagion in subject matter often occurred from one work in progress to another. This applies to decorative motif as well as to content. If one child had introduced a wavy line along the edge of his picture, several more working at the same time would take up the idea and add a similar motif to their own drawings at the top, the bottom, or the sides of the page, afterward interpreting them variously as "mountains," "sky," "road," "coral in the sea," "the edge of the grass," or "irrigation dams in the rice fields." A child of Group B, Gandir, when he had drawn one threatening figure on his page, looked over at Loengsoer (Group A), who had balanced such a threatening figure with a demon, and placed a tree in the center of the battle. Gandir's drawing, when finished, contained a witch (equivalent to a demon) and a tree arranged in the same pattern as Loengsoer's, worked in with his own material, a fisherman, dogs, pigs, etc. In the design the relation of the witch and the tree to his original figure is similar to Loengsoer's, although in technique and in content the drawings are dissimilar. Again, three boys simultaneously produced drawings unlike in design and in characterization but representing the idea *metapa*, ascetic meditation. Two of the nine-year-olds took to pinning their papers on a single drawing board, the edges contiguous. In this position they several times produced drawings so nearly identical, in design, subject, and style, that had I not seen them at work, I should not have known to which child to attribute either drawing. As the skill of these two when working individually was equal and as each seemed to work with equal concentration and attentiveness, without stopping to inspect the other's drawing, one can only consider the influence they exerted upon each other as reciprocal and wonder at the harmony of their common effort. (It is not uncommon to see adult Balinese working in unison on a decorative motif, as, for instance, when two carvers begin at either end of a strip of wall to cut out, without the use of any preliminary sketch, a conventionalized pattern which will join and be continuous when they meet in the center.)

In the interplay of influences between the children, we had cases where the form had been taken over—with or without content—content without form, or the two in combination, producing, when the children had reached the same level of technical development, an almost identical result. Another sort of infectiousness ran through the series, that of purely verbal association, without regard either to form or to content. Dr. Margaret Mead called my attention to this occurrence in her observations of Balinese mountain children, who say "this is a *barong*" when another child announces that he is drawing a *barong*, even though the form may be the same as that which was called a "cake" on a former occasion. Among my children this sort of association occurred most noticeably in the naming of the characters, so that if one child had drawn a more or less recognizable Sangoet, Hanoman, or Bhima, well-known characters from the shadow play, a number of amorphous figures on the pages of other children would be dignified with these names from wajang when the time came for telling the story. Again, a child who was dissatisfied with his drawing might affirm that his not very successful tiger was intended to be a pig. The story told afterward was for this reason not a fair test of what the child had in mind during the actual drawing.

Taken all together, the reciprocal influences between the children produced a "style" to which new members entering the group tended to conform. The children had a common background of experience, and to all of them the materials they used were unfamiliar. Under these conditions, certain individuals stand out as more talented than others. But no one or two could be said to dominate the group, to exert an influence upon it with a force comparable to that of the trend toward uniformity which came about through the interaction of the whole group and which bore upon all its members.

It was evident, as the number of drawings piled up, that shadow-play subjects would be found to predominate. A count of the drawings of Groups A, B, and C over the three months showed 65 per cent which could fairly be classified as wajang drawings because of the clear attempt of the child to depict a wajang scene. The proportion of wajang to non-wajang varied with the individual child; one member of Group A drew 72 per cent wajangs, another only 43 per cent. Of those in Group B who drew sufficiently frequently to make a proportional count of value, one drew 75 per cent wajangs. Not included in this count are the pictures which attempted realistic representation, into which a single wajang figure or detail has crept, or those in which no formal representation of wajangs has been attempted but to which names of wajang characters are given. I have included, however, the pictures predominantly of wajang scenes, to which have been added subsidiary motifs from real life. It is to be noted that, except in the cases of unusual children, even the realistic figures approximate wajang drawing and differ from it chiefly in the lack of a crisp decisive pattern on which the forms are modeled. Whenever possible, the children seemed to find it easier and more satisfactory to represent their subject through the use of a convention already fixed by the culture, and they often drew rocks, trees, even the familiar kris, in a manner taken over from the wajang "properties" or from paintings or temple-carvings which they had seen.

The smaller children, Groups C and D, were more likely to mix indiscriminately wajangs with a rendering of real life. A five-year-old drew a motorcar with a full-fledged wajang, complete with crown and trappings, at the wheel. The car is being "stopped" by another wajang. Below this scene appear four other figures, three mortal and one wajang. Two are doing battle between themselves while the other two, said the child, are forbidding the car-stopping wajang to stop it! The dramatic motif is the same as that in the picture of a nine-year-old, in which a wajang *pedanda* (high priest) is held up by a beast. Compare another subject from Group A: Betara di Loewoer (ancestor god) confronts Betara Soerja (the sun as a god), and causes him to stop. In the center are symbols for the sun, moon, and stars, standing still in their courses. If we recognize this "arrestation motif" as a common one in wajang compositions, we do not know whether to take the motorcar picture as an incident from real life into which wajang figures are introduced, or as the child's idea of a wajang episode in which a motorcar plays a part. The two planes are not clearly distinguished; in fact, they are thoroughly mixed.

The small child brings to the making of his picture an impetus, a desire to create, which carries him over the difficulties of such confusions. Nothing is impossible, and his fancy could fill a dozen pictures. In the work of Groups C and D one generally finds a whole saga crowded onto a single page. In Group B the frame is already closing in, the subject matter is limited to as much of the story as can conveniently be got on the page. Group A, by comparison, has reduced it still further, so that it seems to focus on a single incident, a single moment, in the tale. For this reason, perhaps, the liveliness and activity of the composition reaches a higher point in the drawings of Group B. They have mastered the technique sufficiently to be able to co-ordinate it with an integrated section of the content of their fancy, but have not yet become so technique-conscious as to restrict the subject by the limitations of the style. Where a member of Group B cheerfully draws "little brother" with the crown of a hero, a nine-year-old says, "I can't draw a man"—and sits down to draw a pair of struggling demons, sure of line and complete in detail of physiognomy and trappings. Tradition supplies no accepted "model" for a man, but for a demon it does.

The battle motif, whether of wajangs, beasts, men, gods, or spirits, is the favorite among all these children. We have over and over again a battle scene in which the participants brandish stylistically drawn weapons, the air is filled with flying arrows, enemies transform themselves into strange beasts, and heroes "emanate," through their magic powers, as serpents or fierce birds of prey. I found an average of 66 per cent of the drawings representing a flight or some form of attack. This is not surprising in a group so strongly influenced by wajang, for the battle scenes are indispensable in every wajang performance and constitute the recurrent climaxes up to which less animated passages lead. In some cases the children interpret these scenes as representing themselves. One seven-year-old explained his drawing, "This is me hitting my father, over here I'm hitting my uncle." But in most cases it is difficult to trace an identification. The hero Ardjoena today defeats with magic weapons the giant demon, but tomorrow we find he's had his head cut off. Often the children state of a battle scene, "Nobody wins. They're still fighting." The contest is the subject of the picture, chosen as a dramatic moment.

I shall set down the title and content of a few of the drawings which it is not possible to reproduce, to give some idea of the flexibility with which the stock characters are treated and the variety of protagonists who may take part in the struggles. Animals, both domestic and imaginary: the king fights a *koeplak-kaplik,* an evil spirit said to resemble a goat, but whose ears are so long that they make a sound "koeplak-kaplik" against the ground as he walks; a battle between a mythological bird and a mythological lion, the bird, Garoeda, the lion, Rawana transformed; a cow ridden by a man encounters a *léjak,* a human being transformed into fiendish shape, with wild hair and long projecting teeth—in the center the child of the cow, crying for its mother. A *tonja* pops out of a tree while Ardjoena fights a demon. A *tonja* appears in the river, where an ordinary man is taking his ducks to water; the *tonja* steals a duck. Here is a pair, done by a child on a single day. Scene I: The monkey prince Hanoman comes to tell Bhima that his little brother is lost. Bhima weeps. Hanoman is very angry. He flew through the air, but he did not find him. Scene II: A follower of *rangda,* the witch, hurls herself into the picture from one side, offering in her outstretched hand the head of Bhima's little brother, which *rangda* is about to devour.

Or, if we have as a subject the stealing of a bride, one man with his allies is endeavoring to wrest the girl away from the men of her family. Unrequited love: a lady, almost twice the size of her admirer, refuses to wed him, while he threatens her with drawn kris. A hunting scene: two men with their dogs give chase to a deer, the deer disappears, the dogs mistake their masters for the prey and eat them. In the picture the two men are lying dead, their weapons fallen beside them, one with his leg bitten off. Above are the dogs showing their long-fanged jaws, and all about are the great trees with monkeys in the branches, a common Balinese symbol suggesting danger in a lonely and deserted spot.

What are the scenes not based on fights or acts of violence? The purely pastoral have not occurred—the cows and ducks with which the little boys spend their days are only drawn in combat, perhaps with a mythological lion or threatened by some evil spirit. The nearest approach to lyrical feeling is expressed when two of the children draw temples, with carved gates and decorated walls, over which show the multiple roofs of the little shrines, unprofaned by any human presence. Generally when the children take as their subject a scene from real life, they choose, as from the wajang material, a dramatic moment, a cockfight in action, the communal slaughtering of a pig, a dancing performance at which a crowd has gathered—a *gandroeng,* a *djanger* (favorite dances) or, most popular, a *barong* (dragon). When it is a performance, the orchestra, which adds so much to the gaiety of the actual scene, has always been represented. Two children drew a cremation at its most turbulent point, when the crowds of shouting men mill around the tower in a frenzy to get at the corpse. Only once did a child attempt to depict an actual masked figure of *rangda* which he had seen perform the day before, flanked by trance-dancers pressing krisses into their breasts. In this picture, as in all other attempts at "real life," the execution of the child-artist fell far below the level of his more formalized legendary drawings. This same child had drawn *rangdas* many times, with great conviction, after the model of the wajang *rangda.* It is curious to note that *barongs* have appeared twice in his pictures, not as masked figures supported on the legs of men but with the legs of beasts.

In the discussion of the subject matter of the drawings, I have not made a distinction between the groups according to age, for it seemed to me that the difference was one of treatment rather than of choice of material. I have stated that the field of content narrows as the child grows older, bringing it into line with his skill. Let us see now how the littler ones begin to master the special technique which makes their drawings Balinese. Of the four children in Group D who had not yet lost their first teeth, three did not yet show any signs of the formalized technique. They made round heads, lumpy bodies, and sticklike legs, seen from in front. Their animals were only slightly longer shapes, with four legs to distinguish them from men. The fourth child of this group began at once to draw the head of a man in profile, with the characteristic long nose and slanting eye of wajang. Of eight figures in his picture, seven were drawn in this way, and the eighth, at the bottom of the page, was given a round eye and the rounded horn of a wajang headdress—perhaps a miniature Bhima? Also in the picture are three very large ducks. A child in Group C, who lost his first teeth during the period of the experiment, I was able to catch at his first attempt to draw a wajang. He had been drawing in the manner of the tiny ones when one day he began to put in minute compact wajangs, with horned headdress and extended or bent-at-the-elbow arms, interspersed among the figures of men and beasts drawn in his usual manner. I have reproduced this drawing here (Pl. IX, Fig. 2) so that the aspect of the germ of a style may be known. A month later this child was drawing wajangs with considerable freedom—it was he who put one to drive a motorcar. The other members of Group C were all drawing wajangs, as they had done from the beginning, to the exclusion of all other subjects. They had already attempted a number of complicated headdresses which distinguished the characters (see Kresna and Salja by a six-year-old in Pl. IX, Fig. 1).

It is not often that the observer can put his finger on the exact point which marks a step forward in any given child's development. These children were not seen all day long, nor had any one of them been seen every day. They themselves said that, lacking paper and pencil, they drew only upon the walls. And the walls bore witness to the fact that they did. Except for spatial limitation, the equivalent of a frame, which the edges of a piece of paper provide and which an expanse of wall lacks, I could see no appreciable difference in the style resulting from the change of medium. If the line is looser when the child uses a brush on paper rather than a bit of charcoal on the wall, it is relatively tighter when he uses a pen. Therefore, when a six- or seven-year-old child begins at once to draw recognizable wajangs, one assumes that he has practiced his craft on the walls.

According to the data collected during this period, which cannot be conclusive because of the limited number of children studied, it would seem that the children began to draw in the culturally dictated manner between the ages of five and seven, varying with the precocity and special aptitude of the child. Only two children came under my observation who were over the age of seven and who yet made no attempt to draw in the classical style. Both children were very aberrant types, in all their ways quite unlike their fellows. There are probably many children who do not draw at all, but it seems that those with a touch of ability try very hard to master first the accepted technique. In my Groups A and B, only those who stand out as the most talented ever attempted the more difficult task of portraying a realistic scene. They themselves considered it more difficult and probably less rewarding.

Another point in learning was noted in the case of a nine-year-old when he passed from drawing the hind legs of animals with knees in front like a man's to hocks in back like a beast's. Kantin had been drawing very regularly for a month in the shadow of the wall where hung the classical painting of mythological beasts mentioned earlier. From April 21 to May 14, he had made eight separate drawings containing animals, all with their knees in front. On May 14 and 15, a child of twelve years was seen by Kantin to make a copy of some of the beasts on the wall painting, reproducing their classically drawn hind legs. On May 16, Kantin attempted an animal, was dissatisfied, turned over the page, and drew men. On May 22, he again drew an animal, with knees in front as before. On May 27, suddenly the legs of his animals were changed, forever after to be drawn with the "knees" where they belong. The curious fact is that he did not himself attempt to copy the wall painting, nor did he learn by looking at it. Through the medium of the older boy's drawing, his attention was brought to this problem of animal anatomy, and he seems to have carried the problem in his mind until he had it solved. I have observed children in America becoming concerned with and meeting this problem at very nearly the same age. In spite of the marked conventionalization of Balinese children's drawing, a certain underlying course of their development can be correlated with that of children living under very different conditions.

The drawings themselves bear witness to the fertile imagination which the children bring into play when left to draw what they please. Note with what freedom of treatment the most significant elements have been made to stand out in the *barong* and the cockfight pictures here reproduced (Pl. VIII, Fig. 1, and Pl. X, Fig. 2), simply by magnifying them out of proportion to the scale. From the drawings, too, one can better judge the spontaneous sense of composition and balanced design than from any written description. It is true that whether the composition "comes off" or not depends a great deal on accidental factors. These Balinese children often achieve what seems a masterpiece of design and spoil it afterward by the addition of a wealth of decorative detail—not an unfamiliar trait in the art of adult Balinese. Similarly, the frequent filling-in of space with "mountains," "greenery," "rocks," etc., must be taken over by the children from the decorative conventions of the adults in painting and in temple reliefs. When the children were first given colors, they used them decoratively, not conventionally or realistically. The specified colors of even the most familiar wajang figures—Hanoman, white; Bhima, black; Baladewa, red; etc., which may be seen in Bali by anyone who wanders around to the

PLATE VII. *Balinese Children's Drawing. I*

By I Loengsoer,
age 9

Fig. 1.—*Artist's title:* "Soebali and Soegriwa fighting. They exchange blows and bite each other. They are brothers, Soegriwa is the younger brother." Two monkey princes from the Hindu epic, the *Ramayana*. Note the symmetry of the design.

By I Kantin,
age 9

Fig. 2.—*Artist's title:* "On the right, Tjoepak, with Nang Komoen below him, and above, a Koeoek, who eats people. On the left is Nang Sedahan stabbing Tjoepak, with Paksi [great bird] and Tjèlèng Lelingsen [person transformed into a pig.]" Composition in a circle, overflowing the margins. Tjoepak is the chief character of a cycle of folk plays presented in the shadow play theater.

PLATE VIII. *Balinese Children's Drawing. II*

By I Gandir, age 7

FIG. 1.—*Artist's title:* "A *barong* dancing in the road. People carrying flags, banners, and ceremonial parasols. They are playing *gendèr* [musical instruments], and cymbals, and gongs." A performance of the dance of the dragon is represented. Note the magnification of the size of the dragon mask in relation to the size of the players. (Cf. Pl. I, Fig. 1.)

By I Loengsoer,
  age 9

FIG. 2.—*Artist's title:* "A Tjalonarang story. Pandoeng stabs the Rangda, but she does not die." The Tjalonarang is the story of the witch, performed with the sacred mask, which is the well-known prelude to the ceremonial trance-dance with krisses. The composition renders the balance between the forces of good and evil, in the same manner as the shadow play. (Cf. Pl. III, Fig. 3.)

PLATE IX. *Balinese Children's Drawing. III*

By I Lanoes,
age 6

FIG. 1.—*Artist's title:* "Kresna fighting with Salja." The god Krishna and the hero
Salja, known to the child from the shadow play, are represented in stylized
rendering strongly influenced by the shadow play, in the attitudes of the
personages, the balance of the composition, the distinctive detail of the
headdresses, and the delineation of the features.

By I Dapet, age 5

FIG. 2.—*Artist's title:* "A cow lying down, a man, a bird, a man, Ardjoena, Malen,
Sangoet, a man, a pig, a bird. . . ." Here the figures of ordinary men and
animals appear with wajang figures, which are given the names of heroes
from the shadow play.

PLATE X. *Balinese Children's Drawing. IV*

By I Loengsoer,
age 9

FIG. 1.—*Artist's title:* "Food and drink are brought to Tjoepak by his followers, Panak Sate, Toea Daja, and Nang Sedahan." A typical shadow-play scene, from the Tjoepak cycle.

By I Loengsoer,
age 9

FIG. 2.—*Artist's title:* "A cockfight"

side of the screen where the puppet master is manipulating them—were completely disregarded by these children. They began by applying the colors in stripes along the sides of their lines, a red and a blue stripe down one side of a leg, a green and a yellow stripe down the other side, a purely decorative device. After a month of using color, the children came to painting in solid sections, occasionally even backgrounds, but the leaves of a tree were still likely to be red and the feet of a man sea-green.

As the work progressed, as the child's interest in and mastery over technique increased, the field of content tended to be reduced. Compositions once overflowing, spilling over the margins, became more constricted, the subject matter was limited to what could be adequately handled on a page. There was a loss in compositional dynamism, a widening of margins, and a more meticulous attention to detail. The bold individual expression in the design seemed to diminish, the design became more set, dry, and static. It is only fair to add that early drawings of these children are often their best and that perhaps the lure of the pennies led them to draw at times when they had "nothing to say." It is quite possible that some of these children had drawn too much. I am reminded of the statement of Mr. Bonnet (artist and collector of modern Balinese paintings) that in his experience the work of the young adult painters tended to go down after the first year or two and that their best work was done while they were mastering a new technique. Gregory Bateson and Margaret Mead have told me that in collecting the woodcarvings of adults who were just beginning to make statuettes, the first piece of any individual was usually his most effective, that it often had a quality lacking in his later work. These observations, which corroborate each other, would seem to show that, although the Balinese, adult or child, is never at a loss for a subject, the rich background of legend and the tricks and conventions of a traditional style cannot be depended upon to produce "art" by a formula but that the whole mechanism must be fired from within by some intense feeling of the artist.

CHAPTER 6

Children and Music in Bali

————————————————————————COLIN MC PHEE

The present study is a 1954 revision made for this volume from an earlier article published in Djawa, Vol. XVIII, No. 6, and written in 1938 during the author's residence in Bali when the island was still under Dutch rule. Today, despite many changes under the regime of the Indonesia Republic, Bali, from recent reports, continues to be musically as active as ever.

For a musician, Bali is indeed a special paradise, where music and dancing are not only loved by all but play a most important part in the life of the people. Throughout the year, from one end of the island to the other, hills and valleys relay the echo of gongs, as temples in villages and far-off holy spots hold their annual celebrations in turn. Along the roads drums thunder to the clash of cymbals as chanting processions bear offerings to the sea or follow great cremation towers to the cemetery. From rocky streams rise the voices of singing bathers, while in open fields birds are continually alarmed by the clack of little wind-blown rattles or by the hum of tall bamboo Aeolian flutes that sound with every breeze. In the sky, during the windy months, long kites, furnished with vibrant strings, throb in wiry chorus. Small bells are attached to everything—to oxen's yokes, weavers' shuttles, pony carts, even to the necks of pigeons, along with tiny whistles, to make shrill music when the birds are released to wheel above the trees. Villages ring at night with musical sounds as men, women, and children watch entranced some dance drama or shadow play, while in musicians' clubhouses young men meet each evening to rehearse the swift, intricate music of the *gamelan,* the Balinese orchestra of tuned bronze gongs, gong-chimes, and metallophones, accompanied by drums and cymbals.

The Balinese *gamelan* owes its more direct origin to the similarly composed, but quite different-sounding, *gamelans* of Java. It is a complex orchestra of separate but interdependent instrumental groups, each with its own musical function. These combine to create an elaborate polyphony, sounding, at different pitch levels, the nuclear theme, fully developed melody, melodic paraphrase, and rapid ornamental figuration. The musical sentence is punctuated by gongs. Large gongs mark the main periods, smaller ones subdivide the phrases or accent off-beats. The pair of hand-struck drums combine in complex interplay to lead the ensemble, controlling tempo and dynamics. Cymbals maintain a steady metallic tremolo, reinforcing the drums on important accents.

While a seven-tone scale, inherited from Java, is still found in certain ancient ensembles, preserved solely for playing sacred music, most Balinese *gamelans* are constructed with the more popular five-tone scale system, of which there are various tunings. One type of orchestra, to be discussed in this paper, is limited to a scale of four tones, quite complete in itself. Despite the elaborate orchestration, music survives almost entirely through oral tradition. A rudimentary notation exists to preserve from oblivion the nuclear tones of a composition. It is, however, no more than a bare reminder for the music specialist, not meant to be read from at performance or practice. Balinese musical form shows fine proportion and variety in metric structure, while the underlying rhythm of the drums is highly syncopated. Two-movement ceremonial compositions played on state occasions may take a half-hour to perform. A large repertory of extended suites of contrasting movements exists for the dramatic choreographies of the dance. In the theater, leading characters have each their special theme or leitmotif, and lively, ingenious rondos accompany popular street dances. Modern compositions are tense and restless in their ever changing moods—free fantasias borrowing from classical repertory with brilliant new orchestral effects. While traditional compositions are kept alive through group memory, as young men join the orchestra and older men drop out, new music is taught by the composer through musical dictation. He may be a gifted member of the *gamelan* itself or, famed for his original music, engaged and paid for each composition taught.

The present narrative is an account of how, in 1937, I supplied a group of small Balinese boys in the village of Sayan with a set of *gamelan* instruments, found them a teacher, and how within a period of six months they had mastered the *gamelan* technique sufficiently to make their debut at the anniversary feast of one of the Sayan temples, appearing as a perfectly competent and seriously functioning orchestra. It began as an experiment, for I was curious to see how children who had never played before would learn, if given instruments and a teacher, and how long it would take to produce results. I did not expect that within a year they would become celebrated enough to be called to the local rajah's palace at Gianyar, the head of our district, to play during a great wedding festival, when dancers and orchestras had been summoned from everywhere in the Gianyar district.

But let me first establish the scene. Six years earlier, in 1932, I had built a house in Sayan, a small village in the hills, about thirty kilometers from any large town. The village was chosen partly for its beautiful location on a ridge that overlooked a great valley lined with curving rice terraces, partly for its cool climate, and partly for its quiet and isolation; and when I first came, even the head men of Sayan could speak barely a word of Malay. The villagers were plain farmers, quite poor, and living mainly by a rather leisurely cultivation of their rice fields and vegetable gardens. The Hindu caste system was lightly felt here, for only two or three families had any pretension to rank.

Sayan is relatively new, its inhabitants having settled here within the last century, migrating from the larger village of Pliatan, across the valley to the east, where formerly there had been a large court. The village contains three *banjars* or wards, each with its own administration, a half-dozen temples, no school, and a small, crumbling *puri* or noble residence in Sindu, the *banjar* south of mine, intermittently occupied by Chokorda Rahi, a high-born Satrya descended from the Pliatan aristocracy. My own house stood in Kutuh, the *banjar* to the north, on the edge of the village.

At one time, Chokorda Rahi, carrying on the tradition of princely patronage of the arts, encouraged dance and music in Sayan by forming a *jogèd* club in his *banjar*. This is a popular and rowdy form of diversion, performed in the open street, in which, to the brittle accompaniment of a small xylophone ensemble, a girl, the *jogèd*, trained both to perform solo exhibition dances and engage in coquettish *pas de deux*, solicits dancing partners from the boys and men who form the main part of the surrounding crowd. But the Sayan *jogèd* had married and retired before I arrived. Chokorda Rahi had also trained an *arja* club of youths and girls to give the sentimental singing plays so popular today. But this, too, disbanded the first year I lived in Sayan, as members married and no new talent was found.

As for the village itself, it still possessed most of the instruments belonging to the old ceremonial *gamelan gong*, the customary orchestra to supply music for temple feasts and festive occasions. But since the loss through theft, long ago, of the largest and most valuable gong, the instruments had been locked up in the storehouse of the main temple, to rust and rot. The one active orchestra here is commonly called the *gamelan barong*, since it is intended primarily to accompany the periodic appearances of the *barong*, the local dragon, a masked form reverently guarded in one of the temples, which on occasion, animated by two men, emerges to intimidate and rout the local bad spirits. Should the village need other music for its temple feasts and holidays, it engaged, for a small sum, orchestras from near-by villages.

Before coming to Sayan, I had lived in Klandis, a large village near the sea, with dramatic and music clubs of all kinds that rehearsed continually, so that each night I fell asleep to the music of flutes and gongs and soft reverberating drums that seemed to throb in all directions. But Sayan was already in deep slumber by nine each night, with no light showing in any house. In order that there might be some cheerful sound of rehearsing in the evenings, I bought a set of xylophones, drums, and cymbals. With the help of Lebah, the young man who drove my car, whom I had engaged because of his wide musical experience, I organized a *gandrung* club. *Gandrung* is merely disguised *jogèd*, performed by a boy in girl's costume, with whom the youths and older men from the ring of onlookers dance at will, demonstrating with varying degree of ironic gesture their awareness of the substitution. Although the entertainment was wildly popular in many parts of the island, in Sayan it was a mediocre success. When I left Bali for America in 1934, to remain away two years, I loaned the instruments to a neighboring village, and on my return did not ask for them back.

Instead, I had decided to organize a serious *gamelan* on a large scale. I learned from Lebah that the orchestra used for the *légong* dancers in Tegas, not far away, had only been loaned the musicians by the real owner, my long-time friend, the high-born Anak Agung Mandra of Pliatan, and since the club at the time was inactive, I arranged to rent the orchestra and bring it to Sayan. I had a number of additional bronze instruments made, in order to transform the *gamelan* into a special court orchestra of a type no longer found, romantically called the *Gamelan Semar Pegulingan*, "Gamelan of Semara [the Love God] of the Sleeping Quarters," since it was primarily intended to make sweet music of diversion in the inner palace, in the courtyard known as the *Semarabawa*, "Place of the Love God," where stood the royal sleeping pavilion. Although I knew the music of this ensemble was rather elegant and classical for simple Sayan taste, I hoped to revive it, at least temporarily, because of its great beauty.

A *seka*, or club, of some thirty older boys and men from *banjars* Kutuh and Sindu was formed, the members chosen by Lebah. The club was bound together in the Balinese system through small deposits of entrance money, which would not be refunded if the member dropped out, and various fines for lateness or missed rehearsals. I engaged as teacher an elderly man from the village of Payangan, farther up in the hills, where he had formerly been leading soloist of the *Pegulingan* orchestra in the local palace. Surprisingly, the group took up this recreation with enthusiasm and, though many had never played before, developed in a year's time a finished technique and had memorized a large repertory of classical music. I then engaged more modern teachers from different parts of Bali, partly to keep up club interest and partly in order that the members (and I) might learn other musical repertories and styles. But all this is another story.

The account I have to give here has to do with the small boys of Sayan, the youngsters of from six to eleven or so, who spend their days half in play, half in herding ducks in the rice fields, tending the placid but unpredictable water buffalos, cutting grass for the family cow, or efficiently performing the other thousand-odd tasks given to the *anak chenik* or "small man." Met on the road, they are shy and charming, like gentle, furtive small animals whose hearts beat in alternating rhythms of confidence and alarm. Unobserved, they are lively enough, noisily racing about, full of mischief and malice. They scrawl on village walls the latest scandalous gossip about each other and fill them with drawings of shadow-play heroes and diagrams of sex. In the fields you may hear their bright piping voices lifted in song; the words would make your hair stand on end with their sophistication and hilarious smut.

Their early life is based upon imitation of their elders; their play is partly reproduction in miniature of various adult activities, carried out with great regard for detail. They are devoted patrons of the arts, would rather die than miss a play or *gamelan* performance. One would think, watching them, that the performance was given entirely for their entertainment. Naked, they sit in the best places in swarms, lining the edges of the dance clearing like birds along a telegraph wire. They watch intently every movement of dancer or actor and fall asleep against one another when the action drags. Nothing short of a cloudburst can drive them away before the end of the play, perhaps at dawn, when they wander home to work or sleep. It is up to them, for discipline from the adults is mild to the extreme. Perhaps it is for this reason that they have, from so early an age, so unusual a sense of independent responsibility and are, on the whole, so exceptionally well behaved.

In the 1930's, about 2 per cent of the children in Sayan went through the inhibiting and disrupting influence of the Dutch-directed village schools. For the privilege of learning that the earth is round and how to draw properly with a ruler, five or six urchins from my *banjar* walked a couple of miles each day to the school in Ubud. The happy rest drifted into adolescence with few cares other than the family ups and downs; they all knew how to look out for themselves in money matters, and some of them would pick up reading and writing Balinese script if they were of studious mind.

A *gamelan* such as the lovely-sounding *Semar Pegulingan* that now was heard each night in the pavilion I had built near the road by the garage had probably never been seen by most of the village children. The early rehearsals attracted the small boys from *banjar* Kutuh as honey draws ants. Some even ventured up from *banjar* Sindu. A few begged to be allowed to try the instruments; others simply ran about, disturbing rehearsals with their games. Little by little, as the novelty wore off, they stopped coming. But at odd times of the day, when the club members were off in the fields, I began to hear sounds of ex-

perimental drumming and the chime of metallophones coming from
the pavilion where the instruments were kept. The imitation was surprisingly good. The number of small men who seemed to grow music-
conscious increased, and morning music became a regular thing. But,
finally, I had to put a stop to it, for the parchment of one of the drums
was mysteriously split, hammers got broken or lost, a cymbal disappeared. The club began to complain.

The *Pegulingan gamelan* practiced nightly, the members meeting
at nightfall, after they had bathed in the valley and gone home to eat.
From the different teachers I brought to Sayan they built up a widely
varied repertory—new music and standard compositions with new
orchestration and general interpretation. Each night, from seven to
ten, or later, the air was filled with the shimmer of metallophones and
gong-chimes, swift drumming, and the soft pulsation of deeper gongs
that seemed to float off to infinity. People across the valley said they
could hear the rehearsals. It seemed to give them intense pleasure.
How nice, they said, Sayan was no longer *sepi*, dead silent.

Absorbed in this musical activity and daily engaged in transferring
what could be transferred of this music to the one notation I knew,
I forgot about the children completely. Two of them worked intermittently in the house, polishing knives and spoons, feeding the par-
rots, looking for leaves and roots the cook suddenly wanted for the
daily curry, helping light the lamps at sundown. Between these occupations they would sit down and hammer away at one instrument or
another that I always seemed to have standing about the house. They
discovered for themselves that certain Balinese tunes could be played
on the black keys of the piano, and they improvised astonishing duets.
They had that quick, brief concentration one sees in small monkeys,
doing one thing for five minutes, only to grow suddenly bored and
dart to something else. But every now and then a musical phrase of
extremely complicated rhythm would flash out from some metallophone on the verandah, hammered out with neat precision and quite
unaccountable virtuosity.

What went on in the inner life of these two, what they were thinking
or absorbing, was an utter mystery to me. In true Balinese fashion
they were completely uncommunicative, at least as far as I was concerned, about their real activities. They went home at night; they returned in the morning. What they did when not around was not withheld from secrecy, for we were old friends. It merely did not occur to
either one to mention anything about himself or anything which might
be happening in our *banjar*.

Knowing this, I ought not to have been surprised, as I was, when
sudden proof was given that a number of small boys in Kutuh had
been engaged for some time in an occupation invoking the aid of

nothing less than the muses of music and drama. This was most unexpectedly brought to my attention one sunny morning at *galungan* time, the big yearly festival when the gods descend to earth for a visit, officially a week, but exuberantly celebrated by a month of plays, music, traveling dragons, and sociable gadding-about. As I sat at the typewriter, I grew aware of a gradual crescendo of noise, which seemed to indicate that a procession of sorts was passing through the village. Sounds of strange and lively music drifted down from the road above, in which I could distinguish the vigorous beating of a drum, the crash of cymbals, and the deep jangling rattle of a gong, which sounded badly cracked.

"What on earth . . . ?" I began, when Lebah, coming down from the road, announced it was the children's new *seka barong* making its public debut. They had organized a *gamelan* of their own, got up a play with masked actors, and made their own *barong* to patrol the roads during the *galungan* holidays.

At this point, before reporting further on the children, I should describe the *barong* more fully. It consists of the formidable mask of a mythological beast—lion, said some; bear, said others—and an elongated body covered with fiber or feathers. An elaborate gilded headdress, studded with little mirrors, crowns the mask, while the tail rises high in the air to end in a tassel of tiny bells. It is danced by two men, concealed within the body so that only the lower legs are seen. The front man controls the mask, snapping the movable jaws in fine simulation of demoniac frenzy. Though generally housed in the temple, these creatures are often used in plays to represent the supernatural form of some transformed king or saint. At *galungan*, accompanied by the *gamelan*, they travel from door to door throughout the village, giving a short performance for a small sum of money. They are the Balinese version of the Chinese New Year's dragon.

I went up the road, to find the children's *barong* gathered at the gateway, surrounded by a small but admiring crowd of adults and children, including tots of two or three. The *barong* proved to be a fine imitation, with a body of straw, paper decorations, and a small, rather worm-eaten, but authentic mask. The *gamelan* was reduced to bare essentials, a heavy-keyed metallophone for the melody, a drum for rhythm, cymbals, a large gong (showing a very great crack indeed) for main punctuation, and a small gong to beat time. These, I was told, had been salvaged from various houses in Kutuh—the club was formed of Kutuh boys only—where they had been lying idle and forgotten for years. In addition to the *gamelan*, there were several youngsters, two of them with masks, who formed the acting cast, for a formal *barong* performance often precedes some plays. I let it be known that I wished to engage a performance, and the crowd settled down in agreeable anticipation to witness once more a show they had seen only ten minutes before, a little farther up the road.

The performance was quite astonishing in its general integration and continuity. The musicians played with great spirit, and the drumming, done by one of the older boys, who may have been eleven, was incredibly good in its imitation of the strong, dynamic accents, rapid and syncopated and beaten out at one end of the drum with a drumstick, which mark the *barong's* entrance. The *barong*, operated by two boys of nine or ten, danced with the ferocity of a puppy playing big dog, snapping its jaws in rhythm to the music. When the dance was over, it retired to the background, and the play began.

The story presented was from *Chupak*, the well-known adventures of two brothers—Chupak, the elder, a demonic type, a bully, lazy, boastful, sensual, and cowardly, and Grantang, the younger, gentle, wise, outwardly delicate but inwardly strong, and in the end winning all, of course, after harrowing trials. I have published elsewhere[1] the outline of this tale, which, when played at normal Balinese tempo, can be spread out to last from four to five hours of heroics, romance, and clowning. The children had neatly contracted it to a series of tabloid episodes which reduced the plot to its essence. Poor Grantang! Awful Chupak! The amorous saleswoman (played by a giggling boy of seven) and the lustful farmer who makes uninhibited advances, and, above all, the beloved scene where Chupak makes a revolting exhibition of himself, feasting in Gargantuan fashion on roast pig, sausage, and other delicacies (the stage property here was a small empty basket), gasping, whining, belching, and breaking wind. The actors performed the more ribald moments with great gusto, to the intense satisfaction of the youngest members of the audience. When all was over, I presented the drummer, who seemed to be club manager, with a *kitip*, a Dutch dime (6 cents American, 1938), about the equivalent of seventy-five Chinese cash. The club cheered at the windfall; they had been taken seriously and engaged! Off they trooped, followed by the crowd, to play at intervals down the road until they reached the edge of the village.

I wondered at the time whether the little club would have been formed without the inspiration of the large *gamelan* which they could hear practicing at the house each evening. I felt certain the primary impulse for the children in organizing their club was one of imitating the older boys. They, too, would have their *sekal* As for the music, they must have learned it by ear from the large orchestra. For since the *barong* in our village was rarely seen except on ceremonial occasions, I had, in order that I could write it down, the *gamelan* club learn the complete musical repertory connected with the *barong*, whether it was presented with offerings, marching in the streets, or appearing in some drama of sorcery. For the most part, the music is wild and somber; its violent accents are intensely suggestive to Balinese, pregnant with imagined movement and dramatic situations. Such music, after a silence in the village long beyond the life of these youngsters, was bound, I thought, to stimulate them, and it was indeed shortly after the *gamelan* had been learning the *barong* music that the children's *barong* made its appearance. They were, of course, familiar with the method of presentation, for they had seen many *barongs* in near-by villages.

Chupak they had also seen, either in shadow-play form or given by strolling players, and the music here was reduced to standard theatrical set pieces which also were in the larger *gamelan's* repertory. It was the initiative of two or three boys, I learned, which started the group, and I was not surprised to find that Kantin and Kayun, the two musically minded youngsters who worked now and then at the house, were among the leaders. The others followed with varying degrees of enthusiasm, while a few simply trailed along in order not to be left out. Strangely enough, it was in this condensed performance by the children, in their choice of material and their direct portrayal of the various characters, that I felt the essence of the play for the first time and, through it, caught a new glimpse of the lively Balinese theatrical sense. The love for broad comedy, the sensual delight in being frightened by the supernatural, the gift for creating a vivid general impression (at the expense of a finished performance), and the special talent for exuberant dramatic and musical expression—all this was present in miniature in the performances of these children. Most amusing and impressive of all were the continuity and complete assurance with which everything was done. They were very serious. When an actor suddenly grew self-conscious, lost his *élan* and fluffed his lines in an unreasonable access of shyness, he was sternly reprimanded on the spot by the musicians with, "Go on! What's the matter with you? You're simply rotten!" while the audience laughed unfeelingly at this unnecessary yielding to temperament, which broke the spell.

The club amused themselves in this way for several months, adding to their stock of plays and improving considerably. The drumming grew surer, and a couple of instruments were added to the orchestra. But the Balinese temper is strongly colored by sudden enthusiasms and as sudden reactions. I was therefore not surprised to hear, right after an unusually successful performance, that the *seka barong* had broken up. They were, to use a word one heard a hundred times a day, *med*, bored, fed-up, and through!

I now can turn to the real object of this report, and tell of the deliberate organization on my part of this group of children into a regularly practicing *gamelan* club, with a complete set of instruments of their own. This idea, however, did not occur to me all at once, and before the *gamelan* was finally formed, the group had passed through several phases of musical development. Hating to see the *barong* club break up, I suggested they form a *seka gènggong*, a jew's-harp club. This diverting instrument, cut from the rib of the sugarplum leaf, is heard everywhere, strummed by children and men alike, in quiet solitude or in a companionable little group (Pl. XIII, Fig. 2). The repertory of simple folk tunes known as *gending gènggong*, "jew's-harp pieces," is endless, with amusing titles such as "Yellow Snail," "Croaking Frog," "Golden Dragonfly," "Fighting Cats," "Crow Steals Eggs," and "Monkey Looks at His Reflection in the Water." This idea of a jew's-harp club met with Kantin's and Kayun's instant approval, and they banded the others together again. Lebah suggested for teacher a man from the next village, who had a local reputation for remembering countless jew's-harp tunes. He agreed to come to the house each night, but when I asked him about finding the instruments, he answered in an unexpectedly professional manner, "There's no hurry. They must learn to sing the tunes before they can play them."

Each night the children sat in a ring on the verandah, the teacher in the center, chanting as they learned the wordless tunes. Most of these were brief, repeated over and over without a break. They then began to learn longer pieces, composed of two sections—the first, the *polos* or plain, sung in unison, and the more animated finale, the *chandetan*, a syncopated two-part affair, in which two separate but interlocking rhythms are combined to create an unbroken musical continuity. It sounds complex, and it is, but not to Balinese, who throw themselves into such passages with sheer delight. The children sang the tunes and figurations to a few different syllables, mostly, it seemed, *na* and *no*. I give a purely rhythmic sample of *chandetan* here; a musical example will be found on page 92.

Na No Na　　Na No No　　Na　　No Na　　No Na　　No　　No　　Na

No　　No Na No　　No Na—— Na　　No Na　　No Na—— Na No　　Na

From the composition "Rearing Horse"

It was only after a month had passed, when the chorus knew a dozen or more tunes and had gained some precision in ensemble, that the *gènggongs* were produced. The instrument, a short thin strip of pliant fiber in which a tongue is cut, is held before the mouth by the left hand. The right hand holds a string attached to the right end. A quick tug of the string causes the tongue of the instrument to vibrate, and if the mouth is open at the right degree and you breathe against the tongue, a faint humming tone results. It is a trick any Balinese child knows, one which I could not master. A kind of "breathing" the tune, rather than singing it, against the vibrating instrument is important in amplifying the tones. Within a night or so the *gènggong* orchestra was producing a charming sound, transforming the familiar chanted tunes into an elfin chorus of softly twanging harmonics.

It was another month before I began to notice the well-known signs of waning interest. "What's the matter?" I asked Kayun. "Is the club growing fed-up?" "*Med*," he stated briefly, and that was the end of the *seka gènggong*.

It was about this time that I discovered, while exploring several remote villages to the far east of the island, the survival of an archaic, certainly pre-Hindu, bamboo musical instrument known as the *angklung*, a species of tuned rattle. Three open bamboo tubes of different lengths hang within a light upright frame and fit loosely into separate slots in the transverse base of the framework (Pl. XIV). When the instrument is given a quick sideways jerk, the tubes knock back and forth in their slots and produce, if correctly tuned, a short musical tone. Continued shaking of the instrument produces a steady tremolo, but the preferred method is to agitate the frame briefly, to produce a single note at a time. The three tubes are tuned to sound the same tone in three different octaves. Since the *gamelan* in which the *angklung* is used has a four-tone scale, a set of four instruments is needed, one for each scale tone. Four players are required, each operating a separate *angklung*. They sound their instruments in irregular turn, following the melodic continuity of the rest of the *gamelan*. In *polos* passages this is not too difficult; in the syncopated *chandetan* sections it requires considerable alertness and practice.

In eastern Bali these instruments are still included in a small ceremonial orchestra known as the *gamelan angklung*, since it includes these instruments, whose traditional function in this part of the island is to play only for temple feasts and cremations. In central Bali the special village orchestra bearing the same name, which plays for temple feasts, processions, weddings, and cremations, has not included these ancient instruments for so long that no one has any idea of the origin of the name *gamelan angklung*.

I was fascinated by the tone of the *angklungs*, their special use, and by the unusual tuning of the four-tone scale in the orchestras in which they were found, which lent a further antique tonal color to the music. By chance, I came across a newly made orchestra including these instruments, which was for sale in one eastern village. Although I had no idea what I should do with such an orchestra, I could not resist buying it then and there and had the instruments sent back to Sayan by bus.

I placed the *gamelan*, for the time being, in a small open pavilion near the kitchen. The instruments aroused the greatest interest in Kayun and Kantin, who soon, with several friends, were daily occupied with making experimental music, trying the drums and other instruments, and improvising a little ensemble. The *angklungs* they ignored completely as utterly strange and absurd.

It was on seeing once more the eagerness of these children to make music whenever they had free access to musical instruments that I suddenly had the idea of forming a *gamelan angklung* of small men only. The orchestra I had just acquired all at once seemed ideal for this. The scale was reduced to four tones only, the instruments were all unusually small, and the tone of this ensemble was high-pitched and sweet. Even the drums were miniature in size. One day I told Kayun to call all members of the defunct *seka gènggong*, for I had something important to say, and at sundown some fifteen small boys entered the verandah with polite little bows and sat down on the floor, all attention. I asked them how they would like to form a *seka angklung*; that if they would, I would lend them this *gamelan* and find a teacher. But this time, I said, it would have to be in earnest, and if they learned to play properly, I might let them have the *gamelan* to keep.

My words created an immediate sensation. A *gamelan!* A *gamelan* of their own! They discussed it with each other excitedly. Yes, they would learn. No, they wouldn't grow tired of it. They would practice every day, only give them a teacher! I said the orchestra needed perhaps twenty-five players, and since there were only fifteen present, should we call some boys from *banjar* Sindu? This produced a quick and violent opposition. No, it must be the boys of *banjar* Kutuh alone. They would guarantee more members.

I told them they could take the instruments, all except the fragile *angklungs*, away that night, and keep them in Kayun's house, where they could try them out for themselves. Left alone and under Kantin's and Kayun's direction, they could learn how to hold the hammers, how to strike the metallophones and little gong-chimes. The brightest ones, I knew, would quickly seize the more difficult instruments. They bore off the *gamelan* with joyful shouting, and later that evening I heard sounds of wild and confused music in the distance. This went on each night for a week, when I left for Java and was gone a month.

On returning, the first thing I did was to call the group to the house, to find out what had developed in my absence. I do not think I expected anything in particular, other than to see whether the children had found the instruments they preferred and had perhaps learned to play them well enough to go through a simple tune or so. Every child knows from observation the basic method of playing the *gangsa*, a special form of metallophone used in the *gamelan angklung* (Pl. XV, Figs. 1 and 2, and Pl. XVI). You hold the hammer in the right hand, strike the key smartly, and damp its sound by grasping the end with the left hand as you strike the next key. At slow speed this is easy enough, but at modern Balinese quick tempos it requires great dexterity and quick thinking. The children also know by observation how the *réongs*, a set of four small gongs mounted in a horizontal frame, are played. They also have some ideas concerning the technique of the other instruments, with the exception, of course, of the *angklungs*.

The youngsters file in, carrying their instruments, set them down, and arrange them in proper order: two rows of small *gangsas* in front, flanked at each side by a large metallophone; behind these the *réongs* and two xylophones; behind these again, the large gong, the cymbals, and two drums. There is a little noisy quarreling on the distribution of the hammers—which belong to which instrument, who gets the best —but finally there is silence. Kayun is in the middle of the front row of melody-sounding *gangsas*. Kantin is one of the two at the *réongs*. All look at each other gravely, catching each other's eye. A swift signal is given by Kayun, who raises his hammer a little way and quickly brings it down on the key; with the same seriousness of intention, quite absurd in a group of such small children, they proceed to play a complete and decidedly intricate composition of considerable length, with sparkling *chandetan* toward the end and filled with rhythmic complications, such as syncopations and shifting accents. All this is done with complete assurance, even with style. The music is polyphonic, and there are at least four separate melodic lines, two of which would indeed worry a Western musician. These children, however, sail through all this with ease. True, the tempo falters once or twice, and the drums get out, but the general sound is clear, for there are amazingly few false notes. Changes of tempo are managed smoothly, and some attempt is even made at contrast in dynamics. They finally come to an end with a well-controlled rallentando. I am about to speak, but before I can utter a word they start again. A second piece, shorter this time. And after that a third.

It seemed that they could not wait for my return, when I would call a teacher, but had found one for themselves, the father of a friend from a near-by village, who belonged to the village *gamelan angklung*. Lebah also helped train them. The pieces they learned were not entirely new to them; the tunes were familiar, and the form was fairly simple. But there were various technical hazards which required both practice and natural musicianship. What they had accomplished so far could only have been done through ardor and determination and a youthful precocity peculiarly Balinese.

I learned that the club was now organized on a sound basis. A system of fines had been instituted: one Chinese cash for being five minutes late and more severe penalties for missing rehearsals. They had hung their own *kulkul*, or bamboo signal drum, in a tree near their regular place of rehearsal in Kayun's house (the other club also had a *kulkul*), and they had elected a treasurer and a *klian*, headman and manager. In short, there was to be no nonsense about this undertaking. I began to note emerging personalities, which I will discuss presently.

I had nothing but words of praise for the performance, which they accepted with composure. After such a fine beginning it was indeed up to me to find them a teacher without further loss of time. They firmly demanded a *good* teacher, one who knew plenty of new, up-to-date pieces, saying that the *gènggong* club lost interest because the teacher came from too near by and that his music was out of date. I promised to find them one from Selat, sixty kilometers to the east, famed for musical innovations. I had had this in mind from the start, first of all because the *angklungs*, which the children continued to ignore, were still employed there, and I intended, gently but firmly, to insist that the children learn to play them, and also because the *gamelan angklung* of Selat had a wide repertory of both very old and very new music.

A few days later I fetch the teacher from Selat, I Nengah, a commoner, perhaps forty, shy, gentle, a man of few words, and rather alarmed at the idea of traveling so far from home to a completely strange district. "I have never been to Java," he says, using the one name he knows for the great unknown. He has never taught a group of children, for a *gamelan* composed exclusively of small men is unheard of. To be called to live for some time in the house of a foreigner is stranger still, although we are old friends. His nervousness, however, will wear off in a few days, and he will become very popular with the children.

The first lesson takes place on my verandah, after sundown. The children arrange their instruments in accustomed order, and sit down, quiet for once. I notice that the brightest boys, led by Kayun, are in the front row of *gangsas*, which play the leading melody, and in the second row, which sounds, according to the orchestration, the melody or performs ornamental figuration. Most of the children seem to be about Kayun's age, around eight. Some are younger, and only a few may be several years older. I have already suggested the music I would like them to study first, which I know very well, for I once wrote it out in full while staying in Selat, and later published it in an article on *angklung* music.[2] It is *Jaran Sirig*, "Rearing Horse," and consists of two parts, a first, at moderate speed, in simple unison for everyone but with several tricky syncopations, and a second rapid movement, with melody accompanied by two-part *chandetan* figuration. This last section is complicated, perhaps too complicated for the children, for Selat figuration is difficult. Nevertheless, they asked for it, I thought, and we would see.

Nengah's teaching method in this first lesson seems strangely oblique. He says nothing, does not even look at the children. Without so much as an opening word, he begins by dreamily playing through the melody of the first movement on the *gangsa*, softly, almost to himself. He plays it through again. Then he plays the first phrase only, with more emphasis. He now indicates with a glance at the *gangsa* that they are to begin. Two or three make a tentative attempt to follow him. I notice at once that they do not seem to listen so much as watch the direction his hammer takes along the keys. The phrase is repeated, and they try again. Another joins in, then another. Those instruments which do not play the melody are forgotten for the present, for the melody must be learned first; the neglected players, however, tap out the rhythm of the tune to themselves as they grow familiar with it. Bit by bit the children who are learning the melody are able to extend it, phrase by phrase, forgetting, remembering, gaining assurance. I Nengah remains silent, unless to point out a repeated mistake; generally he is gazing into space. At the end of an hour, however, several can play through the whole melody correctly, and it is a long one, continually going back to the beginning and then taking a new turn. All the children learning it are using the utmost concentration, and I am astonished at their seriousness and patience. But some at least show signs of tiring; the idle ones begin giggling and pinching. It is time to stop. They all go home to eat, although those in the front row can hardly tear themselves away, and come racing back almost immediately to try things out for themselves. One by one, the others return, and the lesson is resumed, to continue until almost ten, a late hour for Sayan people. It is now time indeed to go home and sleep, and the lesson is declared over.

Let us now examine the leading personalities of the group, those who will surely form the backbone of the club and hold it together. The youngest of these is Kayun, about seven. He is quiet, lovable, and popular (his name, Kayun—"*Desiré*," fits him perfectly). He is remarkably independent and goes about the house, industriously putting things in order, doing little things which no one tells him to do, but which he thinks need his attention. He has an unusually quick ear, musically, and the keenest rhythmic sense of the group. He has been sitting next to the teacher, watching every hammer stroke and listen-

PLATE XI. *Children and Music in Bali. I*

Sayan *barong* and *gamelan Semar Pegulingan*

PLATE XII. *Children and Music in Bali. II*

FIG. 1.—The children's *barong*

FIG. 2.—The children's *barong* orchestra; Kantin at the drum

PLATE XIII. *Children and Music in Bali. III*

FIG. 1.—Kayun takes over the drum

FIG. 2.—Gènggongs

PLATE XIV. *Children and Music in Bali. IV*

The children's *gamelan angklung; angklungs* in front

PLATE XV. *Children and Music in Bali. V*

FIG. 1.—Front-row *gangsas;* Kayun in center

FIG. 2.—Second-row *gangsas;* Ada, the youngest member, at right

PLATE XVI. *Children and Music in Bali. VI*

Kayun

ing with every indication of complete absorption in what he is doing. He is the first to get the melody correct; he never forgets it, and Nengah has already recognized him as a star pupil.

Luar,[3] perhaps a year older, is almost as quick. He also is a serious one and runs Kayun a close second in learning the melody. Lungsur[4] is about nine; he hasn't quite the endurance of the first two, but he is eager and willing and learns quickly. Kantin[5] is still older, eleven, I imagine, rather grave and phlegmatic. It was he, however, who gave such spirited drumming to the *barong* performances, although he is considered much slower than the other three. Kreteg, about ten, goes to school, so he is treasurer, and writes down fines in a small notebook. Two new tots, one hardly five, have appeared tonight for the first time, so inexperienced that they came without a stitch of clothes, to the indignation of the others, who sent them home for their *sarongs*. But they have managed to take possession of two *gangsas* in the second row, and in no time at all I will find them hammering out syncopated *chandetan* passages with all the nonchalance in the world. There are two older boys, around fourteen, who don't quite fit in but are needed to fill the quota. They are good-natured but definitely slow at learning, and the younger children have assigned them the easiest instruments to play. The cymbals have been pounced upon by Jati, aged eight. He is a lively, prankful child, not too quick at rhythms, but intensely enjoying what he is doing. He was one of the actors in the *Chupak* cast who forgot his lines. But the cymbals seem to be his true medium; he delights in their continuous and animated clashing, smiling gayly in the loud parts.

During the first lesson, there were several children who sat around rather vaguely, the untalented ones for whom the less appealing instruments had been left to choose from. At the second lesson they still have not made up their minds, and shift from one to another. These are the ones to grow bored first and start small scuffles during rehearsals. Their interest is intermittent and passive; they might easily drop out but for their desire to remain part of the group. They will finally settle down and turn out to be quite good enough for secondary instruments.

The second lesson begins where it left off the night before. Nengah runs through the melody again, to be sure the front row has not forgotten the melody, which they haven't, and is about to turn to other instruments. But I am anxious to introduce the *angklungs* as soon as possible and have them assigned right away rather than waiting until later. The four boys finally chosen to play them must be made to feel that their role is important and a privilege. As Nengah has no idea whatever of how to begin demonstrating their use, I take a hand.

I first ask the club to play the shortest piece they learned while I

was away, in order that we may have some already known music to
which the *angklung* accompaniment can be fitted. They play "Hibiscus
Flower," a short tune with *chandetan*, which repeats over and over.
But since Nengah does not know this tune, the club must teach it to
him. This is a simple matter, however, for before they have repeated
the tune five times, he knows it. We can now turn to the *angklungs*,
which I now bring out. The children are inclined to laugh, but they
are also curious. Kayun and Luar, as the quickest to learn, are each
given an instrument. Nengah takes a third and gives the last to Lebah,
who, although he, too, had never seen an *angklung* before I took him
to Selat, is willing to try, to help me on with this project.

The four *angklungs* are tuned to produce, collectively, the *gamelan*
scale and to sound in turn a series of tones which are, approximately,
f-sharp, *g*-sharp, *b*, and *c*-sharp (see musical examples on pp. 92–93).
In unison passages the *angklungs* follow the melody. In passages with
figuration accompaniment, the *angklungs* either follow the *chandetan*
or the special filling-in patterns played on the *réongs*. As each instrument produces one tone only, the trick is to wait one's turn until the
proper melodic note must sound, then play it by giving the *angklung*
a little shake. Generally *f*-sharp and *c*-sharp are sounded together,
g-sharp is often sounded with *c*-sharp, while *b* is always heard alone.
In simple melodic passages this method is not too difficult, but in fast
syncopated parts this seems to me a hopelessly impossible task.

It isn't, apparently. The children begin the piece again, while Nengah sounds his *angklung* in the right place in the tune. Lebah, quick
to get the idea, joins in as the tune repeats. Before long, Kayun and
Luar have begun to follow, rather awkwardly. They listen intently,
their heads cocked to one side, for their turn. As the melody repeats,
Kayun suddenly gets the feeling for his instrument. He smiles de-
lightedly, looks around, and starts boldly playing, introducing syncopations of his own. On they go until the music has been repeated a sufficient number of times, and the gong is struck on the closing note.
Everyone laughs and cheers. This is new and amusing; the *angklungs*
aren't so bad after all! They continue to practice "Hibiscus Flower" for
a time with the *angklungs*, and then return to "Rearing Horse." I feel
I have won my point. Later we can decide who is to play these instruments. Not Kayun or Luar, of course, for they are too important in
keeping the main melody steady and the *anglungs*, after all, are secondary instruments.

It was not too surprising that Kayun and Luar succeeded as well as
they did on this first attempt. The melodic outline they were following
was already fixed in their minds, since they had already learned it on
the *gangsas*. Furthermore, each note in the fast-moving *chandetan*
recurs in such a way as to create a special rhythm of its own. With

four *angklungs* you have four separate rhythms sounding on the four different scale tones, which, combined, form an unbroken chain of mosaic-like patterns. Rhythm, then, and especially highly syncopated rhythm, forms the basis for their integration.

These four-part *angklung* patterns offer only one instance of the special Balinese feeling for polyrhythmic integration. A dozen boys in bathing will beat out different rhythms on rocks with pebbles and stones, to produce an exhilarating hail of organized flinty sound. In the larger *gamelans*, especially in the older forms, one may find as many as seven cymbal players, similarly integrated. And, it seems to me, it is precisely this exuberant rhythmic sense which, above all, made these rehearsals go, made these children coherent from the very start. And when the second lesson was over, I had the feeling that the *seka angklung* would be a success.

The third night, Nengah begins work on the difficult second move-ment of "Rearing Horse." Melodically, it consists of a straightforward tune of eight measures, ending with a gong stroke, repeated many times without pause, with various changes in speed and force, some-times soft and calm, sometimes loud and agitated. The *chandetan* accompaniment is intricate. Before it can be studied, the melody must first be learned, which should not take long, since it is so short.

As on the first night, Nengah begins by playing the tune through. It has a short introduction, which will later be played solo and which he takes far too fast. Although I know it well, having once written it down, I cannot recognize it, for he seems to upset the rhythmic bal-ance of the phrase by hurrying one or two essential notes which should have the same time value, thus making it impossible to realize where the strong beats of the phrase lie. For the first time during these les-sons Kayun and the others are puzzled. They cannot fall in together on the right beat after the solo, and there is a complete muddle. I tell Nengah to take it slower, more evenly, but he apparently can play it only the way it is inflexibly fixed in his mind. Finally, I take up a *gangsa* hammer and play the solo myself, slowly, distinctly, so that all can hear its correct time values. Nengah's rubato can come later, if the soloist wishes it. The melodic group grasp the time values at once and, from now on, can't possibly be put out by Nengah. The following tune is now quickly learned by the front *gangsas*, and Nengah can now proceed to the *chandetan*, played by the second metallophones, the *réongs*, and the *angklungs*.

Nengah's *chandetan* is essentially the same as that which the chil-dren learned in the *gènggong* club, only far more intricate in syncopa-tion. The *chandetan* playing instruments are divided into two groups, one playing the *molos*, simple (!) part, the other playing the opposing *nyangsih*, differing part. To me, one seems as complicated as the other.

The rhythms, however, are mother's milk to the children. The *molos* part is taken first, since it follows the melody more closely. This takes up most of the lesson. The rest of the time is spent in intermittent rest, with exaggerated complaints from the players of *kéwah!* "difficult!" The next night Nengah runs the *molos* part through, to be sure they have not forgotten (they have been practicing it at home), and then turns to the *nyangsih* players. He also does not forget to run through the first movement, to reassure himself it has not been "lost." The next night is spent mainly in fitting *molos* and *nyangsih* together and playing them along with the melody.

In five days more the club is playing the whole piece through, without teacher and without a break. During this time they have begun to learn another piece. The rhythm now gets out of hand less often, the front rows are less inclined to race. The cymbals are not yet steady, the drumming is still sketchy, and the gong, played by the oldest boy, often comes in at the wrong time. When this happens, the children shout at him in exasperation. They are sharply impatient with one another's mistakes. But the amazing thing in their performances is the freshness and life and the general musical effect, far superior to many *gamelans* I have heard that had been playing together for years. This comes partly from the natural agility of Balinese children in general but more especially from the eagerness of these children to learn and the enthusiasm with which they play. What seems to me most remarkable is their quickness, the rapidity with which they have learned a long, difficult, and completely new piece at the very outset, and the authority and precision with which they already play, especially those in the front rows.

It is now five weeks since the club started lessons. I no longer watch them, and they now rehearse in one of the pavilions near the kitchen. Rehearsals start regularly after sundown, after they have all returned from the fields, bathed, and eaten. The *kulkul* is beaten first, warning tardy ones to hurry. But not one rehearsal has been missed, no one has been absent, and they average about three hours' practice each night. In this time they have learned nine completely new pieces. Nengah has gone home, and another musician from Selat, Purni, a boy of nineteen who is a specialist in new *angklung* compositions, has replaced him. All work together harmoniously. The drumming is better, the cymbals steady, and nuances of shading are being mastered. As they play, I hear, farther off by the garage, the *Pegulingan gamelan* rehearsing, in another key and tempo, and feel well surrounded by music at last. The next temple anniversary is due in a few weeks' time, and the children have been asked by the priest to add to the program of ceremonial music. (The older club has been furnishing most of the music at the temples for some time.) This will be their public debut, and they practice more intensely than ever as the day approaches. But I know from experience that afterward some fresh stimulus will be needed to keep them going at this pace.

Here I would like to stress certain points which can be made from this report and which apply to the general study and practice of music in Bali. It will be seen, first of all, that the teacher here does not seem to teach, certainly not from our standpoint. He is merely the transmitter; he simply makes audible the musical idea to be passed on. The rest is up to the pupils. It is as though, in teaching drawing, a complex design were hung up and one said to the class, "Copy that." No allowance was made here for youth; it never occurred to Nengah to use any method other than that which he uses when teaching an adult group. He explains nothing, since for him there is nothing to explain. If there are mistakes, he corrects them, and his patience is great. But even from the first lesson he played everything too fast, and it was up to the children to follow him as best they could, quite the reverse of our own method of practicing difficult passages slowly at first, then gradually increasing speed.

Yet Nengah's system produced swift results. Perhaps it was because of the alertness of the leaders, though the group as a whole learned more quickly than the older club. This I not only saw for myself but was told by Lebah, who watched their progress with delighted admiration. As for Nengah, he called them, at the start, "sharp as needles." In all fairness, however, let it be said that their music was far simpler than that of the other *gamelan*. The scale had only four tones; no instrument extended in range to a second octave, and pieces were relatively short. But the orchestral fabric was just as complex, and tempos were generally twice the speed of those in the other music.

Then again there is none of the drudgery of learning to read notes in this music, or, worse still, of counting time values; no one to say, "Use the fourth finger . . . did you practice your scales?" The children produced music from the start, in an orchestral group. Learning was fun. Each child took pleasure not only in what he was doing but in the fact that he was doing it in company with his friends. (Hence the opposition to including members from another *banjar*.) And again, no heavy demands were put on any single player. No part was too difficult to be learned with a reasonable amount of application. Each instrument presented a single problem, to which the player could give his whole attention. Combined, the parts produced a full orchestral effect, sparkling with life and movement. This was not children's music they were learning, no mere bong-bong of some progressive rhythm class, but adult music, which, when learned, was fitting to be performed in the temple or at festivals. As a group, the children would practice willingly a far longer time than they would have as isolated soloists. And when a sufficient number had lost interest for the night, they all stopped and, saying they were "very tired," went home. Their teachers accepted this as perfectly reasonable.

While these children are considered to be unusually bright, I do not feel that they were exceptional for Bali, where all over the island one finds boys of eight, nine, and ten taking responsible positions in adult *gamelans,* even playing leading parts. It might be mentioned in passing that girls are never seen in the *gamelan,* since music-making, at least in public, is traditionally man's occupation. In music and in the theater, the role of girls is confined to singing, acting, and dancing.

One last point remains to be made here which concerns both the children's *gamelan* and Balinese *gamelan* methods in general. There is a popular idea that *gamelan* playing is largely improvisational and that the musicians are free to elaborate on a basic theme as they please. This is partly true in Java, but even there to a lesser extent than is commonly imagined. While in older Balinese *gamelans* the leading solo instrumentalist was allowed considerable leeway in melodic interpretation, in modern Balinese music, where the soloist is replaced by a melodic group, increasing emphasis is placed on precision in unison playing. This applies to all sections of the orchestra, where the parts are doubled or redoubled. As for the punctuating gongs, their places are firmly fixed in the metric design. Only the drums seem free, but these, too, are controlled by the metric structure. Ordinarily, the two drums lead the orchestra, urging it forward or holding it back, but in the *gamelan angklung* the tiny drums merely fill in with background rhythms, and the front row of *gangsas,* sounding the melody in unison, are the true leaders. The only time that solo playing is heard is in the free melodic introductions which sometimes precede a piece, and here the performer is at liberty to play as he pleases, as long as the theme is sufficiently recognizable.

The composition is firmly fixed at rehearsal and from then on must be played exactly as learned. Individuality of expression comes into play only at this time, when either teacher or one or two musicians of the group have some new idea, melodically or in figuration, which they would like to introduce into the music being practiced. This is the time when new effects are sought and tried out, with which to surprise and impress some rival club on public appearance. The children of the Kutuh *gamelan* finally accepted the *angklungs* I gave them as something sufficiently new and different to make them worth learning, and later, when they played, as they frequently did, in the large centers of Pliatan and Ubud, they could swell with pride of monopolized possession when they heard the admiring comments on these absolutely novel and therefore utterly desirable instruments. They could hear other clubs' envious declaration to form similar *gamelans.* What, for the moment, could be sweeter. As for me, I was amused to find these ancient instruments, long since discarded in most of Bali as too primitive, suddenly creating a sensation which could possibly restore them to popular use.

It is the opening day of the temple feast, and the children have assembled at the house to carry their *gamelan* to the temple. I give them each a cloth of large black and white check for a headdress, which will mark them as a club, and they all proceed to pick bright red blossoms from the hibiscus shrubs and put them in their hair. They then take up their instruments and go out in dignified single file, while I follow behind. On the way to the temple someone suddenly remembers that the *gamelan* has never been blessed and purified. This is a bad start, but, on reaching the temple, we find that it can be done on the spot, for there are both priest and holy water, and we may have the benefit of offerings already prepared for other purposes. The arrival of the *gamelan* has caused much excited comment. The other club is already there, and the two *gamelans* are set in opposite pavilions. The ceremony of blessing the instruments is performed, and the children are told to play one piece as termination of the rite. They sit down, and people eagerly crowd around, their curiosity aroused by the size of the children and the presence of the surprising *angklungs*. The priest asks them to stand back. It is the children's hour; they dominate the scene. The women pause in their offerings and stand by; the big club watches from the pavilion. The priest says, "*Enggèh, tabuhin!*" "Well, strike up!" and the children begin, while everyone listens in silence, smiling with pleasure. Suddenly, for once, the Balinese seem almost sentimental. There is no doubt that the children are a success.

But the music is soon over, and the program of rituals must proceed. It is now time to go in procession to a distant sacred spring to bathe the gods. The children pick up their instruments as though they had been used to doing this all their lives, and sling them on carrying poles. There is much shouting about getting started. They go out the big gate, followed by the women bearing the god figures on their heads. The *barong*, which is kept in the temple, follows, and the procession is brought up in the rear by a reduced *gamelan* of gongs, *réongs*, drums, and cymbals. The children strike up "Rearing Horse" (their instruments hang before them, from the poles resting on their shoulders), the women chant, and the animated sound of gongs and drums is heard in the rear. Across the fields we go, with waving banners and gilded parasols, through a rushing stream, up the banks, down again into a deep ravine, to wade through one more stream, and up steep rocky slopes. It is getting dark as we approach the next village. At the crossroads everyone has turned out, drawn by the sound of un-

REARING HORSE: reduced score ♩ = m.m. 72

chandetan

melody

large gong

CROW STEALS EGGS; full score. ♩ = m.m. 116

small
gangsas

large
gangsas

bass
genders

xylophones 1

2

angklungs 1
2
3
4

réongs 1
2

drums

small gong

cymbals

large gong

93

familiar music, to watch the procession. We pass through in triumph and finally reach our destination. An hour later it is pitch dark, and torches are lighted. Home we go, the children playing gaily on, losing the rhythm as we step over a fallen tree or scramble down a narrow slippery path. As we return to Sayan, people rush to their doorways with more torches, and children and adults alike join the procession back to the temple. There is a blaze of light in the outer court, where a crowd of men and women move about, gossiping, smoking, eating, and drinking around the refreshment booths, while men and boys are seated about the little gambling tables. Rites have begun in the inner temple, and I decide to go home. I am told the next day that the new *gamelan* club is now famous, people coming from many villages to listen, and that the *angklungs* proved a great success, everyone remarking on their "very sweet" tone. I am also told that the children, apparently drunk with success, could not stop playing but went through their whole repertory several times, until dawn finally announced the end of the first day's celebrations and they suddenly realized they were very sleepy indeed.

POSTSCRIPT ONE: 1938

At the time I originally sent this article in for publication, I learned that both Kayun and Luar had been admitted to the big club. This they had wanted for some time. In spite of their youth, the club was glad to have them, for extra musicians were needed in the figuration section of the *gamelan*. Kayun and Luar were already able to play figuration parts, *molos* and *nyangsih*, to most of the big club's repertory. They simply picked them up by listening, then tried out the passages when the older boys were not rehearsing.

POSTSCRIPT TWO: 1954

When I left Bali in 1939, I formally presented the *gamelan angklung* to the club, with a paper, signed by village witnesses, stating that it was theirs to keep. In 1952, when the Pliatan *gamelan* and dancers, under the direction of Anak Agung Mandra, from whom I had once rented the *Pegulingan gamelan*, arrived in New York for their famous appearances, I asked Lebah, who was one of the group, news of the *seka angklung* in Sayan. "Oh, the boys are all married and have small men of their own," he said, "but they still hold the *gamelan* you gave them. They have added many instruments and play everywhere." He went on to say that *angklungs* became quite the rage after I left and that many clubs include them these days. Even Pliatan had brought a set to New York. "The club," he added, "still likes to remember and laugh about the time you first asked them to play those old-fashioned things."

NOTES

1. McPhee, 1936. References are listed alphabetically in the Balinese bibliography, which appears on pp. 95–98.
2. McPhee, 1937.
3. Drawings by these children are reproduced in an article by Jane Belo (1937) written when these boys were about a year younger. Cf. Jane Belo, "Balinese Children's Drawing" in this volume (p. 52).
4. *Ibid.*
5. *Ibid.*

BALINESE BIBLIOGRAPHY

PUBLICATIONS

ABEL, THEODORA M. 1938. "Free Designs of Limited Scope as a Personality Index," *Character and Personality,* VII, 50–62.

BATESON, GREGORY. 1937. "An Old Temple and a New Myth," *Djawa,* XVII, Nos. 5 and 6, 1–18.

———. 1940–41. "Equilibrium and Climax in Interpersonal Relations." Paper read at the Conference of Topological Psychologists, held at Smith College, Northampton, Mass., December 31–January 2.

———. 1941a. "Experiments in Thinking about Observed Ethnological Material," *Philosophy of Science,* VIII, No. 1, 53–68.

———. 1941b. "The Frustration-Aggression Hypothesis," *Psychological Review,* XLVIII, No. 4, 350–55. Reprinted in *Readings in Social Psychology,* ed. THEODORE M. NEWCOMB, EUGENE L. HARTLEY *et al.,* pp. 267–68. New York: Henry Holt & Co., 1947.

———. 1942a. "Bali: The Human Problem of Reoccupation." New York: The Museum of Modern Art (mimeographed).

———. 1942b. "Comment on 'The Comparative Study of Culture and the Purposive Cultivation of Democratic Values,' by Margaret Mead," in *Science, Philosophy, and Religion: Second Symposium,* pp. 81–97. Published by the Conference on Science, Philosophy and Religion, New York.

———. 1942c. "Morale and National Character." In *Civilian Morale,* ed. GOODWIN WATSON, pp. 71–91. Boston and New York: Houghton Mifflin Co.

———. 1944. "Cultural Determinants of Personality." In *Personality and the Behavior Disorders,* ed. J. McV. HUNT, II, 714–36. New York: Ronald Press Co.

———. 1949. "Bali: The Value System of a Steady State." In *Social Structure: Studies Presented to A. R. Radcliffe-Brown,* ed. MEYER FORTES, pp. 35–53. Oxford: Clarendon Press.

——— (with CLAIRE HOLT). 1944. "Form and Function of the Dance in Bali." In *The Function of Dance in Human Society* (a seminar directed by Franciska Boas), pp. 46–52. New York: The Boas School.

BATESON, GREGORY, and MEAD, MARGARET. 1942. *Balinese Character: A Photographic Analysis.* ("Special Publications of the New York Academy of Sciences," Vol. II.) New York: The Academy.

BELO, JANE. 1935. "A Study of Customs Pertaining to Twins in Bali," *Tidjdschrift vor Ind. Taal-, Land-, en Volkenkunde,* LXXV, No. 4, 483–549.

———. 1935–36. "The Balinese Temper," *Character and Personality,* IV, 120–46.

———. 1936. "A Study of a Balinese Family," *American Anthropologist,* XXXVIII, No. 1, 12–31.

———. 1937. "Balinese Children's Drawing," *Djawa,* XVII, Nos. 5 and 6, 1–13.

———. 1949. *Bali: Rangda and Barong.* ("American Ethnological Society Monographs," No. 16.) New York: J. J. Augustin.

———. 1953. *Bali: Temple Festival.* ("American Ethnological Society Monographs," No. 22.) New York: J. J. Augustin.

COVARRUBIAS, M. 1937. *Island of Bali.* New York: A. A. Knopf.

EISSLER, KURT R. 1944. "Balinese Character," *Psychiatry,* VII, No. 2, 139–44.

GORER, GEOFFREY. 1936. *Bali and Angkor or Looking at Life and Death.* London: Michael Joseph.

GORIS, R. 1936. "Overzicht over de belangrijste litteratuur betreffende de cultur van Bali over het tijdvak 1920–1935," *Mededeelingen Kirtya Liefrinck Van der Tuuk,* Aflevering 5, 1936(?).

HOLT, CLAIRE. 1935. "Les Danses de Bali," *Archives internationales de la danse,* Part I, pp. 51–53; Part II, pp. 84–86.

———. 1939. "Théâtre et danses aux Indes néerlandaises," *Catalogue et commentaires,* XIIIᵉ, "Exposition des Archives internationales de la danse," p. 86. Paris: Masson & Cie.

———. n.d. "Analytical Catalogue of Collection of Balinese Carvings." New York: American Museum of Natural History (unpublished).

KAT, ANGELINO DE, and KLEEN, TYRA DE. 1923. *Mudras auf Bali.* Hagen and Darmstadt (Germany): Folkwang Verlag.

LEKKERKERKER, C. 1920. *Bali en Lombok: Overzicht der litteratuur omtrent deze eilanden tot einde 1919* (Uitgave van het Bali-Instituut). Rijswijk: Blankwaardt & Schoonhoven.

McPHEE, COLIN. 1935. "The 'Absolute' Music of Bali," *Modern Music,* XII, No. 4, 163–69.

———. 1936. "The Balinese *wajang koelit* and Its Music," *Djawa,* XVI, 1–50.

———. 1937 *"Angkloeng* Music in Bali," *ibid.,* XVII, 322–66.

———. 1938. "Children and Music in Bali," *ibid.,* XVIII, No. 6, 1–15.

———. 1939. *"Gamelan*-muziek van Bali, Ondergangschemering van een Kunst," *ibid.,* XIX, 183–85.

———. 1940. "Figuration in Balinese Music," *Peabody Bulletin,* Ser. XXXVI, No. 2, pp. 23–26.

———. 1944. "In This Far Island," *Asia Magazine,* XLIV, 532–37; 1945. XLV, 38–43, 157–62, 206, 210, 257–61, 305–9, 350, 354.

———. 1946. *A House in Bali.* New York: John Day.

———. 1947. *A Club of Small Men.* New York: John Day.

———. 1948. "Dance in Bali," *Dance Index,* VII, Nos. 7 and 8, 156–207.

———. 1949. "Five-Tone Gamelan Music of Bali," *Musical Quarterly,* XXXV, No. 2, 250–81.

———. "Music in Bali, 1931–1939" (in preparation).

MEAD, MARGARET. 1937. "Public Opinion Mechanisms among Primitive Peoples," *Public Opinion Quarterly,* I, No. 3, 5–16.

———. 1939a. "Men and Gods in a Bali Village," *New York Times Magazine,* July 16, pp. 12–13, 23.

——. 1939*b*. "Researches in Bali, 1936–1939; on the Concept of Plot in Culture," *Transactions of the New York Academy of Sciences,* Ser. II, II, 1–4.

——. 1939*c*. "Strolling Players in the Mountains of Bali," *Natural History,* XLIII, No. 1, 17–26.

——. 1940*a*. "The Arts in Bali," *Yale Review,* XXX, No. 2, 335–47.

——. 1940*b*. "Character Formation in Two South Seas Societies," *American Neurological Association Transactions* (66th annual meeting, June), pp. 99–103.

——. 1940*c*. "Conflict of Cultures in America," *Proceedings, Middle States Association of Colleges and Secondary Schools* (54th annual convention, November 23–24), pp. 30–44.

——. 1940*d*. "Social Change and Cultural Surrogates," *Journal of Educational Sociology,* XIV, No. 2, 92–109. Reprinted in *Personality in Nature, Society, and Culture,* ed. CLYDE KLUCKHOHN and HENRY A. MURRAY, pp. 511–22. New York: A. A. Knopf, 1948.

——. 1940–41. "Family Organization and the Super-ego." Paper presented at the Conference of Topological Psychologists, Smith College, Northampton, Mass., December 31–January 2 (mimeographed).

——. 1941*a*. "Administrative Contributions to Democratic Character Formation at the Adolescent Level," *Journal of the National Association of Deans of Women,* IV, No. 2, 51–57. Reprinted in *Personality in Nature, Society, and Culture,* ed. CLYDE KLUCKHOHN and HENRY A. MURRAY, pp. 523–30. New York: A. A. Knopf, 1948.

——. 1941*b*. "Back of Adolescence Lies Early Childhood," *Childhood Education,* XVIII, No. 5, 58–61.

——. 1941–42. "Community Drama, Bali and America," *American Scholar,* XI, No. 1, 79–88.

——. 1942. "Educative Effects of Social Environment as Disclosed by Studies of Primitive Societies." In *Symposium of Environment and Education,* ed. E. W. BURGESS *et al.,* pp. 48–61. ("University of Chicago, Supplementary Educational Monographs," No. 54, "Human Development Series," No. 1.) Chicago: University of Chicago Press.

——. 1943. "The Family in the Future." In *Beyond Victory,* ed. RUTH NANDA ANSHEN, pp. 66–87. New York: Harcourt, Brace & Co.

——. 1947. "Age Patterning in Personality Development," *American Journal of Orthopsychiatry,* XVII, No. 2, 231–40.

——. 1949. *Male and Female.* New York: William Morrow; London: Victor Gollancz.

——. 1954. "Research on Primitive Children." In *Manual of Child Psychology,* ed. LEONARD CARMICHAEL, pp. 735–80. New York: John Wiley & Sons.

MEAD, MARGARET, and MACGREGOR, FRANCES COOKE. 1951. *Growth and Culture: A Photographic Study of Balinese Children.* New York: G. P. Putnam's Sons.

MURPHY, GARDNER and LOIS. 1943. "Review of Balinese Character: A Photographic Analysis," *American Anthropologist,* XLV, No. 4, Part I (October–December), 615–19.

ZOETE, BERYL DE, and SPIES, WALTER. 1939. *Dance and Drama in Bali.* Preface by ARTHUR WALEY. New York and London: Harper & Bros.

FILMS

BATESON, G., and MEAD, M. Films on character formation in different cultures. Institute for Intercultural Studies. Distributed by New York University Film Library, New York 3.

A Balinese Family. 2 reels, sound.
Bathing Babies in Three Cultures. 1 reed, sound.
Childhood Rivalry in Bali and New Guinea. 2 reels, sound.
Karba's First Years. 2 reels, sound.
Trance and Dance in Bali. 2 reels, sound.

MUSIC

Recorded Music

From album of *Music of Indonesia*
Bali:
1. *Ganda Pura* (instrumental with *gamelan and rebab*).
2. *Peperangan Sira Pandji Perabangsa* (classic opera); with notes by RADEN SUWANTO. Information Services, Indonesian Government, No. P-406. New York: Folkways Records, 1950.

Dancers of Bali: Gamelan Orchestra of the Village of Pliatan, Bali, Indonesia, directed by Anak Agung Gde Mandera. ML-4618. New York: Columbia Records, 1952.

McPHEE, COLIN. *Music of Bali.* Album of Balinese flute melodies and *gamelan* compositions, arranged for flute and piano, and for two pianos. Performers, GEORGE BARRÈRE, BENJAMIN BRITTEN, and COLIN McPHEE. G. Schirmer, 1940.

Published Music

McPHEE, COLIN. *Balinese Ceremonial Music: Gambangan, Pemungkah, Taboeh Teloe.* Transcribed for two pianos. New York: G. Schirmer, 1940.
———. Orchestra score of *Tabuh-Tabuhan,* symphonic work for two pianos and orchestra based on Balinese *gamelan* technique. New York: Associated Music Publishers (in press).

CHAPTER 7

French Parents Take Their Children to the Park

————————————————————————MARTHA WOLFENSTEIN

Some of the observations upon which this study is based were made in Paris in the summer of 1947 as preliminary work for a group project on French culture which began in the fall of that year as part of Columbia University Research in Contemporary Cultures (under a grant from the Human Resources Division, Office of Naval Research). Some of the results of that project appear in Themes in French Culture *(Métraux and Mead, 1954). The material presented here has drawn on those findings; also on ideas derived from analysis of French films (Wolfenstein and Leites, 1950); and on Nathan Leites' current, as yet unpublished, researches on France.*

IN PARISIAN families it is a regular routine to take the children to the park. This is a good situation in which to observe how French children play, their relations with one another and with the adults who bring them to the park. In the summer of 1947 and again in the summer of 1953 I had occasion to make such observations in various parks in Paris. As an American watching French children and their parents, I was continuously aware of how they contrasted with American parents and children. I have included these points of contrast in the following account of my observations. The hypotheses about the French which I present draw upon more extensive researches on French culture, of which these observations formed a part.

THE "FOYER" IN THE PARK

For the French each family circle is peculiarly self-inclosed, with the family members closely bound to one another and a feeling of extreme wariness about intrusion from outside.[1] This feeling is carried over when parents take their children to play in the park. The children do not leave their parents to join other children in a communal play area. In fact, there are few communal play facilities—an occasional sand pile, some swings and carrousels, to which one must pay admission and to which the children are escorted by the parents. The usual procedure is for the mother (or other adult who brings the children to the park) to establish herself on a bench while the children squat directly at her feet and play there in the sand of the path. Where there is a sand pile, children frequently fill their buckets there and then carry the sand to where mother is sitting and deposit it at her feet. What one sees in the park, therefore, is not so much groups of children playing together while the adults who have brought them for this purpose sit on the side lines, but rather a series of little family enclaves. In a similar spirit the adults bring food from home for the children's mid-afternoon snack (*goûter*); it is rare for them to buy refreshments in the park (and, in keeping with the small demand, there are few facilities for this).

The adults do not seem interested in friendly overtures between children of different families, showing little of the usual eagerness of American parents that their children should make friends and be a success with their age mates. French adults seem to be much more on the alert for negative behavior of other children toward their charges.

These tendencies are illustrated in the behavior of a grandmother and her two-and-a-half-year-old grandson, Marcel. The grandmother seats herself on a bench facing the sand pile, to which Marcel goes, waving back at her across a few feet as if it were a long distance. He keeps looking at her while he plays, and she praises his sand pies. When a little girl steps on one of them, the grandmother scolds her roundly. Repeatedly the grandmother enters the sandbox and takes the little boy away from the others, telling him to stay in his own little corner. She makes frequent negative comments about the other children, remarking to me: "Have you ever noticed in children how some of them have the spirit of evil [*l'esprit du mal*]? Marcel, however, never destroys other children's things; he is very well brought up [*très bien élevé*]." The little boy, though on the whole he seems friendly toward other children, has the idea of demarcating his own little space and safeguarding it from intrusion. Thus, when another boy sits down on the cement edge of the sandbox where Marcel has a row of prized sand pies that grandmother has helped him make, he is anxious about the other boy getting too close and makes a barrier with his hand between the other boy and the sand pies; then, becoming increasingly uneasy about these fragile possessions, he starts gently pushing the other boy away (Sèvres-Babylone, July 23, 1953). In such little daily experiences the child learns from the attitude of the adult to carry over into the world outside the home the feeling of separateness and the need to guard one's own against possibly dangerous intruders.

There seems to be a continual mild anxiety that possessions will get mixed up in the park. Mothers are constantly checking on the whereabouts of their children's toys and returning toys to other mothers. One woman hands a toy shovel to another, saying: *C'est à vous, madame?* (Sèvres-Babylone, July 21, 1953). Toys seem to be regarded as the possessions of the parents, and mislaid ones are usually restored to them. While parents are concerned to keep track of their own child's toys, they seem particularly upset if their child has picked up something belonging to another and are apt to slap the child for it. This happens regardless of whether there has been any dispute and where the owner may be quite unaware that another child has picked up something of his.

The following incidents illustrate these attitudes. A girl of about two is holding a celluloid fish belonging to a boy of about the same age. Though the boy makes no protest, the attendant of the girl scoldingly tells her to give it to him, pushes her forward, and after the girl has handed the fish to the boy, hustles her back to her own bench (Parc Monceau, September 10, 1947).

A girl of about two has picked up a leather strap from a neighboring group. Her nurse reproves her, takes her by the hand, and returns the strap. A little later a boy of about the same age, belonging to this neighboring family, plays with the little girl, picks up her pail, and keeps it while the little girl is fed by her nurse. The boy's grandmother becomes aware that he has the pail, hits him on the buttocks, scolds, and, taking him by the hand, returns the pail to the girl's nurse. In front of the nurse she repeatedly hits the boy about the head and ears (Parc Monceau, September 10, 1947).

A three-year-old boy has been playing with a borrowed scooter, when his mother notices that the handlebar grip is torn. She takes hold of the scooter with one hand and the child with the other, goes over to the mother to whom the scooter belongs, apologizes, and scolds the boy in front of her (Luxembourg, September 11, 1947).

Among American children issues of ownership versus sharing tend to arise when two children dispute about the use of a toy. What is considered desirable is that the child should learn to share his playthings, which are his property, with others. French children seem to be taught something quite different. Toys are familial property, and those belonging to each family must be kept separate. Just as the children with their parents or other familial adults form a close little circle in the park, so their belongings should remain within this circle. The child who brings into this circle something from outside seems to be introducing an intrusive object, which arouses all the negative sentiments felt, but from politeness not directly expressed, toward outsiders. At the same time it is an offense to the outsiders, whose belongings are thus displaced, and restitution and apologies to them are required. Also, as French adults are much preoccupied with property and with increasing their own, they have to ward off the temptation to do so by illegitimate means. The child's easy way of picking up others' things may evoke in adults impulses to take which they strive to repress in themselves and which they therefore cannot tolerate in the child.

Friendly behavior between children of different families is not encouraged by the adults. A pretty nine-year-old girl is playing with a boy of the same age and his sister, about a year older. The boy clowns a great deal to impress the girl, who is rather severe and unamused. Having finally won a smile from her, he flirtatiously pinches her chin and asks her name. She does not answer. Her grandmother, watching this, remarks humorously to the boy: "She didn't tell you?" The grandmother seems quite content with the girl's aloofness and a bit mocking toward the frustrated little boy[2] (Luxembourg, July 21, 1953).

Adults also seemed apt to interpret children's approaches to one another as more negatively motivated than they were. The mother of a five-year-old boy who is approaching a three-year-old repeatedly calls to him: *Claude, laisse le petit garçon!* It is not clear at first whether Claude is more interested in the other boy or in a ball which he is holding. However, when the ball has been taken by the younger boy's mother, the two children sit in the sand and play together quite amicably. Claude makes the younger boy laugh. At no time had the little one shown any sign of not wanting Claude to play with him (Luxembourg, September 11, 1947). In thus underestimating the children's positive impulses toward one another, the adults may be projecting their own negative feelings toward strangers. It would be mistaken to infer, on the grounds of this adult discouragement, that the capacity for friendship fails to develop in children and adolescents. Other evidence suggests that just the opposite is true.[3] Parental approval or urging does not constitute the only auspices under which the child can find a friend. Sometimes the most intense friendships develop without the encouragement or against the discouragement of the older generation.[4]

SECRET SOLIDARITY OF BROTHERS

In the following incident one can observe the friendly relation of two brothers which becomes more outspoken when they get by themselves, away from the adults.[5] The two boys, of about six and seven, very neat, dressed alike in blue jerseys and white shorts, are playing together in the sand of the path. Their father sits talking with two women, who appear to be friends of the family, and the boys' sister, about a year older, sits on a bench with her doll. As the younger boy moves into the father's field of vision, the father slaps his hands and face, presumably because he has got himself dirty. This puts an end to the sand play; the two boys sit down, subdued, on the bench, and, as the father turns away, the older presents the younger with a cellophane bag—a gesture of sympathy and compensation. After a time the father suggests to the girl that the children take a walk around the park, and they immediately set out. On their walk the boys keep close together, leaving the girl to herself. As they get farther away from the father, the boys begin putting their arms around each other's shoulders. They become much more animated and point things out to each other as they go. As they get nearer to the father again on the return path, they drop their arms from each other's shoulders, drift apart, and again become more subdued. Having returned, they seat themselves quietly again on the bench (Parc Monceau, September 4, 1947).

ACCEPTANCE OF THE LITTLE ONES

French children show a great readiness to play with children younger than themselves, in a way which contrasts strikingly with the behavior of American children. It is typical of American boys particularly to be intolerant of the "kid brother" who wants to tag along and get into the big boys' game when he isn't good enough.[6] An American boy of seven will complain that he has no one of his own age to play with; the neighbors' little boy is six. In America there tends to be a strict age-grading, which the children themselves feel strongly about.

In contrast to this, French children appear interested in younger children and ready to accept them in their games. A boy of eight or nine will play ball with a smaller boy, a five-year-old or even a two-year-old, without showing any impatience at the ineptitude of the younger one. The two children may be brothers or may belong to families that know each other (Sèvres-Babylone, July 21 and 23, 1953). A slender blond boy of about seven seems completely absorbed in a little girl of two or three whom he follows around, bending over to speak to her. The mothers of the two children are acquainted with each other, and the boy and his mother both shake hands with the little girl's mother when she leaves the park. The boy looks quite disconsolate without his little friend; eventually, at his mother's suggestion, he picks up his scooter and slowly pushes off on it (Parc Monceau, September 18, 1953).

Such interest, particularly on the part of boys, in younger children differs markedly from the American pattern, where interest in babies becomes strictly sex-typed for girls only and out of keeping with the boy's ideal of masculine toughness.

On another occasion I observed a group of seven children, ranging in age from about nine to under two, who had been brought to the park by two nurses. They played a number of group games in which the six- to nine-year-olds regularly included a three-year-old little girl, who was given her turn like the rest. In an interval of play, the children sat on a bench, and a couple of the older girls and a boy of about eight took turns in holding and cuddling the baby boy, who was less than two and who accepted their embraces quite complacently (Luxembourg, September 22, 1953).

This sort of grouping which includes a considerable age range may derive from the requirement of staying within the family circle or the circle of children whose parents know one another. Where the American child is expected from an early age to become a member of a peer group outside the family, for the French child the family and the contacts which the adults make with other families remain decisive. While, from the American point of view, this may appear restrictive, it also facilitates friendly relations between older and younger children, including notably affectionate quasi-paternal feelings of older boys toward small children.

It should perhaps be added that in school there seems to be a sharp awareness of small gradations of age. Thus a six-year-old little girl, the child of some friends of mine, informed me that in her class in school the children were seated according to age and that it was mainly the "babies" who were punished by the teacher (who put them in the wastebasket, according to my young informant, or consigned them to the place under her desk). The little girl telling this was evidently not one of the "babies." However, the order of precedence prevailing in the classroom does not seem to carry over outside it.

To the extent to which I was able to observe exclusive groupings, these seemed to be more in terms of sex than of age, though this also appeared much less sharp than among American children. The pair of brothers, of whom I spoke earlier, who were so closely allied but excluded their sister illustrate this. On another occasion I observed a group of girls of various ages (from about four to about seven) playing together at making a garden in the sand of the path (laying down rows of pebbles, etc.) and brusquely throwing out any little boy who intruded ("Boys aren't allowed in the garden. Only girls are allowed in, because we made it.") (Luxembourg, September 11, 1947). This, however, was not frequent; usually boys and girls played quite readily together.

GROWNUPS STOP CHILDREN'S AGGRESSION

French children are not taught to fight their own battles, to stick up for their rights, in the American sense of these terms. If one child attacks another, even very mildly, the grownups regularly intervene and scold the aggressor. The child who is attacked is likely to look aggrieved or to cry, to look toward his mother or go to her. He does not hit back, nor is he encouraged to do so. An attack is thus not a challenge which must be met by the attacked to save his self-esteem. It is a piece of naughty behavior to be dealt with by the adults.

In the following instances one can see how quickly adults intervene in even very slight manifestations of aggression. Among a group of small children playing on a sand pile, a girl of about two and a half takes a shovel away from her four-year-old sister and walks away with it, looking back in a mildly provocative way. The older girl remains seated and simply looks dismayed. The younger one is already going back to return the shovel when the mother comes over and scolds her, calling her *vilaine*. The little one gives back the shovel, and the two resume their digging (Parc Monceau, September 4, 1947).

Two girls about three years old are seated on the sand pile. One takes hold of the other's pail, not removing it but only holding on to the rim. The owner of the pail cries but makes no other defense. An elderly woman, grandmother or nurse of the attacker, intervenes, reprimands, and the girl lets go. The woman reassures the victim, who stops crying. The woman continues to scold her charge, who moves away from the sand pile (Parc Monceau, September 4, 1947).

In an incident cited earlier, where a little girl stepped on a little boy's sand pie, the boy looked toward his grandmother with an expression of amazement and distress. The grandmother promptly launched into a biting verbal attack on the little girl: *Vilaine! Vilaine fille! Tu commences maintenant à faire des sottises!* A little later when another girl was throwing sand into the sand pile, the grandmother scolded her repeatedly, telling her it could get into children's eyes. The girl's mother, a little way off, then chimed in and told the girl to stop. Protective as she was of her little grandson, the grandmother was equally ready to interfere in an aggressive act of his. Thus, when he was pushing another boy, who did not even seem to notice the rather gentle pressure, the grandmother called to him to stop, that he would make the other boy get a *bo-bo,* and the grandson stopped (Sèvres-Babylone, July 23, 1953).

Thus what French children learn is not the prized Anglo-Saxon art of self-defense or the rules that determine what is a fair fight.[7] What they learn is that their own aggression is not permissible.

A consequence of the prohibition against physical aggression is that verbal disputes are substituted for it.[8] Also, in the case of any serious conflict there is a tendency for everything to come to a standstill, for all involved to become immobilized.[9] This was illustrated in a family of five children whom I observed, where a quarrel between two of them brought their play to a complete stop. The four older children (three boys of about twelve, nine, and eight and a girl of about seven) were playing hide-and-seek, while the youngest girl (about six) sat beside her mother, who was knitting. The goal was the chair on which the youngest child was sitting. It happened repeatedly that the second oldest boy, Philippe, a snub-nosed mischievous-looking fellow, did not come out of hiding when he was called. The eldest, a slender, quick, excitable boy, became quite desperate about this, shouting repeatedly: "Philippe! Philippe!" when his brother refused to appear, but not running to look for him. The mother chided him for his shouting, saying, *C'est suffisant*. (Shouting, incidentally, is very rare in Paris parks.) When Philippe finally showed up, in his own good time, smiling provocatively, his elder brother scolded him. Philippe disappeared behind a pedestal against which his mother was sitting; the older boy followed, and evidently hit him, because Philippe was crying when they emerged. The mother appeared to rebuke the older boy. There then followed a prolonged acrimonious dispute between the older brother and Philippe, the game giving way entirely to this dispute. The younger girl and boy, who had participated in the game in a gay and lively way, now became immobile, not joining in the argument or demanding that the game go on or instituting a game of their own, but just standing and gazing abstractedly into the distance. The mother continued to knit, and the father, who had joined them, read his newspaper.

I had the feeling that American children in similar circumstances would, out of a greater urgency for physical activity, have managed to get their game going again. The aggressive feelings would have become dissipated in strenuous action. For the French, the prohibition of fighting seems to extend itself to a general inhibition of motor activity where a conflict has arisen. Everyone becomes immobilized, while protracted and inconclusive verbal hostilities ensue. (This paralyzing effect of conflict is also exemplified in French politics, where *l'immobilisme* in the face of contradictory demands from opposing sides is acknowledged as a central reality.[10])

RESTRAINT IN MOTOR ACTIVITY

To an American visitor it is often amazing how long French children can stay still. They are able to sit for long periods on park benches beside their parents. A typical position of a child in the park is squatting at his mother's feet, playing in the sand. His hands are busy, but his total body position remains constant. Children are often brought to the park in quite elegant (and unwashable) clothes, and they do not get dirty. The squatting child keeps his bottom poised within an inch of the ground but never touching, only his hands getting dirty; activity and getting dirty are both restricted to the hands. While sand play is generally permissible and children are provided with equipment for it, they seem subject to intermittent uncertainty whether it is all right for their hands to be dirty. From time to time a child shows his dirty hands to his mother, and she wipes them off.

Among some children between two and three I noticed a particularly marked tendency to complete immobility, remaining in the same position, with even their hands motionless, and staring blankly or watching other children. A French child analyst suggested that this is the age when children are being stuffed with food and are consequently somewhat stuporous. Occasionally one could see children of these ages moving more actively and running about. But the total effect contrasted with the usual more continuous motor activity which one sees in American children. Also, French children seemed more often to walk where American children would run.

The same French child analyst told me about a "hyperactive" six-year-old child who had been referred to her for treatment. The teacher had brought it to the mother's attention that he was never seated, but constantly moving around at school. I asked whether this was so unusual and was told that the teacher had never seen anything like it, so she knew the boy was ill. Ordinarily, children of this age sit quite motionless in school; as the analyst put it, it is so quiet you can hear a fly flying. As we spoke of the greater activity of American children, the analyst, who had lived for some time in America, remarked that she found many American children *insupportable* in their tendency to keep incessantly in motion.

Thus there appears to be considerable adult intolerance for children's motor activity, which is effectively communicated to the children. The requirement of keeping clean and the inhibition on physical aggression contribute to the restriction of motor activity, and so does the distrustful feeling about alien space, outside the family circle. The relation between restraint on aggression and on large-muscle activity was remarked upon by another French child analyst, who had treated both French and American children.[11] She observed that an American child in an aggressive mood would throw things up to the ceiling, while a French child would express similar angry impulses by making little cuts in a piece of clay.

Forceful activity on the part of children is apt to evoke warning words from the adults: "Gently, gently." Two brothers about nine and six were throwing a rubber ball back and forth. The younger had to make quite an effort to throw the ball the required distance; his throws were a bit badly aimed but did not come very close to any bystanders. His mother and grandmother, who were sitting near him, repeatedly cautioned him after every throw: *Doucement! Doucement!* I had the feeling that it was the strenuousness of his movements which made them uneasy, though they may also have exaggerated the danger of his hitting someone (Sèvres-Babylone, July 23, 1953). Similarly, when two little girls about four and five were twirling around, holding each other's hands, an elderly woman seated near by kept calling to the older girl: *Doucement, elle est plus petite que toi.* To which the child answered that they were not going very fast (Parc Monceau,

September 18, 1953). The implication here seems to be that any rapid or forceful movement can easily pass into a damaging act.

The tendency to talk rather than act appears not only in substituting verbal disputes for fighting but also in prolonged talking, which postpones activity, where the activity is not of an aggressive nature. The preponderance of talk over action was striking in the following incident. The younger of two brothers, about six and eight, has a toy airplane of which he is winding up the propeller. The older boy reaches for the plane, but the younger one keeps it, and the older does not persist. Several slightly bigger boys gather around interestedly (this airplane was the only toy of its sort which I saw in the park). A prolonged discussion ensues about how to launch the plane, whether at this angle or at that. They talk and talk, and the boy with the plane continues to wind the propeller. Watching them, I began to feel rather acutely that there was no action: how about trying actually to fly the plane? Finally, it was set off and was a complete failure, nose-diving about four feet from the takeoff. The interest of the boys, however, did not diminish; they continued their discussion while the owner of the plane again began winding up the propeller. Though a subsequent flight was as bad as the first, no one seemed to draw the conclusion that the plane was incapable of flying. Interest continued, despite failure in action; none of the older boys took the plane out of the hands of the younger one; and the discussion did not lose its zest, despite its lack of practical results (Parc Monceau, September 18, 1953).

On the same occasion the play of another boy whom I observed, with a paper airplane, seemed to demonstrate very nicely the feeling about remaining within a small space. When American boys make planes out of folded paper, these planes are generally long and narrow, with a sharp point, with the aim of their being able to fly as fast and far as possible. In contrast to this prevailing American style, the French boy had folded his paper plane in a wide-winged, much less pointed shape. It moved more slowly through the air and did not go any great distance, but within a small space described many complicated and elegant loops.

Another time I observed a game where an active chase was led up to by elaborate preliminaries in which action was slight. This seemed comparable to the protracted talk postponing action. Five children (of about six to nine) were playing together with a young nursemaid. The nursemaid sat on a bench while the children performed charades in front of her, the performance being preceded by considerable consultation among themselves as to the subject they would enact. As the nursemaid ventured various guesses, the children interrupted their act several times to explain the exact rules of the game to her. When she finally uttered the right word, this was the signal for them to run and her to chase them. Any child she caught before they reached a certain tree then joined her on the bench and helped to guess and to chase the next time round. But before the next brief chase there were again the consultations and the pantomime. Other children's games in which an introductory ritual precedes a chase are common, but I am not familiar with any in which the less active preparatory phase is so elaborate, where talk and small movements occupy such a large part of the game and the chase comes only as a brief finale.

THE CHILD ALONE

French children manifest a greater tolerance for being alone than American children do. Just as they do not show the urge to be incessantly in motion, which one sees in American children, so also they do not show the need to be constantly with other children. When I speak of a child being alone, I mean alone with the adult who has brought him to the park. But this may mean in effect being very much alone, since, as a rule, the adult pays little attention to him. There is usually little interchange in the park between adults and children over one and a half. While mothers and nurses direct a good deal of affectionate talk to a baby in a carriage, they tend to ignore the three-year-old squatting at their feet or sitting on the bench beside them. The child who is able to walk around is, as it were, on his own, even if he is moving around very little. Most of the time the adults read, or knit, or just sit, or talk with other adults of their acquaintance. The child who does not have siblings to play with or other children of families with whom his parents are acquainted may play with a doll or play in the sand or sometimes just sit beside mother without a word being exchanged. There were instances where a mother or a father, a grandmother or nurse, kept up a more lively contact with a child, talking and even playing with him, but this seemed to be the exception rather than the rule.

Where children have others to play with and participate eagerly in common games, they still do not show the need for unbroken social contact. There are intermissions in their play when each may go off by himself. In the group of children of whom I spoke before, seven children of various ages, accompanied by two nurses, a series of organized games (such as charades) were played, which the children seemed to enjoy very much. They could also play in a less organized way, as when they took turns in cuddling the baby or carrying him around. But there came an interlude when they separated. One of the older girls had gone off to take the baby to the toilet, having been given five francs for this purpose by the nurse (this, incidentally, showed an exceptional scruple, as generally children up to six or seven were permitted to urinate in the open). The boy of eight then went a little apart and stood on a chair. He gazed around, looked toward the tennis courts, fingered his collar and his lips, and picked his nose. While in the games he had been lively, smiling, agreeable, and occasionally clowning, he now appeared immobile and abstracted. At a little distance his older sister leaned against a tree, watching one of the younger girls play with a toy that was thrown into the air and caught with a string. While these children came together again shortly afterward, they had chosen for a while to be detached and alone. The moments of detachment, particularly clearly in the case of the boy who was fingering his nose and lips, suggest that the child does not feel so uneasy about autoerotic activities or solitary fantasies that he must be constantly with others to guard against them (Luxembourg, September 22, 1953).

Where there is a choice of either playing alone or with others, playing alone may be preferred (which again I think would be very rare among American children). Three girls of about thirteen were playing near one another, each with the kind of toy which is whirled into the air from a string and caught again, a game requiring considerable skill. The three of them, all quite proficient, continued this play, each by herself, for at least an hour before they joined together and began passing the whirling object from one to another (Luxembourg, September 22, 1953).

For the French child, being alone is partly enforced by the closed family circle, where he is confined with adults, who are often aloof from him. There is some evidence that the child in the circle of adults, preoccupied with their own affairs, may feel painfully abandoned.[12] However, he also seems to achieve a certain tolerance for being by himself, so that, where various possibilities are open to him, he exhibits a range of activities, alternately social and solitary.

It may be added that for the French the mere presence of others, even if there is no overt interaction with them, appears to constitute a valued form of sociability. This would apply to the child who plays by himself alongside other children in the park as well as to the adult who sits alone with his drink and his newspaper at a café table.

LOOKING

Children frequently become absorbed in watching other children. A child walking past where others are playing will come to a standstill and watch. Children sitting on a bench watch others playing ball. A child in the sand-pile becomes immobile, forgets the shovel in his hand and his half-filled pail, as he watches other children. This absorption in looking seems in part related to the obstacles in the way of free contact with others. Sometimes the closest the child can get is to stand a little way off and look. Then, with the inhibition of motor activity, looking may become, in a compensatory way, intensified.[13] But also French children learn by looking more than by doing. They are taught to watch activities for which they are not yet ready but which they will be able to perform later on.[14] This was expressed, for instance, in the way in which parents held up small children to watch older ones on the swings. A mother with a one-year-old boy in her arms stops by the swings and says: *C'est la balançoire, mon petit chéri,* and holds him so that he can watch. A father with a baby of about six months holds the child up to watch, saying, *Regarde. C'est bon?* (Luxembourg, September 23, 1953).

ADULTS ARE ABOVE THE EMOTIONS OF CHILDREN

Adults seem to look down from a considerable height on both the griefs and the joys of children. Childhood and adulthood are two very distinct human conditions. From the vantage point of the adult, the emotions of the child do not seem serious: they are not, after all, about anything very important. The adult is likely to be detached in the face of the child's distress. Where the child is elated, the adult, though sympathetic, may regard the child humorously, perhaps a bit mockingly: how he overestimates these little childish things!

On an occasion when a mother punished a little boy, she appeared quite unconcerned about his rage and grief and was amused when he later came to fling his arms around her. I did not see what it was that provoked the mother's punishment. My attention was attracted when I saw the boy, of about six or seven, running, with his mother, a sturdy, athletic-looking woman, hard at his heels. When she overtook him, she gave him several hard whacks on the behind, and the boy burst into tears. The mother then sat down on the bench beside her husband, who was holding the baby; for her the episode seemed finished. The boy, however, continued crying, his posture very tense, with an expression of raging protest. He stalked off, still crying, looking helplessly angry and hurt, and walked around the playground, where several other children and mothers turned to look at him. His own mother was not looking but after a while glanced in his direction, smiling, seemingly not at him but about him. The boy returned to the parents' bench, stood first in front of his father, then threw his arms around his mother and put his head in her lap. The mother put her arms around him and turned to a woman on the other side of the bench and laughed. The other woman laughed back. The boy remained for some time with his head buried in his mother's lap. The mother had apparently been unperturbed by the boy's stormy tears and by his gesture of walking away, while his return to her, as his love and longing overpowered his angry feelings, seemed to her humorous. In laughing with another adult about it, she seemed to express: that's the way children are; that's all that comes of their little scenes (Sè-vres-Babylone, July 24, 1953). Such discrepancies between the feelings of children and adults, where the adults remain detached while the child is undergoing violent emotions, may produce in the child a sense of painful abandonment.

Where the child is pleased with himself over some achievement, the adults may be more sympathetic, but with a nuance of gentle mockery, expressing a feeling of the smallness of these childish feats. This was the case with the grandmother of the little boy, Marcel, whom I mentioned before. The boy had been trying very hard to make sand molds with his pail. When, after numerous less successful attempts, he turned out a complete one, he threw back his head, beaming with elation. The grandmother was greatly amused by this, laughing and remarking to me: *Il est fier! Comme il est fier!* She was very sympathetic to the little boy, but at the same time found the child's great pride in having made such a thing as a sand pie humorous (Sèvres-Babylone, July 23, 1953). The nuance here is a delicate one. I would say it consists in the adult's never quite putting himself in the child's place but retaining a double position: in part empathizing with the child, but in part seeing the child's concerns as such a small matter that the child's strong feeling about them appears disproportionate and hence comic.

At other times, when children are having fun together, an adult who is with them may be simply unamused, not feeling at all impelled to participate in the children's mood or to smile at what makes them laugh. I observed such a discrepancy of mood where two boys were playing together very gaily while the mother of one of them sat on a bench beside them, reading, very unsmiling, addressing to her son from time to time a slight reprimand and then turning back to her book. Jean, her son, and Michel, his friend, both about seven, were chattering and laughing as they built a sand fort. Jean jumped up to show his mother his muddy hands (he remained otherwise immaculate), saying, *Regarde, maman!* His mother looked up briefly to say in a perfunctory tone, *Quelle horreur,* and continued reading. Jean returned to the fort, jumped up now and then to prance around in a clowning way, then seated himself on the shoulders of Michel, who was squatting over the fort, and playfully bounced up and down. Michel giggled. The mother repeatedly, unsmilingly, told Jean not to do this, without, however, interrupting the play or the good humor of the boys. When the mother announced it was time to leave, the boys began by slow stages to demolish their fort, the operation ending with Michel sitting down on it. The boys thought this very funny (probably the more so since throughout their play they had carefully squatted with their behinds poised an inch or so above the ground). At this final foolishness, the mother smiled for the first time, saying: *Michel, tu es bête* (Parc Monceau, September 18, 1953). In such circumstances as these, the adult's detachment is mingled with disapproval. The children's way of having fun, which here included getting dirty and physical contacts which produced giggles, seems to the adult slightly naughty or at best silly.

I think this latter instance particularly contrasts with the way in which American adults are likely to respond to children's play. For Americans, there is not such a cleavage between childhood and adulthood, nor is adulthood so decidedly the advantageous position. To be able to play like children and with children is a highly valued capacity. The sour-faced adult who is a killjoy to the children's sport is likely to arouse negative reactions not only in children but in adults as well. Adults generally do not like to think of themselves in this role. They are eager to show children that they are good sports, that they have a sense of humor, and this involves falling in with children's playful moods.

CHILDREN MIMIC ADULTS

I observed very little of the sort of make-believe play in which children assume the roles of imaginary characters of drama or story, such as the frequent cowboy play of American little boys. Perhaps such dramatic play is carried on more at home than out in the open. I saw a few little boys with toy guns, but their play was far from aggressive by American standards, and if shooting noises were simulated, they were quite soft. A boy of about seven or eight, holding a gun, told a playmate, *Haut les mains,* in a tone of instructing him how to play the game rather than as a convincing dramatic threat. The second boy obligingly put up his hands and walked smilingly in front of his friend, who held the gun pointed at the other's back (Parc Monceau, September 18, 1953).

More often children mimic the familiar gestures and intonations of adults. Here they show excellent observation, combined with mockery. Their performance has much more zest and vividness than the mild *Haut les mains* of the friendly little gunman. The handshaking ritual of the adults is repeatedly imitated. For instance, as a group of boys pass a brother and sister, one of the boys calls: *Salut!* and the girl takes his hand and shakes it rather hard. Her brother starts shaking hands with the other boys with more show of politeness, saying, *Bonjour, Monsieur* (Parc Monceau, September 18, 1953).

A group of six- and seven-year-old girls who have been working at laying out a garden in the sand of the path take time out to sit on a bench and gossip. After a while, one of them interrupts their talk, exclaiming, like a busy woman who has let herself be distracted from her tasks: "But what are we doing chattering [*bavarder*] like this?" They laugh and return to their work. When smaller children unwittingly get in their way, the girls pick them up and put them to one side, with a *Qu'est-ce que tu fais, petite?* uttered in a tone of simulated amazement, combined with resignation, well imitated from the adults (Luxembourg, September 11, 1947).

At a band concert, a boy of nine, showing off to a pretty little girl, applauds exaggeratedly and cries, "Bravo! bravo!" after every piece. Later, when the concert is over, he mounts the bandstand and imitates the conductor, with autocratic gestures and a grandiose air, while a few other little boys sit in the places of the musicians and pretend to play different instruments (Luxembourg, July 21, 1953).

For the French, adulthood is decidedly the desirable time of life. Simply assuming the role of adults as he knows them is gratifying to a French child; no extraneous glamour need be added. At the same time, the adults in their role of authority rouse impulses of rebellious mockery in children, which they express in parodying the adults among themselves. This motive is liable to persist and to be permitted much stronger expression when the children grow up, in the mockery of authority figures, particularly in the political sphere, which is so prominent in French life.[15]

In contrast to this, for American children the adults they know are far from glamorous. Father is no superman.[16] Cowboys and spacemen provide models that better express the children's aspirations to strenuous and violent activity. The choice of models for children's make-believe play is perhaps reflected in the different styles of adult acting which we find in American and French films. There is little fine mimicry in facial expression, gestures, or tone of voice on the part of the American film hero. As the man on horseback, the man with the gun, fast-moving, triumphant in violent action, he fulfils the small boy's dream, at the same time exemplifying the heroic qualities which daddy lacks. In French films the actors show rather a mastery of small nuances of voice and manner, expressive of different characters that seem to have been unerringly observed. Such acting appears to be the highly elaborated sequel of the children's keen mimicry of adults. The contrast previously indicated between American and French children in respect to large and small movements is also relevant here.

CHILDHOOD IS NOT FOR FUN[17]

For the French, enjoyment of life is the prerogative of adults. Childhood is a preparation. Then everything must be useful, not just fun; it must have an educational purpose. The hard regime of French school children, with its tremendous burden of work, is well known. Probably nothing in later life is such a terrible ordeal as the dreaded *bachot* (the examination at the conclusion of secondary school). It is a real *rite de passage*, a painful test to which youths on the verge of maturity are subjected by their elders.

The attitude that everything for children, even the very young, must serve a useful purpose and not be just amusing is well exemplified around the carrousel in the Luxembourg Gardens. There are various rides for the children, among them rows of large rocking horses. A sign describes these as: *Chevaux hygiéniques. Jeu gymnastique pour les enfants développant la force et la souplesse.*

At the carrousel, as soon as the ride began, an old woman with spectacles and red hair done up in a bun on top of her head and wearing an old-fashioned gray coat (she seemed to me a benevolent witch), handed out to each child in the outer circle a stick (*baguette*). She then held out to them a contraption which dispensed rings and encouraged them to catch the rings on their sticks. Throughout the duration of the ride, the old woman directed to the children an incessant didactic discourse, urging them to pay attention and work very hard to catch the rings. *Attention! Regarde ton travail! Regarde bien, chou-chou! Au milieu,* indicating with her finger the middle of the ring at which the child should aim. *Doucement!* When a child used his stick to beat time instead of to catch the rings, the old woman scolded him for this frivolity. At the end of the ride, she commended a boy who had caught many rings: *Tu as bien travaillé. Tu es gentil.* There was no other premium for catching the rings. On the next ride, a girl of about seven who failed to catch the rings where younger children were succeeding smiled with self-conscious chagrin. The elderly woman who had brought the girl there urged her to do better: *Attention! Regarde bien, Françoise* (Luxembourg, September 23, 1953). Thus, even on the carrousel, children have a task to perform. The elders direct, commend, and rebuke them. They are not there just for fun.

The paradox from the American point of view is that the French grow up with a great capacity for enjoyment of life. The adult enters fully into the pleasures which have not been permitted to the child. There seems to be a successful realization that pleasure is not taboo, but only postponed. The song of Charles Trenet, *Quand j'étais petit,* ends with the triumphant, *On n'est plus petit!*—everything is now permitted. It remains one of the puzzles of French culture how this effect is achieved: that the restraints to which children are subjected have only a temporary influence and do not encumber the adult with lasting inhibitions.

If we compare Americans and French, it seems as though the relation between childhood and adulthood is almost completely opposite in the two cultures. In America we regard childhood as a very nearly ideal time, a time for enjoyment, an end in itself. The American image of the child, whether envisaged in the classical figures of Tom Sawyer and Huckleberry Finn, or in the small hero of the recent film *The Little Fugitive*, who achieves a self-sufficient existence at Coney Island, is of a young person with great resources for enjoyment, whose present life is an end in itself.[18] We do not picture children as longing for adult prerogatives from which they are excluded. Adults tend to feel nostalgic for the carefree times of childhood, or at any rate adolescence. Young adults in their middle twenties may feel old and wish they were back in college. It is in adulthood that the ceaseless round of activities which are means to further ends sets in: the job which is a steppingstone to a better job, the social entertainments which may lead to some advancement, etc. In this continual planning ahead which absorbs adults, the capacity for immediate sensuous enjoyment is often lacking. With the French, as I have said, it seems to be the other way around. Childhood is a period of probation, when everything is a means to an end; it is unenviable from the vantage point of adulthood. The image of the child is replete with frustration and longing for pleasures of the adults which are not for him.[19] It is in adulthood that the possibility of living in the moment is achieved. Not that this precludes much scheming and planning as far as careers or business advantage is concerned. But this is not allowed to interfere with sensuous pleasures, which are an end in themselves. The attainment of these end-pleasures, notably in eating and in lovemaking, is not a simple matter. Much care and preparation are required, and changing stimuli may be needed to keep pleasure intense. Concern with such pleasures and ingenuity in achieving them are persistent in adult life. It is with the prospect of these pleasures that the individual has served his hardworking childhood, and it is now, as an adult, that he can lose himself in the pleasures of the moment.

NOTES

1. Cf. Métraux and Mead, 1954, Part I.
2. Cf. in *The Remembrance of Things Past*, Proust's account of Marcel's long-term childhood attachment to Gilberte, whom he used to see only in the park.
3. Métraux and Mead, 1954, Part I.
4. Roger Peyrefitte's *Amitiés particulières* (1945) recounts a special case of intense homosexual attachment in a strict Catholic school where any meeting of two boys alone together was taboo.
5. The importance of dyadic relations in the family is indicated in Métraux and Mead (1954), Part I.
6. Margaret Mead has pointed out the position of the American "kid brother," whom the older boys regard as a nuisance because he tries to get into their games and he isn't good enough. The recent film, *The Little Fugitive*, gives a vivid instance of this.
7. Margaret Mead describes how, on an American playground, mothers keep admonishing their children to stick up for their rights, to fight for themselves, and to fight fair (Mead, 1942, pp. 141–42).

8. A stock French parental injunction is: *Disputez, mais ne vous battez pas.*

9. Abel, Belo, and Wolfenstein, 1954.

10. Nathan Leites, unpublished research in French politics.

11. Cf. Françoise Dolto, "French and American Children as Seen by a French Child Analyst," in this volume (p. 408).

12. Cf. Prévert, 1951.

13. Abel, Belo, and Wolfenstein (1954) suggest that prohibitions against nocturnal looking intensify the wish to look.

14. French girls, for instance, learn to cook by watching their mothers (cf. Métraux and Mead, 1954, Part I).

15. Cf. the peculiarly irreverent political satire of *Le Canard enchainé*.

16. Mead, 1942, 1949.

17. Cf. Françoise Dolto, "French and American Children as Seen by a French Child Analyst," in this volume (p. 408).

18. Cf. Martha Wolfenstein, "The Image of the Child in Contemporary Films," in this volume (p. 277).

19. *Ibid.*

LIST OF REFERENCES

ABEL, THEODORA M., BELO, JANE, and WOLFENSTEIN, MARTHA. 1954. "An Analysis of French Projective Tests." In *Themes in French Culture: A Preface to a Study of French Community,* ed. RHODA MÉTRAUX and MARGARET MEAD, pp. 109–20. ("Hoover Institute Studies.") Stanford, Calif.: Stanford University Press.

MEAD, MARGARET. 1942. *And Keep Your Powder Dry.* New York: William Morrow & Co.

———. 1949. *Male and Female.* New York: William Morrow & Co.

MÉTRAUX, RHODA, and MEAD, MARGARET (eds.). 1954. *Themes in French Culture: A Preface to a Study of French Community.* ("Hoover Institute Studies.") Stanford, Calif.: Stanford University Press.

PEYREFITTE, ROGER. 1945. *Amitiés particulières.* Paris: Jean Vigneau.

PRÉVERT, JACQUES. 1951. "L'Enfant abandonné." In *Spectacle.* Paris: Gallimard.

PROUST, MARCEL. 1934. *The Remembrance of Things Past.* New York: Random House.

WOLFENSTEIN, MARTHA, and LEITES, NATHAN. 1950. *Movies: A Psychological Study.* Glencoe, Ill.: Free Press.

CHAPTER 8

The Place of Book-Learning in Traditional Jewish Culture

————————————MARK ZBOROWSKI

Adapted from a paper with the same title in Harvard Educational Review, *XIX, No. 2 (spring, 1949), 87–109. This paper is part of a larger study of the culture of Eastern European Jews and of their lives in the small communities of Eastern Europe before World War II. The author grew up in such a community and participated in the Columbia University Research in Contemporary Cultures project, sponsored by the Human Resources Division, Office of Naval Research, which drew upon the memories of Eastern European Jews in the United States, supplemented by selected written materials, films, photographs, etc. One result of this project was the book* Life Is with People: The Jewish Little Town in Eastern Europe, *by Mark Zborowski and Elizabeth Herzog (1952). The author is indebted to Mrs. Elizabeth G. Herzog for her close collaboration and to Dr. Conrad Arensberg for stimulating suggestions, as well as to the group engaged in the study of Eastern European Jewish culture at the time this paper was written: Dr. S. Benet, Dr. T. Bienenstok, Miss N. Chaitman, Dr. N. F. Joffe, and Miss I. Rozeney.*

FOCUS ON LEARNING

THE centuries of Jewish history are centuries of study—millennia of study, in fact, for the cult of scholarship was well established before the destruction of the Temple in A.D. 70. To the tradition-steeped Jew the great landmarks of his history are closely associated with the pursuit of learning. Jerusalem, Yabneh, Babylon, Pumbadita, Spain, Wolozhin, Mir, Slobodka, and Lublin are linked in his mind not only with dramatic events but also with the study of the Law. When the Romans destroyed Jewish national independence, the first thing that Rabbi Jokhanan Ben Zakai did to preserve the Jewish tradition was to create the school in Yabneh. When the Japanese organized the Jewish ghetto in Shanghai, in 1942, one of the first things the Jews did was to organize a *yeshiva* (school of higher learning) and reprint a full set of Jewish scholarly classics. A Jewish community is unthinkable without a center of learning, be it a *kheder,* where the youngest children study, a *talmud tora* for those whose parents cannot pay tuition, a *yeshiva* for higher studies, or a *bes hamidrash* for prayers as well as for study.

The values and patterns discussed here are the ones characteristic of the *shtetl*—the Jewish community in the small town or village of Eastern Europe,[1] i.e., in the Ukraine, Poland (Galicia and Russian Poland), Lithuania, Rumania (Besarabia and Bukovina), Hungary, and Carpatho-Russia. Their effects and their traces are also perceptible among Jews in western Europe and in the United States.

Study is the duty, the privilege, and the joy of the *shtetl* Jew. Young and old, rich and poor, businessmen and manual workers, devote themselves to it. The *bes hamidrash* is never empty, whether it be in the Eastern European *shtetl*, the Lower East Side of New York, or in Brownsville, Brooklyn. In any community that adheres strictly to Jewish tradition, some men are always engaged in fulfilling the divinely decreed obligation of learning. If his occupation does not permit a Jew to devote himself entirely to study, he will study in the morning before work or in the evening after work, or he will devote at least one day a week—the Sabbath—to study.

Study is twice prescribed. In order to be a good Jew, one has to follow the commandments of the Scripture. In order to follow them, one has to know them. In order to know them, one has to study. Moreover, to study is a *mitsva*, that is, a deed commanded by God. To share one's learning is also a *mitsva*.

A Jew without learning is incomplete. He is an ignoramus, an *amorets;* and an ignoramus is the most despised member of the community. There is a saying in the Talmud, "Better a learned bastard than an ignorant priest."

The language itself is amazingly rich in terms for referring to a learned man: *lerner, masmid, kharif, talmid khokhom, ben tora, iluy, lamdan,* are only a few of the terms used in everyday speech.[2] Many more refined and complicated ones are used in writing, to describe the precise degree of knowledge of a learned Jew.

Learning gives prestige, respect, authority, and status. It is, in fact, the primary basis for social stratification, at least in principle. In the *shtetl,* Jewish society is composed of two main groups: the *proste yidn* and the *sheyne yidn,* literally translated the "common Jews" and the "beautiful Jews," although the beauty is based on spiritual values rather than on physical appearance.

The *sheyne yidn* are the "representative" Jews, the "faces" (*pney*) of the community. They are the ones who are given the seats of honor in the synagogue, at the east wall, which the Jews face during their prayers because it is in the direction of Jerusalem. The *proste yidn,* the common Jews, are artisans, workmen—people who in the synagogue are seated farther and farther from the east wall until the very last ones are at the west wall, the place for beggars and strangers.

The learned man belongs automatically to the *sheyne yidn,* since the most important basis for social stratification is learning. A really learned man, a *talmid khokhom,* cannot be a *proster yid;* but a very rich man may be one, if he lacks the background of learning. The three main criteria of status are (1) learning, (2) *ikhus,* or family status, and (3) money. In theory, money is by far the least of these, although in practice it may be given more weight. The ideal combination is learning and wealth—these two together assure *ikhus.* The typical mother's daydream, as expressed in folksong, is to have her son "a *talmid khokhom* and also a clever businessman."

As a learned man he will enjoy all honor in the community. Besides having a seat at the east wall, he will be called more often than others to the weekly reading of the Torah, and he will receive those portions of the reading which are valued most. At social gatherings he will have the place of honor. When he is invited to a feast to celebrate some family occasion, the host will give him his own place at the table, and he will be served first. When he speaks, he will be listened to with deference and not interrupted. In synagogue, during the periods between two prayers, he will always be surrounded by a group respectfully listening to his comments on some passage in the Talmud, or on events in the life of the community, or even on political problems.

The learned man is the pride of the community, and still more of the family. "May he be raised for the Torah, for the wedding, and for doing good deeds." is the wish uttered at the birth of a son. The more learned men a family includes—whether by birth or by marriage—the greater is its *ikhus. Ikhus* may be defined as the sum total of all the values that set the social status of the family, including origin, genealogy, provenience. Among these values the most important is the number of learned men in the past and in the present.

Jewish parents dream of marrying off their daughter to a learned youth or their son to the daughter of a learned father. The marriage broker, who is a very important institution in the *shtetl,* has in his notebook, under the names of the boys and girls, detailed accounts of their *ikhus,* including the enumeration of learned men in their families. The greater the background of learning, the better the match. The sages have said, "A man should sell all he has in order to get for his son a bride who is the daughter of a scholar."

The dowry of a girl is proportional to the scholarship of the prospective bridegroom. Very rich Jews used to go to the *yeshiva* and ask the head for the best student, whom they would then seek as a son-in-law. An outstanding student would receive not only a rich dowry but a given number of years of *kest*—that is, of board at the home of his parents-in-law so that he might continue his studies.

"The Torah is the best commodity" is a popular saying among Eastern European Jews. The father will support his son; the sisters their brother; the father-in-law his son-in-law, in order to give opportunity for study. Moreover, it is correct for the wife of a gifted scholar to earn a livelihood for the family while he remains with his books, and for the community to subsidize the poor student. If a man were not devoting himself to study, he would be scorned as a ne'er-do-well for letting his wife support him, and he would be despised as a beggar if he lived on the community.

Parents seek a learned son-in-law or the daughter of a learned father, not only because of a desire to augment the *ikhus* of the family, but also because of a genuine admiration and relish for intellectual prowess. In addition, learning is viewed as a guaranty of high moral and social standards. An *amorets*, an ignoramus, is not only an unlearned man. He is also a man who does not know how to behave socially, one with low ethical principles, who will treat his wife without due respect and may even beat her. And, above all, he is a man who would not know how to bring up his children.

It is assumed that the child of an *amorets* will probably be an *amorets* also and that a learned man will be a good husband and father. Jewish ethics are learned. One of the basic principles of Jewish education is that the mere fact of learning the rules of behavior causes one to behave accordingly. The wife of a learned man will be treated according to the rules of conjugal relations which are in the holy books. The children will grow up to be learned people. A girl who comes from a family of learned men will be a good wife and a good mother. She will be modest and well behaved, and, most important of all, she will put her husband's learning above everything else because she understands the value of learning.

There is still another advantage in seeking a learned husband for one's daughter. Learning assures the future life, the *olam habo*. A woman by herself has little hope of gaining *olam habo*. She is inferior to men, who daily give thanks to God that they were not created women. Moreover, she does not study—learning is for men only. She, however, reaps part of her husband's *olam habo*. If she is a good wife, especially if she facilitates his studies by taking over such humdrum cares as running the house and earning a living, she will be recompensed for it by a share in her husband's eternal happiness.

All these considerations stimulate parents to dream of a son-in-law who will be a *talmid khokhom,* a dream expressed in a lullaby for girls:

> Under [Baby's][3] cradle
> Stands a snow-white kid.
> The kid went off to trade
> With raisins and almonds;
> But what is the best trade?
> [Baby's] bridegroom will learn,
> Torah he will learn,
> Holy books will he write,
> And good and pious
> Shall [Baby] remain.

The prestige that is linked with learning can be observed also in the relationship between adults and children, for learning erases the difference in age that is so important in Jewish social life. Usually there is a definite separation according to years, and seniority is given all honor. A child is an incomplete member of society, and as such he gets little attention from the male adult. Grownups not only tolerate the presence of children at the synagogue, but even insist on it, because the atmosphere is essential to a Jewish education. But a child is "only a child," and no one expects from him any reasonable, goal-conscious action or attitude.

As long as the child is small, the father pays little attention to his life and activities. But the whole relationship changes as soon as the boy begins to learn, and his prestige increases in proportion to his progress in his studies. The first real mark of respect a boy receives is when he passes the first elementary studies and enters the next stage, the *gemara kheder.*

A boy who is studying the Talmud is considered almost an adult, especially when he shows special aptitude. He may participate in all the debates of adults, and his opinion carries equal weight. A bearded Jew will not be ashamed to bring some difficult talmudic question to a young boy of thirteen or fourteen who is known as a future scholar. A boy who is known as a genius, *iluy,* will be shown the same deference as a learned adult. I have witnessed, for example, the respect shown to a child of eight, son of a famous Ukrainian rabbi, because the little boy knew by heart all the prayers and two complete books of the Pentateuch, together with the accompanying commentary of Rashi.[4]

The Jewish ideal of male beauty again reflects the emphasis on intellect. A man who has a distinguished, beautiful face, ideally has a long beard—symbol of age and therefore of wisdom—a high forehead, indicating highly developed mental abilities; a pale complexion, revealing long hours spent over books at night; thick eyebrows, showing penetration, that jut out over deep-set, semiclosed eyes, indicating weariness from constant poring over books—eyes that shine and sparkle with wit as soon as an intellectual problem is discussed. Very important are the small, pale hands, confirming the fact that the owner is not engaged in any manual trade but has devoted his life to study.

A scholar is easily recognizable in the streets of the *shtetl*. He walks slowly, sedately, absorbed in his thoughts. His speech is calm, rich in quotations from the Bible or the Talmud. A great deal is said by a sound, an allusion, a slight wink, grimace, or gesture.

When he walks, he is greeted first by other members of the community, in deference to his high position. Not only the poor but also the wealthy greet him first, if they are less learned than he. His answer to the greeting will correspond to the intellectual status of the person. If the salutation comes from an *amorets,* there will be just a slight imperceptible wink—and sometimes even that is omitted. If the other person is considered more or less an intellectual equal, there will be an inclination of the head.

A learned man seldom laughs. Excessive laughter is considered the mark of an *amorets.* For the most part, he will react to a joke or a witty saying by a smile or a very short and restrained chuckle. The *talmid khokhom* must indicate his position in the community by his behavior and his appearance.

In view of the advantages attached to scholarship—status, prestige, a rich wife, the joy of study itself—it is natural that to be a scholar is considered the most desirable career of all. From infancy the boy is guided and prodded toward scholarship. In the cradle he will listen to his mother's lullabies:

> Sleep soundly at night and learn Torah by day,
> And thou'lt be a rabbi when I have grown gray.

or

> My Yankele shall learn the Law,
> The Law shall baby learn,
> Great books shall my Yankele write,
> Much money shall he earn.

or

> A boy who'll study the *gemara,*
> The father will listen with happiness and joy,
> A boy who grows to be a *talmid khokhom.* . . .

The whole family—mother, aunts, sisters, everyone who is in close contact with the baby—will watch for anything in his behavior that could be interpreted as a sign of intellectual precocity. A smile, an unexpected gesture, an imitation of an adult's expression, will be considered an indication of exceptional intelligence—and parents and neighbors will exclaim about the little prodigy.

As soon as the baby starts to talk, his mother teaches him religious blessings and sometimes a few simple Hebrew words. More important, however, the child is steeped in the atmosphere and the spirit of learning. Most of the father's time at home is spent over his books. While the father studies, he will take the little boy, even before the child is able to talk, on his lap, to make him familiar with the "black points," or letters. The child becomes used to the melody of learning—the chant always uttered as the scholar reads—to the father's continual swaying as he studies, to the general aspect of a book.

The father does not object if the child turns the page, if he closes or opens the book; but one thing is strictly prohibited—to damage the book or throw it on the floor. From the very beginning the child is taught to respect a book, even to hold it in awe. He is taught to respect the whole process of learning. When father is studying, he must be quiet. No noisy games are allowed, because "father is studying." He sees his mother and the other members of the family avoid the least noise because "father is studying," "father is looking into a book."

When a learned member of the family comes into the house, the child sees the respect shown to him, and a mother will never forget to tell her son, "When you grow up, you must be a *talmid khokhom* like him." As the boy is usually named after some prominent deceased member of the family, he is always reminded to follow his example and become a learned man. Thus learning is a frequent topic of family conversation, of mother's lullabies, of blessings, of wishes, and of exhortations that the child receives from day to day.

Once he starts to school, the boy is the "jewel" of the family. Every Saturday the father will examine him, while the teacher sits by and the mother looks on tensely. Each new step in the curriculum is an occasion for family celebration, at home and in the synagogue. At such celebrations the boy must show his intellectual mettle and his progress by some original interpretation of a sentence from the Bible.

If the boy shows ability and enthusiasm, the family is happy and the parents are proud. If he is indifferent or incompetent, they will reproach him, painting his future in appalling colors: "What will you be? A tailor? A shoemaker? An *amorets!*" The father will try to stimulate his intellect by threats, by punishments, by beating. As one informant said, "When my father beat me for playing hookey from *kheder*, he would say, 'You'll become a *talmid khokhom* even if I have to kill you!'"

A LIFELONG PROGRAM OF STUDY

Formal education begins between the ages of three and five, when the boy is first taken to the *kheder*. It is a curriculum that has a beginning but no end. Jewish learning never finishes because, as the proverb says, "The Torah has no bottom."

Entrance into the *kheder* is a painful moment in a child's life. A mere baby, he is taken away from his mother's familiar presence to spend ten or twelve hours a day at study. The child cries, the mother has tears in her eyes, but, as I. I. Singer says in his memoirs, "No power could oppose the commandment to teach Tora to a boy who is already three years old."[5]

To make the new experience more pleasant, a special assistant of the *melamed,* or teacher, will carry the child to and from school for a number of weeks. This assistant is called the *belfer.* To stimulate the child's interest, at the first lesson candies or coins are thrown from above him onto the open prayer-book from which he is learning his first letters— the letters that spell the Hebrew word for "eternal" and "truth." And the *melamed* will tell him, "Those are angels watching a Jewish boy start his study, and they are throwing the reward from heaven."

But the first steps on the lifelong path of learning are very difficult, both emotionally and intellectually. The *belfer* who carries the small children to and from *kheder* is usually very rough with them and has to be bribed with the sweets and pennies he receives from their mothers. The room in which they study from eight to six, five days a week and a half-day on Friday, is small and poorly furnished, crowded with fifteen or twenty children of assorted ages.

Their teacher, the *melamed,* for the most part is not himself a learned man and has fallen into his profession because he failed elsewhere. He barely manages to live on the meager payment he receives; he and his family are chronically underfed. He seldom has any pedagogical ability or any interest in teaching, is always gloomy and angry because of his miserable life, and never misses a chance to vent his spleen by severe punishments.

The method of teaching demands of the child tremendous intellectual effort. The candies thrown on his first lesson-book sweeten only the very first hour of learning. Thereafter there is no attempt to sugar-coat the subject matter. No textbooks with pictures, no storytelling, no educational games, are used. The only guides to lead the child into the "gates of the Torah" are dingy, tattered prayer-books with incomprehensible letters and words, and old Bibles used over and over again. The centuries-old method is followed of endlessly repeating the incomprehensible Hebrew words, memorizing each letter, each word, the meaning of each word and of the sentence. Yet little by little the child does learn to read and to translate.

The method of teaching by mechanical repetition and memorizing does not demand any understanding of the text. That will come later. Words in the sentences are translated separately, without any reference to grammar or etymology. Sometimes even the true meaning of the word is neglected, especially when in reading the Bible the boy comes across some botanical or zoölogical name. In these cases, instead of translating the word exactly, the *melamed* (who himself does not always know the meaning) will say, "a kind of fish," "a kind of beast," "a kind of tree."

Swaying as one reads and chanting the words in a fixed melody are considered necessary for successful study. Movement and melody are automatically acquired by imitation, as are the appropriate gestures with the index finger and the thumb, sweeping the finger through an arc of inquiry and nailing the point down with a thrust of the thumb. Above all, the students are trained to be attentive to the words of the *melamed* and ready to repeat the reading or the translation of a word the moment he indicates it with the pointer. Inattention and absent-mindedness are severely punished, and very often interest is stimulated by the teacher's cat-o'-nine-tails.

In this small, ill-lit, ill-ventilated room, packed with childish misery, are nourished the roots that will eventually blossom into a veritable passion for study, one in which zest is conspicuous. And from the uncomprehending rote repetition of syllables and words will develop an exuberant virtuosity in interpretation and endless analysis.

The *kheder* is viewed as a training period for the real learning that is to come. In the most elementary, the *dardaki kheder*, or small children's *kheder*, the pupils learn the elements of reading and the prayers. After a few months, when the child has mastered *ivri*—the mechanics of reading, as differentiated from *ivri taytsh*, or "true" reading with translation—he begins to study the Pentateuch or *khumash*. But he does not begin with the first book, Genesis, which could give some joy through its legends and stories. He starts with Leviticus, the dull and difficult theory of sacrifices.

Study of the Pentateuch is combined with study of the commentary of Rashi.[6] It is not enough for the child of four to six to understand and to translate the text of the Bible; there must be comment and interpretation. The words and sentences have, in addition to their simple, direct meaning, another special significance, and in order to understand them it is necessary to study the commentary of Rashi. For example, the Bible says: "When Sarah died, her age was a hundred and twenty and seven years." According to Rashi, the question must be asked, "Why the repetition of the 'and'?" The answer is that not only at the time of her death was she a hundred and twenty-seven years old, but also that at this age she looked as beautiful and young as at the age of twenty; and that at the age of twenty she looked as beautiful and young as at the age of seven years. Thus from the *khumash kheder* the child becomes acquainted not only with direct understanding of direct statements but also with involved interpretations and the search for hidden meanings.

But *khumash* and Rashi represent the most elementary phases of study, in which pupils are taught directly by the *melamed*, as befits small children and beginners. In the *gemara kheder*, the highest *kheder*, where Talmud studies are the main subject, that sort of instruction is gradually replaced by the principle of independent study under the guidance of the teacher.

Talmudic study is a continuous discussion, commentary, and interpretation, with the help of innumerable commentators and interpreters, of the most varied aspects and problems of Jewish life, ancient and contemporary, religious and secular. With equal concentration, the child of eight or nine has to study the holiday ritual in the temple, the problems of man-to-man dealings, the laws of divorce, or the rules governing behavior during menstruation.

It is with the talmudic studies that the true joy of learning is born. In the *dardaki kheder* and the *khumash kheder* the work was routine, mechanical, boring, repetitious, without much understanding and without the true joy of learning. The Talmud opens the opportunity to exercise individual capacities and imagination, to show one's intellectual quality.

The beginning of the talmudic studies, although it is not celebrated so spectacularly as the beginning of the *khumash*, has a tremendous importance for the boy's future. In the *gemara kheder* the boy begins to study the main code of Jewish wisdom. It is here that his abilities meet the real test and it becomes evident whether he will become a *talmid khokhom*, a wise student. Here the boy of ten or eleven begins to display the real caliber of his memory and his power to spend long hours over a difficult problem, using the numerous commentaries and interpretations with penetration and understanding.

The opinion of the teacher about the boy's capacities is not enough. The father may take him from time to time, on a Sabbath, to be examined by some member of the family who is known as erudite, a *lamdan*, or to any famous scholar in the community, and anxiously wait for an opinion. When a learned guest from out of town visits the family, the father will provoke a scholarly discussion in order to find out what the guest thinks about his son's endowment. The whole family listens to the discourse, especially the mother, because the opinion of a learned man means a great deal for the future of the boy. The great question is: Is he qualified to devote his life to his studies, or should he interrupt them and go into trade or business?

If the boy is judged capable of becoming a *talmid khokhom*, he is sent from the *gemara kheder* to the highest institution of learning, the *yeshiva*. There, among hundreds of boys from different towns and provinces, under the guidance of eminent scholars, he will devote all his days and a great part of his nights to study.

The general principle of the *yeshiva* is independence and self-reliance. There is no definite program of studies, no set course. Each student is privileged to study the part of Jewish wisdom that appeals to him most. If he is attracted by mystical problems, he will study the *kabala;* if philosophy is his field, the works of Maimonides are at his disposal; if he is interested in legal questions, he will work on the Talmud. But in all cases the approach is the same: commentary, interpretation, referring of the different texts to the ultimate biblical quotation.

Certain aspects of talmudic study are often called *pilpul,* meaning "pepper," and they are as sharp, as spicy, as stimulating, as the name implies. It means comparison of different interpretations, analysis of all possible and impossible aspects of the given problem, and—through an ingenious intellectual combination—the final solution of an almost insoluble problem. Penetration, scholarship, imagination, memory, logic, wit, subtlety—all are called into play for solving a talmudic question. The ideal solution is a new, original synthesis, one that has never before been offered. This mental activity combines the pleasures and satisfactions of high scholarship and of high sport. It is a delight both to the performer and to his audience. Both enjoy the vigor of the exercise and the adroitness of the accomplishment. And, at the same time, both relish demonstrating their ability to perform on such a lofty and esoteric level.

In the *yeshiva* the teacher is strictly a guide. He will give an assignment from the Talmud, usually some difficult, contradictory problem, which the students have to work out, making use of different commentators and discussing the problem among themselves by way of rehearsal for classwork. The recitation period will be a discussion of the problem between students and teacher, an exercise in which the teacher as well as the student will try to excel. Such assignments are apart from the individual work of the students, already mentioned.

An eye witness describes a lesson in the *yeshiva* as follows:

Every one of [the students] tries to place himself as near as possible to the platform [where the teacher stands] in order to be able to hear the explanation as clearly as possible. They are standing almost on top of each other. . . . The *shiyur* [lesson] usually took two hours but was interrupted many times. . . . Almost every sentence was challenged by the pupils who were placed higher than the others and who were shouting in order to contradict the words of the teacher, who seemed to them to be an angel of God. They did not behave with the *derekh erets* [deference] which forbids several people to speak at once and to interrupt. On the contrary, sometimes they attacked the teacher in groups in order to fight him, and it seemed as if the subject concerned them personally and they wanted to fight him in a struggle which knew no bounds. At this time the great teacher sat calmly and quietly without saying a word, as if he were thinking, "Go ahead, children, go ahead!" He did not like those pupils who were quiet and silent.

In order to be able to devote his life to study, the *yeshiva bakhur,* or *yeshiva* boy, has to be assured of material subsistence. "Without flour [bread] there is no study," says the proverb. Very few of the students have parents who can support them, however. The solution of this problem once more demonstrates the importance attached to learning —the community takes over the burden of supporting not only the *yeshiva* itself but each individual student.

Deputies travel in cities and towns of Eastern Europe raising money to support the *yeshiva;* and members of the community where a *yeshiva* is established board the individual students. At the beginning of the semester each member of the community offers to feed a student one day each week. The great majority of the students subsist by these "eating days" with different members of the community, and it is said that the dream of a *yeshiva bakhur* is: "a house seven floors high; on each floor lives a *nogid* [rich man]; and with each *nogid* I'll have a 'day.'"

Each member offers "days" according to his economic status. A rich man offers several days to several students, a poor man only a scanty meal one day each week to one student. Some, who for one reason or another are unable to feed the student at home, replace the meal by coins to buy food—not always enough. Everyone in some way must fulfil the *mitsva* to support the study of the Law among the people of Israel.

It is, of course, only a small minority who attends the *yeshiva,* that special elite drawn from the outstanding students of the *gemara kheder.* The number is further limited by the distance of many towns and cities from the centers where the *yeshiva* are located.

For all those unable to continue their studies in the *yeshiva,* the place for post-*kheder* study is the *bes hamidrash,* the house of study. It is usually a local synagogue, for the synagogue is as much a house of study as it is a house of prayer. In the *bes hamidrash,* after the periods of daily prayers, students, old and young, study the same subjects pursued in the *yeshiva,* under the same methods of independent and individual study. One of the learned men in the community adopts the role of teacher, helping the students in their work. Since the teacher's role is minimal in advanced studies, the work does not lag or suffer, even when the *bes hamidrash* students are completely deprived of a teacher.

In the *bes hamidrash,* as in the *yeshiva,* poor students are supported by the community through "eating days." The students in the *bes hamidrash,* however, include some not found in the *yeshiva.* One group is composed of men who have interrupted their *yeshiva* studies because of marriage. Supported by their fathers-in-law, they continue their studies in the local *bes hamidrash.* To this group also belong Jews who are devoting their time to study while their wives earn the living for the family. Another group of students consists of workmen, businessmen, tradesmen, who, after their daily work, still strive toward learning, even though they do not belong to the learned men of the community. These nonscholarly students, who are not qualified to study independently, are grouped in associations or teams called *khevras*. Each *khevra* studies a definite segment of Jewish lore, according to the background and training of its members, and each has a name corresponding to the subject studied. There will be a group which studies only the Mishna, or Code of Law without the talmudic commentary; a group which studies only the digest of Jewish laws, etc. The members of the *khevra* frequently hire a *melamed* who helps them through the difficulties encountered in their studies. Often the *melamed* will be a young boy who is famous for his knowledge and learning.

The three institutions of learning—*kheder, yeshiva,* and *bes hamidrash*—and in some larger Jewish communities the *talmud tora,* embrace almost the total male Jewish population of the community, from three-year-old boys to venerable graybeards. The normal expectation for a boy born in the *shtetl* is that, from the *kheder* to the grave, he will devote some portion of his time to study. No matter how long a man lives, he can continue to explore new wonders in the limitless intricacies and vistas of the Law. During his middle years he must spend part of his time making a living—unless he is one of the scholarly elite. But after retirement he may once more devote all his waking hours to study.

Not every Eastern European Jew is a scholar or even a learned man. But intellectual achievement is the universally accepted goal. There are few Jews from Eastern Europe who have not attended the *kheder*, at least for a short time. Even those who have almost completely abandoned the traditional pattern still speak with pride about their childhood in the *kheder*.

THE NATURE OF JEWISH LEARNING

In the traditional Jewish pattern, study is not an optional activity left to the choice of the individual. It is a *mitsva,* a divine command. To observe a *mitsva* is blessed; to violate one is to invite disaster in this life and later. The *mitsva* of learning is stated in the Bible: "Thou shalt teach them diligently unto thy children, and shalt talk of them when thou sittest in thy house, and when thou walkest by the way, when thou liest down and when thou risest up."

Six hundred and thirteen *mitsvos* comprise the totality of obligations, fulfilment of which is the essence of Judaism. The first ten define the direct obligations toward God; the eleventh is the *mitsva* of learning, just quoted.

Not all, or nearly all, of the *mitsvos* are fulfilled even by orthodox Jews. Some are impossible because they presuppose the existence of the ritual in the Temple of Jerusalem and the national independence of a theocratic Jewish state. Some are neglected because their observance is too difficult for even the most devoutly orthodox. But those which constitute the main base of Jewish cultural behavior—ethical rules, social duties, religious beliefs, dietary regulations—remain in force. Among these the *mitsva* of learning has never lost its strong position. On the contrary, during the long centuries of exile its importance has increased, at least for the Jews of Eastern Europe. The persistence and vitality of the emphasis on learning can be understood partly through analysis of its content, its characteristics, and its social significance.

The traditional Jewish concept of learning partakes of infinity and of paradox, leaping the limits of time and space and joining apparent opposites. The process of study itself does not aim at any concrete or immediately utilitarian product. Moreover, it is far from admirable or prestigeful to make a living from one's learning. A Jew looks with scorn upon one who sells knowledge rather than giving or sharing it. To share one's knowledge is among the most "beautiful" of deeds; to sell it is unworthy. The *melamed* who teaches the elementary *kheder* is despised as a symbol of failure, because that is the only way he has found to support himself and his family. Almost every Jew knows enough to be a *melamed*, to teach small children the elements of the Law. But almost any Jew would prefer to carry his own studies further and make his living at some other occupation. Even the rabbi in Eastern Europe does not receive payment for dispensing his knowledge of the Law. The arrangements in the United States, where a rabbi receives a salary for expounding the word of God, are often surprising to the immigrant from the *shtetl*.

The amount of knowledge amassed through continuous study is not officially measured or evaluated. There is no degree marking the completion of a certain phase of study, for such completion does not exist— "the Torah has no bottom." The diploma the student receives after a few years in the *yeshiva* indicates only that he has the right to exercise the function of rabbi. He does not receive with it a special scholarly title. On the contrary, every Jew, from the tailor who studies a chapter of the Talmud weekly in the *bes hamidrash* to the most learned of savants, is called *Reb*, "my teacher," so that this form of address has become equivalent to our "Mister." When scholars use other forms of address, they describe the degree and quality of intellectual excellence, and not the amount of knowledge. The title *Rov*, or rabbi, is functional rather than academic and is acquired only when a man begins to serve in that capacity.

When a Jew has completed a reading of the Talmud, he has a celebration, usually in the *bes hamidrash*. Then he begins all over again. To describe a man's scholarship, people will tell how many times he has gone through the Talmud. The study of the holy books may be interrupted or may diminish in intensity, but it never stops.

Just as there is no limit to learning, so there is no set curriculum. Everyone studies according to his own capacities and background, concentrating on the area most congenial to him. One will study a chapter of the Pentateuch with its commentary, another a portion of Mishna, a third a page in the *gemara*, with the most difficult commentaries. Each is equally proud of the fact that he is studying. Each will celebrate the completion of a portion of his work, whether it be quite elementary or highly advanced.

Nor are there any special textbooks for study. There are merely editions of the Bible, the Talmud, the *Shulkhan Arukh*, which differ only in the amount of commentary added to the original text.

Rigid distinctions of time are blurred and blended in the tradition of Jewish learning. Past and present are linked together. In the *bes hamidrash* in Williamsburg, Brooklyn, the Jew will discuss the sacrificing of a lamb on a holiday in the Temple, and which parts are due to the High Priest. It is of no moment to him that the situation was actually two thousand years ago, that there is no more Temple, nor sacrifices, nor Priests. The problem has not lost its intellectual reality.

In the *yeshiva* the student participates in the discussions between Rabbi Hillel and Rabbi Shamai, who both lived in the first century A.D., examines the arguments of a seventeenth-century rabbi which support one against the other, and arrives at his own original conclusions. There are no dates in Jewish learning, but rather a continuum which embraces and links together Rabbi Akiba, Rashi, Rabbi Joseph Caro, and the student from the *yeshiva* in Brownsville. The *responsa* of the medieval rabbis are used to solve problems dealing with contemporary business transactions.

Not only the past and the present are interwoven in the learning continuum. In the days to come, when the Messiah brings together all the Jews and rebuilds the Temple, the learned Jews will study the Torah together, and the Lord himself will discuss and give the final solution for the difficult problems which could not be mastered and were left pending "until the coming of the Messiah."

Jewish learning effaces the limits of space as well as of time. A page of the *gemara* looks the same now as two hundred years ago, and the same in Vilna as in Shanghai. All over the world Jews are studying the same Torah, the same Talmud, and with the same talmudic chant, the *nigun*. Little children are reciting the same text as they begin their study of the Mishna: "Two have grasped a piece of cloth." No matter

PLATE XVII. *Book-Learning in Jewish Culture. I*

FIG. 1.—*Yeshiva* in Poland

FIG. 2.—*Kheder* in Poland

Pictures from the archives of the Yiddish Scientific Institute—Yivo (New York)

PLATE XVIII. *Book-Learning in Jewish Culture. II*

FIG. 1.—Reading lesson—*Melamed* and pupils

FIG. 2.—The Sabbath examination (painting by J. Kaufman)

Pictures from the archives of the Yiddish Scientific Institute—Yivo (New York)

where the *shtetl* Jew wanders, if he finds a traditional community at all, he will find the same studies being pursued, the same problems being debated with the same zeal and zest, the same texts, the same type of school, the same emphasis on study.

The learned tradition, then, not only serves to transmit Jewish culture but is also a prime factor of cohesion, maintaining unity and continuity in time and space. Deprived of common territory and common national history since the Diaspora, the Jews have maintained a stable realm in the domain of the intellect. When a Jew takes a scholarly book into his hand, he immerses himself in the tradition that reaches from the far past into the living present. Through study he escapes from the dark reality, from home troubles, from persecution, and finds the joy of identification with his own background and his own group.

The content and the command of traditional Jewish learning also defy clear-cut boundary lines. The Torah—which means not only the holy scrolls but all of Jewish wisdom—contains the whole Jewish truth, which is the only truth. Through continuous study of the same texts, over and over, one comes closer and closer to an understanding of Divine Law, which is truth. It is hard, very hard, to understand the whole truth. Only through analysis of each sentence, each word, through commentary and interpretation, through searching out hidden meanings, can one come gradually, step by step, nearer and nearer to the goal. Yet one never achieves full understanding.

Since no one can claim to have mastered the whole of wisdom, there is no final authority. On the other hand, everyone who studies is able to come closer and closer to understanding, and so through his own efforts to become a relative authority; each student or scholar is potentially an expert. Each strives toward a new and original interpretation—and, in doing so, each relies greatly on his own intellectual ability.

Accordingly, learning is not an exclusive privilege of one social class. It may be achieved by the rich or the poor. Every Jew may hope to have his son become a scholar, every Jew in the community is a student, every Jew is potentially a teacher. Moreover, the prestige brought by learning makes an individual only *primus inter pares*. There is no scholar so wise that his words will not be weighed, examined, and questioned.

The Talmud that the boy begins to study in the *kheder* and continues studying until the end of his days embraces all of Jewish life. It is more than a code of laws; it is also a code of ethics and a handbook of daily behavior. Every detail—social, religious, economic, moral —is examined and discussed, and a definite rule and prescription are set for it. To be a good Jew, a man must learn these norms and rulings; if he is unable to learn by himself, he has to be taught by those who have learned. If "culture is learned behavior," in the *shtetl* community this definition takes on the meaning of "learned from books."

A tremendous part of this monumental work is devoted to the problems of the relationship between man and man. Situations which cannot be regulated by decree are discussed in the Talmud—situations involving honesty, love, the ties between man and wife, parents and children. All the Jewish mores and folkways—in fact, the whole of Jewish culture—is the subject of Jewish learning. Thus the content as well as the nature of the process confirms the Jewish tradition. All that the student learns in his daily life is reaffirmed by the holy books, so that study is a continual reinforcement and reintegration of his own culture.

No subject is too large and none is too small to be included in the all-embracing attention of the scholars. Since the basic rules are held to govern all details of life, none is too trivial to merit exercise of the scholar's virtuosity. For example, the Bible prohibits working on the Sabbath, and the Talmud interprets this prohibition as forbidding even the indirect causing of work activity on that day. In good talmudic spirit, a contemporary rabbi may implement this decree by ruling against opening the refrigerator on the Sabbath, because through opening it one causes the motor to work. It is noteworthy that rulings are adapted not only to modern inventions but also to current conditions. Thus the laws of divorce and remarriage are studied and interpreted in the light of special circumstances caused by the breaking-up and destruction of millions of Jewish families during the Nazi invasion.

The learned man becomes the arbiter in the questions of adjustment which history has made a constant and crucial problem for the Jews. It is his task to facilitate adjustment by an appropriate interpretation of eternal law in the light of ephemeral conditions. If the interpretation is clever enough, it can eliminate hardship for all concerned. Such cleverness can go to great lengths without imposing any sense of disrespect to the Law, for to help humanity is an absolute good. For example, a Jew is forbidden to own flour during the eight days of Passover and, accordingly, must sell all his stock before Passover begins. This problem is solved by a fictive sales contract with a non-Jew, carried out in the presence of the rabbi and effective for the holiday period only. Thus the commandment is fulfilled, and the Jewish dealer does not suffer.

This human editing of divine precept often appears paradoxical to a mind not schooled in the tradition of Jewish learning. On the one hand, there is a legalistic preoccupation with the letter of the law, a verbalistic exercise that reaches extremes of virtuosity, until often it seems to be pursued largely *pour le sport*. On the other hand, there is an underlying concern for the spirit of the law as expressed in the holy books. One may twist and reinterpret divine decree about Sabbath-day usage, until one appears almost a scriptural shyster. At the same time, there is a profound belief that the divine will is actuated by intelligence and reasonableness and that under extreme exigency it is necessary to modify the letter of the law in order to conform to the spirit which dictates always the preservation of human life and the fostering of human welfare.

Clearly, although Jewish learning overrides the limits of time and space, it is by no means abstract. Every discussion is geared to a concrete situation, one which may be improbable or imaginary, but is never impossible. When an extreme effort of imagination is needed in order to understand a given problem, an example, a parable, even a legend, will be used to lend concreteness. When a Jewish student studies a problem concerning sacrifices, it is not an abstraction for him, but a concrete situation which has occurred and may occur again when the Temple is rebuilt.

This extreme concreteness again may appear paradoxical in conjunction with the unperturbed disregard of conventional time and space criteria. The assumption is, however, that the essential unity of the tradition is stronger than any break in physical or temporal continuity. If one accepts this assumption, the whole orientation of Jewish learning is seen as practical and realistic rather than abstract and theoretical.

A learned Jew has scant regard for pure science, pure literature, pure poetry. He can see in such studies no *takhlis*—that is, no direct goal. It is immaterial whether you apply them now or in the days to come, in actual dealings with people, or in understanding the motive of an imaginary deed, but they must be applied. There is no pure philosophy, pure aesthetics, pure mathematics, in Jewish learning. Mathematics is studied in connection with agricultural or architectural problems, aesthetics in connection with applied arts in the decoration of the temple, and philosophy in direct correlation with ethics or with understanding the nature of God.

Similarly, a piece of fiction must have a *musar heskl*, a moral. It must be told or written in order to teach. Poetry is not just an aesthetic arrangement of words and sentences, but a beautifully phrased expression of praise for the Lord or of some moral idea. The "Song of Songs" is not regarded as a poetic description of pure love but as an allegorical presentation of the relationship between the Lord and his people, Israel. Solely as a paean of love, the "Song of Songs" would have no *takhlis*.

In the *shtetl* orientation, the usual distinction between secular and nonsecular hardly applies, for Jewish law and the behavior it governs combine in one entity the religious and secular elements. Strictly speaking, there are no secular elements, since there is no realm of life divorced from the truth and the law embodied in the holy books. The Talmud includes subjects not connected with religion among many other groups, but they are always supported by a religious reference.

For the *shtetl* Jew, the opposition is not between secular and non-secular but between Jewish and non-Jewish. When he opposes his learning to the curriculum of schools and colleges, he does not condemn their studies for being secular but for being incomplete, superficial, and lacking in fundamental truth—as all studies must be that do not stem from the holy books. When an orthodox father forbids his son or daughter to attend a secular school, his arguments are: What can they teach you that we do not have in our Talmud? Aren't our scholars greater, deeper, and don't ours have more knowledge than "theirs"? "Their" science and "their" knowledge originate in colleges and universities. It is human science, while our science comes directly from Mount Sinai, from God. Nothing can be learned in the schools, according to this viewpoint, which has not been said long ago by the Jewish seers.

A different and rather contradictory factor may also be present in the opposition to non-Jewish science, namely, a defense against acculturation. Many traditional Jews—even some who may admit the possibility of learning something new in the schools—see in such curriculums a danger to the Jewish tradition. An immature boy does not yet have a strong enough core to withstand the temptations of a learning that lacks the basic enlightenment. As a matter of fact, one principle in Jewish education is that adolescents who have not gone through the talmudic preparation are forbidden to study those works of Jewish scholars which may misguide and mislead—such as *Guide for the Perplexed*, by Maimonides.

The tradition of learning has contributed to segregation as well as to continuity. Devout belief in the completeness and authenticity of the truth embodied in the holy books—and consequent scorn for those who neither knew nor believed—reinforced from the Jewish side the separation enforced by the majority group. In Eastern Europe the intellectual activity of the *shtetl* Jews was contrasted with the illiteracy of the Polish and Russian peasants. Feelings of intellectual and spiritual superiority over those who rejected truth were strengthened by the intellectual backwardness of the non-Jews—the *goyim*—who, to the Jewish minority group, represented ruthless, blind physical force. In this situation, under conditions of persecution, the tendency to identify intellect and virtue were magnified.

Conversely, a rise in the intellectual standards of the local non-Jewish population may coincide with impulses toward assimilation.

The centrifugal cultural trends that began with the "Enlightenment," *Haskala,* and in great cultural centers of Eastern Europe sometimes led toward complete assimilation of the Jews, coincided with the rise of the intellectual standards of the non-Jewish population.

The prevailing orientation toward learning is brought out in the evolution of the Chassidic movement, which began as a revolt of the unlearned against the bookish doctrine. The salient feature of Chassidism was a love for the common man, the *proster yid.* Nevertheless, in the course of its development Chassidism began to produce a literature of commentary and interpretation based on the sayings and parables of the *tsadikim,* or holy men, the leaders of Chassidism. In time the followers came to vaunt the greatness of their rabbi by telling about his knowledge of such books—although this knowledge was viewed as a result, not of studies in the *yeshiva,* but of direct communication with God. During the further development of Chassidism, this attitude changed so that again knowledge was viewed as being based on book learning. The child of Chassidic parents would receive the same education and attitudes toward learning as any other Jewish child.

In their atitude toward authority, these rebels against the cult of book learning provide an interesting sidelight on the pattern that has grown up about it. The Chassidim, the one antilearning group, are the only group of Jews for whom the religious leader represents absolute and indisputable authority. While the *misnagdim* or non-Chassidic Jews would feel free to discuss and to question any statement of any person, the Chassid would accept categorically and without hesitation any act or statement of their leader, the *tsadik.*

Interviews, life-stories, and literature obtained from Eastern European Jews reveal attitudes and thought habits that are obviously related to the learning tradition just described. One of these traits is commonly referred to as "talmudistic." The legalistic interpretation and analysis of rules and prescriptions, the elaborate word play built about them, the ability to reinterpret them according to the exigencies of the moment, are popularly associated with talmudic training.

Also evident in the interviews and written material (obtained chiefly from non-Chassidic Eastern European Jews) is the antiauthoritarian attitude. There is no final and absolute dictum to be accepted without question. Each individual has to weigh every problem himself, using his own judgment and his own brains. He is little impressed by authorities but is always ready to probe the statement of an expert and to compare it with his own opinions or those of another expert.

There is, too, a reluctance to indulge in easy generalizations. Each problem must be analyzed in its own terms, and the solution is not necessarily simple. By using innumerable "if's," all possible pros and cons are weighed before a solution is accepted. A statement must not be taken at face value; it may hold a second, secret, meaning. Accordingly, every item has to be discussed and interpreted. In politics and in business, the meetings of co-workers or of partners show considerable resemblance to the discussion of a problem in the *yeshiva*.

Bound up with this approach is a relativistic rather than a positivistic attitude. Truth, as perceived by the imperfect human mind, is never single and simple; it is never *the* truth, and is always subject to interpretation. The only absolute truth is the Torah, the Divine Law—and that is inaccessible in full to even the most powerful human intellect. This relativistic and provisional approach fosters a tendency to analyze, to probe, to discuss every problem, every phenomenon; to see it not in one aspect but in multiple aspects. There is not the classic opposition between "yes" and "no." Everything contains both elements, negation and affirmation. It is proverbial in Eastern Europe that a Jew will never answer a question by a direct affirmation or negation. The answer has a conditional character. For, according to his tradition, it is the business of the thinker to recognize and to reconcile incompatibles or opposites, in the realm of the spirit and in the practical world—realms which themselves are indivisible.

The learned Jew in Eastern Europe is known also for allusive speech, when he is conversing with his intellectual peers. Incomplete sentences, a hint, a gesture, may replace a whole paragraph. The listener is expected to understand the full meaning on the basis of a word or even a sound. This habit, in contrast to the fluency displayed under other circumstances, is a direct product of the traditional studies. It is assumed that a truly learned Jew is familiar not only with quotations from the Bible and the Talmud but also with the trend that comment or interpretation would be likely to take. Accordingly, in speaking or writing, a scholarly Jew may say only the first few words of a sentence, expecting his hearer to complete it in his mind. Such a conversation, prolonged and animated, may be completely incomprehensible to one not steeped in traditional learning. The pattern may also be embarrassing to younger men who are less learned—or more acculturated—than their elders assume and who find themselves unable to fill in the gaps as the speaker expects them to do.

OUTSIDE THE *shtetl*

The pattern of learning has been described as it appears in its clearest form in the Eastern European *shtetl*, and secondarily in concentrated settlements in European or American cities. Further study will be required to follow the course of the pattern under the impact of acculturation in the United States. It is obvious that certain features remain and certain changes appear. Both the survivals and the changes need to be studied in relation to the old and the new cultures. Fresh insight into the old culture may be gained by analyzing the features of the new that are most readily adopted and the ones that are most strongly resisted. Certain points may be made on the basis of present observations, however. It is clear, for example, that the emphasis on learning, which is so strong in the life of the traditional Jew, has diminished little in intensity on different levels of acculturation.

The objectives of learning and the fields of learning do change, but the keen striving toward intellectual activity remains. Just as the *shtetl* parents-in-law supported their sons-in-law during several years of study at the *yeshiva* or *bes hamidrash,* so the wealthy acculturated families in Russia or Poland supported their sons-in-law at the universities.

In the United States, parents do not necessarily save their money in order to send their children to the *kheder* or the *yeshiva,* but they may struggle and sacrifice in order to provide a college or university education. The professional man, who is, by definition, highly educated, takes the place of the *talmid khokhom* as the ideal son or son-in-law. There is the pattern, too, of a whole family concentrating its effort on training one son for an intellectual career, while the others go into business. Usually the choice falls on either the oldest or the youngest.

Parallel to the institution of *kest* (see p. 121), here as in Europe, parents-in-law support the young couple so that the son-in-law may continue his studies. In many cases the wife works so that her husband can complete his undergraduate or graduate degree. This pattern, too, is in line with the *shtetl* practice. Since it is also found with increasing frequency among non-Jews, however, it cannot be attributed directly to the old tradition.

Acculturation was, of course, already under way in Europe. From one angle, in fact, the history of the Jews since the Diaspora might be regarded as a history of acculturation. If one views the *shtetl* as the Eastern European culture base, there are still strong elements of acculturation not only among Jews who have gone to the city but also within the *shtetl* itself.

The interaction and merging of old and new patterns can be seen in the status accorded to learned professions, as well as in the professions that are classed as learned. In the cities of Eastern Europe, any profession which requires special education is regarded as an intellectual calling, by non-Jews as well as by Jews. The dentist and the veterinary surgeon are professionals and intellectuals. They have studied at a university and so are educated people.

Even within the *shtetl* these professions command honor. As long as one is not involved in the strict tradition of Jewish learning, it is correct and prestigeful for him to exploit his intellectual achievement for money profit, although it is contemptible to capitalize on the study of the Law.

In the United States, Jews from the *shtetl* continue to group the veterinary and the dentist with the doctor and the lawyer as professionals and intellectuals. Even a practitioner in a beauty parlor shares the aura that distinguishes one whose profession requires a special education and degree.

Within the professional category there is a distinct hierarchy of prestige. An *emeser* (real) doctor or "doctor doctor" rates higher than a Ph.D., as does a lawyer; a dentist outranks a veterinary surgeon. Among women a schoolteacher would outrank a nurse, and either would rate above a secretary or cosmetician.

The learning pattern of the *shtetl*, already influenced by European contacts, has combined no less readily with the American success pattern. In the basic *shtetl* culture, learning was for its own sake, and it was contemptible to exploit this *mitsva* in order to gain one's daily bread. In the United States, intellectual activity is used to enable one to earn money in an honorific way—a way that itself is a badge of academic accomplishment. The same tendency would be observed in Germany, where Jews occupied an important place among the professional group.

The tendency to guide one's children into intellectual careers or marriage with an "intellectual" is illustrated by the reports of the most satisfied parents among informants. A father summarized the careers of his children as follows: one daughter teaches music, another has a beauty parlor; the others are married to a dentist, a veterinary, and a businessman. One son studied journalism, another graduated from a technical high school. The father wanted the youngest boy to continue in the Jewish tradition, so he was sent to a *talmud tora* for six years. Then he left and continued his studies at Cornell University, where he became a veterinarian.

Another man had seven sons and one daughter, of whom one became a businessman and one a salesman, while the others became physician, dentist, graphic artist, teacher of Spanish in high school. Others write with pride: "My eldest son got his M.A. from Florida University, the second son is studying chemistry in Florida, a daughter is still in high school."[7] "My eldest son got his diploma [dentistry]. Despite the bad material situation, we have sent him money to give him the chance to study. So did his brother [a railway mail clerk] and his girl-friend."[8]

In blending the American success pattern with the *shtetl* emphasis on book learning, something of the early veneration appears to have remained. It is not merely that to work with the head carries more status than to work with the hands. There is also a feeling that intellectual activity is better than manual activity in the sense of being more enjoyable and also of being morally superior.

In the *shtetl*, the Torah was the fountain of all truth, and every good Jew was obliged to come as close to the truth as he possibly could. Among highly acculturated Jews in the United States, social significance may predominate over religious significance. Nevertheless, not only is the concept of learning surrounded with considerations of prestige, status, and pecuniary gain; it also bears the stamp of human nobility. It is still felt that the learned man has the best opportunity to become the best kind of human being.

NOTES

1. When the present tense is used in describing the *shtetl* culture, for the purposes of this chapter it is to be regarded as the historical present, referring to the period preceding 1939. The general picture given here is based on conditions in Ukrainian Jewish communities before the Russian revolution of 1917 and in the Polish, Hungarian, or Rumanian villages or small towns before their destruction in the years 1939–45. Nevertheless, despite the profound changes brought by war and revolution, enough of the basic attitudes and usages persists to make a clearly defined historical present more accurate than a straight past tense.

2. *Lerner,* studious one; *masmid,* one who is always bending over his books; *kharif,* the acute, especially one who excels in *pilpul* (cf. p. 128); *talmid khokhom,* wise student, learned one; *ben tora,* son of the law, scholar; *iluy,* genius, superior or accomplished person; *lamdan,* erudite one; *gaon,* genius; *oker horim,* "uprooter of mountains," one who excels in *pilpul.*

3. The name of the girl is filled in.

4. The persistence and antiquity of this pattern are suggested by an episode in the life of Christ, described by the Evangelist Luke (Luke 2:41–52). The twelve-year-old Jesus was found in the temple discussing the Law and confounding bearded scholars by his scholarly and penetrating questions. The situation—depicted in well-known paintings by Dürer, Van Dyck, Botticelli, and others—bears a striking similarity to the treatment and behavior of a young *iluy* in the Eastern European *shtetl.*

5. Singer, 1946.

6. I.e., of R. Salomon Itskhaki, the most popular commentator of the Torah and the Talmud, who lived in the eleventh century A.D.

7. "Life Stories of Yiddish Immigrants" (in Yiddish). Unpublished manuscripts for the Archives of Yiddish Scientific Institute, Yivo (New York).

8. *Ibid.*

LIST OF REFERENCES

SINGER, I. I. 1946. *Fun a velt vos is nishto mer.* New York: Privately published.

ZBOROWSKI, MARK, and HERZOG, ELIZABETH. 1952. *Life Is with People: The Jewish Little Town in Eastern Europe.* New York: International Universities Press, 1952.

PART III

Child-rearing Literature

Introduction

THE existence of literature telling parents how to bring up their children is indicative of a changing culture. In traditional cultures, where the same pattern is repeated from generation to generation, the elders are authorities in these matters. But in a changing culture the elders lose their infallibility. American parents, for instance, do not expect to bring up their children in the way they were brought up, any more than they would want to live in the house in which they were raised or to drive around in the family car of their childhood. They hope to bring up their children better than they were brought up themselves. For guidance in this undertaking they turn to the contemporary expert, the pediatrician or family doctor, and to the writings of doctors, psychologists, teachers, and the increasing number of specialists in parent education.

These experts draw upon a growing body of knowledge about children. But the process of transmission of scientific findings in this field is not simple or direct. Findings remain incomplete and their implications for practice often ambiguous. Those who mediate between science and the lay public often draw on their own and currently prevailing moral attitudes to derive practical recommendations. Thus child-training literature is as much expressive of the moral climate of the time and place in which it is written as of the state of scientific knowledge about children. Also scientific studies of children are themselves related to prevailing attitudes and feelings, which influence what is investigated or observed at different times.

In a historical perspective, child-training literature is related to codes of conduct, religious and secular, such as the Book of Leviticus or the *Analects of Confucius.* However, such rules for behavior (whether they prescribe under what conditions a ritual bath is required, when to make a burnt offering, or how a gentleman should dress and in what manner a man may remonstrate with his parents) are directed to the mature individual on the assumption that, when properly instructed, after he has attained manhood he can conduct his life correctly. Child-training literature is based on a different assumption, namely, that whether one lives well or badly depends largely on the experiences of the earliest years. The responsibility for the individual's fate in life falls on his parents. There is an analogy here to the rituals which, in various religions, parents are expected to have performed on their children for their spiritual well-being, such as infant baptism or circumcision. Yet instruction to parents in child-training literature also has a different premise from such ritual observances, which can be carried out without the child's compliance or response. Child-training literature assumes an intimate interaction between parents and child in which the child's response to the parents' behavior toward him is of crucial importance.

In a contemporary context, child-training literature appears related to the vast "how-to" literature, currently produced in America. Instructions on how to perform an extraordinary variety of activities are now available in printed form.[1] The existence of these publications suggests that, for Americans, very nearly every occupation, whether it be work or pastime, physical culture or social relations, is a learnable skill and also that there are a great many people who are eager to gain new skills or to improve those they have and that they do not have the facilities to gain these skills by face-to-face instruction or by apprenticeship, learning by example and the spoken word. Thus they presumably turn to the book or pamphlet by the unknown expert. While child-training literature in some ways resembles older moral codes, it also belongs, at least in America, to the class of contemporary "how-to" books, with their emphasis on impersonal transmission of skill.

The major topics of child-training literature are: a view of the child's nature, his impulses, needs, ways of responding, and how these change as he gets older; an ideal of what the child should become; recommended means of achieving this ideal; and cautionary stories of what may happen from taking the wrong course, the negative counterpart of the ideal, the picture of what it is feared the child might become. As the following papers will illustrate, what is said on each of these topics and also how it is said differ for different cultures and for the same culture in different periods.

One of the most striking changes in American thinking about children from the nineteenth and early twentieth centuries to the more recent past and the present is the radical change in the conception of the child's nature. From the nineteenth-century belief in "infant depravity" and the early twentieth-century fear of the baby's "fierce" impulses, which, if not vigilantly curbed, could easily grow beyond control and lead to ruin, we have come to consider the child's nature as totally harmless and beneficent. In America we tend quickly to forget on the conscious level what we have put behind us or outgrown. Many people are surprised to learn that the *Infant Care* bulletin of the United States Children's Bureau carried as late as 1938 a picture of a recommended patent cuff which would hold the child's arm stiff at the elbow and so prevent him from sucking his thumb. Thumb-sucking, once considered a great evil, expressing the child's intense and dangerous impulses and requiring the mother's militant interference, has become something legitimate or negligible. Yet, however much we turn from the convictions of our parents' generation to the ideas of contemporary experts, it seems likely that our own upbringing retains a lingering effect.[2] Since this effect can probably be dealt with more successfully if we are aware of it, rather than by denying it, the reconstruction of past child-training ideas in our own culture may have a practical as well as a theoretical value.

In the analysis of this literature, its style and imagery are no less significant than its general propositions. Rhoda Métraux brings out, for instance, how recurrent the image of gardening is in German books on parent guidance. The child is likened to a plant that the parents must tend but whose development they cannot wholly control—they are gardeners, not gods. This image may be used in an effort to moderate parental tyranny, suggesting the limits of their powers, the degree to which the growing potentialities of the child should be respected. In a similar way those American writers of advice to parents in the last century who advocated a softening of the traditional severe discipline were apt to liken the little child to a delicate plant. In early twentieth-century American child-rearing literature, the plant image seems to carry not only the connotations of fragility but also those of uncontrollable growth and expansion (a figure for impulses which may grow beyond control). In contemporary American writing in this field the plant image seems to have dropped out, partly, one may suppose, because children have grown sufficiently tough and parents sufficiently tender.

The papers here enable us to compare Soviet ideas on child training with our own. One of the major points that emerges from this comparison is that Soviet ideas resemble much more American nineteenth-century views than those of America today. This is particularly so in the estimation of the moral hazards of the world and the parental vigilance and severity required in guarding against them. Nineteenth-century American parents were warned of the "evil within and without" in the child's nature and in the omnipresent seductions to which he is exposed, so that the only salvation was in keeping the child strictly under the sway of parental rectitude. The view of the moral predicament in recent Soviet child-training literature is not far different. Within the child is the dangerous tendency to follow the line of least resistance, which must be opposed by setting goals for striving and obstacles to be overcome, even for the toddler. External hazards are even more threatening; the moment the child eludes the parents' sphere of influence, he is liable to fall under that of vicious elements. In contrast to both the recent Soviet views and the older American ones, those of America today envisage evils within and without as practically nonexistent.

In Soviet child-training literature, the value of what we would call "compulsive" character traits is strongly urged. Parents must guard themselves against acting in the heat of the moment. They must be controlled, calculating the effects of their acts on their children and giving reasoned explanations instead of blows. The cultivation of a state of mind in which there is continual self-questioning as to whether one did everything as well as possible is highly praised.[3] This is the moral condition to which the well-brought-up young Soviet citizen should attain. In America all this restraint, care, calculation, righteous explanations, and self-questioning are things which in recent years have been strongly disparaged by the experts writing for parents. The trend has been rather toward easygoingness, casualness, being relaxed, and having fun—attitudes rendered feasible by the disappearance of evils within and without. Thus Soviet and American child-training experts seem to have been moving in opposite directions.

Despite such differences between cultures or within a given culture from one period to another, there are, if we consider things from a certain level of generality, some views held in common by the writers of different times and places reported on here. These common points would appear to be ideas diffused throughout Europe and America and persisting over a considerable period, at least among that stratum of articulate persons who have made it their business to instruct parents. One such common belief is that everything parents do every minute of their lives affects their children for good or ill. In the task of bringing up children there are no intermissions. This is equally held by German and Soviet writers on child training, and by American writers today and a hundred years ago. A corollary of this is the explicit or implicit demand that parents control their emotions. Nineteenth-century American parents, for instance, were warned to guard against the secret smile which would give them away while they scolded their child; in revealing that they were actually amused by the child's naughtiness, they would negate the effect of their discipline. Similarly, German parents at the present time are alerted that children will sense the spirit in which parents say things to them; it is no good to say the right words without the right sentiments.

Contemporary Soviet parents are warned not to give way to emotional scenes. They should say nothing to a misbehaving child when they and he are hot with excitement. Only later, in a moment of calm, a few well-chosen words should be uttered. These precepts represent an attempt to cultivate defenses against older Russian tendencies toward wild emotional scenes.[4] They express the disciplined Bolshevik's repudiation of outpourings of emotion which give immediate relief but in which one quite loses sight of the ultimate goal to be achieved.[5] In contemporary America, parents are told they should have fun with their children. Though the emotional atmosphere here preferred is very different from the Soviet one of careful restraint, there is a common general rule, namely, that parents are expected to control their emotions. In both these instances the recommended emotional tone represents a reaction against older tendencies in the culture. In the Soviet case, as already indicated, it is a reaction against scenes of rage, elation, depression, and so on, which made the individual inefficient. In America it is a reaction against a Puritan tradition in which work was good, and fun suspect.

The relation between child-training literature and actual parental practices is not a simple one. Procedures recommended by the experts represent an ideal, and there are always discrepancies between ideals and everyday behavior. That certain things are more or less vehemently urged in child-training literature might suggest that the writers assume the opposite to be often observed in practice, or even mistakenly cherished as right by those to whom they address themselves. And yet it would be questionable to suppose that there is a direct opposition between this literature and practice, as if the writers were regularly opposing what they take to be current errors. In every area of moral utterance there is a tendency to reiterate commonly held values, as an ever renewed avowal of faith. It seems likely, then, that the precepts in child-training literature in part coincide with widely held beliefs of the culture and in part urge reform. Further research is required to determine the relations between the ideas in the literature and what parents of a given time and place hold to be correct and (which may be quite a different thing again) what they are actually doing.

M. W.

NOTES

1. Macdonald, 1954.
2. Cf. Greenson, 1954.
3. Calas, 1951.
4. Erikson brings out how, in the Soviet film *The Childhood of Maxim Gorky*, the boy Gorky is shown as developing into the new type of Soviet man by holding aloof from the intense, violent, suffering, tearful, and repenting family scenes that go on around him (Erikson, 1950, pp. 316–58).
5. Cf. Leites, 1953.

LIST OF REFERENCES

CALAS, E. 1951. "Summary of Conclusions of Research on Soviet Child Training Ideals and Their Political Significance," in MARGARET MEAD, *Soviet Attitudes toward Authority*, pp. 107–9. New York: McGraw-Hill Book Co.

ERIKSON, ERIK H. 1950. *Childhood and Society*. New York: W. W. Norton & Co.

GREENSON, RALPH R. 1954. "The Struggle against Identification," *Journal of the American Psychoanalytic Association*, II, No. 3, 200–217.

LEITES, NATHAN. 1953. *A Study of Bolshevism*. Glencoe Ill.: Free Press.

MACDONALD, DWIGHT. 1954. "Howtoism," *New Yorker*, May 22, pp. 82–109.

CHAPTER 9

Early Nineteenth-Century American Literature on Child Rearing

―ROBERT SUNLEY

Very little has been done as yet in bringing together and analyzing the material on nineteenth-century American child-rearing practices. In the present study, which is part of a more extensive research on American child rearing from Colonial times on, I have drawn mainly on original nineteenth-century sources, including writings on child-rearing practices in parent and family magazines, medical and religious books, journals, biographies, travelers' reports, stories, children's books, and advertisements. Artifacts, such as feeding bottles and children's toys and games, were also considered relevant.

In evaluating the extent to which a given publication may have represented a general trend, consideration was given to such factors as the circulation of a magazine, the number of editions of a book, the number of publications discussing a similar behavioral trend, the nature of the authorship, and references to the publication in other works. When several sources agreed on a point, it was presumed that the attitude or theory in question was probably fairly common. The sources cited in the List of References at the end of this chapter are only a sample selected from the total material assembled, but they give an adequate picture of the types of sources for the period.

The principal secondary sources which I have used are: Max Berger, The British Traveller in America, 1836–60; *A. Calhoun,* A Social History of the American Family; *S. Chown, "Some Notes on the History of Infant Feeding"; S. Fleming,* Children and Puritanism; *M. Kiefer,* American Children through Their Books, 1700–1835; *A. Kuhn,* Mother's Role in Childhood Education: New England Concepts, 1830–60; *F. Mott,* A History of American Magazines, 1741–1850; *E. Wilson,* Hygienic Care and Management of the Child in the American Family Prior to 1860.

The problem of reconstructing actual behavior from material found in the literature is a complicated one, which I do not undertake to deal with in this article.

IN A changing culture like ours, ideas on how to bring up children undergo many transformations through time. If we look at the ideas prevailing on this subject a hundred years ago, we find, together with the beginnings of many current developments in child rearing, concepts which seem remote, alien, and repugnant to us. However, the attitudes of past generations may retain more of a hold on us than we realize. Ideas we are not conscious of may continue to exert influence on the levels of less conscious feeling, transmitted from one generation to another through child rearing itself, as well as through literature. Thus a study of child-rearing ideas of the past century has a practical as well as a theoretical significance. It is a contribution to cultural history. It also can help to make us aware of precedents which remain dynamically related to our own work in the upbringing and education of children.

Between 1820 and 1860, the period which I have chosen for analysis here, the American public showed a markedly increasing interest in the importance of children and in child-rearing problems. For the first time in the United States, a substantial body of literature appeared on the subject, ranging from practical advice on infant care to elaborate theories on the moral training of children. The child-rearing literature suggests some of the reasons for this increased concern over the upbringing of children: an increasing emphasis on the child as the extension of parental ambitions and as the representative of the parents' status in society; a growing belief in man's power to control the environment and direct the future, including the molding of the child; a new need for personal direction, as established patterns of living and child rearing were being disrupted in the rapid shift to industrialization and urbanization. Child rearing, in the literature, was considered a rational process, certain results flowing forth if certain methods were followed. Particularly in the child-rearing theory based on Calvinism, methods were consciously related to the type of adult desired: a moral, honest, religious, independent individual who would take his proper place in society.

IMPORTANCE OF THE MOTHER

The mother's role in child rearing was generally considered paramount. She was regarded as the child's best instructor, the principal person in forming the child's character, a process which was considered to take place largely during the first six years or so of life.[1] "Especially the mother cannot act without leaving an impression on the child . . . by the mother's forming hand it receives its shape to a great extent, for all its future existence."[2] Thus the mother, according to Lydia Child in the 1830's, had to govern her own feelings and keep her heart and innocence pure.[3] Lydia Sigourney, a woman writer of advanced views, spoke of the "immensity of the mother's trust in raising a child" and "infancy [as] the only period of a mother's perfect enjoyment." The mother, she writes, is "to nurture the infant . . . as a germ quickened by Spring, it opens the folding doors of its little heart . . . like timid tendrils, seeking where to twine."[4]

Some authors placed the entire burden of the child's well-being in this life and the next upon the mother: "Yes, mothers, in a certain sense, the destiny of a redeemed world is put into your hands; it is for you to say, whether your children shall be respectable and happy here and prepared for a glorious immortality, or whether they shall dishonor you, and perhaps bring your grey hairs in sorrow to the grave, and sink down themselves at last to eternal despair!"[5] Mothers were charged also with a larger responsibility than that for their individual children, as the following example indicates: "You hold the sceptre in your souls in which, more than in the laws of a legislature, now repose the futurity of the nation, the world, and the destinies of the human race."[6]

The mother represented also the force which protected her children after they had left home. Mother's voice was ever with the child: "In foreign climes the power of the tempter has been dispelled by some word of counsel."[7] An apt motto for these times in which grown-up children were likely to move away to the cities was "A happy childhood is a boy's best safeguard."[8] To insure such results in the adult, however, the mother had to exercise discipline as well as love. One writer inveighs against those who "love their own ease too well to employ that constant care and exertion, which is necessary to restrain children . . . they cannot bear to correct them, or put them to pain, not because they love their children, but because they love themselves, and are unwilling to endure the pain of inflicting punishment and of seeing their children suffer."[9]

The role of the father received little attention, in contrast to the great emphasis placed upon the role of the mother. In many households, especially in the cities and towns, the mother often was seen as devoting herself to the infant, to the neglect of the older children and the father. One writer attributed this shift in wifely and maternal affection to the woman's disappointment in marriage, in failing to receive the love and gratification she had expected.[10] The father in such families, whether from prior disposition or as a result of his wife's absorption in motherhood, then became more occupied with his work. Writers often mention how many fathers spent most of their time away from home and had little to do with their children. The father gave such reasons as the need to frequent bars after working hours in order to make business connections.[11] While some writers on the subject still tried to give the father the position of the instructor of the children, even this function seems to have been declining. The mother not only was taking over the teaching of the young child but also was handling the daily disciplinary problems rather than waiting for the father's presence in the evening. Daily religious observances, previously conducted by the father as head of the family, were less and less practiced, and the mother tended to take over what was left of this function.[12]

Corporal punishment was widespread at this time, although many writers opposed it or felt it was best used as a last resort. Accounts indicate that at home it was most often the father who administered corporal punishment. In the school system, such punishment was universal at the beginning of the period 1820–60. At this time teachers were predominantly male. By 1860, an intensive campaign headed by Lyman Cobb had greatly lessened the use of corporal punishment in schools; and at the same time, the great majority of schoolteachers were now women rather than men.[13]

A similar shift thus seems to have occurred inside and outside the home, with discipline placed in the hands of women and with physical punishment apparently abandoned in favor of other forms of discipline to be administered by the mother or woman teacher.

FEEDING AND THE DANGERS OF STUFFING AND DRUGGING

During this period American mothers could, for the first time, turn for detailed, practical advice on infant care to a fairly large body of literature which was not, as earlier, imported from England. This literature generally urged mothers to breast-feed their children, refuting the current objections that breast feeding would spoil the figure, that it would tie the mother down at home, that mothers were too "nervous" to breast-feed. Doctors did recognize that breast feeding was not desirable for some women for health reasons but, in general, claimed that it was best for baby and mother, both physically and emotionally. Literature directed to fashionable women, however, conceded a point by giving advice on artificial or bottle feeding, although condemning the practice.

Writers on infant feeding generally advised leaving it up to the baby to establish a routine as to time and frequency of breast feedings. Guides on feeding were given for babies of various ages, though with some disagreement among the various writers, but with little insistence upon rigid adherence to a regular schedule.[14] There is insufficient evidence to indicate definitely what the actual practices were, beyond the doctors' advice and the implications as to practice. In general, it appears that the middle and upper economic groups were the ones to use bottle feeding and wet nurses as the alternatives to breast feeding. These same groups entertained the belief that the poor generally nursed their own babies with a plentiful supply of milk for many months. It was also believed that the children of the poor were often fretful as the result of the influence of the mother's ill-governed passions transmitted through the milk.

Medical books, with few exceptions, advocated gradual weaning to preserve the child's temper. However, weaning was to take place within a period of a week or two instead of being dragged out for months. For the completion of weaning it was often considered advisable for the mother to absent herself, to avoid the danger of her yielding to the infant's entreaties. The optimum age for weaning was set variously from eight to twelve months, with no particular change discernible in this time range during the 1820–60 period. The age depended upon other factors also, such as the appearance of teeth, which was a definite signal to begin weaning. Another factor, considered local to the United States, was the season of the year, as weaning in the warm weather was thought to expose the child to "cholera infantum" and other intestinal diseases. Consequently, the time of weaning might be advanced or delayed to avoid the warm weather.[15]

Bottle feeding, known also as "artificial feeding," "raising a baby by hand," or "dry nursing," seems to have been popular first in Continental Europe, then in England, and in the United States only by the beginning of this period, although not unknown before then.[16] Nursing bottles could be purchased inexpensively at drugstores in cities and towns.[17] Many formulas were devised, though it was not until about 1860 that the first good formula, "Liebig's," came into use.[18] Inventors were constantly at work improving the bottle, as evidenced by the steady flow of patents granted; the rubber nipple, for example, was patented in 1845 and was in increasing use from then on.[19]

Wet nurses were drawn primarily from the poor class, and a considerable number appear to have been unmarried mothers. Newspapers in the cities carried listings of wet nurses, even long past Civil War days. Wet nurses, all the books cautioned, should be carefully selected to avoid two dangers: that of the mother losing the baby's love and that of adverse influences on the baby from the wet nurse. Accordingly, the nurse should resemble the mother as closely as possible physically, as well as be in good health, be calm, reliable, and of good morals. Some felt that wet nursing beyond six months tended to attach the baby too firmly to the nurse.

Overfeeding, before and after weaning, was widely observed by travelers from abroad and was soundly condemned by the authors of the child-rearing literature. Babies on the bottle or those receiving supplementary feeding were often given candy, cake, and other food, as well as "pap," which consisted of moistened meal or bread served in bowls resembling modern gravy boats. Sweets were also given to elicit the baby's pleased response, which some parents took as an evidence of "love."[20] The primary reason for overfeeding, as noted by observers, was to quiet the baby, and there was a belief that servants were the most frequent offenders. Observers also commented that some mothers seemed to believe that an infant would starve if it were not crammed with food from birth. Overfeeding continued throughout childhood in some families; and doctors frequently warned against "piecing," that is, eating between meals.[21] Feedings were apparently somewhat irregular, only an occasional writer suggesting that regular feeding hours be instituted as early as possible, for the mother's comfort and convenience as well as the child's.[22]

Drugs were given to infants to stop their crying and put them to sleep. In the form of patent medicines, drugs were given to remedy a variety of illnesses, major and minor, including gripes, flatulence, and irregular bowels. The use of drugs is described by a contemporary writer: "The bane of infants and young children is laudanum [a form of opium] . . . which is the basis of all quack medicine and given almost indiscriminately in this country to infants, from the moment they are born—till—I may say—the day of their death."[23] Another writer comments, regarding a patent medicine based on laudanum: "If improper food has slain its hundreds, Godfrey's Cordial has slain its thousands."[24]

Alcohol was similarly used to quiet a child both in home-made and in patent medicines. Servants, it was believed, often resorted to such drugging to be quit for a time of a troublesome infant or to make sure the child slept while the servant took time off. Laudanum was used by some working mothers to make sure their children slept while they were away, but evidence indicates that mothers of the upper classes also used such drugs.[25] So often is this practice mentioned and so often condemned by medical writers that it may be inferred that the practice was widespread. A number of infant deaths were officially attributed to opium. In 1837–38, for example, inquests showed that fifty-two infants were included in the total of one hundred and eighty-six deaths due to opium.[26]

MOTOR DEVELOPMENT AND INDEPENDENCE

The child-rearing literature of this period favored freedom of movement for the infant. The child was to be helped to gain voluntary control of his activity rather than be the passive subject of adult manipulation. Medical advice favored loose, light clothing and condemned the tight clothing and bands to which many infants were subjected.[27] However, babies generally seem to have been overclothed with layers of flannel and wool. Swaddling seems to have been customary in some regions of the country, possibly depending on the national origins of the inhabitants, but evidence is insufficient to indicate how prevalent swaddling was or in precisely which areas.[28] Modifications of swaddling, however, appear to have been widespread; and, in addition to the heavy clothing, the ends of the garments were often tied to prevent movement of hands and feet.[29] The reason given by parents and nurses for such tight clothing was that it gave the baby a proper shape, made it look nice and feel firm, and kept it warm, "like in the womb."[30]

Babies slept in cradles for the most part and were rocked a great deal. One British observer attributed the restlessness of the American adult to violent rocking in infancy.[31] Some mothers also took their infants to sleep with them, a practice which the child-rearing literature warned against as having two dangers. First, the infant sleeping with its mother was likely to be breast-fed too often. Second, there was the danger of "overlaying," which referred to the mother's rolling over and smothering the baby to death during the night.

Parents apparently often forced infants and young children to perform beyond their physical or mental level. Babies were sometimes required to sit upright before being able to do so. Some babies were not permitted to go through the crawling stage (perhaps to prevent dirtiness), and walkers and leading strings were used to get the baby to walk as soon as possible.[32] Mental precociousness was much admired, children being taught lessons far beyond their years, so that they could be shown off before company.

Encouragement of the child's independent activity was found also in many families where babies were permitted to feed themselves from a cup from a very early age; and at ten to fifteen months they would already be at the family dinner tables in high chairs, the center of attention. Travelers from abroad often considered this practice repellent because of the baby's noise and grabbing for food.[33]

The crying baby was, as always, a problem for parents. During this period the general attitude seems to have been, "Let the baby cry," rather than to rush at once to its side. One school of thought advised the parent to go to the baby, but not immediately; a certain amount of crying was good exercise for the baby, strengthening its lungs.[34] Too prompt attention to the baby might get it into the habit of making constant demands, which, if met, would lead to the baby's becoming the ruler of the family. The other general attitude found in the literature held that the baby should be allowed to cry until it stopped: in this way its "will" would be broken.[35] This second attitude is part of the Calvinist theory on child rearing, of which more will be said in the section on "Moral Development." The use of drugs to halt crying has already been mentioned in the section on "Feeding."

Educational activities for the child up to school age were advocated, to encourage its independent gaining of control. Some authors advised trying to interest the young child in its environment, arousing its curiosity, displaying objects to it, urging close observation, and encouraging nature study and nature collections.[36]

TOILET TRAINING, CLEANLINESS, AND VIRTUE

The child-rearing literature tended to recommend early toilet training, though seldom specifying the exact age when the training was to start or be completed. Early training was advised as a means of establishing "habits of cleanliness and delicacy." One doctor cited with approval the example of a mother who "trained" her child at one month, and he urged other mothers to strive for this ideal.[37] While no specific age was indicated, disgust and disapproval of wetness and lack of control are evident throughout the literature. Training was to be accomplished through frequent changes of the child's clothing, by placing the child on the "chair," and by the example of older children. Some mothers expressed the feeling that success in early toilet training was to the credit of the child and themselves.

Some emphasis is placed in the literature on regularity; failure to "duly" discharge the bowels led to the retention of poisonous matter in the body.[38] Reabsorption would ensue, with dire consequences. Several means to relieve constipation and insure regularity, such as enemas, suppositories, and cathartics, were used with great frequency and for the most part were sanctioned in the literature. One doctor did warn against the "habit" which might be formed by too frequent use of such means, without specifying the precise danger.[39]

Playing with dirt was to be discouraged, according to some writers, as being neither cleanly nor useful; but digging and raking were permissible because they involved learning useful skills. There was much emphasis on cleanliness; soiled clothes should be promptly removed from children, washing should be frequent, and the mother should conduct a daily inspection of the children. Extreme neatness, cleanliness, and orderliness in children met with resounding approval from adults —at least in the literature and in some accounts written by mothers. Cleanliness had a moral counterpart: "For dirt and indelicacy are frequent companions, and a disregard for the decencies of life is a step toward indifference toward its virtues."[40]

Standards of cleanliness for adults, according to observers, were apparently high in regard to care of the person. Americans appeared to several travelers as the cleanest people in the world—not only the prosperous but also the ordinary tradesmen, mechanics, and police always wore clean clothing and even had clean fingernails.[41] An interesting counterpart to this personal cleanliness was the untidy, unkempt appearance of the gardens, yards, streets, and sidewalks.

DANGERS OF SEXUALITY

Masturbation presented a serious problem to the parents of the period. Books warned of the "ruin" consequent upon the child's masturbating—leading to disease, insanity, and even death. It was recognized that the danger applied to younger as well as older children. European doctors whose books were reprinted or read in this country were apparently the originators of such warnings, at least in the literature.[42] Juvenile books, especially the semi-illicit ones, were blamed for exciting children and suggesting possibilities to them.⁴³ The genitals, some writers advised, should be touched only for strictly hygienic purposes.

Among the more prosperous groups it seems to have been widely believed that children did not discover masturbation by themselves or through spontaneous sexual play with other children of their own class but had to be inducted or seduced into such practices by servants, slaves, or depraved school children (presumably of the lower classes). One writer commented: "The coarse hugging, kissing, etc. which the children are sure to receive in great abundance from ignorant and low-minded domestics are certain to develop a blind precocious sexualism of feeling and action, which tends directly to all the evils I have mentioned, on the maturity of those offspring, and sometimes in sudden disease and death to little ones."⁴⁴ Catherine Beecher, a sister of Harriet Beecher Stowe, explained that the difficulties of bringing up children properly "are often heightened by the low and depraved character of a great portion of those who act as nurses for young people. One single vulgar, or deceitful, or licentious domestic may in a single month mar the careful and anxious training of years."⁴⁵ One of the leading doctors and advisers on children, Dr. Dewees, gave the following warning on spontaneous autoeroticism: "Children should not be permitted to indulge in bed long after daylight; as its warmth, the accumulation of urine and faeces, and the exercise of the imagination, but too often leads to the precocious development of the sexual instinct."⁴⁶

Those who adhered to the Calvinist doctrine of "infant depravity," which held that the infant was destined to commit sins unless given thorough guidance by parents, also believed in "external corruption" of their children. These religious groups favored solitary prayer and solitary Bible reading by young children. An incident related by a mother suggests that one reason such solitary activity was favored was to counteract the child's desire to masturbate. The mother entered her little girl's bedroom precipitately one day, and saw the child hastily change her position. The child refused to answer her mother's question as to what she had been doing. The mother said, "But little children who do not like to tell what they are doing, are in great danger of doing something they are ashamed of." Whereupon the child, wounded, answered, "Oh no, mother, I was only going to pray a little while."⁴⁷ Parents and nurses were warned to be suspicious of their children's engaging in masturbation or sexual play with other children. At the same time, adults had to be careful not to be suggestive in their own words or behavior. One writer warns: "A nurse cannot be too guarded in what she says or does in the presence of children, nor must she fancy that they are always infants, or less alive than herself, to what passes before them. At the same time, the precautions taken should be perceived as little as possible, for she will defeat her end, if she excite curiosity, by giving them the idea that there is something to be concealed."[48]

MORAL DEVELOPMENT: "INFANT DEPRAVITY" AND "INFANT CONVERSION"

Religious doctrine played an important part in the moral training of the child, not only in the obvious form of religious training, but even more importantly as the ideological basis for child-raising theory and practice. Foremost among these doctrines during this period was the Calvinist theory, which was adhered to not only by the New England Puritans but also by many of the other Protestant sects, such as the Presbyterians, Methodists, and Congregationalists. The keystone of Calvinist doctrine regarding child rearing was "infant depravity," which, leaving theological subtleties aside, consisted in the belief that the infant was born "totally depraved" and doomed to depravity throughout life unless given careful and strict guidance by the parents and, ultimately, saved through Grace.[49] "No child," wrote one New Englander, "has ever been known since the earliest period of the world, destitute of an evil disposition—however sweet it appears."[50]

Complete obedience and submission were thus requisite if the child was to be kept from sin and evil. The parents were considered responsible and so had to exact such obedience in order to carry out their duty. As a corollary, the safety and health of the child depended upon complete submission. Parents were fond of relating how their child's life was saved because the child obeyed at a crucial moment—by taking medicine upon command, for example. Submission was necessary also so that the child would accept unquestioningly the positive virtues and the truth of religion at an age when it was not considered capable of arriving at such truths through its own reasoning.

Submission was obtained by "breaking the will" of the child—a concept not restricted, however, to those actually members of Calvinist religious groups. "Will" was seen as any defiance of the parents' wishes, at any age. "The very infant in your arms will sometimes redden and strike, and throw back its head, and stiffen its little rebellious will."[51] The child was not to have what it wanted, for its desires were sinful, "depraved." The techniques to be used for breaking the will were widely discussed during the period, especially among groups of mothers belonging to the more numerous Protestant-Calvinist sects. Beginning shortly before 1820, these mothers formed discussion groups to talk over child-rearing problems. The groups, known as "Maternal Associations," were spontaneously organized over much of the country, even on the frontier, and in foreign lands by wives of missionaries. Several magazines, either published by or involving these "associations," gained a very large circulation for those times.[52] The members of the groups belonged generally to the middle-income class. Among the many topics discussed, "breaking the will" and "infant conversion" (referring to a child who became converted to and professed religion as an adult would) were perhaps foremost. In general, breaking of the will or training in obedience was begun by teaching the child to obey every command quickly and completely. Some felt that for the first three months of life, or even the first year, the infant should be tenderly cared for and its wishes granted. But then, "Establish your will, as the law," wrote one woman on the subject, for this would keep the child from experiencing "all those conflicts of feeling of those doubtful as to their guide." She pointed out that George Washington had been trained in this way.[53]

Sooner or later the child would refuse to obey a command, and the issue of "will" was at hand.[54] It was considered fatal to let the child win out. One mother, writing in the *Mother's Magazine* in 1834, described how her sixteen-month-old girl refused to say "dear mama" upon the father's order. She was led into a room alone, where she screamed wildly for ten minutes; then she was commanded again, and again refused. She was then whipped, and asked again. This was kept up for four hours until the child finally obeyed.[55] Parents commonly reported that after one such trial the child became permanently submissive. But not all parents resorted to beatings to gain this end. One mother spoke of "constant though gentle drilling," which consisted partly of refusing to give the child an object just out of its reach, however much it cried.[56] Another mother taught submission and self-denial at one and the same time by taking objects away from the child. Strictness in diet and daily routine was apparently frequently an accompaniment to obedience training. However, many mothers seemed to find it hard to follow out such prescriptions, and the *Mother's Magazine* carried many exhortations to mothers to do their duty toward their children.

"Infant conversion" was considered highly desirable, for it meant that the child had reached the point of accepting on its own the truths of religion and hence was well on the road to being saved from depravity. There were many signs of such conversion—quick conversion not being considered as sound as the more gradual—among which signs were the practices of solitary prayer and Bible reading already mentioned.[57] Little girls were apparently more often converted than boys, and the pages of the magazines contain quite a few melancholy stories of such children who became devoutly religious, submissive, seemingly drained of vitality and desires, and met an early death, often by the age of ten. Such children were held up as models of piety for the others, and a considerable number of children were quoted by their parents as having as a favorite book one of the classic stories of such "infant conversion" and early death.

For the parents of this group, "indulgence" was to be shunned. Presumably, indulgence was more or less equivalent to "spoiling" but carried with it a religious meaning related to "depravity," rather than the merely secular danger of having a troublesome, spoiled child. One writer in the *Mother's Magazine* commented, "Men are made monsters in life by indulgence in infancy."[58] Indulgence abetted natural depravity and jeopardized the child's future. Such a child was likely to become unreasonable in its demands and end up tyrannizing the family.

Somewhat distinct from the Calvinist theory of child rearing, which emphasized the innate tendency toward evil within the child, was a second general theory centered around "hardening" the child and fostering "naturalness" of behavior.[59] This theory, stemming from Locke and to some extent from Rousseau and not rooted in religion, implied that it was the external environment of civilization which was dangerous to the child. Children should become strong, vigorous, unspoiled men, like those in the early days of the country. Cold baths and cold plunges, for example, were considered necessary, in the manner of the Indians. While Locke's writings were apparently rather influential—quotations were printed even in the almanacs and calendars which entered many homes—it is not possible to estimate how widespread this attitude was, though it seemed focused primarily in the East.

A third general theory and body of practice in child rearing can be discerned, apparently widespread, though probably not so prevalent as the Calvinist. This theory advocated gentle treatment of the child and had its roots in English and European movements already afoot.[60] The child was to be led, not driven; persuaded to the right, not commanded. Consistency and firmness were counseled, but with understanding and justice to the child. Encouragements and rewards should be offered; beatings, reproaches, slaps, dark closets, and shaming were to be avoided. Punishment and reward were to be administered not according to the consequences of the child's act but according to the motives. In regard to consistency, one writer even cautioned parents against "the secret smile," in which superficial disapproval of the child's behavior was undone by the tacit approval of the parent in smiling or giving other subtle signs.[61]

Corporal punishment was undesirable, partly because it did not bring about the desired results, partly because the child was felt to be too tender for such treatment. The child was likened to "an immortal bud just commencing to unfold its spotless leaves . . . a beautiful flower opening to the sunshine."[62] The child was ignorant of right rather than bent to wrong. Consequently, the fear of indulging the child and of being dominated by it was not marked, nor was it imperative to "break the will." A firm stand by the parent eliminated obedience problems.

There were also modifications of the Calvinist attitude which approached this third theory. Lydia Child, writing in the early part of the period, denied infant depravity but pointed out the need for a good environment for the child, to keep the child's "bad propensities" down until he was old enough to resist by himself. "Evil is within and without."[63] Other writers did not see corporal punishment as undesirable in itself but felt it should be withheld whenever possible and administered not in anger and the heat of the moment, but dispassionately and with deliberation. By 1844 even the *Mother's Magazine* had begun to admit some moderation of the strict obedience training. Articles appeared encouraging the parents to mingle more with the children, to understand and enter into their feelings. This would not, the writers claimed, result in lessened obedience from the children, nor did it amount to surrendering parental authority.[64]

The main ideas about child rearing in the American literature on this subject in the mid-nineteenth century can be summed up as follows: The mother at this time was expected to take over almost entirely the upbringing of the child, the role of the father declining markedly. Concurrently, the education of the child came more under the direction of women teachers in the schools.[65] With the mother taking over more of the disciplinary functions, it would seem that a major sanction became that of making her love conditional upon the child's obedience and conformity to her standards.[66] This sanction tended to replace, in principle if not in practice, corporal punishment (associated with fathers and male teachers), which was increasingly frowned upon. The exclusive role of the mother was further enforced by a growing suspicion about nurses, who were regarded in particular as seducers of children.

The activity of the child was to be fostered and encouraged from earliest years. In the interests of this activity, writers inveighed against the overfeeding and soporific drugs which made the child stuporous and inert. Similarly, it was urged that loose clothing for the infant replace tight wrapping, so that he might have greater freedom of movement. The moral counterpart to this approved activity was the early internalization by the child of religious and moral principles. It was not considered desirable for the child to remain protractedly dependent on adult authority. Rather he was to became at an early age a self-maintaining moral being. The highly praised "infant conversion" was a striking instance of such achievement. Until such moral independence could be attained, however, the parents bore a total responsibility for the child's moral and spiritual well-being. The world was fraught with extreme moral hazards, and it was the parents' task to guard the child from "evil within and without."

Concepts of the child's nature varied. According to the Calvinist view, the child was born depraved: "No child has ever been known since the earliest period of the world, destitute of an evil disposition —however sweet it appears."[67] It followed that parents must vigilantly guard children against the tendency of their depraved impulses; enforcing absolute obedience to adult demands could alone secure the child's salvation. Breaking the child's will meant freeing him from the hold of his evil nature.

The second general theory, that of the "hardening" school, deriving from Locke and Rousseau, emphasized the importance of bringing out the manly virtues against the weakening effect of civilization. While the danger to the child was here quite differently defined as compared with the Calvinists, some of the recommendations, such as forcing on the child things that were hard for him to take, were similar.

The third school of thought, advocating "gentle treatment," saw the child as having certain needs and potentialities which the parents were not to frustrate or control, but rather were to help fulfil and encourage into full development. The child's sexual and aggressive drives, which were explicitly recognized and handled by the Calvinists, under this theory were minimized as being not basic or strong but rather elicited as the result of erroneous upbringing by the parents. The child was a tender creature who could be harmed by the lack of nurture, kindly care, and gentle discipline. This latter view would seem to be the one most favored in child-rearing literature today, though without the qualification of the child's fragility.

NOTES

1. Fowler, 1847, p. 132; Searle, 1834, p. 260.
2. Allen, 1848, p. 97.
3. Child, 1831, p. 4.
4. Sigourney, 1838, pp. 29, vii, viii.
5. Hall, 1849, p. 27.
6. Howard, 1849, p. 100.
7. Canfield, 1849, p. 123.
8. Bigelow, 1844, p. 28.
9. Allen, 1849, pp. 128–29.
10. Calhoun, 1917, p. 133.
11. Beste, 1855, I, 127; Marryat, 1839, II, 115; Abbott, 1842, p. 148.
12. Kuhn, 1947, pp. 9, 102–3, and 171–72; Sproat, 1819, p. 16.
13. Cobb, 1847; Branch, 1934, p. 54.
14. Kuhn, 1947, p. 138.
15. Combe, 1840, p. 43; Dewees, 1826, pp. 187–88; Donne, 1859, p. 154.
16. Combe, 1840, p. 43.
17. Ireland, 1820, p. 38.
18. Warren, 1865, p. 10.

19. Drake, 1948.
20. Graves, 1844, p. 96.
21. Fowler, 1847, p. 178; "Overfeeding of Children," 1839; Hough, 1849, p. 166.
22. Dwight, 1834, p. 27.
23. Ireland, 1820, p. 5.
24. Searle, 1834, p. 212; Chavasse, 1862, p. 46.
25. Wilson, 1940, p. 35.
26. Chavasse, 1862, p. 124.
27. Dewees, 1826, p. 65; Barwell, 1844, p. 40.
28. Barwell, 1844, p. 41; Kuhn, 1947, p. 141.
29. "Improper Clothing," 1838; Wilson, 1940, p. 128.
30. Alcott, 1836, p. 49; Dewees, 1826, p. 65.
31. Bishop, 1856, p. 122.
32. Wilson, 1940, pp. 105 and 109.
33. Gallaudet, 1839; Duncan, 1852, p. 78; Thomson, 1842, p. 31.
34. Dewees, 1826, p. 115.
35. "What Manner of Child Shall This Be?" 1843.
36. Abbott, 1855; Holbrook, 1838.
37. Dewees, 1826, p. 237.
38. Warren, 1865, p. 15.
39. Donne, 1859, p. 170.
40. Barwell, 1844, p. 53.
41. Beste, 1855, p. 112; Thompson, 1842, p. 16; Baxter, 1855, p. 30.
42. The European works referred to by American writers were by Tissot, Hufeland, and Lallmand, all of whom wrote between 1760 and 1836.
43. Ray, 1849, p. 280.
44. Hough, 1849, p. 160.
45. Beecher, 1846, p. 13.
46. Dewees, 1826, p. 251.
47. "Little Ellen," 1840.
48. Searle, 1834, p. 269.
49. Hyde, 1830.
50. Dwight, 1834, p. 31.
51. Humphrey, 1840, p. 127.
52. *Mother's Magazine*, 1832–76; *Mother's Assistant*, 1841–63; *Parents' Magazine*, 1840–50.
53. Sigourney, 1838, p. 35.
54. Searle, 1834, p. 247.
55. "To Mothers of Young Families," 1834.
56. Warren, 1865, p. 39.
57. Gallaudet, 1838.
58. "Hints for Maternal Education," 1834, p. 115.
59. Dewees, 1826, p. 131; Edgeworth, 1815; Humphrey, 1840, p. 64; Wilson, 1940, pp. 71 and 132; Kuhn, 1947, pp. 54 and 162.
60. De Saussure, 1835; Ackerley, 1836; Bushnell, 1867; Mann, 1863; Barwell, 1844; Cobb, 1847; and Kuhn, 1947, who, in particular, describes the development of this theory in the United States in some detail.
61. Hoare, 1829, p. 86.
62. Taylor, 1849, p. 24; Briggs, 1849, p. 97.
63. Child, 1831, p. 8.
64. Abbott, 1844, p. 119.
65. Geoffrey Gorer in *The American People* (1948) has interpreted the extensive significance for American character of the predominant role of women in the raising and education of children.
66. Margart Mead in *And Keep Your Powder Dry* (1942) has stressed the importance of "conditional love" in American mother-child relations.
67. Dwight, 1834, p. 31.

LIST OF REFERENCES

ABBOTT, JACOB. 1844. "The Importance of Sympathy between the Mother and Child," *Mother's Magazine*, XII, No. 4, 111–19.

——. 1857. *Learning To Talk*. New York: Harper & Bros.

ABBOTT, JOHN S. C. 1842. "Paternal Neglect," *Parents' Magazine*, III, No. 3, 148.

ACKERLEY, G. 1836. *On the Management of Children*. New York.

ALCOTT, WILLIAM A. 1836. *The Young Mother*. Boston: Light & Stearns.

ALLEN, REV. RALPH W. 1848. "A Mother's Influence," *Mother's Assistant*, XIII, No. 5, 97–100.

——. 1849. "Family Government," *ibid.*, XV, No. 6, 126–29.

BARWELL, MRS. 1844. *Infant Treatment*. . . . 1st American ed. with supplement for the U.S. Boston: James Mowatt.

BAXTER, W. E. 1855. *America and the Americans*. London: Routledge.

BEECHER, C. E. 1846. *The Evils Suffered by American Women and Children*. New York: Harper & Bros.

BERGER, MAX. 1943. *The British Traveller in America, 1836–60*. London: King & Staples, Ltd.

BESTE, J. RICHARD. 1855. *The Wabash*. 2 vols. London: Hurst & Blackett.

BIGELOW, ELIZA. 1844. "Make Home a Happy Place," *Mother's Assistant*, IV, No. 2, 26–28.

BISHOP, ISABELLA L. 1856. *Englishwoman in America*. London: John Murray.

BRANCH, E. DOUGLAS. 1934. *The Sentimental Years, 1836–60*. New York: D. Appleton–Century Co.

BRIGGS, CAROLINE A. 1849. "Intellect of Children," *Mother's Assistant*, XIV, No. 5, 97–101.

BUSHNELL, HORACE. 184—. *Christian Nurture*. Reprinted in 1867. New York: Charles Scribner's Sons.

CALHOUN, ARTHUR. 1917–19. *A Social History of the American Family from Colonial Times to the Present*. 3 vols. Cleveland: Clark.

CANFIELD, CHARLES H. 1849. "Never Enter a Theatre," *Mother's Assistant*, XV, No. 6, 121–24.

CHAVASSE, P. H. 1860. *Advice to a Mother*. 5th London ed. 1st American ed., 1862. London: Balliere.

CHILD, LYDIA. 1831. *The Mother's Book*. 2d ed. Boston: Carter & Hendee.

CHOWN, STANLEY. 1936. "Some Notes on the History of Infant Feeding," *Manitoba Medical Association Review*, XVI, No. 9, 177–84.

COBB, LYMAN. 1847. *Tendencies of Corporal Punishment as a Means of Moral Discipline in Families and Schools*. New York: Newman & Co.

COMBE, ANDREW. 1840. *Treatise on the Physiological and Moral Management of Infancy*. Philadelphia: Carey & Hart.

DEWEES, WILLIAM P. 1826. *Treatise on the Physical and Medical Treatment of Children*. Philadelphia: Carey & Lea.

DONNE, ALFRED. 1859. *Mothers and Infants, Nurses and Nursing*. Boston: Phillips, Sampson & Co.

DRAKE, T. G. H. 1948. "American Infant Feeding Bottles as Disclosed by U.S. Patent Specifications, 1841–1946," *Journal of the History of Medicine and Allied Sciences*, III, No. 2, 507–24.

DUNCAN, MARY. 1852. *America as I Found It*. New York: Robert Carter & Bros.

DWIGHT, THEODORE. 1834. *The Father's Book*. Springfield, Mass.: G. & C. Merriam.

EDGEWORTH, MARIA and RICHARD. 1815. *On Practical Education*. 2d American ed. Boston: Wait.

FLEMING, SANDFORD. 1933. *Children and Puritanism*. New Haven: Yale University Press.

FOWLER, ORSON S. 1847. *Self Culture and Perfection of Character, Including Management of Youth*. New York: Fowler & Wells.

GALLAUDET, T. H. 1838. "On the Evidence of Early Piety," *Mother's Magazine*, VI, No. 11, 241–45.

———. 1839. "Domestic Education at the Table," *Mother's Magazine*, VII, No. 4, 73–76.

GORER, GEOFFREY. 1948. *The American People*. New York: W. W. Norton & Co.

GRAVES, MRS. A. J. 1844. *Girlhood and Womanhood*. Boston: Carter & Mussey.

HALL, MRS. ELIZABETH. 1849. "A Mother's Influence," *Mother's Assistant*, XIV, No. 2, 25–29.

"Hints for Maternal Education." 1834. *Mother's Magazine*, II, No. 8, 113–15.

HOARE, MRS. LOUISA. 1829. *Hints for the Improvement of Early Education and Nursery Discipline*. Reprinted from the 5th London ed. Salem: Buffum.

HOLBROOK, JOSIAH. 1838. "Domestic Education," *Mother's Magazine*, VI, No. 8, 188–92.

HOUGH, LEWIS S. 1849. *The Science of Man*. Boston: Bela Marsh.

HOWARD, REV. ORIN B. 1849. "The Mother, an Educator," *Mother's Assistant*, XV, No. 5, 97–100.

HUMPHREY, HEMAN. 1840. "Restraining and Governing Children's Appetites and Passions," *Mother's Magazine*, VIII, No. 6, 124–30.

———. 1840. *Domestic Education*. Amherst: Adams.

HYDE, REV. ALVAN. 1830. *Essay on the State of Infants*. New York: C. Davis.

"Improper Clothing." 1838. *Mother's Magazine*, VI, No. 9, 214–15.

IRELAND, W. M. 1820. *Advice to Mothers on the Management of Infants and Young Children*. New York: B. Young.

KIEFER, MONICA. 1948. *American Children through Their Books, 1700–1835*. Philadelphia: University of Pennsylvania Press.

KUHN, ANNE L. 1947. *Mother's Role in Childhood Education: New England Concepts, 1830–60*. ("Yale Studies in Religious Education," Vol. XIX.) New Haven: Yale University Press.

"Little Ellen." 1840. *Mother's Magazine*, VIII, No. 1, 6–14.

MANN, MRS. HORACE, and PEABODY, ELIZABETH. 1863. *Moral Culture of Infancy and Kindergarten Guide*. Boston: Burnham.

MARRYAT, FREDERICK. 1839. *A Diary in America*. 2 vols. Philadelphia: Carey & Hart.

MEAD, MARGARET. 1942. *And Keep Your Powder Dry*. New York: William Morrow & Co.

MOTT, FRANK L. 1930. *A History of Amercian Magazines, 1741–1850*. New York: Appleton.

Mother's Assistant. 1841–63. Boston.

Mother's Magazine. 1832–76. New York.

"Overfeeding of Children." 1839. In *Lady's Annual Register*, ed. CAROLINE GILMAN, p. 69. Boston: T. H. Carter.

Parents' Magazine. 1840–50. Gilmanton and Concord, N.H.

RAY, ISAAC. 1863. *Mental Hygiene*. Boston: Tichnor & Fields.

SAUSSURE, MME NECKER DE. 1835. *Progressive Education*. Notes, Appendix, and translation by EMMA WILLARD and ALMIRA PHELPS. Boston: Tichnor.

SEARLE, REV. THOMAS. 1834. *Companion to Seasons of Maternal Solicitude*. New York: Moore & Payne, Clinton Hall.

SIGOURNEY, LYDIA H. 1838. *Letters to Mothers*. Hartford: Hudson & Skinner.

SPROAT, MRS. NANCY. 1819. *Family Lectures*. Boston: Armstrong.

TAYLOR, CATHERINE L. 1849. "Education," *Mother's Assistant*, XV, No. 4, 73–80.

THOMSON, WILLIAM. 1842. *A Tradesman's Travels in the United States*. Edinburgh: Oliver & Boyd.

"To Mothers of Young Families." 1834. *Mother's Magazine*, II, No. 4, 53–55.

WARREN, ELIZA. 1865. *How I Managed My Children*. . . . Boston: Loring.

"What Manner of Child Shall This Be?" 1843. *Mother's Magazine*, XI, No. 3, 52–54.

WILSON, ELIZABETH A. 1940. "Hygienic Care and Management of the Child in the American Family Prior to 1860." Unpublished Master's thesis, Duke University, Durham, N.C.

CHAPTER 10

Fun Morality: An Analysis of Recent American Child-training Literature

——————————————————————MARTHA WOLFENSTEIN

This is a slightly revised version of the article which originally appeared in the Journal of Social Issues, *VII, No. 4 (1951), 15–25.*

A RECENT development in American culture is the emergence of what we may call "fun morality." Here fun, from having been suspect, if not taboo, has tended to become obligatory. Instead of feeling guilty for having too much fun, one is inclined to feel ashamed if one does not have enough. Boundaries formerly maintained between play and work break down. Amusements infiltrate into the sphere of work, while, in play, self-estimates of achievement become prominent. This development appears to be at marked variance with an older, Puritan ethic, although, as we shall see, the two are related.

The emergence of fun morality may be observed in the ideas about child training of the last forty years. In these one finds a changing conception of human impulses and an altered evaluation of play and fun which express the transformation of moral outlook. These changing ideas about child training may be regarded as part of a larger set of adult attitudes current in contemporary American culture. Thus I shall interpret the development which appears in the child-training literature as exemplifying a significant moral trend of our times.

The ideas on child training which I shall present are taken from the publications of the United States Department of Labor Children's Bureau. These publications probably express at any given time a major body of specialized opinion in the field, though how far they are representative would have to be determined by further study of other publications. In taking these publications as indicative of certain changing attitudes, I leave undetermined to what extent these attitudes are diffused among parents and also to what extent parents' actual behavior with their children conforms to these ideas. Both these topics would require further research.

The innovations in child-training ideas of the past few decades may readily be related to developments in psychological research and theory (notably behaviorism, Gesell's norms of motor development, and psychoanalysis). However, the occurrence and particularly the diffusion of certain psychological ideas at certain periods are probably related to the larger cultural context. A careful study of the ways in which psychological theories have been adapted for parent guidance and other pedagogical purposes would show that a decided selection is made from among the range of available theories, some points being overstressed, others omitted, and so on.

The *Infant Care* bulletin of the Children's Bureau, the changing contents of which I shall analyze, was first issued in 1914. The various editions fall into three main groupings: 1914 and 1921, 1929 and 1938, 1942 and 1945 (i.e., the most drastic revisions occurred in 1929 and 1942).[1] For the present purpose I shall mainly contrast the two ends of the series, comparing the 1914 edition with those of 1942 and 1945 (the two latter are practically identical) and skipping over the middle period. Thus I shall attempt to highlight the extent of the change rather than to detail the intermediate stages (which in any case show some complicated discontinuities).

As the infant embodies unmodified impulses, the conception of his nature is a useful index of the way in which the impulsive side of human nature generally is regarded. The conception of the child's basic impulses has undergone an extreme transformation from 1914 to the 1940's. At the earlier date, the infant appeared to be endowed with strong and dangerous impulses. These were notably autoerotic, masturbatory, and thumb-sucking. The child is described as "rebelling fiercely" if these impulses are interfered with.[2] The impulses "easily grow beyond control"[3] and are harmful in the extreme: "children are sometimes wrecked for life."[4] The baby may achieve the dangerous pleasures to which his nature disposes him by his own movements or may be seduced into them by being given pacifiers to suck or having his genitals stroked by the nurse.[5] The mother must be ceaselessly vigilant; she must wage a relentless battle against the child's sinful nature. She is told that masturbation "must be eradicated . . . treatment consists in mechanical restraints." The child should have his feet tied to opposite sides of the crib so that he cannot rub his thighs together; his nightgown sleeves should be pinned to the bed so that he cannot touch himself.[6] Similarly for thumb-sucking, "the sleeve may be pinned or sewed down over the fingers of the offending hand for several days and nights," or a patent cuff may be used which holds the elbow stiff.[7] The mother's zeal against thumb-sucking is assumed to be so great that she is reminded to allow the child to have his hands free some of the time so that he may develop legitimate manual skills; "but with the approach of sleeping time the hand must be covered."[8] The image of the child at this period is that he is centripetal, tending to get pleasure from his own body. Thus he must be bound down with arms and legs spread out to prevent self-stimulation.

In contrast to this we find in 1942–45 that the baby has been transformed into almost complete harmlessness. The intense and concentrated impulses of the past have disappeared. Drives toward erotic pleasure (and also toward domination, which was stressed in 1929–38) have become weak and incidental. Instead, we find impulses of a much more diffuse and moderate character. The baby is interested in exploring his world. If he happens to put his thumb in his mouth or to touch his genitals, these are merely incidents, and unimportant ones at that, in his over-all exploratory progress. The erogenous zones do not have the focal attraction which they did in 1914, and the baby easily passes beyond them to other areas of presumably equal interest. "The baby will not spend much time handling his genitals if he has other interesting things to do."[9] This infant explorer is centrifugal as the earlier erotic infant was centripetal. Everything amuses him, nothing is excessively exciting.

The mother in this recent period is told how to regard autoerotic incidents: "Babies want to handle and investigate everything that they can see and reach. When a baby discovers his genital organs he will play with them. . . . A wise mother will not be concerned about this."[10] As against the older method of tying the child hand and foot, the mother is now told: "See that he has a toy to play with and he will not need to use his body as a plaything."[11] The genitals are merely a resource which the child is thrown back on if he does not have a toy. Similarly with thumb-sucking: "A baby explores everything within his reach. He looks at a new object, feels it, squeezes it, and almost always puts it in his mouth."[12] Thus again what was formerly a "fierce" pleasure has become an unimportant incident in the exploration of the world. Where formerly the mother was to exercise a ceaseless vigilance, removing the thumb from the child's mouth as often as he put it in, now she is told not to make a fuss. "As he grows older, other interests will take the place of sucking."[13] (Incidentally, this unconcerned attitude toward thumb-sucking is a relatively late development. The 1938 edition still had an illustration of a stiff cuff which could be put on the infant at night to prevent his bending his elbow to get his fingers to his mouth. The attitude toward masturbation relaxed earlier, diversion having already been substituted for mechanical restraints in 1929).

This changing conception of the nature of impulses bears on the question: Is what the baby likes good for him? The opposition between the pleasant and the good is deeply grounded in older American morals (as in many other ascetic moral codes). There are strong doubts as to whether what is enjoyable is not wicked or deleterious. In recent years, however, there has been a marked effort to overcome this dichotomy, to say that what is pleasant is also good for you. The writers on child training reflect the changing ideas on this issue.

In the early period there is a clear-cut distinction between what the baby "needs," his legitimate requirements, whatever is essential to his health and well-being, on the one hand, and what the baby "wants," his illegitimate pleasure strivings, on the other. This is illustrated, for instance, in the question of whether to pick the baby up when he cries. In 1914 it was essential to determine whether he really needed something or whether he only wanted something. Crying is listed as a bad habit. This is qualified with the remark that the baby has no other way of expressing his "needs"; if he is expressing a need, the mother should respond. "But when the baby cries simply because he has learned from experience that this brings him what he wants, it is one of the worst habits he can learn." If the baby cries, "the mother may suspect illness, pain, hunger or thirst." These represent needs. If checking on all these shows they are not present, "the baby probably wants to be taken up, walked with, played with," etc. "After the baby's needs have been fully satisfied, he should be put down and allowed to cry."[14] (This position remained substantially unchanged up to 1942.)

In 1942–45, wants and needs are explicitly equated. "A baby sometimes cries because he wants a little more attention. He probably needs a little extra attention under some circumstances just as he sometimes needs a little extra food and water. Babies want attention; they probably need plenty of it."[15] What the baby wants for pleasure has thus become as legitimate a demand as what he needs for his physical well-being and is to be treated in the same way.[16]

The question of whether the baby wants things which are not good for him also occurs in connection with feeding. The baby's appetite was very little relied on to regulate the quantity of food he took in the early period. Overfeeding was regarded as a constant danger; the baby would never know when he had enough. This is in keeping with the general image of the baby at this time as a creature of insatiable impulses. In contrast to this, we find in the recent period that "the baby's appetite usually regulates successfully the amount of food he takes."[17] Thus again impulses appear as benevolent rather than dangerous.

Formerly, giving in to impulse was the way to encourage its growing beyond control. The baby who was picked up when he cried, held and rocked when he wanted it, soon grew into a tyrant.[18] This has now been strikingly reversed. Adequate early indulgence is seen as the way to make the baby less demanding as he grows older.[19] Thus we get the opposite of the old maxim, "Give the devil the little finger, and he'll take the whole hand." It is now "Give him the whole hand, and he'll take only the little finger."

The attitude toward play is related to the conception of impulses and the belief about the good and the pleasant. Where impulses are dangerous and the good and pleasant are opposed, play is suspect.

Thus in 1914, playing with the baby was regarded as dangerous; it produced unwholesome pleasure and ruined the baby's nerves. Any playful handling of the baby was titillating, excessively exciting, dele-terious. Play carried the overtones of feared erotic excitement. As we noted, this was the period of an intensive masturbation taboo, and there were explicit apprehensions that the baby might be seduced into masturbation by an immoral nurse who might play with his genitals.

The mother of 1914 was told: "The rule that parents should not play with the baby may seem hard, but it is without doubt a safe one. A young, delicate and nervous baby needs rest and quiet, and however robust the child much of the play that is indulged in is more or less harmful. It is a great pleasure to hear the baby laugh and crow in apparent delight, but often the means used to produce the laughter, such as tickling, punching, or tossing, makes him irritable and restless. It is a regrettable fact that the few minutes' play that the father has when he gets home at night . . . may result in nervous disturbance of the baby and upset his regular habits."[20] It is relevant to note that at this time "playthings . . . such as rocking horses, swings, teeter boards, and the like" are cited in connection with masturbation, as means by which "this habit is learned."[21] The dangerousness of play is related to that of the ever present sensual impulses which must be constantly guarded against. (In 1929–38, play becomes less taboo, but must be strictly confined to certain times of the day. In this period the impulse to dominate replaces erotic impulses as the main hazard in the child's nature, and the corresponding danger is that he may get the mother to play with him whenever he likes.)

In the recent period, play becomes associated with harmless and healthful motor and exploratory activities. It assumes the aspect of diffuse innocuousness which the child's impulse life now presents. Play is derived from the baby's developing motor activities, which are now increasingly stressed. "A baby needs to be able to move all parts of his body. He needs to exercise. . . . At a very early age the baby moves his arms and legs aimlessly. . . . As he gets older and stronger and his movements become more vigorous and he is better able to control them he begins to play."[22] Thus play has been successfully dissociated from unhealthy excitement and nervous debilitation and has become asso-ciated with muscular development, necessary exercise, strength, and control. This is in keeping with the changed conception of the baby, in which motor activities rather than libidinal urges are stressed. For the baby who is concerned with exploring his world rather than with sucking and masturbating, play becomes safe and good.

Play is now to be fused with all the activities of life. "Play and sing-ing make both mother and baby enjoy the routine of life."[23] This min-gling of play with necessary routines is consonant with the view that the good and pleasant coincide. Also, as the mother is urged to make play an aspect of every activity, play assumes a new obligatory quality. Mothers are told that "a mother usually enjoys entering into her baby's play. Both of them enjoy the little games that mothers and babies have always played from time immemorial." (This harking back to time immemorial is a way of skipping over the more recent past.) "Daily tasks can be done with a little play and singing thrown in."[24] Thus it is now not adequate for the mother to perform efficiently the necessary routines for her baby; she must also see that these are fun for both of them. It seems difficult here for anything to become permissible without becoming compulsory. Play, having ceased to be wicked, having become harmless and good, now becomes a new duty.

In keeping with the changed evaluation of impulses and play, the conception of parenthood has altered. In the earlier period the mother's character was one of strong moral devotion. There were frequent references to her "self-control," "wisdom," "strength," "persistence," and "unlimited patience." The mothers who read these bulletins might either take pride in having such virtues or feel called upon to aspire to them. The writers supposed that some mothers might even go to excess in their devoted self-denial. Thus the mothers were told that, for their own health and thus for the baby's good, they should not stay bound to the crib-side without respite, but should have some pleasant, although not too exhausting, recreation.[25] The mother at this time is pictured as denying her own impulses just as severely as she does those of her child. Just as she had to be told to let the baby's hands free occasionally (not to overdo the fight against thumb-sucking), so she must be counseled to allow herself an intermission from duty. (In the 1929–38 period parenthood became predominantly a matter of know-how. The parents had to use the right technique to impose routines and to keep the child from dominating them.)

In the most recent period parenthood becomes a major source of enjoyment for both parents (the father having come much more into the picture than he was earlier). The parents are promised that having children will keep them together, keep them young, and give them fun and happiness. As we have seen, enjoyment, fun, and play now permeate all activities with the child. "Babies—and usually their mothers—enjoy breast feeding"; nursing brings "joy and happiness" to the mother. At bath time the baby "delights" his parents, and so on.[26]

The characterization of parenthood in terms of fun and enjoyment may be intended as an inducement to parents in whose scheme of values these are presumed to be priorities. But also it may express a new imperative: You ought to enjoy your child. When a mother is told that most mothers enjoy nursing, she may wonder what is wrong with her in case she does not. Her self-evaluation can no longer be based entirely on whether she is doing the right and necessary things but becomes involved with nuances of feeling which are not under voluntary control. Fun has become not only permissible but required, and this requirement has a special quality different from the obligations of the older morality.

I should now like to speculate on the connection between the attitudes revealed in this child-training literature and a wider range of attitudes in American culture today. The extent of diffusion with respect to class, region, etc., of the attitudes I shall discuss would be a topic for further research.

The changing attitudes toward impulse and restraint, the changing treatment of play, the changing evaluation of fun which we have found in the child-training literature, would seem to have many counterparts in other areas of adult life. Play, amusement, fun, have become increasingly divested of puritanical associations of wickedness. Where formerly there was felt to be the danger that, in seeking fun, one might be carried away into the depths of wickedness, today there is a recognizable fear that one may not be able to let go sufficiently, that one may not have enough fun. In the recent past there has been an increased tendency to attempt by drinking to reduce constraint sufficiently so that we can have fun. Harold Lasswell has defined the superego as that part of the personality which is soluble in alcohol. From having dreaded impulses and being worried about whether conscience was adequate to cope with them, we have come round to finding conscience a nuisance and worrying about the adequacy of our impulses.

Not having fun is not merely an occasion for regret but involves a loss of self-esteem. I ask myself: What is wrong with me that I am not having fun? To admit that one did not have fun when one was expected to arouses feelings of shame. Where formerly it might have been thought that a young woman who went out a great deal might be doing wrong, currently we would wonder what is wrong with a girl who is not going out. Fun and play have assumed a new obligatory aspect. While gratification of forbidden impulses traditionally aroused guilt, failure to have fun currently occasions lowered self-esteem. One is likely to feel inadequate, impotent, and also unwanted. One fears the pity of one's contemporaries rather than, as formerly, possible condemnation by moral authorities. In our book, *Movies: A Psychological Study*,[27] Nathan Leites and I referred to this new obligatoriness of pleasure as "fun morality" as distinguished from the older "goodness morality," which stressed interference with impulses. We noted a particular type of current American film heroine, the masculine-feminine girl, whose major merit consists in making the achievement of fun not too effortful. She initiates the flirtation, keeps it casual, makes it clear that she does not require excessive intensity from the man. At the same time she supports his self-esteem by implying that she never doubts his resources for having fun, however cool or abstracted he may seem. She affords a relief from the pressures of fun morality.

David Riesman, in *The Lonely Crowd*,[28] has observed how extensively work and play have become fused in business and professional life. Activities formerly sharply isolated from work, such as entertainment, have become part of business relations. Aspects of the personality, such as pleasingness or likability, formerly regarded as irrelevant to work efficiency, have been increasingly called into play in working life. Relations with work associates have become less and less sharply distinguishable from relations outside working hours. Thus there has been a mutual penetration of work and play. Work tends to be permeated with behavior formerly confined to after work hours. Play, conversely, tends to be measured by standards of achievement previously applicable only to work. One asks one's self not only in personal relations but now also at work: Did they like me? Did I make a good impression? And at play, no less than at work, one asks: Am I doing as well as I should?

In the past when work and play were more sharply isolated, virtue was associated with the one and the danger of sin with the other. Impulse gratification presented possibilities of intense excitement as well as of wickedness. Today we have attained a high degree of tolerance of impulses, which at the same time no longer seem capable of producing such intense excitement as formerly. Is it because we have come to realize that the devil does not exist that we are able to fuse play and fun with business, child care, and so on? Or have we developed (without conscious calculation) a new kind of defense against impulses? This defense would consist in diffusion, ceasing to keep gratification deep, intense, and isolated, but allowing it to permeate thinly through all activities, to achieve by a mixture a further mitigation. Thus we would have preserved unacknowledged and unrecognized the tradition of puritanism. We do not pride ourselves on being good, and we secretly worry about not having enough fun. But the submerged superego works better than we know, interspersing play in small doses with work and applying a norm of achievement to play. Instead of the image of the baby who has fierce pleasures of autoeroticism and the dangerous titillation of rare moments of play, we get the infant who explores his world, every part of whose extent is interesting but none intensely exciting, and who may have a bit of harmless play thrown in with every phase of the day's routine. We get the adult whose work is permeated with personal relations and entertainment requirements, the impact of which is far from intensely pleasurable, and whose playtime is haunted by self-doubts about his capacity for having as much fun as he should.

I should like to add a further instance which epitomizes this tendency to fuse work and fun, manifestly to make work more agreeable, but in effect probably reducing the impact of fun. Recently a ten-year-old boy showed me one of his schoolbooks. It had the title *Range Riders* and showed on the cover a cowboy on a galloping horse. The subtitle was *Adventures in Numbers*—it was an arithmetic book. The problems involved cowboys, horses, and so on. The traditional image of the American schoolboy has been that he sits with a large textbook propped up in front of him, a book representing the hard and tedious lessons which he wants to evade. And inside the textbook he conceals a book of Wild West stories, detective stories, or the like, which he is avidly reading. These two books have now been fused into one. I do not know whether this succeeds in making the arithmetic more interesting. But I have a suspicion that it makes the cowboys less exciting.

After I had made the analysis of child-training literature presented in the foregoing pages, a new edition of the *Infant Care* bulletin appeared, in the fall of 1951. This new bulletin contains some points which are worth remarking. While it perpetuates many of the tendencies of the 1942–45 editions, it also shows some changes. Fun morality remains prominent. The new parents are told that they are making a good start if they can enjoy their baby.[29] The child should learn that mother and father are "two people who enjoy each other."[30] Introducing the baby to solid foods will be "fun" and "amusing" for the mother, and the baby will "enjoy the new experience more if you are having a good time."[31] The mother should arrange the baby's bath so that it will be "the pleasant time it should be. . . . If you feel hurried, bath time won't be the fun for either of you that it should be."[32]

The difficulty of achieving fun, which, as we have observed, tends currently to worry adults, is now ascribed to the infant as well (following the general tendency to see the infant as the model of impulse life). The infant now may suffer from boredom. And this has become the main reason for autoerotic activities. The baby may suck his thumb out of "loneliness or boredom."[33] He may rock or bang his head because of "boredom."[34] In toilet training the baby, the mother must take care that it does not become a "hateful bore" for him.[35] Masturbation is mentioned only in the section on toilet training: "sometimes a baby handles his genitals when he is on the toilet, or at other times when he is undressed."[36] While it is not said explicitly that he does this out of boredom, we might infer it on an analogy with thumb-sucking, rocking, and head-banging, since we are told that the baby may also get bored on the toilet. Thus the autoerotic activities which were first derived from fierce impulses, later from less intense exploratory tendencies, now arise as an escape from boredom. The dwindling of impulsive intensity has proceeded further than before.

The exploratory impulse of the baby continues to be stressed. We have interpreted this as an attempt to conceive the child's impulsive endowment in harmless terms. But the puritanical condemnation of impulses seems to be catching up with this displacement. Bounds must now be set to the baby's exploration. "We know that if we leave him free to creep everywhere he'd get into trouble." Thus we must "set a limit" for the baby "while he explores."[37]

There are still more striking signs that the belief in the dangerousness of impulses is breaking through the defenses that have been erected against it. In 1942–45 the view was advanced that the early gratification of the baby's demands led to the subsequent moderation of demands. There is now a conflict on this point. In some areas the precept is maintained, notably in relation to sucking and food preferences.[38] But in respect to the impulse to dominate, it has been reversed. The apprehension of the twenties that the baby may get the upper hand if his parents give in to him reappears. The baby may get the parents "at his mercy by unreasonable demands for attention."[39] Although the baby's need for companionship and for being held when he cries is stressed,[40] the mother is also warned: "If you get in the habit of picking your baby up every time he whimpers, you may do more harm than good." The gratified demand is apt to grow rather than to subside. The mother "may find her baby getting more and more demanding."[41]

Thus the conflict about facing and accepting human impulses is far from solved. On the one hand, the attempt to dilute and diffuse impulses seems to lead to doubts about adequate impulsive intensity, boredom, and the difficulty of achieving fun. On the other hand, the anxiety that impulses in one form or another will tend to grow beyond control has not been successfully warded off.

NOTES

1. My analysis is based on the six editions indicated. I was unable to obtain those of 1926 and 1940.

2. *Infant Care* (1914), p. 58.
3. *Ibid.*, p. 62.
4. *Ibid.*
5. *Ibid.*
6. *Ibid.*
7. *Ibid.*, p. 61.
8. *Ibid.*
9. *Ibid.* (1942), p. 60.
10. *Ibid.*
11. *Ibid.*

12. *Ibid.*, pp. 59–60.
13. *Ibid.*
14. *Ibid.* (1914), pp. 60–61.
15. *Ibid.* (1945), p. 52.
16. In a recent television advertisement, Angelo Patri is quoted as saying: "Youngsters today need television for their morale as much as they need fresh air and sunshine for their health."
17. *Infant Care* (1945), p. 95.
18. *Ibid.* (1914), pp. 60–61.
19. *Ibid.* (1945), p. 30.
20. *Ibid.* (1914), pp. 59–60.
21. *Ibid.*, p. 62.
22. *Ibid.* (1942), p. 41.
23. *Ibid.*
24. *Ibid.*
25. *Ibid.* (1914), p. 34.
26. *Ibid.* (1945), pp. 1, 29, 38, 62.
27. Wolfenstein and Leites, 1950.
28. Riesman, 1950.
29. *Infant Care* (1951), p. 3.
30. *Ibid.*, p. 1.
31. *Ibid.*, p. 32.
32. *Ibid.*, p. 64.
33. *Ibid.*, p. 57.
34. *Ibid.*, p. 56.
35. *Ibid.*, p. 87.
36. *Ibid.*
37. *Ibid.*, p. 76.
38. *Ibid.*, pp. 47, 57.
39. *Ibid.*, p. 55.
40. *Ibid.*, p. 53.
41. *Ibid.*, p. 42.

LIST OF REFERENCES

CHILDREN'S BUREAU, DEPARTMENT OF LABOR. *Infant Care*. 1914–51. Washington, D.C.: Government Printing Office.

RIESMAN, DAVID. 1950. *The Lonely Crowd*. New Haven: Yale University Press.

WOLFENSTEIN, MARTHA, and LEITES, NATHAN. 1950. *Movies: A Psychological Study*. Glencoe, Ill.: Free Press.

CHAPTER 11

Child-training Ideals in a Postrevolutionary Context: Soviet Russia

—————————————————————MARGARET MEAD AND ELENA CALAS

The detailed materials on Soviet child training in this paper are based on the research of Elena Calas between 1947 and 1950, and especially on an unpublished manuscript: "Soviet Child-training Ideals and Their Political Significance" (1949). For a summary of this research see Mead, Soviet Attitudes toward Authority (1951), and for publications of approaches on which I have drawn extensively see Leites, Operational Code of the Politburo (1951) and A Study of Bolshevism (1953); Leites and Bernaut, Ritual of Liquidation (1954); Gorer and Rickman, The People of Great Russia: A Psychological Study (1950); Mosely, "Some Soviet Techniques of Negotiation" (1951); and unpublished researches by Leopold Haimson and Herbert Dinerstein.

For the background materials which I have used in the interpretation—for which I am entirely responsible—I am indebted to the group of specialists with whom I have been privileged to work during the years I have participated in researches on Old Russia and on Soviet Russia: Sula Benet, Elsa Bernaut, Elena and Nicolas Calas, Herbert Dinerstein, Ralph Fischer, Geoffrey Gorer, Leopold Haimson, Nelly Hoyt, Nathan Leites, Philip Mosely, Bertram Schaffner, Vera Schwarz, Martha Wolfenstein, Mark Zborowski, and Rosalind Zoglin.—M. M.

WHEN a revolution occurs which is not merely a palace coup but a conscious attempt to change the institutions of a society, the whole position of child training may be altered. Instead of a series of partially related efforts designed to assist parents, educate teachers, and incorporate new bodies of scientific findings on child development, laws of learning, child psychiatry, nutrition, etc., child rearing may become a conscious instrument of the revolutionary regime. This has been so in small religious revolutions, as that of the Hutterites, where the establishment of religious communities in which goods were held in common was accompanied by communal rearing of young children. It has been so in Israel, where the Kibbutzim have established communal nurseries which free both parents to work and are designed to free children from the traditional close ties of the Eastern European Jewish family and fit them for work in agricultural collectives. Even among the Manus tribe of the Admiralty Islands, who have recently

179

undergone a profound religious, social, and economic upheaval as they attempted to reorganize their entire culture, we find new rules for child rearing, so that along with the attempts to substitute individual responsibility for the former wider kinship ties go admonitions to parents to keep their children at home, to forbid their wandering about to the houses of relatives, and community discussions of such matters as whether a child's body and personality are damaged if he is carried too long on an adult's back.[1] The historical evidence would suggest that such concern with changes in child-rearing practices appropriately appears in such revolutionary contexts.

There has also been a tendency throughout Western history—echoed not only in religious sects in the West, in recent social experiments such as Israel, but in spontaneous socioreligious revolutions among primitive peoples—to revise the sex mores at the same time that political and economic institutions are overhauled. Such revision often takes the form of repudiating whatever controls on sex behavior were most characteristic of the older religious or political regime against which the new movement is directed, so that various new types of sexual freedom, having their reflections in forms of family life and parental control, are likely to be widely mooted. The right for either sex to choose a mate, social disapproval of sexual jealousy, admonitions to women to contribute willingly to the sexual satisfactions of the males, especially the leading males in the group, are frequent accompaniments of revolutionary movements. A further reinforcement is given to this type of relaxation of sex controls by the way in which both unorthodox sexual behavior and unorthodox political behavior are often linked together in the behavior of youth or sexual deviants, sometimes to the extent that political conspiracy becomes surrounded with all the aura of secretly obscene activities—in the behavior of rebellious university students plotting a different world and in the fear of the enthusiastic guardians of the old order that political unreliability and sexual deviation somehow go together.

Furthermore, totalistic revolutions, in which there is an attempt to revise the whole culture, to reorganize the whole society, have, with astonishing frequency, followed practices which have been loosely labeled as the "nationalization of women." These have occurred in such widely scattered settings as in the ancient Inca state, under which girls could be taken from any community and assigned by state officials either to perform manufacturing tasks in segregated communities or as sex partners for Inca officialdom; in Nazi Germany, where measures provided adequate protection and indulgence for unmarried mothers bearing sons to the state; and in the contemporary Admiralty Islands, where the native leader, in an attempt to provide against the spiritually corroding effects of unsatisfied lust, proposed that any man lusting after a married woman should be allowed to sleep with her once, thus ridding himself of his obsession, freeing his mind for higher things, and that she should be recompensed by a fixed fee set by the community authorities. So, while it has been more customary to associate the early Soviet attitudes toward the family, sex, and child rearing with specific Marxian doctrines about the role of the individualistic bourgeois family which had to be eliminated in a socialist state, there seems good reason to suggest that this process of initial loosening of social-sexual restrictions and re-examining of the relationship between sex, family structure, child rearing, and the desired political utopia is rooted very deeply in the mechanisms through which any society maintains its continuity by developing a type of character structure capable of perpetuating its social, political, and economic institutions.

The early days of the Soviet revolution were a conspicuous example of this whole process. The bourgeois family was to be abolished, women were to be free to choose their mates, divorce was made easy, women were to work just as men did, and the state was to assume the care of children, with the dual objectives of freeing women to contribute their labor to the state and rearing children in an institutional setting appropriate to the citizens of a socialist society. Abortion was legalized as a way of giving women greater freedom, and the familiar abuses, in which new forms of sexual promiscuity flourished, developed as women were expected to yield their favors as part of their duty as "comrades" to male members of the party. The relationship between the assumption of authoritarian, totalistic leadership and the exploitation of women, under the guise of giving them freedom, was fully illustrated in the early Soviet revolution.

It is also important to note that Marxian theory had never developed any coherent concept of the relationship between character structure and political institutions, beyond the simple unsupported assertions that a bourgeois character accompanies bourgeois institutions and a socialist character will follow from socialist institutions. These connections are loose and broad. The bourgeois institutions, which produced a bourgeois character, were the possessive, patriarchal family, the institution of private property, the class system, etc., and no attempt was made to trace out the ways in which the character of the growing child embodied—through the patterned minutiae of interpersonal contacts—the forms within which it was reared. There is, on the whole, less sophistication about the relationship between child-rearing practice and character formation in the published literature of the Soviet Union than there is in the present-day Admiralty Islands, among a people who twenty-five years ago were in the Stone Age. This lack of sophistication may be referred partly to Marxian insistence upon economic determinism and failure to root its theoretical approach in any theory of child development, partly to crude theories of conditioning, and partly to Russian optimism about human potentialities.

Early Soviet family legislation and child-rearing practices, therefore, presented a curious medley of rejection of older family forms; attempts to imitate the Western world, whose patterns of industrialization were being welcomed even as their patterns of social, economic, and political life were being rejected; and the extension into the institutional care of children of the kinds of ideas of collective behavior which permeated the whole climate of the day. So, together with rights for illegitimate children and encouragement of crèches for children of working mothers went the importation of the nursery and pediatric practices of the West, stricter and earlier toilet training, an attempt to abolish the swaddling of young infants, and such definitely ideological measures as feeding two babies with alternate spoonfuls or hanging two babies up in a sort of net together as a learning experience in collective behavior. The mélange of child care which existed at this period presented the characteristic revolutionary picture of relaxations, extravagances, and innovations from other cultures. It was during this period that enthusiasm in other countries for the place of the child in society and for the economic and political freedom of women hailed the Soviet experiment as representing a new era, and enemies of the regime accused them of destroying the family, nationalizing women, promoting abortion, approving promiscuity, etc.

Slowly this picture changed. In 1932, the Department of Education proclaimed: "The Soviet state views each child, be it born in registered wedlock or out of it, as a future citizen, necessary to society."[2] Throughout, this insistence on children as future citizens is central; children are not seen as representing a value which society should conserve, but, like the masses,[3] they are an essential resource of the society. The report continues:

It [the state] is interested that this citizen enter life properly prepared, communistically reared, and strong-muscled. It is necessary to rear and teach this future citizen in a corresponding way. The state primarily takes this duty upon itself but does not free the family from it either. . . . The state cannot as yet fully take upon itself the care and support of the child. . . . In case the parents do not properly fulfil this duty or misuse their power over the child, the state reserves the right to take the child away from the parents and, without freeing them from material obligations of support, to designate a guardian. The boundary between those born in wedlock and out of it is effaced.[4]

The legislative acts of Proletarian Dictatorship printed in this book are the laws of a transitory period toward the time when socialistic society takes upon itself in full the care of children and their rearing. As yet, at the present stage, together with the gigantic growth of the Komsomol and Pioneer organizations, which embrace masses in-the-million of children and youths and educate them in the spirit of communism, with Soviet schools teaching all children, with a considerable growth of children's homes, children's colonies, and other such organizations into which children are taken for full rearing, the role of the family is still kept in the matter of bringing up the younger generation. . . . Such a concept as parental rights, still remaining in Soviet legislation, has acquired an entirely different character than it has in bourgeois society. In truth, parental rights may be called rights only in quotes, because their content consists merely in the protection of children's interests and in parental duties toward children.[5]

When we realize that children are important because of their future usefulness to the state, then the role of the family as a state agency for the protection of human raw material is clear. Such positions were not incompatible with the encouragement of children and young people to inform against their parents and to rebel openly when their parents showed traces of "bourgeois attitudes." The parents were not seen as models for their children to follow. Indeed, it was necessary to break down tendencies in children to imitate their erroneously educated parents; at best, most parents could be subordinate caretakers of the physical well-being of the child, who was trained in public institutions to the new attitudes appropriate to a Soviet citizen.

By 1944 the new family code had re-established the importance of the family; divorce was frowned upon, abortion had been abolished, and parents had been restored to the position of models for the conduct and ideals of their children. This restoration of a large number of conditions familiar in Western society was pictured, however, as an advance:

In a class society, there has not been, there is not, and there cannot be a family structure identical in its organization or its character or its interrelations with the structure of society as a whole. Such a family has first arisen under socialism.[6]

So the earlier doctrine in which the family was regarded as a reflector of the economic institutions of an outmoded form of society is here explicitly side-stepped:

The most essential conditions for the organization of the new type of family is the building of all Soviet society on the foundations of labor free from exploitation and the full political, economic, and juridic freedom of women.[7]

. . . As a result of realistic achievements of a socialistic regime of social relations . . . there has been an essential change in the character of relationship between spouses [and] between parents and children. Women, having become masters of the country on a par with men, have acquired great weight in the family. Parental authority has grown in relation to children. Parents, after all, are no longer those rightless toilers, ever fearful of unemployment, humiliated and mistreated by the rich and powerful of the old capitalistic regime. They are fully aware of their dignity as the builders of a new life, appreciated and respected by society and state. Soviet laws establish and strengthen new socialistic relations between parents and children and assist the further welfare of the family.[8]

Now parents have rights again:

> Parents have a right to rear their children. No one can hinder them in
> this. They realize this is their right according to their capacities and oppor-
> tunities. . . . Ideas of rearing children outside the family, rather widespread
> in their time among certain authors and practical workers, are harmful and
> rejected in the USSR. They ignored the rights and interests of parents and
> children and issued from the incorrect thinking that in a socialistic society
> a family, it seems, is unable to give children proper upbringing. Those
> authors forgot that in a socialistic society the family is no longer the same
> as in a capitalistic society, that the very conditions of family upbringing
> have changed at the roots. The practice of socialistic building has shown
> that the family in socialistic society provides an excellent upbringing for
> the new generation.[9]

However, this reliance on the parents as models is still conditional.
In addition to "unremitting effort," the parents are always on trial, always subject to rebuke or rejection by society and by their own children if they do not conform to and live up to the standards set by the
party and the school.

The counterpart of this conditional reliance on parents is faith in
the potency of the system:

> If youths have been brought up in the spirit of Communist morality, if
> they have mastered the principles of Marxist-Leninist philosophy, if their
> main purposeful life-attitude is to give all their strength and knowledge to
> the struggle for communism, one need not worry about their future.[10]

It is within this setting of an initial rejection of family authority and
its later re-establishment that contemporary theories of child rearing
must be interpreted.

A second social condition essential to an understanding of the emphases found in Soviet child-rearing material is the Soviet theory of
leadership and the way the party and the party line function. Under
Soviet theory, children and masses are both a source of strength, zest,
and energy, and a group always in danger of succumbing to evil
"influences." Neutral in themselves, perhaps even intrinsically good,
the children and the masses must be guarded and protected against
evil companions, evil influences, false ideas, false models, and the
smallest traces of bad habits which may rapidly expand into evil behavior of catastrophic proportions. Not only actual political deviation
but no possibility of a political deviation should go unpunished. The
smallest event may lead to the largest and most disastrous consequences.

The establishment of a socialistic society may indeed make it possible to add parents to the set of authority figures through which children are guarded, controlled, and disciplined, but it has not made it
possible to relax. Each new generation of children must be brought up

with equal vigilance, each new generation of masses must be protected from the evil effects of capitalistic propaganda. The way the line functions, in lieu of the kind of political changes which can be introduced where there are several political parties, means that any procedure may be carried to great extremes and then as violently reversed, so that specific theories of education may be repudiated with a change in the line. But the essential position, which includes the family with the party, the Komsomols, the Pioneers, and the schools as a ring of authorities surrounding the growing child and expected to present an absolutely monolithic front, has remained fairly constant since the middle of World War II.

There is a spectacular increase in the bitterness of the complaints against the failure of the family to prevent the spread of juvenile delinquency. Parental overindulgence is singled out for attack.[11] The accompanying cartoon reprinted from *Krokodil* (Pl. XX, Fig. 3) is an indictment of the family as an institution invested with authority. (This tendency to blame the family for failures in the upbringing of children is shared with Western countries, but with a difference. In the United States, for example, the family is also regarded as the principal positive bulwark of character, while in the Soviet Union, the family is blamed for failure while party and state take credit for the successes.)

Within this setting we may now consider the explicit Soviet theories of child training. There is relatively little recognition of stages in development to which qualitatively different methods are appropriate. Soviet training should begin at birth. This training is first a training in endurance: "Precisely in the first days of an infant's existence, training in this important quality [endurance] should begin; naturally at this age one can talk only of training in physical endurance."[12] Parents are warned not to suppose that the passage of time will itself change the child. At every stage intervention is necessary:

An immense responsibility lies with the tutor whose every step is under the steady observing gaze of the little being. Each action, each conversation, each word, either helps the blossoming of the child's *soul* [spiritual] forces, or, on the contrary, breaks and maims his *soul* [spirit]. . . . In upbringing, in this many-sided deep process of personality formation, there is nothing which may be considered a trifle. . . . The older a child becomes, the more heightened becomes parental responsibility for his upbringing as well as for their own behavior.[13]

As the child grows, he becomes one of the ring of exacting authorities which surround the adults: "An adolescent, not to speak of a youth, grows to possess the ability to analyze, evaluate, weigh the conduct of adults, and presents ever higher demands on himself and those around him."[14]

Thus the parent is presented as participating in the task of unremittingly forming the "moral countenance" of the child, so that the child will learn to take control over itself and join the group of authorities who help to maintain external controls on other people. "For the authority of parents to be really high, a strong, well-knit family is necessary first of all. . . . Besides, the atmosphere of the family must be one of comradeship, friendship, mutual help, industry, common political and cultural interests."[15]

There must be friendship between parents and children, in contrast to the classical ideological break between parents and children in pre-revolutionary Russia. "This friendship is not born by chance and effortlessly. It must also be won."[16] Models are presented of school children who ask advice:

"What should one's attitude be if parents want to make an egotist of one?" . . . Each step of the parents is exactingly evaluated by the older children. "My mother graduated from two institutes of higher learning, but does not work any place and does not even read!" In those words of a ninth grader, what cruel reproach, what a serious warning.[17]

But at the same time no upper age limit is placed on the authority of the parent, so a mother, in depicting her exemplary family, says: "All the children obey me. My eldest son, who returned from the front a lieutenant, will do nothing without asking my advice, will go nowhere without having told me."[18] Congruently, a Soviet-educated woman who had emigrated to America and who expressed strong anti-Soviet sentiments, nevertheless took her child out of an American nursery school when she heard another child say "shut up" to a teacher, and, commenting on this to me, she said: "In the Soviet Union it is not permissible to *think* 'shut up.'"

At the same time there are some warnings against the evils of limitless authority, which may stifle the child's development: ". . . the child most of all needs freedom of action, that any oppression and interference in his life by adults can only destructively influence the flowering of his natural gifts." But these warnings are accompanied by even stronger admonitions against the even more dangerous point of view:

Such an advocation of free upbringing, or, more precisely, freedom from upbringing, can lead only, as we have seen proved by the example of homeless children, to moral and mental savagery. Parents must gradually make demands on children in correspondence with the growing level of the development of the child. The line of parental behavior must be determined by the line of the child's development. It is as if it [parental guidance] marches ahead, lighting the way, leading the child from absolute obedience to independence, to the consciousness of responsibility, to conscious discipline, to self-discipline, and, finally, to a courageous defense of the child's right to a free expression of his personality.[19]

Within this training, every detail is important. For pupils whose wills are to be educated,

> ... it is not enough to inspire them with great aims and ideals. ... The best training is the accurate, scrupulous fulfilment of daily, modest, ordinary duties.[20]

> Children must know exactly their bedtime, time of play, and preparation of lessons. ... Children must have a capacity to repress, to control themselves.[21]

The familiar Soviet attitude toward the dangers of the line of least resistance is heavily emphasized. The child should be continually presented with obstacles that he can overcome. Furthermore, these obstacles should separate him from a goal, and the pursuit of harder and harder goals should be part of the educational process. Even the little child just beginning to walk should be given "tasks which he is up to but which are always more difficult, for example, to walk independently an always greater distance from a definite place to a goal set beforehand."[22] The parent or educator must be careful also to help the child

> strengthen his belief in himself, in his ability to become a better person, not to blunt but to sharpen in him the feeling of pride in the achievement that demands work, effort, self-mastery, and emphasize always those large perspectives of social significance which are possible on the condition of such upward movement.[23]

It is these "large perspectives of social significance" which are essential, and only within such an emphasis on a complete acceptance of group goals is individual striving approved or rewarded.

Improvement of personal position is recognized as legitimate only in relation to the social target. Character traits unbecoming to a young Communist are not only stigmatized by the term "petty bourgeois," but as personal preoccupations and selfishness:

> Courage as a general concept implies steadfastness and stoicalness of spirit, an ability to bear personal hardships in the name of a noble and high cause and with sufficient firmness to stand in defense of justice and principles without consideration of personal comfort or peace. This is why we do not call courageous everyone who is patient or persistent in the achievement of a goal. Real courage is incompatible with private strivings. He who has learned to overcome obstacles and be firm, merely to reach a more favorable position for himself, is far from courageous.[24]

The abolition of corporal punishment has been a significant theme. Parents are also warned against frightening children with threats of "a strange man," "black man," "bear,"[25] and against punishing by deprivation of movement. "Not infrequently a mother resorts to beatings, spankings, and scaring. Parents must remember that nothing furthers more the growth of malignancy and stubbornness, on the one hand,

and, on the other, cowardliness, timidity, and shyness."[26] Parents who
say they only spank lightly,

fail completely to take into consideration that a child often feels the insult
from the loved person more than pain; and a spanking, however light, is
no less insulting than a beating. . . . When do parents awaken fears? They
resort to frightening when children are stubborn or behave from the point
of view of adults "indecently," suck their fingers, pick their noses, touch
their genital organs, wet their pants.[27]

All these cautions represent a counterpoint to older Russian practices,
in which excessive immobility and outward decorum were exacted
from children, including very long periods of standing without movement, not as punishment, but as ordinary, expected behavior.

The withdrawal of parental love and group approval are supposed
to replace corporal punishment. The circumstances under which punishment is to be used are discussed elaborately:

If it happens that all measures of influencing the child have been exhausted and the child has not only not corrected himself but each day has
become worse,[28] that he has gotten into some vicious milieu which sucks
him in ever more, tears him entirely from his family and makes him, in fact,
a *bezprisorni* [homeless, unsupervised]—in such a case, constant personal
supervision by parents is necessary. Parents must discuss the supervision
with the managers of their enterprises and ask for a change in shift for one
of them so that the child will be guaranteed constant supervision, without
any loss to the enterprise.[29]

If a son insults his mother, no trick will help. . . . All educational work
must be started anew [30] much may need to be re-examined in your family,
much thought over and, before all else, you should place yourself under the
microscope. . . . Perhaps you were rude to your wife in your son's presence.
Although if you insulted your wife in your son's absence, this, too, is worthy
of attention.[31]

Frequent and severe punishments are disapproved on the ground
that they will lose their effectiveness. Verbal punishments must also
be watched. So the case is cited of Boria, a fourth-grade pupil, guilty
of "self-willed departures duing school hours," "careless preparation of
home assignments," and a "completely indifferent mocking attitude toward all talks, reproaches, and punishments." It is suggested that when
he was six or seven years old, he

. . . constantly heard from surrounding adults that he was impossible, disobedient, wicked, that nothing would come of him, that in school he would
be properly called to account, that his parents expected nothing but grief
from him. . . . The adults not only did not help him master his excitability
and liveliness, but made demands, got angry, and punished. . . . He became
accustomed to those "epithets," his receptivity became dulled.[32]

All forms of verbal reaction, such as scolding, lecturing, grumbling,
moralizing, must be controlled and in no event may be used as catharsis for adult feelings. Verbal reactions not only dull children's re-

sponses, but also they give "a discharge to one's state of mind, to one's dissatisfaction with the children, to anger: 'The heart feels lighter.' "[33] Such lightening of the parental heart is most undesirable, as it prevents the parents from being goaded by conscience into the proper action:

Words must serve only for explanation, for evaluation of behavior, for criticism or approval. One should not permit one's self many-wordedness.[34]

There should be no excessive persuasions or explanatory talks; neither excessive caressing nor excessive administration, excessive giving in or excessive punishments. All in good measure.[35]

Intimate talks which play upon the conscience of the child or the adolescent are recommended. So of an educator it is said she sometimes calls

. . . an older pupil to her study and has a heart-to-heart talk with her, gives her advice and guidance. She knows how to appeal to the very best and dearest that is hidden in each heart—love of motherland, the great Stalin, parents who are grieved when children study badly. In talking with them, M. will talk about everything, will have no mercy—about excessive love of amusement and finery, the absence of true love for their country and their mother, the lack of respect for the collective and for teachers, etc.[36]

Recurrently there is advice that such talks should be postponed until child and adult are calm. (This contrasts with prerevolutionary memories, in which children were able to ward off punishment by showing extreme emotion.) Modern Soviet teaching aims at the control of mood swings, the elimination of emotionality, the substitution of calm, rational control, which, however, while avoiding moments of excitement, is not above advising an adult to utilize

. . . an especially favorable moment when there is between you a warm feeling of mutual trust and closeness. . . . Such verbal influence at a suitable moment leaves a deep and favorable trace in children. . . . A raised, excited voice is like a whip to a fiery horse—a stroke and the horse rears! . . . The raised voice of adults causes some children to flare up like powder, to go into a state of sharp excitation and give in response an undesirable reaction; or strong inhibition occurs, and children fall into a state of stubbornness. As a result children's characters are spoiled.[37]

So a mother who is also a lieutenant colonel and finds her eight-year-old son is being disrespectful takes him to an officers' mess. There he hears these officers say: " 'Permit us to sit down, Comrade Colonel.' Such men ask his mother's permission!"[38] So the little boy is properly impressed and becomes obedient.

Withholding of love is explicitly recommended. In the *Notebook of a Mother,* a woman relates how she handled her boy's use of bad words. This exemplary mother says:

I wanted most of all not to show my son the helplessness I was feeling. I gathered all my strength and said: "Djanik, is your teacher good?" "The

very best," Djanik answered. "You do not want to hurt her feelings?" "No."
"And do you love your mother?" "And how!" "Listen, Djanik, those words
which you have learned are very bad. Schoolboys must not say them. They
are only spoken by drunken *diadki* [uncles] because they do not know what
they are saying. If your teacher finds out she will not let you go to school.
And if I hear them again, I will not love you. Do you understand?" "Yes,"
whispered Djanik. I did not speak about it any more. . . . A few days later
Djanik came to me and asked guiltily: "Mother, you have not stopped loving me?" "Why should I?" "Remember, for the words. Now I am no more
U.'s friend and never listen to what he says." I said: "I knew you would do
as mother asked." He threw himself on my neck and whispered hotly: "I
know you won't stop loving me now."[39]

While punishments which fit the place, circumstances, and conditions
of the misdeed in a logical way are recommended for older children,
"for younger school-age children, a possible measure may be a temporary outward cooling off toward the child."[40] But parents are also
warned: "With preschool children a chilly attitude is not effective;
they very soon convince themselves that father and mother will not
be angry very long, and evaluate the conduct of the parents as a
caprice."[41]

It is interesting here that the difference between measures that are
effective for preschool-age children and older children is seen as a difference in the capacity of the parent to maintain a disciplinary anger
and that the child is credited with the type of omniscience in regard
to parental motives which is such a familiar feature of Russian phras-
ings of human relations. Finally, the adolescent may respond to such
a measure by withdrawing from the parents,[42] and this is regarded as
most undesirable, for "what matters is that parents, by their lives,
their moral qualities, inspire such respect in children that the latter
would not hesitate to seek advice on the most painful problem, to discuss intimately how best to act under certain circumstances."[43] Blind
and indulgent love may also lead to bad effects: "It happens that accepting the independence of a youth borders on blind admiration for
each of his actions."[44]

Within the period when the infant grows into adulthood, parents
are enjoined to modulate their behavior in terms of its effectiveness;
but there is no recognition that adolescents need any period of rebellion or privacy or experimentation. All these are dangerous to the
regime and must be discouraged in children—the future citizens:

The ability of the young Soviet generation to guide their imagination, to
develop it in the necessary direction, to utilize creative force in the interest
of the communistic transformation of our motherland—those are the concrete problems of the psychology of upbringing. . . . [But] in the process
of play, parents should give the child as much freedom of action as possible, but only as long as the play proceeds properly.[45]

So there is approval for children's learning:

How to dream so that the dream does not break with reality. . . .[46]

Development of fantasy is an important task of the educator. For example, children prepare to fly to the moon. They represent in play that which has not taken place in reality. But such play arose as a result of stories of the remarkable flights accomplished by our fliers. These stories have created the conviction in our children that the heroes will accomplish ever new exploits, that they will continue the conquest of cosmic space. . . . Obviously, such make-believe is to be permitted and encouraged by the educator.[47]

However, just as in every other aspect of life, complete control must be maintained:

The educator does not permit inventions which may create in children incorrect representations, incorrect attitudes toward life. If children represent Soviet soldiers, fliers, workers, it is very important that their actions and words correspond to the role they adopt.[48]

A distinction is made between the "creative imagination" and the "narcotic imagination,"[49] the latter recalling the Marxian description of religion:

Religious misery is in one mouth the expression of real misery, and in another a protestation against real misery. Religion is the moan of the oppressed creature, the sentiment of a heartless world, as it is the spirit of spiritless conditions. It is the opium of the people.[50]

There are definite admonitions against the kind of prolonged emotional repudiations and scene-making which were so characteristic of old Russian life.[51] Punishments that act strongly should be reduced in strength, and the father who refuses to greet his erring son and evokes from the son extreme behavior, so that "he cries for a long time, moans, stops eating, or damns the grandmother," has gone too far. Reproaches work when children respect their parents, ". . . but it must not be abused, and one cannot demand from children, especially of eleven- to fourteen-year-olds, that they say they are sorry for every deed of innocent mischief."[52]

There is very little explicit discussion of the handling of sexual attitudes. Makarenko, the most noted of Soviet writers on child rearing, who has been regarded as an authority from the civil-war period to the present, believes that, with a correct regime and proper physical conditioning, early sexual feelings do not arise:

The right time comes for all knowledge and there is no danger if you reply to your child, "You are small yet; when you get older you will know." It must be noted that children have no insistent interest in sexual matters. Such an interest arises only in the period of genital maturation. . . . In adolescence, a talk between parents and children can no longer bring harm because both understand that they are treating an important and secret theme, that the discussion is necessary in consideration of the benefit it will bring, that this benefit [*polza*], while remaining intimate, will at the same time be realistic. . . . Talks must come about in connection with a definite occurrence: a cynical anecdote repeated by the youngster, interest in someone's family scandals, early coquettishness, etc. . . . Wrongdoing and the resultant need for a talk can be avoided if parents comment on the sexual conduct of other persons with an expression of sharp condemnation and disgust, and show their conviction of quite different behavior in the children.[53]

For adolescents, heart-to-heart talks, in which the responsibility of sex relationships in a socialistic society is emphasized, are recommended, with explanations of the need for

many years of friendship to learn what another person is, however attractive the first impression. . . . In some cases it is necessary to make the youth aware that sexual life can be normal only at the full maturity of the organism, for among some of our youths there is a mistaken notion in this area which draws some of them into a false and harmful path.[54]

From the time that children enter school, peers are added to the group which will reinforce the desirable behavior of each individual child. Within the Pioneers, the Communist organization for younger children:

The Pioneer *active* of the brigade [i.e., the activating group within the children's brigade] helped the teacher to watch carefully that the children worked well and conscientiously. The children had their own methods of influencing those who worked badly; they understood excellently the force of a sharp word said, not cruelly, but in comradely fashion, yet hitting not the eyebrow but the eye, and they ably used this distinctive pedagogical instrument. . . . The negligent ones immediately became a target of gay mockery. . . . All these were not chance jokes. In using the joking form, a serious feeling was manifested, exhibiting a new form of morality, and a conscious drive to help the motherland and the Soviet army. By jesting and mockery they tried to influence careless, light-minded comrades, and to force them to work more seriously and purposively.[55]

. Within the family, the value of sibling relationships is emphasized, with stress on the value of large families and the importance of children learning to show friendship and respect for older siblings and to succor younger siblings.[56] So the maintenance of the authority structure is furthered by seeing to it that a younger child is taught that "he is obliged to obey not only his parents but his older sister and brother, to help them according to his abilities, and under no circumstances to hinder them when they are studying or otherwise occupied."[57]

On the other hand, care must be taken not to put too heavy a load on the older children. Here, showing through the excessive demands made on the children, we find a contrapuntal insistence on treating human beings very carefully, on the great danger of doing damage by lack of sensitive handling of human emotions, which is reminiscent of older Russian sensitivity, although the word "sensitivity" itself—as it is stated as a character goal for children—is related to active anticipation of the demands of others. Adults are exhorted not to reprimand and shame children in the presence of siblings[58] and classmates,[59] but derision and a deliberately chosen group situation are used in the treatment of such disapproved behavior as bragging.[60] Throughout the material on sibling relationships and the use of group pressures in school and children's groups, there is the double emphasis on protecting the child's feelings, teaching the children in the collective to be gentle but firm, respecting children's friendships with one another, and at the same time using disapproval by this peer group as a strong incentive. So the teacher says,"If I entrust some task to a child, I explain to him that he is responsible for carrying it out, not only to me but to the collective of children."[61]

For adolescents there is strong approval of friendships in which

both adolescents influence each other positively, mutually help each other to outlive their shortcomings. . . . The problem of parents and teachers consists precisely in developing and strengthening in children feelings of comradeship and friendship on the basis of ideals, in helping children to evaluate one another's actions, in encouraging true comradely relations and uprooting false ones based on covering up wicked anti-social behavior of comrades. . . . If their Pioneer link is working badly, let the two friends struggle with common effort to make it the best of the best.[62]

However, it is important to be alert against the danger of friendships which influence an adolescent adversely.[63] Proper training in courage should enable one to make "a just appraisal of the act of a close friend, even in the case when such appraisal may cause the deep displeasure of the latter."[64]

Model social behavior and solidarity with the collective of peers is placed above personal feelings of friendship, and feelings of comradeliness are thus used to serve the interests of society primarily, whether they develop the individual's self-knowledge or bring him back into line. "The rules of conduct adopted by the collective become binding for the one who feels himself a member of the collective; the evaluation of the collective of various traits of character becomes absolute for each of its members."[65] In difficult cases of discipline, the Pioneers are treated as the executive point for focusing the combined pressure of comrades, teachers, and parents on a single erring child:

A pupil of the sixth grade, Lucy, began to frequent movies in the neighboring town without the knowledge of her parents. She returned home very late and went to bed without preparing her lessons. The problem of Lucy was brought up at the meeting of the link [the smallest Pioneer unit]. The girl, who was indulged by her parents, only laughed at the demands of her comrades to stop her frequent movie-going, which hindered her preparation of lessons. The problem of Lucy was next discussed in the squad soviet [the council of a larger unit]. A comradely "pointing out" was made to her, but this too did not help. Then she was called to the troop soviet [the senior council of a Pioneer group in a given school]. . . . The chairman of the troop put a question to Lucy: Did she have any consideration for the Pioneer group? "Yes, of course," she said. The Pioneers who were members of the troop soviet explained to Lucy how badly she had acted in not having submitted to the demands of her squad. Lucy sincerely repented of her misdeed and gave her word to stop movie-going. She kept her promise and began to study better, faithfully fulfilling her home assignments.[66]

In another model case, the problem of two boys, S. and K., who had been doing bad school work, was first examined in the link meeting, where it was suggested to them that they reform. As this did not help, the parents of the two boys, who had good living conditions but paid little attention to their children's conduct, were approached:

The problem [was] placed before the squad meeting to which the parents were invited. At first the parents were offended—What is this, calling us to attend a Pioneer meeting! But when, one after the other, the Pioneers came out and spoke to S. and K. about all their misdeeds, when the squad raised the question: Should the boys remain in the squad? when the boys pleaded hotly not to be expelled, said the squad was dear to them, and promised to reform; at that point the parents admitted their guilt in that they had not watched and interested themselves in their sons sufficiently. Now S. and K. have changed their attitudes.[67]

Here again we see an instance of the tendency, referred to earlier, to ring each individual with a judging, pressuring group, which for adults also includes children, their own and their children's collective. Congruently, not only are parents expected to be responsible for their own children, but "the bad action of any child in the street or in a public place must immediately bring forth condemnation from adults, who have not the right to pass by indifferently."[68] Praise and reward should be used sparingly, and there are express warnings against the use of money as a reward. There is a frequently expressed fear that children will become conceited, the vice so often pilloried in old Russian literature.

The whole problem of discipline is summarized as follows:

First, there is conscious discipline [*soznatelnaya*], i.e., discipline founded on the inner conviction of pupils of the necessity for conducting themselves in accordance with definite rules and demands, this conviction growing out of an understanding of the sense and meaning of these demands. Secondly, there is discipline with initiative [*initiativnaya*], i.e., it is not the discipline of simple obedience, but a discipline tied to an urge to carry out as well as possible the order, instruction, or commission received, and, even more, tied to a readiness to carry out one's duty without waiting for instruction or a reminder, but on one's own initiative. Thirdly, there is firm discipline, i.e., a discipline of absolute submission [*besprekoslovnoe povinovenie*] and subordination to the instructor, tutor, organizer; without this there is no discipline. Fourthly, there is organized discipline, i.e., a discipline inducing and habituating a person to precise organization of individual work and work in the collective (and also to organization in play and everyday life). Fifthly, there is comradely discipline, i.e., founded on the mutual respect of the members of the collective; and, sixthly, the discipline of overcoming difficulties in order to carry out every matter to the end, which involves the subordination of one's conduct to high motivations and the conquest of motivations of a lowly character.[69]

So far we have dealt primarily with methods which are recommended in the rearing and education of children. The use of these methods is expected to develop such frequently mentioned qualities as ideological purposefulness, strong convictions and principles, sense of duty, perseverance, endurance, courage, unselfishness and selflessness, self-control and discipline, humanism, vigor, optimism and cheerfulness, generosity combined with care of property, and also politeness, modesty, and sensitivity. These are precious, valuable, useful qualities of Soviet man, and it is stressed that the Communist Party cultivates "precisely these qualities."[70] Optimism and cheerfulness are seen as "traits natural to Soviet people," and are explained as follows:

Love of life, joy and cheer, acquired in creative work for the good of the motherland, and in the accumulation of knowledge widening the field of vision and increasing the power of man, are typical traits characterizing the moral countenance of Soviet people.[71]

Here the most important contribution which the parents can make is "the constant ideological growth and political activity of the parents themselves."[72] Everyone must be involved in continuous, unremitting self-improvement: "School is for study, and study cannot be unconstrained. . . . Kindergarten must renounce lack of restraint in activities."[73]

The reward for this continuous activity is presented as spiritual:

Obedience gives rise to a feeling of satisfaction and joy even when a child denies himself strong and legitimate desires. "Calm conscience" as a result of duty fulfilled gives man an immense joy. And terribly oppressed feels the one who experiences "torments of conscience" from a bad action, a breach of social duty. . . . The habit of fulfilling that which he must [fulfil] not only brings joy and satisfaction—calm conscience as is usually said —but develops a special sensitivity, that is, a special anxiety about whether all has been done and done properly.[74]

Thus, from a revolutionary setting originally occupied with the elimination of old values and rebellion against old restraints, with no theory of character structure except a belief in forming good habits, avoiding bad habits, following models, and learning dependence upon the approval of all around one, there has now developed in the Soviet Union a theory of child training internally consistent and showing a point-for-point congruence with Soviet political and social theory. For the pre-Soviet system of many authority figures, each of whom often

carried particular virtues and vices to extremes, we now have a solid
ring of individuals, old and young, at home, in school, in youth organizations, in the work collectives, the party, and the state, all of
whom are expected to express the same values, at all times, in all
places. The educational system now embodies the struggle by the
early Bolsheviks to substitute controlled purposeful activity for the
vague, diffuse, and emotionally toned attitudes toward life.

The child is expected to internalize the values of society and also
to be continuously supervised by outside figures, to whom he is bound
by feelings of love, trust, and respect. Some hint of how this system
works is given in a novel about an adolescent, who, as one of a group
of apprentices in a foundry, had individualistically attempted to distinguish himself, endangering the output of the foundry:[75]

[The day comes when Aleha applies to join the Komsomol. He goes
through many painful apprehensive moments as he asks the old master
(ironmaker) to recommend him and confesses to his *Komsorg* (Komsomol
organizer) that he had lied.] But at the meeting Aleha again understood
that not so easily and quickly could all his sins be forgotten. Having finished
recounting his autobiography, Aleha fell silent, awaiting the further moves
of the meeting. Igor B. took the floor. "Our bureau has decided to accept
the comrade. But this does not yet mean anything. The main thing is you,
fellows, the Komsomol mass. We await your decision. To accept the comrade or to abstain. Let us think. . . ." Aleha listened to these words with
terror. They resounded in his very heart. Igor continued: "Comrade Polovodov [Aleha] has placed himself beyond the collective. He wanted alone to
make use of the success and joy of Komsomol work. And it is unknown, had
everything gone smoothly, how far he would have risen in his pride. Let
him today answer all of us what he now thinks about himself, about us,
about the Komsomol, about life. This moment is such that a man's soul can
be seen even without glasses. So, say everything that you think, Polovodov."
. . . Many noticed that Aleha was trembling. His agitation immediately
transmitted itself to all the others sitting in the hall, quickly from one to
another, as a wave in the sea is stirred by wind. Everyone felt simultaneous
pain and joy. Pain, because they clearly saw a man suffering and understood precisely from what [he was suffering] and already wished that he
might no longer suffer. And joy because he was with them and was not
separated, withdrawn any more. This could be seen by his sparkling eyes,
his quivering lips which were preparing themselves already to pronounce
other words, finally by his hands, stretched out uncertainly, with the fingers
spread apart, as if he wanted to encompass in one embrace all those sitting
there in the hall. . . . No one was indifferent any longer. The soul [of each]
wished to express itself. But the rules of the meeting were rigid, the chairman sat severe, immovable. He gave the floor to no one except Aleha. The
boys wished that Aleha would take courage. He was now their comrade.
They recognized this. After such a sudden frank expression of mutual feeling, Aleha did not really have to continue. Everyone understood what further he wanted to say. But Aleha himself unexpectedly calmed down and
firmly decided to express his intentions to the meeting. "I, fellows, am not
going to lie to you. What is there, is there. I am here in front of you as at

PLATE XIX. *Child-training Ideals—Soviet Russia. I*

FIG. 1.—The Kharkov Suvorov School in Chugu-yevo. Vitya Chegurin—a Soviet boy when he arrives at the school.

ɢ. 2.—The Kharkov Suvorov School in Chugu-yevo. Vitya after he has been issued kit and uniform. Here is what the future officer looks like.

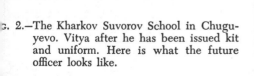

ictures by SOVFOTO. Published in M. Mead's "A Natu-l History Approach to Soviet Character," *Natural History* ʾagazine, September, 1951.

PLATE XX. *Child-training Ideals—Soviet Russia. II*

Ewing Galloway

FIG. 1.—Sporting festival in a Moscow
school

FIG. 2.—An exhibit of modern Russian art held in Odes
School children and th
teacher examining a workin
man, his wife, and their t
children being evicted fr
their home in a capitalis
country.

Acme Photo

(Published in M. Mead's "A Natural History Approach to Soviet Character," *Natural
History Magazine,* September, 1951.)

FIG. 3.—Cartoon from *Krokodil.* "At 2 A.M.
—The doorman: 'Excuse me—your
mother phoned. She's worried over
whether you did your homework.'
Drawing by Boris Yefimov (*Krokodil,* No. 1, January 10, p. 16").

confession. I cannot feel my hands and feet, I feel so good. Do you still think that I like it better alone than with you? It is not so. Alone, I suffer, that is all. I am not glad to be by myself. But now it will be a completely different matter. Now I'll begin to work even better. . . . Forgive me if I said anything to affront you." On this his speech ended, and the meeting prepared to vote. Aleha felt that he was experiencing in himself some yet incomprehensible grace which affected all his feelings, urges, wishes. He had never imagined that it could be so pleasant. It was as if all were changing in him, each little vein becoming stronger.[76]

The preparation for such a scene is allowed for in such pedagogical instructions as these:

> Give him time to think and torment himself over the solution, but in the end, if necessary, point out to the adolescent that there is but one way, that of duty [in this case, to confess before his teacher and schoolmates].[77]

The likenesses and differences between the old type of Russian motivation and the new Soviet type are brought out very strikingly in these examples. Under the old system, a child was reared and admonished by the very large number of persons of different castes and was given different sets of standards, which were very loosely tied together by the teachings of the Orthodox Church, and were reinforced, in the teachings of peasants and nurses, by a large number of miscellaneous supernatural fears. Fear of being cut off from one's own group, fear of supernatural punishments, confusion among the many standards of conduct which were illustrated and enjoined, a diffuse sense of guilt which was willing to take upon itself a variety of sins committed perhaps only in thought—these characterized this earlier type of character.

During the development of the early intelligentsia, with their rigorous revolutionary ideals, there seems to have been some narrowing of these multiple authority figures in the life of the child and the emergence of the demand, which we now characterize as Bolshevik, for a more rigidly defined, focused, and unyielding character in which forgiveness played much less of a role and a man judged both himself and his fellows more harshly. At the same time, theories of what community and collective life meant, the substitution of the social group for a supernatural, priest-mediated authority, seemed, in the early days of the Soviet Union, to be placing all the emphasis outside the individual and encouraging a type of education in which the feeling of shame, if one were discovered and rebuked, was the behavior type which was most likely to result. This was particularly so during the period in which the family was regarded as unimportant, and the group alone, whether it was in kindergarten, of Komsomols, or of fellow-workers, was supposed to hear confessions and to administer public rebukes.

Today the literature suggests that the Soviet Union is moving toward a type of education which resembles (but, as we shall see, also differs from) the older Russian form of many authority figures operating upon an individual sense of general guilt and unworthiness. The authority of the parents has been re-emphasized after the attempts to reduce it during the first fifteen years of the regime, and parents are now recognized as the principal figures in the early life of the child, which means the reintroduction of persons of greater age and status as authority figures, and this is conducive to the formation of internalized standards of conduct. Furthermore, parents are seen as only one part of a completely harmonized attempt to bring up the young in the way they should go.

"What does it mean," asks Likhacheva, "to bring up a fighter for communism? It means that the school and the family and the society must bring up the young man."[78]

This bringing to bear of all available forces upon the target is a familiar Bolshevik theory of tactics, here applied to education. Instead of the old inconsistencies between standards and sanctions presented by many individuals in the environment, one set of standards is to be presented. When the parents fail, the Komsomol steps in, or the school may even apply to a trade-union to persuade an erring father to take an interest in his son's report card.

Aiding the strengthening of family relations and ties, socialist society thereby makes fast in the people many of those high qualities which characterize the moral countenance of the Soviet citizen.[79]

And, in comparing the old and the new, a Soviet student of education puts his finger on the greater concentration on a unified effort:

Belinsky wrote [about the prerevolutionary school] that the family must make a man out of the child; the school, an educated citizen ready to struggle for the best ideals. . . . Now the school and the family are joined in one wish: to nurture in us the traits of a real Soviet man, make us educated persons devoted to our people, to our mother country.[80]

All the agencies which impinge on the child are to put their entire effort, all their thought, into doing the same thing. This should produce a type of motivation and will power which does not occur in Western democracies, where there is a variety of different courses presented to a child, in whom, ideally, the will to choose among them has been cultivated. Nor was such a character structure cultivated in pre-Soviet Russia. Instead, educational experiences tended to develop a diffuse sense of guilt and of responsibility, not for acts of will, but for the merest thought or intention.

Under this new Soviet character structure, the will should be developed, without, however, any sense of the possibility of choice. If the child looks into himself, he should find only the same standards as those expressed all around him. All authority figures converge upon him, and he, like Aleha, is to feel completely at one with and submissive to this standard, which is both inside him and outside him:

> Soviet man feels himself an indivisible part of the industrial or social collective to which he is bound, with which he labors. Soviet man experiences achievements or lack of them in communal matters as his own personal successes or failures. He feels his moral responsibility for communal matters and thus he develops a sense of duty. . . . The personal interests of Soviet man must combine harmoniously with communal interests; the personal must always be subordinated to the social.[81]

It must be recognized that in such an ideal there should be no need for force, for physical coercion. The conception of character is one in which the individual himself is able to receive grace from a group whose standards he shares—the secular Soviet version of forgiveness—and so go on to a higher moral level. It is self-evident that this ideal, which would need no reinforcement by coercion or by political police, is incompatible with the Soviet demand for total control over every detail of the life of children. A character structure such as that described here is congruent with a complete respect for all human beings in a society, with a lack of hierarchy, and with a lack of any sense of gulf between a group ruling and a group ruled. But the leadership of the Soviet Union seems to have inherited and developed, from sources of its own, a deep contempt for the mass of the people and an attitude toward children which does not provide the necessary conditions for development of the kind of ideal character structure described here.

In conclusion, it is interesting to consider how present-day Soviet practice, like earlier Soviet practice, can be related to the general history of cults. A cult is distinguished initially by the extreme stand which its members take, the sense of absolute rightness and determination to revise all the details of life to fit its tenets. As such a cult develops, it may become an integral and transforming agent in the next phase of the whole culture, it may become a world religion, or it may dwindle into the rigidly held dogma of a small unimportant segment of society. In this last event, it is customary still to speak of such groups as cults. They maintain their meager numbers and their narrow cultures by systems of education which unfit their children for participation in the wider society and which build into the personalities of each generation the defensive hostility to the outside world on which the cult relies to preserve its existence. From this point of view it is possible to distinguish between cults and cultures by the degree to which such groups feel safe in leaving children and adult members open to communications, appeals, and temptations offered by the rest of the world.

Seen in this way, the Soviet Union, with its rigid training of children, its sedulous attempts to protect all its citizens from any contaminating contact with, or information from, the outside world, and its intolerance of the type of change which varieties of human gifts and experience naturally introduce into a cultural system, the Soviet Union —despite its great size and power—still exhibits the characteristics of a cult rather than those of an inclusive, flexible, national culture. The ideals of education which have been discussed here are not only incongruent with the methods which are prescribed to attain them, but also this ideal character and these ideal educational methods, taken together, are designed to produce a character structure equipped for a rigid acceptance of a doctrinaire view of the world, unreceptive to outside influences, energetic in the pursuit of Soviet national purposes.

NOTES

1. Mead, 1954.
2. Perel and Lyubimova, 1932, Introduction.
3. Mead, 1951, pp. 79–88.
4. Perel and Lyubimova, 1932.
5. Perel, 1932, Introduction.
6. Kolbanovsky, 1947*b*.
7. *Ibid.*
8. Tadevosian, 1947, p. 5.
9. *Ibid.*, pp. 7–8.
10. "Training in Purposefulness," 1948.
11. *Current Digest of the Soviet Press*, December 23, 1953, and May 26, 1954. See also the April 11, April 25, and December 30, 1953, issues.
12. "Training in Endurance," 1948.
13. Yudina, 1946.
14. *Ibid.*
15. *Ibid.*
16. "Education in Comradeship and Friendship," 1948.
17. Raskin, 1948.
18. Alekseyev and Andreyeva, 1948.
19. Arkin, 1940.
20. Makarenko, 1937.
21. Yudina, 1946.
22. Liublinskaya, 1948.
23. *Ibid.*
24. "Training in Courage," 1948.
25. Speransky, 1941.
26. Simson, 1932.
27. *Ibid.*
28. Note the sense of retrogression here, balancing the earlier statement demanding continuous progress.
29. Raskin, 1941.
30. This is a familiar echo of each campaign in the Soviet Union to re-reform some part of the society.
31. Pisareva, 1946.
32. Liublinskaya, 1948.
33. Pisareva, 1946.
34. *Ibid.*
35. Prozorov, 1948.

36. Sapirstein, 1947.
37. Pisareva, 1946.
38. Bershanskaya, 1946.
39. Mahova, 1948.
40. Raskin, 1941.
41. *Ibid.*
42. *Ibid.*
43. "Education in Comradeship and Friendship," 1948.
44. Raskin, 1948.
45. Makarenko, 1937, "Lectures on the Upbringing of Children."
46. Raskin, 1948.
47. Mendzherritskii, 1948.
48. *Ibid.*
49. Shneerman, 1949, p. 61.
50. Marx, 1926, p. 12.
51. Versaev, 1913.
52. Raskin, 1941, pp. 21–29.
53. Makarenko, 1937.
54. Raskin, 1948.
55. Pechernikova, 1948.
56. Alekseyev and Andreyeva, 1948.
57. "Report on a Conference on Moral Education," 1946.
58. Mahova, 1948.
59. "From the Notes of a Teacher," 1946.
60. Svadhovsky, 1947.
61. Golosnitskaya, 1948.
62. "Education in Comradeship and Friendship," 1948.
63. *Ibid.*
64. *Ibid.*
65. Liublinskaya, 1948.
66. Katina, 1948.
67. *Ibid.*
68. Makarenko, 1937.
69. Goncharov, 1947, chap. viii.
70. Svadkovsky, 1947; "Training in Courage," 1948; "Training in Sense of Duty," 1948.
71. "On Cheerfulness and *joie-de-vivre*," 1948.
72. Kolbanovsky, 1947*a*.
73. Kornilov, 1948.
74. Svadkovsky, 1947.
75. The remainder of this article, except for the last two paragraphs, is reprinted with minor changes by permission from *Soviet Attitudes toward Authority* by Margaret Mead, pp. 75–78. Copyright, 1951, McGraw-Hill Book Company, Inc.
76. Kurochkin, 1947.
77. "Training in Sense of Duty," 1948.
78. Likhacheva, 1948.
79. Sverdlow, 1946.
80. *Stories by Graduates of Moscow School,* 1947, p. 8.
81. "Training in Sense of Duty," 1948.

LIST OF REFERENCES

ALEKSEYEV, A., and ANDREYEVA, M. 1948. "Report of a Working Mother," *Family and School* [*Sem'ya i Shkola*], No. 4.

ARKIN, E. A. 1940. *Letters on the Upbringing of Children.* Moscow: Uchpedgiz.

BERSHANSKAYA, E. D. 1946. "After the War," *Family and School,* Nos. 4–5.

CALAS, ELENA. 1949. "Soviet Child Training Ideals and Their Political Significance." Unpublished manuscript.

Current Digest of the Soviet Press. 1953. Vol. V, No. 9 (April 11); No. 11 (April 25); No. 45 (December 23); No. 46 (December 30).

———. 1954. Vol. VI, No. 15 (May 26).

"Education in Comradeship and Friendship." 1948. An editorial in *Family and School*, No. 4.

"From the Notes of a Teacher." 1946. *Family and School*, Nos. 7–8.

GOLOSNITSKAYA, N. 1948. *My Work in Upbringing Children.* Moscow: Uchpedgiz.

GONCHAROV, N. K. 1947. *Foundations of Pedagogy.* Moscow: Uchpedgiz.

GORER, GEOFFREY, and RICKMAN, JOHN. 1950. *The People of Great Russia: A Psychological Study.* New York: Chanticleer Press; London: Cresset Press, 1949.

KATINA, L. 1948. "Laying the Foundations of Cultural Behavior in Kindergarten," *Preschool Education* [*Doshkol'noe Vospitonie*], No. 6.

KOLBANOVSKY, V. N. 1947a. "Ideological-political Education in the Family," *Family and School*, No. 10.

———. 1947b. "For the Further Strengthening of the Soviet Family," *ibid.*, No. 11.

KORNILOV, K. N. 1948. "Role of the Family in the Rearing of Preschool Children," *Preschool Education*, No. 7.

KUROCHKIN, V. 1947. "Brigade of the Smart," *Oktyabr'* ("October"), September, No. 9.

LEITES, NATHAN. 1951. *Operational Code of the Politburo.* New York: McGraw-Hill Book Co.

———. 1953. *A Study of Bolshevism.* Glencoe, Ill.: Free Press.

LEITES, NATHAN, and BERNAUT, ELSA. 1954. *Ritual of Liquidation.* Glencoe, Ill.: Free Press.

LIKHACHEVA, N. F. 1948. "Mother-Tutoress," *Family and School*, No. 3.

LIUBLINSKAYA, A. A. 1948. "On the Misdeeds of Children," *Family and School*, No. 1.

MAHOVA, K. V. 1948. *Notebook of a Mother.* Moscow: Academy of Pedagogical Sciences.

MAKARENKO, A. S. 1937. *Book for Parents* [*Kniga dlya roditelei*]. Moscow: Gospolitizdat (out of print). Moscow: Academy of Pedagogical Sciences, 1949.

———. 1948. "Lecture on the *Book for Parents*," given in 1938, published in *Family and School*, No. 11.

MARX, KARL. 1926. *Selected Essays.* Translated by H. J. STENNING. London: Parsons.

MEAD, MARGARET. 1951. *Soviet Attitudes toward Authority.* New York: McGraw-Hill Book Co.

———. 1954. "Manus Restudied: An Interim Report," *Transactions of the New York Academy of Sciences*, XVI, No. 8, 426–32.

MENDZHERRITSKII, D. 1948. "Children's Play," in *Play of Children* (collection of articles from the magazine *Preschool Education*). Moscow: Uchpedgiz.

MOSELY, PHILIP E. 1951. "Some Soviet Techniques of Negotiation." In *Negotiating with the Russians*, ed. RAYMOND DENNETT and JOSEPH E. JOHNSON, pp. 271–303. Boston: World Peace Foundation.

"On Cheerfulness and *joie-de-vivre*." 1948. *Family and School*, No. 5.

PECHERNIKOVA, I. A. 1948. *Teaching the Schoolboy To Share in the Family Work.* Moscow: Uchpedgiz.

PEREL, I. (ed.). 1932. *Property Rights of Children.* Moscow: Uchpedgiz.

PEREL, I., and LYUBIMOVA, B. 1932. *The Legal Position of the Child in the Family,* Introduction. Moscow: Uchpedgiz.

PISAREVA, L. V. 1946. "The Word in Upbringing," *Family and School,* Nos. 4–5.

PROZOROV, G. S. 1948. "A. S. Makarenko on Pedagogical Tact in Family Upbringing," *Family and School,* No. 8.

RASKIN, L. E. 1941. "Discipline and Culture in the Conduct of School Children," *Young Guard.*

———. 1948. "High-School Students in the Family," *Family and School,* No. 6.

"Report on a Conference on Moral Education." 1946. *Family and School,* Nos. 4–5.

SAPIRSTEIN, L. 1947. "School Direction E. V. Mart'ianova," *Family and School,* No. 3.

SHNEERMAN, A. L. 1949. "Problems of the Psychology of Upbringing in the Course of General Pedagogy," *Soviet Pedagogy* [*Sovetskaya Pegagogika*], Vol. IV.

SIMSON, T. P. 1932. *Nervousness in Children and Measures for Preventing It.* Moscow: Izd. Mosoblisolkoma, Zdravotdel.

SPERANSKY, G. N. 1941. *The Young Child.* Moscow: Zdravotdel.

Stories by Graduates of Moscow Schools. 1947. Moscow: Detgiz.

SVADKOVSKY, I. F. 1947. "Training in Obedience, Politeness, and Modesty," *Family and School,* No. 3.

SVERDLOV, G. M. 1946. *Marriage and the Family* [*Brak i sem'ya*]. Pamphlet. Moscow: Uchpedgiz.

TADEVOSIAN, V. S. 1947. "Rights and Obligations of Parents in the Soviet State," stenogram of a lecture read in Moscow, May 29, 1947.

"Training in Courage." 1948. An editorial in *Family and School,* No. 2.

"Training in Endurance." 1948. An editorial in *Family and School,* No. 1.

"Training in Purposefulness." 1948. An editorial in *Family and School,* No. 3.

VERESAEV, V. 1913. *The Image.* St. Petersburg.

YUDINA, N. V. 1946. "Parental Authority," *Family and School,* Nos. 4–5.

CHAPTER 12

Parents and Children: An Analysis of Contemporary German Child-Care and Youth-Guidance Literature

—————————————————————RHODA MÉTRAUX

This chapter was prepared in 1953 as part of a study of German national character, made in collaboration with Nelly Schargo Hoyt, under the auspices of the American Museum of Natural History ("Studies in Contemporary Cultures, B," conducted under a contract with the Office of Naval Research). The writer is indebted to Dr. Hoyt for insights of importance in this paper (cf. Métraux and Hoyt, 1953).

CONTEMPORARY German child-care and youth-guidance literature written by the specialist for the layman—parents, especially mothers, teachers, youth leaders, and others concerned with the education of children and adolescents—spans a period of more than twenty-five years and gives an impression of clear continuity from post–World War I to post–World War II thinking about the aims of education and the need for new methods of bringing up children. Some of the authorities of the 1920's are still writing; some of the older books are still popular.[1] Discussions of the intervening years of social upheaval and disruption are significantly absent from recent writing. In the experts' presentations it is as if a curtain had been dropped, shutting off from view the images of the immediate past.

Although there is concern for the special problems of uprooted adolescents who have lost or left their homes, the primary concern of the guidance literature is the child in its home. Discussions of the problems of homeless children or of children with broken homes are extremely rare. The authors, even of recent books, write rather as if every child had a home and a full complement of relatives and seldom pause to glance at "times like these" or deal with life outside the home except to describe, as examples of faulty or neglected upbringing, the misadventures of problem children. How to bring up children in the home is the main consideration in these books on childhood and youth education for the lay reader.

Modern German educators emphatically agree that all aspects of the growing child must be treated as parts of the total personality and that each aspect—the body, the mind (*der Geist*), the spirit (*die*

Seele),[2] and the character—must be educated with equal conscientiousness. This total education must begin in earliest infancy:

From the first days of life, care for the spiritual [*seelische*] health of the child is as necessary as is painstaking physical care. Its future life is extraordinarily dependent upon the physical and spiritual care given the child in its first months and years of life. In infancy and early childhood the foundation is laid for the adult's health and ability to face life, through a suitable direction of health which must always visualize the whole person, that is, body *and* spirit. Contrariwise, disregard of the challenge of managing health [*Gesundheitsführung*] has, as its result, vulnerability to shock, weakness, and defective ability to carry things through [*mangelnde Durchschlagskraft*] in the battle of life.[3]

One of the purposes of early education is to armor the child to face "the battle of life." Another is to prepare the child to fulfil life's tasks. It is the duty of the adult from the very beginning to see that "the growing powers of the child are guided toward the fulfilment of the tasks [*Aufgaben*] which it must master [*bewältigen*] in life."[4] Thus, from the first, the goal of education is impersonalized: the child must be educated to face life and the problems and duties (*Aufgaben* has this double meaning) imposed by life.

Life also is a teacher. German parents say, especially to adolescents: "Life will teach you. . . ." And the experts urge parents to prepare the child to meet the challenges of life's lessons. For life sets tasks and prepares tests which the young person can only master by displaying the autonomy (*Selbständigkeit*) learned in the course of his upbringing. At all ages, facing a situation depends upon firmness of character (*Halt*); mastery—which may consist either in overcoming or else in accepting circumstances—is possible if one can *will* something sufficiently. Ideally, the manner of meeting difficulties is summed up in the proverb, *Wer es will, kann es auch* ("Whoever wants—wills—to do something, can do it"). From this point of view, character formation —the training of the will—is primary and central in German education.

Germans formally distinguish between two aspects of the educational process: upbringing (*Erziehung*), which is concerned with the development (*Entwicklung*) of the child, and instruction (*Unterricht*), which has to do with imparting information and with teaching skills on which later technical and intellectual development are dependent.[5] Ideally, the two aspects of education are united in the concept of *Bildung*, for the cultivated man (*der gebildete Mann*) combines discipline of the mind and of the spirit. Not everyone can achieve *Bildung*, since this requires higher education, but *Lebenstüchtigkeit* (the ability to meet life's problems) is an educational goal which almost everyone can reach, since it concerns character and therefore is the result of correct upbringing. The child-care specialists are almost exclusively concerned with teaching parents how to bring up children who are *lebenstüchtig;* in their view, all else in their future life depends on this.

Traditionally, upbringing is primarily the responsibility of parents, while instruction is the responsibility of teachers outside the home. Each adult complements the other, and, if each is thorough and successful, there is little need or occasion for the two—parent and teacher —to meet or to compare their experiences with a child.[6]

Upbringing is thought of as a lengthy process that continues into young adulthood. In German thinking, *die Jugend* (youth, with reference to an age group) is a rather elastic term that includes both adolescents and an older group of those from about eighteen to twenty-five years. In the experts' view, upbringing is still incomplete at a time when young individuals begin to regard themselves as autonomous and when, depending on their social class and occupation, they may be partly or wholly economically independent.[7] Discussing the legitimate demands of adolescents to be regarded not as children but as a group with their own characteristics, demands, and needs, Spranger comments:

> The high flights of self-valuation and the demands on life [made by a young person] are screamingly incongruent with the true situation of the youthful person. As yet he is in truth nothing. Even given the greatest freedom, he would still be nothing as yet. His productivity is limited to presentiments. His will is not yet firm, his judgment is not sure, his feeling is not balanced. He dreams of world travels and returns from his first job "outside" after a quarter of a year, disillusioned. His adventurous plans are stranded on the disenchantment of his helplessness.[8]

In a word, the young person is not yet able to face life and, in spite of his high self-valuation, he "is in truth nothing." To become something, to become an adult, he must still be educated until his character (will, judgment, feeling) is finally determined. The child is no more than a potentiality and becomes "something"—a person—only through long, conscientious upbringing.

The central importance of the home for character formation is emphasized even in recent discussions of the destiny of the homeless youth of West Germany—the youth-without-ties (*die bindungslose Jugend*), who are living and working or looking for work far from their homes and the influence of their families. Writing about these masses of young people who are living in various types of institutional "homes" as refugees, job-seekers, apprentices, trainees, young industrial workers, etc., Bondy and Eyforth describe the effect of their homelessness on their character:

> We call them "youth-without-ties," for many are lacking not only home and work but also ties to the family and, indeed, true ties with people altogether, ties to their work and to spiritual worth; in the final analysis, they

are lacking a sense of the meaning of their lives. They have become mass-people with all their characteristics: their isolation and lack of direction, their pleasure-seeking and restlessness, their fear and hopelessness. They are unhappy even if they do not know it.[9]

And further:

They are incapable of making their own decisions; they have no firmness of character; they show no readiness to take over responsibility; they lack the will to come to terms spiritually with the affairs of their life; and they are unaware of the motives of their actions. So in many respects, they show the characteristics of mass-people.[10]

Without further educational care, they foresee a dark future for this youth:

Our concern is that the youth without work and without home will develop into people-fully-without-ties. That would mean that they would lead a meaningless, impulse-directed, unfulfilled life, that they would only too readily be ruined [*verwahrlosen*] and would become criminals and that later, perhaps, their children would grow up just like their parents.[11]

To prevent this personal and social tragedy, these writers see an urgent need for the development of youth leaders who would combine the role of parent and ideal educator and who would undertake to turn the various institutional homes into true familial homes by fostering personal relationships and shared activities and values. These youth leaders, men and women, would so incorporate in their own personalities the desired forms of behavior that, having by frankness and shared interest won the confidence of the young people, these would want to take on the responsibility of becoming persons like them. Thus the first step in the re-education of the youth-without-ties would be the re-education of the educators themselves, so that they could turn institutions into homes, where these young people could complete their upbringing while they were being integrated into working life.

Family life and the parents are, in German thinking, almost exclusively decisive in the education of the child, and family education is a necessary preparation for all else, in that character education takes precedence over all other kinds of learning. Therefore, parents must take the responsibility for learning correct educational methods. Thus Plattner addresses the mothers of young children:

Many people are of the opinion that there is "much too much bringing up." They would rather "not bring up" their children at all. Clearly, by "upbringing" they understand the attempt to form the child but forget that there is no such thing as "not-bringing-up." Every word, every act, whether in dressing, at housework, in earnest or in fun, everything the child sees and hears of us in the course of the day, works on it—well or badly, it works. As long as we breathe, as long as we live, we educate our children for better or worse, as long as our child lives with us.[12]

The blame for the child's misbehavior or misery is placed on the parents, whose methods have made the child ineducable, in any good sense, in and outside the home. Concluding his study of sexual education, Seelmann describes, as a cautionary example for parents, the miseducation of youthful criminals who go on to corrupt and seduce other lonely, unwanted, overcurious, oppressed, or problem children:

Most of these perpetrators were badly or wrongly brought-up children. They gave those who brought them up various kinds of difficulties. They were reproved and often severely punished. But all this had no effect, because they received no real understanding and, above all, did not have the educational climate they needed. They felt themselves pushed out of the way, misunderstood, and without help. And so they developed a striving toward secretiveness and experienced the benefits which they were denied in abnormal ways because they could not obtain them in normal ways. If today a large proportion of these culprits are between fourteen and twenty-five years, it is because these young people were denied, during the war and postwar period [World War II], an orderly family atmosphere, goal-oriented education [*Erziehung*] and direction [*Führung*], and loving guidance to the right life.[13]

For good or for bad, children become what their parents make them —this is an underlying theme of the experts' books.

The first lesson parents learn by reading these books concerns themselves rather than their children: parents must educate themselves to become educators. Although some few people are instinctive mothers or educators, others—by implication, most parents—must be educated for their task. This is where the expert comes in, not to supplant the parent, but to help the parent to self-education and to rescue and re-educate the erring parent and the child whose education has gone amiss.

Like the authors of cautionary tales (e.g., *Der Struwwelpeter*[14]), the child experts educate in large measure by means of the warning example and by promising parents that they can learn without suffering by knowing about the difficulties and sufferings of others whom they will not emulate. Parents are taught how to do it by learning how not to do what others have done. In the Foreword to her book on "Mistakes in Education" Hetzer tells the reader:

[In this book] an attempt is made to show how mistakes in upbringing are made in life and to advise ways in which these mistakes can be avoided. Not all the many mistakes in upbringing could be discussed, but only a small number of them which, because of the frequency with which they occur and the seriousness of their consequences, deserve special attention. That which is important—namely, the right understanding for questions of upbringing—can be wakened by such a sample from the totality of mistakes in upbringing.[15]

And Plattner recommends her advice to her readers because

one can learn a lesson through the harm that has come to others and, through this, avoid much that is wrong; one can make useful for one's self the good ideas of other people and thereby lighten one's own burden; both to the advantage of the children.[16]

In these books most of what is mistaken, harmful, and wrong is illustrated by the behavior of ordinary parents; "the good ideas of other people" are, for the most part, the experts' own, illustrated by their casework and their care for their own children. By describing how other parents and children behave, inviting disaster from which they can be saved only by the intervention of the expert, who sets them on the right track, and by showing how the expert has been a successful parent and educator, the guidance books indicate how, if parents educate themselves to be educators, they will have a happy family life and a healthy child and therefore, by implication, will need no help from outside the home.

Unlike the experts, who can produce rapid and lasting changes in the relationships between parents and children which alter the behavior and character of the children, the ordinary parents pictured in their books are neither omnipotent nor omniscient. On the contrary, the opportunities for making errors are so numerous ("not all the many different mistakes in upbringing could be discussed") that parents who depend on their own methods and insights will certainly go astray unless they conscientiously educate themselves to be educators.

Education of the educator does not consist merely in learning procedures and precepts—for people are too different from one another for hard-and-fast rules to apply alike to all—nor merely in applying learned principles—for knowledge alone is an impediment to "natural" relationships. It is more than this:

There, where . . . there is no real life-relationship [between mother and child], even the most tested methods of education are of little help. The child will somehow be stunted, even though one attempts to do the right thing as far as fulfilment of precepts is concerned. For in these circumstances the child lacks the ground of common life with the adults in which, in order to succeed in later life, it must strike deep roots.[17]

The parent who has only learned is no better off than the parent who does not know; both are likely to bring up a problem child. The parent's self-education must be such that what is learned is completely assimilated and "natural." Then the parent need not think what to do but can react automatically and totally to every situation. This is the basis of trust of the parent by the child, and so the beginning of good education.

The German parent is not invited to learn skills which the expert is prepared to teach but rather is expected to modify her own character.

In this respect German child-care and youth-guidance literature differs in aim and content from that written by and for Americans. For where the American mother is given a great many explicit directions about what she is to do in carrying out the daily routine of care for her child (e.g., in such books as that by Spock[18]), detailed information on such subjects as nursing, weaning, diet, toilet training, etc., which is necessary for learning specific skills, is almost wholly lacking in comparable German books. (There are, however, some exceptional areas, e.g., sexual education, where parents are taught how to inform their children as well as how to inculcate correct attitudes.) The subject matter of German expert books is not *what* to do but rather *how* to do it and how to get the child to do it. And where the image of the mother is implicit in American books, the German mother is told what she must, and must not, be like, in order to succeed.

In the question of upbringing, content is secondary to method. So mothers are told that a child should be given a good "natural" diet of healthful foods, but only a few examples of such foods and no instructions for preparing them are given. The emphasis of the teaching is rather on how to get the child to eat well at the proper time. Or, in a chapter on "First Lessons in Upbringing" for the child in its second year,[19] weaning and cleanliness training are discussed briefly as examples of a method of teaching by gradual, continuous adaptation suitable to children of this age. And the first three chapters of Plattner's book[20]—about half the book—are concerned with (1) obedience and how to obtain it—with examples; (2) punishment and how to administer it—with examples; and (3) autonomy and how to foster it—with examples.

One of the reasons that the assimilation of principles into the personality of the parent-teacher is so important is that children are able to see through mere knowledge and outward appearance: "[Children] will sense behind all the [adult's] knowledge, behind all the interesting details, the uncertain, unclear, compromising attitude of the educator and, because of this, will be unable to take over and build upon the natural attitude which the educator is only acting out for them."[21] The parent who would educate the total personality of the child and hold the child's trust must incorporate learning into the whole of her (his) own personality, because insight on the part of the child, when this involves recognition of a discrepancy in the adult, is fatal to the educational relationship. The parent, not the child, should have insight into others.

The central character in the child-care literature is the mother. (This is, of course, by no means peculiar to the German literature on the subject.) In the books written by women there are two mothers to choose between: the lay-mother, cited in innumerable examples, who invariably makes mistakes with her children, and the expert-mother (the author), who sets things straight for others and who, in caring for her own children, has already learned what is correct and effective. (Sometimes the expert-mother first learned from her own mother or grandmother or a beloved aunt, a gifted woman with the right instincts, but it is assumed that the reader-mother will not identify herself with this untaught expert.)

In the youth-guidance literature, which may be written by a man and which concerns somewhat older children, the erring lay-mother also appears, but the central character is likely not to be the expert-parent, but someone else, usually a man (the author) of rather indeterminate age and great experience, who is able to achieve wonders through a quasi-comradely relationship to the child or adolescent who is in trouble.[22]

Thus in the current literature on child care and youth guidance, some of it newly written, some of it dating back to the 1920's, the views expressed are not so much those of two parental figures (mother and father) as they are those of a mature, motherly, feminine figure (the child-care expert) and of a somewhat younger, emotionally more distant, masculine figure (the youth-guidance expert). Though both stand in a complementary relationship to those being educated (erring parents and misguided children), the experts are not, in their self-images, on the same generation level. Father, as an immediately influential expert figure, has been eliminated from the picture.[23]

The family, as it appears in the pages of these books, is truncated. Although the experts formally emphasize the importance of parental unity and of a full family life, the father appears only rather distantly and indistinctly as a co-educator or, in examples of parental misguidance and juvenile difficulty, either as the worried, angry, outraged companion of the mother or as a minor villain who disturbs the peace of the home, who excites, spoils, or spanks the darling or the naughty child, who interferes with proper education. Siblings and other relatives appear in even more shadowy form. The books about upbringing in the home are directed toward the mother and are concerned with the relationship between one mother and one child, who is presumably one of several in a family rich in children (*eine kinderreiche Familie*). Occasionally the several children of the expert-mother furnish her, the writer, with a chorus of comment on the behavior of an erring mother and child, illustrating implicitly the unity of good parent and good child.

One image of the relationship of the German parent and child is that of the gardener and the plant.[24] Plattner uses this image to stress the inviolability of the child's personality:

As little as we could make the smallest blade of grass grow if wonderful powers of life did not work in it without our actions, as little as we can turn grass into weed, just so little can we form our children. We are gardeners, not gods.[25]

She uses it elsewhere to describe the role of the parent:

Educators are not to be compared to artists but to gardeners, who, with much knowledge and experience, prepare the ground and protect from harm, but for the rest must patiently wait to see how their plants develop of their own accord, following their own rules of growth. . . . Our care should not lead to overfeeding, and the protective hedge around the paradise of childhood must not turn into a hothouse.[26]

Or Hetzer, urging parents not to postpone education, writes:

This putting off is just as nonsensical as if a gardener were to wait with the care, for instance, the watering, of a bed which he has sown until the plants growing out of the seed had broken through the earth or until the plant's buds and leaves were clearly recognizable.[27]

Or Seelmann asks:

What about vulnerability to seduction? Must not the ground on which the seed of seduction falls be specially prepared in advance . . . ?[28]

The adult is the gardener. Sometimes the whole child is likened to a plant (as in the first two quotations and, more doubtfully, in the last two). At other times the child is the ground which is tended or the container in which plants grow, and the plants are character traits, good and bad, inborn or sown in the child. The following three images from Plattner treat the child as ground or container:

Only when we sense that our child is moved, that it is opening the little door of its heart and is listening to our words with all its senses, only in such moments can we lay seeds in the childish heart which later perhaps will grow.[29]

In early childhood the ground is prepared on which later the riches of the spirit can unfold. . . . Not on what we say but much more on what we are does it depend whether the roots of belief in God reach down into the dreamlike experience of earliest childhood.[30]

Pride holds down the underbrush of vanity and prepares the ground on which the love of truth can grow.[31]

Sometimes development and growth result in an alteration of the image:

Everything that helps the healthy thriving of the child helps prepare the ground on which later the love of truth can grow. It is particularly important not to damage the little child's pride. For the love of truth is nourished by pride . . . without any educational intention proud people spread around them an air in which the love of truth can grow and thrive. What comes to life under their protecting hands is the spark of the courage of conviction. . . . This spark, in pioneering people, becomes a flame which nothing, not even death and torture—in a real or in a symbolic sense—can extinguish.[32]

Here Plattner treats the child as the container, and the love of truth as a plant, which, as it grows and flowers, turns into a flame.

A second type of image associated with childhood and growth is that of the steps (*Stufen*) which must be ascended to reach adulthood. In contrast to the image of the living plant (which can thrive or be stunted, can be implanted or uprooted, can pine away in artificial light or respond to the natural sunlight), the image of steps is entirely, or almost entirely, a mechanical one. According to ideas to which this image is related, the child inevitably goes through stages (up steps) of growth which are essentially independent of experience or training. Each successive step must be ascended, but the child's ascent can be hindered, halted, or facilitated by training.

These two images—of the plant and of the steps—are not only used alternatively in the literature but also appear together in single contexts, as if there were no conflict between the conceptions of development which these metaphors express.

A third type of image is that of unrolling, unfolding, or externalizing. The usual term for development and maturation is *Entwicklung*, which literally means an unrolling (and which also is used in photography to refer to the development process).[33] It is sometimes used together with the image of steps, i.e., *Entwicklungstufen* ("stages of development"), but the two terms also are used separately, with somewhat different connotations. Related terms are *entfalten*, "to unfold or develop," and *enthüllen*, "to unveil or to reveal."

The image of the steps or stages is one of automatic growth. The image of development is one of the gradual revelation of existing qualities. Both are used in close conjunction with the plant-gardener image. We are therefore given a total image—a kind of metaphoric mosaic— of the child who is born with certain predispositions and innate qualities (*Keim*, "sprout," is sometimes used to refer to these), who goes through stages (*Stufen*) of predetermined growth, in the course of which there is a process of opening up, of revealing (*Entwicklung*) and during which the parents work on the child—preparing the ground, fostering some qualities, implanting some qualities, removing and uprooting others (innate or implanted), even creating ground (i.e., the ground of common personal relationships) in which roots can take hold and grow—so that the child will reach a kind of ripeness at each stage and, finally, the ripeness of adulthood.

These images suggest that while parents as educators may—or may not—be able to alter the qualities with which a child is born and while the stages of growth are more or less predetermined, the development of a good character is wholly dependent upon parental guidance. How the character will develop and what will be revealed depend upon the way in which parents prepare the ground, implant or uproot traits, tend the plant, stunt or foster qualities inherent in or planted in the child. Left to itself at any point, the child almost invariably will make the wrong choice, do the wrong thing, come under the wrong influence.

Parents who are anxious about the ineffectiveness of their educational methods are granted only one possible escape: the assurance that there are a few, a very few, children who are born with only bad traits and who must therefore be treated differently from others. With these rare exceptions, whatever potentialities for good or evil a child may have, the good potentialities can be developed only by the unremitting effort of parents who have incorporated in their own personality the same or complementary character traits. Bad potentialities, on the contrary, are activated by single events; one mistake, one omission, one neglected occasion, or one inconsistent act by the parent is sufficient to encourage a "weed" to grow in the child, which can then be uprooted only by further unremitting effort.

There are several educational themes that interweave in the child-care literature. (1) The child must learn to obey, so that it can be trusted to be alone without endangering itself and so that it can master the tasks set by life. Obedience must become exact and automatic; it must be accepted as a matter of course, as natural. (2) The child must learn to become autonomous, so that it can meet the trials of life and so that it can both face life independently of others and enter into relationships with others. (3) The child must develop a sense of itself without ever becoming the center of attention. (4) The child must be loved and protected from danger, but it must not be spoiled or weakened by overfeeding it with tenderness or protecting it from difficult reality. Neither too great nor too few demands must be made upon its growing powers. (5) Education must take place in an atmosphere of self-disciplined, insightful love—expressed impersonally—which fosters the child's trust in the adult.

The young child lives in the world of "the children's paradise" (*das Kinderparadies*), which is surrounded by a high hedge. The parents control how much of reality shall be permitted to enter. "The children's paradise" refers simultaneously to the home and family in which the child lives and to the child's own internalized vision of the world, half fairy tale or "dream," half real. Here the child lives, happy and sheltered (*geborgen*, a word with overtones of sentiment lacking in the English word), if it is well brought up, but also gradually moving toward reality and school. During this period the child both finds itself and gets a sense of itself as a member of a group:

The way in which this first fitting of the ego [*das Ich*] takes place is important for future life. If the little one feels its ego, of which it is first becoming conscious, to be part of a larger "we" in which it knows that it is secure [*geborgen*], in that it receives what it needs and is allowed to give what it can, and so grows toward a personal life [*Eigenleben*], then it has everything necessary for a childhood paradise.[34]

To become part of the "we-group," the toddler should have its own play corner in the mother's room and should accompany her in her work, both as a form of companionable play and as a way of gradually learning to take over small duties. The child has already learned, from the first days of its life, to be alone, so that the mother need not be at its beck and call and can go away without fearing that the child may be in danger. This is one of the early lessons that lead to autonomy: the child must learn to be alone *and* completely with people.

As a first step in this direction, mothers are urged to let the young infant "cry it out," so that it learns to control itself and then to enjoy food and companionship when they appear. Mothers are warned, for instance, that the five- to seven-week-old child is naturally a "screamer" because of the many new impressions impinging upon it; they are assured that the screaming will stop "of its own accord" as soon as the child "masters" these new impressions, if the adult will endure and wait.[35] In this way the parent, now as later, makes use of a stage of growth to train the child for the whole of its life. For the child learns to accept companionship and care at specific times in an orderly way. The young child also should be cared for by one person, who systematically does the same things at the same times in the same way. This is part of the program of training by habituation and is regarded as essential to the development of trust, on which the winning of obedience is said to be based. Thus trust, regularity, and consistency, on the one hand, and distrust, irregularity, and discrepancy, on the other, are thought of as linked, contrasting sets. The child is believed to react with trustful obedience to consistency and regularity and with distrust and disobedience to a single discrepancy in adult performance.

The successful training of the child depends on the adult's being orderly, consistent, quiet, and patient (repeating the same sequence until the child can take over and do what is required of its own accord). In beginning this training, the parent can build on the child's own inborn need for order:

The behavior of the newborn child very much favors habituation to a definite order; one could almost say that the child obeys this orderliness before we begin our upbringing to orderliness and that, if we do not insist on maintaining order [i.e., a schedule] in the first days of life, we take it out of this [natural] order. . . . It is therefore understandable that the child learns to accommodate itself quickly to the order we prescribe for it and that, where we destroy the natural order through irregularity, the child is brought out of order so that one succeeds only with difficulty later in accustoming it to regularity.[36]

Thus the infant, in its first stage of life, is prepared to accommodate itself to orderliness (*Ordnung*) and regularity (*Regelmässigkeit*) and to trust and enjoy the adult by whom these values are inculcated.

German experts feel strongly that for each stage in the child's development there are (1) things which can be done only at that stage, or most easily at that stage, and only with difficulty later (e.g., habituation to systematic regularity in early infancy); (2) things which *cannot* be done at that stage (e.g., attempting to teach a child under eighteen months by word alone or by punishment); (3) things which must be done at that stage because a later stage has not yet been reached (e.g., linking word and action in training the very young child who does not yet know that a word stands for an action; at this stage the mother must be willing to repeat each command on many occasions and must insist that the child match word and action so that it will become habituated to the relationship between word and deed); and (4) things which are done at each stage to prepare the child for stages still to come, sometimes in the distant future (e.g., the parent "prepares the ground"—for the love of truth, the development of pride, the life of the spirit—long before these may be said to develop).

In learning obedience, the child progresses from the first passive stage in which it learns to accept prescribed order, to the next stage (up to about eighteen months), during which it learns to respond in word-action situations. At this stage, when the child cannot yet respond to words alone, the mother is urged to train the child by the repeated use of consistent word-action combinations, in which the mother systematically helps the child to carry out the action as she says the words, e.g., "Knives you may not touch," always patiently removing the child's hand. At about eighteen months, the child begins to understand commands and the meaning of "No," but cannot yet be expected to obey prohibitions in the absence of an adult.

At two, it can carry out simple verbal requests and begins to obey prohibitions of its own accord. Then the child says to itself (as its mother has said innumerable times): "Knives you may not touch," and it leaves the knife (or the cake or mother's bright-colored pins) on the table.

Then gradually it becomes possible to combine a series of desired actions in one order. The mother says: "It is time to go to bed," and the child begins the series of activities involved in "going to bed" without being told each separate detail. After a time, only a few commands are necessary, and the child acts without realizing that it is being obedient:

So with increasing age the single order more and more takes the place of many specific commands. An obedient child is not overburdened with orders, while orders and prohibitions fall like hail on other children: "Leave that alone!"—"You know you should not do that!"—"Sit properly at table!" The obedient child sits properly without thinking about it and without even knowing that he was once told to do it.[37]

Obedience, for which the child began to take responsibility at two years, is accepted as a matter of course, and the single command starts an automatic chain reaction. The future of the obedient child is pictured as a pleasant one:

> With this upbringing, at a later age, when will and consciousness are fully developed, a simple and friendly word—for instance, "Do your homework now"—will be obeyed and taken for granted, and the wish to play more will be overcome. How beautiful the life of the school child can be if we have laid the right foundation in the small-child age![38]

Automatic obedience can be furthered also if, instead of thwarting the small child who wants a forbidden object, the mother encourages the child to do what the mother herself would do, i.e., if she lets the child put the pretty pins or Daddy's gold watch out of sight and temptation.

Moreover, the pedantry characteristic of the two- to three-year-old child helps the parent teach obedience. For it is recognized that at this age the child itself needs to have everything exactly as it should be and is disturbed by change and by the unusual. Knowing how things should be, the child itself takes over the task of keeping them exactly the same:

> One can observe in two- and three-year-olds a readiness for obedience that is almost unbelievable to an adult—a painstaking exactness, a peculiar longing for conformity, which takes amiss every deviation from the rule. Little children will fly into a delicious rage (*köstliche Entrüstung*) if one of a row of drawers is not entirely closed or if the usual places at table are changed or, indeed, if there is any change from a rule which has once been made. "But you said . . . ," they say reproachfully. This peculiar childish pedantry makes it possible to accustom the small child to particular rules which give firmness and order to everyday life.[39]

Thus a stage which is regarded by Americans as an especially difficult one to get through comfortably is given very positive and constructive meaning by the German expert, who is so deeply concerned with the problem of how the child is to take over the task of enforcing its own good behavior. (It is not clear in these formulations whether this pedantic stage precedes or is another aspect of "the stubbornness phase," discussed below.)

The three-year-old has progressed to the stage at which it can carry out simple repetitive tasks—setting the table, watering the plants. It should therefore be given small household duties for which it assumes responsibility. In this way another use is made of the child's pedantry to incorporate it actively into the household and to introduce it to the real world of duty.

At three, when the child knows what it may and may not do, when it is able to obey of its own volition, it must be punished if it is disobedient:

Everything has to be learned. Therefore, the child has a right to make mistakes and a right to punishment, which helps it to overcome mistakes.[40]

The child has a "right to punishment" because punishment helps it to learn self-control. (In certain circumstances physical pain is intended to have the effect of a challenge.) Therefore, hurt or not, the disobedient child must be punished so that it will not come to grief in later life:

Some years later the young person will test the ice and will himself know that he must not go on it if it is not strong enough. If he has learned as a child to obey, he will now obey his own insight. But if he was disobedient and obeyed only when he was watched and forced to do so, if he has never learned to overcome a forbidden desire of his own volition, then he will walk on the ice and break through it.[41]

Neither threats nor promises of reward are useful in teaching obedience. Mere threats, especially unrealizable ones, leave the child in a state of uncertainty and promote disobedience, for, knowing what the punishment may be, the child can choose whether to obey or to continue the forbidden pleasure and accept the consequences.

Rewards distract the child's attention from the thing to be done. After a while it becomes "accustomed" to rewards and turns into a "cool calculator who works only for the sake of rewards."[42] Nor should a child be reasoned with; the child's "Why?" is only a means of escape and may become a source of danger when the child insists on a reason when action—avoiding an oncoming car—is imperative. It must learn first to obey and then to find out why, to act and then to understand the reason. Knowing why should be the happy consequence of following out a command.[43] Through simple commands, uncomplicated by "unless" (threats) and "so that" (rewards), and through constructive punishment, the child soon learns that obedience is self-evident. The child who has accepted the idea of obedience before it has developed self-consciousness remains happily unaware of alternative possibilities.

Such obedience is regarded as essentially impersonal. In keeping with this, the good parent phrases directions and orders "impersonally": "One doesn't do such a thing" (*So was macht man nicht*), or "Who opens the door, must close it" (*Wer die Tür aufmacht, macht sie auch zu*). This is consistent with the feeling that it is "life" that sets the tasks, tests the performance, rewards, or punishes. Both the mover and the moved act for impersonal reasons. The parent must treat her own word "like one of the Commandments" or "like a law of nature." She must never break her word, change her mind, make an exception, or make a mistake which must be corrected by a change of order. If she makes a single exception, takes back her word only once, is caught out in one mistake, the child will discover, first, that it can get its own way by begging, fighting, or stubbornly resisting (i.e., that it can be stronger than the parent) and, second, that the adult, in making demands, is acting out of sheer arbitrariness or caprice (*Will-kür*). Then the child will become resistant. It is apparent that the "law-of-nature" definition of a command is lost as soon as personal wishes become a basis for action for parent or child.

Education in obedience for the preschool and school child has, as one of its goals, the taking-over of this same task, in some measure, by the adolescent. Thus Spranger describes the developmental changes that take place during adolescence:

> The deeper the glimpses into one's own self become, the more frequent is self-judgment, and in self-judgment also lies self-education. In few young people does the belief in their own accomplishment go so far that they themselves have the opinion that they do not need any more upbringing. But their relationship to upbringing is different from that of the child, in that they themselves begin to choose what effect an educational influence should have upon them. As soon as this selectivity is paired with self-discipline and conscious work on one's own character, education by outsiders has irrevocably gone over into self-education. No miracle can make intentional educational measures have an effect on the youth if he does not will it himself. Therefore, upbringing during this stage consists basically in *waking* the will for self-education.[44]

In a word, the adolescent's own will is to be placed at the service of further education of the self, and the adolescent is being prepared to become the adult self-educating educator.

The training of the will for self-education is also fostered by a subtle change in the relationship between the educator and his charge. Although rules, commands, and prohibitions may be phrased as impersonally as before, the adult must now adopt a genuinely "frank" and "open" and "comradely" attitude if he is to win and hold the confidence of the self-conscious adolescent. To protect his role as educator, he must lessen the distance between the young person and himself by increased self-revelation. Thus at the very time when the adolescent has become self-aware, when he has achieved a measure of independence and is able to have a private, "secret" life of his own, he is encouraged to be frank and self-revealing by the more comradely attitude of the educator. By this means the educator is enabled to continue his watchful, insightful supervision, and the adolescent—voluntarily giving the educator clues to his secrets—is helped to become more independent, to enter into new relationships, and to better his still faltering efforts at self-discipline and correct behavior.

During the years when the child is learning obedience, it is also being trained in self-reliance and personal autonomy. This training begins when the infant learns that "crying accomplishes nothing." But true education in autonomy commences when the child begins to move around and walk. Then parents must encourage the child to experiment with and practice using its own body. Anxious protection at this stage will injure the child's character for

the child must learn through the harm that comes to it; that is, one or another accident, e.g., falling down, is an unavoidable necessity.[45]

And

. . . without bruises and scratches, no child can become a real person. What the mother forbids [in the way of physical experimentation] out of anxiety, an inborn pressure forces the child to do, to test out its powers. The order given by the forward-driving will to life is stronger than the mother's prohibition. With such prohibitions, one drives the child to disobedience.[46]

Where physical experimentation is concerned, parents are warned that prohibitions are likely to endanger their educational program, for, on the one hand, the strong child may be driven to disobedience or, on the other hand, the obedient child may fail to learn the lessons of self-inflicted pain. The child learns through pain, but where punishment deters and so promotes obedience, self-inflicted pain challenges the sufferer to try it again and so promotes autonomy.

The mother who protects her child and who does things for it which it can very well do for itself is turning her child into a helpless sissy (*Muttersöhnchen,* "Mother's little boy") who bullies and tyrannizes over its parents and others. "As long as I *cannot,* Mother *must*" is the conclusion reached by the protected, fearful, and now demanding child. Through helpless dependence, this problem child compels its parents to continue their personal care and minute supervision. Later, the way to independence must be "battled with endless effort."

The child who, on the contrary, is allowed to experiment with jumping and running and climbing and who learns to take no notice of the painful incidents that are part of the process is also prepared to face the difficulties of life and to master them. Concerning the value of physical pain, an expert-mother explained to her own daughter who was suffering with toothache:

"In all growth there are difficulties to overcome. Also when you children grew in me and I bore you, I had to bear hardships and pains as you do now because you are getting a new tooth. But as a result I had you. Don't you want to have children sometime too? The tooth is a good preparatory exercise for getting through such a pain."[47]

Significantly, congruence between types of experience is established not through similarity of content but through the person's attitude toward a variety of experiences, which are, in this instance, classified as "painful." In theory, learning to bear one kind of "pain" prepares the sufferer to bear all other kinds, and, in effect, one kind of pain or suffering can be equated to any other kind.

Also significant is the contradiction between the education of adults and children proposed by the experts. Addressing themselves to parents and urging them to educate themselves, the experts say that they can learn without suffering by contemplating "the harm that has come to others." Addressing themselves to the same parents in regard to the education of their children, they insist that "the child must learn through the harm that comes to it."

The small-child period of life culminates when the child is "ripe" for school, but the climax of this period comes at about mid-point— when the child is two and one-half to three years old. Earlier and later the small child is easy to lead and ready to learn, but at mid-point it suddenly becomes conscious of its self and of its own will and then, for about six months, it goes through the stubbornness phase (*Trotzperiode*) so well known and so abhorrent to German mothers. The experts explain that consciousness of self and of its own will are central to the small child's life but that, after a brief and stormy appearance, it will die down and will rise to a new climax only in the middle of adolescence. The first climax prefigures the second. Both are necessary for the development of will and pride in the adult, and both are periods of difficulty for the child and the responsible adult. The stubbornness phase of the small child is, by implication, one of the inevitable steps in the child's development, which can be well managed but cannot be avoided.

The child is born with a readiness for order and, if it is well brought up, has a new kind of readiness to undertake tasks when it reaches the school-child stage. During the climax of self-will or stubbornness, it attempts to act on its own, to set its own goals—a prefigurative characteristic of this stage which will be lost if the adult attempts to "break the child's will." At this time parents have two tasks: to conserve what has already been achieved (i.e., obedience) and to protect what is still to come (autonomy). However, they are given little instruction about how to make constructive use of this stage. They are told that they must not punish the child "too much"; they must only see to it that ordinary rules are kept. The child's previous upbringing will help carry it through the stubbornness phase. If it has already learned to obey, it will continue to think that obedience is natural and will not exercise its new-found will by refusing to go on with ordinary daily activities. But if parents have to use force, because they have put off necessary measures of education, there will be "conflict with the world around it and scenes of stubbornness." Yet if it is given no opportunity to exercise and display its self-consciousness and will—and for this it must have achieved some autonomy—it will grow up into a "weak-willed, characterless person."[48] At worst, this is a period of misery and futile scenes; at best, it is a waiting period for adults who will be able to go on with upbringing if they are but patient: "In the next period of willingness-to-undertake-tasks, everything can be done without difficulty that could not be accomplished during the period of stubbornness."[49]

The *Trotzperiode* is only a shadowy prefiguration of adolescent *Sturm und Drang*. And, in contrast to the almost incidental treatment of the first climax in the child-care literature, the management of the second—of the problems and difficulties and tragedies of the adolescent period of self-will and self-recognition—is a major preoccupation of the writers on youth guidance. For, from the German point of view, this climax in the midst of the period of "youth" is a high point in the whole of life.

Although a child will be stunted in its development if it lacks attentive love, and will be endangered and dangerous if it is neglected, and will become a rebel or a sycophant or a will-less slave if too great demands are made and too great pressures are put upon it, and will come to grief if it fails to learn self-discipline through obedience, and will be unable to face and master life if it has not achieved autonomy, the greatest anxiety expressed by experts is connected with the idea that the child may be weakened and spoiled, may become unsocial and prematurely sexually aware (*frühreif*) through parental over-attentiveness, overcarefulness, and overfeeding with foolish affection. Such a child is enfeebled and made unable to exercise self-control or to subject itself to guidance. Since overfond parents are portrayed as waverers who first give in to everything and later rue the inevitable results, this child has no basis for trust in people. Since it sees itself at the center of the stage, the cynosure of admiring eyes and later perhaps the central figure in a drama of punishment and tragedy, it gets an utterly false sense of its own importance.

The only child is, of course, believed to be especially endangered by the too loving miseducation of its parents and possibly doting grandparents, aunts, uncles, and other relatives. Except at the cost of a long and painful struggle, such a child may never achieve independent adulthood or find a place in a group of people.[50] Giving a child, especially a young child, too great a sense of its own self and personality makes impossible its integration first into the family circle and later into any other group. And if one goal of upbringing is to make the child into a whole person, the other goal is to make him into a group member. Thus Seelmann formulates the duality of the human being: "The human being is a self-inclosed unit. But as such, he is also a member of a larger community."[51]

To prepare the child for social life, parents should have a family rich in children. Then, as they must divide their attention among all the children, they must learn to moderate their demands, to remember that each child is different from each other one, that each must be differently educated to obtain the same results (i.e., the content—not the method—of their education must be different), and to control their expressions of fondness. They must take the middle course of exactness for the sake of their children's character development.

Part of the child's education in autonomy and in social life consists in playing with other children, especially siblings. Here, too, in its relations with its play-fellows, the child learns by experiencing difficulties and suffering frustrations. The following suggests how social learning is expected to take place:

Five-year-old Karl and four-year-old Fritz jointly have a tricycle. Fritz is riding on it; Karl "wants to too." Fritz doesn't want to give it up. Karl tries to take it away. So neither one can ride. They get into a fight. The mother hears their furious howling and comes.

She judges the quarrel according to the immediate situation and insists that Karl give the tricycle to Fritz, because Karl's fury and stubbornness are obvious. Karl feels unjustly treated, because Fritz has ridden already. Full of opposition to his mother, he determines to get back at his brother. Still worse is the little devil that has awakened in Fritz's soul. He did not let Karl ride and now he and not the stupid Karl is riding again. Wasn't it sly to get appearances on his side. He has the advantage and Karl has the disadvantage. How Mother let herself be fooled! He had thought she knew everything. In spite of this triumph, Fritz has an uncomfortable feeling. The pleasure in the tricycle is spoiled. . . .

[The writer then supposes that the mother gave the tricycle to Karl instead of Fritz, and indicates that this would have had equally bad results.]

It is not the duty of the mother to be a judge but to be the representative [*Vertreterin*] of the laws of life. . . . But the law of life does not say: "If two quarrel, the one who is right gets the advantage." It says rather: "If two quarrel, both have disadvantage." This disadvantage even the small child should feel. Therefore, the mother should take away the toy about which they were quarreling. . . . If the mother acts in this way in every instance of a quarrel, quietly, as if it were a foregone conclusion, then the child—at an age when intellectual understanding is still impossible—grasps how foolish quarreling is.[52]

Explicitly, the reader is shown that children who have learned the disadvantages of quarreling, of envy and jealousy, and who have been punished by deprivation will also learn the advantages of getting along with one another. But there is also an implicit lesson, namely, that social relations require a kind of impersonalization of everyone involved. The children's wishes and motives cannot be taken into account, the mother must not judge—lest her judgment be wrong and her authority over the children be impaired, to the disadvantage of the children themselves. Thus the child who, as an individual, is brought up to face and master "the battle of life," should also discover that social relationships are controlled by impersonal "laws of life." And, in a happy family, where the mother fosters personal relations by impersonal means, the child—it is said—will be able to find a foundation for all future social relations in and outside the family.

Thus the German child is prepared in the home to become an independent individual, who, through the practice of willing obedience to parental rules, has learned to obey all rules of his own accord and who, through painful experience, has trained his will to master the problems of life. The fact that this education takes place in the family setting of parents and siblings also prepares the individual to take his place outside the family as a member of other groups. The intention of this education is not to prepare the individual to make choices but rather to know what is right and to have the strength and fortitude to do it.

Significantly, the child-guidance specialists believe that this education can be made easy and pleasant if training in obedience begins early enough—before the child is aware that choice is possible—and is totally consistent and impersonally phrased, and if parents recognize that the process of education is a long one which must be adapted to each stage of growth through which the child goes. Punishment then becomes a method not of handling disobedience but of correcting childish mistakes. At the same time, since the child is not prohibited from experimenting with its own physical capacities and is not protected from inevitable mishaps, it learns to control its own will.

Parents, especially mothers, must carry out this education in a "natural" way, i.e., they, too, must incorporate in their personalities the qualities which they are teaching, in such a way that they, too, can act without having to make choices or having to dissemble in any way. To learn to do what is right, they must learn to be right. The method of teaching used for parents, however, differs from that advocated for children—for, with the greatest consistency, the experts teach parents what is right through examples of what is wrong, as well as by encouraging examples of success achieved by the right means.

With rare exceptions, the child at birth is neither good nor bad but is pictured as having unformed potentialities. Misguided or left to its own devices at any point, the child is believed to be incapable of developing its own good potentialities, but with guidance the bad ones can be eliminated. This is the basic justification for total parental authority over the child and for self-education of the educator himself.

Changes in the future education of the child, therefore, are regarded as dependent upon changes in the past education of the adult. There is, however, an underlying optimism in the child-care literature. For bad traits can be changed by good influence, and even the misguided adult, who is suffering because of a problem child and who determines to do better, can, with help, re-educate himself or herself to be a good parent. Consequently, the educators set a limit upon the retracing of steps necessary to become and to help others become persons of good character in their assurance that the educator can educate himself, that parents can learn from the experiences of others how to bring up children who later can take up their own adult self-education.

NOTES

1. The books included in this study were selected in the summer of 1952 from those available to West German readers in bookstores and said, by booksellers and others consulted, to have a popular sale. All the books cited were written within the last thirty years; with one exception (Franzen-Hellersberg, 1932), all have appeared in new printings or new editions or have been first published since 1947. Eduard Spranger's study, first published in 1924, continued to appear in new printings during the Nazi regime and has been reprinted since the war. Some of the authors, e.g., Hetzer, were trained and published influential studies in the period of the Weimar Republic and are continuing their work today. Since this analysis considered only publications available to readers in West Germany, the study has immediate relevance only to this area.

2. *Geist* and *Seele* are essentially untranslatable terms, both of which refer to inner or spiritual life.

3. Hetzer, 1947*a*, p. 5.

4. *Ibid.*, p. 7.

5. This dichotomy is by no means peculiar to German thinking. Thus the French also distinguish between upbringing (*formation*) and instruction (*instruction*). But the aims and methods of French and German educators differ in fundamental ways (cf., on France, Métraux and Mead, 1954).

6. In modern German school-guidance literature it is assumed that teachers must supplement the upbringing begun and carried on in the home, especially as regards education for citizenship. However, in practice schoolteachers are likely to refer failures in instruction to failures in home upbringing, and there is a sharp division of feeling among teachers today between those who say that the school must carry out the tasks which parents cannot or will not undertake and those who say that the teacher's task is confined to instruction.

7. For a discussion of the educational needs of proletarian youth in the 1920's cf. Franzen-Hellersberg, 1932. In this pioneering study of the problems of working-class girls, the author concludes that the failure of the girls and women to comprehend the conditions of their vocational life goes back to failures in education in the home itself.

8. Spranger, 1951, p. 134.

9. Bondy and Eyforth, 1952, p. 5.

10. *Ibid.*, p. 55.

11. *Ibid.*, pp. 53–54.

12. *Plattner*, 1951, p. 6.

13. Seelmann, 1952, p. 187.

14. Hoffmann, [1845].

15. Hetzer, 1947*b*, p. 5.

16. Plattner, 1951, p. 6.

17. Hetzer, 1947*b*, p. 4.

18. Spock, 1946.
19. Hetzer, 1947*a*.
20. Plattner, 1951.
21. Seelmann, 1952, p. 20.
22. The comradely male educator is also a stock character in the juvenile fiction of the last thirty years (cf. the novels of Kästner and Speyer). In such stories he is typically not in a position of great formal authority (e.g., he is not the principal, but the beloved teacher who remembers his youth; he is not the father, but a younger bachelor uncle; or he is a somewhat mysterious outsider without standing in the community), but he is nevertheless a man who wields great influence for good, sometimes by the most unorthodox means. Cf. in this volume, "A Portrait of the Family in German Juvenile Fiction" (p. 253).
23. Spranger (the first edition of whose book appeared in 1924), who writes from a lofty philosophical position, is an exception. The other male writers are likely to put another, older expert in a fatherly position. Thus Seelmann (1952) continually quotes "my teacher, Dr. Leonhard Seif" (now dead), to whom his book is also dedicated, as a source of his ideas.
24. For a discussion of the English version of this image cf. Mead, 1948, and of the French version cf. Métraux and Mead, 1954.
25. Plattner, 1951, p. 65.
26. *Ibid.*, pp. 162–63.
27. Hetzer, 1947*a*, pp. 5–6.
28. Seelmann, 1952, p. 175.
29. Plattner, 1951, p. 105.
30. *Ibid.*, p. 155.
31. *Ibid.*, p. 125.
32. *Ibid.*, p. 136.
33. It is appropriate also to mention here that the young infant is referred to as *das Wickelkind* ("the rolled-up–swaddled–child").
34. Plattner, 1951, p. 111.
35. Hetzer, 1947*a*, p. 13.
36. *Ibid.*, p. 14.
37. Plattner, 1951, p. 12.
38. *Ibid.*
39. *Ibid.*, pp. 10–11.
40. *Ibid.*, p. 52.
41. *Ibid.*, p. 44.
42. Hetzer, 1947*b*, p. 84.
43. Plattner, 1951, pp. 16–18.
44. Spranger, 1951, pp. 161–62.
45. Hetzer, 1947*a*, p. 28.
46. Plattner, 1951, p. 31
47. *Ibid.*, p. 76.
48. Hetzer, 1947*b*, pp. 28–29.
49. Hetzer, 1947*a*, p. 63.
50. In addition to the situation of the only child whose adult life is ruined by its parents' "senseless and immeasurable spoiling," another type of situation is described involving an only child who—if it is a boy—is predestined to become a homosexual, the product of a witch woman and a rabbit man:

"Everyone knows the particular type of woman who is usually haggard and narrow-featured, cool, devoid of feeling, calculating, avaricious, untender, domineering, irritable, uncommunicative—in short, a type who, as an old woman, could be regarded as a 'witch.' . . . Only one type of man is susceptible to these women as long as they are still young and attractive. These are the men who, in the jargon of the clinic, are called 'little rabbit men': soft, gentle, shy, big-eyed, poorly endowed by Nature, mostly spiritually not very independent, but orderly, conscientious, passive natures. . . .

"[Such couples never have more than one child.] If the only child is a boy, it grows up from the beginning of its life in the following situation: mother—bad, cold; father—soft, good, tender. In the earliest period of development, long before any conscious memory, this child has had the experience of one sex as good, the other as bad. We have already pointed out that every person develops from a plantlike existence in childhood, through a childish sexual preoccupation with the self and a youthful preoccupation with others of the same sex, to a full person. This break-through to becoming a full person is possible only when the woman becomes something worth striving for, for the man, [when she] becomes a goal of desire. This is not the case for the type of child pictured here. On the contrary. The image of the woman, the bad mother, is deeply bound up with fear, refusal, hate, opposition, stubbornness, and so on. In the depths of the unconscious of this person there will be no inclination to break out of the homosexuality of the boyish and youthful period into adult life with its responsibility. What is the result? When the child of such a couple comes into the period of youth and adulthood, it remains bound up in its tender and sexual impulses to itself and to its own sex (to the father); we have before us a homosexual" (Schultz, 1951, pp. 99–101).

51. Seelmann, p. 35.
52. Plattner, 1951, pp. 78–80.

LIST OF REFERENCES

BONDY, CURT, and EYFORTH, KLAUS. 1952. *Bindungslose Jugend: Eine sozialpädagogische Studie über Arbeits- und Heimatlosigkeit.* Munich and Düsseldorf: Verlag Wilhelm Steinebach.

FRANZEN-HELLERSBERG, LISBETH. 1932. *Die jugendliche Arbeiterin: Ihre Arbeitsweise und Lebensform. Ein Versuch sozialpsychologischer Forschung zum Zweck der Umwertung proletarischer Tatbestände.* Tübingen: Verlag von J. C. B. Mohr (Paul Siebeck).

GRAMPER, HANS BEAT. 1952. *Handbuch für Lagerleiter.* Frankfort: N. R. Sauerlander Verlag.

HESTER, HILDEGARD. 1947a. *Seelische Hygiene lebenstüchtige Kinder.* 8th ed. Lindau/Bodensee: Verlag "Kleine Kinder." 1st ed., 1930.

———. 1947b. *Erziehungsfehler.* 4th ed. Lindau/Bodensee: Verlag "Kleine Kinder." 1st ed., no date.

HOFFMANN, HEINRICH. [1845.] *Der Struwwelpeter: oder lustige Geschichten und drollige Bilder.* Liepzig: Insel Verlag.

Leherbildung für Württemberg-Baden (Esslinger Plan). 1949. Stuttgart: Verlag von Ernst Klett.

MEAD, MARGARET. 1948. "A Case History in Cross-national Communications." In *The Communication of Ideas,* ed. LYMAN BRYSON, pp. 209–29. New York: Harper & Bros.

MÉTRAUX, RHODA, and HOYT, NELLY SCHARGO. 1953. "German National Character: A Study of German Self-images." ("Studies in Contemporary Cultures, B.") New York: American Museum of Natural History. (Dittoed.)

MÉTRAUX, RHODA, and MEAD, MARGARET. 1954. *Themes in French Culture: A Preface to a Study of French Community.* ("Hoover Institute Studies.") Stanford, Calif.: Stanford University Press.

PLATTNER, ELISABETH. 1951. *Die ersten Lebensjahre: ein Erziehungsbuch.* Heidelberg; Quelle & Meyer.

SCHULTZ, J. H. 1951. *Geschlecht, Liebe, Ehe: Die Grundtatsachen des Liebes- und Geschlectsleben in ihrer Bedeutung für das menschliche Dasein.* 5th improved ed. Munich and Basel: Ernst Reinhart Verlag.

SEELMANN, KURT. 1952. *Kind, Sexualität und Erziehung: zum Verständ-nis der geschlechtlichen Entwicklung und Fehlentwicklung vom Kind und Jugendlichen.* 2d ed. Munich and Basel: Ernst Reinhardt Verlag.

SPOCK, BENJAMIN. 1946. *The Pocket Book of Baby and Child Care.* (Pocket Books, No. 377.) New York: Pocket Books.

SPRANGER, EDUARD. 1951. *Psychologie des Jugendalters.* 22d printing. Hei-delberg: Quelle & Meyer. First printing, 1924.

THIELICKE, HELMUT. 1952. *Die erzieherische Verantwortung der Hoch-schulreform: Grundfragen der Hochschulreform.* Tübingen: Verlag J. C. B. Mohr (Paul Siebeck).

WENKE, HANS. 1952. *Wissenschaft und Erziehung: Beiträge zur Pädagogik und Kulturpolitik.* Heidelberg: Quelle & Meyer.

PART IV

Fantasies for and about Children

Introduction

Songs and stories, pictures, dances, and theatrical shows are among the gifts which a child may receive from his culture. What the child is given of this sort is subject to wide variation, depending on the artistic productivity of the culture and on the prevailing relations between adults and children. We shall only indicate here some points in the range of possibilities and mainly stress literary productions.

Stories, dramatic performances, and the like may be presented for a combined audience of adults and children. Here we have works which are not specially produced for children, in relation to which children are incidental hearers or onlookers. They are brought to the performance by their elders, and they may attend to parts of it and sleep through other parts. The dances and shadow plays of Bali are an example of this. Similarly, folk tales in Europe and America, as originally transmitted by oral tradition, were listened to equally by grownups and children. Many television programs at the present time are watched by the whole family. On another level of self-consciousness in respect to cultural heritage, children may be required to study the works prized by their elders. They are made to learn poems by heart. The works of the most honored writers of the past become part of the school curriculum. There are courses on art and music appreciation and so on. In a variant of this kind of transmission, special versions of adult literature are produced for children, ranging from Lamb's *Tales from Shakespeare* to the comic-book *Hamlet*. In contrast to the compulsory and often reluctant assimilation of adult masterpieces in school, there is an opposite way in which children may share adult literature, namely, in their clandestine reading of books forbidden by the adults.

Sometimes stories which were originally for adults or shared by all ages become the special possession of children. This has happened with European fairy tales after they passed to a large extent from oral tradition and were written down in the nineteenth century. They were then brought out (and increasingly, as time went on, with many illustrations) to be read by children or by adults reading aloud to children. Adult readers became limited to professional folklorists.[1] Joseph Jacobs in his famous collection of English fairy tales indicates this division of his audience. At the beginning of his section of notes and references for students of folklore, there appears the notice: "Oyez. Oyez. Oyez. The *English Fairy Tales* are now closed. Little boys and girls must not read any further."[2] *Robinson Crusoe* and *Gulliver's Travels*, written for adults, have come to be regarded as children's stories, usually appearing for this purpose in simplified and shortened versions. Similarly, *Monkey,* the famous Chinese novel of the sixteenth century, became a favorite book of children. Originally *Monkey* was a political satire, which presented earthly bureaucracy under the guise of a hierarchy of mythological personages.[3] However, the analysis of *Monkey* as a children's favorite which is presented here (p. 246) shows that children can greatly enjoy this story, responding to the rebellious and irreverent antics of Monkey in terms of their own relations to familial authorities. Among the many rich layers of a great story, those corresponding to adults' or to children's experience are emphasized at different times. This migration of stories from the adults' to the children's domain raises interesting questions, which will only be suggested for further exploration. Under what conditions does a division of adults' and children's literature develop? And which stories, originally for adults, become children's stories?

Turning to stories which are specially produced for children, there is one category of these which we may call the "adults' secrets." These are fictions which adults transmit to children to veil their own activities. So, for instance, there is the story, widespread in Western cultures, of the stork bringing the babies. French children are told that girl babies are found in a rose, boy babies in a cabbage. Among the Zuñi, parents tell their children that they will be punished by supernatural visitors. When masquerading fellow-tribesmen appear to accuse the child of all the misdemeanors with which the parents have primed them, the parents put on a drama of pleading to save their children from terrible punishments. In this way they deflect from themselves the children's resentment for blame and discipline. The story and play of the visit of Santa Claus cloak parental generosity in a similar mythological disguise.

Another form of expression which is meaningful only in relation to children is the lullaby. It is interesting that many lullabies contain threats to the infant.[4] In "Rockabye, Baby," for instance: "When the bough breaks, the cradle will fall / And down will come baby, bough, cradle, and all." Perhaps the mother releases in this way a component of hostility toward the baby, expressed in words he does not understand and belied by the gentle tune, while she reassures herself that such catastrophes cannot befall the infant safe in her arms.

In the nineteenth century in Europe and America an extensive literature developed which was produced expressly for children. Much of it was moralistic and cautionary, as in the German *Struwwelpeter,* which related how children who play with matches were burned to a crisp, boys who sucked their thumbs had their thumbs cut off, and so on. In an exceedingly attenuated and mild way, the contemporary

American story for young children, *Tootle*, which David Riesman analyzes (p. 236), serves a similar purpose of warning the child and guiding him aright. Stories of a different sort were written by adults who retained or gladly revived within themselves the imaginings of childhood—Robert Louis Stevenson, for instance, in *Treasure Island*.[5] Sometimes intensely attracted to children and longing to please them, such writers evoked the strange irrationality of the child's mind. Thus Lewis Carroll produced his marvelous *Alice* books, and Edward Lear his nonsense verses. This escape into nonsense expressed a covert revolt against the constraining moral atmosphere of the Victorian age.[6] Sympathetic understanding of children provided a vantage point for defying logic as an adult convention or, alternatively, for showing up the self-important adults as foolish and unreasonable. More explicitly, Lewis Carroll parodied the didactic literature for children of his time, in the verses which Alice found came out all wrong when she tried to recite them. The homily about the busy bee was transformed into: "How doth the little crocodile / Improve his shining tail," and so on.

Many less talented and less deeply motivated writers also turned to producing books for the increasing public of child readers. Some of these works, often appearing in endless series, while absorbing to children, are sharply age-typed and mainly unreadable by their elders, as, for instance, *The Bobbsey Twins, The Rover Boys*. There are, however, many books for children which, though they are not what an adult would choose to read by himself, are intended for adults to read aloud to children. The German stories for children about family life, which Rhoda Métraux analyzes (p. 253), are largely of this sort.

The development of a literature specially for children (together with special songs, pictures, plays, television programs) is related to many complicated factors in adults' relations to children. In western Europe toward the end of the eighteenth century and concurrently with revolutionary social philosophies and political movements, there arose a changed image of the child. The child came to be regarded not as an incomplete adult to be subjected and subdued as quickly as possible to the adult mode but as a being of rich inner resources, often corrupted by adult tutelage. An emotionally intense, sensuously acute, spiritually elevated, imaginatively charmed life was attributed to the child by some writers. Wordsworth spoke movingly of the constriction of these vital and noble forces which the child suffers in growing up:

> Shades of the prison-house begin to close
> Upon the growing boy,
> But he beholds the light, and whence it flows,
> He sees it in his joy.[7]

There was doubtlessly a wide discrepancy between such feelings about childhood, diffused among the literate and cultivated but per-

haps confined to moments of poetic elevation, and the attitudes of
parents and teachers toward their charges in everyday life. Nostalgia,
regret, and reproach about one's own lost childhood are not necessarily conducive to tenderness toward, or even interest in, children. However, in the course of the nineteenth century there developed among
certain writers a longing for contact with the charmed age of childhood. Another important factor in this was the growing impetus of
scientific thought, which tended increasingly to exclude magical thinking from adult consciousness. A recapturing of the dreamlike and
magical could be permitted and justified in communication with children, in making stories for them. Certain sectors of adult consciousness, otherwise muted and denied, could find expression in telling tales
for children. Kingsley's *Water Babies* and Barrie's *Peter Pan* evoked a
magical world in which children would never have to grow up.[8] The
child became the guardian and repository not only of the fanciful
(fairy tales old and new being typed as children's stories) but also of
the romantic: tales of chivalry, old wars, and explorations of a world
not yet completely mapped out. Making stories specially for children
thus arose out of an adult necessity, a discovery of a new important
role of the child in relation to the adult.

Another related area where we can see varying interpretations of
childhood is in the representation of the child in adult art and literature. Sometimes children are not represented here at all; at other times
they become major figures. Many mythologies include childhood episodes in the lives of heroes, attributing to the child marvelous feats,
which foretell his later greatness. The nature of these precocious
achievements varies according to what is most admired in a given
culture. In ancient Greece, where strength and courage, the virtues of
the warrior, were prized, the infant Hercules was depicted as strangling serpents with his bare hands. The boy Jesus, in a Jewish culture
setting high value on words, confounded the elders in the temple with
his masterly arguments. In cultures where artists are sufficiently admired to become figures of legend, their life-stories are likely to include
episodes in which they produce remarkable works at an early age.[9] In
the roster of powerful infants a peculiarly malign one appears in the
Russian folk tale of "Prince Ivan and the Witch Baby," that of a girl
baby born with iron teeth, who in three days grows to the size of a
house and eats up her mother and father. In contrast to these mythological strong children, the child protagonists of nineteenth-century
European literature, notably in Dickens and Dostoevsky, were distinguished by their weakness and vulnerability. In tear-provoking scenes,
they often died young. Their heroism consisted in an almost super-
human goodness and sweetness of character.

Just as the nineteenth century in Europe and America witnessed a growth of a large literature for children, so during this time children became increasingly important protagonists in adult literature. At the present time child characters occupy a significant place in adult novels, plays, and films. In the last chapter of this part, Martha Wolfenstein explores some of the ways in which children are depicted in current films of different countries.

M. W.

NOTES

1. *The Jack Tales*, collected by Richard Chase (1943), are an example of this. Recorded from oral tradition in the southern mountain regions of the United States, where admired storytellers were listened to by young and old alike, these stories became a book for children, with large print and many illustrations and, at the same time, a well-documented source for folklorists. Cf. Martha Wolfenstein's analysis of "Jack and the Beanstalk" in this volume (p. 243).
2. Jacobs, 1898.
3. See the Introduction to the translation of *Monkey* (Waley, 1943).
4. Micheline Guiton has made an analysis of the frequent occurrence of fantasies of damage to the baby in French lullabies, in an unpublished paper on "Le Bercement."
5. A psychoanalytic analysis of Stevenson's work, with special reference to his poems and stories for children, will be found in Kanzer, 1951.
6. This point was suggested by Ernst Kris in an oral communication. For a detailed study of the works of Lewis Carroll and Edward Lear cf. Sewell, 1952.
7. William Wordsworth, "Ode: Intimations of Immortality from Recollections of Early Childhood."
8. For a psychoanalytic study of Kingsley, with special reference to *Water Babies*, cf. Deutsch, 1948.
9. Kris, 1952.

LIST OF REFERENCES

CHASE, RICHARD (ed.). 1943. *The Jack Tales*. Boston: Houghton Mifflin Co.

DEUTSCH, FELIX. 1948. "Artistic Expression and Neurotic Illness," *Yearbook of Psychoanalysis*, II, 140–71.

JACOBS, JOSEPH. 1898. *English Fairy Tales*. New York and London: G. P. Putnam.

KANZER, MARK. 1951. "The Self-analytic Literature of Robert Louis Stevenson." In *Psychoanalysis and Culture*, ed. G. B. WILBUR and W. MUENSTERBERGER, pp. 425–35. New York: International Universities Press.

KRIS, ERNST. 1952. "The Image of the Artist." In his *Psychoanalytic Explorations in Art*, pp. 64–84. New York: International Universities Press.

SEWELL, ELIZABETH. 1952. *The Field of Nonsense*. London: Chatto & Windus.

WALEY, ARTHUR (trans.). 1943. *Monkey*. New York: John Day.

CHAPTER 13

"Tootle": A Modern Cautionary Tale

DAVID RIESMAN

Adapted from The Lonely Crowd, by David Riesman, with the collaboration of Reuel Denney and Nathan Glazer (New Haven: Yale University Press, 1950), pp. 107–11.

IN AN earlier day, American parents and other authorities held out to children certain objective goals: they should get rich, for one thing, or become great scholars or maybe even become president. And parents drove their children toward these goals. The traits of character which mattered were such things as diligence, honesty, and thrift—the injunctions of Ben Franklin's Almanac. If the child delivered the goods according to these reasonably clear criteria, it mattered rather less what he was like as a person; parents neither knew enough to observe his psychological makeup, nor were they very interested in it. As a member of society's work-force, the child would be expected to produce rather than to be a particularly well-adjusted or even happy person. Thus both his character, with its implanted goals, and his situation, as he turned to make his living or his mark, combined to intensify the demands made on him as a producer, while the demands made on him as a person were slight. This gave him a certain freedom to be different, provided he did his work adequately.

What matters about the individual in today's economy is less his capacity to produce than his capacity to be a member of a team. Business and professional success now depends much more than ever before on one's ability to work in a team in far-flung personnel networks; the man who works too hard or in too solitary a way is, by and large, almost as unwelcome in the executive offices, the universities, or the hospitals of urban America as he would be in a union shop. He cannot satisfy society's demands on him simply by being good at his job; he has to be good, but he has also to be co-operative. When translated into child-rearing practices, this means that parents who want their children to get along and to succeed will be quite as concerned with their adjustment in the school group as with their grades or with their industry on an after-school job.

I don't mean to suggest that parents consciously calculate their children's job-chances and train the youngsters accordingly. Rather, the same great and still not fully understood social changes that have altered the nature of attitudes toward work and the worker have also influenced the home (the parents, or at least the father, are also workers), the school, the movies and radio, and other institutions which divide among themselves, in none too friendly a fashion, the tasks of defining the goals for modern children.

These goals are no longer clear-cut. The older goals—such as sheer moneymaking—were often shallow and have been to a considerable degree abandoned. New goals—such as a full and happy life—have not yet had a chance to become more than vague mandates that cannot guide a parent or a child from day to day. Consequently, there is every opportunity for one goal, namely, popularity, to outstrip all others in importance. This is a means of rating the child when there is no other means available. Parents can no longer prefer to have a child who is diligent to a child who is "one of the gang." So parents, too, though perhaps with some misgivings, share the concern with popularity. Unlike their predecessors of the Victorian age, they know—from the teacher, the P.T.A., their own children—what the popularity score is.

Matters would be relatively simple for parent and child if the market demanded complete conformists. Then, at least, expectations would be clear—and rebellion against them equally clear. But matters are not simple. What is expected of children and adults, in the middle and upper educated strata at least, actually *is* difference—but not too much. That is, one must be different enough to attract attention, to *be* a personality, to be labeled and tagged.

Progressive parents, taught for the last several decades to "accept" their children, have learned to welcome a certain amount of rebelliousness or difference. Likewise, business and the professions, especially perhaps in the growing number of fields catering to consumption and leisure, welcome a certain amount of eccentricity, if this goes together with a co-operative team spirit. Thus children often find themselves in the paradoxical position in which their "difference" is simply evidence that they are conventional and up-to-date. Perhaps more important, they are compelled to learn to find their way among exceedingly subtle expectations on the part of others. They are expected both to be spontaneous and not to disrupt the mood of a particular group; to a degree they must conform and yet maintain the personality they have already built up.

And the parents themselves become concerned and anxious, and understandably so, if the child's age mates reject him; they fear his differences are of the wrong sort and perhaps, too, that their differences from their neighbors are of the wrong sort. Are they to defend their child's differences, then, at the cost of his undoubted present and possible future misery?

In this new setting, there seems to have been a definite shift in the attitude toward what books should and do mean to a child. Ever since Lucy Sprague Mitchell started writing the "Here and Now" books, parents and teachers have been told that imaginative books and fairy tales are bad and disturbing; that they may impart false values; that in dealing with princesses and giants they are trivial and unreal. In place of such fare it is said that children should have books that will enlighten them about the world, about reality. Reality turns out to be how things work, how water gets into the bathtub, for instance, or milk onto the doorstep; the human meanness of ogres and stepmothers is definitely not reality.

This whole development assumes that we know more than we do know about the consequences of reading one or another sort of book. There is always an element of indeterminacy in art; in the relation of a reader to a book many things—many unintended things—can and do happen. It seems possible to argue, for instance, that *Huckleberry Finn* is a more serious book on race relations than any of the recent crop, among other reasons because of the artistic ambiguities in the reflections of Huck on the problem of helping Nigger Jim escape. Likewise it seems possible to argue that people need to read less that deals with the present and more that deals with the past and future. The very expense and solidity of the hard-cover book—its quality as furniture—may bear some relation to the long-run timetable of its impact, as compared with those media that cannot as readily be preserved, annotated, reread, or inherited. And among such things it is perhaps precisely the more "escapist" ones which for many can nourish the longer perspectives and the detachments that this country, with its abundant resources of people and goods, can afford even—or especially—in wartime.

True, there is no necessary conflict in principle between the "escape" book which is a craftsmanlike treatment of literary themes and the topical book which is a tract for the times. It follows from what I have said that what is a liberating book for one person may not be so for another—a point often overlooked by those who, nostalgically overestimating the uncorrupted tastes of an earlier day, assume that all those who read good books in the eighteenth century or saw Shakespeare's plays in Elizabethan days found the good things in them. (In her excellent historical study, *Fiction and the Reading Public*,[1] Q. D. Leavis does present some evidence, such as material from letters and diaries as well as analysis of best sellers, to indicate a decline of English taste in the last century and a half, but it is terribly difficult to be sure of any such judgment about a dead audience when we cannot even tell much about a live one.) In *The Road to Xanadu*[2] John Livingston Lowes traced some of the kaleidoscopic influences which had seeped into the mind of Coleridge, but similar detective work has not been done to trace the impact of books in the lifespan of less notable figures. Beyond the well-thumbed indexes of reading by age, sex, and previous condition of social-class servitude, research, I must repeat, can so far tell us very little about the subtle interplays between books of different kinds and people of different kinds. Reading a sheaf of book reviews is evidence enough that any book of moment can be interpreted in a fantastic variety of ways.

I recall, for example, the hue and cry among many parents and teachers, already leery of comics, when the story appeared about the boy who had jumped from an apartment-house window wearing a Superman cloak and been killed. It was naturally assumed that children identify themselves with Superman and with other heroes of the newer media. But a careful study of comics readers[3]—one of the very few sophisticated studies we have of any sort of reader—shows that perhaps the majority of children do *not* identify themselves with Superman or other potent wizards of the comics. The reader's fear of being a sucker; the fear of seeming to make ambitious, envy-arousing claims; the here-and-now interest in aviation coupled with disinterest in imaginative "flying"—all these things may inhibit the child's power and willingness to identify with a fictional hero.

Tootle[4] (text by Gertrude Crampton, pictures by Tibor Gergely) is a popular and in many ways charming volume in the "Little Golden Books" series—a series for children, with a circulation of well over two million, an audience which includes, it seems, all classes of children. It is a cautionary tale, even though it appears to be simply one of the many books about anthropomorphic vehicles—trucks, fire engines, taxicabs, tugboats, and so on—that are supposed to give a child a picture of real life. Tootle is a young engine who goes to engine school, where two main lessons are taught: stop at a red flag and "always stay on the track, no matter what." Diligence in the lessons will result in the young engine's growing up to be a big streamliner. Tootle is obedient for a while and then one day discovers the delight of going off the tracks and finding flowers in the field. This violation of the rules cannot, however, be kept secret; there are telltale traces in the cowcatcher. Nevertheless, Tootle's play becomes more and more of a craving, and, despite warnings, he continues to go off the tracks and wander in the field. Finally, the engine schoolmaster is desperate. He consults the mayor of the little town of Engineville, in which the school is located; the mayor calls a town meeting, and Tootle's failings are discussed—of course, Tootle knows nothing of this. The meeting decides on a course of action, and the next time Tootle goes out for a spin alone and goes off the track, he runs right into a red flag and halts. He turns in another direction only to encounter another red flag; still another—the result is the same. He turns and twists but can find no spot of grass in which a red flag does not spring up, for all the citizens of the town have co-operated in this lesson.

Chastened and bewildered, he looks toward the track, where the inviting green flag of his teacher gives him the signal to return. Confused by conditioned reflexes to stop signs, he is only too glad to use the track and tears happily up and down. He promises that he will never leave the track again, and he returns to the roundhouse to be rewarded by the cheers of the teachers and the citizenry and by the assurance that he will indeed grow up to be a streamliner.

The story is an all too appropriate one for bringing up children in today's society. They learn that it is bad to go off the tracks and play with flowers and that, in the long run, there is not only success and approval but even freedom to be found in following the green lights. The moral is a very different one from that of *Little Red Riding Hood*. She, too, gets off the track on her trip to the grandmother; she is taught by a wolf about the beauties of nature—a hardly veiled symbol for sex. Then, to be sure, she is eaten—a terrifying fate—but the tables are eventually turned, and she and grandmother both are taken from the wolf's belly by the handsome woodchopper. The story, though it may be read as a cautionary tale, deals with real human passions, sexual and aggressive; it certainly does not present the rewards of virtue in any unambiguous form or show the adult world in any wholly benevolent light. It is, therefore, essentially realistic, underneath the cover of fantasy, or, more accurately, owing to the *quality* of the fantasy.

There is, perhaps, a streak of similar realism in *Tootle*. There the adults manipulate the child into conformity with the peer group and then reward him for the behavior for which they have already set the stage. Moreover, the citizens of Engineville are tolerant of Tootle; they understand and do not get indignant. And while they gang up on him with red flags, they do so for his benefit, and they reward him for his obedience as if they had played no part in bringing it about. The whole story, in fact, might have been written by a student of learning theory, so palpably does it deal in terms of conditioned responses.

Yet with all that, there is something overvarnished in this tale. The adult world (the teachers) is *not* that benevolent, the citizenry (the peer group) *not* that participative and co-operative, the signals are *not* that clear, nor the rewards of being a streamliner that great or that certain. Nevertheless, the child may be impressed because it is all so nice—there is none of the grimness of *Red Riding Hood*. There is, therefore, a swindle about the whole thing—a fake like that which the citizens put on for Tootle's benefit. At the end Tootle has forgotten that he ever did like flowers anyway—how childish they are in comparison with the great big grown-up world of engines, signals, tracks, and meetings!

While the antagonistic and rebellious elements may be veiled in a folk tale, the children who read *Tootle* or have it read to them are manipulated away from rebellion and taught the lesson of obedience to signals. Strikingly enough, moreover, the story also bears on one principal topic of peer-group co-operation: the exercise of consumption preferences. Those middle-class children who read the tale are not going to grow up to be railroad engineers; that is a craft followed by more old-fashioned types from the working class. But, while neither *Tootle* nor its readers are concerned about what it really means to be an engineer, the book does confirm one of the consumption preferences of today: big streamliners—if one cannot go by plane—are better than old coal-burning engines.[5] To be sure, *Tootle* has something to teach about train lore. It indicates that there are tracks, signals, round-houses, just as fairy tales indicate that there are forests, woodchoppers, wolves. On the whole, however, children are attuned to the magic of travel, of communications, not in an adventurous way but in what educators are pleased to call a "realistic" one.

More impalpably, the humanized grimacing engines in *Tootle* symbolize the effort characteristic of contemporary society to cover over the impersonal mechanisms of production and transport with a personalized veneer—what we might term "false personalization." For there is sufficient abundance not only for the luxuriant growth of service trades per se but for allowing even the nonservice trades to deliver "service with a smile." Today the conductors on Vanderbilt's old railroad are trained on the Twentieth Century Limited and other major runs to remember faces and give service "especially for you." The very books, such as *Tootle* or *Scuffy the Tugboat*,[6] by the same writer and illustrator, that are intended to acquaint children with the objects and forces of the industrial society, turn out to condition them to their role in the "consumer's union."

We come, finally, to the theme of winning. Tootle does, after all, win; with his winning ways he will grow up to be a big streamliner. The reader's identification with the consumption of others' winnings is, therefore, not betrayed. But it is not made clear in the story what happens to Tootle's schoolmates in engine school. Do they *all* grow up to be streamliners, too? The peer-group relations of Tootle, either to the other engines or the other citizens of Engineville, are entirely amiable, and Tootle's winning does not mean that others fail. It is akin to the "benevolent conspiracy" of progressive parents and teachers, who see to it that every child is a leader and that no one is left out or conspicuous, thus reinforcing the tendencies toward "antagonistic co-operation" of the peer group itself. Who can be sure that Tootle would want to be a streamliner if others were not to be streamliners too?

If this were all, we would have to conclude that the peer group, as one of the mediating agencies in child readership and listening, is simply open to manipulation by the professional storytellers. But I want to raise very briefly the alternative possibility: namely, that the peer group may have a relatively independent set of criteria which helps it maintain not only marginal differentiation but even a certain leeway in relation to the media. Put the question this way: While the self-confirming process of the peer group pushes preference exchange to the point of parody, has the peer group any way of reminding its captives that they are, also, individuals?

We must go further and ask whether there may be areas of privacy which children learn to find inside a superficial adjustment to the peer group and under the cover of a superficial permeability to the mass media and to such stories as *Tootle*. In other words, we must re-explore the assumption made so far that the child is almost never alone, that by six or seven he no longer talks to himself, invents songs, or dreams unsupervised dreams.

NOTES

1. Leavis, 1932.
2. Lowes, 1930.
3. Wolf and Fiske, 1948–49.
4. Crampton, 1945.
5. This preference is so strong that it influences directorates of railroads in coal-mining territory, concerned not only with public relations but with their own feeling for their road. A fine study could be made of railroad management's belated conversion to glamour, and the influence on this of the development of a new generation of consumers—more eager to be told that their conveyance is up to date than to be comfortable—or, more accurately, eager to be *told* they are comfortable.
6. Crampton, 1947.

LIST OF REFERENCES

CRAMPTON, GERTRUDE. 1945. *Tootle* (*Story of a Locomotive*). ("Little Golden Books," No. 21.) New York: Simon & Schuster.

———. 1947. *Scuffy the Tugboat.* ("Little Golden Books," No. 30.) New York: Simon & Schuster.

LEAVIS, Q. D. 1932. *Fiction and the Reading Public.* London: Chatto & Windus.

LOWES, JOHN LIVINGSTON. 1930. *The Road to Xanadu.* Boston: Houghton Mifflin Co.

WOLF, KATHERINE M., and FISKE, MARJORIE. 1948–49. "The Children Talk about Comics." In *Communications Research*, ed. PAUL F. LAZARSFELD and FRANK N. STANTON, pp. 3–50. New York: Harper & Bros.

CHAPTER 14

"Jack and the Beanstalk": An
American Version

————Martha Wolfenstein

I am indebted to Sylvia Brody for her compilation and classification of variants of this story.

Jack and the Beanstalk" is a variant of a widespread folklore theme: the boy who steals the giant's treasure. The occurrence of the beanstalk as the means by which the boy attains his purpose is a distinctive English invention.[1] Tales of English origin have become a part of American folklore. While these tales retain many of their original elements, they have to some extent been transformed. If we take the version of "Jack and the Bean Tree" as told in the mountains of North Carolina and as recorded by Richard Chase, we can see how the English tale has been modified to assume a characteristic American flavor.[2]

The main outline of the plot remains: there is the wonderful beanstalk which Jack climbs, the giant and his wife, the danger of being eaten by the giant, the wife's hiding of Jack, Jack's three thefts of the giant's belongings, the eventual chase, Jack's chopping down of the beanstalk, and the giant's fatal fall. As to the variations, we may note first that the English version begins with the dire poverty of Jack and his mother, the mother's unhappiness, and some reproach against Jack, who is spoiled or lazy or cannot hold a job or who has carelessly exhausted the family substance.[3] This reproach against Jack, who makes his poor mother suffer, is intensified when he makes the apparently foolish bargain with the man who trades him a handful of beans for the cow. The mother is in despair and enraged against Jack, and the boy then frees himself of this burden of guilt by his heroic feats and the gifts which he brings the mother.

In the American tale Jack is a small boy running at his mother's heels while she is trying to clean the house. She sweeps up a big bean and, to keep the boy occupied, tells him to go out and plant it. Next day Jack finds the beanstalk already knee-high, the second day as high as a tree, and the third day grown out of sight. Each time he tells his mother about this remarkable growth, and each time she slaps him for telling lies. This is followed by her confirming each time that he has told the truth and making it up to him by giving him something good to eat. Thus, instead of Jack's being in the wrong, he is falsely accused by the mother. This sequence embodies a major theme of American fantasy in which the hero (or heroine), while innocent, may appear guilty and have to clear himself of false suspicions rather than redeem himself from sin. Comparison of American and British films has shown this tendency to substitute conflict between the hero (or heroine) and false accusers for the inner conflict in which the protagonist struggles with self-accusations.[4]

Another aspect of the American version is that of the little boy exhibiting the marvelous growth of his bean tree to his mother. The beanstalk generally may be taken to have a phallic significance: it is a possession of the boy's which has extraordinary erectile powers. In the episode peculiar to the American version, Jack boasts to his mother about the springing-up of his bean tree and gets first a rebuke and then a reward. There is the fantasy here that the mother will welcome and admire the little boy's phallic showing-off, that her scolding for it may give way to affectionate acceptance. In the English tale Jack uses the beanstalk to obtain presents for his mother; the American emphasis is more on masculine exhibition.

The things Jack steals from the giant are also different in the American and English versions. Instead of the moneybags and the hen that lays the golden eggs, the American Jack steals a gun and a knife. These are again symbols of masculine prowess, and they are things that the boy can play around with to amuse himself. "Well, he played around with that knife a right smart while." There is not the element of giving something to the mother but of the boy's winning male accouterments for himself. The theme of giving and getting is considerably played down in comparison with the English version. Thus, also, the exchange of the cow for the beans does not occur here. The things the American Jack takes differ in another way from the English Jack's booty. They are not magical sources of supply, like the hen that lays the golden eggs, in relation to which the possessor can assume a passively receptive attitude. They are rather tools with which the owner can, by the active exercise of skill, do something. While a gun and a knife may have associations of magical power for a small boy, as manifestly presented in the story these objects are nonmagical.

The third thing which the American Jack steals is the "coverlid on the old giant's bed [that] had little bells sewed all over it." This jingling coverlid is the equivalent of the harp that plays by itself. Both may stand for the strange sounds which the child hears in the night and which he takes as signs of his father's sexual prowess. The American Jack, in snatching the coverlid off the giant's bed, boldly exposes and mocks his antagonist. There is an analogy here to another of the "Jack Tales," in which Jack crowns a series of ingenious feats of robbery by stealing the shimmy off the back of the rich man's wife after she has retired for the night.[5] There is an emphasis here on male rivalry, not so much for the woman's favors as to discomfit and outdo a rival of big pretensions.

The English version, with its emphasis on giving and getting, its golden treasures and magical sources of supply, as well as the theme of a boy making things up to a mother whom he has made to suffer, has many more prephallic components than the American one. The latter takes the springing bean tree more as the dominant theme and, in keeping with this, provides other elements of masculine prowess: showing off to mother, getting a gun and a knife. The American tale ends: "And the last time I was down there Jack was gettin' to be a right big boy, and he was doin' well." Thus the concluding image is that of the boy growing to be fine and big, after the model of the springing bean tree.

NOTES

1. Chase, 1943. Notes on parallels to "Jack and the Bean Tree," p. 190.
2. The "Jack Tales," which Chase (1943) recorded in the 1930's, had been transmitted by oral tradition among the inhabitants of the mountains of western North Carolina, elsewhere in the southern mountains, and in parts of Virginia. Chase's informants acknowledged as the major source of their tales an admired storyteller of their region, Council Harmon, who lived from 1803 to 1896.
3. Joseph Jacobs' version of "Jack and the Beanstalk," in his *English Fairy Tales*, first published in 1890, is the best known. Jacobs recorded the tale as he recalled having heard it when he was a boy in Australia. The reproach against Jack as a boy who was unable to hold a job appears in this version. Variants of this theme, in which Jack is described as lazy, a dreamer, spoiled, extravagant, and so on, occur in the following: Tennyson, 1886; Cruikshank, 1911; Scudder, 1919; Craik, 1923; Steele, 1924; De la Mare, 1927.
4. Wolfenstein and Leites, 1950.
5. Chase, 1943, pp. 195–97.

LIST OF REFERENCES

CHASE, RICHARD (ed.). 1943. *The Jack Tales as Told by R. M. Ward.* Boston: Houghton Mifflin Co.

CRAIK, DINAH MARIA (Mulock). 1923. *The Fairy Book.* New York: Macmillan Co.

CRUIKSHANK, GEORGE. 1911. *The Cruikshank Fairy Book.* New York: G. P. Putnam's Sons.

DE LA MARE, WALTER. 1927. *Told Again.* New York: A. A. Knopf.

JACOBS, JOSEPH. 1898. *English Fairy Tales.* 3d ed. rev. New York: G. P. Putnam.

SCUDDER, HORACE E. 1919. *The Book of Fables and Folk Stories.* New Illustrated ed. New York: Houghton Mifflin Co.

STEELE, MRS. FLORA ANNIE (Webster). 1924. *English Fairy Tales Retold by Flora Annie Steele.* New York: Macmillan Co.

TENNYSON, HALLAM. 1886. *Jack and the Beanstalk, in English Hexameters.* London and New York: Macmillan Co.

WOLFENSTEIN, MARTHA, and LEITES, NATHAN. 1950. *Movies: A Psychological Study.* Glencoe, Ill.: Free Press.

CHAPTER 15

"Monkey": A Chinese Children's Classic

This study has been selected and edited by the editors of the present volume from a more extensive unpublished essay on Chinese children's literature, which was prepared by a Chinese anthropologist as part of a study on Chinese culture under the direction of Ruth Bunzel, in the Columbia University project, Research in Contemporary Cultures, under a grant from the Human Resources Division, Office of Naval Research.

THOUGH not originally written for children, Monkey[1] has for long been the favorite book of Chinese children from six to ten, an age when belief in magic is particularly strong. The novel is based on an actual historical event: the journey of the monk Hsuan-chuang to India, during the Tang Dynasty, to obtain the Buddhist scriptures—but it is a folkloristic account, far different from the realistic record left by the monk himself.

Monkey is of supernatural origin, yet his character is quite humanly aggressive and assertive. He is extremely self-confident, fearless, and reckless, with a strong urge for activity. He is also very frank in stating his opinions and uninhibited when speaking to his superiors, since he has no sense of status difference or of behavior adjusted to status difference, and, least of all, of "face" (*mien-tzu*). Being highly intelligent, he manages very early in his existence to equip himself with all the powers necessary to assure him victory in any kind of struggle. He is very proud of his superior physical and mental abilities, which he believes entitle him to a dominant position in the universe. His sense of justice and fairness is based upon this belief.

Monkey has an insatiable desire for prestige and power. He has little difficulty in winning the allegiance of the little monkeys who inhabit his native mountains or in fightng the hordes of animal spirits that beset them and reducing them to submission. But when he ventures outside his native territory in search of greater conquests, he comes into conflict with the paternal authority that controls the universe. This authority is represented by the three father-figures with whom Monkey has to contend at various times in his life: Buddha Tathagata, the supreme ruler of the universe; the Jade Emperor, the ruler of the heavens; and the saintly monk Hsuan-chuang, who is known in the story as Tripitaka. The Jade Emperor, who stands at the apex of the hierarchy that controls both heaven and the invisible side of the world (known as *ying*), refuses to recognize Monkey's claim to a dominant place in his court but, in order to appease him, confers upon him a minor title, which is represented to Monkey as very high-sounding. Monkey sees through the deception and is infuriated by it; he returns to heaven with the intention of wrecking it. There he engages in battle with the warriors of the Jade Emperor, who, when they find they cannot control him, appeal to Buddha Tathagata for aid. But Monkey is not intimidated even by the supreme ruler of the universe. Buddha Tathagata finds it necessary to put Monkey in his proper place by disciplining him; he imprisons him under a mountain for five hundred years.

Monkey is released from his imprisonment through the intervention of Kuan-yin, the goddess of mercy, who urges him to repent and offers him a means of redemption by assigning him the mission of guarding the monk Tripitaka on his journey to the Western Heavens to obtain the holy scriptures from Tathagata. Tripitaka is the third father-figure. He is a virtuous and learned man, but he lacks physical prowess and does not know how to deal with the practical problems they meet on their journey. He is concerned solely with the salvation of the soul. For this reason, he insists that Monkey observe the moral code of a good Buddhist, which Monkey finds so distasteful that he deserts his master. Although he has nothing but contempt for the good monk, Kuan-yin persuades him to return and furnishes Tripitaka with a magic spell by means of which Monkey can be controlled. Monkey is thus forced to remain on the path to salvation, and in time he even learns to appreciate his master's unswerving devotion to his purpose.

Kuan-yin is the ideal mother-figure. All creatures look to her for salvation. She has great patience with Monkey and is able to persuade him to resume his task when he wants to give it up. She has so firmly convinced him she has only his salvation at heart that he never harbors any resentment against her, even when she gives Tripitaka the spell to control him or deliberately places obstacles in the pilgrims' path. Whenever he meets with insurmountable difficulties, his first thought is of Kuan-yin, and he immediately somersaults through the heavens to her abode in the South Seas to seek her aid. The narrative leaves no doubt of the fact that, of Tripitaka's three disciples, all of whom have sins to redeem, Monkey is Kuan-yin's favorite, even though he is the worst offender against the authority of heaven. It should be noted that the goddess Kuan-yin not only is depicted as the succoring mother-surrogate; she is also pictured as a young and charming woman.

The plot of the narrative dramatizes the conflict of the child with paternal authority, an authority that is exercised by virtue of the father's position in a well-ordered social structure. The child, in so far as he resembles Monkey, believes that his own aggressiveness entitles him to a high place in his social world. Only after he has suffered severe frustration does he learn that in order to merit the acknowledgment of his elders, he must modify his aggressiveness in such a way that it can be utilized for the benefit of the family.

The age period of six to ten is an important stage in the socialization process of the individual. From interviews with Chinese informants, it appears that Chinese children experience great difficulties at this time. It is the time when, following the comparatively great permissiveness and constant attention of the early years of his life, the child is suddenly weaned from the care of his mother, or mother-surrogate, and placed under the tutelage of his father or a father-surrogate. Usually, the father-surrogate (e.g., a teacher) is preferred because it reduces the possibility of conflict with the father. Thus, in conformity with this pattern, Monkey has very little contact with either Buddha Tathagata or the Jade Emperor; he earns his redemption by following Tripitaka.

It is generally agreed among Chinese that children of this age group, and boys in particular, are difficult to handle. They have a strong repressed hostility toward adults, which manifests itself in avoidance of contact with grownups and, above all, in resentment against interference in their affairs. They are exceedingly active, whereas adults like quiet, sedate behavior; they often get themselves into dangerous situations, which is highly resented by their parents, since the bodies of the children belong to the families and must be shielded from harm; and very frequently they perpetrate mischief which seems wholly meaningless to the adult. It is apparent from this how closely the character of the child resembles that of Monkey and how effective it must appear to the child to punish Monkey by immobilizing him for a long time.

In this usually unexpressed conflict with paternal authority, the mother plays an important role, urging the boy in his own interest to accept the values and attitudes which the father (or father-surrogate) prizes, in order that he may gradually earn the attention and appreciation of the grown-up world, which as a baby he received without effort. She does not shield him from punishment; indeed, she will on occasion punish him herself. Nor does she suppress his natural tendencies; rather she encourages and helps him, through moral support, guiding him as Kuan-yin guides Monkey in the use of his own resources in order that he may attain his goal.

Of Tripitaka's other two disciples, the most original figure is Pigsy, whose character is the very opposite of Monkey's. As his name implies, he is a pig by nature. He is slow and sluggish in mind and body, has an inordinate love of food and sleep, and cannot resist any female. Many times on their journey, Pigsy falls prey to the wiles of some female evil spirit, bringing himself and his companions to the brink of destruction. Monkey is able to recognize the aura of evil spirits, but Pigsy always falls into their traps. Pigsy is a caricature of the man who lives for his appetites. Monkey will also gorge himself on occasion, but only for a real purpose, as, when he discovers that the Jade Emperor has neglected to invite him to a feast, he steals all the peaches of long life from the garden of the Empress-Mother. The Chinese commentator remarks, and with good reason, that Monkey symbolizes the mind of man, and Pigsy his carnal appetites. Monkey can be guided along the road of higher achievement because he has intelligence and ambition, but Pigsy has neither the mental capacity nor the steadfastness of purpose to enable him to achieve salvation without constant exhortation.

The relationship between Monkey and Pigsy, with its constant teasing and heckling, is reminiscent of that between siblings. There is considerable rivalry between them; Pigsy often tries to arouse their master's anger against Monkey. But despite the inconveniences and additional work which Pigsy creates for him, Monkey is forced to accept his brother-disciple in much the same way as the child must learn to accept younger siblings as part of the we-group.

The females in this narrative are of two types: the succoring mother-surrogate as symbolized in the goddess Kuan-yin and the lewd female spirit who tries to tempt Tripitaka with her charms in order to bring him into her power. Evil spirits often pose as alluring young girls and try to play on Tripitaka's emotions. Monkey, who has no licentiousness in his character and who has had experiences with the spirit world, always recognizes the tricks of the evil spirits and tries to warn Tripitaka and Pigsy against them. But his words always fall on deaf ears. Time and again, one or the other of them falls into a trap, and Monkey has to extricate their entire party. This is often a very difficult task, since some of these evil spirits possess strong magic powers. The Princess of the Iron-Fan, for example, can start a fire with her fan at a moment's notice. When she obstructs the pilgrims' path with one of her fires, Monkey makes three fruitless attempts to quench it, and only by posing as her husband is he finally able to defeat her and put out the fire. The sexual implications of this incident are quite clear. Sex is described as a powerful weapon with which to capture a man; an intelligent man avoids such dangers.[2]

The narrative also contains a great deal of information on attitudes toward the body. Monkey commands in his body good resources for implementing his aggressiveness. He is familiar with both the every-day world in which mortals live and the world of spirits and divinities. His aggressiveness has won him such widespread fame that all spirits have heard of him—a reputation which proves very useful, since he often has occasion in the course of the journey to seek the assistance of some divinity in extricating his party from some difficulty. And the good spirits, who formerly feared him as a creature of boundless vio-lence, are now willing to help him, since his mission is one of high purpose.

Monkey has the capacity to see beings of the other world that are hidden from the eyes of ordinary mortals. His master usually disbe-lieves him when he insists that there is an aura of evil spirits around a certain place, but it alway turns out that Monkey was right. This power of detection by the eye exemplifies a recurrent theme of Chinese fantasy.

Monkey achieves immortality early in his life by training under a teacher, then strengthens it by eating the peaches of long life from the Empress-Mother's garden and the pills of long life of the Heavenly Alchemist. In addition, when he is pushed into the stove of the Heav-enly Alchemist, his body hardens to a metal-like consistency and be-comes indestructible. Through these various means, he has made his body impervious to attack. He loves to show off this indestructibility in engagements with his enemies by permitting them to pound on his head.

His companions are not so fortunate; they are, on the contrary, ex-tremely vulnerable. All along the way they are preyed upon by spirits who have learned that, by devouring the pilgrims, they will attain im-mortality in the flesh. We find expressed in this an anxiety concerning the destructibility of the body—an anxiety which led to the search of the "pill of long life" by alchemists. Chinese folklore contains innu-merable stories and legends of priests and recluses who attained im-mortal life in the flesh. It is significant that in *Monkey* there is hardly any mention of the world of the dead. The fear is not for what will happen to the soul after death, but that body and soul may be sep-arated.

Monkey's body is capable of taking on any shape at a moment's no-tice; even the hairs of his body can be transformed at will into any-thing he desires. By plucking a handful of hair from his body, he is able to conjure up a horde of little monkeys equipped with weapons, with which he can rout the enemy he happens to be fighting. A hair can serve as a good substitute for any magical weapon he takes from his enemy; and after they have served their purpose, the hairs can be taken back and restored to the body. Monkey's chief weapon is a cudgel of enormous weight which can be expanded or shrunk to any size he desires. Habitually, it is carried in his ear, thus forming a part of his body. In all these fantasies of conflict, the hero's own body furnishes him with all the necessary instruments. It is all-powerful in defense as well as in offense.

Yet, although he has been able to render his body as resistant as rock or metal, Monkey still has fears of being destroyed. This danger is closely allied to orality. Only one type of magic instrument can destroy him, and it brings him very close to annihilation. This is a container in the shape of a gourd, vase, or bag, which has the capacity of sucking in any creature and causing it to disintegrate. The gourd is a favorite symbol of the Taoist immortal, and many stories tell of evil spirits that were defeated by this means. The shape is that of the human body without the limbs, for the gourd or vase has a constricted neck, a small head, and a big belly. Its potency is analogous to that of the human body in digesting food, except that it is much magnified. When Monkey happens to be sucked into the gourd, he is really frightened, for he fears his body will disintegrate before he has been able to find a way of getting out. This emphasis on sucking and digesting is apparently a memory of the nursing stage in the life of the young individual, which in China frequently lasts for two years and even three or four years. At this age the child has become conscious of his own will and his ability to manipulate his environment. The breast is the first property he can command, and he commands it through sucking. When the aggressiveness of the child of six to ten grows intense, it is very likely that guilt feelings arouse in him the image of a sucking body bent on destroying him.

We have seen that orality is the chief danger confronting the pilgrims. The animal spirits are eager to absorb the substance of their bodies, because the pilgrims have attained a certain degree of sanctity which permits their bodies to impart immortality. In fact, on several occasions, Tripitaka and his disciples are actually on the verge of being cooked before they are rescued.

Orality likewise furnishes Monkey with his most potent weapon. If he finds himself unable to defeat an evil spirit in open combat, he will assume a form that will make it easy for the enemy to swallow him. Then he will attack the enemy from the inside. The excruciating pain which Monkey inflicts by tugging at his victim's heart, liver, entrails, etc., and, in the case of a female spirit, by tramping on her womb immediately reduces the enemy to abject submission. The inside of the body can thus be very potent in destroying an enemy and can also be the most vulnerable spot for attack.

Monkey, the favorite story of Chinese children between the ages of six and ten, presents a grandiose counterpart to their own life-situation. The child of six to ten is assertive, very active, and proud of the physical skills he has mastered, but he finds himself severely frustrated by parental authority. Inwardly, if not outwardly, he rebels against the entire adult world. The only one who understands him at this stage is his mother, who protects him from frequent encounters with the supreme paternal authority and shows him how he can achieve the recognition he craves from his father. The father-surrogate, the teacher, with whom she provides him does not conform to his idea of a capable person, but he has the responsibility of inculcating in him an appreciation of adult values which will help him to attain maturity. At this stage, also, oral aggression is the cause of considerable anxiety.

Monkey's aggressiveness is, above all, a means of self-assertion. There are three father-figures in *Monkey:* the supreme father who punishes, the Jade Emperor who withholds recognition, and the teacher whose authority is derived from the mother-surrogate. In the second part of the book, Monkey learns that physical violence per se does not receive applause, but, when employed in the service of the group, it may lead to salvation, i.e., to a status close to that of the supreme father.

NOTES

1. In the original: *Hsi-Yu-Chi*, by Wu Ch'en-en. There is a good translation by Arthur Waley (1942), but unfortunately it includes only thirty out of the one hundred chapters of the original text, and many of the most significant episodes have been omitted.

2. Cf. Heyer and Muensterberger, 1948.

LIST OF REFERENCES

Heyer, Virginia, and Muensterberger, Warner. 1948. "A Character Analysis of Chinese Men from a Thematic Study of Folk and Literary Tales." Columbia University Research in Contemporary Cultures (unpublished).

Waley, Arthur (trans.). 1942. *Hsi-Yu-Chi*. London: Allen & Unwin.

CHAPTER 16

A Portrait of the Family in German Juvenile Fiction

RHODA MÉTRAUX

This chapter was prepared in 1953 as part of a study of German national character, made in collaboration with Nelly Schargo Hoyt, under the auspices of the American Museum of Natural History ("Studies in Contemporary Cultures, B," conducted under a contract with the Office of Naval Research). The writer is indebted to Dr. Hoyt for insights of importance in this paper (cf. Métraux and Hoyt, 1953).

THIS portrait of the German family is based on an analysis of novels about home and school written between 1880 and 1939 and read in Germany today.[1] These novels about familiar life, which purport to be accounts of the experiences of young heroes and heroines not too different from the readers themselves, are but one of several types of fiction popular among German adolescents.[2] A contrasting type, read by girls as well as boys, is the adventure story in which the hero, usually a solitary figure, struggles to ultimate fame and glory in countries far from home.[3] In the adventure story the exotic setting—the desert, the jungle, some vast unexplored area—is itself a chief attraction. Younger children are given folk and fairy tales and nature fantasies, as well as stories about everyday life; older readers may turn to more serious folklore, legends, and epics. Still other books, some read by younger and others by older readers, are cautionary tales or give a comic or satiric view of the world; *Der Struwwelpeter* and *O diese Kinder* are classic examples. In addition, there are the great works of fiction, such as Schiller's *Wallenstein* and some translations of foreign classics, which have been familiar to generations of readers. Thus the novel of familiar life is but one of the sources on which the young German can draw for his interpretations of personal relationships and for his imaginative comprehension of the world about him, and this study analyzes but one type of available imagery.

The novels discussed here are generally known. The older stories have been read since well before World War I, the newer ones by readers who grew up during the latter part of the Weimar Republic and during the Nazi regime, as well as by readers now growing up. The audience for some types of stories has altered somewhat over time.

A recent survey[4] indicates that the "young girl's book" (the novel of family life) is nowadays read more by younger readers than formerly, and reaches the height of its popularity among readers eleven and twelve years old. Some of the others—the novels by Speyer and some by Kästner—are read by boys and girls in their early teens.

Most of these novels are intended not only to entertain but also to instruct their youthful audience and perhaps, indirectly, adults too. Some are intended for family reading. Thus Agnes Sapper's books are described in a recent jacket blurb: "These agreeable stories are of high educational value; may they continue to find their way into every German family." Sapper herself, in the original dedication of *Die Familie Pfäffling* to her mother, refers to her didactic intention:

You have shown us what a blessing accompanies throughout life those people who have grown up in a large circle of brothers and sisters and in simple circumstances under the influence of parents who, with trust in God and in a joyous frame of mind, have understood how to do without the things that were denied to them. . . . I would like to present not your family but one animated by the same spirit in this book about the German family.[5]

In the Foreword to a later edition, Sapper hopes that this book and its sequel will find their way "to all those who have an understanding of genuine German family life." In a somewhat similar mood Schumacher addresses her readers at the conclusion of *Das Turm-Engele*:

I think you will have learned one thing from this story—that true happiness does not consist in [having] beauty, riches and a life without worry and least of all in pretending to be more than one is. When one is young, one does not quite believe that, but older people can at once differentiate between genuine and ungenuine people.[6]

Most of the novels present highly idealized and moral versions of family life and of the problems set for and solved by the young heroes and heroines, whose experiences—whether during some crucial period in their development or throughout a long life depicted from early childhood to grandparenthood—are central to the plots. The ideal of family life alters little in over fifty years of story-writing. The differences between the earlier versions of family life (e.g., *Das Turm-Engele*, the stories of the Pfäffling family, the Wildfang series) and the later ones (e.g., the Nesthäkchen and the Trotzkopf series) are rather in the explicitness with which the ideal is stated, in the means by which the ideal life is to be attained, and (particularly in Kästner's stories) in the recognition of adult, especially parental, fallibility. This is reflected to some extent in the authors' conceptions of the relation between the real and the ideal.

Sapper, in the Foreword already quoted, written at the turn of the century, intimates that the ideal German Pfäffling family was based on reality. Ury, writing somewhat later, plays between fiction and reality when, in the conclusion to *Nesthäkchen und ihre Küken,* she writes:

> Yes, my Nesthäkchen lives. She lives wherever a child is the sunshine of a harmonious parental home. Where a grannie mirrors herself in her grandchild. Where warmhearted friendships live on through childhood and adolescence. Wherever one works and strives, wherever one wins the produce of the German home-earth, in the city and the country, wherever anyone spreads happiness and joy in his own home. Everywhere there my Nesthäkchen is at home.[7]

Kästner, writing in the 1920's and 1930's, insists that his fiction is fiction—as when he gives a fanciful account of how *Das fliegende Klassenzimmer* came to be written or intersperses the telling of the story of *Pünktchen und Anton* with chapters of author's comments; or that the reality of his fiction has not yet been achieved—as when, in *Pünktchen und Anton,* he comments on the happy ending:

> Now you could perhaps conclude that things in life come out as justly as in this book. That would be a fatal mistake. It ought to be so, and all reasonable people take pains to have it so. But it is not so. It is not so yet.
> We once had a school companion who regularly denounced his neighbors. Do you think he was punished? No, the neighbor whom he denounced was punished. Do not be surprised if in life you are sometimes punished for the crimes of others. See to it, when you are grown up, that things are better. We ourselves have not quite achieved it. Become more decent, more honest, more just and reasonable than most of us are.[8]

Thus the ideal of the novels alters over time from one which is believed to be based on the behavior of living people to one which living people, fallible as they are, might achieve if they learned to behave well.

Yet in these juvenile novels it is not so much values that alter over time as the recognition and acceptance—in the world of fiction and, by implication, in reality—of adult behavior that is less than the ideal. This is particularly well illustrated by changing attitudes toward adult fallibility.

Stinde, in *Die Familie Buchholz,* a family novel written in the 1880's for an *adult* audience, counterpoints the solemnity of popular contemporary novelists (e.g., the nineteenth-century *Gartenlaube* writers)[9] in his humorous presentation of a naturally clever but fallible mother. Yet he, no less than other contemporary writers for adults or the authors of earnest and sentimental didactic stories for children (of which Schanz's *In der Feierstunde* is a minor example), values the family as the center of life and emphasizes the importance of family training for the attainment of good character. Likewise, Kästner, writing for a *child* audience in the 1920's and 1930's, mocks the straightforward seriousness of slightly earlier juvenile writers, but he, too—taking fallibility as one theme—supports and re-creates their

values. In the 1880's, a writer could convey to adults—through humor—
the idea that good parents are fallible (though, being of good character, they could bring up satisfactory children); in the 1920's, a
writer could convey to children—through humor—the idea that adults
are fallible (but that, nevertheless, they could help one to grow up
to have a good character). Speyer in a sense begs the question, in
that in his books the adult authoritative figures remain in the shadows
until they step forward to recognize the children exhibiting their own
solutions to moral problems.

Spanning the period between Stinde, on the one hand, and Kästner
and Speyer, on the other, authors of juvenile novels such as Haarbeck,
Sapper, Schumacher, and Ury, describe families who are patterns of
perfection, at least in the older generation. In these novels the shift
from infallibility to fallibility takes place as the fictional children grow
up and in turn become parents. Here the shift is internal to the stories:
the authors indicate that the heroes and heroines (with whom the
young readers are meant to identify) are fallible as children and later
as adults—but still are mainly good people and have good children
themselves.

In most of the stories the families portrayed are middle class; some
are well to do, others are poor and struggling. Most are professional
families in modest circumstances. The father in the Buchholz family
is a small businessman; Turm-Engele's father is a worthy bell-ringer
in a small town; the Pfäffling father is a struggling music teacher who
becomes the respected director of a music school; in the Wildfang and
Nesthäkchen series the fathers are doctors, one in a small town, the
other in Berlin; the father in *Gunhild die Reiterin* (the scene of which
is laid in Norway) is a small landowner. The children likewise grow
up to become teachers, nurses, doctors, lawyers, engineers, pioneer
farmers in Africa, estate owners, etc.—sometimes slightly improving
on their parents' positions but, in general, remaining well within the
"good middle-class" orbit in which they grew up. And, like their parents, most become the parents of a new generation.

The stories focus upon the life of the family to the exclusion of
most other events. The boundaries of the story world are at their
widest when an author (e.g., Wildhagen) apostrophizes *German*
youth in the person of a little boy who dares not own up to a misdeed,
or when an author (e.g., Sapper) invokes the unique *German* Christmas. Where home (*die Heimat*) is concerned, the boundaries narrow
to the scene visible from the windows of the parental house. In the
Introduction to *Die Familie Buchholz,* Stinde sets the essential scene:

> Whoever is interested in knowing about intimate family life in the soli-
> tude of a great city [Berlin] will participate in the worries and joys of Frau
> Wilhelmine and will regard her letters [the book is written as a series of let-

ters to the editor of a newspaper] as sketches of the life of the capital city, which consists not only of asphalt streets and long rows of houses but also of many, many homes, the doors of which remain closed to strangers.[10]

The two boundaries come together when, as often happens, a family is referred to as "the German family."[11]

Sometimes in these stories we are given the name of the city or town where the family lives, sometimes only its general location, e.g., "a small town in southern Germany." Sometimes we are given definite, though incidental, clues to the period when the story takes place, as when the author of *Nesthäkchen und ihre Küken* explains: "Each one had his own worries. In the bitterly expensive period that followed on the world war, it was not easy for a young doctor to found his own hearth."[12] Even so, we can only place this story in the late 1920's because we already know (from earlier volumes) that Nesthäkchen was a schoolgirl in the immediate postwar period. In other stories the reader can infer period and the passing of time only from minor details. So in Haarbeck's Wildfang series the father first goes out on calls in his carriage, and later, when the children are grown up, someone has a car. In Speyer's *Kampf der Tertia* the children chew gum (an American importation)—a detail referred to several times by German informants as something that impressed them when they read this book in the late 1920's—and there are cars and motorcycles, and one boy has a flier hero. As the heroes and heroines grow up, we may follow them to a school or a university, to another place away from home where they take up their professions, even (though rarely) overseas to faraway places—as when two of the Pfäffling children go to German Africa, one as an engineer and the other as the bride of a pioneering farmer.

Thus in these novels we are given a general idea of place and time and, mainly because the characters themselves grow up and age, of the passing of time. Yet essentially we live in a timeless and eventless world bounded by the garden surrounding the family home. Outside events, heard there only as faint echoes, can perhaps be meaningfully interpreted by the reader but scarcely affect the lives of the family within. In these stories, most of which are deeply concerned with problems of character building and fulfilment, children are brought up to face "reality" and "life" and "the world" effectively. But the reality which, eventually, they do face—especially in the series that take the protagonists from childhood to adulthood or old age—is the reality of the family world, of courtship and marriage and home and the upbringing of the next generation.

In some stories the end contains the beginning. Wildfang, who in effect became the mother of her younger siblings, marries a widower and becomes a successful stepmother. Wildfang's youngest brother

becomes a small-town doctor like his father and eventually rehabili-
tates the family home. Nesthäkchen, who studied medicine to become
her father's assistant, marries a young doctor, who becomes her father's
assistant. The youngest Pfäffling boy (the real hero of this series),
whose father was a music teacher, becomes not a professional musician
but a musical instrument maker. Gunhild and her brother, whose
parents are killed and whose ancient homestead is destroyed by a
catastrophic landslide, re-create the home and the property but double
it as they both marry and settle down beside each other. So in these
stories the life of the family tends to turn back upon itself and to
re-create itself in new generations, essentially unaffected by and having little effect upon external events in time and space. The world of
the family is a closed world, with its own private hazards and trials
and eventual solutions and triumphs.

Public and official life hardly touches upon the characters in these
novels. Most of the adult men have the kind of work that assures
them a measure of autonomy. They are not officials but doctors and
lawyers and gentlemen farmers, and the details of their professional
life do not enter very significantly into the stories. If Turm-Engele's
father (the town bell-ringer) has official duties, he fulfils them punc-
tually and unfailingly because he is a dutiful and methodical man.
If Pfäffling doubts that he will be chosen to be the head of a music
school, it is because the new school is in a strange city where he is
unknown and people may not judge him in terms of his real merits.
If a doctor has a hard time establishing himself, it is because times
are hard. People act and fail or succeed in terms of their own merits—
or because of circumstances that are clearly outside any reasonable
control.

Germany exists as an idea—as a beloved way of doing things, as a
series of landscapes, as the summation of a kind of character—but
hardly as a political entity. References to government are few, incidental, and limited to a locality. A *burgomeister* may appear as a
minor character, some boys may have a snowfight and get into difficulties with the police. But on a larger scale government and politics
neither trouble nor adorn these books.

Nor, although some of the writers are piously Christian, do differences in religion appear significantly in these stories. There are min-
isters, and people pray and go to church, but never once does the
reader follow a character into a specific church during a religious
service. The characters in these novels are good Christians and good
Germans, but there are few, if any, references to religious dogma or
political opinion.[13] Christianity and Germany are symbolic wholes in
which each family very generally participates.

The underlying theme of these stories is character development, and the plots, often episodic in their construction, reach minor and major climaxes in terms of character rather than of external event. So, for instance, in *Das Turm-Engele,* we follow the heroine, Engele, from childhood to young womanhood and learn first how she was made into a pretty and spoiled young girl and then, in a series of adventures, how through suffering and re-education following upon suffering she was made into an appreciative, loving, capable young woman, ready for romance and reintegrated into her home. In *Die Familie Pfäffling* the unifying plot turns upon the difficulties of a poor but respectable large family and upon the problem of whether or not the father becomes the head of a music school, but each of the episodes of the plot illustrates an event that tries and proves the character of one or more of the children in the family: Can one son overcome his social cowardice? Can another control his love of music? In the first volume of the Wildfang series we see, first, how the tomboy heroine, Wildfang, eludes her responsibilities as the eldest daughter of a widowed father, then how she comes to grief through disobedience (swinging on a forbidden swing, she falls and becomes paralyzed), and, finally, how, having learned to accept and so to master her physical suffering, she recovers and becomes the responsible, self-sacrificing foster-mother of her own siblings.

The family of the juvenile novels is likely to be "the family rich in children." The Pfäfflings, the Röders (in the Wildfang series), and the Brauns (in the Nesthäkchen series) are all large families, and many of the children when they grow up in turn have large families. In *Kampf der Tertia* and *Die goldene Horde* a class of boys functions as a group of siblings with a single girl, whose position as an only child or as a member of the sibling group remains unclear. Two children appear to be minimally necessary for the safe upbringing of a child. An only child (e.g., Turm-Engele, Pünktchen, and Anton, and a host of minor characters) is likely to be a problem child whose parents are regularly exceptional in their handling of the child's upbringing. Sometimes the only child is brought through a critical period or is permanently saved by contact with children and parents in larger families, i.e., a child prodigy is able to perform at a concert after he has played with happy children; the erring son of a widowed hotel owner reforms when he is sent to live a simpler life with a family of relatives in the country; a young flirtatious girl is saved from becoming *frühreif* (prematurely sexually aware) by living in a large family; Pünktchen and Anton, both only children, select each other as friends and eventually create a complete family for themselves. The only child may be cherished or neglected—its fate is always uncertain.

In the first generation the stories concentrate upon the family in a single household, but later—as the children grow up and marry and found households of their own—the family as a whole consists of numerous households, each independent of the others and bound to the others only by ties of affection that are likely to be renewed on ceremonial occasions or during crises: birthdays, marriages, christenings, holiday visits, sickness, and death. The separation of the households is symbolized by their being scattered not only in one city but quite regularly in different parts of Germany—in country and city, in north and south. The novels suggest repeatedly that, while deep attachment to home (*die Heimat* and, more narrowly, *das Elternhaus*) is necessary and good, residence too close to home may be a sign of dependence. The child who, as an adult, does not move away has not achieved autonomy. Maturation involves *physical* removal from one place to another but not a breaking of the emotional tie to the family and the parental home. Thus maturity is achieved by partly reversing the childhood situation when everyone lived under one roof and sat at one table. At the same time, recognition of the unbreakable emotional tie to home is itself a sign of maturity. So, for instance, Turm-Engele, sadder and wiser for tragic experiences away from the childhood home she wanted to deny, finally returns there and looks out of a window:

> With enchantment she looked out over all the known houses and hills. Distance no longer had a lure for her. Engele had returned gladly, so gladly, to the homey, inclosed nest and now knew that happiness does not come from outside but rather from within the heart.[14]

The table is a symbol of the unity of the single household and of the larger family. In these stories the table provides a place where the individuals in a household or the members of the larger family can meet together and where, when they are together, they are visibly one united group. When the several households that make up a family meet, they are likely to be pictured around a table: grandfather and grandmother, father and mother, aunts and uncles, children and grandchildren and cousins draw up around a table for Sunday dinner, for a holiday meal, meet at the coffee table set for a birthday or an anniversary celebration. The table reappears in various situations, for now we see the family gathered in the dining-room and now, on another occasion, at the coffee table in another room or in an arbor or under a shady tree or, when a large family goes on an excursion, at an inn or in the woods.

For the single household, the central table also serves as a symbol of the united family. We see the family gathered together at meals; the same table (or another like it) holds a separate pile of Christmas presents for each member of the family; or in the evenings the family sit together, each person busy with his own work. So, on a winter evening, we are shown the Pfäffling family:

What kinds of work were done in the Pfäffling family at the big table under the hanging lamp that was lighted as early as five o'clock! Of the four brothers, one was doing his Greek, the other his Latin, the third his French, the fourth his German lessons. One stared into the air and sought clever ideas for his composition, the other thumbed his dictionary, the third murmured conjugations, the fourth scratched arithmetic on his slate. . . . Mother sat with her sewing basket at the head of the table and next to her sat little Else, who was supposed to busy herself quietly but did not always succeed in doing so.[15]

The table is a device for drawing the family together, but it does not necessarily unite them in their occupations.

Away from the table, each member of the family has an appointed place where he or she is likely to be found, which is special to that person. Father has his study, which is sacred to him. Mother has her sewing table, sometimes at a window, sometimes in an alcove, sometimes in a corner of father's room. The children have their rooms or one playroom which, especially as small children, they share. If by chance another relative—a grandfather or grandmother—lives in the household, this person is likely to have a room apart and, except at meals (and sometimes even for meals), will live there—not joining the evening group around the table but occasionally inviting everyone to join him (or her) in this semiseparate residence. Thus ideally the German home provides the individual with a place where he is a member of a group and a place where he is at least semi-independent of all others.[16] The parental home itself provides a safe place ("a nest") within which the family forms a group "closed to strangers"; the table provides a meeting place where the individuals in the family become "members of a larger community"; a room, a nook, or a special chair gives each one a chance to be a separate personality.

Ideally, mother and father have entirely separate responsibilities within the household: mother runs the household, and father provides for it. Mother exhibits her responsibility by having a perfect household, perfectly prepared to receive father whenever he comes home and perfectly arranged to care for and control the children. In these stories, the difficulties of *young* marriage (in the second generation) may center on the problem of how the inexperienced wife does or does not manage to realize this ideal. In the older stories, the bride finally achieves her goal (or, more rarely, the marriage is recognized to be a failure). In the more modern ones, the ideal is recognized but seldom attained. The heroine—Nesthäkchen or Trotzkopf—remains a well-meaning but comparatively inefficient housewife, but nevertheless is a successful wife and mother because she is the right kind of person.

Yet, despite their separate responsibilities, mother and father form a single unit before their children and in facing the outer world. In all decisions and expressions of opinion about family decisions, they must be at one, must be of a single mind. This does not mean that they must be alike. On the contrary, parents in these stories may be markedly different from each other. If the father (*Die Familie Pfäffling*) is active and outgoing and quick-tempered, the mother is quiet and reserved and patient and seldom gives way to impulse. If the mother (*Nesthäkchen*) is quick and gay and foolish, the father is steady and patient and more farseeing than his wife. Ideally, mother and father support each other with their particular talents and strengths and together form one balanced whole. At the same time, mother as a matter of course adapts herself to father's personality and needs. Where she cannot or will not do this (as is sometimes the case in a marriage in the younger generation), the marriage and the family run into difficulties which can be overcome only when and if the wife solves the problems that prevent her from doing her part correctly.[17] In *Werden und Wachsen* an older woman advises a bride about the responsibilities of a wife:

". . . Many a violin maker is a simple artisan or businessman. My husband conceived of his work as an artist, and we were taken up in cultivated circles, as you too will be. But in spite of this, exactly in this situation, the woman is important, the man wins or loses through her."

"But the wife is much more under the influence of her husband?"

"I hardly believe so. The whole running of the household, the outer appearance, the social tone, and later the upbringing of the children depend more upon the woman; through her the man is raised up or pulled down."[18]

Yet in these stories, neither mother nor father is a dominating or a dominated person. Rather they are at one. Good parents make decisions together behind closed doors: father calls mother aside, mother calls father aside, when there is news, when a decision is to be made. The decision, when it is announced, is one in which they concur. Children learn about the *news* only when the *decision* that follows has been made. Or the parents together prepare surprises for the children: mother and father (or, as in Wildfang's story, father and the responsible eldest daughter who replaces the mother) prepare the Christmas tree in the Christmas room. The children enter the situation only when everything has been arranged for them. This means not only that the parents present a united front but also that the children can only guess at the preparatory steps, at the process of decision-making. In *Die Familie Pfäffling* a crucial scene is one in which the eldest son, an adolescent boy, is permitted to sit with his parents at the family table while they make a difficult decision. As a witness (not a participant) who enjoys his parents' confidence, he now is somewhat separated from his siblings, for he is expected not to discuss the problem with the younger children.

The mother is so important that she is replaceable, and one of the things the reader learns is that mothers are, in one sense, multiple. The mother may die—but there must be a mother in the home. Fears about an unloving mother are played off in the fictional children's fears about the stepmother. Yet there is in these stories no example of a stepmother who is not a loving mother. The reader knows that the stepmother is good; the story problem is for the fictional children to discover it.

One of the characteristics of the good stepmother is that she does not deny the true mother; on the contrary, she keeps the image of the mother bright and clear in the children's memory. Initially, the children may doubt the stepmother and believe her to be too strict and exacting; eventually they learn that she is really kind and loving and cares about their well-being and happiness. Then (sometimes early in the relationship, sometimes only after a protracted struggle) she becomes "mother" (*Mutter* or *Mutti*) in the fullest sense, but without displacing the true mother.

In Kästner's *Pünktchen und Anton* there are three maternal figures: Pünktchen's well-to-do inattentive mother, Pünktchen's weak and silly governess (who lets the little girl make friends with Anton while she herself is being seduced by a thief who eventually gets the housekeys from her), and Anton's poor but worthy mother, who cannot manage the difficulties of life alone with her little boy. In this story the problems of how to have a complete household run by a perfect mother and how to get rid of a failing mother are solved when Pünktchen's busy father, apprised of the true situation, has the governess jailed and asks the good mother (Anton's mother) to take over the upbringing of both children in the well-to-do home. The ineffectual mother (Pünktchen's mother) remains but is divested of responsibility.

The positions of mother and stepmother are exemplified in the following passage from a letter written by a young girl soon after her father's remarriage:

In the house itself Father led us both [daughter and stepmother] into his study to the portrait of my first mother, who died when I was still very young. He was deeply moved; I could see it. Then he gave me a kiss and said softly: "Lu, if your mother can see us now, she will be very happy that you have a mother once more."[19]

The relationship of dead mother, stepmother, and children is made explicit in scenes of conciliation, such as the following, in which a little girl, who has refused to accept a stepmother, suddenly discovers her worth:

Altogether she [the stepmother] was completely different from what Brigittchen [the child] had thought. How loving and careful she was with little Willie. Not at all like a stepmother! And how good she had been to

Paul when he had stolen! If she had not been there, he would in the end have been beaten by Father. And it had made a great impression on the little girl that now on Gisela's birthday she had gone with Father and the stepchildren to the cemetery to the grave of their dead mother and that she had taken the wreath of forget-me-nots from Gisela's basket and had laid it on Mother's grave and had said: "Children, never forget your good first mother." And how happy Father had been. Yes, at Mother's grave, that was beautiful![20]

The little girl, Brigitte, then decides to call her stepmother "Mother." The new mother gives her a necklace which had belonged to the first mother and which the father had wanted to give his second wife:

She [the stepmother] put the necklace around the little girl's neck and said: "Father agrees that I cannot wear this jewel because it belonged to your mother and you will be the first one to wear it after her."

"Until I am grown up and married you can wear it, Mother," Brigitte said smilingly.

"No, you will be the first one to wear it after your mother, as is the family custom. Father will keep it for you and you will have it as a remembrance of the hour when Tante Grete [the stepmother] became your second mother who never wants to push the first one out of your heart."[21]

In these stories the ideal family is able to include the dead among the living, and the good stepmother *re*places the true mother without *dis*placing her.

Unlike the mother, the father is unique. He may die, but he is not replaced by any other man inside the home who takes over responsibilities within the family as does the necessary stepmother.

As long as the parents are living and are in charge of their children, other relatives—grandparents, aunts, and uncles—play roles entirely different from parental ones. The relationship is also a complementary one, but where parent and child are linked together by responsibility and obedience, other relatives—especially grandparents—attach themselves to children mainly through permitted indulgence and "spoiling." Grandparents win their grandchildren through play and sunny understanding and with cake and sweets and other luxuries unobtainable from parents. So, for instance, a grandmother calms her screaming grandchild at a family birthday party:

But what are grandmothers for in this world? Grandma lovingly overpowered the raging little child and even before everyone sat down little Urzel was sunshiny again.

"You are spoiling the child, Mother dear." Dr. Hartenstein [the father] did not entirely agree with his mother-in-law's educational methods.[22]

Or a grandfather plays with his grandson:

When Grete [the mother] had not time . . . she carried little Willie into Grandfather's room. Then he shouted and rejoiced because no one could play so beautifully and quietly as Grandfather. Willie was allowed to sit on his knees and play with his watch chain or listen to the tick-tock, or

Grandfather sang him a little song or let him tear a big newspaper into little pieces. That was wonderful, for there was a marvelous mess and it made a lovely noise.[23]

With a grandparent, a child may even be safely destructive.

Similarly, aunts and uncles—except when they replace parents—are expected to be affectionately indulgent and to help their nieces and nephews. Kästner, in his fantasy story, *Der 35. Mai,* plays with the possibilities of such a relationship:

Uncle Ringelhut was Konrad's father's brother. And because the uncle was not yet married and lived all alone, he could call for his nephew at school every Thursday. Then they ate together, conversed, drank coffee together, and only toward evening did the boy return to his parents. These Thursdays were very funny. . . . He and Konrad ate all sorts of crazy things. Sometimes ham with whipped cream. Or pretzels and bilberries. Or cherry pie with English mustard. . . . And if they then felt sick, they leaned out of the window and laughed because their neighbors thought that Pharmacist Ringelhut and his nephew had, alas, gone mad.[24]

Mother's friends and father's friends are assimilated to aunts and uncles and, indeed, any person with whom the young child may have some relationship of trust and confidence may become a pseudo-aunt or pseudo-uncle, i.e., Uncle-Doctor (the child's doctor), Aunt-Schmidt (the landlady of the house)—irrespective of whether or not this person is on intimate terms with the parents. Thus the child grows up surrounded by loving and indulgent relatives who visit the parental home but who do not live as members of it. As far as the child is concerned, the world is made up of familiar people—relatives and pseudo-relatives—but the child learns to differentiate between the roles of responsible adults in the household and that of indulgent adults outside it.

All siblings are assumed, in these stories, to get along with one another, and the sibling group pictured is generally coherent and friendly, the core of friendship groups whether of boys and girls, or of boys or girls alone.[25] In many cases brothers' friends and sisters' friends eventually marry into the family. The closest and most affectionate relationship between siblings is that of brother and sister. The warmth of this relationship is expressed epecially in the sister's tender concern and attentiveness to her brother's needs and wishes; it is the sister rather than the brother who is careful and insightful.

The tender love of brother and sister is echoed in the relationship of the bride and young wife to her husband's family. From the first moment that a young man brings home his fiancée, she enters into the family—calls her prospective parents-in-law "mother" and "father" and becomes a sister to the other children. So, for instance, a mother awaits the arrival of her son's fiancée, a girl whom the family have never seen:

Mrs. Pfäffling stood upstairs, heard happy laughter and called down, "Welcome!" Two gay brown eyes looked up. "That must be Mother!" called a happy voice in a somewhat Bavarian accent and, hurrying ahead of her fiancé, the bride . . . came upstairs and gave Mrs. Pfäffling her hand. "May I say 'Mother'?" She found herself drawn warmly and feelingly to a mother-heart.[26]

The bride becomes a visiting child in the family, but one who lives in another household and makes her own decisions (sometimes with the devoted help of a sister-in-law) about ministering to the welfare of her husband and children.

Scenes of this kind set the stage for the beginning of a new cycle in which the parents become grandparents (and eventually die) and the grown-up children begin to bring up their own children, usually with greater difficulties than their own parents experienced but, for the most part, with no less success.

Following the heroes and heroines through childhood, the reader learns that parents (but by no means all parents or all adults) are almost perfect and that children have difficulties and problems to solve. Following the same characters into marriage and parenthood, they discover that parents, too, have difficulties. Yet, as they follow the grown-up children in their independent careers, it becomes clear that the relationship of parent and child has continuity, even as it changes over time:

Just as the parents formerly were pleased when the little ones took their first steps, so now they also were [pleased] when their big children took their first independent steps in life; and just as they were happy when a new word appeared in the child's vocabulary, so now also as new ideas and ambitions awoke in the young people. For they do not regard themselves as finished, these two parents, and for this very reason they are not [finished], but go ever further onward. With this difference from their youth that now they have clearly recognized and can keep to the main direction in which they want to go. Because of this they exercise an often unconscious leadership over their children. For in an unknown land—and that is what life is—we gladly follow those whom we see striding ahead quietly and with dignity, with courage and a cheerful countenance. And so the grown-up Pfäffling children followed [*folgten* also means "to obey"] willingly and in all freedom of movement the direction taken by their parents.[27]

From this it would appear that the individual, moving from childhood and adolescence into adulthood, becomes, in the ideal world of juvenile fiction, both perfectly autonomous and perfectly dependable. The young adult goes his own way, following "new ideas and ambitions," and yet his parents, from whom he has moved away, are still his guides, "striding ahead quietly and with dignity, with courage and a cheerful countenance," until they are removed by death.

Since these stories are implicitly or explicitly concerned with problems of character development, the reader is given considerable information about methods of upbringing and the characteristics of a good person. One of the main themes in the novels is that the harmony and happiness of the family and the well-being of the children grow out of complete, natural obedience.[28]

Reward and punishment play an unimportant part in these stories. Rather, disobedience, disregard of rules, failure to be the kind of child one's elders expect, carry their own punishment. The disobedient child, the child who does not follow directions, the child who looks for interstices between the rules ("no one said *not* to do that"), inevitably gets into trouble.

For instance, a young girl insists on making friends with an undesirable young woman who gives her shoddy romances to read and encourages her in a secret flirtation with her scapegrace brother:

Physically Lu [the young girl] had not yet suffered. But she ran the danger of losing the breath of attractiveness and youth which is peculiar to untouched, pure girls and which alone creates the wonderful magic which, unknown to her, surrounds the young girl. Hede [the undesirable friend] had long since lost this breath of youth, this flower magic, and she now busied herself with taking it away from little Lu. Rosy as a peach blossom when she came to Buchingen, it now seemed as if the delicate petals were fading. . . . She had been introduced to all the secrets of flirtation and trifling, and her great fault was that she had not followed her conscience and turned away. She had played with wrongdoing, and now wrongdoing played with her.[29]

Lu is saved because the father of a good friend (in whose home Lu is living) sees through her and traps her into discovery and confession. In this situation, as in many others in these stories, confession and remorse on the part of the child and forgiveness by the responsible, insightful adult are the way back to the right path—the way to "make good" again and to gain happiness.

Occasionally a parent must make a child suffer for its own good. In *Die Familie Pfäffling* the youngest son, Frieder, is a passionate and highly gifted musician who cannot stop playing his violin, although he has been warned to limit the number of hours he practices every day. One day he plays long past the time—deliberately. Frieder tells his father he is sorry, but this is not enough:

"You must be made sorry," said the father. "If you had just forgotten in your enthusiasm that you had played over the time, I could easily forgive it, but if you remembered that you should stop and did not want to obey, if you did intentionally what I had expressly forbidden, then your violin playing is at an end. What do you think would happen if all you children did not obey, if everyone did as he thought best? That would be as if in an orchestra no one followed the director, but played when and what he pleased. No, Frieder, my children must obey; your violin playing is at an end, I will not say forever, but for a year and a day. Give it to me!"

[Frieder refuses to give up the violin. The father insists that he give it up of his own free will.]

But the child did not let go. From all sides, loudly and softly, his brothers and sisters said: "Give it up." And as the mother saw how passionately he pressed the instrument to himself, she asked painfully: "Frieder, do you love the violin more than Father and Mother?" The little boy stayed still.

"Then keep your violin," called out the father. "Here is the bow as well, you can play as long as you like. But you will be our child only when you give it to us!" And, opening the door to the entry, he called out loud and threateningly: "Go out, you stranger child!"

[After several hours of lonely exile in the dark entry, Frieder brings his father the violin wrapped up "like a little corpse."]

The father took the package away from him quickly and put it aside, took hold of his little boy and drew him to himself and said in a warm tone: "Now everything is well, Frieder, and you are our child again." Frieder cried his pain away in his father's arms.[30]

Later, in connection with the same incident, Frieder's father, himself a musician, enlarges on the necessity for self-control and obedience:

"You cannot stop [playing], Frieder? It is only that you do not want to because it is hard for you. But don't you see that we can all stop if we must? Do you think I would not rather go on playing than give a music lesson to Miss Vernagelding when she comes? Do you think that Mother would not rather go on reading her lovely books after supper than stop after half an hour and mend stockings? And that your big brothers would not pefer to play rather than do their lessons? And that the swallows would not rather get food for themselves than go out and get food for their nestlings, as God has ordered it? And Frieder Pfäffling wants to stand all alone in the world and say: 'I cannot stop.' No, he would have to be ashamed before all animals, before all people, before the dear Lord himself. . . . There are no exceptions, Frieder, whoever has a firm will can stop in the middle of a bow stroke on his violin, and that you must learn too. Take pains and when you feel that you have acquired a firm will, then I will let you play your violin every Sunday for an hour."[31]

In the end Frieder tells his father that he has learned how to have a firm will. He has practiced it at meals: " 'Three times. I stopped when I had the greatest hunger. Even when we had pancakes!' "[32] He is then given the violin. This is an event that follows Frieder throughout his life.

Thus the child learns to do the right thing—or *not* to do the wrong thing, the preferred, the pleasant but forbidden thing—"of his own free will" and learns that love and warmth and security in the family are dependent upon such willing obedience.

Just as controlling his hunger for pancakes helps Frieder control his desire to play the violin, so later the firm will he acquired by not playing the violin helps him in solving the problems he has as an adult. Similarly, for the little tomboy heroine, Wildfang, a fall from a forbidden swing (which she had not been told was broken) is the pathway to suffering but also to reform and to a life of sacrifice and, in the end, of happiness and contentment. The young readers of these books can learn a double lesson from the trials of the heroes and heroines. First, obedience leads to harmony and happiness; and, second, disobedience leads to suffering but makes a good person out of the sufferer. The rewards of suffering are very great.

The suffering which is rewarded is of very different kinds, serves very different purposes: making right a wrong, accepting sacrifice for the sake of others, overcoming a personal desire, mastering a weakness. An important aspect of this conception of suffering is the recognition of its value by the sufferer. So Wildfang, now a contented young woman, looks back on a period of self-sacrifice:

> Yes, there had been a time when she had thanked God because she knew only joy and no sorrow and [then] there was a night . . . when sleep fled because there was only pain and misery on earth for her. Today when she looked back at that time, it was nevertheless beautiful and rich and she would not have wanted to miss it in her life. "Poor is a life without sorrow, without pain, without sacrifice and without love," she whispered.[33]

Or a teacher comments on a little boy who has just made a suicidal jump from a gymnastic apparatus in order to master his cowardice and to impress the other boys with his daring:

> "Well, that he has succeeded in doing," said Justus [the teacher]. "And pull yourself together! Don't forget that breaking a leg is less bad than if the little fellow had gone through the whole of his life fearing that others did not respect him. I really believe that this parachute jump was not so idiotic as I thought at first."[34]

An alternative, safer mode of behavior is suggested by a fellow-pupil, who, challenging the popular opinion that the reckless child had proved his courage, insists that he jumped only out of despair and shame at his timidity and says to the other boys:

> ". . . Have you ever considered whether I have courage? Has it ever occurred to you that I am fearful? Never. Therefore, I shall tell you that I am, in fact, unusually fearful. But I am shrewd, and I don't let you notice it. My lack of courage doesn't disturb me particularly. I am not ashamed of it. And that is because I am shrewd. I know that everyone has faults and weaknesses. It is only important that these faults do not show."
>
> "I prefer the person who is ashamed," said [another boy]. "I, too," answered Sebastian softly.[35]

Shrewd concealment of a character fault is, then, a possible alternative to eradication of the fault. But even the advocate of concealment believes that the other course of action is preferable. Implicit in this are both the belief that people and things should be what they are "entirely" and the gnawing doubt that they may not be what they seem.

The single reckless act proves not only that the person can act in a courageous way on one occasion but also that he is altogether a courageous person. This principle of the indicative value of the single act works in both directions. A single act can show a person to be a coward; another single act can show him to be a brave "hero." In *Die Familie Pfäffling* an adolescent boy deserts his younger brother on the street in a difficult situation because he fears he will be laughed at by his classmates. His father brands him as a coward, and his mother tells him:

"Yes, Otto, he had to consider you a coward because you were—and on other occasions in the same way. You must always be independent of what others think about you. Asking for forgiveness does not help, only fighting against cowardliness helps, demonstrating that you can also be brave."[36]

Otto reverses his behavior—returns and does what he had refused to do earlier, allowing himself to be laughed at. The father then reverses his judgment:

Mr. Pfäffling gave his son a happy, warm look and said, "There are many kinds of heroism. That was one kind. No, child, you are no coward."[37]

Since the whole person is continually judged in terms of single acts, it would seem that judgment of character would be subject to continual swings from good to bad and back again. There are, however, two related beliefs—repeatedly demonstrated in these stories—that affect the swing of judgment. On the one hand, there is the belief that the person who acts out of weakness or error or deliberate choice of wrongdoing will continue in such acts until he is forced out of them. Unguided or misguided children, illustrated by a host of minor characters, come to a bad end. So, for instance, Lu's would-be seducer (*Wildfang als Backfisch*) fails his examinations and is thrown out of school. On the other hand, there is the belief that once a person has been induced to act in a good way (either because of initially correct training or because of learning through suffering), he has become good and cannot fall back permanently into evil ways. The little boy who can control his hunger can also control his violin playing and, later in life, can make sacrifices for distant satisfactions. The little boy who has once demonstrated that he can be brave assures others and himself that he is brave and will act bravely on all other possible occasions. This sets an automatic limit to the number of times a person need suffer in order to be rewarded, in order to achieve a good character.

The idea of the value of suffering carries with it a way of looking at things in which one detail can be substituted for another and any detail can stand for the whole. Suffering in one kind of situation prepares one to manage suffering in totally different situations; what one has learned to manage is suffering itself. Mastering fear in one situation means that one has mastered fear itself. Disobedience in one detail is a sign of total disobedience (and vice versa). Making the point that children grieve and suffer no less than adults do, Kästner comments:

> There is no difference whether one cries because of a broken doll or, at some later time, because one has lost a friend. In life it is irrelevant what one grieves about, what is relevant is how much one grieves.[38]

Congruence, proportion, and relatedness are, in this sense, irrelevant.

In these stories the educational value of pain and suffering is dependent upon shared knowledge. For only if the child is guided through the maze of wrongdoing and consequent pain by a wise and insightful adult, can it profit by the experience. Unlike the neglected or misguided children who come to a bad end, others are saved from the predicaments of misguidance or disobedience by adults who know what they have done and who may have to force the children to do the right thing (not to do the wrong thing) until they can behave well of their own free will. There is, however, a difference between the older and the more modern stories in this respect. In the older stories the parents or wiser parent-substitutes see through their children, discover wrongdoing and labor to correct it. In the more modern stories (e.g., the Nesthäkchen series), the parents may be equally insightful, but, instead of punishing the child, they may merely say: "I ought to punish you for this." The words alone are effective.

Or the knowing adults may seem to be mainly observers. In Speyer's *Kampf der Tertia*, the head of the school, and in Kästner's *Das fliegende Klassenzimmer*, the head of the school and, to a lesser extent, the beloved teacher stand aloof and allow the children to prove that, in spite of appearances, they are being good. (In both these stories there are, however, secondary adult characters who share completely in the children's secrets and help them to carry out their plans.)[39] In *Das fliegende Klassenzimmer* a major episode and in *Kampf der Tertia* the central plot turn on situations in which the child protagonists commit forbidden acts in a good cause; plot tension arises from the question of whether the children will be punished for wrongdoing or rewarded for success in achieving their ultimate goal. In Kästner's story punishment is turned into reward. In Speyer's story the children are punished when they fail to carry out certain necessary steps successfully, but they are in the end very fully rewarded. Then recognition of their success involves a public exhibition of the wounds of battle. The children, adolescents in a boarding school, have fought a mighty battle with the town children to rescue the town cats from destruction. Their success assured, they march in review before the head of the school (who now appears for the first time), their teachers, and their comrades in other classes:

> The Third Form [Tertia] is marching. In front the Great Elector [the class leader] breathing heavily, bruised and asthmatic. A half step behind him the honorary leader [a girl who had rescued all the boys], fresh, rosy, white-gold and brown, uninjured, unwounded and unchangeable, with an impudent smile and a proudly lifted head.
>
> In the first row Reppert, Lüders, and Borst—Borst who had changed from a fearful, clumsy rabbit-boy into a hero of the Iliad. . . .
>
> And all the others followed . . . scraped, flayed, limping, and bandaged in the most peculiar parts of their bodies.
>
> But no one had said that he was sick; no one had stayed away from the parade. . . .
>
> So the band marched across the court. When they passed the granary door, the Doctor [head of the school] raised his cap from his crown, from his blowing gray hair.
>
> Rapidly the young teachers followed suit and reluctantly the older ones also. . . .
>
> And all the pupils on parade, all without exception, pulled off their caps and held them in the air with stiffly outstretched arms. No longer with noise and hurrahs, but silently they now greeted their comrades of the Third Form.[40]

Thus the activities which the children appeared to be carrying out in secret are in the end openly acknowledged by the children and the adults.

In these stories, secrecy in general is inimical to a good character. There are, in fact, only four kinds of acceptable secrets, and even these are likely to be shared by at least two persons: the secrets that concern a happy surprise for another person, the secrets that conceal suffering and self-sacrifice for another's benefit, the secrets that insure the success of a plan for another's benefit, and the secrets of decision-making—the process by which parents become one for the welfare of the family. Mother and father share in the preparation of Christmas for the children (as the children also share in preparing surprises for the parents and one another), the parents keeping everything hidden until, the scene set, the moment of happy revelation comes. A young woman confides only in a trusted family servant that she has sacrificed her hoped-for marriage to care for her own family; years later, when the lovers are reunited and the sacrifice becomes known, the old servant praises God and drops dead with joy. The schoolboys make a complicated secret plan to save the town cats from the greedy boy bullies in the town. Mother and father meet behind closed doors before telling the rest of the family what is going to happen. The safe secret— and it is safer if it is shared—is one that is kept not for the person's own benefit but for another person's benefit.

Otherwise, secrecy and concealment carry with them the possibility of danger for the person—usually a child—who is not open. The fact that parents usually can see through their children may serve to avert the danger in time. In other situations, confession of what has been kept secret is a first step in "making good" again, in doing right and being good.[41] There is, therefore, double assurance that parents can bring up their children correctly: parents can look at their children and see what is happening, and children learn to confess to their parents. The eyes, more than any other feature, reveal the immediate situation and the person's character. A little girl looks at her father and sees that his eyes are twinkling, even as he scolds; she recognizes the affection with which he speaks. A child's head droops; he cannot look at his parent—he is concealing a misdeed. Someone looks out at the world with clear, blue, laughing eyes—this is the good and happy person, a little child with a clear conscience, a grandparent who has mastered life's problems.

The family world of the story-book is not altogether a happy one. People age and die and are mourned. Children sicken or die in fatal accidents. Families have to struggle and learn to do without. Dreams have to be revised and hopes postponed or sacrificed. Friends and lovers sometimes disappoint, are not what they seem. Nevertheless, for the person who controls his own will, so that he can give up what he desires and do what he dislikes, who (as a child) can obey willingly or (as a parent) can lead unfalteringly, who has learned by and accepts suffering, who is what he is entirely and without concealment (except for the sake of others), this family world offers security and warmth and completeness, irrespective of the troubles in the world outside. Then parents can be fond and children can be happy, and the German family can live in harmony—and Germany is well off.

NOTES

1. With one or two exceptions, the books discussed here are standard books, available in bookshops in West Germany in new printings or editions prepared since 1945. The novels were selected from among those discussed by German informants or referred to as perennial favorites in recent German book reviews of juvenile fiction. Speyer's two books, *Der Kampf der Tertia* and *Die goldene Horde,* and one of Kästner's books, *Das fliegende Klassenzimmer,* all of which are novels of school life, have been included primarily because they were regarded as important by German informants speaking about their own adolescence. The books differ considerably in their appeal to young German readers, i.e., sophisticated admirers of Speyer and Kästner might deny any interest in the more obviously sentimental stories (but were familiar with at least some of them); but the readers of "girls' books" were likely also to enjoy Kästner. For the novels included in this study see the List of References at the end of this chapter.

2. For a recent survey of German juvenile tastes in reading, based on a sample of children in Berlin, cf. Haseloff, 1953.

3. Based on discussions with German informants and with an American informant who interviewed German children in Germany. The most popular adventure stories still seem to be the series by Karl May, whose hero—known as "Kara-ben-

Nemsi" in his travels to the Near East and as "Old Shatterhand" in his wanderings in the American West—has become the prototype of the adventurer for generations of German readers, juvenile and adult. A large body of research and philosophical writing has grown up around these books and their author, who, even in his lifetime, tended to merge his identity with that of his hero (cf. Nelly Hoyt, 1953a).

4. Haseloff, 1953.

5. Sapper, 1951; first published in 1908.

6. Schumacher, 1951. No date for original publication; the setting is pre–World War I.

7. Ury, 1950. No date for original publication; the setting is post–World War I.

8. Kästner, 1949, pp. 168–69.

9. Cf. Hoyt, 1953b.

10. Stinde, 1951, p. 5.

11. One of the major contrasts between the family novel and the adventure story is in the imagery of horizons. See, for instance, the wide horizons continually described by Karl May. There is, however, a common boundary to the two worlds —the symbolic one of "Germany" and all that is "German" (cf. Hoyt, 1953a).

12. Ury, 1950, p. 10.

13. In this study I have deliberately avoided the specifically politically oriented literature of the 1930's and also specifically religious books intended for a special audience.

14. Schumacher, 1951, p. 222.

15. Sapper, 1951, pp. 22–23.

16. In this respect the home in the family novel illustrates the duality of the individual personality as it is sometimes described in German psychological literature and as it is summed up, for instance, by Seelmann (1952, p. 15) writing about youth guidance: "The human being is a self-inclosed unit. But as such he is also a member of a larger community."

17. There is also the implicit point in these stories that when the man takes the initiative in making a change, he gets a new wife. In the Wildfang series, a young widower marries his childhood sweetheart (Wildfang) to continue the work of a good wife. In *Das Turm-Engele*, the father—who permitted his first wife to spoil their only child—later marries a strict, good mother. In *Pünktchen und Anton*, the father introduces a foster-mother into the home without actually getting rid of the neglectful true mother. An alternative to a woman's changing herself is a man's bringing in a new woman.

18. Sapper, 1952, p. 103.

19. Haarbeck, n.d., *Wildfang als Backfisch*, p. 205.

20. Haarbeck, n.d., *Wildfang als Mutter*, p. 55.

21. *Ibid.*, pp. 55–56.

22. Ury, 1950, p. 34.

23. Haarbeck, n.d., *Wildfang als Mutter*, p. 69.

24. Kästner, 1933, pp. 5–6.

25. The siblings are likely to be divided into an older and a younger cluster. Occasionally one child does not quite fit into the group of "the big ones" or "the little ones"—and this child may die (cf. Wildfang series).

26. Sapper, 1952, p. 54.

27. *Ibid.*, p. 110.

28. To a certain extent both Kästner and Speyer work on a reversal of this statement. The children in their stories are likely to work for good goals with formally inacceptable means, but when they arrive at their goals the means turn out to have been acceptable, partly because the protagonists have learned through the suffering they endured and overcame on the way.

29. Haarbeck, n.d., *Wildfang als Backfisch*, pp. 78–79.

30. Sapper, 1951, pp. 214–19.

31. *Ibid.*, pp. 272–73.

32. *Ibid.*, p. 273.

33. Haarbeck, n.d., *Wildfang als Tante*, p. 222.

34. Kästner, 1938, p. 131.

35. *Ibid.*, pp. 136–37.

36. Sapper, 1951, p. 115.

37. *Ibid.*, p. 116.

38. Kästner, 1938, p. 15.

39. The role of these secondary adult characters appears to parallel that of the psychiatrically trained youth-guidance expert in the youth-guidance literature, in that they have the children's confidence and advise and help them in situations where other adults in positions of authority would necessarily hinder or stop them. In both stories these confidential guides are rather solitary, unmarried men without ordinary adult responsibilities, who are attracted to children and who, as one said, never forgot being young.

40. Speyer, 1927, pp. 240–42.

41. On this point, cf. also "The Consequences of Wrongdoing: An Analysis of Story Completions by German Children," in this volume (p. 306), which describes situations in which the child writers indicate how children—by blushing, stammering, etc.—reveal themselves to adults.

LIST OF REFERENCES[1]

Böttichen, Georg, *et al.* n.d. *O diese Kinder.* Munich: Braun & Schneider.

Haarbeck. L. n.d. *Wildfangs Schulzeit. Wildfang als Backfisch. Wildfang als Braut. Wildfang als Tante. Wildfang als Mutter.* Ensslin and Laiblin: Verlag Reutlingen.

Haseloff, Otto Walter. 1953. "Was die Jugend heute liesst," *Neue Zeitung,* March 11, 12, and 24.

Hoffmann, Heinrich. [1845.] *Der Struwwelpeter: oder lustige Geschichten und drollige Bilder.* Leipzig: Insel Verlag.

Hoyt, Nelly Schargo. 1953a. "Karl May: Living a Dream: An Exploration of the 'Karl May Frage,'" *in* "German National Character: A Study of German Self-images," by Rhoda Métraux and Nelly Schargo Hoyt. ("Studies in Contemporary Cultures, B.") New York: American Museum of Natural History. (Dittoed.)

———. 1953b. "The *Gartenlaube:* An Exploration of Popular Nineteenth Century Fiction." *Ibid.*

Kästner, Erich. 1933. *Der 35. Mai.* Zurich: Atrium Verlag.

———. [1938.] *Das fliegende Klazzenzimmer.* Zurich: Atrium Verlag.

———. 1949. *Pünktchen und Anton: ein Roman für Kinder.* Zurich: Atrium Verlag.

Métraux, Rhoda, and Hoyt, Nelly Schargo. 1953. "German National Character: A Study of German Self-images." ("Studies in Contemporary Cultures, B.") New York: American Museum of Natural History. (Dittoed.)

Roebel, Suse la Chapelle. [1937.] *Trotzkopf als Grossmutter.* Authorized translation from the Dutch by Anna Herbst. Basel: Münster-Verlag.

1. The dating of German books presents a bibliographical problem, in that many are not dated, while some give only the date of the present edition or printing and others (which may have been reprinted many times) give only the original date of publication. Dates in brackets here are the presumed date of original publication; some of the books with recent dates, e.g., those by Sapper, are merely recent printings.

SAPPER, AGNES. 1950. *Das kleine Dummerle und andere Erzählungen.* Stuttgart: D. Gundert Verlag.

——. 1951. *Die Familie Pfäffling: eine deutche Wintergeschichte.* Stuttgart: D. Gundert Verlag.

——. 1952. *Werden und Wachsen: Erlebnisse der grossen Pfäfflingskinder.* Stuttgart: D. Gundert Verlag.

SCHANZ, FRIDA. n.d. *In der Feierstunde: Erzählungen für kleine Mädchen.* Stuttgart: Verlag von Gustav Weise.

SCHUMACHER, TONY. 1951. *Das Turm-Engele.* 32d printing. Stuttgart: Harold-Verlag.

SEELMANN, KURT. 1952. *Kind, Sexualität und Erziehung: zum Verständnis der geschlechtlichen Entwicklung von Kind und Jugendlichen.* 2d ed. Munich and Basel: Ernst Reinhardt Verlag.

SPEYER, WILHELM. 1927. *Der Kampf der Tertia.* Munich: Drömersche Verlaganstalt.

——. 1931. *Die goldene Horde.* Berlin: Ernst Rowohlt Verlag.

STINDE, JULIUS. 1951. *Die Familie Buchholz.* Hamm: G. Grote Verlag.

URY, ELSE. 1950. *Nesthäkchen und ihre Küken.* Düsseldorf: Hoch-Verlag.

——. 1951. *Nesthäkchen fliegt aus dem Nest: Erzählung für junge Mädchen.* Düsseldorf: Hoch-Verlag.

——. 1952. *Nesthäkchen Backfischzeit: eine Jungmädchengeschichte.* Düsseldorf: Hoch-Verlag.

WILDHAGEN, ELSE. 1937. *Trotzkopfs Ehe.* Basel: Münster Verlag.

WUSTMANN, ERICH. 1951. *Gunhild die Reiterin: ein Mädchenleben in Norwegen.* Ensslin and Laiblin: Verlag Reutlinger.

CHAPTER 17

The Image of the Child in Contemporary Films

MARTHA WOLFENSTEIN

CHILDREN as they appear in art, literature, drama, or films embody a complex mixture of fantasy and reality. They represent memories and dreams of adults about their own lost childhood, as well as feelings about those mysterious beings, their own children. These feelings and fantasies often undergo elaborate transformations. Mythologies abound in figures of divine children.[1] In ancient legend, there was Eros, the son and constant companion of Aphrodite, the capricious boy who brought confusion into the lives of mortals by his well-aimed arrows, inspiring unassuageable passion. The divine child of Christianity was a god of love of a less earthly kind and the son of a virgin mother. In the art of different countries and times he has assumed a variety of appearances. In Italian Renaissance painting, for instance, we find the plump and beatific infant, with his hand on the rich maternal breast, the first and adored son of a young mother. Flemish painters, in contrast to this, portrayed a thin, anxious-looking infant, already devoted to an ascetic ideal.

Earthly children similarly assume a variety of guises as they appear in literature and art. The ways in which they are portrayed express a complex of feelings about children prevailing in a given culture at a given time: the legend of the childhood one had or should have had, the image of the ideal child or of the demonic child, models and hazards for relations between adults and children. The story of Tom Sawyer and Huckleberry Finn expresses certain characteristic American attitudes about children. These boys are resourceful and independent and repeatedly prove that adults' alarms and anxieties about them are unfounded. The adults, whether Huck's drunken father or Tom's good, fussy Aunt Polly, are superfluous. The boys pursue their own adventurous existence and, despite appearances of waywardness, are fine, noble-hearted fellows. This legend of the good, strong, self-sufficient child expresses an American ideal: that the child should from an early age sally forth and join his peers and be able to hold his own. Dependence and weakness in the child tend to be played down or disparaged.

The image of the child in Dickens' novels is a very different one. While children appear as exceedingly noble, they are vulnerable and weak and need the protection of kindly adults. Without it they become helpless, suffering victims of wicked and cruel characters. A major theme in British culture is the danger of cruelty to the weak; a major corresponding character trait is a defense against this temptation, the cultivation of gentleness. The weak, who represent a temptation to cruelty and who must be protected from it, include women, children, and animals. In Dickens' novels there is a rich evocation of the sufferings of the weak and good, particularly children, and an appeal to adult pity and protectiveness. This contrast between British and American attitudes is epitomized in the endings of *Oliver Twist* and *Huckleberry Finn*.[2] Oliver, after having undergone many gruesome experiences, as a helpless, unprotected child, finally enters into the haven of a good home into which he is adopted. Huck, faced with a similar prospect of adoption, decides to light out for the open road.

In the films of contemporary cultures we find a series of contrasting images of children. I shall deal with those that appear in recent Italian, French, British, and American films. This account is not intended to be exhaustive. Rather I shall concentrate on certain distinctive themes which recur in the presentation of the child in the films of each of these cultures. In Italian films there is an image of the child as a saviour; in the French, an evocation of the disappointments of childhood; in the British, the issue whether the adults are worthy of the child's trust; in the American, a quest of the child for an ideal man. These themes relating to children are connected in a variety of ways with other major and distinctive themes in the films of each of these cultures. I shall try to indicate some of these connections. Finally, I should like to bring out a quality of the child, namely, his nobility and his function as a touchstone of virtue, which is common to the child protagonists of all four groups.

ITALIAN FILMS: THE INFANT SAVIOUR

The image of the infant saviour continues to shine forth from the walls of Italian cathedrals and churches. Other pictures, close by, evoke the fated role of the beautiful and beloved child as he becomes the bearer of the cross, the crucified one, and the judge of mankind.

Child heroes in Italian films are likely to retain something of this aura. The burden of saving the erring people around them falls upon their slight shoulders, and they may die to save or die because the task is too great for them. They recall corrupt adults from their misguided ways. The adult feels himself judged when the sad gaze of a noble child falls upon him like an accusation, and the adult becomes aware of his weakness and sinfulness.

In *The White Line,* the Christlike role of the boy hero is most explicit. The scene is laid in a town on the Italian-Trieste border. Following the war, a boundary line (the white line of the title) is drawn through the town, dividing it in two. Animosities arise among the townspeople as some cross back from the Trieste side to remain Italian, while others renounce their Italian allegiance. There are disputes about property as farms have been cut in two; a farmer can see his ancestral property being expropriated by a turncoat on the other side of the line, and so on.

The hill down which the boys used gaily to coast in their wagons has also been cut in two by the line. Having become involved in the hostilities of their elders, the boys gather in two gangs on either side of their old coasting hill and exchange insults. Someone throws a stone, and the hero is hit on the forehead. The boy who hit him, suddenly overwhelmed with what he has done, bursts into tears, The hero, with his head bleeding, walks slowly across the line to comfort his old friend. With this the boys all become friends again. In a gesture of revolt against the boundary, they uproot a boundary post and throw it down a ravine.

The townspeople now react strongly to the disappearance of the boundary post. There are accusations of each side against the other as to who has removed it. The boys become alarmed and hold a secret meeting. They decide that someone of them must confess. The question is raised: Whose father will not beat him for it? The boys agree that the hero's father will not beat him. Thus the beloved of his father must take the common sin upon himself and become the sacrifice.

The hero, disconsolate, wanders around the town that evening. He sees through lighted windows how men are getting out their guns, to guard the boundary against further depredations. Then he decides to restore the boundary marker rather than confess. He descends the slope and takes up the burden of the heavy, cross-shaped marker, and struggles up the hill with it. One of the night watchers spies him and shoots. The boy falls, fatally wounded. Later he is found and carried home. The townspeople are sad and sobered, ashamed of their senseless quarrels. The boys come, across the line, to visit their dying comrade. Shortly after this farewell visit, he dies.

The boy hero of this film embodies the essentials of the Christ-legend. He forgives his enemies, he bears the cross, he dies for the sins of others; by his example he teaches his fellow-men that they should love instead of hate one another.

In the somber and tragic *Germany, Year Zero* (made by Rossellini in Berlin), the boy hero is also called upon to save, but the task exceeds his powers; he fails and is crushed by it. The boy has to support his aging, invalid father and his elder brother, who is in hiding from the authorities because of his Nazi past. He is also the sole protector of the virtue of his older sister. In his struggles to find a livelihood, the boy appears as the only noble character in a totally corrupt city. When he seeks help from a former schoolmaster, the teacher tries to seduce him into homosexuality. His family is close to starvation, and the boy assumes the terrible task of deciding who shall be saved; there is not enough for all. He decides to kill his sick and helpless father so that his brother may live. Having given poison to the father, the boy climbs to the top of a ruined building and jumps down. He has tried to save; he has taken the terrible role of judging and of meting out life and death. In his inability to save, he has become a destroyer. And he dies self-condemned for his crime. His fate is a testimony to the wickedness of a world that corrupts the goodness and subverts the noble impulses of a child. The boy has been prevented from fulfilling his destiny as a saviour by a world that appears beyond redemption.

In a more hopeful vein, *His Last Twelve Hours* shows a child, this time a girl, who succeeds in saving. The girl's father, unknown to the other characters in the film, has been run over and killed. Having been called up to a higher sphere, he is informed by a woman judge that he is damned. But she yields to his pleading to grant him twelve hours in which to redeem his bad life. Returning to earth and in haste to seek virtue, he is surrounded by cold and selfish people who do not understand his sudden impulses of generosity and think he has gone mad. Only his little daughter, a beautiful, serious-looking child, feels that something fateful is happening to her beloved father. And it is she who leads him to find salvation. The father has been directed by the otherworldly judge to concentrate his efforts on a poor man whom he has unknowingly wronged. The father makes this poor man rich, sets him up in the mansion of his dreams, and strives to satisfy all his whims. The man then begins to put on airs, tries to break up the engagement of his niece to a poor workman, and demands an aristocratic husband for her. The father in desperate haste arranges this, with the result that the niece and her lover are miserable and the household into which he was to bring happiness is torn by dissension. When the little daughter enters the scene, she sees at once what should be done. She is moved by the plight of the young lovers and urges her father to help them. The father, exasperated with the demanding old man who has given him so much trouble to no avail, makes an impulsive, generous gesture and gives the mansion to the young couple. He is sure that thereby he has lost his chance of heaven. But when his time is up and he again faces his judge, he learns that this last act, to which his child prompted him, has achieved his salvation.

In other Italian films, the saving role of the child may be less fully elaborated. But repeatedly it is a hurt look on the face of an innocent child which recalls an adult from the wrong path, or makes him aware of the depth of his fall from grace. So the ignominy of the father in *The Bicycle Thief*, who is reduced to becoming a thief himself, is underscored by the fact that his devoted little son is the witness of his shameful act. In *Father's Dilemma*, an egotistical, overbearing man is meanly belaboring a poor dressmaker for an unfinished task. Suddenly he notices the dressmaker's little girl, who is looking at him silently with big, sad eyes. The man is at once conscience-stricken and attempts to be placating toward the child and to win her forgiveness. In the same film, the tears of an innocent child save her parents from committing a degrading act. The egotistical man, who is very rich, is desperate to obtain a first communion dress for his little girl (as he has lost in the meanwhile the dress he got from the tardy dressmaker). He attempts to bribe a poor neighbor to give up the communion dress of his daughter. The poor man and his wife are about to yield, but they cannot withstand the tears of their little girl. They are later seen beaming with happy pride as their child kneels angelically at the communion rail.

I can indicate only briefly some connections between this presentation of the child and other themes in Italian films. Saving and more often sacrificial and unsuccessful attempts to save constitute major motifs in these films. The would-be saviour, the one he attempts to save, or both, may perish in the attempt. In *Il Bandito*, the hero is about to rescue his sister from a house of prostitution, into which she has fallen while he was away at the war. Their path is barred by her procurer, who draws a gun. The hero struggles with the other man, the gun goes off, and the sister is killed.[3] The mother of a young man, in *Under the Sun of Rome*, runs out into the street when she hears her son is in danger and suffers a fatal heart attack. In the same film the young man's father learns that the son is about to participate in a robbery. He rushes to the place where the planned robbery is to occur, in the hope of dissuading his son, and is shot in the cross-fire between the robbers and the police. In *Without Pity*, a Negro GI attempts to rescue a girl who has been forced to become a prostitute. In their flight, she is shot, and he also perishes. Rescue in these plots involving adult characters seems often to stand in place of a love act for persons who are forbidden to each other. In the fatality precipitated by the rescue attempt there may be a final embrace in death. The hero of *Il Bandito* clasps his dead sister in his arms. The last shot of *Without Pity* shows the joined hands of the dead Negro soldier and the white girl he loved.

Forbidden wishes and their noble counterpart, the wish to save, combine in a single protagonist where the plot deals with adult characters. Where the innocent child appears, he may embody purely the motive to save as over against the sinfulness of the adults. However, the purity of the saving motive in the child is not without exception. Its evil counterpart breaks through when the little boy who cannot save, in *Germany, Year Zero,* murders his father.

Another distinctive feature of Italian films is their idealization of the pure young girl, the virgin. It is she alone whom men love, toward whom they turn adoringly, and in favor of whom they scorn and repudiate alluring but bad or tarnished women. This is in contrast to American, French, and British films, in all of which a bad woman, or at least one who looks bad, is likely to triumph over a girl who is simply and sweetly good.[4] In Italian films it is regularly the good girl who wins out over her more experienced and seductive rival. The bad woman who despairs because no man can really love her is filled with hopeless yearning at the sight of the virgin bride.[5] An older ideal of womanly purity and virtue, which seems to have lost its hold on other Western cultures, remains in the ascendant in Italy. The blessed and beloved virgin retains her place beside the infant saviour.

FRENCH FILMS: DISAPPOINTMENTS OF CHILDHOOD

Of the cultures under consideration here, the French are least concerned in their films with issues of good and evil. Rather they are preoccupied with the ironical or tragic discrepancy between human wishes and the way the world goes. A lover is taken away by the police just as he is about to join his beloved. When he gets out of jail, he finds she has become the sweetheart of another man (*Sous les toits de Paris*). A moment after an innocent man dies, the police discover the evidence that would have cleared him (*Panique*). Things do not turn out the way men would wish, and their dreams of justice are as unrealistic as their dreams of happiness. This is the recurrent burden of French films. Their aim appears to be that of mastering past disappointments and of inuring one to those of the present.[6]

If one wants to re-evoke disappointments rather than deny them, it is not difficult to find a wealth of material in childhood. It is the time in life when the most impossible wishes are cherished, when one has yet to learn how unsatisfactory the world is, and when one is therefore most vulnerable. Children in French films are not innocent in the sense of being free of amorous or destructive impulses. They are replete with human longings. And they are exemplars of human disappointment.

In the episode entitled "Lust" in *The Seven Deadly Sins,* a girl of thirteen, a prim and serious child in pigtails, thinks she is pregnant. When her mother, a handsome widow, demands to know who the man is, she names an attractive artist who is staying at the inn which the mother runs. There follows a confrontation of the mother and daughter with the man. In amazement, he denies what the girl says. She then tells the mother he was really not to blame, he did not even know it happened. As the adults, with growing skepticism, question her further, she admits that she had sat in the man's armchair just after he had left it, while it was still warm from his body—that is how she became pregnant. The mother and the man laugh with relief, assuring her that she will not have a baby. The girl angrily demands that they leave her alone and, when they have left, throws herself on her bed in a storm of tears.

To complete the little girl's frustration, her mother succeeds where she has failed. The child's fantasy stimulates the mother and the man, who have already been flirting with each other, and serves to precipitate an affair between them. The mother goes that night to the artist's room. She seats herself in his armchair and they joke about how risky this is. As he sits on the arm of the chair and caresses her, she recalls her own girlhood, how she had believed you could get a baby from being kissed, and how at twelve she had had a hopeless love for a man of forty who had not even known she existed. The artist persuades her to spend the night with him. The girl, in her high-necked nightgown in the room above, looks down from her window to see them closing the shutters. The lovers turn on the phonograph so as not to be overheard. The needle gets stuck in a groove and the same phrase plays over and over intolerably as the girl listens. The servants of the inn gather in the hall, wondering whether the phonograph has been left on and there is no one there; perhaps they should go to turn it off. The girl rushes downstairs to warn her mother and save her from being found by the servants. Restless and despairing, the girl then wanders through the dark and vacant inn parlor and out alone onto the country road.

The girl in this film is moved by deep longings which the adults do not take seriously.[7] This is the recurrent fate of children. The mother recalls a similar hopeless love of her own childhood. Stimulated by her daughter's dreams, the mother is impelled to have the affair with the older man which the daughter cannot have and which she herself had been unable to have when she was twelve. But it is not the dream of magic love that transforms the adoring beloved with a touch which she now achieves. It is a light and easy affair. By the time one can gratify the wishes of childhood, they no longer mean what they had meant. There is here an implicit complaint about how badly things are timed, which constitutes a recurrent theme of French films. The situation in which the one who is most filled with longings is the ex-

cluded onlooker at the pleasures of others, as in the case of the girl
in this film, is also many times repeated in French movies.[8]

The Male Brute relates a similar story of a child's intense and disappointed love. The hero is an eleven-year-old boy whose mother is
a prostitute. She has had him reared in the country, but now she
brings him to live with her in Marseilles. There is at first an idyllic interlude, as the adoring little boy happily brings his mother her morning coffee and they have breakfast together. But he soon feels how
much he is excluded. From the door of his room, on the floor below
hers, he sees men entering her room, and, looking out the window, he
sees her closing her shutters. He becomes increasingly pushed aside
as his mother forms an attachment to a small-time crook with whom
she falls hopelessly in love. The abandoned and jealous little boy sees
his mother constantly with this man, whom he detests. The man is
very impatient about having the boy around, and the mother defers
to his wishes. The boy overhears how his mother plans to send him
away to school and to redecorate his room for her beloved man. The
man cynically takes money from the mother, is unfaithful to her, and,
when enraged, smashes her belongings and beats her. The boy, over-
hearing the fight from his room, rushes to the mother's defense, attacking the man with a knife. Later, when the man tries to beat the
boy, the boy threatens to expose him for passing counterfeit money,
which the boy has found out about by chance. The man becomes
placating and tries to find out what he can do to please the boy. The
boy then says that he wants to have dinner with his mother alone.
This long-postponed dream is realized, but the wonderful evening
is spoiled in the end as the mother shows her incessant preoccupation
with the man and tries to persuade the boy to give up the counterfeit
bill which he is holding as evidence. The boy becomes obsessed with
getting rid of the man and makes an unsuccessful attempt to shoot
him. The man meanwhile, alarmed at the danger of exposure of his
connection with the counterfeiters, goes to the police and buys his
immunity by giving information about the gang. This is discovered by
the gang, and they shoot their betrayer.

Earlier in the film, when the boy had been in despair at his mother's
desertion, he had tried to drown himself and had been rescued and
befriended by a kindly ship's captain, who offered to take him on as
cabin boy. After his unsuccessful attempt on the life of his mother's
lover, the boy takes refuge on the ship. The mother learns he is there
and speaks with the captain just before the ship is about to sail. The
captain explains that the boy loves her. She says she loves him, too
(and indeed she has been shown as always charming to the boy when
she was not preoccupied with more important things). The captain
says: "But he loves only you. That is what love is like at the age of

eleven." At the end of the film the mother, not knowing that her lover is dead or that, if he had lived, he was about to go off with another woman, is patiently waiting for him. The boy, as the ship sails out to sea, stands at the prow with a fresh, elated face.

That is what love is like at the age of eleven: exclusive, uncompromising, gallant, violent—and doomed to disappointment. The little boy would like to be the only man in his mother's life, and this is impossible. It is a major theme of French films that intense longings arise under circumstances, or at a time in life, when it is impossible to satisfy them. The predicament of the child is one instance of this. Another which frequently recurs deals with the other end of the life-cycle—the comedy or tragedy of the aging man who is overwhelmed with love for a woman young enough to be his daughter. This theme of French films has been dealt with at length elsewhere.[9] *Symphonie pastorale* and *Le Silence est d'or* are among the many illustrations of it. In French films the bad timing of events in relation to human wishes appears repeatedly. This bad timing may be a matter of accidental circumstances. But the basic instances of it, those of the aging man and of the child, express the belief that it is rooted in the nature of life itself. Desires are not synchronized with the capacity to satisfy them: they arise both too early and too late.

BRITISH FILMS: ARE THE ADULTS WORTHY
OF THE CHILD'S TRUST?

Turning to British films, we enter an atmosphere where moral issues are again in the ascendant. Here it is not a question of whether life is disappointing but of whether one is measuring up to the proper standards. British films alone, among those of the cultures considered here, contain an image of a perfect father. This is a father who has complete control over his impulses and presents a model of such control to his son. Conversely, there are fathers who fail to control bad impulses and who therefore do not provide an adequate model. A heavy reproach is leveled against them.[10] A murderer bitterly blames his father, who was a public hangman and who took a perverse delight in his work; the father has made the son what he is (*Wanted for Murder*). The impulses which must be controlled are particularly those of cruelty toward the weak, toward women and children. As the child is particularly vulnerable, he represents a test of the adult's virtue: the ideal adult will treat him gently, as the wicked one treats him cruelly. The child thus makes a double demand on the adult: to provide a worthy model and to treat him with gentleness.

The children are likely to look up to adults with worshiping eyes. The danger that the adult will fall short of the child's expectations is summed up in the title of *The Fallen Idol*. In this film a little boy is intensely attached to his parents' butler, whom he takes as his ideal. The parents are away throughout the action of the film, so that the butler and his wife stand in the place of parents to the child. In contrast to the kindly butler, his wife is the epitome of everything the adult should not be to the child. In a fit of wicked rage she seizes the little boy's pet snake and burns it up in the stove. Relations between the butler and his wife are strained, as the butler has fallen in love with the beautiful secretary of his employer. There is a violent quarrel between the butler and his wife, following which the wife, trying to spy on the husband and the secretary, climbs onto a high window ledge, loses her balance, falls, and breaks her neck. The frightened little boy has glimpsed part of these events and mistakenly pieces them together, imagining that the butler has pushed his wife down the stairs. The idolized man thus appears to have failed to control his destructive impulses toward women. The boy strives, nevertheless, to remain loyal to him. When the police come to investigate, the boy lies in a way which he thinks will protect the butler but which in effect tends to implicate him. So, unwittingly, the boy's suspicions and reproach break through. The man's fate appears to depend on the boy's faith in him. As this faith wavers, the man's very life is at stake. In the end, of course, the butler is exculpated (Scotland Yard, another embodiment of ideal authortiy, is always just). The little boy's parents return, and he escapes from the nightmare in which the idolized man seemed to turn into a destroyer of women.

In *The Browning Version*, a man's faith in himself depends on the genuineness of a boy's belief in him. The man is an unsuccessful schoolmaster. While he is devoted to classical learning, his teaching of it remains dull. Excessively reserved, unable to express positive feelings, he cannot compete with the more hearty and jovial masters for the boys' affections. Among the boys, who generally dislike or are indifferent to him, there is, however, one, more scholarly and sensitive than the others, who feels an affectionate admiration for him. He is not put off by the teacher's aloofness, and his responsiveness and interest are of great value to the teacher. At the end of the term, this boy comes to the teacher's house to give him a fine edition of a book which they had discussed together. The teacher is moved to tears and has difficulty concealing his emotion. Subsequently the teacher's wife, who is contemptuous of him and unfaithful to him, disillusions him with the boy's motives in giving the present, suggesting it was given for some self-seeking purpose. The teacher is then deprived of the one thing in his life, this boy's admiring devotion, which made him feel not quite a failure. Eventually, the teacher finds the courage to break with his wife. And he gains the happy realization that the boy's attachment to him was genuine. With this he is able to resume a piece of work that he had long abandoned and which the boy's interest encourages him now to complete.

The Stranger in Between shows how a man is moved to self-sacrifice in response to a child's devotion to him. The man has committed a murder and is running away. By chance he encounters a little boy who is also running away. The boy has accidentally set fire to the curtains in his foster-parents' home and fears a terrible beating. The boy attaches himself to the man, who at first finds him a nuisance, then decides it will be a form of disguise if he travels with a child. In the course of a long and desperate flight, these two become close companions. The man grows increasing fond of the boy, who responds with intense love to this the first person who has been kind to him. They finally reach their goal, a small boat on the coast in which they can make their escape. They put out to sea, but by this time the boy, from sleeping in fields and having little to eat, has become sick. As the man sees him feverish and weak, he is torn between the urge to escape and the need to get the requisite care for the child. He turns back. We see him at the end, walking up the quai, carrying the sick child in his arms, to save the boy and to forfeit his own life.

In *The Man Between*, a boy is intensely attached to a man of dubious character. The man is involved in shady machinations in postwar Berlin, while the boy, dashing about on a bicycle which the man has procured him, is his messenger, his spy, his aide, and his vassal. When the man finally decides to abandon his operations, he dismisses the boy from his service, telling him to go back to school. The boy is terribly sad, and the man tries to tell him kindly that he is not really worthy of such devotion. Yet in the end he proves himself worthy—he dies gallantly to save the woman he loves.

In these plots the crucial relation seems regularly to be between a man and a boy. The man is called upon to justify the boy's idealizing devotion. A girl does not seem to require the same nobility: it is possible for her to love a man who treats her cruelly (*The Seventh Veil*). Reversing the situation, women in relation to children are often cruel, like the butler's wife in *The Fallen Idol*. This image of the wickedness of women gives a clue to the destructive impulses of men toward them, impulses which the ideal man holds firmly in check while he substitutes the picture of the weak woman for that of the cruel one. In *The Stranger in Between*, it is his wife whom the man has murdered, a vicious woman who has wrecked his life. But the fact that he is capable of great kindness is subsequently demonstrated toward the little boy. The child provides the possibility for the man to prove that his gentleness is stronger than his violence.

In British films the issue of whether a protagonist measures up to his own ideal standards is of major importance. The child is an external embodiment and also an activator of these internal moral demands. In his idealizing faith he calls upon the adult man to be worthy of it. In his vulnerability he makes an appeal and provides an opportunity for the demonstration of the crucial virtue of gentleness.

AMERICAN FILMS: SEARCH FOR AN IDEAL MAN[11]

Where the child in British films easily finds among the adults around him someone to idolize and it then behooves the adult to deserve this trust, the child in American films longs for an ideal man to appear from afar. Father is not a hero, though great-grandfather may have been. The child's capacities for hero worship lack an object. A stranger must come from afar, the child must journey away from home, or visions of a remote past must be conjured up to provide the missing hero.

In *Shane,* a boy lives with his parents on a lonely frontier farm. The father is a good, hardworking man, who lacks any aura of grandeur. The boy longs to be endowed with masculine powers, to learn to shoot a gun, but the father is always too busy with his farmwork to teach him. Then appears the mysterious stranger, Shane, dressed in buckskin, with a gleaming gun hanging from his belt. The boy is immediately fascinated with him, wonders whether Shane could beat his father in a fight, secretly and in awe handles Shane's gun, and confesses to his mother that he loves Shane almost as much as his father. Shane stays on at the farm as a hired man. A conflict is brewing between the group of homesteaders, to which the boy's parents belong, and the cattle ranchers, who want to dispossess them. While Shane is at first quiet and in the background, slow to react to minor provocations, it is evident that he is to be the protector of the homesteaders against the powerful ranchers. In the meantime Shane satisfies the boy's long-standing wish to be taught how to shoot and demonstrates his extraordinary quickness with a gun.

As the conflict between the two factions becomes increasingly aggravated, the leader of the ranchers invites the boy's father to a parley. When his wife pleads with him not to go, the father indicates that if anything happens to him she will have a better man to take care of her. He has understood that she, like the boy, cannot help preferring the heroic Shane to him. Shane has been warned that the parley is really a trap and means to go in the father's place, as he knows that he alone would be able to handle it. The father is obstinately intent on going to the dangerous encounter, and Shane can only dissuade him by knocking him out. In the fight, Shane fights unfairly, clubbing the father over the head. The boy becomes for the moment disillusioned with Shane and calls after him that he hates him. The mother then explains to the boy that Shane had to do this to save the father. The repentant boy runs after Shane to say he is sorry and follows him to the saloon, where the showdown is to take place. The ranchers have hired a notorious gunfighter, but Shane is, of course, quicker on the draw, shoots him and the leader of the ranchers too. As another, concealed enemy is about to shoot Shane, the watching boy cries a warning, and Shane also eliminates him. His work done, Shane will go away. He gives the boy a message for his mother. The mother had been against guns and fighting. Shane, the great fighter, wants her to know that now there will be no more guns in the valley; he has silenced them. The boy weepingly pleads with Shane to stay, but Shane has to travel on. He does not belong to this good, tame world of the homesteaders, but to a world of the past. He is a bad gun fighter turned good, who has put himself briefly into the service of the new workaday life in which he cannot share.

It is significant that when the boy is disillusioned with Shane for fighting unfairly, this is a misunderstanding. There does not have to be a transformation of the man's character to make him worthy of the boy's trust, only an explanation which clears up the misunderstanding. This is a general rule in American films. Instead of inner changes of character, from sin to redemption (as in the British *The Stranger in Between*), there are temporary false appearances, which may make a hero look bad when he is good all along and in the end succeeds in proving it.

The boy in *The Little Fugitive* has no father. On an adventurous journey away from home, when the seven-year-old boy goes all alone to Coney Island, he finds an ideal man, a "cowboy" in charge of the pony concession. This man is for the boy replete with the skills and accouterments of longed-for masculinity, with his aura of the Far West and his knowledge of horses. There is a brief interlude when the boy thinks it will be possible for him to work for the "cowboy," to learn how to handle horses, and to gain all the admired powers of the man. However, this plan proves unfeasible, and in the end he has to go back to the flat in Brooklyn and the shadowy cowboys of television.

This film exemplifies a number of major American themes. The little boy's flight to Coney Island is precipitated by his older brother's friends playing a trick on him. They are tired of having this kid brother always tagging along and trying to get into games which he is not yet up to.[12] To scare him off, the older boys offer him the privilege of shooting a rifle, then fool him into thinking he has killed his brother. The boy then runs away. Like the heroes of many American movie melodramas, he has been framed, appears guilty, is really innocent. At Coney Island, after he has used up all his money, he wanders disconsolately on the beach. There he finds another boy picking up bottles and turning them in for refunds—five cents a bottle. The boy immediately goes into the bottle business, makes enough for repeated rides on the ponies, and so attracts the interest of the "cowboy." With his successful bottle enterprise the boy could apparently have maintained himself until the end of the season.

This is the American legend of the self-sufficient child. However, this dream of getting along on his own is shown to be in part the little boy's illusion. When the "cowboy" offers him a job, he is only fooling. It is a ruse to get the boy's name and address so that he can see that the boy gets back home; the man gets the information by saying he needs it for the boy's social security card. The man then phones the boy's older brother to come and get him. The boy, however, runs away again when he sees the "cowboy" exchanging a casual remark with a policeman; the boy thinks, of course, that he will be turned over to the police for his supposed crime. When the brother comes to find the boy, there is a long search through Coney Island, but the brother succeeds in finding the boy without having recourse to the police. He is like the private investigators in the melodramas. While the boys have been having all these adventures, their mother has been away. They succeed in getting back just before her return, and when she supposes they have been watching television the whole time she was away, they exchange a knowing wink and do not disabuse her. The grownups do not know and do not need to know about the enterprises and hazards of their children's lives which the children can handle quite well on their own.

Returning to the search for the ideal man, *When I Grow Up* presents a vision of such a man in a flashback to the days when grandfather was a boy. The father in the contemporary scene is an ineffectual bank clerk, uninspiring and unable to handle or to understand his son. But grandfather's father—there was a man. He was strong and awe-inspiring, and he whipped his son in the woodshed. But he could be tender and understanding and evoke great love. When his son is sick with typhoid fever, he nurses him, exchanges confidences and jokes, and a real intimacy blossoms between them. In the crisis of the son's illness the father drives out in his buggy in a terrible rainstorm to bring the doctor to save the boy's life. And as a result of the strain and exposure of the night drive, the father becomes ill and dies.[13] Just before the boy learns of his father's death, as he himself begins to recover, he has two dreams about his father. In one of these dreams, father and son are engaged in an amorous, laughing tussle in the hay, in the course of which each playfully spanks the other. In the second dream, father and son lie side by side next to a pond, with their fishing rods hanging out over the water. The boy turns affectionately to the father to clasp his hand. The image of a strong and tender father who can be loved like this appears in a dream within a flashback about great-grandfather.

In an interlude in this film when the boy of the past turns against his father for having whipped him unfairly, the boy and his ragamuffin pal go off to join a circus. There the boy finds one of the away-from-home heroes who can teach a boy such marvelous tricks, the star clown, who becomes his friend.

One of the reviews of Geoffrey Gorer's book, *The American People* (1948), bore the title "Sometimes I Feel Like a Fatherless Child."[14] In American culture, fathers who are strong, admirable, and lovable do not seem to be the rule. Rather there are two alternate father-types: the strong, severe father (rather old-fashioned), who is feared, not loved, and the nice, likable father who is a pal and falls short of the masculine ideal.[15] These two images of the father as they appear in American films have been discussed elsewhere.[16] In American life, children are expected to surpass their parents. The father is not the model that the son will follow when he grows up. But the boy longs for a man who can induct him into the mysteries and powers of masculinity, who has the strength and skill to which the boy aspires, and who can show him how.[17] Thus we have seen how the boy heroes of these American films are drawn to men other than their fathers to whom they can look with admiration, men who are masters of wonderful skills—the gun fighter, the cowboy, the acrobatic clown—who might impart to the boy the masculine prowess which he longs to attain. And we have also seen the dream of a father who could be both strong and tender projected into the past—great-grandfather—not the father of today.

The children in films that I have been discussing are heroes or heroines. Malign children sometimes appear in films, but they are rare.[18] When wicked impulses are dramatized, it is much more likely to be through adult protagonists. Children in the films of the four cultures considered here all have something in common. They are noble characters, usually nobler than the adults around them. They are not the embodiment of impulses which, by adult tutelage, must be brought under control. Rather, in one way or another, they represent moral demands and ideals. This is the adults' image of the child, to which two major factors would seem to contribute. First, there is the infantile amnesia of which Freud speaks, in accordance with which adults forget the intense impulsive desires of their own childhood.[19] Second, there is the appeal which the child makes to adult goodness, to be an ideal model and to exercise kindness and protective love. This adult goodness, which the child evokes, is then projected onto the child; it is he who appears as the exemplar of virtue.

There are different nuances to the nobility which the child manifests in the films of these different cultures. In Italian films, the child appears as a saviour. By his suffering and sacrifice, or it may be simply by the unerring reactions of his pure soul, he recalls men from wickedness to redemption. The child's virtue in French films is rather a counterpart to his immaturity. It is a virtue of necessity; he is not yet capable of fulfilling his desires. The sad and yearning child, whose dreams of love are bound to be disappointed, appears to the audience as a touching contrast to the adult characters, but he does not affect them; he cannot divert them from their impulsive pursuits. In contrast to this again, the child in British films appeals to the adult to whom he gives his trust and worship to be worthy of it. The adult is sensitively responsive to this demand, which echoes or strengthens that of his own conscience, and may sacrifice himself in order not to betray the child's trust. In American films the child is the bearer of the hero image. In a prosaic world, he dreams of a man surpassing his father, who would combine masculine strength and tenderness. And, happily, the film may provide an appearance of this hero, who illuminates at least for a time the life of the child.

NOTES

1. Jung and Kerényi, 1949.
2. Auden, 1953.
3. Cf. "Themes in Italian Culture: A First Discussion," 1953.
4. Wolfenstein and Leites, 1950.
5. Wolfenstein, 1953*b*.
6. Wolfenstein and Leites, 1950, also 1953.
7. Cf. Martha Wolfenstein, "French Parents Take Their Children to the Park," in this volume (p. 99).
8. Wolfenstein, 1953*a*.
9. Wolfenstein and Leites, 1950, 1953.
10. Wolfenstein and Leites, 1950, 1951.
11. For studies of American culture relevant to the following discussion see Mead (1942 and 1949), Gorer (1948), and Erikson (1950).
12. Margaret Mead (1948) has pointed out this characteristic American relationship between older and younger brothers.
13. This mortality of fathers is a recurrent theme in American films. In *So Big*, there is a very similar episode, in which a big strapping father falls down and dies after a long wagon ride on a stormy night. Children in American films appear to be much tougher and more viable than fathers. There would seem to be a contrast here to cultures like the Eastern European Jewish and the pre-Soviet Russian, where anxiety about probable death from being out in the rain and similar common hazards was concentrated on children.
14. Kazan, 1948.
15. Frenkel-Brunswik, 1952.
16. Wolfenstein and Leites, 1950.
17. Bibring, 1953.
18. The following are among the relatively exceptional bad children in films. In the Italian *Germany, Year Zero* and *Sciusca*, vicious children appeared as products of an impoverished and callous society. In French films a child may be evil or a bringer of evil for various reasons. The tragic little girl in *Forbidden Games* is an

PLATE XXI. *Image of the Child in Contemporary Films. I*

Italian: *The White Line*

● THE CHILD AS SAVIOR.

PLATE XXII. *Image of the Child in Contemporary Films. II*

Courtesy of Paramount Pictures

FIG. 1.—American: *Shane*

Courtesy of Joseph Burstyn

FIG. 2.—American: *The Little Fugitive*

● THE CHILD'S SEARCH FOR THE IDEAL MAN

PLATE XXIII. *Image of the Child in Contemporary Films. III*

Courtesy of Joseph Burstyn

FIG. 1.—French: *The Male Brute*

*Courtesy of Arthur Davis
Associates, Inc. & Arlan Pictures*

FIG. 2.—French: *The Seven Deadly Sins*

● DISAPPOINTMENTS OF CHILDHOOD

PLATE XXIV. *Image of the Child in Contemporary Films. IV*

British: *The Fallen Idol*

Courtesy of Selznick Releasing Organization

● IS THE MAN WORTHY OF THE CHILD'S TRUST?

instance of the dangerous intruder in a family circle. The malign twelve-year-old girl in *Le Corbeau* is a bad counterpart to the girl in *The Seven Deadly Sins;* being a frustrated onlooker at adults' pleasures impels her to vindictive acts. In *Ballerina,* a little girl injured a dancer who had replaced the one she adored. In British films, children are sometimes whimsically naughty, as in *Tony Draws a Horse.* In American films, where children are usually uninterested and unenvious in relation to adults' affairs, an exceptional bad child appeared in *The Children's Hour,* the little girl who spread malicious gossip about her teachers. A wicked, though eventually redeemed, boy figured in *Tomorrow the World,* a child of Nazi upbringing.

19. Freud, 1938.

LIST OF REFERENCES

AUDEN, W. H. 1953. "Huck and Oliver." British Broadcasting Company Third Programme Broadcast, October.

BIBRING, GRETE L. 1953. "On the 'Passing of the Oedipus Complex' in a Matriarchal Family Setting." In *Drives, Affects, Behavior,* ed. RUDOLPH M. LOEWENSTEIN, pp. 278–84. New York: International Universities Press.

FRENKEL-BRUNSWIK, ELSE. 1952. "Interaction of Psychological and Sociological Factors in Political Behavior," *The American Political Science Review,* XLVI, No. 1, 44–65.

ERIKSON, ERIK H. 1950. *Childhood and Society.* New York: W. W. Norton & Co.

FREUD, SIGMUND. 1938. "Three Contributions to the Theory of Sex." In *The Basic Writings of Sigmund Freud,* pp. 553–604. New York: Modern Library.

GORER, GEOFFREY. 1948. *The American People.* New York: W. W. Norton & Co.

JUNG, C. G., and KERÉNYI, C. 1949. *Essays on a Science of Mythology: The Myth of the Divine Child and the Mysteries of Eleusis.* New York: Pantheon Books.

KAZAN, ALFRED. 1948. "Review of Geoffrey Gorer's *The American People,*" *New Yorker,* May 20, pp. 108–10.

MEAD, MARGARET. 1942. *And Keep Your Powder Dry.* New York: William Morrow & Co.

———. 1948. "A Case History in Cross-national Communications." In *The Communication of Ideas,* ed. LYMAN BRYSON, pp. 209–29. New York: Harper & Bros.

———. 1949. *Male and Female.* New York: William Morrow & Co.

"Themes in Italian Culture: A First Discussion." 1953. In *The Study of Culture at a Distance,* ed. MARGARET MEAD and RHODA MÉTRAUX, pp. 131–40. Chicago: University of Chicago Press.

WOLFENSTEIN, MARTHA. 1953a. "Movie Analysis in the Study of Culture," *ibid.,* pp. 267–80.

———. 1953b. "Notes on an Italian Film, *The Tragic Hunt,*" *ibid.,* pp. 282–89.

WOLFENSTEIN, MARTHA, and LEITES, NATHAN. 1950. *Movies: A Psychological Study.* Glencoe, Ill.: Free Press.

———. 1951. "Movie Psychiatrists," *Complex,* No. 4, pp. 19–27.

———. 1953. "Plot and Character in Selected French Films: An Analysis of Fantasy." In *Themes in French Culture: A Preface to a Study of French Community,* by RHODA MÉTRAUX and MARGARET MEAD, pp. 89–108. ("Hoover Institute Studies.") Stanford, Calif.: Stanford University Press.

PART V

Children's Imaginative Productions

Introduction

O^{NE} of the most striking developments in the study of human behavior of the last thirty years has been the systematic use of projective materials, ways of evoking from children and adults pieces of
creative behavior which could then be analyzed with the help of our
developing understanding of psychological dynamics. Attention to projective behavior began with attempts to investigate the way in which
the normal child developed his understanding and mastery of the
world, to construct theories of social evolution or developmental psychology, and to establish a background for therapy and education
through attention to the art of the insane, the typical play behavior of
children, etc. These naturalistic observations developed, in the climate
of opinion of the twentieth century, into attempts to obtain more comparable and controlled materials. Projective tests, of which the Rorschach and the Thematic Apperception Test are the outstanding examples, came into existence, and individual subjects are now being
asked to project into partly structured materials such as a symmetrical
"ink blot," an ambiguous drawing, a segment of their own idiosyncratic way of interpreting themselves and their relationship to the
world around them.[1]

Parallel to this development, the use of play in therapy has become
a form of communication with child patients. Disturbed children are
given miniature life-toys; toys which in size and shape make it possible
to act out or demonstrate their distorted or overspecialized interpretations of the functioning of their bodies, their relationships to other
people and to the natural and social universe in which they live. The
use of play in therapy provides a varied set of materials—"mini-toys,"
Margaret Lowenfeld's world constructions,[2] etc.

A close interrelationship has developed among these methods, so
that a test devised to measure intelligence may be used to give more
insight on a child's affectivity, as in the picture-interpretation item on
the Stanford-Binet; or a test designed to measure brain injury, like the
Bender-Gestalt, may become a projective test. Children's spontaneous
productions may be analyzed with insight derived either from the
widespread statistical material on Goodenough's Draw-a-Man Test or
from the experience of the therapist who uses art; and experience in
child analysis may provide the model for research on individuals of a
given sex or age group.

These three methods—naturalistic descriptions, tests, and play materials—of evoking and analyzing have been used also in the study of cultural differences, in studies of art and ritual, and in testing large groups of individuals from another culture, either by a standardized, partially structured, test situation or by using the freer methods developed in therapy in which children or adults are asked to draw or model, compose a story or construct a dramatic scene from a variety of specially provided materials.[3]

When methods like these are adapted to the study of cultural regularities, certain adjustments have to be made. If partly structured materials are used, care must be taken not to make the materials too complex. For the study of individual differences within a culture, the richer the materials, the better the delineation of each individual personality; but such a complete delineation of the idiosyncratic makes it more difficult to see the cultural regularities.

The following chapters in Part V illustrate these three approaches to projective materials. The French children's paintings were assembled in an art exhibit, from the original work of French children in France, on the basis of aesthetic criteria and were analyzed in a study of French culture conducted in the United States. The story-completion test given to German children in Germany by Harold and Gladys Anderson, subsequently analyzed by Rhoda Métraux as part of a study of German culture at a distance, is an example of the use of a test situation projectively for the study of cultural characteristics. Erik Erikson's study of sex differences in the play productions of a group of California children utilizes play materials to elicit culturally regular sex differences in preadolescents. In the study of the French children's paintings, nothing was known about the individuals except age and sex. For the German children, school grade and locality were carefully specified, and in the California group the children were part of a longitudinal study in which a large number of individual characteristics were known from observational and interview material, so that a knowledge of the individuals made it possible to handle the regularities with optimum authority.

The two chapters in Part II by Jane Belo and Colin McPhee are examples of the combination of observation, interviewing, and use of the materials which the children produced and may be referred to for illustrations of placing children's fantasy productions within the complete cultural context—a context which can be partially taken for granted only when the production is part of a familiar Western culture, where the art, architecture, and plot style are known.

M. M.

NOTES

1. Frank, 1948.
2. Lowenfeld, 1935, 1939.
3. For discussion and bibliography see Abel, 1948; Dubois, 1944; J. and Z. Henry, 1944; W. Henry, 1947; Mead, 1954; Mead and Métraux, 1953.

LIST OF REFERENCES

ABEL, THEODORA M. 1948. "The Rorschach Test in the Study of Culture," *Rorschach Research Exchange and Journal of Projective Techniques*, XII, No. 2, 79–93.

DUBOIS, CORA. 1944. *The People of Alor*. Minneapolis: University of Minnesota Press.

FRANK, LAWRENCE K. 1948. *Projective Methods*. Springfield, Ill.: Charles C Thomas.

HENRY, JULES and ZUNIA. 1944. *Doll Play and Pilaga Indian Children*. ("American Orthopsychiatric Association Research Monographs," No. 4.)

HENRY, WILLIAM E. 1947. "The Thematic Apperception Technique in the Study of Culture-Personality Relations," *Genetic Psychology Monographs*, XXXV, No. 1, 3–135.

LOWENFELD, MARGARET. 1935. *Play in Childhood*. London: Gollancz.

———. 1939. "The World Pictures of Children: A Method of Recording and Studying Them," *British Journal of Medical Psychology*, XVIII, Part I, 65–101.

MEAD, MARGARET. 1954. "'Research on Primitive Children." In *Manual of Child Psychology*, ed. LEONARD CARMICHAEL, pp. 735–80. New York: John Wiley & Sons.

MEAD, MARGARET, and MÉTRAUX, RHODA (eds). 1953. *The Study of Culture at a Distance*. Chicago: University of Chicago Press.

CHAPTER 18

French Children's Paintings

————————————————————————MARTHA WOLFENSTEIN

This study was originally done as part of the work on French culture in the Columbia University Research in Contemporary Cultures, conducted under a grant from the Human Resources Division, Office of Naval Research.

A FRENCH color-manufacturing firm, that of J. M. Paillard in Paris, holds yearly painting competitions for children. Children in all French schools where painting is taught are eligible. Each year a different subject is given, such as streets, the seasons, fairs, churches and monuments, sports, work on the farm, waterways, the Liberation, trades, cities and villages. A jury of noted artists and art critics selects from the thousands of paintings submitted from all over France those which are to appear in the annual exhibition, to be shown first in Paris, then in other French cities and abroad. At the beginning of 1948, the Museum of Modern Art in New York presented a selection of these French children's paintings, which had been collected over the preceding twelve years. The following observations are based on the paintings which appeared in that exhibition. They were the work of children between the ages of eleven and sixteen.

The work in all these pictures was careful and precise, almost pedantic. The most striking thing about them was the absence of wide vistas and of energetic human action. Landscapes were divided up into small bounded spaces, in which details were painstakingly worked over. Human figures tended to be immobile, or if some action was portrayed, it was incompletely shown. One could see fishing rods, but the fishermen were concealed behind trees. One could see the oars of a rower, but the oarsman himself was cut off by the boundary of the picture; within the picture was his companion who sat inactive in the boat. These characteristics of the pictures seem related to an aspect of French child training in which aggressive impulses and large-muscle activity generally are drastically interfered with.[1] The pictures which these French children painted express the visual counterpart of such curtailment of aggressive and muscular tendencies. The wide view to the open horizon is the pictorial correlate of the impulse to move actively into space. Conversely the landscape without a distant horizon and with many boundaries and barriers corresponds to more confined movements. Small and delicate applications of paint, as against wide sweeping strokes, have a similar significance, indicating a concentration on small-muscle activity.

The aspect of the visual world which is emphasized is that of providing agreeable stimuli: the bunches of grapes on the vines in a country scene, the gay café umbrellas in the city, the minutely detailed cakes in a *pâtisserie* window, and the humanized landscape in which nature has been sufficiently transformed by civilizing influences so that it can be contemplated with equanimity.

I shall now attempt to describe the paintings in more detail.

1. Landscapes tend to have high horizon lines, preferably above the top margin of the picture. The effect is that of the ground being tipped up, with a relative absence of linear perspective, of objects diminishing in size with distance, or of atmospheric effects. The most remote objects in this way are brought close and seen clearly and distinctly. There is a preference for inclosed spaces, a courtyard or a farm- or chickenyard with the view beyond closed off by buildings. Waterways are inclosed by arching bridges or stopped by a town cozily nestled at the far end, instead of reaching into the distance or in free expanse from border to border. Scenes are broken up into patches with many repetitive elements within them, such as grapes and grape leaves, sheep, haycocks, identical tree silhouettes, bricks, roof tiles, café umbrellas, loaves of bread. There is frequently a patchwork-quilt effect, with fine detail, but relative absence of an over-all whole effect.

Some of the tendencies manifested here seem obviously derived from familiar aspects of modern French painting. The tipping-up of horizontal planes, reducing a three-dimensional vista to a flat two-dimensional design has been a prominent tendency in French painting, particularly of still life, since near the beginning of the century. This tendency has been interpreted by Meyer Schapiro[2] as expressing a diminution of energetic striving; everything is brought close, so that one hardly has to raise one's hand to reach it, and the favored still-life subjects have been those of private amusement and self-stimulation: bottles of wine, pipes, fruit, musical instruments. These children's landscape paintings have a similar effect of reducing the distance which appeals to energetic movement. As compared with paintings of American children of the same age, this absence of push to a distant horizon is marked. Where American adolescents seem concerned with mastering a large vista, with the use of linear perspective and a grasp of the total view, these French adolescents, in a more painstaking way, fill each small area with a delicate pattern.

The tipping-up of the horizontal plane, bringing everything near, together with the elimination of atmospheric effects, serves another important purpose—everything can be seen clearly and distinctly. This corresponds in visual terms to a major French striving, traditionally expressed in the Cartesian emphasis on "clear and distinct ideas" and exemplified in the prized intellectual trait of "lucidity."

The characteristic French image of landscape as humanized rather than as wild nature is also illustrated here. The field is broken up into many small areas, and there are always houses, though not always human figures, in the scene. The avoidance of the unbounded and irregular expresses a French attitude toward nature, whether it be in the form of human impulses or in their counterparts in moving water, rolling countryside, or windy sky. Whether in the internal or the external sphere, the unbounded and irregular must be brought under control. Hence expanses of land and water are inclosed by humanly introduced boundaries. The fact that the expanse of sky cannot be so bounded may be one reason why so little sky is shown. For the irregularities of external nature (corresponding to the unpredictability of impulse) the orderly, repetitive bricks, haycocks, tree rows, etc., are substituted. This recalls also the French manipulation of real landscape, the persistent clipping of trees to produce uniform and regular outlines, the planting of trees in rows, etc. The tendency in these pictures to fill up every space with organized detail may also be interpreted as a defense against the free expression of impulse: in the empty unorganized space, who knows what might happen? It is like the need of compulsive individuals to fill up every moment of their time with some busy task, so that there will be no interval into which wayward impulse may intrude. One may recall in this connection the heavy burden of school tasks imposed on French children, which allows them few free moments.

2. There is little human action in these pictures. The most active figures are an incidental diver and swimmer in a river scene. In the one sports picture, tennis players are standing still waiting for the game to begin. Animals show livelier activity: in a circus scene, horses (without riders) gallop around a ring, horses and dogs do acrobatic stunts, while a clown and a ringmaster delicately raise a finger or a whip to direct their movements. The most rapidly moving human figures are people being swung by a revolving swing at a fair: they are not moving on their own initiative but are being moved by an outside agency.

This absence of forceful human movement is indicative of the strong restraint imposed on energetic outward drives. One sees a connection here between the elimination of distance in landscape and the immobilization of human figures. On both scores there is a strong contrast between French and American children's art, since in the latter we find not only the push into the distance in landscape but also an interest in violent human action, for instance, boxers and football players.

Pictures on the subject of the Liberation give further evidence of restraint of human movement. Here the general tendency toward immobilization may be reinforced by a feeling on the part of the French that they failed to be sufficiently energetic in this operation. One picture on this topic shows French civilians standing in the streets looking at tanks, tents, and khaki-clad soldiers. Another shows a parade of tanks, between masses of people with flags and banners, lining the streets. These bystanders smile, but their hands are on their hips or in their pockets. In the one picture that shows fighting, a Frenchman has captured two German soldiers, who walk in front of him with arms raised while he walks behind holding a gun. A third German lies dead on the ground. Thus the result of a violent action, the immobile corpse, is shown, but not the action itself. From behind the closed shutters of a house in the background, guns spit fire, but the gunners remain unseen. The man who appears with the gun (escorting the prisoners) is only holding the gun; those who are shooting are offstage.

A similar tendency to substitute an immobilized image for a violent act appeared in Rorschach responses of French adults.[3] There was a tendency in these subjects, as soon as they saw the possibility of some activity or aggression, to freeze the figure, pin it down, or turn it into a statue. Similarly, the targets of aggression were seen as dead, skinned, crushed, but the acts which would have produced these results were excluded. On another projective test a French child drew a picture of an arrow with the explanation that a hunter was shooting at a bird but missed. Neither hunter nor bird was shown, and the fantasied violence was further repudiated by denying that anything would come of it.

A related defense against aggression appeared in the artwork of some French children which I saw at a little gallery for children's art in Paris in 1953. The children, about ten years of age, had made "tapestries" by cutting out small pieces of colored cloth which they glued to a background, producing a kind of cloth mosaic. One of these portrayed the assassination of Henry IV and another Joan of Arc being burned at the stake. While the subject matter in this case was explicitly violent, the way of expressing it, not in bold sweeping strokes, but in the long-drawn-out labor of carefully cutting out and pasting all the little pieces of cloth, would presumably have the effect of considerably toning down aggressive feelings in the process. Also, the aggressive acts chosen were outstandingly condemnable ones: the killing of France's greatest heroes.

3. Returning to the paintings of the Museum of Modern Art exhibit, in those dealing with different trades there was a striking tendency to show the working person as isolated. A shoemaker, a dressmaker, a baker, a drygoods salesgirl are shown, each entirely alone. A painter appears in a scene with unrelated figures. The isolated working person

occasionally comes in contact with a customer. A woman flower-vendor, accompanied by a small child, offers flowers to a passing man. A single clerk in a ladies' hatshop waits on a lady customer. Three customers wait for the services of a single *coiffeur*. Only in one instance, in a butcher-shop, do two butchers appear, each engaged with a separate customer. These French adolescents seem to picture working life, their own future existence, as peculiarly lonely. Their view seems to have coincided with the then current trend of existentialism in its emphasis on the isolation of the individual. In other pictures, figures shown in recreational activities also tend to appear alone. As incidental to a waterways scene, a figure appears rowing alone or fishing alone. In one scene a woman in a rowboat appears at the bottom of the picture; she presumably has a companion, but he is not seen—only the tips of his oars appear above the bottom margin. The main athletic activity shown is swimming, an individual rather than a group sport. This is, of course, in keeping with a general French preference in respect to sports activities (e.g., bicycle racing).[4]

4. In two pictures funeral processions appear. In one the funeral cortège passes through a busy street with a restaurant in the foreground and an elaborate *confiserie* in the background. The delicacies in the shop window are depicted with the same care and detail as the wreaths on the coffin; the latter bear the inscriptions, *à mon père, à mon époux, ses collègues*. The other funeral has a village setting; a *mairie*, with flag flying, fills in the background. Behind the coffin walk young men and boys, followed by younger and older black-clad weeping women (this would seem to be also the funeral of a father). These French adolescents do not avoid thinking of death, but they do not think of it in a melancholy, romantic way. They see a funeral in the same ironic manner in which the adult French have been picturing it since the mid-nineteenth century in painting and more recently in films. The ordinary details of ongoing life obtrude themselves; the funeral appears as an almost casual incident in the larger scene. It provides a *memento mori*, reminding the lover not to lose a moment in kissing his aging sweetheart (in the film *Extenuating Circumstances*, he raises his hat to a funeral passing below the balcony and does not interrupt the kiss); it impels the adolescent painter to conjure up the image of the huge *confiserie*.

5. Several pictures show crowds, at a parade, in a market, at the circus. There are many tiny figures, none of them standing out. One must look very closely to see that some effort has been made to maintain individual differences, in different colors of clothes and hair, different postures, etc. There seems to be a feeling that the individual is easily lost in the crowd and, at the same time, a resistance to this merging with the group.[5] The alternative life-situations which occur to these

PLATE XXV. *French Children's Paintings. I*

Courtesy of Museum of Modern Art, New York

Water color by a fourteen-year-old French girl. Visual counterpart to restraint on motor and aggressive activity.

PLATE XXVI. *French Children's Paintings. II*

Courtesy of Museum of Modern Art, New York

Tempera by a sixteen-year-old French girl. *Memento mori* and the pastry shop.

young painters seem to be either being completely alone or lost in the crowd.

The over-all impression of this collection is one of a subdued, almost a resigned, attitude, with little of the youthful rebelliousness or grandiose dreams sometimes associated with adolescence. However, it must be remembered that these paintings were produced and selected for a competition, so that more spontaneous and possibly nonconforming work would not appear. That some of the tendencies shown in these pictures exemplify more general French traits is suggested by their coherence with other aspects of French culture. Thus the interference with aggression and strenuous movement finds pictorial expression in the partitioning of space and the immobilization of figures. As to the sobriety and diligence which these French adolescents show in their paintings, we may in part relate it to the French view of what is appropriate to different phases of life. Childhood is not for fun; it is a hard-working probation, while in adult life there are interludes of pleasure not permitted to children.[6] Correspondingly, in adult French painting more freedom is often apparent than in these children's paintings.

NOTES

1. Cf. Martha Wolfenstein, "French Parents Take Their Children to the Park," in this volume (p. 99).
2. Schapiro, 1936.
3. Abel *et al.*, 1954.
4. Observations of French children at play suggest that they play alone much more than American children do. Cf. Martha Wolfenstein, "French Parents Take Their Children to the Park," in this volume (p. 99).
5. In French films crowds are usually pictured as obstructive or dangerous (cf. Wolfenstein and Leites, 1954).
6. Cf. Martha Wolfenstein, "French Parents Take Their Children to the Park," and Françoise Dolto, "French and American Children as Seen by a French Child Analyst," in this volume (pp. 99 and 408).

LIST OF REFERENCES

ABEL, THEODORA, BELO, JANE, and WOLFENSTEIN, MARTHA. 1954. "An Analysis of French Projective Tests." In *Themes in French Culture: A Preface to a Study of French Community*, by RHODA MÉTRAUX and MARGARET MEAD, pp. 109–18. ("Hoover Institute Studies.") Stanford, Calif.: Stanford University Press.

SCHAPIRO, MEYER. 1936. "The Social Bases of Art." In *First American Artists' Congress*, ed. JEROME KLEIN *et al.*, pp. 31–37. New York: American Artists' Congress.

WOLFENSTEIN, MARTHA, and LEITES, NATHAN. 1954. "Plot and Character in Selected French Films: An Analysis of Fantasy." In *Themes in French Culture: A Preface to a Study of French Community*, by RHODA MÉTRAUX and MARGARET MEAD, pp. 89–108. ("Hoover Institute Studies.") Stanford, Calif.: Stanford University Press.

CHAPTER 19

The Consequences of Wrongdoing: An Analysis of Story Completions by German Children

—————————————————————————RHODA MÉTRAUX

This article was prepared in 1953 as part of a study of German national character, made in collaboration with Nelly Schargo Hoyt, under the auspices of the American Museum of Natural History ("Studies in Contemporary Cultures, B," conducted under a contract with the Office of Naval Research). The writer is indebted to Dr. Hoyt for insights of importance in this paper (cf. Métraux and Hoyt, 1953).

PRESENTED with a hypothetical situation in which a child is pictured as having done something wrong, what does a child foresee will happen next? The answers to a series of such problems by one child can, at best, give us some insight into the imaginative reworking of experience by that child. From the anwers of a group of children we can derive something else: the pattern of expectation about a type of experience and, by inference, the organization of attitudes toward such experiences in a culture.

This study is an analysis of German children's attitudes toward wrongdoing by children, expressed in a series of story completions. The plots of six situations, each involving a possible incident of wrongdoing, were presented to German school children, who were asked to write an ending to each story. The study was made for purposes of comparison with books on child care and youth guidance by German educators and with juvenile fiction by German authors, in which each type of material was regarded as one source of information on contemporary German attitudes, especially toward upbringing.

The Story Completion Form, which was the basis for the study, was developed by two American social psychologists, Dr. Gladys L. Anderson and Dr. Harold H. Anderson, and the test was administered under their direction to children in schools in a West German city in the summer of 1952. Thus the plot situations were not specifically German, but only the children's story completions. This study is based on a sample of the total material, consisting of the answers given by 150 ten- and eleven-year-old children (56 boys and 94 girls) in classes in three schools.[1]

The method of analysis, an adaptation of pattern analysis developed for studies of public opinion,[2] was open-ended and qualitative. The procedure followed was to synthesize the several plot solutions given for each of the six stories and to analyze these in terms of the organization of significant detail and of emergent themes.[3] In this presentation I shall discuss, first, the children's handling of plot and, second, the dominant themes.

STORY PLOTS AND PLOT SOLUTIONS

The plot situations—the stories presented to the child writers for solution—are variations on two themes: loss and accidental damage. In five of the stories the child protagonist is faced with a situation where something has gone wrong through the child's fault or by accident; one is an ambiguous situation where an adult may blame a child. Thus the range of situations is a limited one. In most of the stories the child is or may come in conflict with an adult; in two there may be conflict between children. Thus the plot situations present some possibilities for comparison of adult-child and child-child relationships.

For each of the stories I shall give a translation of the German text of the plot situation and then a summary of the writers' story endings.

1. The Lost Cap[4]

Plot situation.—Peter and Franz are going to school. Suddenly Franz grabs Peter's hat and throws it high into the nearest tree, so that Peter cannot get it down with his hand. Franz had never done anything like that before. Franz and Peter did not have a quarrel the day before. Why did Franz do this? What does Peter do? What does Franz think? What does Peter think?

Three main solutions are given by the children:

a) Franz (who threw the cap) gets the cap down again[5]—sometimes only after Peter has exerted pressure by crying or by bringing in or threatening to bring in an adult (own mother or father, Franz's mother, teacher); sometimes with the help of another person (a passer-by, a bigger boy, Peter himself). *The friends are then reconciled and go on to school together.* Rarely, Peter gets angry and goes away, the boys quarrel, or the friendship is ended; this ending crosses over into plot *b*.

b) Peter has to get his own cap down. Where the victim must singlehandedly recover his own loss, *Peter is likely to get angry, and there are usually unpleasant consequences for Franz:* Peter tells his mother, who forbids him to play with Franz; Peter tells the teacher or Franz's mother, who punishes Franz—or Franz fears she will do so, etc. In these versions, *the friendship comes to an end:* Franz (or Peter) must look for a "new friend." Alternatively, Peter decides *not* to tell the teacher, *not* to take the episode seriously—*not* to jeopardize the friendship. There may also be mitigating circumstances. If Franz helps Peter and/or apologizes, he has made good again. Then Peter may not get angry or may overcome his anger, and the friendship is resumed as in plot *a*.

c) *Peter retaliates and the friendship is resumed*. In these versions the main point is not getting the cap back but getting even with Franz: Peter boxes Franz's ears, throws Franz's cap into the tree; hits Franz (who perhaps strikes back). When the two have got even, they are again friends. However, Peter may take his revenge by telling someone—e.g., the teacher, who punishes Franz. Then the story may slip over into plot *b*. In one case the teacher fetches the cap, and Franz and Peter thank him and go off happily.

There are also a few other plot variations. A teacher was passing by; Peter did not take off his cap and therefore Franz threw it into the tree (i.e., the victim is turned into the wrongdoer). Franz was envious of Peter's new hat (in one story both boys get new caps). Franz was not angry at Peter but at Peter's brother (one victim stands for another).

The suggested motivations vary but occur in all story versions: Franz did it as a joke; out of high spirits; to tease Peter; to make Peter late for school; to make Peter angry; to see what Peter would do, etc. The motivation does not necessarily affect the outcome, i.e., Peter may or may not react angrily to a joke, or he may or may not accept a provocation.

In this story of an incident between friends, the main point appears to be keeping a kind of balance between equals. The positive solutions turn on the questions of whether (plot *a*) the wrongdoer makes good or (plot *c*) the victim gets even. Where those alternatives are not chosen, the friendship is likely to break down (plot *b*)—unless the victim values the friendship too much to let one incident spoil it (or, in another case, unless the friendship itself is a secret and forbidden one).

The solutions suggest that friendship is limited to two persons and that possibly a boy has only one friend at a time. The writers say: "Now Franz has to look for a new friend"; or "Now Peter has no friend." Either boy may be pictured as the solitary one.

Friendship can be endangered from within: Franz refuses to make good again; Peter regards the incident as a provocative one. Or it can be endangered from without: Peter will be blamed (by his parents) for losing his cap, etc.

Although this story concerns two boys, adults (or older persons) may become involved in three different ways. The wrongdoer asks an older person to help him set things right, and he does so (Franz gets assistance in getting down Peter's cap). One boy or both become *afraid* when the cap gets caught in the tree; one or both fear the scolding that will follow upon the loss of the cap, and this motivates their further acts—Peter cries, Franz decides to help Peter, etc. The victim calls on an adult to force the wrongdoer to set things right. The boys' solidarity is protected by adult help and survives the fear of adult intervention, but when the victim turns this fear into a reality, the boys' relationship is likely to break down.

The two boys may get angry at each other, or one may turn stubborn and the other angry; this may result either in a temporary rift, until the stubborn one relents or the angry one gets even, or else in a permanent break. Equally important, one or the other of the boys or both become afraid: Peter is afraid that he will be punished for losing his cap or that he will spoil his clothes if he climbs the tree; Franz gets a bad conscience when Peter cries or gets frightened when Peter threatens him. Fear is used by Peter as a threat, as retaliation, as punishment. In calling for help, the weaker person endangers the whole relationship—but he does so. Sometimes when the weaker person calls on someone stronger than the bully to set things right, this is a person by whom the victim himself feels threatened (as when Peter—afraid of being scolded—calls on his own parent to punish Franz); he deflects a punishment which he himself fears.

2. The Lost Sausages

Plot situation.—The mother sends Michael to the butcher. He is to buy two pairs of fresh sausages. On the way home he lays the package of sausages on the curb and plays with his friends for a little while. Suddenly a wolfhound runs up and pulls a pair of sausages out of the package and runs away with them. Michael wraps up the rest of the sausages and takes them home. What does Michael say to his mother? What does the mother do? What does Michael think then?

From the viewpoint of the writers, this story seems to involve two acts of wrongdoing: playing while on an errand and losing part of the sausages. Three plot solutions are proposed by the children:

a) Michael comes home and tells the truth.

b) Michael modifies the truth to omit the circumstances of playing, thus attempting to turn himself into a victim of the dog.

c) Michael tries to get out of the whole situation, usually by telling a lie, a preposterous lie that is easily uncovered.

Irrespective of the solution proposed, *Michael is likely to be scolded and usually is punished in other ways;* in some cases he has to go and buy more sausages with his own money. Thus the children accept the idea that wrongdoing must be made good both by suffering and by actual restitution. The only Michael who completely gets away with the loss is one who *secretly* gets his own money and buys more sausages; it is then said that Michael's mother was "content." In two cases the truth-telling Michael suffers in advance—is afraid—but "nothing happened." In one case the mother did not believe the truth. But in most cases, whether he tells the truth, prevaricates, or lies, Michael may be scolded, threatened, punished by slaps, earboxing, whipping, house arrest.

Irrespective of whether he lies or tells the truth, Michael is likely to suffer in advance. Two images appear in these stories that refer to this suffering: *Michael is red in the face* and *Michael is or becomes afraid* at some point—before he arrives at home, when his mother looks at him, when she looks at the sausages, when she scolds him, when she has seemed to accept the lie, etc. Blushing and stammering are signals to the parent that something is wrong. But what is feared does not necessarily happen, and the true cause of the blushing may not be divulged; in some cases Michael gets away with it at least in part—more often when he prevaricates than when he has been truthful. A lie *may* pay off.

Additionally, if Michael promises never to do it again as he tells his story, the mother may be more lenient. Or if he lies and is then forced to admit the truth, he may be entirely forgiven because "now he told the truth." That is, the original fault is covered by the more recent virtue of confession. Irrespective of the story that Michael tells and its consequences for him, there is likely to be a resolution by Michael henceforth to obey. Nevertheless, in one case the mother does *not* accept the promise of reform and then the boy is enraged; in another story, after Michael promises henceforth to obey and is forgiven, he is still "sad" and "helpful to his mother" all day long.

In this story, the *mother* who accepts the child's offer to make up for badness by goodness (or promise of goodness) is rewarded: Henceforth she will have an obedient child. But the *child* who lies successfully or who manages to conceal what happens is best off.

Other characters are brought into only a few of the stories. Two mothers threaten to denounce Michael to his father or do so. A neighbor tells the mother that her dog has brought home some sausages. The grandmother comes in and takes Michael into her protection when the mother boxes his ears. Michael fears that a friend may betray him (but he does not).

3. The Lost Money

Plot situation.—The teacher (a man) suddenly discovers that two marks have disappeared from his desk. He looks up and sees that the whole class are quietly working on their arithmetic lesson. He considers what has happened to the money and what he should do. What does the teacher do? End this story with some sentences. Tell what happened to the money, and also exactly what the teacher thinks and what he does.

The solutions to this story turn on the writers' assumption that, rightly or wrongly, *the teacher will believe there is a thief.* There are, however, several variations on what happens next:

a) *There is, in fact, a thief in the class. The teacher searches and catches the thief.* Alternatively, in a few cases, *the teacher searches but does not catch the thief; or the thief is allowed to make an anonymous return.*

b) *The outcome is inconclusive. The teacher searches for a thief but does not find one*—and it is not stated whether or not there is a thief.

c) *The teacher searches and does not find a thief.* Later he finds the money—the accusation is turned back against the accuser.

In most cases where the writers state that there is a thief, he is apprehended and dealt with (usually punished in some way); anonymous return is rarely permitted. In the few cases where the thief is not caught, the whole class may be involved in the theft; they accept punishment and later enjoy themselves.

The main point of the story is the teacher's belief that someone has stolen the money, and the main emphasis is upon his increasingly angry search for the supposed thief. The children do not assume that the teacher is omniscient or that he is necessarily able to discover the culprit.

The descriptions of the teacher's behavior—irrespective of the plot solution—follow a definite pattern (although not all steps are given by all writers):

The teacher looks around, gets suspicious, asks the class about the money—sometimes at once, sometimes waiting until the end of the lesson. The class says nothing or no one says anything (no one announces himself). The teacher threatens to search the class or to punish the whole class. No one says anything. He searches the class—opens books and bags and rummages through desks and pockets; he is very angry. (He finds the money in various places. Or later the money drops out of a pupil's pocket.) He goes to the principal. He punishes the whole class. (Later he finds the money on the desk, in a book, etc.)

The thief may be caught, may give himself away (by blushing), or may be given away by a frightened pupil at any stage in the search. The fate of the thief is not always discussed, but there are alternative solutions: the thief is caught or confesses under duress and is punished; or the thief is forgiven and does not steal any more.

The thief who is caught publicly is punished in various ways, and the circle of punishment spreads beyond the schoolroom to principal and parents. In contrast to the children, the teacher who finds that he himself has mislaid the money is unlikely to make a public statement.

In a few cases the thief is allowed to make a private confession and extenuating circumstances are invoked (his mother was sick); then the thief (except in one story where he did not confess the same day) is completely forgiven. In contrast, those who were caught had a bad purpose in taking the money—the culprit wanted to buy a ball or candy, etc. Thus it is suggested that the person who confesses wrongdoing has a good reason and will be completely protected by the fact of confession. Furthermore, the confessing thieves henceforth reform. The story goes no further.

Voluntary confession and forgiveness are likely to be paired; the thief is a poor boy, the teacher understands and gives him the money; the teacher likes the boy because he is now honest, and the boy does not steal again; no one held it against the boy, because he was a fine boy. In one case it is said that poverty is not a reason for stealing, and the boy is mildly punished (although the teacher would have given him the money, had he asked). In another the confession does not have the usual beneficial effect because it is made tardily.

The children in the stories hang together (although it is seldom made clear whether or not they know who the thief is, or if there is a thief) until the teacher brings great pressure to bear; then one child may accuse another. In a number of stories they mutely accept joint punishment when the thief is not discovered; in a few they later enjoy themselves.

4. The Ink Spot on Mother's New Coat

Plot situation.—Elisabeth is sitting in the living-room doing her lessons. She thinks about her mother's new coat. She would like to see whether it is becoming to her. When she takes it off again, she notices that she has got ink spots on her mother's new coat. Just as Elisabeth is rubbing out the spots, her mother comes in the door. What does her mother say? What does each think? What does Elisabeth say? What does each do?

In this story there are two possible misdeeds: interrupting lessons to play and trying on mother's new coat. An accident follows. The child gets ink spots on the coat.

The girls' and boys' stories differ somewhat in their emphasis. The girls emphasize the emotional situation—the scoldings that follow upon discovery and the punishments threatened and given. They are also more concerned with what happens to the coat. The boys' answers are more matter of fact, and they are more likely to emphasize the interrupted lessons as the main misdeed.

There is little plot development of this story: *Elisabeth is scolded and punished;* sometimes (more often boys) the ink spot is taken out, sometimes not. Sometimes the child has to pay for having the coat fixed. In a few cases the mother threatens to tell the father. The emphasis is upon punishment. There is no story in this set that deals with reconciliation. At best, the mother gets the spot out and life goes on, or they both try to forget the incident.

There are a few reversals. Occasionally Elisabeth is said to become afraid, but in one story it is the mother who "gets a fright." In one story the mother believes a lie, thanks Elisabeth, and helps her remove the spot. In another involving a lie, it is the mother who "sobs."

In these stories there is some repetition of the blushing reaction; here it typically accompanies a plot version (usually told by boys) in which Elisabeth is trying to get out of her predicament: ". . . Elisabeth gets red in the face and looks for an excuse."

5. The Broken Window

Plot situation.—Manfred and Karl are playing football. They know that they should not kick the ball on the little street in front of the house. Manfred kicks the ball, and it flies into a windowpane, which gets a big crack. Karl thinks that someone came to the window. No one could have seen who kicked the ball into the window. End this story with some sentences and describe what you think both boys thought and did.

In this story, as in "The Lost Sausages" and "Mother's New Coat," an accident follows on a misdeed. The two boys play ball on a forbidden street; one of them cracks (or breaks) a window. Two practical questions shape the solutions: *Have the boys been seen? If the boys run off, can they get away with it?* In most stories it is assumed that they recover the ball; if they do not, the ball itself may become central: *how explain the loss of the ball?*

In almost all versions, *the boys run away and hide.* There are then three main alternative conclusions:

a) They are red and fearful, but they get away with it and decide henceforth to play ball in the ball field.

b) They are seen, are found out, and get punished. Sometimes it is a neighbor, sometimes the house-owner (man or woman), sometimes the mother, who sees or finds out. The boys fall to quarreling (in some stories) and are punished—have to pay for the window, pay a police fine, are punished at home (are whipped, etc.).

c) Fearful and trembling, they decide to confess voluntarily and to make restitution—using their own money or working for it. Nothing further happens.

In this story the alternatives are clear cut. Those who confess voluntarily and who arrive with money in hand, ready to make good the loss, have no further troubles. They may even be rewarded: the owner decides not to tell their parents; the owner has another window and does not take their money. Those who are apprehended *before* they have a chance to run to safety or to confess are punished in several ways: by having to pay for the window and/or a fine, by scoldings and whippings at home.

The boys may or may not get away with a lie. In one case they do—they tell the house-owner they are searching for the culprits. In another they do not—they lie successfully to the house-owner, but then a storekeeper gives them away. Confession and restitution, if they are to be effective, must be voluntary, personal (paying with own money), and immediate. Delay spoils the effect; the boys are punished if they admit their deed when they have been seen or are under duress. But a lie may be effective.

As in "The Lost Money," the boys stick together until pressure is applied; then they begin to blame each other. Otherwise, the writers are likely not to differentiate between the boy who kicked the ball and the one who was playing with him. When the boys confess and pay, they share in the cost.

Significantly, the boys who get off scot free are the ones who learn the objective lesson: they decide never to play ball on the street again, but to play ball on the ball field. This is *explicitly* stated in the stories. The implicit lessons in the other two versions are: if you voluntarily confess and offer to make reparation, you will be forgiven and may be rewarded; if you are caught, you will be punished in addition to having to make good the damage.

6. The Lost Composition Book[6]

Plot situation.—Else often turned her compositions in late to the teacher (woman). This time it was a particularly important composition, and she had written it on time. On the way to school, she lost the composition book and could not find it anywhere. What did Else say to the teacher? What did the teacher say?

The plot, as it is outlined by the writers, turns on two questions. *Does Else tell the truth about the loss* (or, rarely, is the story of the loss true)? And, irrespective of whether Else tells the truth or invents a lie, *does the teacher believe her?*

Two main solutions are proposed for this story:

a) Else goes to school and tells the truth. (In contrast to "The Lost Sausages," most of the children expect Else to be truthful. They do not question how she lost the book, but accept the story as one of simple, accidental loss. In "The Lost Sausages," Michael's prevarications are an attempt to turn the story into one of accidental loss.) *In about half these stories, the teacher does not believe her.* And, whether she is believed or not, *Else gets no sympathy and is punished.* The teacher scolds and "has no pity"; calls her names; shames her before the whole class; gives her a bad mark; makes her write the composition again after school; writes to her parents, and Else is slapped or beaten, etc.

b) Else tells a lie—often an improbable lie that worsens her situation, for, as in "The Lost Sausages," the improbable lie gives the liar away. In about half the stories, *the lie is believed.* Nevertheless, in most cases, *Else is punished* and the punishment spreads from school to home.

There are three minor contrasting plots. *Another pupil returns Else's lost book, and Else is vindicated* (again, as in "The Lost Money," the accusation is turned against the teacher). *The teacher forgives Else, and henceforth she is a model pupil* (a repetition of the theme of getting away with it). *The whole story of the loss is a lie, but Else gets away with it and so goes on without interference to even more reprehensible acts* (unlike the children in "The Broken Window," who reform voluntarily when they have got away with their misdeed).

The handling of this story suggests that there is no certainty that the truth told by a child will be more acceptable to an adult than a lie, and, as in "The Lost Money," the adult is not thought to be omniscient (the teacher is as ready to disbelieve the truth as she is to believe a lie). An underlying assumption seems to be that a child who has done wrong in the past will be suspected and punished in the present. One child quotes the proverb: "Who once has lied is not believed, even when he tells the truth (*Wenn einer lügt, dem glaubt man nicht, Und wenn er auch die Wahrheit spricht*). This conclusion suggests that, contrary to the belief that forgiven sins are forgotten, the children expect past misdeeds to affect present troubles.

Irrespective of the particular plot, Else's situation is an unpleasant one, for the accident—if it was one—is symptomatic of bad behavior. One writer comments: "That is what happens to disorderly children." Whether the protagonist tells the truth or a lie, is believed or disbelieved, she is likely to be punished.

There are, however, two interesting alternatives. In one story, the *writer* denies Else's past delinquencies—all was well because Else was the best pupil in the class. (This echoes the situation in "The Lost Money," where the thief was said to be a good boy and so no one held the theft against him.) In another story the teacher gives Else a new composition book, and henceforth Else is a model pupil. (This echoes versions of "The Lost Money," in which the teacher gives the thief, a poor boy, the stolen money—to buy food or medicine for a sick mother—and the thief reforms because good is returned for evil.) In another story the teacher, after doubting the truth, is persuaded of it and finds that Else really wrote a good composition; she then says: "Always be as industrious as this and you will be a good pupil." The implication is that Else does reform. Thus where the teacher displays her own virtue through forgiveness or praise (where, in fact, she is the one who should apologize for her earlier doubts), there is a total reversal of effect.

What the children suggest in their handling of this story is that any wrongdoing leads to punishment, especially of the habitual sinner; but free forgiveness leads to reform.

EMERGENT THEMES

Each of the plot situations involves a child who commits, or who may have committed, a misdeed. Each presents a limited cast of characters—two friends (boys), mother and son, mother and daughter, teacher (man and woman) and pupil or pupils; in all but one, the culprit is identified. The dominant explicit theme—the handling of wrongdoing—and the main characters are, therefore, specified. The themes and characterizations discussed here are those that emerge from the child writers' interpretations.

Outstanding in the children's management of the denouements is their moral attitude toward the consequences of misdeeds and their preoccupation with the idea of punishment. Their major expectation is that wrongdoing will be followed by punishment, and, in terms of the punishments meted out, they do not differentiate sharply between deliberate misdeed (the thief), an accident that follows on a misdeed (Michael, Elisabeth, Karl and Manfred), and an accident (Else). Except in "The Lost Cap" (where the main characters are two boys), the climax scene, which is likely also to be the concluding scene of the story, is most commonly that in which the culprit is punished.

The moral atmosphere of these stories is entirely secular. Moral values are enforced by adults (parent, teacher, school principal, the police) or by the child itself. There is no reference in these stories to supernatural agents of punishment or of protection against punishment, irrespective of whether the culprit is caught or gets away with it. Children recognize and may involuntarily betray their own misdeeds: the guilty (but sometimes also the innocent) are fearful, blush and stammer. But their conscious anxiety is related to the possibility of discovery and of expected punishment by others—adults. The one guilty adult (the teacher who has lost his own money and who has accused the children) may conceal the discovery of his error.

Punishment appears to be inescapable if the culprit is discovered—if he is immediately confronted by an adult who can or who does know what has happened. In this connection, it is worth recalling a statement made by German adult informants, that for children there is an eleventh commandment: "Don't let yourself get caught" (*Du sollst dich nicht erwischen lassen*).

Nevertheless, some of the child culprits attempt to improve their situation by modifying the circumstances in which the misdeed occurred. Thus in one version of "The Lost Sausages," Michael tells his mother about the dog episode but omits any mention of loitering and playing (which the more astute mothers then fill in); in so doing, Michael tries to present himself as a victim. The dog episode itself plays into a very common threat made by German mothers to small children: "Watch out! Don't do such-and-such or the dog will bite you!" It is also a recurrent episode in German comic and cautionary literature (e.g., *Der Struwwelpeter, O diese Kinder*, etc.). It is a threat which child-care specialists use as an example in telling parents not to educate their children through the use of threats. Thus in manipulating this story situation, the writers have Michael turn himself into a victim, using a device that covertly suggests that punishment has already taken place. Yet, neither in this story nor in "The Lost Notebook," when Else tells the truth, does the victim get much sympathy; some form of punishment still is likely to follow.

The expectation of punishment is reflected in indicators that give adults definite clues that all is not well: the culprit blushes, has a red face, stammers, cannot look at his mother. Michael, the thief, the boys who break the window, Elisabeth, and Else, all exhibit these symptoms of anxiety or guilt. Or the culprit tells a preposterous lie (Michael, Elisabeth, Else) which is easily uncovered. Occasionally, in spite of the signal, "nothing happens." More often, the adult is thereby alerted.

This signaling of wrongdoing is also recurrent in German juvenile fiction.[7] It seems to tie into two themes important in German education: (1) the omniscience of parent and educator (nowadays, in child-care and pedagogical literature this is phrased as a need for the parent to learn what is right and to make himself—or herself—omniscient; the counterpoint—that parents do not know, that children do keep secrets—is recurrent in informants' statements) and (2) the high valuation of immediate, voluntary confession as a way of making good again.

There is little discrimination in the kind of punishment administered in specific situations: shouting, scolding, threatening, slapping, boxing ears, beating, house or school "arrest," using the child's own money to make good a loss, telling another person who then also punishes, are standard for the various misdeeds described. Parents' responses are pictured as noisy, impulsive, and immediate.

In German child-care literature, parents are repeatedly told that (1) every misdeed *must* be followed by punishment and (2) the punishment should be appropriate to the misdeed. What children appear to have learned is that punishment follows discovery.

Although children are likely to give themselves away, adults are not pictured as omniscient. They are likely to believe the worst, but they cannot always ascertain the truth ("The Lost Money"), and they cannot certainly distinguish between truth and falsehood (Michael, Manfred and Karl, Else)—sometimes to the disadvantage, more often to the advantage, of the child.

For discovery is not the only solution to these stories. Alternatively, the culprit voluntarily confesses and makes good and/or is rewarded, or the culprit gets away with it.

The idea of confession as a solution is most clearly worked out in "The Broken Window," where the boys (in one version) run away and hide and then decide to confess and to replace the cracked or broken window, paying the cost themselves. In the face of possible exposure and punishment, voluntary confession is chosen as the safest and cheapest course of action. (In one story the boys make a condition in their confession—that the house-owner is not to tell their parents; in another, the boys decide it is cheaper to pay for the window than to be caught and also to pay a police fine.) Voluntary confession is also one solution in "The Lost Money." The thief who confesses (in contrast to the one who is caught) has a "good" reason—he is a poor boy who needed money for medicine or food. Thus confession suggests that the person is really good and should not be blamed for the incident.

It is significant that mere truth-telling is not equivalent to confession. In some versions of the different stories the culprit (Michael, Elisabeth, Else) tells the truth and is nevertheless punished. Telling the truth combined with a promise "never to do it again" may—or may not—have the effect of modifying the punishment (e.g., Michael) but does not carry with it the rewards of confession.

For the child who confesses may, in fact, be rewarded, e.g., the teacher gives the thief the already stolen money; the house-owner tells the boys that he has a spare window and they need not pay. Confession of a second misdeed may carry with it absolution from the first, e.g., Michael admits that he has lied about the sausages, and his mother decides not to punish him because "now you are telling the truth."

Confession seems to be most effective when the culprit might have got away with it, e.g., the teacher has not found out who took the money, the boys (who confess to breaking the window because they may be caught) have not yet been caught. Voluntary confession seems to be valued to the extent that (from the child's viewpoint) discovery is forestalled and that (from the adult's viewpoint) discovery might not have been effected. Confession is one way of handling the problem of the parent who ought to be, but is not, omniscient and of the child who depends upon an omniscient adult to set and keep things straight.

In these stories there is a third alternative: the culprit gets away with his misdeed. This is, in an objective sense, the most effective solution in that, in the stories told by the children, the *culprit himself* resolves to do the right thing henceforth. The culprit who gets away with it exercises his own moral judgment. (This is counterpointed by rare cases in "The Lost Money" and "The Lost Composition Book," where the culprits escape discovery and then go on to worse deeds or, sometimes after being punished, enjoy themselves.)

In one respect, voluntary confession which is followed by forgiveness and getting away with it have like consequences. The child who is forgiven and perhaps rewarded by the adult (the teacher gives the thief the money, the teacher gives Else a new composition book) resolves to reform. Likewise, the child who gets away with it decides to reform. The difference between the two situations, as presented in these stories, is that confession presupposes a forgiving adult and has the effect of re-establishing a warm relationship between child and adult, whereas getting away with it presupposes a punishing adult and leaves the child solitary and apprehensive (e.g., in one story Karl and Manfred go home "sad and lonely").

In one story that involves equals (the two boys in "The Lost Cap"), the handling of the plot is different, but the themes appear to be related to those of the other stories. If Franz, who threw the cap, restores it and/or apologizes to Peter, the boys continue to be friends. Here, restitution and apology to an equal parallel confession and freely making good to an adult. If Franz refuses to get back the cap, he may be punished through adult interference. Or, alternatively, if Peter has to get the cap down, Franz may be left without a friend; i.e., he gets away with it, but the human relationship breaks down. In this context the loss of the friend makes explicit what was left implicit in the child-adult getting-away-with-it theme, and the rewards of getting away with it are here omitted. The third solution, in which Peter gets even with Franz and then the two boys are again friends, suggests that retaliation is at least implicit in versions of the stories where the teacher ("The Lost Money," "The Lost Composition Book") is proved to be wrong and where the teacher ("The Lost Money") is himself the guilty one. In the adult-child situation, the retaliation is indirect: the child who *writes* the story knows the truth, not admitted by the adult in the story.

Both the stories involving adult and child and those involving two boys suggest, in some versions, that punishment sets in motion a process that has no necessary end. In some, though not in all, stories it is not sufficient for one person to punish the child. Mother tells father, teacher tells principal and also tells mother, etc. Each of these persons then begins to punish the culprit. Thus an ever widening circle of strong, punishing persons presses in upon the young wrongdoer. The process can be triggered either by discovery by an adult (Michael, the thief, Elisabeth, Karl and Manfred, Else) or by the complaint of a victim, who calls on a stronger person for help (Peter). It can be prevented by restitution or by confession—before discovery. The weaker person, the child culprit, can save himself from punishment only by admitting his fault and asking for compassionate forgiveness; the culprit who is an equal (Franz) can save himself by tacit admission, by restitution and/or apology.

In contrast, the weaker person, who is defined as a *victim*, may, after suffering, be saved by someone stronger than the bully, i.e., Peter asks an adult for help, and Franz is punished; Michael tries to turn himself into a victim, and in one story grandmother enters and stops mother from boxing Michael's ears; Else is sometimes pictured as a victim of the teacher's disbelief and is vindicated when a "bigger girl" returns the lost composition book or when her mother confirms her explanation.

Thus the complementary relationship of child and parent and the endless hierarchy of the weak, the slightly stronger, and those still stronger are invoked in the punishment of wrong, the restoration of goodness to the wrongdoer, and the protection of the victim. From the viewpoint of the child writers, the only escapes from this system for the comparatively weak are in the maintenance of exact equality with equals (as when Franz makes restitution to Peter or Peter gets even with Franz) or in the secrecy and solitude of the wrongdoer, who, undiscovered, resolves to do right and to be good. A counterpoint to solitary reform is enjoyment of the fruits of wrongdoing by a group of children who have stuck together to face adult pressure and group punishment. From the viewpoint of the child, only the strong adult (the teacher) gets away with things with impunity.

The plot situations include only two of the three generations that are part of the German family system. Given the two, parent or parent-surrogate and child, and a situation in which the child is involved in a misdeed, the parent is pictured as someone who acts impulsively to stop something which has already happened, who may bring in another agent of punishment, and who becomes kind only when the child exhibits obedience and knowledge of what would have been right. But weakness has its own strength, for by exhibiting obedience after the event (promising to reform, confessing wrongdoing), the child can turn the parent from punishment to forgiveness and reward.

It is significant that "The Broken Window" (which is open to interpretation as a conflict between two boys) is treated as a two-generation problem, as, in some versions, is "The Lost Cap." Thus there is a tendency for difficulties to be phrased as problems not of equals but of persons in complementary positions.

The parent involved in these plot situations is the mother ("The Lost

Sausages," "Mother's New Coat"), and the parent to whom difficulties are referred in the plot solutions is more likely to be the mother than the father—the father is likely to be drawn in by the mother. However, the writers differentiate little in their descriptions of the behavior of the man and the woman teacher or of mothers and fathers who do appear. The one contrast figure (who occurs only once in one story, "The Lost Sausages") is a grandmother who protects her grandson from excessive punishment.

Descriptions of adult behavior and of children's responses differ in the degree of emotional intensity injected into the stories by individual writers. Stories vary all the way from straight unemotional statements (e.g., "Elisabeth's mother took out the spot and then she went on with her lessons") to tearful, emotionally fraught dialogues (e.g., " 'Dear, dear Mummy, please, please don't be angry, I will never do it again, oh please, please don't tell Father or else I'll be beaten, oh please!' "). And there is a tendency for one mood to persist throughout the stories told by a particular child. In these fantasy portraits of parents, there is little sex differentiation (except that the mother is more immediately concerned with the child); differences are rather in intensity and in over-all expectations of harshness or indulgence expressed by individual child writers.

In describing the relations between children (two boys in both stories), the boys (especially in "The Lost Cap") keep a straighter story line than do the girls. The slight tendency for girls to mix different plot elements (e.g., Peter gets angry although Franz gives back his cap) may, however, be attributed to the greater ease of identification with the situation by boys and, perhaps, to a real lack of detailed knowledge about boys' friendship behavior among the girls.[8]

The picture of the world which emerges from these story solutions is a very fragmentary one, but one which has consistency in terms of the children's attitudes.

They recognize clearly that a misdeed, whether accidental or intentional, carries with it a penalty which may take various forms—punishment by one or more persons, following on discovery or forced confession or even when a child tells the truth; making good out of one's own resources either voluntarily or forcibly; fear and anxiety even when "nothing happens"; or a private decision to reform by a miscreant who has got away with it.

The emotional focus is on fear of discovery and its consequences. To deal with their fears and to forestall discovery, the child protagonists may confess what they have done and offer to make good. The implication is that a person who confesses is not bad but good and therefore should be forgiven—as, in most cases, he is in these stories. Similarly, a person who has wronged a peer and who has made good the wrong should be forgiven. Alternatively, anxiety may move the culprit to decide henceforth to do the right thing. The implication is that, left to his own devices, the wrongdoer will reform himself—punishment is not necessary or perhaps even beneficial. In rare cases, a child writer suspects that the wrongdoer might not benefit by escaping punishment but would go on to even worse behavior. If punishment does not insure reform, it does prevent bad from getting worse. The children try to escape and usually only succeed in making things worse for themselves—e.g., when they tell preposterous lies. But escape does not carry with it any enjoyment, except in the rare cases where a whole group of children is involved who can still enjoy the fruits of their misdeeds after they have been punished as a group.[9]

The child writers believe that it is children's own weakness which betrays them to adults. Their bodies betray them—they blush and stammer, even when they are innocent of a particular accusation. They cannot tell convincing lies; the truth as they tell it is unconvincing. (But lies may also be as effective as the truth in avoiding punishment.) Adult pressure can break down juvenile solidarity. But they also make use of their weakness—when a child victim calls on an adult to deal with a child bully, sometimes deflecting possible punishment from himself to the bully.

The child writers suggest that, in contrast to children, adults get away with misdeeds with impunity. Adults are not assumed to be omniscient but are likely to believe the worst and to act impulsively in all situations where misdeeds are suspected or discovered. It is not assumed that adults will necessarily make good a false accusation against children when it is found that the fault lies elsewhere. On the contrary, children's suggestions that this may be so provoke the adult to even greater anger. Also in contrast to children, adults are assumed to have very considerable solidarity where a child has done something wrong. Parents, teachers, principals, neighbors, bystanders—all are assumed to be ready to join in discovering and punishing an erring child. One is given a sense, in these stories, that from the child's point of view, once discovery is effected, there is no way of knowing when punishment may end. The child's only method of controlling penalty is immediate voluntary confession and making good. Confession restores the child's relationship to the strong adult world. In contrast to this, private decisions to reform—the ability to do what is right of one's own accord—leave the child "sad" and alone, still fearful of possible discovery. In this sense wrongdoing and its consequences, seen from the viewpoint of children, are, on the one hand, a way of achieving lonely independence or, on the other hand, of keeping alive—through discovery and punishment or through confession—relationships between children and adults.

NOTES

1. I am indebted to the kindness of Dr. and Mrs. Anderson for permission to work with this sample of their material. As this study was made without knowledge of their analysis and conclusions, the responsibility for the conclusions presented here is my own.

2. Métraux, 1943.

3. The detailed steps of analysis are omitted here. Preliminary analysis showed that, with one or two exceptions, there were no consistent differences in the answers given by boys and girls, by children of Protestant and Catholic backgrounds, or by children in different classes or different schools. Consequently, the material was handled as a unit in the final analysis, except on one or two points, which will be specified.

4. The story titles were added for convenience in identification.

5. Main points in the plot solutions are italicized.

6. In considering the implications of this story, it is necessary to bear in mind that in German schools the composition book is a permanent document. Each mark is entered into it, corrections are entered into it, and the final mark is based on it. Consequently, its loss—whether voluntary or involuntary—is a very serious matter for the student.

7. Physical appearance is also used as an indicator of character in popular German novels and films. There the *audience* is, as it were, made omniscient, by being given unmistakable clues to "good" and "bad" persons. One way of building audience tension is to raise the question of when and whether the fictional characters will recognize what the audience already knows (cf. Nelly Schargo Hoyt, "The *Gartenlaube* and the *Gartenlaube* Novel," in Métraux and Hoyt, 1953).

8. This may be in part an age factor of the children writing the stories. In Germany the mixed play group tends to break into groups or pairs of boys or of girls somewhere between ten and twelve years.

9. German child informants also take pride and pleasure in describing occasions when a whole class, rather than one or two guilty individuals, was punished as a group. The pleasure in such a situation is in having maintained solidarity in the face of adult pressure.

LIST OF REFERENCES

HOYT, NELLY SCHARGO. 1953. "The *Gartenlaube* and the *Gartenlaube* Novel: A Magic Mirror for Society." In "German National Character: A Study of German Self-images," by RHODA MÉTRAUX and NELLY SCHARGO HOYT. ("Studies in Contemporary Cultures, B.") New York: American Museum of Natural History. (Dittoed.)

MÉTRAUX, RHODA. 1943. "Qualitative Attitude Analysis of Public Opinion." In *The Problem of Changing Food Habits*, pp. 86–94. (National Research Council Bull. 108.) Washington, D.C.: Government Printing Office.

MÉTRAUX, RHODA, and HOYT, NELLY SCHARGO. 1953. "German National Character: A Study of German Self-images." ("Studies in Contemporary Cultures, B.") New York: American Museum of Natural History (Dittoed.)

CHAPTER 20

Sex Differences in the Play Configurations
of American Pre-Adolescents

ERIK H. ERIKSON

Adapted from a larger paper published in the American Journal of Ortho-psychiatry, *XXI, No. 4 (1951), 667–92.*

I

IN PREVIOUS publications,[1] the writer has illustrated the clinical impression that a playing child's behavior in space (i.e., his movements in a given playroom, his handling of toys, or his arrangement of play objects on floor or table) adds a significant dimension to the observation of play. And, indeed, three-dimensional arrangement in actual space is the variable distinguishing a play phenomenon from other "projective" media, which utilize space either in two-dimensional projection or through the purely verbal communication of spatial images. In an exploratory way it was also suggested that such clinical hints could be applied to the observation of older children and even of adults; play constructions of college students of both sexes[2] and of mental patients were described and first impressions formulated.[3] In all this work a suggestive difference was observed in the way in which the two sexes utilized a given play space to dramatize rather divergent themes; thus male college students occupied themselves to a significant degree with the representation (or avoidance of) an imagined danger to females emanating from careless drivers in street traffic, while female college students seemed preoccupied with dangers threatening things and people in the interior of houses, and this from intrusive males. The question arose whether or not such sex differences could be formulated so as to be useful to observers in a nonclinical situation and on a more significant scale; and whether these differences would then appear to be determined by biological facts, such as difference in sex or maturational stage, or by differences in cultural conditioning. In 1940 the opportunity offered itself to secure play constructions from about 150 California children (about 75 boys and 75 girls), all of the same ages.[4] The procedure to be described here is an exploratory extension of "clinical" observation to a "normal" sample.[5] The number of children examined were, at age eleven, 79 boys and 78 girls; at age twelve, 80 boys and 81 girls; at age thirteen, 77 boys and 73 girls. Thus the majority of children contributed three constructions to the total number of 468 (236 play constructions of boys and 232 constructions of girls), which will be examined here.

On each occasion the child was individually called into a room where he found a selection of toys such as was then available in department stores (122 blocks, 38 pieces of toy furniture, 14 small dolls, 9 toy cars, 11 toy animals) laid out on two shelves. There was no attempt to make a careful selection of toys on the basis of size, color, material, etc. A study aspiring to such standards naturally would have to use dolls all made of the same materials and each accompanied by the same number of objects fitting in function and size, and themselves identical in material, color, weight, and so on. While it was not our intention to be methodologically consistent in this respect, the degree of inconsistency in the materials used may at least be indicated. Our family dolls were of rubber, which permitted their being bent into almost any shape; they were neatly dressed with all the loving care which German craftsmen lavish on playthings. A policeman and an aviator, however, were of unbending metal and were somewhat smaller than the doll family. There were toy cars, some of them smaller than the policeman, some bigger; but there were no airplanes to go with the aviator.

The toys were laid out in an ordered series of open cardboard boxes, each containing a class of toys, such as people, animals, and cars. These boxes were presented on a shelf. The blocks were on a second shelf in two piles, one containing a set of large blocks, one a set of small ones. Next to the shelves the stage for the actual construction was set: a square table with a square background of the same size.

The following instructions were given:

I am interested in moving pictures. I would like to know what kind of moving pictures children would make if they had a chance to make pictures. Of course, I could not provide you with a real studio and real actors and actresses; you will have to use these toys instead. Choose any of the things you see here and construct on this table an *exciting* scene out of an *imaginary* moving picture. Take as much time as you want and tell me afterward what the scene is about.

While the child worked on his scene, the observer sat at his desk, presumably busy with some writing. From there he observed the child's attack on the problem and sketched transitory stages of his play construction. When the subject indicated that the scene was completed, the observer said, "Tell me what it is all about," and took dictation on what the child said. If no exciting content was immediately apparent, the observer further asked, "What is the most exciting thing about this scene?" He then mildly complimented the child on his construction.[6]

The reference to moving pictures was intended to reconcile these preadolescents to the suggested use of toys, which seemed appropriate

only for a much younger age. And, indeed, only two children refused
the task, and only one of these complained afterward about the "child-
ishness" of the procedure: she was the smallest of all the children examined. The majority constructed scenes willingly, although their enthusiasm for the task and their ability to concentrate on it, their skill
in handling the toys, and their originality in arranging them varied
widely. Yet the children of this study produced scenes with a striking
lack of similarity to movie clichés. In nearly five hundred constructions,
not more than three were compared with actual moving pictures. In
no case was a particular doll referred to as representing a particular
actor or actress. Lack of movie experience can hardly be blamed for
this; the majority of these children attended movies regularly and had
their favorite actors and types of pictures. Neither was the influence of
any of the radio programs or comic pictures noticeable except in so far
as they themselves elaborated upon clichés of western lore; there were
no specific references to "Superman" and only a few to "Red Ryder."
Similarly, contemporary events of local or world significance scarcely
appeared. The play procedure was first employed shortly before the
San Francisco World's Fair opened its gates—an event which dominated the Far West and especially the San Francisco Bay region for
months. This sparkling fair, located in the middle of the bay and offering an untold variety of spectacles, was mentioned in not more than
five cases. Again, the approach and outbreak of the war did not increase the occurrence of the aviator in the play scenes, in spite of the
acute rise in general estimation of military aviation, especially in the
aspirations of our boys and their older brothers. The aviator rated
next to the monk in the frequency of casting.

It has been surmised that in both groups the toys suggested infantile play so strongly that other pretensions became impossible. Yet
only one girl undressed a doll, as a younger girl would; she had recently been involved in a neighborhood sex-education crisis. And while
little boys like to dramatize automobile accidents with the proper
bumps and noises, in our constructions automobile accidents, as well
as earthquakes and bombings, were not made to happen; rather, their
final outcome was quietly arranged. At first glance, therefore, the play
constructions cannot be considered to be motivated by a regression to
infantile play in its overt manifestations.

In general, none of the simpler explanations of the motivations responsible for the play constructions presented could do away with
the impression that a play act—like a dream—is a complicated dynamic
product of "manifest" and "latent" themes, of past experience and present task, of the need to express something and the need to suppress
something, of clear representation, symbolic indirection, and radical
disguise.

It will be seen that girls, on the whole, tend to build quiet scenes of everyday life, preferably within a home or in school. The most frequent "exciting scene" built by girls is a quiet family constellation, in a house without walls, with the older girl playing the piano (see Pl. XXVIII). Disturbances in the girls' scenes are primarily caused by animals, usually cute puppies, or by mischievous children—always boys. More serious accidents occur too, but there are no murders, and there is little gun play. The boys produce more buildings and outdoor scenes, and especially scenes with wild animals, Indians, or automobile accidents (see Pl. XXVII); they prefer toys which move or represent motion. Peaceful scenes are predominantly traffic scenes under the guiding supervision of the policeman. In fact, the policeman is the "person" most often used by the boys, while the older girl is the one preferred by girls.[7] Otherwise, it will be seen that the "family dolls" are used more by girls, as follows functionally from the fact that they produce more indoor scenes, while the policeman can apply his restraining influence to cars in traffic as well as to wild beasts and Indians.

The general method of the study was clinical as well as statistical; i.e., each play construction was correlated with the constructions of all the children as well as with the other performances of the same child. Thus *unique elements* in the play construction were found to be related to unique elements in the life-history of the individual, while a number of *common elements* were correlated statistically to biographic elements shared by all the children.

In the following three examples, the interplay of manifest theme and play configuration and their relation to significant life-data will be illustrated.

Deborah,[8] a well-mannered, intelligent, and healthy girl of eleven, calmly selects (by transferring them from shelves to table) all the furniture, the whole family, and the two little dogs, but leaves blocks, cars, uniformed dolls, and the other animals untouched. Her scene represents the interior of a house. Since she uses no blocks, there are no outer walls around the house or partitions within it. The house furniture is distributed over the whole width of the table but not without well-defined groups and configurations: there is a circular arrangement of living-room furniture in the right foreground, a bathroom arrangement along the back wall, and an angular bedroom arrangement in the left background. Thus the various parts of the house are divided in a reasonably functional way. In contrast, a piano in the left foreground and a table next to it (incidentally, the only red pieces of furniture used) do not seem to belong to any configuration. Taken together, they do not constitute a conventional room, although they do seem to belong together.

Turning to the cast, we note, within the circle of the living-room, a group consisting of a woman, a boy, a baby, and the two puppies. The woman has the baby in her arms; the boy plays with the two puppies. While this sociable group is as if held together by the circle, all the other people are occupied with themselves: clockwise, in the left foreground, the man at the piano, the girl at the desk, the other boy in the bed in the left background, and the second woman in the kitchen along the back wall.

Having arranged all this slowly and calmly, Deborah indicates with a smile that she is ready to tell her story, which is short enough: "This boy [in the background] is bad, and his mother sent him to bed." She does not seem inclined to say anything about the others. The experimenter (who must now confess that, at the end of this scene, he permitted himself the clinical luxury of one nonstandardized question) asks, "Which one of these people would you like to be?" "The boy with the puppies," she replies.

While her *spontaneous story* singled out the lonely boy in the farthest background, an *elicited afterthought* focuses, instead, on the second boy, who is part of the lively family circle in the foreground. In all their brevity, these two references point to a few interpersonal themes: punishment, closeness to the mother and separation from her, loneliness and playfulness, and an admitted preference for being a boy. Equally significant, of course, are the themes which are suggested but not verbalized.

The selective references to the boy in disgrace and to the happier boy in the foreground immediately point to the fact that in actual life Deborah has an older brother. (She has a baby brother, too, whose counterpart we may see in the baby in the arms of the mother.) We have ample reason to believe that she envies this boy because of his superior age, his sex, his sharp intellect, and his place close to the mother's heart. Envy invites two intentions: to eliminate the competitor and to replace, to become him. Deborah's play construction seems to accomplish this double purpose by splitting the brother in two: the competitor is banished to the lonely background; the boy in the foreground is what she would like to be.

We must ask here: Does Deborah have an inkling of such a "latent" meaning? We have no way of finding out. In this investigation, which is part of a long-range study, there is no place for embarrassing questions and interpretations. Therefore, if in this connection we speak of "latent" themes, "latent" cannot and does not mean "unconscious." It merely means "not brought out in the child's verbalization." On the other hand, our interpretation is, as indicated, based on life-data and test material secured over more than a decade.

But where is Deborah? The little girl at the desk is the only girl in the scene and, incidentally, close to Deborah's age. She was not mentioned in the story. She is, as pointed out, part of a configuration which does not fit as easily and functionally into a conventional house interior as do the other parts. The man at the piano, closest to the girl at the desk, has in common with her only that they share the two red pieces of furniture. Otherwise, they both face away from the family without facing toward each other; they are parallel to each other, with the girl a little behind the father.

In life, Deborah and her father are close to each other temperamentally. Marked introverts, they are both apt to shy away in a somewhat pained manner from the more vivacious members of the family, especially from the mother. Thus they have an important but negative trend in common. Just because of their more introvert natures, they are unable to express what unites them in any other way than by staying close to each other without saying much. This, we think, is represented spatially by a *twosome in parallel isolation*.

In adding this theme to the two verbalized themes (the *isolated bad boy* and the identification with the *good boy in the playful circle*), we surmise that the total scene well circumscribes the child's main life-problem, namely, her isolated position between the parents, between the siblings, and (as yet) between the sexes. In a similar but never once identical manner, our clinical interpretation arrives at a theme representative of that life-task which (present or past) puts the greatest strain on the present psychological equilibrium. In this way, the play construction often is a significant help in the analysis of the life-history because it singles out one or a number of life-data as the *subjectively most relevant* ones and adds a significant key to the dynamic interpretation of the child's personality development.

We may ask one further question: Is there any indication in the play constructions as to how deeply Deborah is disturbed or apt to become disturbed by the particular strain which she reveals? Here a clinical impression must suffice. Deborah uses the whole width of the table. She does not crowd her scene against the background or into one corner, as according to our observations, children with marked feelings of insecurity are apt to do; neither does she spread the furniture all over the table in an amorphous way, as we would expect a less mature child to do. Her groupings are meaningfully and pleasingly placed; so is her distribution of people. The one manifest incongruity in her groupings (father and daughter) proves to be latently significant; only here her scene suffers, as it were, a symptomatic lapse. Otherwise, while there is a simple honesty in her scene, there certainly is no great originality and no special sparkle in it. But here it is necessary to remember the surprising dearth of imagination in most constructions and the possibility that only specially inclined children may take to this medium with real verve.

In one configurational respect Deborah's scene has much in common with those produced by most of the other girls. She places no walls around her house and no partitions inside. In anticipation of the statistical evaluation of this configurational item, we may state here an impression of essential femininity, which, together with the indications of relative inner balance, forms a welcome forecast of a personality potentially adequate to meet the stresses outlined.

In addition to the arrangement on the table and its relation to the verbalization, clinical criteria may be derived from the observation of a child's general approach to the play situation. Deborah's approach was calm, immediate, and consistent; her selection of toys was careful and apt. Other typical approaches are characterized by prolonged silence and sudden, determined action; by an enthusiasm which quickly runs its course; or by some immediate thoughtless remark such as, "I don't know what to do." The final stage of construction, in turn, can be characterized by frequent new beginnings; by a tendency to let things fall or drop; by evasional conversation; by the need to find room for all toys or to exclude certain types of them; by a perfectionist effort at being meticulous in detail; by an inability to wind up the task; by a sudden and unexplained loss of interest and ambition, etc. Such time curves must be integrated with the spatial analysis into a space-time continuum which reflects certain basic attributes of the subject's way of organizing experience—in other words, the ways of his ego.

In the spatial analysis proper, we consider factors such as the following:

1. The subject's approach, first, to the shelves and then to the table, and his way of connecting these two determinants of the play area.

2. The relationship of the play construction to the table surface, i.e., the area covered, and the location, distribution, and alignment of the main configurations with the table square.

3. The relationship of the whole of the construction to its parts and of the parts to one another.

Let us now compare the construction of calm and friendly Deborah with that of the girl most manifestly disturbed during the play procedure. This girl, whom we shall call Victoria, is also eleven years old; her intelligence is slightly lower than Deborah's. She appears flushed and angry upon entering the room with her mother. A devout Catholic, Victoria had overheard somebody in the hall address this writer as "Doctor." She had become acutely afraid that a man had replaced the Study's woman doctor at this critical time of a girl's development. This she had told her mother. The mother then questioned the writer; he reassured both ladies, whereupon Victoria, still with tears in her eyes but otherwise friendly, consented to construct a scene in her mother's protective presence.

Victoria's house form (she called it "a castle") differs from Deborah's construction in all respects. The floor plan of the building is constricted to a small area. There are high, thick walls and a blocked doorway; and there is neither furniture nor people. However, there seems to be an imaginary population of two: "The king," says Victoria, letting her index finger slide along the edge of the foreground, "walks up and down in front of the castle. He waits for the queen, who is changing her dress in there" (pointing into the walled-off corner of the castle).

In this case the "traumatic" factor seems to lie, at least superficially, in the immediate past; for the thematic similarity between the child's acute discomfort in the anticipation of having to undress before a man doctor and, in the play, the exclusion of His Majesty from Her Majesty's boudoir seems immediately clear. High walls and closed gates, as well as the absence of people, all are rare among undisturbed girls; if present, they reflect either a general disturbance or temporary defensiveness.

One small configurational detail in this scene contradicts the general (thematic and configurational) emphasis on the protection of an undressed female from the view even of her husband. In spite of the fact that quite a number of square blocks were still available for a high and solid gate, Victoria selected the only rounded block for the front door. This arrangement, obviously, would permit the king to peek with ease if he were so inclined, and thus provides, for this construction, the usual (but always highly unique) discrepant detail which reveals *the dynamic counterpart to the main manifest theme* in the construction. Here the discrepant detail probably points to an underlying exhibitionism, which, in this preadolescent girl, may indeed have been the motivation for her somewhat hysterical defensiveness; for her years of experience with the Study had not given her any reason to expect embarrassing exposition or wilful violation of her Catholic code. We note, however, that Victoria's construction, overdefensive as it is in its constricted and high-walled configuration and theme, is placed in the center of the play table and does not, as we have learned to expect in the case of chronic anxiety, "cling" to the background; her upset, we conclude, may be acute and temporary.

Lisa, a third girl, has to deal with a lifelong and constant problem of anxiety: she was born with a congenital heart condition. This, however, had never been mentioned in her interviews with the workers of the Guidance Study. Her parents and her pediatrician, although in a constant state of preparedness for the possibility of a severe attack, did not wish the matter to be discussed with her and assumed that they had thus succeeded in keeping the child from feeling "different" from other children.

Lisa's scene consists of a longish arrangement, quite uneven in height, of a number of blocks close to the back wall. On the highest block (according to the criteria to be presented later, a "tower") stands the aviator, while below two women and two children are crowded into the small compartment of a front yard, apparently watching a procession of cars and animals. Lisa's story follows. We see in it a metaphoric representation of a moment of heart weakness—an experience which she had never mentioned "in that many words." The analogy between the play scene and its suggested meaning will be indicated by noting elements of a moment of heart failure in brackets following the corresponding play items.

"There is a quarrel between the mother and the nurse over money [anger]. This aviator stands high up on a tower [feeling of dangerous height]. He really is not an aviator, but he thinks he is [feeling of unreality]. First he feels as if his head was rotating, then that his whole body turns around and around [dizziness]. He sees these animals walking by which are not really there [seeing things move about in front of eyes]. Then this girl notices the dangerous situation of the aviator and calls an ambulance [awareness of attack and urge to call for help]. Just as the ambulance comes around a corner, the aviator falls down from the tower [feeling of sinking and falling]. The ambulance crew quickly unfolds a net; the aviator falls into it, but is bounced back up to the top of the tower [recovery]. He holds on to the edge of the tower and lies down [exhaustion]."

Having constructed this scene, the child smilingly left for her routine medical examination, where, for the first time, she mentioned to the Institute physician her frequent attacks of dizziness and indicated that at the time she was trying to overcome them by walking on irregular fences and precipitous places in order to get used to the dizziness. Her quite unique arrangement of blocks, then, seems to signify an uneven fencelike arrangement, at the highest point of which the moment of sinking weakness occurs. That the metaphoric expression of intimate experiences in free play "loosens" the communicability of these same experiences is, of course, the main rationale of play therapy.

These short summaries will illustrate the way in which configurations and themes may prove to be related to whatever item of the life-history, remote or recent, is at the moment most pressing in the child's life. A major classification of areas of disturbance represented in our constructions suggests as relevant areas: (1) family constellations; (2) infantile traumata (for example, a twelve-year-old boy, who had lost his mother at five but had seemed quite oblivious to the event, in his construction revealed that he had been aware of a significant detail surrounding her death; this detail, in fact, had induced him secretly to blame his father for the loss); (3) physical affliction or hypochrondriac concern; (4) acute anxiety connected with the experiment; (5) psychosexual conflict. Naturally these themes interpenetrate.

II

We shall now turn to a strain which is by necessity shared by all preadolescents, namely, sexual maturation—a "natural" strain which, at the same time, has a most specific relation to the clearest differentiation in any mixed group, namely, difference in sex.

Building blocks provide a play medium most easily counted, measured, and characterized in regard to spatial arrangement. At the same time, they seem most impersonal and least compromised by cultural connotations and individual meanings. A block is almost nothing but a block. It seemed striking, then (unless one considered it a mere function of the difference in themes), that boys and girls differed in the *number* of blocks used as well as in the *configurations* constructed (see Pls. XXVII and XXVIII).

Boys use many more blocks, and use them in more varied ways, than girls do. The difference increases in the use of ornamental items, such as cylinders, triangles, cones, and knobs. More than three-quarters of the constructions in which knobs or cones occur are built by boys. This ratio increases with the simplest ornamental composition, namely, a cone on a cylinder; 86 per cent of the scenes in which this configuration occurs were built by boys. With a very few exceptions, only boys built constructions consisting *only* of blocks, while only girls, with no exception, arranged scenes consisting of furniture exclusively. In between these extremes the following classifications suggested themselves: towers and buildings, traffic lanes and intersections, simple inclosures, interiors without walls, outdoor scenes without use of blocks.[9]

The most significant sex differences concern the tendency among the boys to erect structures, buildings and towers, or to build streets (see Pl. XXVII); among the girls, to take the play table to be the interior of a house, with simple, little, or no use of blocks.

The configurational approach to the matter can be made more specific by showing the spatial function emphasized in the various ways of using (or not using) blocks. This method would combine all the constructions which share the function of *channelizing* traffic (such as lanes, tunnels, or crossings); all elaborate buildings and special structures (such as bridges, boats, etc.) which owe their character to the tendency of *erecting* and *constructing;* all simple walls, which merely *inclose* interiors; and all house interiors, which are without benefit of inclosing walls and are thus simply *open interiors.*

In the case of *inclosures,* it was necessary to add other differentiations. To build a rectangular arrangement of simple walls is about the most common way of delineating any limited area and, therefore, is not likely to express any particular sex differences. But it was found that, in the case of many boys, simple inclosures in the form of front yards and back yards were only added to more elaborate buildings or that simple corrals or barnyards would appear in connection with outdoor scenes. In this category, therefore, only more detailed work showed that (1) significantly more boys than girls build inclosures only in conjunction with elaborate structures or traffic lanes; (2) significantly more girls than boys will be satisfied with the exclusive representation of a simple inclosure; (3) girls *include* a significantly greater number of (static) objects and people within their inclosures; (4) boys *surround* their inclosures with a significantly greater number of (moving) objects.

Height of structure, then, is prevalent in the configurations of the boys. The observation of the unique details which accompany constructions of extreme height suggests that the variable representing the opposite of elevation, i.e., *downfall*, is equally typical for boys. Fallen-down structures, namely, "ruins," are exclusively found among boys,[10] a fact which did not change in the days of the war when girls as well as boys must have been shocked by pictorial reports of destroyed homes. In connection with the very highest towers, something in the nature of a downward trend appears regularly, but in such a diverse form that only individual examples can illustrate what is meant: one boy, after much indecision, took his extraordinarily high tower down in order to build a final configuration of a simple and low character; another balanced his tower very precariously and pointed out that the immediate danger of collapse was in itself the exciting factor in his story, in fact, *was* his story. In two cases extremely high and well-built façades with towers were incongruously combined with low irregular inclosures. One boy who built an especially high tower put a prone boy doll at the foot of it and explained that this boy had fallen down from its height; another boy left the boy doll sitting high on one of several elaborate towers but said that the boy had had a mental breakdown and that the tower was an insane asylum. The very highest tower was built by the very smallest boy; and, to climax lowness, a colored boy built his structure *under* the table. In these and similar ways, variations of a theme make it apparent that *the variable high-low* is a *masculine variable*. To this generality, we would add the clinical judgment that, in preadolescent boys, extreme height (in its regular combination with an element of breakdown or fall) reflects a trend toward the emotional overcompensation of a doubt in, or a fear for, one's masculinity, while varieties of "lowness" express passivity and depression.

Girls rarely build towers. When they do, they seem unable to make them stand freely in space. Their towers lean against, or stay close to, the background. The highest tower built by any girl was not on the table at all but on a shelf in a niche in the wall beside and behind the table. The clinical impression is that, in girls of this age, the presence of a tower connotes the masculine overcompensation of an ambivalent dependency on the mother, which is indicated in the closeness of the structure to the background. There are strong clinical indications that a scene's "clinging" to the background connotes "mother fixation," while the extreme foreground serves to express counterphobic overcompensation.

In addition to the dimensions "high" and "low" and "forward" and "backward," "open" and "closed" suggest themselves as significant. Open interiors of houses are built by a majority of girls. In many cases this interior is expressly peaceful. Where it is a home rather than a school, somebody, usually a little girl, plays the piano: a remarkably tame "exciting movie scene" for representative preadolescent girls. In a number of cases, however, a disturbance occurs. An intruding pig throws the family in an uproar and forces the girl to hide behind the piano; the father may, to the family's astonishment, be coming home riding on a lion; a teacher has jumped on a desk because a tiger has entered the room. This intruding element is always a man, a boy, or an animal. If it is a dog, it is always expressly a boy's dog. A family consisting exclusively of women and girls or with a majority of women and girls is disturbed and endangered. Strangely enough, however, this idea of an intruding creature does not lead to the defensive erection of walls or to the closing of doors. Rather, the majority of these intrusions have an element of humor and of pleasurable excitement and occur in connection with open interiors consisting of circular arrangements of furniture.

To indicate the way in which such regularities became apparent through exceptions to the rule, we wish to report briefly how three of these "intrusive" configurations came to be built by boys. Two were built by the same boy in two successive years. Each time a single male figure, surrounded by a circle of furniture, was intruded upon by wild animals. This boy at the time was obese, of markedly feminine build, and, in fact, under thyroid treatment. Shortly after this treatment had taken effect, the boy became markedly masculine. In his third construction he built one of the highest and slenderest of all towers. Otherwise, there was only one other boy who, in a preliminary construction, had a number of animals intrude into an "open interior" which contained a whole family. When already at the door, he suddenly turned back, exclaimed that "something was wrong," and with an expression of satisfaction, rearranged the animals along a tangent which led them close by but away from the family circle.

Inclosures are the largest item among the configurations built by girls, if, as pointed out, we consider primarily those inclosures which include a house interior. These inclosures often have a richly ornamented gate (the only configuration which girls care to elaborate in detail); in others, openness is counteracted by a blocking of the entrance or a thickening of the walls. The general clinical impression here is that high and thick walls (such as those in Victoria's construction) reflect either acute anxiety over the feminine role or, in conjunction with other configurations, acute oversensitiveness and self-centeredness. The significantly larger number of open interiors and simple inclosures, combined with an emphasis, in unique details, on intrusion into the interiors, on an exclusive elaboration of doorways, and on the blocking-off of such doorways seems to mark *open and closed* as a feminine variable.

The most significant sex differences in the use of the play space, then, add up to the following picture: in the boys, the outstanding variables are height and downfall and motion and its channelization or arrest (policeman); in girls, static interiors, which are open, simply inclosed, or blocked and intruded upon.

In the case of boys, these configurational tendencies are connected with a generally greater emphasis on the outdoors and the outside, and in girls with an emphasis on house interiors.

The selection of the subjects assures the fact that the boys and girls who built these constructions are as masculine and feminine as they come in a representative group in our community. We may, therefore, assume that these sex differences are a representative expression of masculinity and of femininity for this particular age group.

Our group of children, developmentally speaking, stand at the *beginning of sexual maturation*. It is clear that the spatial tendencies governing these constructions closely parallel the morphology of the sex organs: in the male, *external* organs, *erectible* and *intrusive* in character, serving highly *mobile* sperm cells; *internal* organs in the female, with vestibular *access*, leading to *statically expectant* ova. Yet only comparative material, derived from older and younger subjects living through other developmental periods, can answer the question whether our data reflect an acute and temporary emphasis on the modalities of the sexual organs owing to the experience of oncoming sexual maturation, or whether our data suggest that the *two sexes may live, as it were, in time-spaces of a different quality*, in basically different fields of "means-end-readiness."[11]

In this connection it is of interest that the dominant trends outlined here seem to parallel the dominant trends in the play constructions of the college students in the exploratory study previously referred to. There the tendency was, among men, to emphasize (by dramatization or avoidance) potential disaster to women. Most commonly, a little girl was run over by a truck. But while this item occurred in practically all cases in the preliminary and abortive constructions, it remained a central theme in fewer of the final constructions. In the women's constructions, the theme of an insane or criminal man was universal: he broke into the house at night or, at any rate, was where he should not be. At the time we had no alternative but to conclude tentatively that what these otherwise highly individual play scenes had in common was an expression of the sexual frustration adherent to the age and the mores of these college students. These young men and women, so close to complete intimacy with the other sex and shying away only from its last technical consummation, were dramatizing in their constructions (among other latent themes) fantasies of sexual violence which would override prohibition and inhibition.

In the interpretation of these data, questions arise which are based on an assumed dichotomy between biological motivation and cultural motivation and on that between conscious and unconscious sexual attitudes.

The exclusively cultural interpretation would grow out of the assumption that these children emphasize in their constructions the sex roles defined for them by their particular cultural setting. In this case the particular use of blocks would be a logical function of the manifest content of the themes presented. Thus, if boys concentrate on the exterior of buildings, on bridges and traffic lanes, the conclusion would be that this is a result of their actual or anticipated experience, which takes place outdoors more than does that of girls, and that they anticipate construction work and travel while the girls themselves know that their place is supposed to be in the home. A boy's tendency to picture outward and upward movement may, then, be only another expression of a general sense of obligation to prove himself strong and aggressive, mobile and independent in the world, and to achieve "high standing." As for the girls, their representation of house interiors (which has such a clear antecedent in their infantile play with toys) would then mean that they are concentrating on the anticipated task of taking care of a home and of rearing children, either because their upbringing has made them want to do this or because they think they are supposed to indicate that they want to do this.

A glance at the selection of elements and themes in their relation to conscious sex roles demonstrates how many questions remain unanswered if a one-sided cultural explanation is accepted as the sole basis for the sex differences expressed in these configurations.

If the boys, in building these scenes, think primarily of their present or anticipated roles, why are not boy dolls the figures most frequently used by them? The policeman is their favorite; yet it is safe to say that few anticipate being policemen or believe that they should. Why do the boys not arrange any sport fields in their play constructions? With the inventiveness born of strong motivation, this could have been accomplished, as could be seen in the construction of one football field, with grandstand and all. But this was arranged by a girl who at the time was obese and tomboyish and wore "affectedly short-trimmed hair"—all of which suggests a unique determination in her case.

As mentioned before, during the early stages of the study, World War II approached and broke out; to be an aviator became one of the most intense hopes of many boys. Yet the pilot shows preferred treatment in both boys and girls only over the monk, and—over the baby; while the policeman occurs in their constructions twice as often as the cowboy, who certainly is the more immediate role-ideal of these Western boys and most in keeping with the clothes they wear and the attitudes they affect.

If the girls' prime motivation is the love of their present homes and the anticipation of their future ones to the exclusion of all aspirations which they might be sharing with boys, it still would not immediately explain why the girls build fewer and lower walls around their houses. Love for home life might conceivably result in an increase in high walls and closed doors as guarantors of intimacy and security. The majority of the girl dolls in these peaceful family scenes are playing the piano or peacefully sitting with their families in the living-room: could this be really considered representative of what they want to do or think they should pretend they want to do when asked to build an exciting movie scene?

A piano-playing little girl, then, seems as specific for the representation of a peaceful interior in the girls' constructions as traffic arrested by the policeman is for the boys' street scenes. The first can be understood to express *goodness indoors;* the second, a guarantor of safety and *caution outdoors.* Such emphasis on goodness and safety, in response to the explicit instruction to construct an "exciting movie scene," suggests that in these preadolescent scenes more dynamic dimensions and more acute conflicts are involved than a theory of mere compliance with cultural and conscious ideals would have it. Since other projective methods used in the study do not seem to call forth such a desire to depict virtue, the question arises whether or not the very suggestion to play and to think of something exciting aroused in our children sexual ideas and defenses against them.

All the questions mentioned point to the caution necessary in settling on any one dichotomized view concerning the motivations leading to the sex differences in these constructions.

The configurational approach, then, provides an anchor for interpretation in the ground plan of the human body: here, sex difference obviously provides the most significant over-all differentiation. In the interplay of thematic content and spatial configuration, then, we come to recognize an expression of that interpenetration of the biological, cultural, and psychological, which, in psychoanalysis, we have learned to summarize as the *psychosexual*.

In conclusion, a word on the house as a symbol and as a subject of metaphors. While the spatial tendencies related here extend to three-dimensionality as such, the construction of a house by the use of simple, standardized blocks obviously serves to make the matter more concrete and more measurable. Not only in regard to the representation of sex differences but also in connection with the hypochrondriac pre-occupation with other growing or afflicted body parts, we have learned to assume an unconscious tendency to represent the body and its parts in terms of a building and its parts. And, indeed, Freud said fifty years ago when introducing the interpretation of dreams: "The only typical, that is to say, regularly occurring representation of the human form as a whole is that of a house."[12]

We use this metaphor consciously, too. We speak of our body's "build" and of the "body" of vessels, carriages, and churches. In spiritual and poetic analogies, the body carries the connotation of an abode, prison, refuge, or temple inhabited by, well, ourselves: "This mortal house," as Shakespeare put it. Such metaphors, with varying abstractness and condensation, express groups of ideas which are sometimes too high, sometimes too low, for words. In slang, too, every outstanding part of the body, beginning with the "underpinnings," appears translated into metaphors of house parts. Thus, the face is a "façade," the eyes "front windows with shutters," the mouth a "barn door" with a "picket fence," the throat a "drain pipe," the chest a "bone house" (which is also a term used for the whole body), the male genital is referred to as a "water pipe," and the rectum as the "sewer." Whatever this proves, it does show that it takes neither erudition nor a special flair for symbolism to understand these metaphors. Yet, for some of us, it is easier to take such symbolism for granted on the stage of drama and burlesque than in dreams or in children's play; in other words, it is easier to accept such representation when it is lifted to sublime or lowered to laughable levels.

The configurational data presented here points primarily to an unconscious reflection of biological sex differences in the projective utilization of the *play space;* cultural and age differences have been held constant in the selection of subjects. As for *play themes,* our brief discussion of possible conscious and historical determinants did not yield any conclusive trend; yet it is apparent that the material culture represented in these constructions (skyscrapers, policemen, automobiles, pianos) provides an anchor point for a reinterpretation of the whole material on the basis of comparisons with other cultures. In such comparisons *houses again mean houses;* it will then appear that the basic biological dimensions elaborated here are utilized at the same time to express different technological space-time experiences. Thus it is Margaret Mead's observation that in their play Manus boys who have grown up in huts by the water do not emphasize height, but outward movement (canoes, planes), while the girls, again, concentrate on static houses. It is thus hoped that the clear emphasis in this paper on the biological will facilitate comparative studies; for cultures, after all, elaborate upon the biologically given and strive for a division of labor between the sexes and for a mutuality of function in general which is, simultaneously, workable within the body's scheme and life-cycle, meaningful to the particular society, and manageable for the individual ego.

NOTES

1. Erikson, 1937, 1938, 1940.
2. Erikson, 1938.
3. Erikson, 1937; see also Rosenzweig and Shakow, 1937.
4. The author is indebted for this opportunity to Dr. Jean W. Macfarlane, director of the Guidance Study, Institute of Child Welfare, University of California, Berkeley. The Guidance Study, in the words of its director, is "a 20-year cumulative study dedicated to the investigation of physical, mental, and personality development" (Macfarlane, 1938). Its subjects were "more than 200 children arbitrarily selected upon the basis of every third birth during a given period in Berkeley, California." The children were matched at birth on certain socioeconomic factors and divided into a guidance group and a control group. The study thus provided for "cumulative observation of contemporaneous adjustments and maladjustments in a normal sample."
5. At the time of this investigation, the author was not familiar with the much more comprehensive "world-play" method of Margaret Lowenfeld in England (Lowenfeld, 1939).
6. The emphasis on the element of "excitement" warrants an explanation. In the exploratory study mentioned above (Erikson, 1938), Harvard and Radcliffe students had been asked to build *"a dramatic* scene." All English majors educated in the imagery of the finest in English drama, they were observed to build scenes of remarkably *little dramatic* flavor. Instead, they seemed to be overcome by a kind of infantile excitement, which—on the basis of an extensive data collection—could be related to *childhood traumata.* Conversely, a group of psychology students in another university, who decided to employ a short cut by asking their subjects to build *"the most traumatic scene* of their childhood," apparently aroused resistance and produced scenes characterized by a remarkable lack of overt excitement of any kind, by a dearth in formal originality, and by the absence of relevant biographic analogies. These experiences suggested, then, that we should ask our preadolescents for *an exciting* scene in order to establish a standard against which the degree and kind of dramatic elaboration could be judged, while this suggestion as well as the resistance provoked by it could be expected to elicit lingering infantile ideas.
7. Honzik, 1951.
8. All names are, of course, fictitious, and facts which might prove identifying have been altered.
9. An analysis of the sex differences in the occurrence of blocks and toys in the play constructions of these preadolescents has been published by Dr. Marjorie

PLATE XXVII. *Play Configurations of American Pre-Adolescents. I*

FIG. 1.—Construction of towers built by a boy

FIG. 2.—A second view

(Published originally in the *American Journal of Orthopsychiatry*)

PLATE XXVIII. *Play Configurations of American Pre-Adolescents. II*

A girl's construction of furniture. (Published originally in the *American Journal of Orthpsychiatry*.)

Honzik. For a systematic configurational analysis and for a statistical evaluation see the original article (Honzik, 1951). The writer is indebted to Dr. Honzik and also Drs. Frances Orr and Alex Sherriffs for independent "blind" ratings of the photographs of the play constructions.

10. One single girl built a ruin. This girl, who suffered from a fatal blood disease, at the time was supposed to be unaware of the fact that only a new medical procedure, then in its experimental stages, was keeping her alive. Her story presented the mythological theme of a "girl who miraculously returned to life after having been sacrificed to the gods." She has since died.

11. For an application of the configurational trends indicated here in a masculinity-femininity test cf. Franck, 1946. See also Tolman, 1932.

12. Freud, 1922.

LIST OF REFERENCES

ERIKSON, ERIK HOMBURGER. 1937. "Configurations in Play," *Psychoanalytic Quarterly*, VI, No. 2, 139–214.

——. 1938. "Dramatic Productions Test." In *Explorations in Personality*, ed. H. A. MURRAY. New York: Oxford University Press.

——. 1940. "Studies in the Interpretation of Play. I. Clinical Observation of Play Disruption in Young Children." *Genetic Psychology Monographs*, XXII, 557–671.

——. 1951. "Sex Differences in the Play Configurations of Preadolescents," *American Journal of Orthopsychiatry*, XXI, No. 4, 667–92.

FRANCK, K. 1946. "Preference for Sex Symbols and Their Personality Correlation," *Genetic Psychology Monographs*, XXXIII, No. 2, 73–123.

FREUD, S. 1922. *Introductory Lectures on Psychoanalysis*. London: Allen & Unwin.

HONZIK, M. P. 1951. "Sex Differences in the Occurrence of Materials in the Play Constructions of Preadolescents," *Child Development*, XXII, 15–35.

LOWENFELD, M. 1939. "The World Pictures of Children: A Method of Recording and Studying Them," *British Journal of Medical Psychology*, XVIII, Part I, 65–101.

MACFARLANE, J. W. 1938. *Studies in Child Guidance. I. Methodology of Data Collection and Organization*. ("Society for Research in Child Development Monographs," Vol. III, No. 6.)

ROSENZWEIG, S., and SHAKOW, D. 1937. "Play Technique in Schizophrenia and Other Psychoses," *American Journal of Orthopsychiatry*, VII, No. 12, 32–47.

TOLMAN, E. C. 1932. *Purposive Behavior in Animals and Men*. New York: Century Co.

PART VI

Interviews with Parents and Children

Introduction

I NTERVIEWING is a phenomenon of the twentieth century[1] which testifies to the extension of the domain of science into human affairs. It is a special development of human intercourse, a new mode of conversation for purposes of investigation. Nonscientific analogues of the interview range from the talk of lovers eager to know all about each other to police interrogations. The scientific interview has a more impersonal motivation and is also designed to safeguard its subjects. There are numerous varieties of interviewing, differing in purpose and in method. There is the kind of interviewing which aims at knowing a few things about a large number of persons, as exemplified in public opinion polls, where contact between the interviewer and his subject is transient. At an opposite extreme we find the protracted work of an anthropologist in the field with an informant, from whom a wealth of information about the culture is gradually elicited and evaluated in terms of the concurrently obtained knowledge about the informant himself.

We may distinguish two main kinds of subjects of interviews: (a) the one who gives information about external matters in which he is knowledgeable and (b) the one whose statements are significant as expressions of his subjective processes. In the first case we have, for instance, the informant whom the field worker questions about linguistic forms or social customs or political intrigues, where the responses obtained contribute to the researcher's gradually accumulated knowledge on these topics. In the second case, what is learned is something about the person interviewed, whether it be what candidate he favors or the content of his dreams and fantasies. What the researcher obtains here are not factual statements but data to be analyzed. The division between these two kinds of subjects, or two kinds of objectives, in interviewing is not hard and fast. The same subject may provide material of both sorts, facts about external states of affairs and expressions of his own feelings. However, the emphasis of the researcher is often likely to be on one side or the other. When the informant who is sought as a source of knowledge about customs and events reveals tendencies toward distortion, this is important in qualifying the truth value of his statements. On the other hand, where a person whose subjective processes are the focus of study offers items of factual information, these may be of interest mainly as contributing to the picture of his mental functioning, establishing the degree of his orientation in reality.

The interview which focuses on the subjective processes of the person interviewed may be undertaken for purposes of pure research or for purposes of therapy. Where research is the aim, the results of the interviewer's analysis and interpretation of the material obtained are not necessarily communicated to the subject. In therapy it is integral to the work that the therapist's interpretations of the material which the patient brings be sooner or later communicated to him. Since findings derived from therapeutic interviews have constituted major scientific discoveries, procedures from this field have been applied, with various modifications, in interviewing for purely research purposes. One of the major discoveries about human nature and how to investigate it which were made in therapeutic interviewing is that nothing is irrelevant. In the early years of Freud's treatment of neurotics, he tried to get the patient to concentrate on the circumstances of the onset of his or her symptoms. When a patient rambled from this given theme, Freud recorded: "She produced all kinds of things that could not be relevant."[2] It was some time later that he developed the method of free association, based on the realization that whatever comes to a person's mind, however incoherent or trivial it may seem at first, is meaningful and bears an emotional connection to what has preceded and what follows. Similarly, matters which had not been included in the sphere of science, love affairs which had been subjects for gossip and novels, dreams which had been considered nonsense, became material for serious investigation. Interviews for research purposes have developed to a considerable extent on this model, in their variety of topics and encouragement of undirected and free-flowing talk. There is evidently a range here, too, from the interview based on a fixed questionnaire to the one which approximates free association.

Various skills are required on the part of the interviewer, depending on the form and purpose of the interview. In any interviewing which allows for some freedom in the pursuit of its questions, the sensitivity of the interviewer to the trend of the subject's thoughts, to what he is most ready to talk about, is highly relevant to the quality of material which will be elicited. In interviewing for research purposes, the interviewer need not possess the skill of interpreting the material he obtains and may in any case postpone interpretation to sometime after the interview. In therapeutic interviewing, on the other hand, interpretation (whether or not it is communicated to the subject at the moment) must keep pace with the accumulation of material.

The subject's image of the interviewer is also significant and affects the results, increasingly so with more intensive interviewing, and constitutes a factor of which the interviewer must remain aware. A displaced person, for example, may mistake a research interviewer for a police agent. American Jewish parents, who were being interviewed by a college student on their methods of bringing up children, took the interview as a test situation and wanted to study their books on the subject before answering the questions. The interviewer's own reactions to his subjects also affect the results and require awareness and control on his part. In therapeutic interviewing the patient's image of the therapist and the therapist's reactions to the patient are of central importance and must be continuously observed and analyzed by the therapist.

The studies of interviews with parents and children which follow are based on directed interviews (where a certain set of questions was asked but free elaboration of answers was encouraged). The subjects are regarded mainly from the point of view of what they reveal about themselves. Interpretations were applied to recorded interview material, there being more or less a division of functions between the interpreter and the interviewer. The kinds of questions asked and the interpretations of results show the influence of psychoanalytic hypotheses. Both these studies are concerned with the transmission of moral and social attitudes in the parent-child relation. The material collected consists of paired interviews with parents and their children, by means of which the responses of both to the same questions can be studied. In the second paper, interviewing has been supplemented by written questionnaires and projective tests.

The first paper, on variants of moral training, is a cross-cultural study, in which an attempt is made to find a basic coherence in the reported attitudes and practices, for instance, in relation to punishment, in each of several cultures, to point up the contrasts between them, and to relate them hypothetically to alternative structurings of the mother-child relationship.

The second paper, on differential patterns of social outlook and personality in family and children, deals with contrasting extremes of social attitudes of parents and children within the same culture and connects each of two types of social outlook with associated personality traits and perceptual responses. Any complex culture is likely to exhibit such ranges of attitudes as Else Frenkel-Brunswik here indicates by illustrating the two extremes of the authoritarian and the liberal family in contemporary America. As she brings out, the liberal family is closer to the American ideal and probably to the mode. What is characteristically American throughout the range is the crucial importance of attitudes about equality. One may be for or against or indifferent on questions of equality (between ethnic groups, adults and children, boys and girls), but whatever position one takes is affected by the fact that issues of equality have been and are a central theme of American culture.

In this book the writers are more often concerned with the regularities in a given culture than with the range of variants within it. These are differences of focus; one does not deny the other. The distinctive quality of a complex culture may be seen in the variables which are important in it, not in a uniform adherence to one point on a variable.[3]

M. W.

NOTES

1. For a detailed account of work with informants and the use of interviews generally in cultural studies see Margaret Mead on "The Single Informant," and Rhoda Métraux on "Informants in Group Research," in Mead and Métraux, 1953.
2. Freud, 1954, p. 139.
3. Bateson, 1953.

LIST OF REFERENCES

BATESON, GREGORY. 1953. "Formulation of End Linkage." In *The Study of Culture at a Distance*, ed. MARGARET MEAD and RHODA MÉTRAUX, pp. 367–78. Chicago: University of Chicago Press.

FREUD, SIGMUND. 1954. *The Origins of Psychoanalysis: Letters to Wilhelm Fliess, Drafts and Notes: 1887–1902*, ed. MARIE BONAPARTE, ANNA FREUD, and ERNST KRIS; trans. E. MOSBACHER and J. STRACHEY. London: Imago.

MEAD, MARGARET, and MÉTRAUX, RHODA (eds.). 1953. *The Study of Culture at a Distance*. Chicago: University of Chicago Press.

CHAPTER 21

Some Variants in Moral Training of Children

—————————————————————MARTHA WOLFENSTEIN

The material on which this study is based was collected by a special group in the Columbia University project, Research in Contemporary Cultures (under a grant from the Human Resources Division, Office of Naval Research), which made a cross-cultural study of child training. Families were interviewed by researchers of their own cultural background, the parents being interviewed in their native languages. I am indebted to the work of Mrs. Edith Lauer, Miss Naomi Chaitman, Dr. and Mrs. Stephan Toma, and a Chinese colleague in this connection. I have also drawn on materials from the larger research project as they related to the cultures discussed here. The report which appears here was published earlier in The Psychoanalytic Study of the Child, *V (1950), 310–28; some of the footnotes have been amplified in the present version.*

IDEAS about good and bad are common to all cultures; what specifically is good or bad varies. Parents use different methods to induce their children to do what they consider good and to desist from what they consider bad, methods which also vary with time and place. In discussing variants in the moral training of children, I shall draw on material provided by a series of interviews with parents of diverse origins (mainly Chinese, Czech, Eastern European Jewish, and Syrian) and their American-born children. The interviews explored the ideas of these parents and children on a number of questions: What is a good child and what is a bad child? How do they get that way? How should children be rewarded or punished? What will a good child grow up to be like? What will become of a bad child? What is a good mother, a good father, and their bad counterparts? What effects do they have? What should a child do, and what should a parent do, when faced with certain specified moral dilemmas? and so on. These questions were taken as a starting point for eliciting recollections of familial experiences and, on the part of the adults, memories of their relations with their own parents. I shall not attempt here to give all the findings from these interviews. Rather I propose to take certain differences in attitudes or reported behavior as a basis for some general hypotheses about parent-child interaction in the process of moral training.

Parents usually do not begin to apply conscious moral conceptions and disciplinary techniques to their children from the moment of birth.

An interval of varying length elapses before the conscious moral code of the parents and its sanctions are applied. Speculations about very early experiences of the infant have suggested that he may feel every deprivation imposed by the mother as a punishment for his destructive impulses. It is equally possible to assume that this is a retrospective transformation of early impressions in conformity with later experiences. However we may reconstruct the feelings of the infant, from the parents' side certain early deprivations which they impose are consciously distinguished from later deprivations which are introduced as moral sanctions. Thus the mother who does not feed her crying infant because she is adhering to a schedule or who later weans the child from the breast or the bottle is consciously behaving in a different way from that in which she may behave later on when she deprives the child of candy or some other desired object because he has been naughty. In this sense we may speak of an early premoral phase in the parent-child relations.

The premoral, or (as we may also call them) nonmoralized, relations appear as such from the parents' point of view; we are not at present able to say what differential impact parental treatment has on the child, depending on whether it is consciously felt by the parents as morally justified. While premoral feelings are likely to be most prominent in early phases of parent-child relations, the term is not intended in an exclusively temporal sense; premoral maternal attitudes may continue side by side with later moralized behavior toward the child. We should also not overlook the case where the mother's relation to her child may have a moralized quality from the moment of the child's birth or even before.

The parents probably feel their moral relations with the child as different from, and disconnected with, the premoral relations. However, we may take it for granted that there are close connections between the two. Certain aspects of the premoral relations may serve as models for the moral relations. Differences in moral ideas and sanctions may be related to different premoral experiences.

We may start from the consciously moralized behavior of the parents and proceed to speculate about its antecedents. Punishment is an incident in the moral drama of parents and children which may be enacted in a variety of ways. The form of punishment, its tools, the time and place and agent of punishment, the emotional reactions of the punisher and the punished, admit of many variations. If we consider the tools of punishment, we find, for instance, that Czech mothers whom we interviewed consider it traditional to use (or threaten to use) the wooden kitchen spoon for spanking their children. This brings to mind the stock implement for spanking supposedly preferred by American mothers, namely, the hairbrush. We may ask what differences in the mother-child relation are expressed in one mother's choosing to punish with a spoon and another with a hairbrush. What premoral situations are suggested by these implements, both of which have other uses? The kitchen spoon evokes a feeding situation, and specifically the preparation and giving of solid food. The hairbrush suggests the mother's concern to make the child clean and neat and her efforts to elicit from him responsiveness to these demands. Thus our first tentative guess is that something in the mother-child relation having to do with the giving of solid food is repeated in the choice of the kitchen spoon as the spanking instrument, while where the hairbrush is chosen the antecedent situation is one of cleanliness training. The guess that Czech mothers tend to model punishment on something in the feeding situation (that is, something to do with giving and withholding) seems to be supported by further information. The Czech mothers to whom we spoke, who all knew about the kitchen spoon as a traditional punishment tool but who were inclined to say that they themselves merely threaten to use it, tended to prefer as an actual punishment the withholding of something which the child very much wants.

Let us see whether a like connection suggests itself in other choices of means of punishment. Our Syrian and pre–Soviet Russian sources portrayed occasions of punishment in which children were beaten with a whip or belt which wrapped itself around the body and where the child might be tied down before being whipped. If we look for a premoral antecedent to this, we find that in both cultures the swaddling of infants seems to be prominent, that is, something is wrapped around the body and the child is immobilized.

A variety of modes of punishment is, of course, chosen within any given culture, as also within any particular family. According to Syrian informants, the pinching of the ear is another preferred Syrian form of punishment. Schoolteachers have special metal implements with which to pinch the ears of their pupils. The manifest rationale for this attack on the ear is that the child has not listened to the words of his mentor; the punishment is directed against the refractory organ. The presumable relation to an earlier model is somewhat complicated in this case. A characteristic style of nursing in Syrian culture seems to be for the mother to bend over the infant, who is bound down in his cradle, and to thrust her nipple into his mouth. Even the older child may have pieces of food thrust into his mouth (and the same procedure is practiced with guests). The relation between the immobilized infant into whose mouth the breast is thrust and the school child who is required to receive with equal docility the words of the teacher is indicated by explicit formulations. The child is supposed to receive his character from his mother's milk. Of the older child who is resistant to the moral teachings of his elders it is said: his head is dry. Thus words replace milk and the ear replaces the mouth as the orifice through which the character-formative stream is to be admitted. The punitive attack on the ear is related to a prepunitive situation via a displacement from the mouth to the ear.

The foregoing examples have suggested that punishments tend to repeat some earlier phase in parent-child relations not only in the choice of implements but also (where the punishment is corporal) in the part of the body to which the punishment is applied. A further illustration indicates a similar connection in the attitudes expressed in the punishment situation. A Chinese informant tells how her little brother at the age of four, having done something wrong, spontaneously took down his trousers and bent over a stool waiting for his mother to come and spank him. The other children ran to tell the mother that brother was waiting. A contrasting picture is presented in an account by a mother of German origin: when she was threatening to spank her little boy of about the same age, he put his hands over his buttocks and shouted: "It's mine, don't you dare touch it." Punishment which focuses on the buttocks may be supposed to be related to antecedent experiences in toilet training. In the two instances cited, differences in the method of toilet training seem to correspond to the different attitudes expressed by the children toward spanking. The German mother had toilet-trained her child by demanding that he voluntarily submit a function of his to her control; the issue of whether it was his or hers was contested. The little boy repeated apropos of the spanking the sense of protest which he had felt earlier about his excretory functions. The Chinese mother had begun toilet-training her child between one and three months and had not expected that he could voluntarily do what she asked or obstinately resist her. She had picked him up at a likely moment, so that the child's excretory activities almost from the first were associated with the mother's presence and might be felt to be hers as much as they were his. In offering his buttocks for the spanking, the little boy seemed to be expressing: it is yours—just as the other child asserted the opposite.

If we suppose that punishment repeats an earlier, premoral situation, we must ask what could be motivations for this repetition. A preliminary hypothesis would be the following. In the early care of the child the mother, of necessity, imposes numerous deprivations. Her empathy with the child re-evokes in her (probably mainly unconsciously) the feelings of rage and resentment which she felt toward her own mother in similar circumstances and which she now feels are directed toward her by her own child. If later when the child has been "bad," she symbolically repeats the earlier deprivations in the guise of punishment, she communicates to the child in effect that it is his own "badness" which has provoked the deprivations and requires that he redirect his blame of her into self-blame. As a result, the earlier deprivations are reinterpreted, or in so far as the child has a spontaneous tendency to feel that the original deprivations were punishments for his bad impulses, this feeling is now confirmed. Hence punishment may tend to re-enact those early experiences, which were felt (presumably by both mother and child) to have a strong deprivational impact on the child. Where this is the case for weaning or the introduction of solid food, a favored punishment would be likely to be withholding, and the spoon might become an instrument of punishment. Where toilet training has been a major focus of interference with impulse, the related punishment which in a moralized way attacks the same body area would be spanking. Where early interference with motor activity through swaddling has had a strong deprivational impact, the related punishment may be a renewed immobilization as the child is bound and a lashing of the body in which the whip replaces the swaddling bands.[1] Of course, as we have already remarked, a variety of punishments is usually chosen in any particular family or group, which would then commemorate a variety of early deprivations.

We might guess that, other things being equal, the prominence of a particular punishment device would tend to be proportional to the intensity of the early deprivation repeated in it. Where deprivations in a certain area tended to be minimal, as seems to be the case with our Chinese subjects in respect to oral satisfactions, there would be little or no reference to this area in chosen punishments. Thus our Chinese parents showed very little inclination to withhold food or any other desired thing as a punishment. We might suppose that the mother is loath to impose as punishment what she did not previously wish to impose as a premoral deprivation. In other words, in the area where the mother is, from the start, most gratifying, she tends to remain so.

While this hypothesis enables us to connect various phenomena in a meaningful way, it raises a number of further questions, which we probably cannot answer here. We do not know why in some cases one or another early deprivation has a particularly strong impact, or why, where this impact seems related to specific details of maternal handling (in the manner of weaning, toilet training, etc.), the mother (or group of mothers) should choose these procedures. Moreover, we have not indicated how the father's disciplinary role may be related to the moral and premoral mother-child relations. Even in respect to the mother, there is evidence to suggest that there are other (though not necessarily conflicting) factors operative in the development of her moral relations with the child. Thus it seems possible that one of the circumstances relevant to the mother's choice of punishment is what she finds most difficult or painful in the care or training of the child. These areas of difficulty may be individually idiosyncratic or, as in the instances which we have been considering, possibly traditionally regular. Suppose, for instance, that mothers find cooking especially burdensome (which may be a stock way of regarding this function in a particular culture). When their children are "bad," the righteous resentment of these mothers may be reinforced by the accumulated (though non-moralized) annoyance related to their cooking duties. Such a factor may overdetermine the appearance of the cooking spoon in the punishment situation, where it may represent a reproach ("After all that I have done for you!") and also a reversal of hardships (what the child has imposed upon the mother is now turned against the child). In the case of a masochistic mother the re-enactment or re-evocation in punishment of the pains which the child causes her may have a (probably unconsciously) gratifying effect as well. This is illustrated in the behavior of some of our Jewish mothers, who use as their most severe punishment a more or less prolonged refusal to speak to the child. Among the motivations of this probably highly overdetermined behavior, the following is relevant in the present connection. These Jewish mothers are likely to reproach their children with having damaged and weakened them through the ordeal of childbirth, the depletion of nursing, etc. There is some evidence to suggest that this suffering imposed by the child and the fantasy of being destroyed by the child are sources of strong gratification to the mother, though it may only be expressed in complaints and conscious dysphoria. When the mother, injured yet again by the child's badness, refuses to speak, she is behaving as if dead, that is, acting out the fantasy that the child has destroyed her.

This further hypothesis, that the mother re-evokes in punishment what she feels as the greatest hardships that the child imposes on her, is quite compatible with the previous hypothesis that punishment repeats what to the child have been major early deprivations. It seems likely that what the mother experiences as the greatest hardship in relation to the child may be experienced by the child at the same time as the greatest deprivation. The way the mother handles him in what to her is the least enjoyable aspect of their relation may very well convey to him negative and distressing feelings.

We have so far taken the situation of punishment as an illustration of possible connections between moral and premoral parent-child relations. Let us now proceed to consider a larger range of details, including, together with punishment, reward and other moral actions and ideas; and let us see whether these may be systematically interrelated and also point to premoral prototypes.

We may take as illustrative some of the material obtained in our interviews with Czech mothers and children. One of the distinctive features of the disciplinary technique of these mothers is their tendency to combine reward and punishment. A promised reward is likely to be inextricably involved with a threatened punishment. Thus, as one mother describes her procedure, she promises her children long in advance that if they are good they will get some present or outing. In the intervening time, whenever they are bad she threatens to withhold it. Thus the same object figures in both a reward and a punishment context, according to whether the mother will give it or withhold it. This contrasts with parental procedures in which rewards and punishments are mutually independent, where the child is separately rewarded for good behavior and punished for bad. Thus our Chinese parents tend to say that they spank their children when they are bad and may buy them new clothes when they have been good. The tendency of our Czech parents to mingle reward and punishment was reflected also in what their children told us. Two sisters, aged nine and five, agreed that the best thing that could happen to them was to break a leg: then they wouldn't have to go to school. The fantasy of being exempted from school without any attendant penalty was apparently not accessible to them. (In this instance, another factor seems also to be operative, namely, the need to pay in advance for a forbidden gratification.)

The tendency for reward and punishment to be mutually involved is further illustrated in the way in which our Czech parents are likely to praise their children. Praise frequently also carries a connotation of blame. When a child has behaved well on a visit to friends of the parents, the father or mother may say: "You see how well you can behave!" According to these words of praise, the child has, as it were, unguardedly behaved well on this occasion and thus supplied ammunition in support of the parents' argument that he could behave well at other times. The commendation for this instance of good behavior reminds the child of less good behavior on other occasions. In a similar way a mother asks her little girl: "What did I say when we were visiting last Saturday and you behaved so nicely?" The little girl replies: "That you were proud of me." The mother continues, "Yes, but I have to say more often, 'Don't do that, I will have to be ashamed of you.'" These mothers also show a similar tendency in the opposite direction, starting with criticism and shifting to commendation. One mother says that children should obey, then immediately qualifies this by saying, "I mean within reason." (This group of parents tends to qualify the demand for obedience with "I mean seventy-five per cent of the time," or "Of course, I would not like a child not to show any opposition.") The mother continues that she has, of course, still to remind her children to do many things. However, "I have to say it myself—they are really good children." This is again followed by her calling to mind another cause for reproach: "I tell them that they should not waste food—this is something I really cannot stand."[2] A combined or alternating reward and punishment value seems also to attach to "explanations" as used by our Czech parents. Explanation is a frequently cited disciplinary device but is also referred to as a positive form of parent-child relation, as when a mother says that a father is needed to explain things to his sons.

The tendency for a positive expression to be followed by a qualifying negative one and vice versa appears not only in praising and blaming children but in other contexts as well. This tendency is manifestly explained as a fear of exaggeration. A positive statement seems to call to mind at once negative, nonconforming instances, and so to be one-sided and inaccurate; when the necessary negative points have been expressed, positive feelings again emerge, and so on. The need to avoid exaggeration does not seem adequately to account for this oscillation between positive and negative feelings, since exaggeration may also be avoided by cautious phrasing or consistent understatement. What we see here is rather a continuous giving (the positive statement), taking back (negative qualifications), restoration (renewed positive expressions), and so on. Such a series of alternate withholding and giving is illustrated in the following statement of one mother apropos of adult misbehavior: "I have no sympathy for a bum or a drunk. I want to help people—though I'm very poor. But a drunk or a bum—I don't say no one should help them. But somebody who has more money, or an agency. . . . I would even take a seventh child into my house."

This pervasive tendency, of which the interlocking of reward and punishment is an instance, may be related to a premoral phase in the mother-child relation, namely, the feeding situation and particularly the preparation of solid food. As we would reconstruct this situation, the mother feels resentful at the imposition of having to cook for the family, she counteracts this resentment with conscientious and exhausting efforts in the kitchen, which then evoke more resentment, which in turn is atoned for by further efforts. An episode in a recently published Czech children's story, *Zuzanka Discovers the World*,[3] seems to confirm this reconstruction. A princess offers to cook dinner all by herself for her prince and sends the servants away. However, when she goes to the kitchen, she finds that there is only one egg, and in her unskilfulness she drops it on the floor. She has nothing to feed her prince, and she weeps thinking how she would even give her heart for him. At this her heart flies out of her breast and into the frying pan. She cooks it and serves it to the prince for dinner. Afterward, however, she is very mean to him—because she has no heart.

Our Czech mothers seem perpetually to complicate their cooking tasks while at the same time they manage to precipitate reproaches from their children about the food. Each member of the family is encouraged to develop special idiosyncrasies of taste, so that sometimes the mother is cooking the same thing in as many different ways as there are members of the household. However, in some cases the favorite dishes of one member or another of the family must be served in alternation. This becomes the occasion for reproaches: "You have cooked daddy's favorite dish twice since you have cooked mine"—and so on. In the food-giving situation, the mother's withholding tendencies are not overt but can only be inferred from what appears to be a reaction-formative overpreoccupation with and complication of cooking, by the mother's provoking reproaches from her children for insufficient giving (which may be an indirect way in which the mother achieves the expression of her own self-reproaches), and by such fantasies as that of the princess with her heart.

Recollections of these mothers about their own mothers tend to express a reproach that their mothers did not give them enough. Such reproaches are likely to be expressed with the characteristic qualifications, so that the mother who is described seems partly giving and partly withholding, and the daughter who describes her repeats the same behavior. Thus a mother will say that her own mother was a very good mother, only she did not show enough affection; she really loved the child, only she did not understand that sometimes you must show appreciation; and so on. Another mother will say: "My mother did not have much time for us, she was always busy with the housework." Shortly afterward she makes up for this reproach by saying that sometimes she can even understand and sympathize with the mothers one reads about in the newspapers who abandon their children; perhaps it was too much for them, with maybe five children and the husband in the hospital or drunk, etc. These mothers also express strivings for autonomy so that one becomes the source of gratification for one's self and is not dependent on others who may be disappointing. These autonomy strivings are indicated as having both good and bad potentialities. One may become a drunkard, which is one of the worst things; or one may become an omnivorous reader, which is one of the best. One mother quotes her own mother as saying: "A good book never disappoints you." An eleven-year-old son of one of these mothers responds to a TAT card which pictures a woman looking into a room: "She is looking for some person, or maybe for a book."

It is a truism that parents tend to repeat the behavior of their own parents. However, the mechanisms involved in such repetitions are, it would seem, far from simple. Assuming that our Czech mothers repeat an oscillation between withholding and giving which they felt in their own mothers, we might find a variety of motivations which combine to keep this oscillation going. The mother's identification with her own mother's withholding might tend to evoke her own resentments as a child, which she now attributes to her children and wants to avoid; her own pity for herself as a child, which she now directs toward her children; and her reproaches against her mother, which arouse guilt and evoke the alternate image of the giving mother ("my mother was a good mother . . . she really loved me"). These and probably other feelings impel the mother from withholding to giving. But the grudgingness which she has felt in giving to her own mother, evoked by her mother's insufficient giving to her, and her displacement to her children of what she felt were unfair demands of her mother impel her again into a withholding position. Some of the alternations of feelings about giving, as a mother shifts from thoughts of her parents to thoughts of her children, are suggested in the following remarks: "Children have no obligation. They certainly should obey, but they have nothing to do with their coming, so it's up to you to do your share, and children have no obligation." Here the mother is probably expressing mainly her feelings toward her own parents. Shortly afterward, when asked what is the worst thing children can do, she says, "If they only take without thought. When they make a big fuss when they can't get something they want." We would guess that she is now thinking more of her children. However, she again quickly shifts the balance of blame and adds, "But this is often the fault of the parents."

Let us now return to our earlier general proposition about a possible relation between the mother's moral and premoral handling of the child, and see how this can be applied here. According to our hypothetical reconstruction of these mothers' behavior in regard to feeding, a conflict over giving and withholding is expressed mainly through an intensified expression of the positive sector, which serves to repress the resentment for having to give what is felt to be too much (the meanness of the princess after having cooked her heart), and the indirect expression of doubts whether the mother gives enough via the complaints of the children, which, despite all her apparent efforts, she manages to evoke. If we turn to the moral relation in reward and punishment, praise and blame, we find that the withholding tendency is much more outspoken. The intimate involvement of giving and withholding impulses which we suspected in the feeding situation is here clearly dramatized. Rewards are held out to the child as something which the mother alternately promises to give and threatens to withhold; words of praise are half taken back again by counteracting expressions of criticism.

We are now led to a possible refinement of our general hypothesis about the relationship of moral to premoral maternal behavior. In the premoral relation the mother may tend to repress or otherwise interfere with her impulses of annoyance toward the child. These accumulate and are able to find "justified" expression when the child is bad.[4] Thus our Czech mothers are able to express in the sphere of reward and punishment the withholding component of the giving-withholding complex which they restrain in the feeding situation. A similar observation can be made in the case of our Chinese mothers, who show so much patience and tolerance in toilet training, which they begin so early and in which they accept slow progress and late completion with seeming equanimity. However, when the child is naughty, the little buttocks are beaten freely and frequently. We may leave it unsettled here whether the mother's greater restraint in expression of negative feelings in premoral relations is the general rule or observable in certain cases only. We may note in this connection that there are mothers who use spanking as a major punishment who are much less restrained in the expression of disgust, impatience, etc., in connection with toilet training than our Chinese mothers seem to be.

Let us now turn to other moral variables. We may consider some of the adult beliefs about the probable results of meritorious behavior or its opposite in this life. We may take a type of behavior which is widely regarded as meritorious, namely, effort. What relations are supposed to exist between exerting one's utmost efforts and the occurrence of success? Roughly, there are four possible combinations: effort and success, effort and no success, no effort and success, no effort and no success. Of course, an individual or group may regard one or both of these variables as of no value and accordingly be unconcerned with their probable relations. Where effort and success are regarded as morally relevant, it is possible to stress one or the other of their alternative relations. There may be, for instance, strong belief in the efficacy and irresistible force of effort; that is, the combination of effort and success may be emphasized: if one tries hard enough, one will succeed. The converse may also be held: if one has not succeeded, it is a sign that one has not tried hard enough. This would seem to correspond to one type of older American moral ideology. On the other hand, it is possible to stress the other pair of alternatives. Success may seem to be mainly a result of chance. One may regard the successful with doubts as to whether they have made any effort commensurate with their success and award the greatest praise to those who, without succeeding, have exerted themselves the most strenuously. This seems to be maintained by some of the Czechs whom we have interviewed.

If we examine this position a little further, we find that it seems to imply a higher valuation on effort than on success. A Czech woman tells us how badly her father felt when her Gymnasium teacher told him: "Your daughter is doing excellent work, but we know that she is preparing her homework a few minutes before class." The father, reproaching the girl, told her how much he would have preferred to hear that she was making a less brilliant record but had tried harder. The idea of the combination of effort and success is not prominent here. Success tends to appear as undeserved, while great effort is imagined as combined with lesser success. We somehow get the impression that it is not only the demonstration of effort but also the lack of success which has positive value.

To consider an early experience in the life of the child in which effort and success and their opposites occur, we may return again to toilet training. If we consider what would correspond to the combination of effort and no success, it would be the situation where the child gives demonstrations of trying without producing anything. If we ask further why this situation might be highly valued, we would guess that in this case the child wishes to frustrate the mother, or rather to give and withhold at the same time; thus he gives his effort but withholds the feces. This might then be a prototype of the moral situation favored by our Czech informants. Relating this to what we said earlier about the conflict over the giving and withholding of food which we ascribed to our Czech mothers, we might infer that in toilet training the child responds in a similar way about giving and withholding of excreta. The greatest feeling of gratification would attach to the instance which combines giving and withholding. In subsequent elaboration this would lead to attaching the most positive moral feeling to effort without success. Of course, there are undoubtedly many factors from later experience as well which contribute to such an attitude.[5]

To turn to another, not unrelated, item of moral ideology, there may be various beliefs as to the probable outcome of careers which have started off in a good or bad direction. There are numerous and widely diffused sayings to the effect that the initial direction determines or is prognostic for the whole life-course ("As the twig is bent," etc.). One class of these sayings has to do with the influence of the parents (e.g., "The fruit does not fall far from the tree"). In contrast to these beliefs, the views of our Czech informants tended to be that one can make no such predictions. When asked what a bad child would grow up to be like if not corrected, they answered: "You can never tell." If we asked what effect does a good mother have on her children, the answer was likely to be: "I often wonder." This would be followed by reflections about women who seemed to be very bad mothers, but whose children turned out well. The children of these Czech families expressed similar uncertainty. A girl of nine replied to the question, What makes some children good and others bad? by saying: "You can't tell. Once I got such a lot of presents for my birthday and then I was very bad. . . . I really don't know. Sometimes it looks as if being left alone and getting no presents makes children good. I have a girl friend . . . she is really a good girl, and she is left so much alone and never gets presents for her birthday. But I don't know."

This belief about the uncertain determination and development of goodness and badness, which probably has a very complex derivation, may be in part related to some of the tendencies which we have already observed in our Czech informants. The tendency toward alternate giving and withholding is perhaps expressed in the moral evaluation of others. As soon as one calls a person bad, one then veers to the other side: he may still turn out all right. And, conversely, if one calls someone good, who knows whether in the end this goodness will amount to anything? The tendency to oscillate between positive and negative feelings is illustrated in a series of associations which proceed by opposites. Sequences in the moral world may thus seem devoid of meaningful connection; the bad may be unpredictably superseded by the good, and vice versa. If we consider a contrasting picture of the moral world in which sequences are meaningful, we might imagine in a simplified way some such emotional process as the following underlying it. When anything turns out badly for one's self or someone else, one thinks spontaneously of previous mistakes or sinful acts, forgetting for the moment anything good or creditable. The present event seems congruous with a long past history; a univocal mood and set of associations are then expressed as a belief in a causal inevitability. The process of association in our Czech subjects is different from this. If a child seems to be turning out badly, one tends to think of all the evidence for the mother's having been a good mother. One sector of the ambivalence does not become exclusively absorbing, but very quickly evokes the opposite sector. This emotional sequence is then expressed in a judgment about the sequence of events in the moral world.

The tendency to react by opposites which we have noted in our Czech subjects may have an interpersonal as well as an intrapersonal application. As illustrated in the mother-child relation, the child may tend to behave in a way opposite to, rather than congruous with, the mother's behavior toward him. One mother remarked, for instance, when we asked what makes a child good: "I really don't know. Sometimes you wonder. . . . Sometimes I slap Mary and she will be as good as gold, and sometimes I am nice and good and she's unbearable." The same mother also remarked on her little girl's reaction to punishment: "When I put Mary in the corner and then say she can come out, she says, 'Thank you, now I like it here.'" We have already cited the other little girl who recalled how badly she behaved on her birthday. In remarking on the supposed withholding tendencies of these mothers, we have made the guess that their children may tend to react by wanting to disappoint the mother in turn. This impulse may take the form of reacting in the opposite way from that which the mother expects. The child thus demonstrates that he cannot be controlled, just as he felt that his mother could not be controlled by his wishes. This feeling of uncontrollability may then contribute to the reactions: I wonder what effect a good mother has; you can't tell what makes a child good or bad.

The tendency to mingle reward and punishment may also contribute to this uncertainty as to the outcome of moral careers. In so far as the child sees a wished-for reward alternately offered and withdrawn, he remains in doubt as to whether he will turn out to have been good or bad. Since children seem susceptible to measuring their goodness or badness in terms of the deprivations or indulgences they receive, parental indecision in the latter respect would be conducive to the child's being uncertain as to his moral status. The parents' tendency to mingle blame with praise would reinforce this uncertainty. When we asked how a bad child might turn out well in later life, a frequent answer was: "He could be changed by love; a good woman can have a great influence." This would seem to express a fantasy of finding a more rewarding mother-figure who could relieve the man's uncertainties about his goodness and also provoke less contrary reactions.[6]

Despite the doubts which our Czech subjects expressed as to whether good treatment makes a child good, etc., they were not inclined to generalize from the contrary instances either. They did not cite any such maxims as the old American "Spare the rod and spoil the child." We have the impression here of an endless oscillation of ambivalence so that the image of a well-behaved but badly treated child also evokes contrary images, namely, of children who turned out badly because of neglect or of good children of good mothers.

A different pattern of reaction by opposites seems to be illustrated by our Syrian subjects. While interpersonal relations may be characterized by contrary reactions, these are taken as sufficiently reliable to make prediction and control feasible. Thus in some cases children may learn: if you ask the parents for anything, they will refuse it; if you do not ask, they will give it. One informant gives an illustrative recollection from her childhood. Every evening after supper her mother used to buy ice cream for her and her brother. One evening on the walk to the store, the children were talking of the anticipated treat, and the mother overheard them. That evening they got no ice cream. "When we were alone, my brother and I talked about it, and we decided that the reason was that mother had heard us talking about it and she wanted to teach us a lesson not to ask for anything. . . . I have never forgotten it, and ever since then my brother and I never asked for anything. I am going to do that with my baby too." The justification for this contrary behavior, as understood by this informant, is that "to give a child everything he asks for will spoil him." A less conscious motivation would seem to be that of the parents maintaining an active position while holding the child in a passive one. If the parent gives when asked, he becomes subject to the control of the asking child. We may recall the position of mother and child in nursing as described by some of our Syrian informants: the child remains bound in the cradle while the mother bends over it and thrusts her nipple into its mouth. Subsequent withholding by the mother in response to the child's active asking would then aim at a re-enactment of the earlier situation, in which the mother was exclusively active.[7] This would not seem to express the same sort of conflict over giving which we ascribed to our Czech mothers and does not lead to the same endless alternation of giving and withholding.

Let us briefly summarize the main hypothetical connections which we have sketched between certain premoral mother-child relations and certain forms of moral behavior and beliefs. Starting with a conflict in the mother about giving and withholding of food, we have seen giving and withholding tendencies repeated in reward and punishment. We were led to suppose that the mother's combined giving and withholding tendencies in relation to food were taken over by the child in toilet training, where he could disappoint the mother in his turn by giving a demonstration of effort and still withholding his feces. This seemed to be related to the adult moral position which awarded the highest valuation to the person who tried the hardest without achieving success. Uncertainty as to moral causation (e.g., What makes a child good or bad? What is the effect of good or bad parents? etc.) appeared to be related to a number of factors: alternate giving and withholding in the moral estimation of others; uncertainty as to one's own moral score in connection with the parents' tendency to alternate or combine reward and punishment; the tendency of children to behave in a contrary fashion; and the fantasy of a purely rewarding mother in relation to whom one could become entirely good. Thus a variety of moral beliefs and behaviors seemed to be mutually interconnected and to have common ties with certain mother-child relations.

Let us now proceed to consider further variants of premoral experience and the moral attitudes which appear to be associated with them. We spoke previously of the very early inception of toilet training reported by our Chinese informants. The mother is said to pick up the infant from as early as one month on; she does not expect him to call or come to her, or to cede to her direction a function of which he has gained control, since none of these things applies to an infant of this age.[8] She assumes the responsibility of discovering the proper time, of learning to interpret the involuntary sounds and movements of the infant. In so far as she stimulates him, it is by little sympathetic sounds, of hissing or grunting, which simulate the sounds of urination and defecation. One apparent derivative of this early toilet training for which the mother assumes the responsibility appears in the following custom which our subjects report. Instead of asking the children at a later age to make good resolutions at New Year's, the parents come to the bedside of the sleeping children at night and wipe their lips with toilet paper; this is supposed to wipe away the effects of all the bad things they have said in the year which has passed. Another related point may be the connotation of certain words for naughtiness which emphasize receptors rather than effectors. One such term is literally translated as "obstinate skin"; a term for obstinate is "dead eye of the heart." The image here seems to be nonreceptivity to stimuli rather than tensed muscles and active resistance (contrast our "stubborn as a mule"). This seems congruous with the method of training in which the mother asks the child to respond to sensory stimuli coming from her rather than calling on him for more active, voluntary co-operation.

The participation of the mother in the infant's excretory processes from such an early age may help to perpetuate the child's feeling that his body is connected with his mother's. He may be particularly encouraged to feel that the contents of his body are continuous with those of his mother's body. That the food he receives comes from inside the mother's body may seem confirmed not only from nursing but by the fact that mothers frequently chew the first solid food which they give and transfer it from their own mouths to the children's.[9] The mother maintains her interest in these products of hers after they have entered the child's body and may be felt as presiding over their journey through the alimentary tract, since she is almost always there to receive them back when they are excreted. The feeling of the identity of the mother's and child's body products is suggested in a folk belief reported by some of our informants. Mother's milk is supposed to have a restorative value for adults suffering from certain debilitating illnesses; the urine of a breast-fed boy baby is supposed to be equally efficacious. Related to such beliefs there seems to be a tendency not to devalue excretory products very much; the journey through the alimentary tract does not wholly divest the good food of its virtues. Where the child feels for the moment on bad terms with the mother, he may feel that, in charming his excreta out of him, she is weakening him. Such a fantasy seems to be displaced to dangerously amorous women in later life, who are said to drain the man of the milk of his virility. In a story which expresses this fantasy, "The Mandarin-Duck Girdle,"[10] the unhappy hero becomes the lover of several insatiable young nuns who so exhaust him with their amorous demands that he wastes away and finally dies. (Contrast the story in Boccaccio where the hero succeeds in surviving a similar danger.)

The feeling of continuity between the inside of the mother's body and that of the child's seems to be expressed in beliefs of mutual influence. Just as the mother controls the contents of the child's body, so the child is accused when he is bad of causing destructive effects inside the mother's body. Thus a reproach which, according to our informants, mothers are likely to make against bad children is: "You fill me with gas." This gas is supposed to be generated inside the mother and to produce stifling sensations in response to the child's badness. The mother may say: "You kill me with gas"—thus presenting to the child the fulfilment of his bad wishes via the medium of his control of her insides. One derivative of this belief is the stress which some of the children of our Chinese parents placed on the danger of leaving the gas on in the kitchen. A ten-year-old boy, when asked to write a story about a bad child, titled his story "The Frightened Boy," and related: "His name was Tommy Lee. One day he did something very bad. He opened the gas by mistake and can't close it. So the gas went under the door and everybody in the house got infected by the gas. Later when his parents came home they found everyone on the ground. They called the police and told them the story. After that he tried to be good and most of the time he was." In a similar way, a nine-year-old girl mentioned that it would be a specially meritorious act which she would want everyone to know about if she found the gas accidentally turned on and turned it off. This suggests that the choice of physical hazards most warned against in various instances of child training is related to other fantasied dangers which are thus indirectly represented.

The feeling of continuity between the child's body and the mother's which is encouraged in the early handling of the infant seems to fit in with a major Chinese moral requirement that the child should perpetuate his family. His body belongs to his family and is the instrument of its perpetuity. If he injures or endangers his body, he is punished for having thus damaged or exposed his parents' property. The image of several bodies combining to form a single body is expressed and reinforced in several Chinese children's games described by our informants. In these games a number of children form a composite body, and the point is to keep this composite intact. Thus in the Walking Pagodas the boys of each team form a pyramid by climbing on one another's shoulders; the two pagodas attack each other, and that side wins whose members maintain their positions in the composite figure without being dislodged.

The continuity of mother's and child's bodies emphasized in infancy may be utilized in the later requirement that the child continue the family line. The greatest filial impiety is for a son not to have any offspring. The pre-oedipal relation to the mother may provide a base for the later relation to the father. Just as the infant is led to feel that he receives the products of his mother's body and that she maintains her interest and property rights in these valuable products as they pass through his body, so the son may later fantasy that he receives and transmits generative substances from his father. The docility and submission of the son to the father might be based on passive oral fantasies combined with the feeling that the son's genital activity is directed by the father on the model of body-as-transmitter derived from the relation with the mother.[11] Obviously, there are, in general, many different ways in which the son's oedipal opposition to the father may be mitigated and resolved. In the case which we have been considering it would seem that the early infantile feeling of the child's body as recipient and conveyer of the valuable products of the mother's body may contribute to the reconciliation in the oedipal phase of the son's genital activity with that of the father. The father replaces the mother as the source of the valuable body products which the son is asked to receive and to transmit.

NOTES

1. Whether swaddling has a deprivational impact has been questioned by Phyllis Greenacre (1944). Ruth Benedict has suggested that swaddling may have a variable impact, depending on the intent of the swaddler (Benedict, 1949).

2. This close association or rapid alternation of reward and punishment may have the further function of insuring the moderation of punishment. Parents of different cultures vary in respect to this, whether they are more concerned to confine punishment within certain bounds, lest it be too destructive to the child, or whether their main concern is that punishment should be forceful enough to control the child. Our Chinese and Jewish informants seemed concerned with delimiting the severity of punishment. They frequently specified that punishments were not so extreme as they might be or that precautions were taken not to damage the child. Thus some Chinese informants remarked that the mother is usually the one to punish the child "because her hand is lighter." Similarly, a nine-year-old boy of Chinese parents said that his mother hit him with anything, then added smilingly, "Not with iron, of course." Jewish informants repeated that in hitting a child they took care not to strike the head. They also mentioned that they would never withhold as punishment anything necessary to the child's health, such as food.

An opposite attitude toward punishment appears among Syrian parents: no moderation is necessary; the only problem is to punish sufficiently. A Syrian informant cites a traditional paternal saying: "I do not want my neighbors to say I have done well when I beat my son; if they say I have done too much, then I will be satisfied." When Syrian parents bring a child to school for the first time, they are supposed to urge the teacher to beat him properly, by saying: "The skin is for you, the bones for me." This apparent lack of anxiety about the destructive possibilities of punishment seems to be related to a strong libidinization of punitive violence. This is illustrated in the following account which a nine-year-old daughter of Syrian parents gives of how her mother beat her: "My mother was going out, and I refused to kiss her because—I don't remember why. My mother took me across her knee and gave me a beating. I cried and then I kissed her. She said to me that I could have done that before and saved myself a beating. Then I kissed her, and I have never stopped kissing her since." It remains a question under what conditions the libidinization of aggression serves to make aggression seem less dangerous, and under what conditions such a fusion of impulses tends to make sex seem more frightening.

3. Chvojkova, 1946.

4. The converse of the mother's feeling seems to be expressed in the fantasy of an eleven-year-old boy of a Czech family. Asked to tell a story of a good boy, he tells about a film he has seen. "It was in the Middle Ages, and there was a boy,

he robbed bakeries. The bakers were chasing him, but they did not get him." The interviewer, thinking that he has misunderstood and told about a bad boy, asked whether he wanted now to tell a story of a good boy. The child said: "But this was a story of a good boy. . . . You see this was the Middle Ages and then the bakers were very rich, and the boys were very poor and had to work hard." Thus in the boy's fantasy, where food is withheld, the child's taking is justified (becomes good). This is the reverse of the mother's feeling: when the child is bad, withholding is justified.

5. In this connection Czech informants have brought up their image of Austrian rule: a Czech who was successful might be supposed to owe this more to having ingratiated himself with Austrian officials than to hard work. There were also tendencies toward noncompliance with the officials (cf. the image of the good soldier Schweik), which consisted in giving the greatest demonstrations of zeal while producing none of the required results. Whether these were mainly adult realities confirming early experience or fantasies deriving from it, they are congruent with the syndrome which we have described.

6. Another factor which may contribute to uncertainty as to whether one will turn out to be good or bad is disagreement among adult authorities. Our Czech mothers seemed quite outspoken in criticizing their children's teachers in front of the children. In contrast, our Chinese mothers were inclined to feel that the teachers were right, and they further specified that a good parent is one who accepts all criticisms about his children. In keeping with this agreement of authorities, there seemed to be greater certainty about the probable outcomes of various moral careers.

7. What seems to be a high degree of outspokenness about ambivalence in our Syrian subjects may be related to the method of nursing which we have described. This ambivalence was expressed, for instance, in proverbs which these subjects cited: "From the time I saw you, my children, I ceased to enjoy my bread." "I am against my brother; my brother and I are against our cousins; but cousin, brother, and I are against strangers." "Beware of your enemies once, beware of your friends a thousand times." A possible connection between pronounced ambivalence and an experience in nursing, where the child feels that he is being aggressively penetrated by the mother's breast, has been suggested by Edmund Bergler (1948). While Dr. Bergler was inclined to doubt whether actual differences in maternal handling contributed to these oral fantasies, our Syrian material suggests that they are relevant.

8. Related to this method of toilet training, there seems to be a relatively slight value placed on punctuality. When we asked our Chinese children what they would do if they were on their way to school and saw they were in danger of being late, they were little inclined to stress hurrying. One said: "I would tell the teacher I had to get dressed and eat my breakfast." Hurrying appeared more as a possible hazard to safety or health than as a virtue. Another child said: "I would run; when I came to a red light I would stop, of course." Another remarked: "I run; when I get out of breath, I walk." This is in keeping with a traditional polite remark of adults to departing guests: "Walk away slowly"—which may be interpreted as referring to the dangers of hurrying.

9. The pleasure of eating food which has been prechewed by the mother and the possibly related fantasy of eating the mother's body contents would seem to be perpetuated in the Chinese custom of having food chopped very fine in the process of preparation before it is brought to the table. Numerous dishes in which finely chopped food is enveloped in a doughy covering may be related to a fantasy of eating the mother's body as well as its contents. At the same time, the fact that the food is cut into small pieces before it reaches the table, that no cutting or strenuous biting occurs in the process of eating, may also be regarded as a defense against oral destructive tendencies. Chinese informants reported that a meat fast was sometimes observed on the day sacred to the protection of mothers. Also, when a parent was extremely ill, a child might as a last resort serve him or her a soup in which he (the child) had cooked a piece of his own flesh.

10. Acton, 1947.

11. The intellectual counterpart to this transmission is expressed in the traditionalism of Confucius, quoting Mo Tzu: "I have 'transmitted what was taught me without making up anything of my own'" (Waley, 1945). The apparently very gradual development of moral autonomy may also be related to the feeling of continuity with the parents. The individual remained, up to an advanced age, accessible to moral guidance of parents and other critics, with relatively little opposition of his judgment to theirs. A traditional phrase was: "If you have it [the fault attributed to you], change it; if you don't have it, be warned against it." Tendencies to resentment, self-justification, or counterattack in response to criticism seem to have been little in evidence. The tendency to continue early childhood relations with parental moral authority was expressed by the Chinese children of prepuberty age whom we interviewed. We asked them: "If a child did something bad and no one found out, would he tell anyone?" Our Chinese children tended to say that the child might tell his parents; it would be better for the parents to know, so that they could correct him; also, otherwise someone outside the family might find out. Children from other groups, e.g., our Czech children, were more inclined to say that the child might tell another child, a trusted friend, in case the bad deed weighed on his conscience. They thus expressed a transfer of moral role from the parents to age mates, which was less evident in the Chinese children.

LIST OF REFERENCES

Acton, Harold, and Yi-hsieh, Lee (trans.). 1947. "The Mandarin Duck-Girdle." In *Four Cautionary Tales*. London: Wyn.

Benedict, Ruth. 1949. "Child Rearing in Certain European Countries," *American Journal of Orthopsychiatry*, XIX, No. 2, 342–50.

Bergler, Edmund. 1948. "Three Tributaries to the Development of Ambivalence," *Psychoanalytic Quarterly*, XVII, No. 2, 173–81.

Chvojkova, Hlena. 1946. *Zuzanka Discovers the World*. Prague.

Greenacre, Phyllis. 1944. "Infants' Reaction to Restraint: Problems on the Fate of Infantile Aggression," *American Journal of Orthopsychiatry*, XIV, No. 2, 204–18.

Waley, Arthur (trans.). 1945. *The Analects of Confucius*. London: Allen & Unwin.

CHAPTER 22

Differential Patterns of Social Outlook and Personality in Family and Children

————————————————————————————ELSE FRENKEL-BRUNSWIK

The first of the two case studies presented here has previously been reported in a paper, "Patterns of Social and Cognitive Outlook in Children and Parents," which appeared in the American *Journal of Orthopsychiatry, XXI, No. 3 (1915), 543–58.*

MOST investigators who have written about the American family agree that at present we witness a weakening of the family as an institution and that this change runs parallel to the weakening of many other social institutions. It is pointed out by these writers, especially by Ogburn,[1] that the dilemma of the modern family is due to the loss of some of its functions, such as the economic, the educational, or the religious function. But in the interpretation of this loosening of the older, more rigid forms of family organization the writers disagree. Some, such as Zimmerman,[2] see in this change signs of disintegration and point to divorces, delinquency, revolt of youth, and increased individualism as proof of their contention. Others, such as Burgess,[3] find that the increased relaxation of authority and regimentation within the family leads to greater stress on companionship and affection. Instead of regarding it as a sign of disintegration, he sees in the replacement of old-time family structures a phenomenon of growth and increased adaptability, brought about by greater democracy, freedom, and opportunity for self-expression within the family. A cogent analysis of the American family can be found in Mead.[4] In view of such comprehensive collections of the different views on the American family as that by Winch and McGinnis,[5] we need not expand on the subject further.

Although the trend toward democratization of the family is, without doubt, an outstanding development in this country, the old-type authoritarian family with its unquestioned parental rule, even though deviant by modern standards, has not vanished altogether. In the present paper one example each of the two opposite extremes of American families is presented. In each case the presentation is centered about one of their children. It was the children who were the basis of the selection of the two families; they represent the authoritarian and the democratic attitude and personality structure in their purest forms. Neither of them can be considered representative in the statistical sense. To paraphrase a statement of Woodworth, they are so typical that they can be considered to be atypical. They exhibit most of the trends found statistically to be prevalent in their respective groups, to be introduced below, but rarely present in such completeness in a single individual. In accordance with our general findings, existing differences, if any, in sex, intelligence, or size of family may be considered of but secondary importance in the choice of paradigms for our present purpose, which is the concrete demonstration of the authoritarian versus the equalitarian syndrome. As will become evident to the reader, there are rather striking differences in the educational and intellectual levels of the two families. The question as to whether these differences are primary or whether they are secondary effects of the general inaccessibility to experience which is so characteristic of even the more intelligent authoritarian individuals cannot be fully discussed here, although some light will be thrown on this issue by the present material.

The first of the two families belongs to a pattern obviously less frequent in the present American culture than the second. It mirrors the old-fashioned authoritarian type of family structure in its most rigid form. Our second, democratic-minded example, even though by no means free of internal tensions, represents an orientation geared toward the realization of basically equalitarian principles; these are pursued in this family with relentless devotion and without compromise. It must be stressed that neither of the two families presents an ideal from the standpoint of perfect adjustment, as generally both the authoritarian and the nonauthoritarian personality are sometimes associated with their own particular brands of neuroticism.[6]

Since we are describing two individual families, we cannot generalize to the culture as a whole. In fact, our examples stress the variety rather than the uniformity of family life and individuals that can be found within one and the same culture. Furthermore, in the present context we are not primarily interested in social and economic determinants and, therefore, in the origin and structure of such social institutions as the family; rather, our main emphasis is on the influence of such institutions upon the outlook and personality structure of children and adolescents. However, we shall not neglect to point out the ways in which the family patterns described here seem to be rooted in some aspects of the complex institutional structure of our society.

Although our start is from the children and other individuals concerned and our method is a clinical one, with special emphasis on depth interviewing, our eventual concern is with general problems of social psychology. Under this aspect we explored the ways in which parents and children relate themselves to shared norms and values, their feelings of belongingness, their conception of parent-child relationships, of occupational roles and sex roles, and their religious and social outlook in general. Over and above this we tried to probe into the underlying patterns of motivation and emotions.

In a child-family study begun in 1944 and still under way at the Institute of Child Welfare, University of California,[7] approximately fifteen hundred children and adolescents, most of them between the ages of ten and fifteen, were given questionnaire-type tests dealing with attitudes toward minority groups as well as attitudes toward political and economic issues in general. From some of these instruments an over-all ethnic prejudice or "ethnocentrism" score was derived. Among those scoring extremely "high" and extremely "low" on ethnocentrism (that is, scoring within the uppermost or lowermost 25 per cent), one hundred and sixty-one were interviewed and given a specially designed variant of the well-known Thematic Apperception Test.[8] The interviews, conducted in 1946 and 1947, concerned attitudes toward minority groups and the social scene in general, toward school, discipline, work, parents, friends, and the opposite sex, as well as the child's conception of the self. With respect to these procedures, our methods and results are analogous to those of a separate project on "The Authoritarian Personality,"[9] of which this writer was one of the authors and in which the relationship between ethnocentrism and a more generalized authoritarianism was ascertained for the case of adults. Over and above these procedures, one or both of the parents of forty-three of our children were also interviewed concerning their attitudes and child-rearing practices; in addition, the socioeconomic family history was gathered. A further distinguishing phase of our child-family study consisted of an exploration of the children's cognitive mastery of reality by having them perform various experimental tasks in perception, memory, and thinking.[10]

The use of children as subjects in the study of social beliefs offers both advantages and disadvantages. Children are generally more direct and uninhibited; they openly express attitudes and feelings which, though no doubt still alive in adults, are manifested by them with greater reserve and restraint. On the other hand, children's attitudes are less structured and less consistent than those of adults. But even in children we found that the social beliefs held by an individual, though varying in degree of crystallization, tend to fall into a coherent pattern and that this pattern seems to be related to the personal "fate" he had met in his early interpersonal relationships within the family.

A body of data has now been accumulated by various investigators which shows that different socioeconomic classes vary a great deal as to the pattern of child rearing. Since our study was not primarily oriented toward class differences, we tried to select two families which are not too different as far as their economic locus is concerned. In fact, the two families are even matched in the sense that both are objectively moving downward on the economic ladder when compared with the grandparents; yet we find a profound difference in the reaction to the loss of objective status. Although approximately matched economically, the two families differ widely with respect to many other social indices, such as education and prestige. These differences, without doubt, in addition to the differences observed in the personalities of the parents, will explain a good part of the radically different atmospheres prevailing in the respective homes.

CASE STUDY OF AN AUTHORITARIAN FAMILY AND CHILD

One of our most ethnocentric child subjects is an eleven-year-old boy whom we shall call "Karl."

Parents and home atmosphere.—Karl's father comes from an authoritarian family and is a mechanic. Karl's father and paternal grandfather were born in this country, whereas the child's paternal grandmother came from Germany. The paternal grandparents died when Karl's father was four years old, and the father was reared by the great-grandparents, who owned a large farm and a wholesale store and "who were rich but not generous with their money."

Karl's mother was born in this country, and so was her father, while her mother was born in Scotland. Karl's maternal step-grandfather was a notary. Karl's maternal grandmother had divorced her husband shortly after Karl's mother was born. In fact, Karl's mother had a succession of stepfathers, one of whom, a combination of musician and laborer, also played an important role for her. She finished the eighth grade, whereas Karl's father's education stopped even before he had reached this level.

The interviewer describes the home as crowded with overstuffed and dreary oak furniture, with lace doilies on the tables. All this perhaps represents a concerted effort on the part of the parents to stress their middle-class identification and to avoid the possibility of being grouped with the underprivileged. This anxiety stems at least partially from the fact that the socioeconomic history of the family is unstable and that there was some loss of status as compared to the previous generation. There is, however, no evidence of poverty. The family lives in a six-room flat and owns a car and two radios.

The mother's background has much less stability than the father's. "I grew up in big cities and in one hotel after another." Generally, such geographical instability seems relatively common in ethnocentric homes. Both parents, furthermore, report their own parents as foreign-born. This, too, is significantly more often the case with parents of prejudiced than of tolerant children. As a group trend, it may be taken to indicate that the parents still see themselves entangled in the process of assimilation. Apparently as a counterbalance, they stress their "belonging," through both their social aspirations and the rejection of what is considered socially inferior.

Both of Karl's parents had been exposed to strict discipline. The father does not like to talk about his own father, whom he describes as a drunkard and psychopath who deserted his family. He is much more ready to discuss his grandfather, by whom he was raised:

"My grandfather was really strict. He had thirteen children, and even when they were grown up, there wasn't one of them that would talk back to him, and he could handle any of them."

The father of our boy grew up knowing little but work. His grandfather was anxious to see his grandson go to school and even to have his voice trained. Karl's father did not live up to any of his grandfather's ambitions, doing relatively simple work, although he still believes he will one day accomplish a great deal by an invention. He asserts that his occupation is only temporary, since he is likely soon to make a big mechanical invention. This aspiration remains on a fantasy level, since there is little evidence of any concrete work toward the goal.

The idea of achieving fame some day is still alive in the fantasies of Karl's mother as well. Though having worked mainly in factories and being a waitress at the time of the interview, she prides herself on her talents, such as photography, composing, and writing. There is here the same kind of unrealistic fantasy to which attention will be called in discussing Karl himself.

In discussing their children, Karl's parents emphasize that they made rules for them which had to be strictly obeyed. For instance, the children had to be in bed "sharp at six without fail." Asked whether the children ever have tantrums, the mother says:

"I should say not. They had better not. If they got mad, I just sat them on a chair and said to stay there until they could behave. I guess they never really had tantrums."

This is at variance with Karl's own statements, according to which he has outbursts of temper. Either this is mere boasting on his part, or the mother's denial of his ever deviating from what she considers good behavior is a distortion of fact; we are inclined to favor the latter interpretation. Apparently along the same line is the mother's statement about Karl, who is obviously a rather weak child, that "he has a strength but he hides it."

Both parents also report that they have used spanking as a disciplinary measure. To quote the mother: "The boys are more afraid of their father than of me; I guess because he is stronger." She seems not to realize that her children are overtrained and welcome the more severe punishment by their father. The father appears considerably worried about what the interviewer might have guessed about the children's relation to him: "It seems like Karl is afraid of me."

It is the father who represents in the family the rigid dichotomizing of the sex roles, which is, as we shall see, one of the characteristics of the authoritarian milieu: "Boys shouldn't do work in the home, though it's all right for a man to be a chef or a baker. The best of them are men." He apparently feels that it is considered appropriate for a man to be a chef and thus to enter the field of women only if there is assurance that he will excel.

The mother, in explaining her children's personality, relies heavily on astrology. She tells us that the personality of Karl's brother, whom we shall call Bill, can be explained by the fact that "he was born under the sign of The Twins." About Karl she says: "He is a dreamer of far places. He will go far and wide. The stars show that." The dependence on fate and the feeling of a mystical connection with supernatural forces has been found typical of the ethnocentric milieu,[11] the exaggerated ideas of self-importance going hand in hand with an underdeveloped self-reliance.

Both parents are ethnically extremely prejudiced. They consider the Negroes America's biggest problem, and the father adds: "Dig up Roosevelt and let him help settle it." He is concerned that the Negroes "want to go everywhere." The mother tells how, at the time she was a waitress, she personally took it on herself to put Negroes in their place. She would give them a glass of water and then ignore them:

"When they went out, we smashed the glass behind the counter good and hard so they were sure to hear it. The Chinese and Japanese should be separate too."

About the Jews the mother says:

"The Bible says they will always be persecuted. You know it wasn't a small thing they did—crucifying Christ—God said they would be punished till the end of time."

This line of argument is the more surprising because in the discussion about religion it is not the mother but the father who stresses the importance of religion, as does Karl himself.

Karl's social beliefs.—Karl is an unusually fat and passive boy with a history of many illnesses. The parents' ethnocentrism is shared by Karl, who in many other respects mirrors fascistic attitudes. We begin with quotations from that part of his interview record that deals with attitudes toward minority members. Karl says about Negroes:

"They make trouble, start wars. I wouldn't mind having all the Negroes in Oakland and all the white people in a different state. I would like to have a couple for good fighters. They are good fighters when they fight with a

knife. Like somebody starts a fight and you have a gang with some Negroes to fight with you on your side with knives and guns."

Like most of the ethnocentric children, Karl is in favor of segregation of the outgroups, and, like some of them, his statements show implicit envy of characteristics ascribed to minority groups. Karl admires the physical power, strength, and aggressiveness of the Negroes. He rejects them and does not want them to mix with his own group, but he wants them as protectors—we might almost say as bodyguards—in fights against other boys. His passivity and relative immobility also give direction to the stereotype he has about the Jews:

"They think they are smart and go anywhere they please. They think they are hot. They dress up in all kinds of jewelry. Some just kidnap girls and boys and use them for slaves."

Some characteristics of this image of the Jews, such as their alleged social dominance and their exhibitionism of wealth, are common in ethnocentric children. We find, however, in Karl's statements some emphases and elaborations which, as we shall see, are rooted in his own specific conflicts. Thus the mobility and the enslaving motif is very personal with Karl. We have just heard him express the desire to use Negroes as his fighting slaves. The theme of fighting recurs again and again in Karl's description of minority groups. Although children not uncommonly ascribe aggressiveness to Negroes, it is most unusual for them to mention this quality in descriptions of the Chinese. Karl, however, stresses the point that Chinese are "good fighters"; and about the Filipinos he says: "They are good fighters and definitely good to go through jungles with." As we shall see, the preoccupation with jungles, where one can be lost and subject to deprivation, and the preoccupation with animals dominate Karl's fantasy in general.

Like many of the ethnocentric children, Karl sees general avarice and acquisitiveness as the cause of the last war, while the democratic-minded children specify in greater detail the wants of the different countries. Most of the children in our study think that there will be wars in the near future, but Karl, along with a great many of the ethnocentric children, takes this fact as natural and inevitable: "I think so because there's always going to be a war." As do over two-fifths of the high-scoring and a considerably smaller proportion of the low-scoring children, he thinks that we won the last war because of the atom bomb, ascribing a magical quality to its destructive potential. Equalitarian children refer more often in this context to better resources and the better equipment of America in general.

It is evident that Karl is at least in partial sympathy with Hitler and that his concern is only about the wrongs Hitler might have done to Americans. He states: "He was a little bit O.K. Sometimes he got a

little bit too mean and did dirty stuff like putting lighted matches in the toenails of Americans." This partial sympathy with Hitler does not prevent Karl from exercising his extreme punitiveness toward the Germans: "We should put all the Germans and Japs on an island and put an atom bomb to it."

He considers America's biggest problem the fact that "a lot of people are getting mad because everybody is starting war against each other." This is the recurrent fighting theme, this time in the form of an assumption of an almost chaotic war of all against all.

In Karl's response to another interview question we find a further dominant theme—fear of deprivation, especially food deprivation. Karl is against strikes because "if grocery stores go on a strike, we won't have no food. Farmers can go on a strike, and there will be no food, and we will have to grow our own food." Ethnocentric children frequently manifest this particular fear. It is especially exaggerated in Karl but has, as we have ascertained, no basis in real food deprivation.

Karl's attitude toward the social scene and his role in it is best characterized by the one-sidedness of his answer to the interview question, "How would you like to change America?":

"I would like to have a filling station every couple of blocks or so and palm trees and grass along the streets and lawns in front of people's houses and have the back yards all cleaned up and flowers growing. Every store should have all kinds of candy and bubble gum. They wouldn't have no fights in the neighborhood. The cops would take them all in. At Fleishacker's [an amusement park] have nice warm water [in the swimming pool] and the zoo cleaned up. Every day there would be hay for the animals that eat hay and the lions would have lots of meat every day for breakfast and lunch."

As are many of our ethnocentric children, Karl is concerned with cleanliness and external beautification, the removal of aggressive groups, and with having a constant flow of supplies. The only beings for which he shows concern are, characteristically, animals rather than people. His emphasis on rigid order as well as on the regularity in the appearance of streets and other objects contrasts sharply with his emphasis on, and even open advocacy of, turmoil and chaotic aggression, as noticed above.

Equalitarian children, on the other hand, are better able to remove themselves from the pressure of overanxiety about immediate needs. They are more likely to penetrate to such underlying and more general aspects of human welfare as justice and equality, lower prices and higher wages, and moral and ethical values in general.

Before leaving the topic of Karl's beliefs, we should like to point to the similarity between his statements on this subject and those of his brother Bill, older by one year. These differences exist in spite of the

fact that the two boys had no opportunity to discuss the subject between the respective interviews. Like Karl, Bill thinks that "we should
kick out the colored people from San Francisco" because they get
drunk and kill people. He feels that the German war criminals "should
all have been hanged and not put in prison." Like his brother, he wants
to put "the Japs on an island and throw bombs on them." He considers
food to be America's biggest problem, and his main concern in this
context is the problem of the rationing of sugar.

Karl's and his brother's attitudes toward school, family, and sex roles.
—The stereotypical approach to social and ethical challenges, with all
its inherent inhibitions, carries over into such related, more specific
areas as the conception of teachers, parental roles, sex roles, and so
forth. The ambivalent submission to authority, found to be typical of
ethnocentric children, is revealed in Karl's statement about teachers.
An initial stereotyped denial of criticism, "I like everything about
teachers," is followed by the mention of victimization and unjust treatment by teachers: "A lot of them make you go to the principal's office
or out of the room for something you didn't do. I had that happen lots
of times."

When asked in another context to describe the perfect boy, Karl
starts off with a request for obedience to teachers. The craving for a
complete surrender to authority is also exhibited in his brother Bill's
statement about the kind of teacher he doesn't like: "Those who tell
you in a nice way instead of being strict and then don't make you
mind." Bill's ideal teacher would be "a man who would be strict," or,
as second choice, a woman if "she was very strict." While the emphasis
on negative aspects or on strictness seems to be a specific characteristic
of ethnocentric children, the tolerant, by contrast, tend more often to
emphasize positive traits in the ideal teacher, such as being helpful,
laughing at jokes, and the like.

The attitude of ethnocentric children to the teacher appears to be
but one of the aspects of a more generalized hierarchical conception of
human relations, according to which the weak are expected to exhibit
a self-negating surrender to the strong. Karl seems unaware of the fact
that he himself succeeds only very partially in fulfilling the strict requirement of submissive obedience. Obviously, he is possessed by destructive and by no means dormant forces which are in part directed
toward the very authorities to which he demands allegiance but which
are, to an even larger extent, diverted to objects considered by him
as underdogs.

In discussing the pupils he likes and dislikes, Karl seems exclusively
concerned with the possibility of being attacked by one of the other
boys, whereas his brother Bill stresses conventional values, such as
politeness and obedience, values also emphasized by Karl in other con-

texts. Equalitarian children, such as our second major case, Peggy (see below), on the other hand, stress companionship, fun, common interests, and understanding as traits desired in friends.

Both Karl and his brother Bill stress, as do a relatively large proportion of the ethnocentric children, that money helps one to have friends. For Bill, money possesses magical evil attributes:

"It is the root of all evil. It's bad luck to be born with money. If your parents tell you to put it in a bank and you keep it until you are grown up, it's bad luck."

Bill proceeds to describe the disaster which befell several of his acquaintances after they saved their money. This is in line with the general tendency prevalent in the ethnocentric subjects to subscribe to all manner of superstitious statements, to see evil forces at work everywhere, and readily to anticipate doom and catastrophies.

Karl is one of the very few children who would prefer to have a private tutor rather than go to school. He explains that he would like to avoid the effort involved in getting ready to go to school, "to have to pack a lunch and hop a bus." Bill, however, rejects the idea of tutors as "just for rich people, and they are no good." This latter quotation exemplifies the resentment, frequent in ethnocentric subjects, against what they consider oppressors from above, a view which goes along with their fear that those below, such as the minority groups, may rise some day and take over in a fearful revenge.

Both boys have a rigid conception of sex roles, stressing politeness in girls. As Bill points out, "If a boy is talking, they shouldn't butt in." For him the best friend for a boy is a boy, for a girl, a girl. They both reject girls who are discourteous or aggressive toward boys, for example, "If she pulls a boy by the arm and tells him to take her to a show or some place." Although dichotomizing of sex roles is to a certain extent general at this age, children scoring low on ethnocentrism do so to a much lesser degree, stressing more the point that boys and girls should behave naturally with each other. They also do not differentiate their descriptions of a perfect boy from that of a perfect girl as much as do the prejudiced children.

Asked what he would consider a perfect father, Karl, in line with many of the ethnocentric children, speaks mainly of the material benefits this kind of father would provide: "He will let you do anything you like and let you get any kind of food you like and let you take a girl out. Will give you about two dollars every day." Asked how he would like to change his own father, he states emphatically that "my father is good to me" but then goes on immediately to say that he would like to get more money from him to be able "to go to a show or dinner or any place I want." In almost every context he manifests this exploitive-manipulative approach to people.

As is often the case in ethnocentric boys, Karl's hostility is more directly expressed toward the mother than toward the father. When asked how he would like to change his mother, he starts off with "to make her nice," then proceeds to tell what he wants from her, such as "a car." That he is, on the whole, more oriented toward his father is probably related to the fact that the father is more powerful, in a position to provide more goods, and also better able to protect. This kind of dependency is often found to reduce open feelings and expressions of hostility.

While Karl sees people, and especially those in authority, primarily as "deliverers of goods," to use a term of Fenichel's,[12] Bill expects mainly regimentation from them. Thus a perfect father is for him one who, if asked for something, "ought not to give it to you right away." Bill denies that he has any desire to change his parents. There is ample evidence, from his interview and especially from his Thematic Apperception Test stories, of Karl's underlying hostility toward the parents. On a "blind" over-all interview rating of attitudes toward parents, Karl earns the extreme rating of "6" with respect to both parents, representing the rater's impression that he is obsessed by the feeling of being threatened and victimized by their hostility. Bill receives a rating of "5"; this is only one step closer to the opposite extreme, "1," which would indicate an affectionate, secure, companionable relationship as seen by the child.

Both boys are assigned an extreme rating on "externalizaton of values," a category covering opportunism, conventionality, status-concern, and explicit condemnation of those who do not conform.

Both boys tell of corporal punishment at home, and both of them prefer to have their father rather than their mother punish them. Bill comes out with the explicit explanation that his mother "is a little too soft-hearted." In discussing this topic in general, both boys favor very severe punishment of children for relatively minor misconduct and seem only too ready to advocate intervention of the juvenile court in such cases. According to Karl, children should be punished for "talking back to grownups" and for breaking windows: "You should go to Juvenile one year for that."

In Karl a greater readiness toward explosive fits of aggression is revealed in his descriptions of how he reacts in anger: "I do anything I can—bite, pull hair, kick, tear into them." Bill, however, reports that he tries to control his anger as well as he can, mostly by going out of the field. Both explosive outbursts and frantic efforts of control are typical of our ethnocentric children.

Though both boys have shown some tendency to idealize their parents stereotypically and to stress their goodness, neither of them chooses any of the members of the family as companions on a desert island. Karl, of course, stresses first food and water and also that he would take along a girl. From the dreams that Karl relates, as well as from the Thematic Apperception Test, it is evident that he connects the idea of a girl with feeding her or being fed by her and, furthermore, that a girl means to him safety and absence of possible threats felt in connection with boys or men.

Along the same line are Karl's recurrent dreams, "it's about going with a girl for dinner," and about people getting murdered and hanged. The childhood memories he relates are full of mishaps and catastrophes. He remembers having fallen in a pond, recalls seeing his father kill a chicken that ran about without its head, seeing men killing turkeys, and seeing a crate of eggs broken under a truck.

Among his fears he lists his fear of wild animals, of high buildings, of drunken men, of "death in some dark night." He mentions that usually it is the girls who are especially afraid of the dark. When asked whether he wants to be a girl, he denies it but adds the stock projective answer: "Some guys want to be girls." The feminine identification which can be discerned behind much of the aggressive façade is apparent in the interviews and is especially evident in the Thematic Apperception Test.

Karl's Thematic Apperception Test stories.—The rigidification of the child's personality originally induced by the stress on self-negating submission and on the repression of nonacceptable tendencies not only leads to stereotypy; eventually the inherent pattern of conflict may result in a more or less open break between the different layers of personality and in a loss of control of instinctual tendencies by the individual. This contrasts rather sharply with the greater fluidity of transition and intercommunication between the different personality strata which is typical of the child in the more permissive home. The emotional makeup and the rigidity of defense, lack of insight, and narrowness of the ego of the authoritarian personality even carries over into the purely cognitive domain. Here, too, ready-made clichés tend to take the place of realistic spontaneous reactions.

Karl's TAT stories are full of murder and gore, much more so than the usual stories of children of his age. In practically every story a murder is committed under quite extraordinary circumstances. For example, a man who won in a race is "shot in the back five times" while he was "laying in bed, tired from his hard job." Two of the stories, to be further interpreted later, follow:

"It looks like murder. I saw a couple of murder pictures. A girl is down at the dock at night watching them unload freight. There is a man with a cane that is the girl's friend, and he is walking behind her. She had been gambling and won $200. This other man was trying to get the money off her. It was hid somewhere on her. The man with the cane presses on the cane, and a knife comes out. He stabs the man with the gun in the wrist, and the girl calls the cops, and they come and take him away in the patrol wagon to jail. He tries to break away but can't. That night he went to the electric chair, and the girl had the money safe to keep the rest of her life."

"Oh, gads! Sure is murder [cheerfully]. The man was in gambling. He believed the gambling table was crooked. He said it was, and the man behind the gambling table said it wasn't, and he had a whip and started whipping the other in the face. The U.S. Navy guy came in. It was a friend of his. He had a gun, and he shot the bull whip out of the man's hand. The cops came, and the Navy guy told the cops what happened. The guy that owned it was arrested for having a crooked place, and it was turned into a big Safeway store and people went there and bought stuff. And the army guys got $250 for finding out the man had a crooked wheel. The guy in the middle died from bleeding too much."

Usually it is the men who are shot, and only in one story "a lady is hit in the back with a knife." In this case the woman is killed because she betrayed a man. In most of Karl's stories, however, the women manage to be safe and to get food and money.

In almost every one of Karl's stories food is mentioned in a general way or specifically, for example, peanuts, waffles, double-decker cones, etc., and there is reference to specific amounts of money, such as $200, $25, $250, $550,000, $400, 10¢. Usually the person who has the money is in great danger of being deprived of it and of being killed in the process.

Neither the role of the aggressive man nor that of the passive man seems to be workable in these stories. The man who is passive and in possession of some fortune is usually attacked in some surprising way, from behind or while asleep, and is destroyed. The aggressive man, on the other hand, is regularly caught by the police and sentenced at the least to life-imprisonment; more often, he is executed in the electric chair. The earlier story, in which the "crooked place was turned into a big Safeway store," obviously reveals Karl's deep-seated longing that all the dangerous men will be removed and that he will be allowed to be passive and surrounded by food, without fear of aggression and without the ensuing necessity for being aggressive himself. This is also the way he imagines girls to be. Even though the girls are, in the stories, in the more enviable position, not even they are always safe.

Here again we find the preoccupation with animals. In the stories they are being fed, as they were in Karl's projected ideal of America which was quoted earlier. The feminine identification is apparent in the description of the "mother ape that had just laid a baby." Not even the animals and not even the baby ape are safe, since a man tries to "sock the baby ape with his gun."

Of the two types of men, the passive and the aggressive, Karl basically seems to feel closer to the former. In one story he describes in detail how a passive boy who always is being hit by a tough boy "had taken exercises from a guy that helps you make muscles." It is this same passive boy who feeds the animals. We thus have evidence both of insecurity about masculinity and of feminine identification, also manifested in the occurrence of many phallic symbols and castration threats and in an apparent embarrassment about body build and genital organs. In a swimming scene described by Karl he is careful to point out that the boys have swimming suits under their clothes and thus do not have to undress. Karl's stories are not only exaggerated versions of the stories common in ethnocentric boys in general but also have similarities to the stories of overt homosexuals.

Concerning the formal aspects of Karl's stories, the following can be said. They are long and flowing, presenting no necessity for probing on the part of the examiner. In spite of this fluidity, however, the form level of the stories is very low. They are neither coherent nor structured, and what seems like imagination is really a kind of ruminative repetition of the same themes over and over again. Karl is at times aware of this repetitiveness, and he starts one of his stories with the words, "another murder story." One of our foregoing stories begins, "Sure is murder," and the interviewer comments here that Karl makes this introduction with evident cheerfulness. The repetitiveness extends even to such details as numbers: the number $250 occurs in several stories, and other numbers are similar to it. The stories are, furthermore, utterly unrealistic as far as general plausibility is concerned, and they stray away to a marked degree from the content of the picture, which, after the first few sentences, is frequently lost from sight entirely.

The image of the world found in Karl and in most of our ethnocentric subjects—the projection of the hostility they feel toward their parents, and their feeling that the world is a dangerous and hostile place—coincides with the image of the world which Wolfenstein and Leites[13] found in American movie melodramas. This may represent a common fantasy which in the more "typical" Americans, for whom the powerful father is more imaginary than actual, is present at the most archaic levels only.

Bill's stories contain topics similar to those of Karl, such as quarreling, food, money, ambivalence toward the mother, catastrophes, and unhappy endings. But he is at the same time more constricted, and a great deal of encouragement and probing are necessary to lead him away from a mere description of the picture.

Remembering the evidence from the interviews, it appears that Bill is the more disciplined, not to say regimented, of the two boys and the more cautious, even though perhaps the one who will put his biases more readily into action if the opportunity is offered. On the other hand, social upheavals of a major order may be necessary to bring an individual such as Karl to the fore. Lacking these, he may very well lead an inconspicuous, unsuccessful life, ridiculed and baited by his fellows, and possibly even passing over into a state of slow disintegration.

Discussion of family influence.—From this material we gain the impression that the total outlook, just described, seems to a very appreciable extent to have its root in the authoritarian home. Family relationships in such homes are commonly based on roles clearly defined in terms of demands and submission. Execution of obligations rather than affection is the basis of smooth functioning in such homes. Furthermore, there is a stress on stereotyped behavior and on adherence to a set of conventional and rigid rules. The intimidating, punitive, and paralyzing influence of an overdisciplined, totalitarian home atmosphere may well exert a decisive influence upon the thinking and creativity of the growing child. The impoverishment of imagination seems to be analogous to that apparent under totalitarian social and political regimes. At the same time, the consideration of the responses to threats in childhood may reveal much about the ways in which individuals react to threats in adult life.

Intensive experiences in later life are undoubtedly in themselves capable of superseding both earlier influences and the individual predispositions to a certain extent, however, so that no direct or exclusive causal relationship between family structure, attitudes of children, and rise of totalitarianism may be assumed. We must also bear in mind that social conditions and institutions have, in turn, an impact of their own on the family structure.

It is primarily the fact that the home discipline in authoritarian homes is experienced as overwhelming, unintelligible, and arbitrary, demanding at the same time total surrender, which makes for the apparent parallelism with authoritarian political and social organizations. The similarity becomes even more evident if we consider that the child, by virtue of his objective weakness and dependence, is entirely at the mercy of the parental authorities and must find some way to cope with this situation. We found that parents in the authoritarian group frequently feel threatened in their social and economic status and that they try to counteract their feelings of marginality by an archaic and frequently unverbalized need for importance. It is noteworthy that what seems to matter is not so much the actual status on the socioeconomic ladder or the objective marginality within a certain class; what seems decisive in this respect is, rather, the subjective way in which these conditions are experienced and allowed to build up to certain vaguely conceived aspirations. Recent data further suggest that the status concern of individuals susceptible to authoritarianism is quite different from a realistic attempt to improve their position by concerted effort and adequate means-goal instrumentality. An example was given earlier by the rather naïve hope of Karl's father of becoming an "inventor." In addition, we frequently find such aspirations taking the form of an unspecific expectation that help will come from a sudden change in the external situation or from an imaginary person who is strong and powerful.

Authoritarian disciplinary rules seem to have one of their major roots in such vaguely anticipatory, yet inefficient, states of social unrest on the part of the parents rather than in the developmental needs of the child. The parents expect the child to learn quickly certain external, rigid, and superficial rules and social taboos. At the same time they are impatient, demanding a quick execution of commands that leaves no time for finer discriminations and in the end creates an atmosphere comparable to acute physical danger. The rules to be enforced are largely nonfunctional caricatures of our social institutions, based on a misunderstanding of their ultimate intent. In many ways one may even speak of a defiance of culture by external conformity. In any event, the rules are bound to be beyond the scope and understanding of the child. To compel the child into an obedience of the rules which he is thus unable to internalize may be considered one of the major interferences with the development of a clear-cut personal identity.

The authoritarian form of discipline is thus "ego-destructive," in that it prevents the development of self-reliance and independence. The child, being stripped of his individuality, is made to feel weak, helpless, worthless, or even depraved. Parents and parental figures, such as teachers or other authorities, acquire the threatening, distant, and forbidding quality which we have observed in the case of Karl. Disciplining, controlling, and keeping one in line are considered to be their major role. It seems to be largely the resultant fear and dependency which discourage the child in the authoritarian home from conscious criticism and which lead to an unquestioning acceptance of punishment and to an identification with the punishing authority. As we have seen, this identification often goes as far as an ostentatious glorification of the parents. As we have learned from psychoanalysis, however, repressions of hostility cannot be achieved without creating emotional ambivalence, at the least. Thus children who seem most unquestioningly to accept parental authority at the same time tend to harbor an underlying resentment and to feel victimized, without becoming fully aware of this fact. The existing surface conformity that lacks genuine integration expresses itself in a stereotypical approach devoid of genuine affection, so that the description of the parents elicited by interview questions is more often characterized by the use of exaggerated clichés than by expressions of spontaneous feelings. In ethnocentric subjects the range of responses tends to be generally rather narrow and without the variations commonly found in the description of real people. Only the more palpable, crude, and concrete aspects are mentioned.

CASE STUDY OF AN EQUALITARIAN FAMILY AND CHILD

For contrast, we shall present the case of a twelve-year-old girl, whom we shall call Peggy. She scores extremely low on the ethnocentrism scale and generally exhibits the democratic outlook upon life and society in a particularly clear-cut form. The fact that she is of the opposite sex seemed of little bearing on our comparison; our material shows that boys and girls generally seem to be distributed over the same patterns so far as sociopolitical outlook and its relation to personality and family are concerned. Just as Karl manifested almost all the traits which we find prominent in the highly ethnocentric group as a whole, Peggy exhibits a similar concentration of features characteristic of the low-scoring group, thus highlighting the syndrome under discussion.

Parents and home atmosphere.—The socioeconomic backgrounds of the two families show certain similarities. The difference between the present economic situation of Peggy's and of Karl's parents is not too great. And in both cases there is indication of higher social position and greater wealth in the case of the grandparents as compared with the parents. But the two families react very differently to this change. In addition, there is an appreciable difference in the purely social situation of the two families. There is a radical difference between the personalities of Peggy's mother and Karl's mother and certain differences in their social background, including a much greater stability of the family of Peggy's mother.

While Peggy's mother is American born and of American-born parentage, the father was born in Italy, the son of a small-town doctor. At the time of our interview he had just sold a small restaurant which he had come to consider a bad investment. His professional history includes being a salesman, a clerk, and a waiter. He is a college graduate, as is his wife, who is a social worker. Peggy's maternal grandfather was first a small-town lawyer and "a dictator and patriarch to the population. He entered the army . . . and liked the opportunity which it gave him for expressing authority." Peggy's mother apparently received a great deal of warmth from her own mother, but she rebelled against her father.

Although the father's occupational history, especially as compared with that of his parents and that of the parents of his wife, could have led to a feeling of socioeconomic marginality, this family actually does not seem to be dissatisfied with its present status; much of the time of its members is devoted to such pursuits as supporting the causes of the community, participating in discussion groups, and so forth. Both parents are interested in reading, music, and art, and the mother has even written some poetry. Instead of resenting their marginality, the family makes constructive use of the greater freedom given them by their position. They have more time to follow the pursuits in which they are really interested, and they enjoy a great deal of respect among their friends. Although Peggy's parents are divorced, they are on good terms and see each other frequently.

Both parents feel strongly about equality between racial groups, and the father described how shocking the discovery of racial prejudice was to him when he came to this country "after reading Lincoln and Jefferson and men like that." Both parents declare in their interviews that greater tolerance and more education are the direction in which they would like to see America changed. At the same time, they are explicitly opposed to any radical movement.

Affection rather than authority or the execution of obligations dominates the general attitude of Peggy's parents toward the child. The perceptiveness and psychological insightfulness of Peggy's mother are reflected in her answer to the question concerning the positive ideal she holds for her daughter:

"I do hope that she will do something that will make her happy and at the same time be constructive. I hope the girl will have experience early enough that she can integrate it and lead an outgoing, constructive life; that she won't have to spend so long working out her aggression that she finds herself no longer young—not that I wish to spare my daughter the suffering and experience necessary for development, but I hope she may get it early and fast. I feel that I can help by giving a lot of trust and confidence in the girl. I do feel that at times in the past I may have expected too high a performance for the sake of my own gratification, and that may have troubled Peggy. The child has always been given more responsibility than the average, but as a rule it hasn't seemed to be a strain."

This quotation reflects the mother's concern with the inner life of her daughter, with her internal satisfactions, and it reveals how far removed she is from espousing a conventional ideal for her daughter. This absence of stereotyped conventionality becomes even more evident in the mother's response to the question as to what she considers the negative ideal for her daughter. She states that she would hate to see her daughter take a job she didn't like for the sake of money or caring too much for the acquisition of material things so that her ideals would be sacrificed.

Along similar lines are the statements of Peggy's father, in his separate interview. He wants his daughter "to grow up to have an all-around personality in such a way that she can get the best out of herself, be happy with herself and with other people. Whatever work she wants to choose—that is her business. If we can bring her up with self-assurance and not to give up at the first obstacles, we will be doing something."

Both parents stress again and again in varying formulations how much they enjoy the child. The mother considers as the strongest traits of her daughter "her sensitivity and receptivity to artistic things and to people. . . . She has a philosophical interest in people and seems to have a good idea of the interrelationship of people and nations." The father thinks Peggy's strong points are "strength of character and being intelligent and liberal." At the same time, he is aware of some weaknesses in his daughter, such as her insecurity, her exhibitionism, and her interest in boys; the latter he considers as typical of adolescent girls, however.

The handling of authority in the equalitarian home.—The idea has been promoted in many homes and in some educational systems and political circles that, in order to avoid authoritarianism, all authority must be forsworn. Against this excessive view it must be held that total permissiveness would verge upon anarchy. Respect for the authority of outstanding individuals and institutions is an essential aspect of a healthy home and society. It does not as such lead to total surrender to, or to an absolutistic glorification of, the given authorities. This is especially true if their leadership is limited to specialized fields or to special functions. Rather than authoritarianism or else anarchy, there must be "guidance," especially when this is combined with acceptance and thus strengthens the moral functions of the child and helps him to overcome the impulses toward selfishness and aggression. By guidance, therefore, we mean the encouragement of the child to work out his instinctual problems rather than repress them, thus avoiding their later break-through; this encouragement, in turn, must be rooted in a frank understanding of the child's particular needs and developmental steps. The child is treated as an individual and is encouraged to develop self-reliance and independence. His weakness is not exploited. He is allowed to express his likes and dislikes without the threat of losing love and the basis of his existence.

The statistical data which we gathered on adults[14] as well as on children[15] suggest that the way of handling discipline is indeed a crucial factor in the laying of the foundation for an authoritarian or a democratic outlook in children. As we have just said, the way in which parents handle discipline reveals the constructive use or misuse of parental authority and the degree to which a genuine socialization of the child and his adoption of cultural values are made possible.

According to Peggy's mother, everything was explained to the child, and very little active exercise of discipline was necessary. The mother still feels quite guilty that she spanked the child on a few occasions and thinks now that it was because she herself was angry. The father's independent statement, very similar to that of the mother, is as follows:

"I don't know that we ever tried to discipline her very much. I was guilty of spoiling her when she was a baby sometimes, but I don't remember ever trying to discipline her. Oh, I have given her a few times a spat on the rear when I was mad. I shouldn't do that, I know. I think the girl is a little obstinate, hot-headed, and not disciplined as much as she should be now, but maybe that's because she is an adolescent."

In reading the interview of the mother it becomes quite evident that she has, and always has had, a warm and unconditional acceptance of her child. In fact, she is quite outstanding in this respect as far as our total group is concerned.

However, she confesses that in her eagerness to do the right things she has used many techniques which she now would reject. She feels that she had been "too much influenced by Watson." Thus she thinks that it was wrong to have started toilet training as early as she did. Further inquiry reveals, however, that all she did was to hold the child on a pot after meals when the child was six months old; but no pressure was used, and the child was allowed to regulate her own training, which was complete at two years of age. Furthermore, nursing was discontinued after three months, since the mother's milk failed. When the child was put on the bottle, she began to suck her fingers and continued to do this at bedtime until she was six or seven years old. The child never had tantrums, but she did express her objections and wishes emphatically. This is just the pattern of aggression which has been described as typical of individuals scoring low on ethnocentrism. There was never any evidence of nightmares, and the child called her mother during the night when she needed her. The mother always answered these calls because she remembered so keenly her own childhood fears at night. These details reveal that Peggy's mother, who tends toward intrapunitiveness, has not followed Watson as closely as she thinks she has. Apparently she also remembered well how comforting it was to have her own mother when she called for her.

Concerning the family atmosphere in the childhood home of Peggy's mother, she reports that her own mother had a similar attitude toward her child as the latter has toward Peggy. There seems never to have been any gross punishment. However, the father of Peggy's mother is described by her as a stern and authoritarian person. She thinks that her struggle for independence from her father played an important part in her development. She explains the fact that she, unlike her brothers, was able to rebel against her father, by virtue of her being away from her father during the first years of her life. We would add that, as the only girl in the family, Peggy's mother had a better opportunity to identify with her mother than with her father. On the whole, her identification with her mother, whom she describes as "loving and gay when my father was gone," was a positive one. However, in one respect her mother furnished her with a negative example. She considers her mother as "completely cowed by my father, whom she never opposed."

Thus the negative identification of Peggy's mother with her own mother seems to have led to an attempt to have a more independent life which would not imply submission to an authoritarian husband. She realized these aims by attending college, pursuing a profession, which consisted in work with subnormal children, and marrying an utterly unauthoritarian man. As we have said, this marriage did not work out, however, and she blames this at least partially upon the difficulties which she had had with her own father. Peggy's mother needed a long time and the help of a psychoanalyst to work out her problems of feminine identification. In spite of the fact that Peggy's parents are divorced, they and the child do many things together as a family. The parents speak with a great deal of respect about each other, and the father credits the mother with the satisfactory development of their daughter.

Peggy's social beliefs.—Concerning minority groups, Peggy emphasizes in her interview that no one race is better than another:

"The Chinese can do really beautiful art work, the Germans have really intelligent and well-known scientists, and things like that. Every race has a certain amount of skill. They are pretty well equal. I go to parties at a Negro girl's house. I wouldn't mind going with a Negro boy to a party, but it would probably be better to go with a white one because the other kids would tease me, and the Negro boy and I would both feel funny."

This opinion is in sharp contrast to what the majority of the children feel along these lines. In the interviews, a staggering 96 per cent of the children scoring high on the ethnic scale, 83 per cent of the middle scorers, and even as many as 22 per cent of the low scorers express ethnocentric attitudes toward Negroes by ascribing negative traits to them and by favoring segregation;[16] about 60 per cent of the high scorers and middle scorers and 18 per cent of the low scorers express similar attitudes toward the Chinese. Peggy, as we have seen, goes all out for an equalitarian view of the various ethnic groups.

While Karl thought that most of the foreign countries are against us, Peggy things that America is "really very friendly with many countries," except for Russia, which "doesn't understand our ways and she doesn't understand us." While Karl was at least partially sympathetic toward Hitler, Peggy thinks that "he was crazy with power." Asked what a regular American is, Peggy answers that everyone who has citizenship papers "is an American in his own way. There is some foreign blood in every one of the Americans. The first people were foreigners."

To an interview question, "How would you like to change America?" Peggy responds with the following statement:

"Try to have people be more understanding about the Negro problem. . . . Another thing is to have better schools and teachers; nice schools that kids would really like. Give them a chance to change the subject often so it wouldn't be so boring. Also a better department for juvenile delinquents. Not treat them as if they did it on purpose; and a better home for these kids. They really don't want to be bad, but they just don't know what else to do."

Note the contrast with Karl's emphasis on the beautification of streets and on a plentiful supply of food in response to the same question.

Peggy's concern for the welfare of the population is also expressed in her ideal of the President of the United States, whom she considers to be a man who "really thinks of others, not of himself; thinks of them as friends; is always kind and works hard for the people."

Peggy's attitude toward school, parents, and sex roles.—In discussing her teachers, Peggy does not show much evidence of an exaggerated submission to authority. She does not demand strictness and supervision from the ideal teacher. Rather, she thinks that the ideal teacher is one who can "understand you, be a friend to you, someone you can confide in, someone you like." The unprejudiced children tend to emphasize positive things in the ideal teacher, whereas the prejudiced children more often offer negative formulations, such as not playing favorites. The teachers whom Peggy doesn't like she describes as "dumb, and scream at the kids and tell them to shut up," and she adds very perceptively: "The kids always answer this kind of teacher back."

In discussing the girls she likes, Peggy stresses companionship and mutual liking. She dislikes girls who are "silly, stupid, giggle all the time and never get their work done but say they do."

The pattern of Peggy's aggression is one which is mild and not repressed, in contrast to that of the prejudiced children, in whom we find suppression of aggression interspersed with violent break-throughs. Thus Peggy confesses that she really tries to like everyone, but she just can't do it. "Nobody can." She seems to have some mild guilt about her occasional hostile feelings that alternates with a readiness to accept them as unavoidable.

These guilt feelings may also be connected with the feeling of acting against her mother's apparent wish to imbue the child with a far-reaching tolerance toward everybody. Peggy reports that the only occasion on which she and her mother disagree is "when I criticize someone who looks stupid and funny. My Mommy and Daddy both think that I shouldn't do this, since people don't know any better, but I think they really do." Her strong identification with the underdog is revealed by the type of occasions on which she reports that she tends to get angry:

"When people pick on someone, even dogs or animals, or when they tease Negroes and call them dirty names."

Peggy thinks of a perfect father as one who "is a good friend to you, understanding and nice. Just a person." We recall here that prejudiced children tend to think of the ideal father mainly in terms of punishment, as either being too little strict or too much so, whereas unprejudiced children tend to stress companionship, as Peggy does. She describes her real father pretty much in the same words as she does the perfect father, and the same holds for her description of her mother. She reports (and this is substantiated in the direct interviews with her parents) that she has never been punished or scolded: "My mother just talks to me. Children should never really be punished, but have things explained to them."

Peggy's flexibility is also carried into her conception of the sex roles. Like the unprejudiced children in general, she does not tend toward a dichotomous conception of sex roles. To the question, "How should girls behave around boys?" she answers: "Not silly but act like herself. Having a boy friend is just like having a good friend." She also thinks that boys "should not try to show off, should not try to show the girls how strong they are so the girls will be impressed." Furthermore, unlike most ethnocentric children, she does not make any marked differentiation between the best profession for a man and the best profession for a woman. Her description of the best profession for a man shows absence of hierarchical thinking in terms of social status: "Whatever he wants to do, whether it is a shoe clerk or a chemist or anything at all. Nobody else should decide for him." Concerning the worst profession for a man, she replies: "To have his life planned, to be what he doesn't want," and to the question about the best or worst profession for a woman she answers: "Same as for a man." Incidentally, Peggy's own professional ambitions are to be "an artist, a poet, a writer, and a dancer."

In spite of Peggy's equalitarian orientation in relation to authority and sex roles, she is far from being uninterested in boys. When asked about her daydreams, she reports that they are concerned with the wish to have a boy friend and that her real dreams are also mainly concerned with boys. She usually dreams about one special boy and that he takes her to the movies. In fact, in a fond and understanding way, her father calls her "a little boy crazy," and he adds that Peggy occasionally shows exhibitionistic impulses. We have evidence for that in Peggy's childhood memories also. Asked for her earliest memories, she reports one, according to which—at the age of about three—she ran to the top of a near-by hill before her mother had finished dressing her, with only her pants and her shoes on. "The people were shocked by that kind of thing." This may be a projection, since she probably was too small at the time to shock people by her scanty clothes. She also reports that when she was a year and a half or two years old, she "ran out naked to say goodbye to Daddy." These slightly erotically tinted early memories are in decided contrast to Karl's early memories, which are preoccupied with death and violence and carry a distinctly sadistic flavor.

Peggy's Thematic Apperception Test stories.—Peggy's creativeness and imagination are reflected in her TAT stories. While Karl is obsessed with primitive, archaic themes, as evidenced by his rumination about the topics of food and destruction as if flooded by his unconscious, Peggy seems to be at ease with her unconscious trends, which find expression in stories possessing an artistic flavor. In her case the unconscious problems seem to contribute to imagination in a positive manner. Her stories flow freely and at the same time are cognitively disciplined. While Karl's stories were stereotyped and at the same time chaotic, Peggy's stories show a colorfulness of thought which can come only from ease of communication between the different layers of her personality. Although she is by no means aware of all her problems, she possesses an unrepressed approach to life. Her basic self-acceptance has a disinhibiting effect on her productions, without leading to disintegration.

There are several distinct themes in Peggy's stories. The major motif is the same we encountered in the interviews, that is, a protective feeling toward those who are different or who appear weak. While Karl is contemptuous of the weak and the "sissy," Peggy reveals considerable psychological insight in trying to demonstrate that he who is considered a sissy is often the real hero. She describes, in one of her stories, a nine-year-old boy

"whom all the kids in school used to tease and say he was a sissy. Tommy cried when he went home. Next day the boys dared him to fight the biggest bully of the class. The bully hit Tommy in the face, and it made him mad. Tommy had to fight, and he licked the bully. After that he was liked. There was one boy that was a leader that hadn't liked him before that invited him to have a soda. And after that all the boys liked Tommy."

The picture to which Peggy refers here, and which was specially selected for our study, is that of a cruel-looking white boy hitting a Mexican boy. While Karl has nothing but derogatory statements to make about this boy, some children—mainly the equalitarian ones—express some pity for this boy. But it is only Peggy for whom he becomes a hero.

Here are some passages from Peggy's story in response to the picture of a Negro boy who is being maltreated:

"He [the Negro boy] wondered why people could be so ignorant and not know that everybody is created equal, and that people could believe what people say that isn't true. Someone threw something at him and blinded him. Two kids from the army started beating up on him. Yet in the army you are supposed to learn to stand for what is right. . . . He went back to where he came from and thought that someday he would do something about all this."

Another story deals with two young Japanese men, approximately college age:

"Well, there was a Sunday school in San Francisco and, uh, this boy is named Bill. Well, he came here many years ago when he was a little boy. He has grown up here and is proud of it and liked everyone and everyone liked him. Several years later he planned to go to college and get an education as a doctor. When he enrolled for college, people became very prejudiced. They thought he shouldn't go to the same school as white people. Bill felt bad because he liked everyone. So he dropped out of school. A few years later a cousin came from Japan to visit him. The cousin had just started his college education in Japan. He asked Bill why he wasn't going to college. Bill told him why. The cousin wasn't so sensitive as Bill and said the way to lick it was to show people you don't care. And so both of them enrolled for a four years' term, and Bill made friends with several of the professors and some boys and girls, and so did his cousin.

No one knew Bill was a very good pianist. One night at a dance the pianist walked out on them, and Bill offered to play. Everyone was surprised and liked him after that. Finally Bill finished medical school and became an M.D."

This story is quite typical of the way Peggy manages to give a constructive turn to almost every situation. In her reactions to her fellowmen she is generally and genuinely imbued with the spirit of Christian ethics. Thus in still another story she describes a man who was entirely devoted to his success and almost "went to Hell" but was given an opportunity to change his ways, thus being finally saved:

"Well, there was this man named Mr. Benson. He was hard working and very successful, but was not liked by many, because he was an old crab. One day his son got mad at him because he was so mean, and the son told him so. When the man went home, he felt bad and lay down. He fell asleep and dreamed he went down to Hell—to the middle of the world. They go either there or to Heaven. The spirit in charge looked in the book and said he was not registered in either place. Mr. Benson told the spirit what he had done—thinking only of his business. The spirit said, "I think if you go back and change your ways, you can then go to the other place." He woke up on the floor. Next morning he went to his office and did something he never did before. He said a pleasant "Good morning" to everyone in the office. Pretty soon his son came in, expecting the father to be mad when he told him about his plan to marry one of the secretaries. His father surprised him and said, "I hope you will be happy and have many children." He gave his son a present, and the father and son were friends after that, and it all turned out well. When Mr. Benson died, he went to Heaven. Though I don't believe there is any Heaven—we just stay in the earth and turn into little pieces."

Aside from Peggy's consideration for the weak, there is another outstanding theme in her stories, love. Significantly, Peggy often uses a fairy-tale type of approach in these stories, not losing her grip on the structure of the story, however. Oedipal conflicts are revealed in these stories, although she is obviously not aware of them. In one of her stories she tells about a "giant" who wants to keep a beautiful girl for himself while the girl wishes for a "prince." At the same time the two male figures are mixed in her fantasy:

"A giant found her and took her to his cave and raised her. She grew up to be beautiful. Finally a prince came along and said he would rescue her from the giant. She told the prince that the only way to do that was to go down to the river and rescue the giant's heart which he lost there long ago. . . . The prince found the heart and took it to the cave and put it in the giant's supper. When the giant ate his supper, the heart went into his body and he became kind. He let the girl go and the prince married her. And they lived happily ever after."

While most of Karl's stories end in disaster, murder, or death, all of Peggy's stories end well. Every one of them constitutes an attempt to demonstrate positive ways of overcoming external or internal obstacles, including prejudice, selfishness, and possessiveness. It is difficult to say whether Peggy's aggression is merely repressed or whether it is not very strong to begin with. We are inclined to believe the latter. In any event it must be stressed that there is very little discrepancy between the overt level of Peggy's verbalized self-perception and her personality as revealed in the projective stories.

RELATIONS TO PERCEPTION AND THINKING

Perceptual patterns, especially the mechanism of projection, were brought into the foregoing picture by the Thematic Apperception Test. But the relationship between social attitudes, personality, and the general cognitive mastery of reality seems to go far beyond that. Experiments in perception, memory, and cognition were thus added in order to investigate more systematically the matter of how far basic personality trends found in the emotional and social sphere may be reflected in this area. Their purpose was to investigate the pervasiveness of ways of functioning within the authoritarian personality. The shift from the social and emotional to the cognitive area has the added advantage of removing us from the controversial social issues under consideration. So long as we remain under the potential spell of certain preconceived notions, the evaluation of what is reality-adequate or reality-inadequate may be difficult. The authoritarian may accuse the equalitarian of distorting reality, and vice versa. Some of the experiments are as yet in a preliminary stage while others have already led to statistically significant results.

In a memory experiment,[17] the children were read a story which described the behavior of pupils in a school toward newcomers to their class. In the fighting that developed, some of the older pupils were described as being friendly and protective of the newcomers, while others were pictured as aggressive. The children were then asked to reproduce the story in writing.

Ethnocentric children tended generally to recall more of the aggressive characters, and the democratic-minded, tolerant children more of the friendly characters. In addition, 43 per cent of the former, as contrasted with only 8 per cent of the latter, recalled the fighting theme exclusively, without mentioning any of the other themes of the story.

It is further to be noted that in the tolerant children the ratio of friendly to aggressive individuals was closer to the ratio occurring in the story as first presented. That is to say, the tolerant children adhered, in this respect at least, more closely to "reality" than did the ethnocentric. A general tendency on the part of the ethnically prejudiced children to stray away from the content of the story is combined with a tendency to reproduce faithfully certain single phrases and single details of the original story. Thus the stimulus is in part rigidly adhered to, while its remaining and perhaps major aspects are altogether neglected in favor of subjective elaboration. This odd combination of accuracy and distortion also characterizes Karl's general cognitive approach as presented earlier in this paper.

Another experiment consisted in presenting the picture of a familiar object, such as that of a dog, and then leading through a number of vague or transitional stages to the picture of, say, a cat. The subjects were asked to identify the object in each picture. If tentative results with small groups are borne out, the stimuli less familiar and lacking in firmness and definiteness would seem to be more disturbing to the ethnocentric than to the unprejudiced children. Ethnocentric children tend to persist in using the name of the familiar object shown in the first picture, ignoring the changes in the successive pictures. Or they seem to fall more often into a spell of guesses, trying to inject known and structured objects into the vague stimulus, again relatively little concerned with reality. It is probably the underlying confusion and anxiety which compel these children to make a desperate effort to avoid uncertainties as much as possible, resulting in "intolerance of ambiguity."[18] The nonethnocentric children, on the other hand, being generally more secure, are apparently better able to afford facing ambiguities openly, even though this often may mean facing, at least temporarily, increased conflicts.

In another preliminary experiment a picture was presented showing four vertically striped zebras standing together and facing a lone, horizontally striped zebra left in a corner by itself. An inquiry as to the cause of the isolation of the horizontally striped zebra brought out interesting material about the attitude of some ethnocentric children to what is "different." Among other things, it appears that any difference setting off a minority from a majority of objects—even though the given difference may not in itself be emotionally tainted—tends to be conceived of by them as automatically establishing a barrier against social contact.

Rokeach[19] has investigated rigidity as related to intolerance of ambiguity. He used a problem in thinking developed by Luchins[20] which involves the manipulation of three water jars. A mental set was first established by presenting the subjects with a series of problems solvable only by a relatively involved method. There followed problems which could be solved either by maintaining the established set or by using more direct and simple techniques. The ethnocentric children tended to persist in using the first, more complex method rather than shift to the more direct approach.

In recent years, experiments of the types described have multiplied in number and kind and generally have borne out the earlier findings.

We have already noted that Karl's cognitive makeup can be fitted into some of the categories found typical of ethnocentric children in these experiments. Karl's material further reveals that he tends to alternate in his perceptual and cognitive approach between sticking to the familiar and being overly concretistic, on the one hand, and a chaotic, haphazard approach, on the other. Peggy, by contrast, shows considerable flexibility in her perceptual and cognitive approach, although it must be added that she did exhibit rigidity on the water-jar test just described. Here she used an established set without changing to the more functional, faster method. This may well be due to her general weakness in handling arithmetic problems. We have found that even flexible children may be rigid on tasks in which they show little ego involvement. Such tasks remain peripheral for them, and they do not bring out the best of their ability, so that there is regression to a more mechanized approach. There can be no doubt that everyone has areas of rigidity. In some cases we just find rigidity more pervasive than in others.

SUMMARY AND CONCLUSION

Out of a sample of children and their families studied by a variety of methods, two cases were selected which represent opposite extremes as to ethnocentric, as contrasted with democratic, outlook, other social beliefs, cognitive organization, personality, and family structure and atmosphere.

In describing the minority groups and the social scene in general, our paradigm of an ethnocentric, authoritarian child, Karl, exhibits rigid dichotomizing, aggressiveness, fear of imaginary dangers or threats of deprivation, and exaggerated adherence to conventional values, such as cleanliness and order. The same themes also occur in his stated attitudes toward parents and friends as well as in the projective material, especially his Thematic Apperception Test stories.

Our example of a democratic-minded, equalitarian child, Peggy, is much less given to dichotomizing and other forms of rigidity and intolerance of ambiguity than is Karl. This is evidenced, among other things, in her attitude toward minority groups and in her view of sex roles. In both cases differences are de-emphasized, quite in contrast with Karl. While at the surface level Karl emphasizes rugged masculinity and is very much concerned with what is masculine and what is feminine, he is covertly engrossed in passivity and dependency; Peggy, with her lesser insistence on the dichotomy of sex roles, is basically much more feminine than Karl is masculine. A similar discontinuity between the manifest and the latent level had been found in Karl's attitude toward his parents; Peggy, on the other hand, reveals a genuine, personalized love for her parents which is not endangered and undermined by occasional eruptions of deep-seated aggression. Karl and his parents had been found to manifest an odd combination of unrest and predilection for chaos and total change with an uncritical, distorted glorification of existing institutions and social conditions; Peggy and her parents, on the other hand, show a certain healthy medium distance to these institutions in the sense of basically identifying with their aim, yet being concerned with seeing them properly executed, as in the case of ethnic equality. They would like to see some improvement and progress, but total upheavals and radical changes of the social scene do not have the same appeal for them that they do for Karl's parents. All these differences are related to the fact that the definition of an American is much more narrowly conceived by Karl and his parents than it is by Peggy and hers and that the former exhibits some preoccupation with what they consider American values which at the same time presents a shrinkage and oversimplification of these values.

Toward parents, teachers, and authorities in general Karl at the surface demands total submission, and he approves of whatever they do; but underlying resentment and hatred against them are only too apparent in the projective material. This discrepancy is but one of the many breaks and discontinuities found in Karl and in ethnocentric children in general. Another discrepancy is evident in Karl's explicit stressing of conventional values, which is combined with an implicit leaning toward destructive and chaotic behavior. In fact, there seems to be vacillation between a total adoption and a total negation of the prevalent values of our society.

Still another conflicting set can be discerned between Karl's strained effort to appear as a masculine boy interested in girls and his underlying identification with the opposite sex. Instead of being oriented toward girls as objects of cathexis, he envies them because he thinks of them as less in danger of being attacked and as being fed and given other material benefits. As becomes apparent especially in the Thematic Apperception Test, to be a boy or a man means to him to be in danger. If a man is passive, he may not get the necessary supplies and is helplessly exposed; if he is aggressive, he is punished. Doom is thus inevitable for him. All through the material produced by our ethnocentric children there is evidence of panic lest food or money run short. In persons possessed by such fears, human relations are liable to become unusually manipulative and exploitive. Other persons, authorities, and even the magic forces of nature will, of necessity, be seen mainly as deliverers of goods. Aggression against those considered strong and powerful must then be repressed; at least in part, this aggression will be diverted toward those who can neither deprive nor retaliate.

While Karl thus shows many discrepancies and discontinuities in his personality makeup, Peggy is obviously more integrated. Karl fails to face some of the important emotional tendencies within himself, such as ambivalence toward the parents, passivity, and fear. His conscious image of himself contradicts the tendencies which are revealed in the projective material and which he projects onto others, such as minority groups. Peggy, on the other hand, accepts hers more fully, although this does not mean that she is not critical of herself. This basic acceptance of herself makes it possible for her to face her own weaknesses; it also leads to a greater acceptance and tolerance of other persons and peoples, although again she is very free in expressing her dislikes. But, on the whole, the world is for her a benevolent one, interesting and challenging, whereas for Karl it is a dangerous and hostile place, to be viewed with distrust, suspicion, and cynicism.

In spite of the ready flow of fantastic ideas about a wide range of topics, Karl's story productions show little evidence of creative imagination. His repetitive rumination in stereotypes, general diffuseness, and distortion of reality are obviously in the service of warding off anxiety.

This rigidity and lack of imagination is in line with results obtained on ethnocentric children in the experiments on perception and other cognitive functions. Ambiguous and unfamiliar stimuli often seem to be disturbing to these children. They tend to respond either with a spell of haphazard guessing, imposing something definite and definitive upon the indefinite, or with a clinging to a response once established. Both these reactions seem to mirror frantic efforts to avoid uncertainty, that is, an "intolerance of ambiguity," even though the price is distortion of reality. In addition, the recall of given stories by ethnocentric children shows distortion in the direction of greater emphasis on aggressive themes.

In analyzing and interpreting our material, extended use has been made of psychoanalytic hypotheses. Depth psychology has challenged the dominance of the phenotype and has sharpened our eyes to the underlying dynamic patterns. Because of this shift, we can discern in Karl the passivity behind his aggressive violence, the feminine identification and latent homosexuality behind the protestation of his heterosexual interests, the chaos behind his rigid conformity. But since the façade is also an essential part of the psychological makeup, we must think of personality in terms of "alternative manifestations."[21] These are quite self-contradictory in Karl, as they are in most prejudiced children. It is the inherent conflict and anxiety concerning the social, sexual, and personal role of the individual which must be seen at the root of the ensuing desperate avoidance of all ambiguity with its dire consequences for the fate of man.

It should be kept in mind that while our chosen paradigms exhibit nearly all the traits which were found statistically prevalent in the respective groups as a whole, such marked personality consistency is not the rule. Furthermore, the over-all immaturity which Karl, our paradigm of an ethnocentric child, has been found to exhibit is to a certain extent shared with younger children, both authoritarian and equalitarian; some of the trends which are connected with ethnic prejudice or authoritarianism must be considered natural states of development, to be overcome if maturity is to be reached. Some of the test items correlated with ethnocentrism are at the same time subscribed to more often by the younger children than by the older ones. The difference is that our ethnocentric children continue to exhibit many trends which in equalitarian children are limited to the younger age levels and are later outgrown. To a notable extent this is independent of the purely intellectual aspects of development. Other factors, such as especially social background, are modifiers of the distinction between ethnocentric and equalitarian children. Important subtypes may thus be identified in both groups. For example, in ethnocentric children coming from distinctly upper-class backgrounds there is more genuine conformity to society, combined perhaps with a certain rigidity in the total outlook, but little of the psychopathic, destructive, and manipulative coloring which characterizes Karl and many other prejudiced children rooted in the lower social strata.

Karl's parents reveal the feelings of "social marginality" which are so common in the ethnocentric family. It is obviously in defense against the possibility of being grouped with the underprivileged that they rigidly identify with the conventional values of the class to which they try to hold on. The strict home discipline they are trying to enforce is in part in the service of these narrow social goals; beyond this, it is perhaps a revengeful repetition of the situation to which they themselves were exposed in the unstable socioeconomic history of the family. We have also seen how much more constructively an objectively similar socioeconomic family history is handled by the parents of Peggy.

Both the families which we have discussed in this paper are American families. At the same time, they are so different that in many ways they appear as opposite ends of a psychological continuum, a continuum which ranges from rigidity and authoritarianism to affectionate guidance and acceptance.

In the context of American culture, Karl and his family are deviants. Fat, fearful Karl is certainly the opposite of the ideal American boy. Most of his and of his family's attitudes are counterpoints to prevailing or consciously espoused American attitudes. Externalization and hostile exclusion are features which they adopt from the wide variety of possibilities, offered within the culture as a whole. Other features contrasting with the major American pattern are their emphasis on hierarchical rather than equalitarian relations, their anxiety about the availability of material goods, and their belief in mystical forces and apprehension about catastrophes as against confidence in one's own efforts and in the collaboration of the environment.

To understand all this, we remember that Karl and his family are caught in an unsuccessful struggle for social status, a status they cannot achieve through their own efforts. Thus they adhere rigidly to some absolute status values which oversimplify the social and cultural realities of our civilization. This renders them helpless and perverts their view of the social scene, making them susceptible to totalitarian propaganda.

It must be specially emphasized that the compulsive type of conformity with its all-or-none character which we have observed in the family of Karl differs in several ways from genuine and constructive conformity. It is excessive, compensating as it does for feelings of marginality and the attendant fear of becoming an outcast and serving the function of covering up the resentment toward the social system as a whole, unconscious as this resentment may be. The lack of a genuine incorporation of the values of society in the authoritarian milieu accounts for the rigidity of the conformity. At the same time it accounts for a certain unreliability, the readiness to shift allegiance altogether to other authorities and other standards. The adherence to the letter rather than to the spirit of the social institutions, which further characterizes the compulsive conformist, issues from his distortion and simplification of the system of norms and commands in the direction of what one may call unidimensional interpretation.

Evidently, Peggy and her family are infinitely closer to the real values of the American civilization in the ways in which parental authority and child-parent relationships are handled and the democratic outlook is being realized in word and action. They are in search of intrinsic and flexible and at the same time basically more consistent principles. Understanding, emphasis on internalization, thoughtfulness, empathy, compassion, insight, justice, individualism, reason, and scholarship are the values they admire. The core of the human institutions inherent in our culture which must be called upon to explain Peggy and her parents is the democratic tradition, with its protective attitude toward the weak.

NOTES

1. Ogburn, 1953.
2. Zimmerman, 1948.
3. Burgess, 1948.
4. Mead, 1949.
5. Winch and McGinnis, 1953.
6. Frenkel-Brunswik, 1954.
7. Frenkel-Brunswik, 1949a; Frenkel-Brunswik and Havel, 1953.
8. Murray *et al.*, 1938.
9. Adorno *et al.*, 1950.
10. Frenkel-Brunswik, 1951.
11. Adorno *et al.*, 1950; Frenkel-Brunswik, 1949a.
12. Fenichel, 1945.
13. Wolfenstein and Leites, 1950.
14. Adorno *et al.*, 1950.
15. Frenkel-Brunswik and Havel, 1953; other reports in preparation.
16. *Ibid.*
17. For details see Frenkel-Brunswik, 1949b.
18. *Ibid.*
19. Rokeach, 1943.
20. Luchins, 1942.
21. Frenkel-Brunswik, 1949b.

LIST OF REFERENCES

ADORNO, T. W., FRENKEL-BRUNSWIK, E., LEVINSON, D. J., and SANFORD, R. N. 1950. *The Authoritarian Personality.* New York: Harper & Bros.

BURGESS, W. 1948. "The Family in a Changing Society," *American Journal of Sociology*, XIII, No. 6, 417–23.

FENICHEL, O. 1945. *Psychoanalytic Theory of Neurosis.* New York: W. W. Norton & Co.

FRENKEL-BRUNSWIK, E. 1949a. "A Study of Prejudice in Children," *Human Relations*, I, No. 3, 295–306.

———. 1949b. "Intolerance of Ambiguity as an Emotional and Perceptual Personality Variable," *Journal of Personality*, XVIII, No. 1, 108–43.

———. 1951. "Patterns of Social and Cognitive Outlook in Children and Parents," *American Journal of Orthopsychiatry*, XXI, No. 3, 543–58.

———. 1954. "Social Research and the Problem of Values: A Reply," *Journal of Abnormal and Social Psychology*, XLIX, No. 3, 466–71.

FRENKEL-BRUNSWIK, E., and HAVEL, J. 1953. "Prejudice in the Interviews of Children: Attitudes toward Minority Groups," *Journal of Genetic Psychology*, LXXXII, No. 1, 91–136.

LUCHINS, A. S. 1942. *Mechanization in Problem Solving: The Effect of "Finstellung."* ("Psychological Monographs," Vol. LIV, No. 6.)

MEAD, MARGARET. 1949. *Male and Female.* New York: William Morrow Co.

MURRAY, H. E., and WORKERS AT THE HARVARD PSYCHOLOGICAL CLINIC. 1938. *Explorations in Personality.* London: Oxford University Press.

OGBURN, W. F. 1953. "The Changing Functions of the Family." In *Marriage and the Family*, ed. R. F. WINCH and R. McGINNIS. New York: Henry Holt & Co.

ROKEACH, M. 1943. "Generalized Mental Rigidity as a Factor in Ethnocentrism," *Journal of Abnormal and Social Psychology*, XLVIII, No. 2, 259–78.

WINCH, R. F., and McGINNIS, R. (eds.). 1953. *Marriage and the Family.* New York: Henry Holt & Co.

WOLFENSTEIN, MARTHA, and LEITES, NATHAN. 1950. *Movies: A Psychological Study.* Glencoe, Ill.: Free Press.

ZIMMERMAN, C. C. 1948. *Family and Civilization.* New York: Harper & Bros.

——————————————————————————————PART VII

Clinical Studies

Introduction

THERAPEUTIC work has a double aspect. On the one hand, it provides treatment for the individual patient. On the other hand, it affords insights into human nature which are of general scientific interest. Freud's great psychological discoveries were made in the course of his treatment of neurotics. The extent to which the findings made possible by therapeutic work are used to make contributions to psychological science has varied with the interests and preoccupations of different therapists. At the present time an increasing number of projects are under way which aim to utilize more systematically for scientific purposes the findings obtainable from therapy.

The therapist occupied with the treatment of his patient focuses his attention, understandably enough, on the individual, on his distinctive ways of reacting and his particular life-history. The characteristic habits of feeling and fantasy, thought and behavior, of the patient, as they gradually become clear, are understood by the therapist in terms of general concepts of impulses and mechanisms of defense (which do not constitute a closed system but may themselves be amplified and refined on the basis of each new case). The patient's life-history is reconstructed against a general frame of reference of phases of development. The individual case becomes intelligible in terms of concepts assumed to have general human application. The individual represents a series of variations on common themes, variations depending on the particular events of his life (the birth of a younger brother when he was five, the presence of a devoted grandmother in the home, the way he was punished for a childish misdemeanor, his father's having been unfaithful to his mother, etc.) and the ways he reacted to them. While, theoretically, the individual thus appears as a variant of the commonly human, in the actual work of piecing together all the innumerable details of his psychic life the focus is on the individual, on building and rebuilding an exceedingly complex psychological portrait. General concepts function as tools for this labor.

When the therapist, in his thinking about a case, groups the individual patient with other patients, it is likely to be in terms of diagnostic categories, in terms of certain commonly noted combinations of disturbances. It is also possible for theoretical purposes to group patients together in terms of similar cultural backgrounds. To do this requires a shift in the focus of attention and evidently an interest in cultural variables. The therapist must have experience with patients of two or

405

more cultures, which may be supplemented with extra-clinical observations of the cultures in question. The therapist who is in the best position to utilize clinical findings for purposes of cultural studies is the one who has in the course of his professional career moved from one culture to another, so that he has not only had patients from these different backgrounds but has experienced in a more pervasive sense the differences in life-atmosphere.

Psychoanalysts of European origin who have taken up practice in America have been struck by characteristic differences in parent-child relations in this country as compared with those in European cultures. Erik Erikson has drawn on clinical experience, supplemented by other data, to elucidate distinctive features of emotional development in America.[1] Grete Bibring has derived some similar inferences from her analytic work.[2] Both stress, among other things, the consequences of the mother's assuming the major authority role in the family, a phenomenon frequently acknowledged (and contrasting with the European pattern of paternal authority, in the kind of family which produced the classical oedipus complex), and on the basis of clinical material they illuminate the subjective counterparts of this arrangement of familial roles. Taking a different variable, that of cultural changes through time, René Spitz drew on clinical data to elucidate the preference for a certain type of woman, the "baby" type, who was the erotic ideal of the twenties and thirties in both Europe and America.[3] Therapeutic work may also be undertaken for the purpose of supplementing the understanding of a culture obtained by anthropological research, as in George Devereux's study of a Plains Indian.[4] Yet another relation between therapy and the study of cultures appears when a psychoanalyst applies his clinical skills in anthropological field work as Géza Róheim did.[5]

In the first paper in this part, Françoise Dolto, a French child analyst, reports her observations about the characteristically different ways in which French and American children whom she has treated in Paris behave in a therapeutic situation and the different attitudes of their parents in bringing the children for treatment. Supplementing her clinical material with extra-therapeutic observations and impressions, she elaborates some hypotheses about the contrasting sequences involved in growing up for a French child and an American child. The second paper in this part is based on observations made in a child-guidance clinic in New York where psychotherapy is carried on with children and mothers of Jewish families. Contrasting patterns of mother-child relations are noted in families where the mother is of Eastern European origin and in those where the mother is American born. Extra-therapeutic research is utilized to clarify what is culturally regular and what is individually idiosyncratic in these cases and to fill in the background of customs and life-habits, while the clinical material provides insights into the corresponding emotional relations.

M. W.

NOTES

1. Erikson, 1950, pp. 244–83.
2. Bibring, 1953.
3. Spitz, 1937.
4. Devereux, 1951.
5. Róheim, 1950.

LIST OF REFERENCES

BIBRING, GRETE L. 1953. "On the 'Passing of the Oedipus Complex' in a Matriarchal Family Setting." In *Drives, Affects, Behavior,* ed. RUDOLPH M. LOEWENSTEIN, pp. 278–84. New York: International Universities Press.

DEVEREUX, GEORGE. 1951. *Reality and Dream: Psychotherapy of a Plains Indian.* New York: International Universities Press.

ERIKSON, ERIK H. 1950. *Childhood and Society.* New York: W. W. Norton & Co.

RÓHEIM, GÉZA. 1950. *Psychoanalysis and Anthropology.* New York: International Universities Press.

SPITZ, RENÉ. 1937. "Choix objectal masculin et transformation typologique des névroses," *Bibliothèque psychoanalytique.* Paris: Les Éditions Denoël & Steele.

CHAPTER 23

French and American Children as Seen
by a French Child Analyst

───────────────────────────FRANÇOISE DOLTO

Translated by Nathan Leites

THE International Congress of Psychoanalysis, held in London in
1953, gave me the occasion for friendly talks with American colleagues. We began by discussing the nature of jokes characteristic of
children of different ages, and quite naturally we came to consider
the similarities and the differences of our respective experiences with
American and French children. The colleagues with whom I talked
asked me to put down some of the points I had advanced that evening.
We had had one of those chats characteristic of evenings during scientific meetings when the participants, happy about the rare occasion to
communicate with one another and delighted with one another's ideas,
remain together until a late hour. In the hotel lounge in which we were
sitting the "God Save the Queen" of the midnight hour had already
been played for quite some time when we were still conversing in a
more or less psychoanalytic style about the sociopsychological subject
which fascinated us—the reactions and the behavior of children on the
New Continent and on the Old. This is the origin of the pages which
follow.

I should like immediately to note that my experience with American
children is much more limited than with French children. Also my imperfect knowledge of the English language may have distorted some
of my observations. This, I believe, is an important point. Almost all
the American children whom I have seen in Paris were living in an
American milieu and going to an American school; it is through them
that I have received my impressions of the life-atmosphere of their age
group in school and outside it. Many of them had been in France for
only a short time and told me quite recent memories of their life in
America. On the other hand, I had to concern myself with French children who during the war had spent a part of their childhood in the
United States and, while there, lived the life of little Americans to the
extent of, in some cases, not learning, or forgetting, their mother-
tongue. For all these reasons, my experiences have largely gone beyond
the consulting room; they include numerous extra-therapeutic observations, conversations, contacts, stories, and reading. But I have never

been in America. No doubt a trip to America, and particularly some professional activity there, would permit me to revise views which some readers may find hasty.

DIFFERENCES IN INITIAL CONTACT WITH AMERICAN AND FRENCH CHILDREN

The approach of American children both in life and in the psychoanalyst's office seems very different from that of French children. The American child does not, to start with, distrust adults; he expects a grownup, even a woman doctor, to be benign or perhaps indifferent to his interests but not unfavorably disposed. This sense of security in social contact is an undeniable fact, all the more impressive as it is present also when neurotic anxiety is important among the symptoms for which the child is being brought to the analyst. It seems to me that the American parents' confidence in analysis is not the only reason for this. While resistance to analysis is much more widespread in France, some parents do have real confidence in the analyst to whom they bring their child. But the child does not. It is not so much that he fears the doctor as that, for a French child, every adult is at least boring, probably disagreeable, and in any case mysterious and hence disquieting. The French child is on guard against the adult, particularly if he knows that the adult is a doctor.

My typical French child patient thus first adopts a posture which I would call that of a disturbed snail. Then he begins silently to take up contact with the analyst. He begins to live with some sense of ease in the analyst's office, acting by himself and for himself and at the same time observing the adult; he plays, draws, models. If he directs himself at a certain moment fully toward the adult, it is entirely on his own initiative; if he addresses himself to the adult and talks to him, it is because he already feels that he knows him very well. And if he wants to play with the adult, this signifies that he has gained real confidence in him. On the other hand, the American child, very much at ease and all excited by his new experience, tries to attract the adult's attention. He questions the adult or wants right away to play some motor game with him. In the first contacts between the analyst and the French child it is, I believe, the child's facial expression which plays a great role, while it is the whole body of the American child which expresses his confidence or his emotional interest. At this point the American child's face shows little expression, and his words are trite. But if he does not attempt to play with the analyst, this means that he distrusts him; when he wants to play and the adult accepts being his partner, then he begins to show a lively facial expression which conveys a true feeling of security. It is rare, however, for him to seek a deeper contact, for which he does not feel the need.

At first sight, the contrast between the ease of the American child and the reserve of the French child, which borders on distrust, might make one believe that the American child enjoys a greater autonomy. But my experience has, I think, shown me that this is not really so; the energetic and resourceful (*débrouillard*) behavior of the American child derives much more from social usage and the important protection and privileges conferred upon American children in relation to the population as a whole. With all his spontaneity, the American child is much more fragile and much more subject to psychological influence than is the French child.

To sum up what I have said: in contact with an adult, a French child starts with distrust. As trust develops, he begins to live for himself and with a sense of ease at the adult's side, and finally he will enter into communication with the adult, which will then establish a real interpersonal relation. On the other hand, the American child will immediately test the adult in whose presence he finds himself. He will concentrate on the manipulation of objects and on movements; for the American child, words are much more movements than expressions of feelings and thoughts. Feeling and thinking will become prominent in his contact with the adult only when he becomes aware of the fact that the adult wishes for a contact not exclusively mediated through material objects and movements. But if he feels no such further demand in the adult, the American child will not himself desire a more emotional kind of interpersonal communication.

To put it in still another way: an American child is content to act with somebody. He will then have the impression of knowing the other and of being known by him. A certain surface communication is established. The fact of doing things together confers value on each of the partners. A French child needs to be acknowledged as a being that feels rather than as one that acts. But he must first know that his activity is tolerated by the adult so as to be able to enter into emotional contact with him. Once this contact is established, the child does not require an accompanying activity of the body. The American child may very well act in a fashion which disturbs a near-by adult without any awareness of having this impact; all he knows is that he is having fun himself. He is enjoying life. But for a French child, such behavior would express a negative and aggressive attitude toward the adult, a special way of seeking for emotional contact, of provoking the adult. In psychoanalytic terms the American child identifies the ego of any adult with his own ego and the id of an adult with his own id, and this as late as the age of ten or twelve. On the other hand, the French child feels himself to be different from the adult, whom he identifies with his superego or with his ego-ideal.

THE ATTITUDES OF AMERICAN AND FRENCH PARENTS
TOWARD THEIR CHILDREN

We shall understand the difference between American and French children better when we consider the attitudes of their parents toward them.

When one is accustomed to the certainty which French parents of all strata have that they are correct in the way they are bringing up their children, one learns with surprise, in talking with American parents, that they are not at all sure about themselves as educators. They know that psychology is a technique which has its specialists; they really *consult* the physician, both about the child and about their own attitudes toward the child. But when French parents, after long hesitation, finally have recourse to a specialist, they come to *show* their child and ask that the physician *act on the child,* influence him, correct him, lead the child onto the path on which the parents have decided and with respect to which their efforts have failed. The parents feel that, by virtue of their very position, their conduct and their demands are faultless. They do not believe in the analytic method, they come to *see* what the physician will say. This attitude is, by the way, similar to the French feeling about medicine at large. One goes to see a doctor in order to receive a diagnosis, but one is extremely skeptical about his prescriptions. The incidence of what one might call an "innocently illegal" practice of medicine is exceedingly high. One comes back home with the doctor's prescriptions, and one takes the medicine recommended by the concierge or one's acquaintances. Thus every French person engages for at least half an hour every day in the illegal practice of medicine.

Americans, on the other hand, have a faith in the technician with a diploma which is surprising to the French. The French resistance to the analyst is thus not so much one to his particular kind of treatment as a special expression of a general ego-attitude. This attitude is often called one of "individualism"; but this is erroneous. If everybody is convinced of the value of his own judgment, it is because this judgment issues from early family experiences, from a family belief in itself and the family member's belief in the family.

To be sure, the educational behavior of parents is everywhere unconsciously determined by the oedipal phase. But in America the parents' conscious motivations are dominated by their identification with, and the influence of, the immediate social surroundings. In France these motivations have almost nothing to do with the immediate social surroundings, but everything with family tradition. "In my family," says the father or the mother. In the name of his own family he behaves toward his child as his father or mother behaved toward him.

Behind this, there is a devaluation of the mores of the present moment, a parental distrust of the young and of their initiative, a parental lack of respect for the personality of their child, his personal ambitions, his judgment, his act of choice, and even his social milieu. True enough, French child training looks toward the child's adulthood and his adult independence; a French child is being told every day, "prepare your future." But in the parents' belief the best development of this future personage is insured by coercing the child into conformity with precepts which were formulated one or two generations back.

Take the typical example of the pocket money which a father gives his child; in three families out of ten, the number of francs allowed by the father at present is still the same as the amount he received when he was his child's age, without any regard for comparative purchasing power. (The mother is sometimes more generous without letting the father know about it.) And even when the father grants the child a sum which corresponds better to the child's needs and the family standard of living, he has a nostalgic feeling of guilt: "At your age, I was quite content with one franc fifty a week, and you are not satisfied with twenty francs!" He is simply forgetting that when he was a child it cost fifteen centimes to mail a letter while it costs fifteen francs today and that a loaf of bread which now costs twenty-five francs could then be had for thirty-five or forty centimes. When the child, tired of these nostalgic memories, recalls the parent to reality, the father condemns that reality as difficult and bad and pronounces the young generation's insatiable and culpable appetite for pleasure responsible for the steady rise of the price level during the last decades.

Not only do the parents convey by their behavior in money matters that the children are not worth very much in the parents' eyes, they also impress on the children a strong sense of the sacrifices which their parents are assuming on their behalf. I do not know any French parents (they may exist, of course, but I have not encountered them) who implicitly or explicitly tell their children that they, the parents, are happier by virtue of the existence of their children. In the American families which I have come to know, the parents do not seem to feel the burdens which the existence of their children impose on them as very difficult ones. Even when the care or the schooling of their children involves expenses which the parents find it hard to meet, the American child feels that the joy about the benefits conferred on him outweighs for his parents the expense or the disturbance which he occasions.

THE AMERICAN FEAR OF TRAUMATIZING THE CHILD
AND ITS FRENCH COUNTERPARTS

American parents try not to traumatize their child. From the predigestion and premastication of food to the untrammeled freedom of initiative and the public disapproval of corporal punishment, the American child enjoys all sorts of rights. From the point of view of French children, the American child's life is a paradise. But to French grown-ups American children appear "badly brought up" (*mal élevés*). The French child's education consists largely in a coerced and precocious learning of adult behavior without any compensatory award of adult prerogatives. Even in the most liberal French families, child training is largely an affair of imperatives ("don't do this," "don't do that") and of duties, with very few rights. The so-called "liberal" families are a bit more understanding about behavior of the child of which they really disapprove (*font un peu plus "la part du feu"*). There is the "duty" to eat, not to soil one's self, not to play. The only justification for playing—an activity which the parents consider rather contemptible and useless—is to leave the parents in peace when one plays. (The parents would be very impatient with the child if he disturbed them, and in any case would not respond to his demands.) There is the duty to give a good example to one's siblings, the duty to love, etc.

What about the rights of the child? He has the right to obey, to work in school, and to help at home—even his rights are duties. He has the right to a present on his birthday and on New Year's Day, but often this present is immediately taken away from him again and put into a cupboard because it is too precious to be damaged. In fact, French parents like to give presents which are too beautiful and too expensive. They buy them, show them, and don't give them. The money which an uncle or a grandfather may have given the child on one of the feast days is also taken away from him and put into his money box, out of his reach until the moment when he will have grown up—a habit which is perhaps even more widespread among the rich than among the poor.

The French child must constantly "prepare his future"; he must not have fun because he must learn how to live. Once a child told me: "I don't care about my future. I don't want to live, I want to play." Society takes part in this continuous intimidation. Every hardware store sells the instrument of punishment called the *martinet*, a kind of whip. Policemen are glad to threaten, upon the parents' request, children on whom the *martinet* has lost its effectiveness or to whom the parents don't dare give hard spankings. It is not that French parents are child-torturers (*bourreaux d'enfants*); they do love their children, but they feel that they have to learn proper habits after all (*il faut bien les dresser*). "Who loves well, punishes well," is a frequently used prov-erb. In some families it is the gendarme whose name is pronounced as that of a punishing agent; in others it is God. Terrifying threats such as these are made in connection with the child's disobedience of any kind of absurd command, whose violation would damage only the prestige of the adult who has issued it, for whatever motive—most often from apprehension of some kind of risk or of incurring a bad reputation.

In France it is an accepted procedure to frighten the child in order to make him obey. If one does not succeed by physical force, one threatens the child with serious illness or other catastrophes which his disobedience would magically induce. For a small child there is the wolf, the bad man to whom the parents are going to give the child, the kidnapper who is going to come, the policeman, the commissioner of police, etc. A week ago I was told that a physician from the provinces had written his eighteen-year-old daughter—who, of course, was terribly upset—that the medical association had deprived him of the right to practice for six months because the daughter had been seen entering her boarding house in the company of a young man! Girls are, in fact, terrorized much longer than boys. Often policemen lend themselves to the appropriate play-acting. This is called "upholding paternal authority," and one does not consider the impossible climate which the parents create. Children are thus severely punished for leaving the apartment without permission on days when there is no school and when the parents demand that they stay at home. Grave sanctions may be imposed if they steal minimal sums of money, the counterpart of which—given the income of their parents—they should have received from them in any case.

I am not exaggerating. If one often hears the gloomy diagnosis that French children don't fear their parents any more, it is not because the parents don't try to make themselves feared. But more and more women are working and more and more children are in early contact with society at large without the protecting and frightening parental buffer. The children are thus in a position to learn by themselves that the police and the kidnappers are not interested in their domestic life and tiny sins. As many adults put it, "Now that children know as much about life as we, why should they still fear us?" Mothers in parks often say, "Too bad that they grow up so quickly. When they enter school, it's finished. Then you cannot do anything with them any more. They believe they are important and become impossible at home."

In fact, the preschool child in France is not even an individual, he is a parasitic fragment of his mother. It is only rarely that one sees preschool children in psychiatric consultation. But social developments will finally liberate this marsupial nursling. As he sees that school is not the concentration camp his parents made it out to be, he is going to lose confidence in them and also to shed the entire false adjustment to his own impulses which his mother had skilfully constructed. The majority of French children build up for themselves one *modus vivendi* for school and another for the home. This split of the personality continues in the case of many adults who are appreciated, creative, alive, at ease, and smiling in the mixed milieu in which they work but are glum, demanding, boring, and bored at home. They never fuse their two lives except by bringing work home and thus enabling themselves to escape yet again the heavy climate which they are compelled to create there.

This is entirely due to unconscious factors: the first years of life in their family, vacations spent at home and boring Sundays there, have imposed on them the monotonous and reassuring style of life which I have sketched. Religion and observance of the Sunday rest have nothing to do with this. While every Frenchman who visits England finds British Sundays very boring, he is also bored at home on Sunday. But in France every family is bored in its own fashion, as a traditional agglomeration of people who intimidate one another. The one who is most repressed, in the psychoanalytic sense of the term (impulses being blocked without gaining access to consciousness), inhibits the dynamism of those who tend to depart from the so-called "traditional" familial style of life. To be well brought up (*bien élevé*)—in the sense of the constantly employed terms "a well-brought-up boy," "a well-brought-up girl"—means to be able to be bored in the family circle without protesting overtly.

Thus the French do not fear to traumatize children. If traumatization is defined as a combination of permanent and selective inhibitions which are violently imposed in order to block actions oriented on the pleasure principle, then it may be said that *by virtue of tradition and educational principle, children are being traumatized daily* in France.

A CRITIQUE OF THE TWO ATTITUDES

I wonder whether this is not a good thing for the future adult. This seems like a joke. In any case we are not concerned here with what is good or bad but with facts and their consequences. Let us therefore look at some facts more closely and, in doing so, follow the stages of the libido indicated by Freud.

During his first years, the French child *must* eat. If he refuses nourishment (in the countryside this includes wine, cabbage, and alcohol, from the first months on), his mother gets depressed. What is good for the mother is good for him. From a very early age on, he must be clean. Nourishment and sphincter control are imposed to the accompaniment of maternal shouts, spanking, and threats. He *must* say *bonjour* and *au revoir*, even when these words have no meaning for him. It is customary to say in psychoanalysis that the child's feces are his first present to the mother. But in France the child acquires cleanliness not, or almost never, because he receives compliments for every bowel movement conforming to maternal orders. Such conformity is a matter of course. According to her character, the mother is furious or depressed if the child does not perform correctly, but she pays him no compliments if he does. In the latter case, there is simply no trouble. In order to satisfy the mother, the child must swallow all that she gives him to eat, all she wants to give him, but only that. The famous jar of jam illicitly approached by the child creates a maternal cataclysm comparable to that induced by the fact of not eating all of the soup. When the mother comes home she asks the maid: "Has he eaten well? Has he behaved well [*a-t-il été sage*]?" That is, has he obeyed you, whoever the "you" is. To defecate in one's pants is not *sage*, but to defecate on the pot has no positive value; it is just normal. The mother is pleased when the child has eaten everything, even if he looks like someone who has finished a hard day's labor. But not having eaten everything puts you automatically into conflict with authority.

Sagesse, thus, first means to perform the movements and to adopt the rhythms imposed by the adult; for example, to tolerate being covered excessively or insufficiently, etc. (In these matters the father is sometimes even more exacting than the mother). Later there is added the requirement not to "answer back," which means not to express one's opinion if it is contrary to that of an adult. A child who "answers back" is in a state of revolt, even if he is perfectly obedient in his movements. The adult expects that the child will not discuss commands emanating from his sacrosanct authority; if the child does, there will be trouble in store for him. But, on the other hand, the child is incited to the crime of "answering back" by what he perceives to be the relation between his parents, who constantly discuss each other's requests or desires in the name of their divergent family traditions. Even if the families of mother and father belong to the same social level, there are differences in the nuances of their categoric imperatives. But if the child "answers back," he trespasses on a domain reserved for the adults.

This is the age when the child enters school. He finally receives the right, during recess, to be physically active with little surveillance. While the parents forbid a child to fight with another child when he is with them, they are depressed if the child does not fight at school, as the other children are fighting and as one must not let one's self be beaten.

At the oral age the child *had* to swallow without defending himself. At the anal age, he *must* know how to defend himself, which means that he must attack an attacker. But he must not say dirty words, which would be bad-mannered. He must listen in class and never chat. In public school, children of six, seven, and eight expose themselves to bad marks and the principal's thunder if they exchange as much as one word among themselves. They must neither move nor talk, but listen and write. They must not look at their neighbors and must even hide their own notebooks from the indiscreet eyes of their classmates. A good school should be boring. Thus progressive education is little accepted in France and only in the educated groups. The best school, the most "serious" school (*sérieux* is something of solid worth, about which one doesn't smile), is the one in which children are sad and in which they learn in the same fashion by which the child has earlier learned to eat—they sadly swallow verbal knowledge and excrete well-presented exercises (*devoirs*) which they have produced without pleasure.

I have had cases in which I advised parents to send their child to a progressive school because the child was developing an obsessional neurosis and because his superior mental and verbal intelligence was accompanied by an inhibition of motility and of affects. Invariably, the parents feel that I have inflicted a narcissistic wound on them. To their minds, progressive schools are for morons, for poor little ones of whom no work can be demanded. A progressive schoolteacher from the suburbs of Paris tells me that the parents of her pupils—workers, employees, and artisans—cannot tolerate the fact that the children prefer school to home and that they do not have to write pages and pages during the hours of the evening. These parents all express the same fear—the child will never learn how to live if he does not fear his teacher and if his cheeks don't become pale by dint of study. What is true for this lower-class milieu is also true for employees in more comfortable circumstances, whom one might call petty bourgeois, and for many well-to-do members of the bourgeoisie, industrialists and merchants. A satisfying son or daughter is a little obsessive who prepares his future while glancing furtively at the children who have fun (or, better yet, without glancing at them), who is closely attached to a bookish school program and submissive to the parent who has the more authoritarian superego. The future of the child who thinks of playing is in grave danger.

All this must be surprising to the American reader. The young men and women of France seem so free, the Americans say. To be sure, but this is precisely the result of their strictly confined childhood. Life begins when one leaves childhood, and all of childhood is passed in waiting for the end of adolescence. The diploma which certifies the end of studies suddenly liberates the child from familial constraints. Here there is a small difference between boys and girls. The boys who don't have fun, or don't look for fun (*qui ne "s'amusent pas" ou ne "cherchent pas à s'amuser"*), after the end of puberty, make their parents uneasy. All the coercion of French education is, at least in the case of the boy, directed against the pregenital stages of the libido. A young man must sow his wild oats (*jeter sa gourme*). In order to be respected, he must seek, or at least appreciate, sexual pleasure. If one should be *sage* in childhood and work well in adolescence, an overserious student is not well regarded. If he does not act like a youth (*si jeunesse ne se passe pas*), he won't be a good husband. If he is not after women at eighteen, he will be after them, once he is married; a husband should be experienced.

The masturbation of a small boy makes mothers, and sometimes fathers, uneasy; it is actively combated. From the age of fifteen on, masturbation is simply ridiculed among boys, as well as in general talk. The young man's sexual vigor is viewed as an indication of his general quality (*est bon signe*). Running after women or having a girl friend with whom one has regular sexual relations (*avoir une petite amie*) is not only tolerated but enhances a young man's status—if he does it without arousing too much attention and without spending his parents' money. Thus the young man who begins to earn his livelihood by that very fact puts an end to his family's coercion over him. And as, in the course of his childhood, he has acquired a strong internal discipline, he will usually retain self-control in his new freedom. Except in rare cases, he will impose upon himself a rule of sexual conduct somewhere between the pleasure principle and the so-called reality principle.

It is the young student and intellectual, still financially dependent upon his family, who has the greatest difficulty in affirming himself sexually. The difficult *concours* and examinations require great intellectual effort; and the atmosphere of the schools through which the young man has passed before arriving at the upper levels of the educational system has not prepared him to mix pleasure and study and to balance them. He is thus fearful of everything that might upset his equilibrium; he is tempted to use sports—which are becoming increasingly mandatory at this age—to discharge his sexual tensions. But this leads to a chronic state of emotional upset (*désarroi affectif*), and he feels inadequate because he stagnates in his sexual life on a level which he senses to be regressive—all the more as his family is likely to picture the young student as leading a wild life.

Thus we see that the parental superego and the entire society first systematically inhibit the libidinal expression of the boy during the pregenital phases and adolescence and then abandon all conscious coercion of the young adult—who will therefore only very rarely regret the passing of his childhood.

For girls things do not run in quite the same fashion, as I have already noted. Parental concern continues in lower-class milieus until about twenty-one and elsewhere until marriage. Afterward one says of a young girl or of a woman to whom a good deal of premarital or extra-marital sexual activity is attributed that she is old enough to know what she is doing. The fear of having a child is a dominant motive for the coercion imposed upon young girls. France with its tradition of Salic law does not grant women the same freedom which it gives men. Women must be protected against themselves, that is, against the sexual attraction they exercise on young men, who would court them without "serious" intent, just to have fun. It is rather paradoxical that the reputation of young men is enhanced if they engage in sexual intercourse, while the reputation of young girls is strengthened if they resist love making; but that is the situation. Those girls (usually frigid ones) who allow sexual approaches but not full intercourse are the most satisfactory from the point of view of society. Those who are not frigid must be married quickly so that the parents are discharged of a responsibility, which is thus transferred to the husband. But the girls sought as brides of well-situated young men are those who have not been awakened sexually and who expect of marriage the right to consider themselves adult, both socially and sexually. Thus the young girl waits for marriage just as impatiently as the young man waits for his eighteenth birthday—that is, for liberation from coercion and the right to the pleasure principle.

In contrast, after an American childhood comparatively free from all coercion, from all threats of corporal violence at the hands of parents, school, and society, the first direct threats to the freedom of the growing American occur precisely in connection with the activation of genital wishes. The pleasure principle is king until the arrival of genital maturity. All sorts of pregenital satisfactions—oral, motor, aesthetic, and prestige—are more than tolerated; they occasion the parents' affectionate pleasure. It does not seem to me that early masturbation is fought against as much as it is in France. Thus a young human being emerges who has never really assumed responsibility for those of his acts which restrict the freedom of others. For instance, American children are allowed to play ball in the middle of a city street and thus to hinder traffic; the adults impeded by them can only verbally ask them for permission to proceed. In France any driver would feel it his right to box the ears of a child in this situation. But, once the young American has arrived at the age of genital maturity, he is immediately held responsible for all the possible consequences of completed intercourse. I believe this is the dominant fact which distinguishes these two types of Western civilization. American young girls are protected by the society as American children are protected against the possible violence of their parents. Young men, therefore, feel guilt for desiring normal intercourse, while every young girl feels she is within her rights in provoking a young man without consenting to intercourse. The young girl comes to prefer young men who only want to touch (*les froleurs*), who only wish to dance, to perform gallant gestures, and who tolerate long sexual tension without complete release.

Thus it is pregenital childhood which appears most enviable in America. The adults dream of their lost childhood—the golden age which they can find only in regression. For them, difficulties begin with full genital relations, with marriage. I do not mean to say that it is preferable to impose coercion very early, but I do believe it is traumatizing to begin to impose it at the stage of adult genitality. The fact that this is being done in America may explain what appears to the French as so characteristic of American adults, who are usually called "big children" in France.

THE FRENCH AND AMERICAN VARIANTS OF
THE OEDIPUS COMPLEX

Before concluding, I would like to turn to the differences which I have been able to observe in the evolution of the oedipus complex among French and American children. It seems to me, in fact, that American children do not at all structure their oedipus complex in the same fashion that French children do, and the differences are related to some points which have already been made. The classical oedipus complex consists of a desire for the parent of the other sex, which involves rivalry with the parent of the same sex and leads to identification with that parent. But in American culture such a classical development encounters enormous obstacles. First, it is rare that American parents show an emotional and sensual attachment to each other in a way which the child can perceive. American parents who have good relations with each other are likely to be associates rather than lovers, comrades rather than a *couple* in the French sense. Often the father is not the dominating authority. In their educational conduct the parents are more influenced by the standards of the surrounding society than by what has been held to be right for boys in a tradition transmitted from father to son and held to be right for girls in a tradition transmitted from mother to daughter. Thus it is the entire group of the adults of his sex, rather than the individual parent, that tends to become the ego-ideal of the American child. Instead of being jealous of her mother, an American girl may be jealous of a woman friend of her mother; instead of being jealous of his father, an American boy may be jealous of his job. The mother is likely to appear related to a variety of men—with which of her men friends does she seem the happiest?

Rivalry requires a rival, but the father is generally felt as being more maternal than paternal; he is a providing figure rather than a directing and authoritative one—a role which is fulfilled by society at large. The father, as we have seen, does not oppose himself to the child's initiative or to the child's imitation of his own behavior. He becomes simply somebody who prevents the boy from going to bed, or rather from sleeping, in the same room as the mother. But the parents' intimacy does not seem mysterious; it even appears less pleasant than that which is permitted between children of different sexes. There remains the desire to earn a lot of money quickly, to be admired as the rich are. The American child always assumes that love is bought with presents for which one pays, that it is obtained by the appearance of virility and by social success. As the child really understands only what happens in relation to himself and as, for him, the good adult is one who never hits him, the direct contact of bodies (*les corps-à-corps*) are to him more or less socialized games relating to material objects but not to women. On the contrary, in the child's eyes women belong to the men who excel in gallantry and in maternal solicitude, the men who help their wives in the performance of domestic chores, and who are the most attractive according to the canon of masculine beauty, with visibly strong muscles and easy joviality.

The American child does not sense how a woman could be sexually attached to a man who is neither rich nor desired by other women because of his splendid appearance. The aggressive component of pregenital or genital sexuality is not felt as belonging to the ideal behavior of the father, and this fact greatly modifies the oedipal schema. The male appears as passive, on the one hand, and as one who has potency with regard to the acquisition of money, on the other. If the boy does not succeed in sublimating his entire aggressiveness in motor behavior and in the social struggle, he develops an ideal of the tough guy and of the gangster. For, by definition, the gangster gets hold of money and thus of women, in successful rivalry with constituted authority. The gangster thus becomes the substitute father of American boys. If a man does not have the means of obtaining a woman by his good looks or by his money, he can only get her by compromising her. But perhaps there are ways, though regressive ones, to evoke the interest of a woman without compromising her sexually, and even to become rich thereby. Hence the fantasy theme of the upper-class lady interested in charities who is exploited by her masculine protégés, a theme which is popular in America (one may recall the film, *The Lady and the Mob* —*Madame et son Clochard* in the French release) and which has no counterpart in France.

The following theme would be felt to be absurd by young American men. A young girl is sexually aroused by her lover; she attaches herself to him; she challenges social prohibitions; she renounces material happiness represented by a suitor with an excellent social situation, and who also appears to be more attractive. But this is one of the most frequent French plots. The differences between the French and American attitudes toward such a plot are related to the differences in the nuances of the oedipus complex which we have indicated.

What do we observe when we mix with American boys and girls? They constantly use pseudo-adult words among themselves and affect to be flirting. At the age of ten, boys speak of the glamour of their feminine classmates; boy friend and girl friend overtly choose each other. But it seems rather to be a matter of using genital words for narcissistic and orally dependent feelings. This is how you have to be in order to be up-to-date. Threesomes abound. The girls are not faithful, one runs after them; they are difficult, one has to merit them by compliments. And if one has got a girl, one has really got nowhere, as she gives you only as much as will enhance her prestige when she can tell a girl friend about it. The threesome is never resolved; the girl friend's girl friend is the boy's rival. And if a young girl is really in love, she must be sure to hide it, for she would lower herself were she to show it; in order to be desired by the boy, she must remain difficult, etc.

American parents give their girls full freedom to go around with boys, and thus seem to deliver them to their impulses. In fact, this attitude stems from the parents' feeling that the girl should take advantage as fully as possible of the age when relations with boys do not yet have serious consequences. They also believe that if their girl were to become pregnant, she could not remain without a father for her child, as the law protects women. This protection will lead the girl toward becoming the wife of a man who does not love her, or whom she does not love, but who has desired her at one time and to whom she yielded as her controls failed. What kind of father and mother will these two become after the usual ceremony is over? This will not be a couple that will insure a classical oedipus complex in their children.

It seems to me, in conclusion, that for young Americans the adult is not a sexual, but a social, ideal. For the adult, however, the child is the incarnation of his nostalgia for a paradise lost. For the young boy, his mother is not connected with his sexual desire but with his aspiration toward being comrades with a woman for whom others will envy him. Later on he will suffer if by virtue of his character he cannot live out this type of relation. His virile sexual wishes lead, above all, to fantasies and are told to other boys who are not rivals but comrades in hardship and rejection. As for the girl, the object of her desire is disparaged (without being overtly combated) rather than exalted. To the extent to which there is a struggle, it takes place exclusively on the plane of social success, of smart tactics, and of compromising the other socially. In the eyes of her girl friends and of society, a girl is all the more accomplished if she is emotionally cold (or successfully simulates coldness), but at the same time full of charm and bodily seduction. These are the attractions which girls use to tempt boys. The more uitors the girl has, the more timid and insecure they are; the more she feels herself admired, the more her value seems confirmed.

We thus perceive a dominance of pregenital attitudes according to which the real joy of life lies at the stage of reciprocal seduction before there is reciprocal surrender. It is this emphasis which we encounter again in the striving of American adults to look as young as possible, in the conformity of styles of life, and the powerful impact of external signs of knowledge and wealth. By these extra-genital trends, deriving as they do from anal sublimations, American men try to console themselves for the failure of their genital emotions. But this failure, does it not stem from the strangling of these emotions in their oedipal bases? And is this strangling not connected with an emotional situation of the parental couple, where full sexual satisfaction is rare and emotional immaturity frequent? The child often seems to perceive the parental couple as a big brother and sister. Because of this, the child unconsciously fears to adopt a genitally more satisfactory style of life. To do so would make him fall into the insecurity of an orphan, a situation fraught with unconscious hostility.

There is no conclusion to these notes. All I wanted to do was to submit my reflections to the reader and to arouse his interest in the application of psychoanalysis to sociology.

CHAPTER 24

Two Types of Jewish Mothers

————————————MARTHA WOLFENSTEIN

The cases reported here were observed in the Child Guidance Institute of the Jewish Board of Guardians in New York City. I saw both Mrs. L and her daughter Karen in psychotherapy once a week for two and a half years. Mrs. S was similarly in treatment with me for a period of two years. Her son Stan was treated by another therapist, whose detailed case notes were utilized for this study. I am greatly indebted to the Jewish Board of Guardians for their kind permission to use the material from these cases.

I SHOULD like to present here the picture of two mothers, one of Eastern European Jewish origin and the other of an American Jewish family. Markedly different mother-child relations appear in the two cases, which can be regarded as expressing different cultural patterns. These mothers were seen over a period of two or more years in a child-guidance clinic, where their children were also in treatment, and both were primarily concerned about quarrelsome relations with their children. It would have been ideal if these two cases could have been matched in respect to age of the mother, age and sex of the child, socioeconomic status of the family, and so on, so that the cultural background would have been the main variable. Unfortunately, the clinical material which comes one's way is not so neatly arranged for research purposes. However, in assessing the culturally characteristic aspects of the two cases, I have drawn on considerable antecedent research on Eastern European Jewish culture,[1] as well as on other observations of American and Jewish mothers,[2] research on old American non-Jewish families,[3] and an analysis of American child-training literature.[4]

Mrs. S is a stout, ruddy-faced woman of fifty-one who speaks with a marked Yiddish accent. She came to this country as a young woman. Born in Russia, she was the fourth of a family of eleven, three of whom died in childhood. She had little schooling, which she regrets; her intelligence appears to be superior. She retains close ties to her family of origin, sharing a house with her older sister, who is "like a mother" to her. Her husband, also of Eastern European origin, is a workingman, whom she describes as excessively good-natured—everyone takes advantage of him—and for whom she has considerable contempt. She has three sons to whom she is intensely devoted. It is on account of her youngest son, Stan, who is fourteen, that she has come to the child-guidance clinic. Stan has frequent violent quarrels with his mother, cursing and insulting her, after which he cries and implores her forgiveness. Mrs. S weeps when she talks about these scenes, exclaims how it hurts her, how it is killing her, speaks of her intense feelings as a mother and her life of sacrifice for her children.

Mrs. L is a slender, youthful-looking woman of thirty-four. She is second-generation American (her parents having been of Eastern European origin) and the eldest of a family of five, all of whom are living. She is a college graduate. Her family unit excludes her family of origin; she feels that involvement in the affairs of her mother, brothers, or sisters would conflict with giving proper attention to her husband and children. Her husband was born in Eastern Europe, came to this country as a boy, got his schooling here, and is also a college graduate. He is an office manager. They have two little girls. The elder, Karen, who is nine, is brought for treatment. The parents are concerned about her hostility toward her mother. Mrs. L speaks of Karen's "negativism," then reproaches herself for her "rejection" of Karen during her early years. When Mrs. L relates family upsets, she usually assumes a humorous tone as if she would like to turn it all into an amusing anecdote.

I should like to consider certain contrasting attitudes of these two mothers, first in respect to the image which the mother has of the child. Children pass through various stages of development, as, for instance, the helpless infant, the school child bent on acquisition of skills, the rebellious adolescent. Cultures differ in their emphasis on one or another phase of development, taking the characteristics of the child in a particular phase as constituting his essential nature. The way in which the mother conceives her own role varies accordingly. If the image of the helpless infant predominates, the mother must feed and care for him and guard him from harm; she cannot leave him to take care of himself. This conception of the mother-child relationship may persist through all phases of the child's development. If, on the other hand, the phase or aspect of the child's life which has to do with acquisition of skills is most strongly emphasized, the mother's role is more that of an educator, and the child is encouraged to be independent from an early age.

Mrs. S continues to think of her adolescent son as a helpless infant, who cannot be trusted to do anything for himself and who, if left to his own devices, will injure himself, probably irreparably. She is constantly worried about his health: he is in danger of catching cold from not buttoning up his jacket or not wearing his scarf or sleeping with the windows open. When she cautions him about these things, he flies into a rage, yelling that he is not a baby. (Her anxieties reinforce his own adolescent fears about himself, that he may have damaged himself by masturbation. This contributes to making the mother's expressions of worry about the son's health intolerable to him.) To this mother her big athletic boy is still as fragile as an infant, just as vulnerable to the hazards of the environment, and just as dependent on the mother's vigilant care in order to survive. Similarly, when it comes to buying clothes, which he would like to do by himself, she is sure that he will be cheated if she does not go with him. When he wants to get a summer job, she is convinced that he is too young, that the only possible job for him would be one which she would arrange for him to get in her sister's store. About his studies, she again expresses mainly fears that he is damaging himself, either endangering his future prospects by not studying or ruining his health by studying too late at night.

If we attempt to relate this maternal attitude to the Eastern European Jewish background, we can see factors there which made for the fixation of the mother-child relation on the earliest infantile phase. In the traditional Jewish community the mother was not the educator of her dearly beloved sons. At about the age of three the little boy was snatched from the arms of his weeping mother and sent to school. Learning was the province of the men exclusively.[5] The time when the mother could have her son to herself, to love and care for, was when he was a baby, before the world of men and of learning claimed him. For the older boy she had no comparably important role to play. Her image of the child remained complementary to her own role, which was not that of an educator but one of feeding the infant, anxiously protecting his fragile organism, aware of his helplessness, his inability to survive without her constant care.[6] One might say that just as a child tends to become fixated on a certain phase of development if it is extremely gratifying or to regress to it if a later phase is too frustrating, so similarly a mother may remain fixated to the maternal role corresponding to that phase of the child's development which was most gratifying for her and to regress to this in the face of frustration in later phases.[7]

The Jewish religion has as a major motive the consolidation of father-son relations through the submission of the son to paternal authority. There is one god, the father, not the son or the mother deified by Christianity. The custom of the Eastern European Jewish community of separating boys from their mothers at such an early age was in the interest of inducing submission to paternal elders. Before the development of the oedipal phase, with its rebellious impulses toward the father, the boy was already subjected to the tutelage of men, the rod of the teacher, and the word of God. The separation from the mother curtailed opportunities for expression of the oedipal attachment to her.

As a result, the mother knew her little boy much better in the pre-oedipal phase, when he was passive to her ministrations, than in the oedipal phase, in which boys develop more active impulses toward their mothers; and the boy on his side had more opportunity for expressing the earlier than the later strivings toward the mother.

A reality factor in the European Jewish situation which contributed to the mother's anxiety about her child was the high infant mortality rate. In Mrs. S's case, three of her siblings had died in childhood. Such experiences reinforce anxiety about the fragility and vulnerability of the infant.[8]

While Mrs. S's sons were born in this country and brought up under different conditions of life from those of her original community, it would seem that Mrs. S perpetuates the model of her own mother, from whom she learned the maternal role. This role, as the mother of babies, did not include educational functions, and even less could Mrs. S assume those in a strange country where she knows little of what her children must learn.

From Mrs. L, on the other hand, we hear: "When will Karen grow up? Why is she still so babyish?" When she feels less dissatisfied with her daughter, she reports that Karen is beginning to assume some responsibilities. Mrs. L is greatly concerned about skill and accomplishments. She complains that Karen is clumsy, that she lacks manual dexterity, and also that she is not socially adept. When Karen is nine, her mother is already thinking about her independent adult life. If Karen's relations to her family are disturbed, then she may not have good relations to the opposite sex later on. That is why Mrs. L feels that Karen should have treatment. Later Mrs. L is thinking about sending Karen away to college, though she is only at this time in the sixth grade.

The American family has been characterized by Margaret Mead as a "launching platform," the place from which the children take off for their own independent existence. The mother is not supposed to hover protectively over her little one but to speed him off on his tricycle to join his age mates. Recent American child-training literature has stressed the motor and exploratory impulses of the infant, his tendency from a very early age to get going and master his environment.[9] Mothers who study Gesell check whether their children are demonstrating the appropriate skills from month to month. The aspect of the growing child as one who acquires skills is strongly emphasized. The mother's role is to facilitate the acquisition of skills, to preside over the child's learning. In America the role of teacher is to a high degree a woman's role, both at home and in school.[10]

Mrs. L exemplifies this maternal attitude. She is troubled because her child does not show so much skill or so much independent activity as the mother expects. We do not hear from Mrs. L the anxieties about the child wearing enough sweaters or possibly catching cold and so on which so constantly haunt Mrs. S.

Another major question in respect to which maternal attitudes vary is this: How vulnerable is the mother in relation to the child? How much can the child's behavior hurt or wound her? In the case of Mrs. S, the thought is repeatedly expressed that her children can kill her. Though she sees her son Stan as a helpless and fragile baby, who needs her constant care to stay alive, she also sees him as terribly strong and powerful, capable of killing her. When he quarrels with her, she tells him that he is "aggravating" her to death. The doctor has said that, because of her high blood pressure, aggravation could kill her. She frequently tells Stan about a woman who lived across the street whose son actually aggravated her to death. On one occasion when Stan was angry at her, she went out on the porch without a coat and thought she caught cold. In his rages, he tells her to drop dead. She answers him that she will; if he is like that, what does she have to live for? Following a quarrel she often feels sick. She retires to her room and lies down. When Stan comes in and tries to mollify her, she does not speak; she acts as if she were dead.

Death wishes toward the parents, who are at the same time deeply loved, are inevitable in human childhood. And with the child's illusions of omnipotence there is the fantasy that these wishes can kill. In the S family this is not just a guilt-ridden fantasy of the child, it is even more a firm belief of the mother. By his show of anger against her, her son is attacking her very life. The quarrel itself is an act of murder.

A number of factors contribute to this maternal reaction. Mrs. S deeply represses any negative feelings of her own toward her mother and toward her children. She would never have behaved toward her mother the way her son behaves toward her. Recalling her own childhood and how the children would never have dared to answer their mother back, Mrs. S remembered how her sister, after having been punished by their mother, muttered to herself: "It should happen to me"—meaning that what she wickedly wished to the mother should fall on her own head. Hostile feelings were turned back against the self. Perpetuating her strong positive ties to her mother, Mrs. S still lives with her older sister, who is like a mother to her. In relation to her children she also denies any negative feelings; she is never aware of anything but self-sacrificing love toward them.[11] The fate of these unacknowledged hostile feelings would seem to be that they are projected onto her children. The hostility which she dared not admit toward her mother assumes terrifying proportions in her son and is directed toward her. The unadmitted negative feelings which she has toward the son are similarly projected and contribute to her belief that he will fatally damage himself.

Mrs. S is vulnerable not only to the attacks of her son against her but to his tendency to damage himself, which is equally destructive to her.[12] If by not following her admonitions he catches a cold and makes himself sick, who will suffer? She will. The two of them are inextricably bound together in life and death. Mrs. S has also told her son that if she dies, he dies. Presumably he could not survive her, either because of his helplessness or because he would die of guilt and grief.

If we look for a model of the mother-child relationship as Mrs. S experiences it, a situation in which the child is at the same time most vulnerable and most capable of killing the mother, we may find this in childbirth. It is then that the child's life is most endangered, while the child in turn causes the mother intense suffering and endangers her life. For Mrs. S every emotionally fraught scene with her son would seem to be a repetition of childbirth. We may ask what circumstances make for such a strong fixation on this experience. For a mother who is impelled to relive it in this way, we may guess that it represents a very deep gratification. In the Eastern European Jewish community the importance attached to having children was tremendous. A wife who produced no children could be divorced.[13] Mrs. S expresses the traditional pride in maternity. She frequently clasps her hands to her large bosom and exclaims: "I am a mother." However, the high value attached to being a mother does not necessarily carry with it such an intense emotional fixation on the act of birth itself.

In trying to account for this, I would propose the following hypothesis. Traditional Jewish life involved strong defenses against sexual impulses. The preponderance of rituals and avoidances hedging every act strongly suggests a compulsive character structure, profoundly impressed with the dangers of sexuality. At the same time it was recognized that complete genital abstinence was not feasible. Sexual thoughts could obtrude themselves and disturb serious occupations, particularly the ideal pursuit of the man, that of constant study. Thus the sexual act was to be performed to free the man's mind from disturbing thoughts. It seems likely that sexual relations were thus carried out as quickly as possible, to get the thing done and out of the way, that sex was brief and isolated from the rest of life. It was shameful, for instance, for a man and wife to see each other naked.[14] There can have been little erotic elaboration under such circumstances, and one may suppose that the aim of satisfying the woman was absent.

For the sexually unsatisfied wife the great genital experience was childbirth. Then she received from her son the intense and prolonged genital stimulation which she did not get from her husband. But, since she also participated in the regression from full genitality, her image of sex was a sado-masochistic one. Thus her great sexual experience, that of childbearing, was fraught with the dangers of killing and being killed. (While these dangers are actually present in childbirth, they do not under other circumstances assume such emotional importance.) If we suppose that these hypothetically reconstructed relations are exemplified in the case of Mrs. S, we can understand why she is impelled to repeat painful scenes with her son, scenes which have the conscious significance that he may kill her and thus also bring about his own death and which unconsciously reproduce the experience of childbirth.

In contrast to this, Mrs. L does not attribute to her children the power to destroy her. They can be a terrible nuisance and annoyance, but they are not that dangerous. Quarrels are less climactic, more trivial, and imminence of fatality does not haunt the daily routine. Mother and child are less isolated in intense struggle with each other; quarrels as recounted by Mrs. L appear to revolve around many external details and circumstances and to include other persons.[15] Thus Karen comes home from school and complains about her teacher; Mrs. L tries to justify the teacher, and Karen becomes enraged with the mother for taking the teacher's side. Karen and her sister get into a dispute about which one finished her milk first, and Karen shouts so loudly that her mother threatens her with the strap. On another occasion the little sister calls the mother an ass, and the mother spanks her. Karen yells that her mother is mean and cruel until the mother spanks her, too. There are daily quarrels about Karen's not getting dressed promptly enough in the morning, and so on. Mrs. L is exasperated with Karen, but she does not express the thought that Karen could aggravate her to death.

What are the emotional factors in this mother which make for this more moderate estimate of her child's power to damage her? Unlike Mrs. S, Mrs. L does not completely repress her own hostility toward either her mother or her children. She has many outspoken reproaches against her own mother. She does not maintain the same high level of filial piety which we noted in Mrs. S, who still lives on the closest terms with a good mother-figure, her older sister. Mrs. L frequently wards off with resentment what she takes to be unfair claims of her mother on her. She recalls how little her mother has helped her and holds many things against her mother from childhood days. Thus she justifies the negative feelings which she acknowledges toward her mother. Similarly in relation to her daughter, she admits that the child was, to begin with, a terrible burden which she resented. While she blames herself for having felt this way, she readily acknowledges how much of a burden Karen remains for her, and on one occasion confessed that she sometimes wishes that Karen were dead. Since these hostile feelings toward her own mother as well as toward her daughter are to some extent consciously acknowledged, they do not have to be projected onto the child. Thus the child is not invested with mother-killing or with self-destroying tendencies from the mother's own unconscious. As we noted before, Mrs. L is much less concerned than Mrs. S with her child's health and does not see Karen as wilfully exposing herself to colds or in other ways endangering her life.

Mother and child in the L family are not a symbiotic pair, with their fates inseparably intertwined, but two mutually independent persons. The mother is not fixated on the phase of the child's helpless infancy or the situation of childbirth but is urging her child toward increasing independence and looks forward eagerly to the greater independence she herself can enjoy, for instance, when she gets the children off to camp for the summer. Also, the mother's anger is less turned back against herself and less libidinized. When Mrs. L gets annoyed with Karen, she seethes inwardly until she cannot restrain herself from hitting the child; then she feels relieved. She experiences a catharsis. This seems to be in keeping with major American patterns about aggression. There is the feeling that aggression should be turned outward, that it is good to get things off your chest, and that an overt fight clears the air. The venting of anger seems to be experienced as a simple excretory act: something is got rid of, and one feels relieved. Anger here appears to be relatively uninvolved with sado-masochistic fantasies. Neither of the combatants is pictured as weak. The relation between parent and child is felt to be a symmetrical one. (When Karen's mother calls her a "nitwit," Karen calls her mother an "idiot." Karen also calls her mother a "brat.")

Karen, on her side, has the inevitable wishes, fantasies, and fears of her mother's death. But these are isolated from the day-to-day quarrels with the mother. They are expressed in reactions to movies and television shows which fascinate and sometimes frighten her, in which the wife dies and the husband marries his girl friend. Karen writes a play in which a grown-up married daughter becomes enraged with her mother for trying to make her get a divorce (Karen has frequently urged her father to divorce her mother), and the daughter murders the mother. However, her actual quarrels with her mother do not appear to be a manifest dramatization of such fantasies. It is not as in the case of Stan who shouts "Drop dead!" to his mother and so induces in the mother an access of illness, when she retires to her bed and acts as if dead. Karen's mother remains upright and active; she does not comply with the child's unconscious fantasies.

In so far as the thought of killing enters into the quarrels between Karen and her mother, it takes the form of the child's fantasy that the mother is killing her. When the mother hits her, Karen sometimes screams: "You're killing me!" and in the next breath, "You can't hurt me!" Thus the child's death wishes toward the mother are projected onto the mother. It is again the reverse of the S family, where the mother's hostile impulses (toward both her mother and her child) were projected onto the child, who was seen as killing her. (We may also suppose that Mrs. S really believes that her son is bringing her to an early grave, while Karen has less of a serious anticipation of her own death when she accuses her mother in this way.) The projection of the child's bad wishes onto the parents has been observed to be a typical motive of American film plots. There, in oedipal dramas, a mother-figure tries to seduce the hero, and a father-figure tries to kill him. To take one example out of many, in *Gilda*, the beautiful wife of the hero's boss sought to win the hero's love, and the boss made an attempt on the hero's life. The hypothetical connection which we have suggested between this type of film plot and American family life is the following. American children are expected to surpass their parents. As the children see themselves as potentially on a higher level than their parents, they are more easily able to ascribe to the parents the bad impulses which they repudiate in themselves.[16] Karen seems to exemplify this American pattern in her projection of her bad impulses onto her mother. In the S family, on the other hand, where the European image of parental sanctity persists, bad impulses are seen as concentrated in the child.

While parents are inevitably moral authorities for their children, there are many variations in the manner of expressing and acknowledging this authority. Parents may be regarded with awe as righteous judges, or their fallibility may be unmasked. They may demand ceremonial respect, or they may feel uneasy in the role of authority and play it down. For Stan, his mother retains the power to pardon or condemn. After he has quarreled with her, he pleads for her forgiveness. If there have been angry words over breakfast, he cannot leave for school until she gives him a forgiving kiss. This reconciliation and pardon seem to have the effect of undoing the crime implicit in the quarrel. He is not only freed from the burden of his wickedness, but he is reassured that his mother does not remain in deathlike withdrawal. When his mother condemns him, he is liable to feel that this is a just sentence. In yelling dirty words at her he feels that he is implicitly confessing his masturbation and his bad sexual thoughts. The mother responds by calling down the punishment of God on him, and the boy feels that this is what he deserves. Thus his mother remains an external conscience for him, confirming the state of his soul. Mrs. S has no doubts about her own righteousness. She never alternates condemnations of her son with self-accusations. She recalls the respect she had for her own parents and cannot understand the lack of equal respect in her son.

Mrs. L is much less sure of being in the right. She acknowledges that her tolerance or intolerance of Karen's annoying behavior varies with her mood, whether she feels sick or well, or whether she has had a quarrel with her own mother. Karen is outspoken in her conviction that her mother's punishments are not an expression of superior justice but of impulsive feelings. When Mrs. L hits the children, Karen shouts that her mother is a maniac, "She hits because she likes to hit!" Karen never asks for her mother's forgiveness following a quarrel but after a short time "forgets" it (according to the mother) and is affectionate and cheerful again. The mother here is neither a just punisher nor a source of absolution. Just as the quarrel does not assume the significance of a crime, so also it is not a moral drama involving repentance and pardon.

It has been observed that in American families and in American life generally, no one likes to assume a role of authority.[17] A superordinate position makes one feel uneasy. There is a tendency to make all relationships approximate to symmetry. President Eisenhower's favorite news photograph of himself shows him laughingly shaking hands with his small grandson, who bows as the grandfather bows to him.[18] In American families the parents listen to the children rather than requiring the children to listen to them in quiet deference.[19] Parents who do not like to arrogate to themselves a superior authority tend to minimize moral justifications in their handling of their children. This is again reflected in the images of parent-figures in American films. Manifest parents of the hero or heroine are likely to be mild, ineffectual background figures. Characters who stand for the parents in a more disguised way, such as the hero's boss and the boss's wife, are often dangerous, violent, and immoral. Thus the punishing aspect of the parents is separated off as an attack without moral justification.[20] It is in this spirit that Karen takes the occasional angry blows of her mother: "She hits because she likes to hit."

The strong emotions engendered in family conflicts may be a source of intense (though unadmitted) gratification, or they may be felt as a disruption of a desirable façade of calm and efficiency, as senseless and exaggerated reactions, deprecated in retrospect as much ado about nothing. As might be inferred from what we already know, our two mothers differ greatly in their reactions to emotional scenes. Mrs. S preserves and repeatedly relives the intense emotions evoked by familial happenings. As she relates a quarrel with her son, the scene is alive for her, no word or gesture is forgotten, and her tears flow afresh as she exclaims: "I can't stand it, it hurts me, it's killing me." On the manifest level she suffers, but less consciously she enjoys these scenes and is thus impelled to re-evoke them so that she can feel again the gratifying pain which they arouse.

The emotional atmosphere of Mrs. L's discourse is quite different. There are no tears. Mrs. L's characteristic expression is an amused smile, and the tone she assumes as she recounts family upsets is a humorous one. The emotional quality of quarreling scenes is not re-evoked but is transformed in the retelling. In retrospect the feelings of anger and distress (especially of the child—the mother tends to minimize her own) appear unreasonable, disproportionate, absurd. Mrs. L strives to turn upsetting scenes into comic anecdotes. There is less enjoyment here of the painful feelings which a quarrel produces; to derive pleasure from it in retrospect, Mrs. L must transform the emotional tone of the scene and reduce its intensity by treating it humorously. Probably also Mrs. L experiences less pain in the quarrel itself than Mrs. S does, since Mrs. L assumes more the role of an aggressor than of a victim. In so far as quarrels are disturbing for Mrs. L, she tends to blank them out in memory. In her reports there is a displacement of emphasis from the central emotional drama to trivial peripheral details. Thus, if she and Karen have quarreled because she wanted Karen to try on a skirt she was making for her and Karen did not want to interrupt her play, Mrs. L goes into great detail about the pattern and the material she used for the skirt but forgets what she and Karen said to each other in their anger. The angry episode is like an alien thing which has obtruded itself into the reasonable and unemotional tenor of life; Mrs. L rectifies and smoothes over this break by eliminating it in memory.

Suffering is the major theme of Mrs. S's life. When she is not preoccupied with Stan's attacks on her, she recalls the misfortunes of her second son, who, after having started on a brilliant career, got into trouble and ruined his chances. Again and again she remembers with tears his early successes and re-evokes the tragedy of his downfall. "It hurts me, I have such pity on him, I could die." At other times she speaks of her eldest son, who has never caused her any trouble and who is doing quite well. But his wife makes unreasonable demands on him and does not understand him, and he is very hard pressed financially, and again it hurts Mrs. S. When family parties are organized on various occasions, there are always some painful repercussions as someone was not invited who should have been, or someone did not come who should have come, and Mrs. S participates in the hurt feelings which are thus engendered. Every encounter, fraught as it is with intense emotion, assumes a dramatic quality in Mrs. S's telling of it.

There is little of this dramatic quality in Mrs. L's account of her life. As she details the external aspects of events, playing down their emotional undertones, nothing seems very important. One wonders, What really matters here? If one looks for a pervasive theme, one finds it perhaps in the issue about order and disorder. Mrs. L feels that in her parents' house everything was in disorder. Her mother was a bad housekeeper. Innumerable relatives trouped in and out. The family was constantly moving. Nobody ever knew how much money they had. The father gambled. Escaping from this disorder, Mrs. L married an extremely meticulous, fussy, precise, methodical man. However, she is unable to meet successfully his requirements for perfect order; in her there persists an unresolved conflict on this issue. While she does not overtly rebel against her husband's standards, she derives great covert gratification from her daughter Karen's messiness. Over and over she relates Karen's feats of sloppiness. When Karen gets undressed, she leaves one shoe under the kitchen table, the other in the middle of the living-room floor, and so on. Karen eats mashed potatoes with her fingers. When she is supposed to take a bath, she sits in the tub reading a comic book and forgets to wash herself. These and other similar habits of Karen's exasperate her father. While Mrs. L repeatedly complained about them, she laughed so genuinely at the same time that when it was pointed out to her that she vicariously enjoyed Karen's sloppiness, she was able to acknowledge this to be true. Karen's inability to conform to time schedules (getting dressed in the morning, getting to bed at night) is a source of daily conflict, especially with the father.

The mother herself has residual difficulties about punctuality. But she finds relief from her inner conflicts about orderliness by externalizing them; Karen acts out disorderly impulses while the father embodies restraints against them. Mrs. L gives the impression of strong, persistent ambivalence toward early cleanliness training. On the one hand, she rebelled against it, this rebellion being justified by later disillusionment with her parents, who failed to live up to a high standard of orderliness. On the other hand, she felt impelled to strive toward such a standard and sought reinforcement for this striving in her husband. In Karen, understandably enough, there are similar conflicts. At the same time that she is so messy at home, she always has the job of the housekeeper at school. She manifests some very finicky reactions, becoming disgusted to the point of nausea at excretory smells, even her own, and expressing similar disgust at the sight of her little sister picking her nose.

I would suggest the following hypothetical basis for the emotional orientation of these two families. In both cases there seems to be a considerable concentration on motives of the anal phase.[21] But in the S family the sector of these motives which is emphasized is the sadomasochistic one. There are strongly libidinized fantasies of killing and being killed, with the mother's predominant image of herself as suffering and dying because of what her children do to her. In the L family, another sector of anal motives is in the ascendant, namely, those having to do with dirt and messiness and the defensive struggle toward cleanliness, neatness, and order.[22] This conflict between messiness and order lends itself less to melodramatic expressions. It is likely to take the form rather of endless, nonclimactic nagging about petty details. Instead of the tragic maternal reproach, "You are killing me," it is, "Take your bath, Karen. It's already quarter to nine. . . . Karen, take your bath. It's five minutes to nine."

In traditional Jewish culture, strong defenses were erected against aggression. Innumerable rituals guarded against the break-through of aggressive impulses.[23] One may suppose that the impulses thus warded off had a strong sadistic quality. These impulses were to a large extent turned inward. The Jews underwent endless sufferings, which they accepted in a spirit of exalted masochism as inflicted by a God who loved them above all others. This submission to paternal authority was haunted by rebellious impulses which appeared as doubts about religious rules, to which exceptions could always be found; and the doubts were in turn fought back by ever more refined formulations of the rules. The Jewish religion concentrated on regulating relations between men, between a sole father-god and his sons. There are covert indications of sadistic impulses of children toward mothers which also had to be held in check. Thus one motive behind the taboo against eating meat with milk may have been a defense against the impulse of the infant to bite and eat the milk-giving breast. Adam and Eve were expelled from Eden for having eaten the apple (a breast symbol). However, the major emphasis of religious ritual and observance was on male relationships. Women, excluded from study and argumentation about the law, may thus have expressed the same sado-masochistic motives, which men elaborated in highly ritualistic ways, in more free-flowing emotional relations with their children. Men accepted their sufferings from God, women from their children.

This sado-masochistic concentration appears to be absent in American culture. Opportunities for turning aggression outward have been manifold, nor does aggression seem fraught with terrible dangers. The possibility of injuring women has little plausibility where women appear as very strong.[24] On the other hand, cleanliness has been an outstanding American value. Current advertising for soaps and deodorants plays on the doubt about ever achieving perfect bodily cleanliness and the belief that one must be utterly clean in order to be loved. The emphasis on cleanliness training, which here seems so major, is one which involves, on the side of the mother, the image of the child as one who can learn and, on the side of the child, strong conflicts in relation to strict maternal demands.[25] These conflicts have in the past been notably resolved in reaction formations against the original messy impulses, giving rise to the clean, orderly, methodical, hard-working individual, who got things done when they had to be done. At present there is less maternal resoluteness in the demand for cleanliness, and the traditional reaction-formative type of character is no longer in the ascendant. However, I would suggest that there is a certain basic attitude toward excreta which remains the same. Excreta are impersonal things which one has to dispose of in appropriate ways. The relation between mother and child in which things play a major role provides a model for other relationships which are not sheerly between persons, but where persons are mutually involved in the management of things. I would speculate further that where a more sado-masochistic relation prevails, excreta are often equated with beloved persons who have been incorporated and who are being destructively got rid of.[26] This would fit the Eastern European Jewish pattern, in which there are few impersonalized quarrels about the orderly or disorderly management of things but where conflicts tend to have the significance of destroying the opponent.

I have tried to present here two contrasting pictures of some aspects of Eastern European Jewish and American Jewish mother-child relations. The question arises as to how the transition is achieved from the one to the other. Further investigation would be required to provide the answer to this. I have relatively little information about the mother of Mrs. L. From what I know, although she came to this country as a young girl, she seems to have perpetuated the Eastern European model of maternity less than Mrs. S. For instance, she was less anxious about her children and left them more to take care of themselves. As far as the S family is concerned, we can see a marked transition from the Eastern European Jewish pattern in the behavior of the son, in his overt expressions of aggression against the mother. Stan suffers severe conflicts about aggression. He strives to deny the mother's belief that his aggression can kill her. "Nobody ever died of aggravation," he argues. At the same time he tries to justify his aggressive feelings against his parents in terms of what he considers mistreatment in his childhood, and so on. He is striving for the American position that it is permissible to rebel against one's parents. But this remains difficult for him, since in the culture from which the parents come such rebellion is tantamount to murder.

In discussing the L family I have throughout referred to presumable general features of American culture. The question may be asked: What is Jewish in the L family? Here I must bring in the character of the father, whom I have dealt with very little. This father, of Eastern European Jewish origin, appears to exemplify a strong identification with his mother.[27] Thus, since he has been in bad health in recent years, he reproaches Karen for the aggravation she causes him by saying that it will shorten his life. However, he seems to have some conflicts about this, attempting at times to conceal from Karen that he feels exhausted after a prolonged dispute. Mrs. L is outspoken in her condemnation of her husband for attempting to impose such a burden of guilt on the child. Perhaps he realizes vicariously for her her residual masochistic tendencies, which she consciously repudiates. She denies any thoughts that annoyance with Karen can affect her health, and she does not recall any comparable reproaches from her own mother. We may note further that the strong mother–weak father combination which we find in the L family corresponds to a frequent American family constellation.[28] However, the specific qualities of this father, who is physically weak while he remains intellectually superior, have a marked Jewish aspect.

To sum up, we have seen here, in a fragmentary way and with much admittedly speculative interpretation, two contrasting maternal patterns. The Eastern European Jewish mother sees her child at any age as terribly vulnerable, a baby incapable of taking care of himself, who would perish without her constant vigilance. At the same time the baby appears as terribly strong, capable of killing the mother. We saw in this a fixation of the mother on the earliest phase of the child's life, and particularly on the experience of giving birth, and also a tendency to project onto the child the mother's unacknowledged hostility toward him and toward her own mother. The mother is a righteous figure, capable of damning or giving absolution. She is a suffering person, being incessantly wounded and killed and deriving her major unacknowledged emotional gratification in this masochistic way. The American Jewish mother here described sees her child mainly as an independent being, who should stop as quickly as possible being babyish and proceed to acquire skills. A different aspect of the growing child is emphasized, that having to do with learning, and the child is not seen as fragile. The mother acknowledges hostility toward the child and toward her own mother and does not project them onto the child, who is accordingly not seen as self-damaging or as destroying the mother. In the conflicts between mother and child, the mother appears as less surely righteous, and the child can attribute gross unmoralized aggressive impulses to her. This is in keeping with American parents' avoidance of a dominant authoritative role, the tendency toward symmetry in parent-child relations, and the possibility for children to ascribe their own condemned motives to the parents. Instead of the sado-masochistic image of the quarrel as a murder, a central issue is the more impersonalized one about order and disorder. One of the foremost unsolved problems raised by this essay, as a subject for further research, is the question of how the transition from the Eastern European Jewish to the American Jewish family is achieved.

NOTES

1. Zborowski and Herzog, 1952; also unpublished material in the files of Columbia University Research in Contemporary Cultures.

2. I refer to observations made during several years as a school psychologist in private schools in New York City, where the large majority of the families were American Jewish; also to other cases at the Jewish Board of Guardians.

3. Unpublished material in the files of Columbia University Research in Contemporary Cultures.

4. See "Fun Morality" in this volume (p. 168); also Wolfenstein, 1953.

5. Zborowski and Herzog, 1952.

6. An alternative has been observed to the tendency of this type of mother to see the child as always the same, namely, for the mother to hark back to the time of his early childhood as a golden age from which he has subsequently declined. It would seem that these two attitudes can also coexist: the child appearing invariant as far as health is concerned (always fragile and needing vigilant care) but changing in respect to goodness, becoming less loving toward the mother, less exclusively preoccupied with pleasing her.

7. Cf. Coleman, Kris, and Provence, 1953.

8. Infant mortality, however, is not decisive for the view that children are very fragile. Many deep-lying fantasies contribute to the image of the child as weak or strong (cf. "Image of the Child in Contemporary Films" in this volume, p. 277).

9. *Infant Care*, 1945 and 1951.

10. Gorer, 1948.

11. Information about Eastern European Jewish mothers indicates much verbal expression of ambivalence toward their children. "In the mother's moods, opposites are almost simultaneous. If the child pesters her . . . her sharp 'devil take you!' or 'go into the ground!' will merge swiftly into a blessing, 'you shall grow strong and healthy for me!' " (Zborowski and Herzog, 1952, p. 334). Presumably in such swift undoing of the expression of a hostile wish, the mother did not allow herself to become aware of its significance. When the child turns such expressions of hostility back toward the mother (this being apparently an American development), her overwhelming sense of the seriousness of these words derives some of its force from her own unacknowledged hostility toward the child (as well as toward her own mother) which she projects. When the child says, "Drop dead!" the mother's reaction that this can kill her may not be a direct attribution of magical force to the words but rather the feeling that if the child is hostile toward her, this so wounds her to the heart that she can die. In the case of Mrs. S, it seems that she does on her side curse her son when provoked, but she does not acknowledge any feeling but that of wounded love toward him; her curses do not carry the force that his do.

12. This fantasy, that the mother will suffer and die if the son's self-damaging tendencies are carried through, may express an expiation: as if the mother unconsciously acknowledges her projected hostile tendencies and feels she must pay for them.

13. Zborowski and Herzog, 1952.

14. *Ibid.*

15. In contrast to this, typical quarrels in the S family are more narrowly focused in her mother-son relation. At a word from the mother—"Button your jacket" or "You should get some sleep now"—Stan flies into a rage—"Don't treat me like a baby!"—and the fight is on. Where, as in the L family, a larger sector of the external world is likely to be included in the terms of the quarrel, a greater sense of reality guards against the intrusion of melodramatic fantasies.

16. Wolfenstein and Leites, 1950.

17. Gorer, 1948.

18. *New York Times Magazine*, 1954.

19. Bateson, 1942.

20. Wolfenstein and Leites, 1950.
21. Freud, 1942*a*; Abraham, 1942; Jones, 1948.
22. In a similar way Rudolph Loewenstein (1951) contrasts German and Jewish characters, finding in the Germans a preponderance of defenses against dirtiness, in the Jews the concentration of defenses against aggression.
23. Freud, 1942*b*.
24. Similarly, one may contrast the attitudes toward women in British and American films. The British preoccupation with the danger of unleashing sadistic impulses toward women and the need to guard against such impulses find no counterpart in American films, where women are more than able to take care of themselves (cf. Wolfenstein and Leites, 1950).
25. Wolfenstein, 1953.
26. Cf. the little boy cited by Karl Abraham (1942, p. 427) who, when angry with his nurse, threatened to "ka-ka" her over the river. "According to the child's view the way to get rid of a person one no longer liked was by means of defecation."
27. As indicative of Mr. L's maternal identification, he says that he feels tied to Karen by an umbilical cord (when she is very demanding of his attention and he feels he cannot get away from her) and that he feels as if she had drained all the milk out of him (when he is exhausted by her demands).
28. Bibring, 1953.

LIST OF REFERENCES

ABRAHAM, KARL. 1942. *Selected Papers of Karl Abraham*. Translated by D. BRYANT and A. STRACHEY. London: Hogarth Press and Institute of Psychoanalysis.

BATESON, GREGORY. 1942. "Morale and National Character." In *Civilian Morale*, ed. GOODWIN WATSON, pp. 71–91. Boston: Houghton Mifflin Co.

BIBRING, GRETE. 1953. "On the 'Passing of the Oedipus Complex' in a Matriarchal Family Setting." In *Drives, Affects, Behavior*, ed. RUDOLPH LOEWENSTEIN, pp. 278–84. New York: International Universities Press.

COLEMAN, ROSE W., KRIS, ERNST, and PROVENCE, SALLY. 1953. "The Study of Variations of Early Parental Attitudes." In *The Psychoanalytic Study of the Child*, VIII, 20–47.

"Eisenhower's Favorite Picture of Himself," *New York Times Magazine*. January 10, 1954, cover photograph.

FREUD, SIGMUND. 1942*a*. "Character and Anal Eroticism." In *Collected Papers*, Vol. II. London: Hogarth Press and Institute of Psychoanalysis.

———. 1942*b*. "Obsessive Acts and Religious Practices," *ibid.*

GORER, GEOFFREY. 1948. *The American People: A Study in National Character*. New York: W. W. Norton & Co.

Infant Care. 1945 and 1951. Children's Bureau, Washington, D.C.

JONES, ERNEST. 1948. "Anal-erotic Character Traits," *Papers on Psychoanalysis*, pp. 413–37. London: Baillière, Tindall & Cox.

LOEWENSTEIN, RUDOLPH. 1951. *Christians and Jews: A Psychoanalytic Study*. New York: International Universities Press.

WOLFENSTEIN, MARTHA. 1953. "Trends in Infant Care," *American Journal of Orthopsychiatry*, XXIII, No. 1, 120–30.

WOLFENSTEIN, MARTHA, and LEITES, NATHAN. 1950. *Movies: A Psychological Study*. Glencoe, Ill.: Free Press.

ZBOROWSKI, MARK, and HERZOG, ELIZABETH. 1952. *Life Is with People: The Jewish Little Town in Eastern Europe*. New York: International Universities Press.

PART VIII

Epilogue

CHAPTER 25

Implications of Insight—I

————————————MARTHA WOLFENSTEIN

WITH the great increase in our understanding of children in the present century, there has naturally gone the urgent wish to incorporate knowledge gained into practices of child rearing. However, there are many difficulties involved in this process. The practical implications of our findings are often far from being unambiguous. In the transmission from experts to parents and teachers, there may be misunderstandings, distortions, one-sided emphases. The resolve to change when one thinks one has learned a better way is not so easy. Behavior in adult-child relations is deeply rooted in strong and incompletely conscious feelings, not readily controllable by conscious good intentions. Optimistic espousal of a better way of doing things may be followed by backslidings and self-reproach.

One of the too confident expectations of educated modern parents has been that, having become aware that certain experiences involve emotional hardship for a child, they have hoped by proper management to make these experiences completely painless. Mothers, for instance, who have learned that the coming of a new baby makes the older child feel excluded have adopted devices by which the child can feel he participates—in letting him take part in preparing the bassinette and baby clothes beforehand, in telling him that it is "our baby—yours and Daddy's and mine," and so on. Such awareness and such efforts on the part of the mother may indeed help to mitigate the child's sibling rivalry. But what some mothers find it hard to accept is that they do not succeed in totally eliminating these feelings in the child. The understanding, sensitive, and sympathetic adult can help the child to master his emotional conflicts, to achieve constructive solutions of them, but cannot with any amount of understanding and management vouchsafe the child exemption from the emotional difficulties which are part of his development.

In discussing the emotional development of children with both graduate students in psychology and young psychiatrists in training, I have found the same recurrent reaction. In confronting the emotional complications of each phase of development, they repeatedly raise the question whether somehow—say, if the mother is sufficiently "accepting" or sufficiently "relaxed"—the child might not slip through this phase without any intense feeling about it. A life-model seems to be envisaged in which development might be free of conflict, smooth and bland. This view is related partly to a one-sided emphasis on the hazards of morbidity which early conflicts entail. The complementary point is less well realized: that it is just the successful resolution of these conflicts which provides the basis for normal, socially useful, happy, and creative character.

Does this mean that our insight into the exigencies of development has no practical application? If through understanding of the child's difficulties we can help to mitigate them or help him toward constructive solutions, such an achievement, though more modest than a total elimination of problems, is not to be despised. The successful incorporation of insight into practice involves a recognition of the limits within which human nature can be altered. With such recognition, the unconscious demands which parents and educators make on themselves to be omnipotent can be moderated in the direction of the reality principle. This is an outcome which can reduce much disappointment of the adult in himself and in the child. The ability to accept certain human limitations can contribute to tolerance, patience, and affection.

The tolerance which is based on insight, however, is the hardest to achieve. What is easier is a tolerance made possible by closing one's eyes to what is difficult to accept. In recent years there has been a drastic reduction of severity in adults' handling of children's impulsive tendencies. But this increased benevolence has been achieved on the basis of a peculiarly bowdlerized conception of the child's nature. We have here the phenomenon of tolerance operating to ward off insight or being purchased at the expense of insight. In the early part of the century, children's pleasure drives, as expressed, for instance, in autoeroticism, were estimated as being intense and vehement, at the same time that an unremitting struggle against these impulses was advocated. At present we find a tendency to reverse both these positions. Children's pleasure strivings should not be interfered with. The vigilant fight which used to be waged against thumb-sucking, for instance, is regarded as an archaic cruelty. But such benevolence is made safe by a revised view of the child's nature. The child's impulses are described as diffuse, moderate, and harmless. Autoerotic activities are an incident in the child's "exploration of his world." The advice, "Give the child a toy to play with, and he will not have to play with himself," assumes that the intense and focalized strivings for erogenous pleasure, formerly acknowledged and forthrightly stigmatized as "wicked," do not really exist. Thus we have had severity combined with a truer recognition of the force of children's impulses, followed by a rejection of severity which is accompanied by a denial of the intensity of children's impulse life.

The rapid changes in attitudes toward children which have occurred in the present century have involved an equally quick forgetting of rejected beliefs and practices. When one recalls these developments, as, for instance, the changing attitudes about thumb-sucking, college students ask in amazement why thumb-sucking was ever considered wrong and find it hard to believe that stringent measures against it were being advocated by major authorities only fifteen years ago. This forgetting of fairly recent history is of the same order as the repression of painful experiences of one's own childhood. Many of the shifts in attitudes and practices in child rearing bear witness to unresolved ambivalence, where first one side and then the other of conflicting feelings comes to the surface. In a changing culture like our own, many things, particularly in the sphere of material artifacts—outmoded home furnishings, the old car that has been traded in for a newer model—are easily relegated to disuse. But in the sphere of human relations what is rejected of the past is liable to leave continuing residues, which work in us in ways which are the more difficult to control the less we recognize their presence. From this point of view, awareness of past trends in child rearing in our own culture is a prerequisite to the working-through to real conviction of reasoned preferences, a potential safeguard against oscillation and inconsistency.

If we recall the cliché that love is likely to be associated with a rather low degree of realism about its object, it may help us to understand the apparent paradox that benevolence toward children frequently works against insight into their needs. A further illustration of this paradox appears in connection with the very sympathizable trend toward increasing respect for children which has appeared so markedly in the present century. Infants have rights. Children are people. Their interests, their wishes, their dreams, must be cherished and fostered, not crushed under the weight of extraneous adult standards. Their first paintings proudly brought home from nursery school are accorded a place of honor on the living-room, or anyhow the dining-room, wall. Growing respect for children is a complicated development. It is involved with the wish on the part of adults to distinguish themselves less and less from children (the look-alike look in mother's and daughter's dresses, etc.). If one compares photographs of nineteenth-century and twentieth-century American men in public life, one is struck by the deeply lined, ponderous, old look of the former as against the bland, smooth boyishness of the latter. The degree of transformation from child to man has become markedly reduced. One could cite many evidences of this, as in the continued role of play at all stages of life.

Respect for children and decreasing differentiation of child and adult combine with another tendency: the increasing unwillingness of adults to assume a role of authority. "Authority" has become almost a derogatory term. Father wants to be a pal; teacher, a friend. What has been in the past, and still remains in other cultures, a complementary relation between adult and child tends to approximate a symmetrical one. This again is a very complicated phenomenon. The values on which firm adult authority was formerly based have been becoming more uncertain. Adults have been growing more sensitive to, and intolerant of, the anger and rebelliousness which restrictions they impose provoke in children. There follows a solicitous attempt to comply with children's wishes. If it is felt that children would rather read comics than the Scriptures, religious comics are produced and made the texts for Sunday school pupils.

Some of the practices of modern nursery schools, in which many teachers have shown an admirable sympathy and feeling for children, have also exemplified a specious egalitarianism, which belies the true relation between child and adult. Since the teacher calls the children by their first names, she tells the children to call her by her first name. Going a step further, one nursery-school teacher invited the children to call her by a nickname, which was a mocking play on her real name. This precipitated an avalanche of still more mocking nicknames which the children, with this encouragement, readily improvised. Such a teacher seems to express a fear of children's solidarity among themselves against even a loved authority. If the children are going to make fun of her, she wants to be in on it, and even to initiate it. There is a convention of nursery-school parlance according to which rules are formulated in terms of "we"—"We don't hit," for example. Implicit in this formulation is the adult's inclusion of himself in the rules he communicates to the children, as if to say: I am not imposing something on you, we are in this together. But this is in effect a falsification of the relation of child and adult.

The findings of psychoanalytic child psychology stress that the child needs and wants the adult's help in controlling his impulses (even though he often protests against the same restraints). He needs the assurance that his incompletely established inner controls will get firm external support against impulses which he fears will run away with him. And he needs to feel that the adult has achieved a more sure mastery of impulses. The adult is not in the same position as the child in relation to the rules, nor does the child want him to be. Thus the egalitarian tendencies of adults express a one-sided perception of children's feelings toward authority. They show a hypersensitivity toward children's rebelliousness, a wish to be exempted from it, together with an insufficient awareness of children's need for strong adult support in their struggle to achieve inner mastery. (These remarks are not intended as in any way a complete account of current nursery-school practices—the necessity of "setting limits" has been increasingly acknowledged since the earlier days of progressive education. Certain tendencies in nursery-school procedures, which are by no means peculiar to this area of education, are simply cited as illustrative of a significant trend.)

I have been speaking of the tendency for benevolence to entail a certain blindness. I should now like to consider an opposite tendency, that of the overuse or misuse of insight, often in the service of covert hostility. Psychoanalytic psychology has sharpened our awareness of complex and incompletely conscious motives in the persons around us. The better part of discretion in most relationships is not to communicate to the objects of our observation what we have perceived or think we have perceived in them. Insight or presumed insight can be damaging if communicated indiscriminately. An instance of this is a certain type of mother who has picked up a smattering of psychoanalytic psychology and hastily applies it to her child.[1] She proceeds to give interpretations like: "You hate Mother," whenever the child is resistant or angry. This is utterly bewildering to the child, who consciously feels that he loves his mother, who is struggling to hold down the negative sector of his ambivalence toward her, and needs the support of her confidence in his love. The child broods about the unintelligible dicta of his mother, becomes lost in uncertainty and terrified of the whole sphere of feeling. He may later choose narrowly mechanical occupations as the only ones secure against emotional hazards.

We might suggest that the making explicit of insight about another person is risky in any situation where the person has not sought it and where the relationship is not a free and voluntary one. A therapeutic situation is safeguarded in this respect because it is one where insight is sought, if not welcomed, and where there is a free choice about pursuing the relationship. The relationship between friends is also a free one in this sense, and one in which at times insight may be sought and found. But relations between parents and children or husbands and wives are, in the first case, not chosen and, in the second, of more or less lasting commitment. To use as an example the kind of insight mentioned before, the exposure of one partner by the other as being hostile, in ways he himself does not recognize, works against the stabilization of positive feelings. Such communications are liable to be experienced not as a gain in insight but as a hurtful accusation, an expression of the overeager interpreter's own hostility.

To combine insight with discretion and kindness is a difficult accomplishment. Good feelings do not necessarily increase understanding. Rather, as I have tried to indicate, they often involve blind spots or distortions. On the other hand, perspicuity about concealed traits may occur in combination with negative sentiments toward the persons observed. Freud was remarkable, among other things, for the respect he expressed for his patients as well as for the strange tendencies of the human mind which he uncovered. In his case histories he is sometimes outspoken in his good opinion of the human qualities of his patients—a way of feeling less noticeable in many more recent analytic writers. As to the underlying motives in human nature, the obscure dream world so opposite to conscious reason and morality which he illuminated, he saw in it the stuff of great tragedy and high comedy. Here clarity of vision and positive feeling for human nature were combined.

If I have spoken of some of the difficulties of assimilating insight into practice, it is not with any discouraging intent. It is only by a clear awareness of problems that we may be able to solve them.

NOTES

1. I am indebted for the following observations to an unpublished paper of Mary O'Neil Hawkins, read at a psychoanalytic convention in Atlantic City in the spring of 1952.

CHAPTER 26

Implications of Insight—II

————————————————————————MARGARET MEAD

W E MAY approach the question of the implications of insight from the standpoint of theory and research: What are the unsolved problems, the next steps in research, the untapped possibilities for analysis by present methods, etc? Or we may approach it from the standpoint of practice: How will this kind of insight enable us to alter our cultural practices in relationships within the family between parents and children and among brothers and sisters, in pediatrics, in nursery schools and elementary schools, in clinic and hospital, in the production of children's books and children's programs, in educating for membership in a world community, in ways in which we introduce children to religion, and in the ways in which we cherish and cultivate the creative responses of all children and the creative abilities of the specially gifted?

The last half-century has been a period of insight into the dynamic processes of growth and character development,[1] into the involvement of the whole organism in any particular activity or expression. We have realized that reading retardation might be due to fear or unanswered questions, that allergies might result from psychological conflicts,[2] that psychological conflicts might result from a physical defect in sphincter control, and that the whole familial process was a transactional one in which the "rejecting baby"—due to a physiological inability to attain satisfaction—was as real as a "rejecting mother," with the response system of each suffering, regardless of whether one was an infant and the other an adult.[3] Gradually also our thinking about the way in which character was formed expanded from the immediate influences of parents face to face with an intractable organism, to a realization that these parents were themselves part of larger wholes which could be analyzed into neighborhoods, communities, the wider society. From these wholes, in turn, particular situations could be identified, peculiar constellations of individuals, neighborhoods, school groups, which were the necessary—but not the sufficient—conditions of special kinds of behavior, in children and in adults.

We learned to recognize the child who chose a criminal career that put him at odds with society, but who did so not because he himself was at odds with parents and companions but because he was so much in tune with them. We saw that, born in a criminal neighborhood, he wanted to be like those around him;[4] and we learned to distinguish such a delinquent child from one who entered delinquency through his conflicts with his human environment or through extra degrees of energy for which there was no outlet or by fantasies elaborated in loneliness leading ultimately to crime.[5] We learned also to recognize the child—or the adult—who responded to special combinations of circumstances by becoming obese[6] or refusing to eat, and to recognize the especially maternal woman who, frustrated in her desire for children and finally becoming a mother, became an overly protective one. The special conditions for development created by the position of only, oldest, youngest, middle child, by the presence of grandparents in the home, by accidents of relative size and strength between brothers and sisters, have been explored. The interweaving between constitutional factors, chronological age, and social pressures and expectations for a given age and type of child have been charted, with special emphasis on the implications for adolescent development of being physically retarded or accelerated.[7]

As these fields of research have been opened up and the knowledge so gained has been fed into the groups of practitioners, physicians, educators, journalists—most of whom are also parents, so that their experience as parents is fed back into their professional practice—people's ability to use the new knowledge has been continuingly refined. The first response to any of these new insights is often crude and wholesale. If children learned with such incredible plasticity at an early age, shouldn't all their learning be carefully controlled from the start so that children would be conditioned not to want to break dishes or cry when it was inconvenient? If children were worried about sex, wasn't the answer simply to tell them the truth? If infants who were separated from their mothers or exposed to a whole discontinuous series of mother-figures or left alone in a strange hospital showed identifiable signs of emotional damage, wasn't the answer to tie mother and child so firmly together that they were never separated? If there was certain behavior characteristic of "the sixes," wasn't it sufficient to tell parents to expect six-year-olds to kick other people under the table and substitute bedroom slippers for shoes? If constitution was the clue to the age at which a child could read, wasn't the proper response simply diagnosis and waiting for the right age rather than changing the methods of teaching reading? If every adult individual who was subjected to psychoanalysis showed unmistakable signs of having been traumatized by his attempt to deal with some of his childhood experiences which had become unconscious—unavailable except through certain specified operations—wasn't the answer to have all children analyzed young or, if this was impracticable, to construct educational situations in which the early conflicts could be "acted out," as biters were per-mitted to bite, head-bangers to bang at the nursery-school teacher, ex-hibitionism given full play? There were even bolder suggestions: that, as parental upbringing was obviously the cause of most of the trouble in human character, the less there was of it, the better—a point of view which was vigorously defended from the parents' side by George Ber-nard Shaw and adopted as a revolutionary tactic in totalitarian coun-tries seeking artificially to hasten the development of a generation with a different character structure.

All these one-sided proposals—enthusiastic attempts to apply the new knowledge, to free the next generation, to prevent the present adult generation from making the mistakes their parents had made—were particularly congruent with the values of those societies which were oriented forward toward the children of the future, and in which the parents were conceived as able to do almost anything they willed with the child. As expected, there was more widespread acceptance of these ideas in the United States and Germany than in England and France.

Only gradually have we come to realize the complexity of such ap-plications of insight to changed social procedures, the extent to which the whole culture and the whole society must be taken into account, the limitations on innovation given by the extent to which the innovat-ing adults are genuine members of their own culture, able to reinterpret and reorganize the more drastic recommendations.[8] We have slowly come to realize also that insights which are based on trauma, failure, casualties of all sorts are at best only half the story; that we can make no complete plans without a second set of insights based on blessing, gift, success, upon a study of those happy combinations which produce something more than mere "adjustment"; and that from experience the growing child gains not only wounds and vulnerabilities but also extra strengths and blessings.[9]

We are coming to a new appreciation of the relationship between "culture" and "nature," of the ways in which our systems of learned behavior are safer than a reliance upon biological equipment, as well as to an appreciation of the hazard in the denial of the biologically given—as in a refusal to recognize the sexual awareness of the young child, its ability to receive lasting impressions in early infancy, or the differences among children in their readiness to use their eyes for read-ing, or to leave home. So even though there is evidence that breast feeding is extremely felicitous for some mothers and some children, bottle feeding increases the survival potential for all babies. Even though children, especially in extreme circumstances, may be able to select a good diet[10] or find a missing chemical on which their lives de-pend,[11] a culturally patterned diet, with a wide allowance for individual differences built into it, is the best safeguard for the nutrition of all children.[12] Even though some children thrive alone in a home with their mothers in a perfect rhythm of interaction, most mothers need a rest from their children, and most children need the safety of several parental substitutes to widen their world of choice and increase their sense of a world which is not so vulnerable as the individual home.

The comparative study of cultures has played a significant role in introducing this sort of balance into our enthusiastic attempts to revise our methods of child care. Anthropologists have pointed out that problems arising from the conflict between a child's impulses toward a parent of opposite sex, while important, can be solved in a variety of ways and that each way—by extending the family, placing the mother in a mother-role to her husband, elevating the small boy into a position of real rivalry to his father, introducing grandparents or siblings as buffers—carries with it its own rewards and its own penalties.

Studies of culture have emphasized the use of comparative studies to separate the biological uniformities from the cultural elaboration of those uniformities and so have made it possible to avoid the kind of naïveté of the twenties which could invoke a child's biological need for a "wet diaper." As the economists have played a useful role in stressing the economic consequences of any change in home life or educational practice, the need for looking at the costs and the practicability of any plan as well as its advantages, the cultural anthropologists and the sociologists who take culture into account have stressed the importance of balancing losses and gains,[13] of not misconstruing the effects of a certain procedure at a given time and place as universal.[14] They have warned—and clinical studies have borne this out—that attempting to introduce a rigid mother to a permissive routine may do more damage than permitting her to continue her more congenial routinizing of life[15] and that any procedure which is too far from the accepted behavior of the members of a culture will be subtly reinterpreted and bowdlerized. So we have such instances as the mothers who objected to reading their children stories about birth because they had told them all that and there "was no need to bring it up again";[16] the grandmother of twenty-four grandchildren who described "self-demand" feeding and getting rid of all that trouble about schedules so that babies now "eat three meals a day like everybody else"; the nutritionists who rejected well-documented proof that people could be induced to eat the right food by clever arrangements of cafeterias, menus, prices, and ordering devices because people *ought* to learn to want the right food.[17] In the Soviet Union a concerted governmental attack on swaddling was accompanied by such devices as cutting holes in a large nursery table and inserting the babies in the holes;[18] in Germany the new nursery-school practices of greater premissiveness in toilet training were accompanied by tying the child's little potty to a table leg, as a way of making the child sit still.

As cultural change became a systematic field of study, we realized also that it was necessary to use the cultural approach to think several steps ahead of any change in practice. We were able to identify such fiascos as the application of nursery-school techniques—designed to free the overneat children of middle-class urban homes by letting them mess with finger paints—to the deprived children from the disorderly, patternless homes of migrant workers. What these children really needed were the satisfying routines of the old kindergarten—itself an institution invented to deal with deprived children and which, when imported into middle-class education, had proved too mechanical and too routinized.

As we endeavored to develop an ethic which would guide our attempts at altering cultural practice, the insistence upon taking responsibility for all foreseeable events became a model.[19] So clinicians developed self-precautionary measures against giving parents or teachers more raw insight than they could take,[20] learned how to work indirectly through literature and the gradual building of a climate of opinion, how to rely on the strengths in the culture, especially on the alteration which takes place in parents who practice small changes in procedure, and in the strengths which appear in the children who have been exposed to these slight changes and become, in turn, the carriers of the new approach. So the mother who knows that her child's cold *may* be related to her child's not wanting to go to school and takes the trouble to investigate the situation at school a little more fully is a factor in her child's becoming less guilty about having such a cold. Her inquiry stimulates the teacher to consider aspects of the schoolroom situation which have been neglected; the safety of this child and other children is increased. But the mother who has just learned that colds are "psychosomatic," which she thinks means psychic in origin, thus quite effectively destroying the usefulness of a word which was coined to represent the circular processes within the body, runs the risk not only of her own child's developing pneumonia but, by the one-sidedness of her approach, of stimulating countercurrents of resistance in parents, teachers, and physicians, who then insist that no cold is ever psychic in origin.

The magnificent promise of progressive education has been dimmed by those who incorporated a rebellion against and hatred of their own society into their plans for freeing children to learn more spontaneously. Pediatricians who share the cultural belief in the need to teach self-control have twisted the invention of a self-regulatory schedule—a genuinely new invention by which, with modern recording instruments, we could adjust schedules to the baby's rhythm instead of forcing a premature adjustment to ours—to a method of spoiling the baby by giving it its own way.

I should like now to discuss three experiments, of varying degrees of success, which attempted to interject insights on the psychobiological development of the child into the main streams of the culture.

The first was a project called "Modern Children's Stories,"[21] which was designed to produce children's books in which text and illustration would be written by genuinely gifted, creative people, embodying the prescription of a group of specialists, child psychiatrists, psychologists, and cultural anthropologists interested in children and the arts. It was in this project that Dr. Wolfenstein and I first worked together. Our premises were these: We know a great deal about children's needs today which will ordinarily not filter into the general climate of opinion for another fifteen or twenty years. By that time the children themselves may need something quite different. Couldn't we short-cut this situation by translating directly from the most advanced insights, based on clinical work with children in 1945, into publications for children in 1946–47? There was recognition that good books are not written to prescription; the plan was that we establish liaison with writers and artists through individuals at home in both the arts and the social sciences, who would absorb the theoretical prescriptions and translate them into ideas which would be stimulating to the artistic imagination. The expert group selected the preparation of a little girl for the birth of a younger sibling as the first topic and wrote a thoroughly pedestrian prescription of what the child should be told, what problems should be dealt with—like the mother's shrinking lap space and shortening temper, the child's enjoyment of being left alone with her father while mother was in the hospital. The story when written was a charming fantasy in which the routine prescriptions were well buried beneath the story of a little girl who consoled herself with a mythical creature called a "rampatan"—her parents could have a baby, but she could have a rampatan, and a rampatan could be anything she wished: it could swim, it could fly, it could have the head of one creature and the body of another.

We then arranged to test this story out with a group of mothers and children. The children were studied first in play situations; the mothers, after group preparation, read the story to the children. Children and mothers were reinterviewed separately and in groups. The children responded positively to the story, but the mothers were critical. Alterations in the story were made to meet the mothers' objections—they objected particularly to any indication that pregnant women were ever tired and cross, and they wanted more emphasis on what the mother could do to get the child to prepare for the baby. During this experimental phase it became clear that a story which met the fantasy needs of the child did not meet the fantasy needs of the mother. We wanted to help the child by telling it a story in a warm atmosphere in which the mother herself read about mothers being cross, and to help it accept its mother's irritability, but the mothers wanted stories about women who were never irritable, who did a perfect job of pregnancy.

The story itself presented a further complication; it was really a father's fantasy, the expression of a man's ability to create in art rather than through childbearing. This gave the story its charm, but it complicated responses. When we reached the next stages, more trouble developed. The artist who could do delightful drawings of the rampatan couldn't produce equally satisfactory illustrations of real people. The members of the interested institutions who had never borne children, both men and women, said the story would frighten women because it would suggest that a woman might bear a monster (women who had borne children did not advance this objection). Furthermore, for general acceptance of the project it was clear that a children's department of a publishing firm, equipped to meet the high standards of text and art which we had set, would have to accept the story, and also that children's librarians and advisers on children's reading from various lay and religious organizations and agencies would also have to understand and indorse the project.

As we tried the story out at these various levels, it became increasingly clear that, after all, five-year-old children don't buy books and that the children's needs or preferences had to be mediated by layers of other people—mothers, fathers, grandmothers, aunts, librarians, publishers, bookstore buyers, experts—all of whom had a full quota of fears and hope and a much more substantial quota of firmly intrenched values and prejudices than the children for whom the story had been designed. Even with accurate diagnosis of these problems in all their psychological and cultural depth, it was not possible to cut through them, to design a story, consciously and intentionally, which would deal with them. The cultural process by which artists and writers, sensitive to changing values, prefigure those values in their work and the guardians of public taste and morals accept and reject what they produce had proved to be too complex and sensitive for such self-conscious activity.

A comparable and more successful attempt at combining specialist insight with production was made by the Community Players of the American Theatre Wing. This was a wartime invention in communication which has developed into a valuable adjunct to community education programs. It began with the preparation of plays to be presented by volunteer actors and actresses which would stress some part of the volunteer effort. A committee was formed which included specialists in psychological and cultural problems, and this group worked with the script writers and actors in developing themes and suggesting ways of handling them. The final plays were professionally written and professionally acted but usually presented to groups who knew one another, church groups, union locals, etc., thus keeping some of the type of audience response associated with community amateur theatricals while preserving the high standards to which radio and screen have accustomed the American public. Later a mental health series was developed, which included planned discussion after the play. Since the war, the Community Players have developed plays which stress particular educational needs, such as information about cancer or tuberculosis, which serve the public relations interests of particular fund-raising organizations, and other plays on problems of adolescence, parent-child relations, family relations, etc., which, combined with discussion, have proved exceedingly successful.[22]

At first sight, this venture looks very much like the "Modern Children's Stories" plan. But there are certain significant differences. The whole procedure was less formal, there was more reliance on teamwork which involved all the stages of the process, the cultural and psychological experts worked directly with the script writers, with the producers, and, in the case of plays written for organizations, with the educational specialist involved. In the "Modern Children's Stories" project there was teamwork in developing the prescription, but the writers and artists were not involved in the initial process. Secondly, the directed spontaneous discussion after the presentation of the play reduced the amount of contrived, articulate self-consciousness involved and permitted each presentation and discussion a degree of freedom which was not possible with a book which had to stand alone in a minimum edition of 25,000 copies. Without the discussion, these carefully and creatively planned plays also miscarry. The play on cancer had as its plot the theme of a young mother who is told she has cancer; in her despair she tells her brother, who then tells her that medical therapy is possible, that his own wife has had cancer, and that it has been arrested. When a large group of students saw this play and reacted to it without discussion, they simply displaced the secrecy point against which the play was directed and insisted that the young woman should have been told but that she should now keep it secret from her husband and children.

It is possible to build in checks on such miscarriages when discussion is used, but a very large number of uncontrollable factors remain, such as how to evoke emotions which will not in turn arouse defenses. Presentations in which only conscious and approved social purposes are dealt with and there is no invocation of the fears and wishes which have been relegated to the unconscious as the child grew up are characteristic of most literature designed to admonish and instruct—in education, public health, mental hygiene, etc.—and are responsible for the typical audience response of boredom and apathy, which is only relieved, as it is in the average modern church, for those who share the exact purposes and enjoy listening to a preacher telling them that their conscience structure is functioning. In contrast, these Community Players' projects may be said to be a constructive, dramatic attempt to introduce an insight in such a way as to leave the imagination of writer, producer, actor, and audience partly free and spontaneous.

A third attempt to relate increased insight into the psychological needs of parents and children to practice was made at the International Seminar on Mental Health and Infant Development which was held at Chichester, England, in the summer of 1952.[23] In this seminar, a multidisciplinary team of psychiatrists, anthropologists, psychologists, nurses, and social caseworkers from three cultures—English, French, and American—using case materials collected by multidisciplinary teams in each of these three cultures, led a seminar of child specialists from many countries, ranging in type from Thailand to Britain, Puerto Rico to France, Turkey to the United States. The participants represented a variety of disciplines, many different statuses, from heads of national services to junior research workers; their training was at many different levels of scientific sophistication. There were psychiatrists who had come to learn, who found instead that they must learn how to impart their insights to other disciplines; there were organically oriented medical men who had never considered the importance of cultural conditioning; there were representatives of countries newly sharing in the scientific traditions of the West; and there were pediatricians, proud of a profession which would supersede the hit-or-miss character of maternal care.

The principal theme of the conference was the mental-health implications of the mother-child relationship, especially as it was expressed in formal arrangements surrounding pregnancy, preparation for motherhood, delivery, breast feeding, and care during the early months of the child's life. The issues on which the seminar might have foundered were many and various: by the pediatricians resenting the emphasis on the mother, the medical specialists resenting the inclusion of nonmedical specialties, by the less industrialized countries either resenting the dominance of the more industrialized or insisting rigidly on newly learned procedures, male specialists resenting women specialists, European countries opposing the United States, and vice versa. Yet, although all these tensions were present, none of them assumed sufficient proportions to threaten the success of the seminar. Instead it became an instrument for diffusing rapidly the most recent insights on mother-child relations, of warning countries which had no hospital care for obstetrics and pediatrics against repeating the mistakes of the United

States and the United Kingdom, of broadening and deepening the perceptions of the Westerners by contacts with the East.

This success can be laid in part, I believe, to the way in which the cultural approach was imbedded in the planning and the way cultural materials were used throughout the seminar. The faculty was designed to be tricultural, with an explicit recognition of the dangers which could arise if two cultural groups confronted each other and the safeties that could be built in by embodying in the leadership group different types of cultural understanding and contrast, as the Americans and English communicated on the basis of language, the English and French as Europeans, etc. The materials of the seminar were organized with explicit cultural reference, each individual child firmly placed in his culture and society. The use of two languages—English and French —with simultaneous interpretation, kept us continually aware of the extent to which every concept we used was culture-bound and culture-limited, while the use of films made us equally aware that all children shared a common humanity.

The seminar was opened by a short comparative film on *Bathing Babies in Three Cultures*[24]—in New Guinea, the United States, and Bali—which dealt definitely, but not explicitly, with the questions of racial and cultural differences, which had to be combined with an emphasis on the common elements in child development everywhere. There was no need to preach about the importance of cultural learning when "savages," traditionally supposed to be so much more "natural" than modern man, were shown going through routines which were obviously traditional and learned. There was no need to discuss the comparability of nations of different levels of civilization when a film of a nearly naked mother bathing a baby in a crocodile-infested river was placed side by side—on a basis of strict comparability—with bathing a baby in an American middle-class bathroom.

Toward the middle of the seminar, as counterpoint to the emphasis on scientific analytical procedures, I presented a film on *Dance and Trance in Bali*, with music, showing how the Balinese ritual fitted together with and re-enhanced the experience of Balinese childhood.[25] At the end of the seminar, the students presented a skit on this film in which they, as the Balinese do, treated their problems symbolically. The implicit resentment of the main theme of the great and neglected importance of the mother-child relationship—a theme difficult for experts, all of whom were in one way attempting to replace the mothering role—was elaborated under the heading of the neglected father. By increasing the emphasis on the pregnant woman and the witch—which are both played by men in Bali—they produced a pregnant father and a powerful male figure. By their final decision not to have someone play me, but instead to ask me to play myself—anthropologist with a coffee grinder instead of a movie camera—they tied their fantasy solution back to reality. And so the circle from study of culture, through students of culture, to experts working in culture, was rounded out.

Seen another way, we had least success when we tried to develop communication from expert to child where there was a series of intractable production steps associated with large-scale book publishing in between and where the end-product was a finished object which had to be sent out alone into the world. The Community Players represent a much more flexible form of communication from expert to lay audience—a script can be altered to include a new insight, the emphases of sensitive actors may shift in the middle of an actual performance. But even here the finished form has been found to be somewhat intractable without the associated discussion in which each audience has a chance to make the problem presented its own. In the Chichester experiment, the communication was from expert to expert, and the whole onus of interpretation and use was shifted to those who received the communication.

These three instances of applied cultural insight suggest that the more a recognition of culture and a knowledge of culture contrasts can become part of the way we structure groups, part of the materials with which we work, and part of the climate of opinion, and the less we engage in direct manipulation of persons and events, the more deeply useful this new form of awareness of ourselves may become.

NOTES

1. Frank, 1948.
2. Mead, 1947.
3. Mead, 1954c.
4. Thrasher, 1936.
5. Alexander and Healy, 1935.
6. Bruch and Touraine, 1940.
7. Keliher, 1938; Zachry, 1940.
8. Mead, 1954a, 1954b.
9. Mead, 1952.
10. Davis, 1935.
11. Wilkins and Richter, 1940.
12. Mead, 1955.
13. Dollard, 1937.
14. Mead, 1928, chaps. xiii and xiv.
15. Soddy (in press).
16. Wolfenstein, 1946.
17. Committee on Food Habits, 1943.
18. Mead, 1951.
19. Bateson, 1942; Mead, 1942, 1949a, 1950; Mead, Chapple, and Brown, 1949.
20. Mead, 1949b, Appendix II, "Ethics of Insight-giving."
21. Wolfenstein, 1946.

22. A catalogue of the currently available plays and their distribution sources, 1954–55, can be obtained by writing to the American Theatre Wing Community Players, 351 West Forty-eighth Street, New York 36.
23. Soddy (in press).
24. *Bathing Babies in Three Cultures* (film).
25. *Dance and Trance in Bali* (film); *Karba's First Years* (film).

LIST OF REFERENCES

ALEXANDER, FRANZ, and HEALY, WILLIAM. 1935. *Roots of Crime.* New York: A. A. Knopf.

BATESON, GREGORY. 1942. "Social Planning and Deutero Learning." In *Science, Philosophy, and Religion: Second Symposium,* ed. LYMAN BRYSON and LOUIS FINKELSTEIN, pp. 81–97. New York: Conference on Science, Philosophy, and Religion. Reprinted, 1947, in *Readings in Social Psychology,* ed. THEODORE M. NEWCOMB *et al.,* pp. 121–28.

Bathing Babies in Three Cultures (film, 1 reel, sound). Produced by GREGORY BATESON and MARGARET MEAD in series entitled "Films on Character Formation in Different Cultures." Institute for Intercultural Studies. Distributed by New York University Film Library, New York 3.

BRUCH, HILDA V., and TOURAINE, G. 1940. "Obesity in Childhood. V. The Family Frame of Obese Children," *Psychosomatic Medicine,* II, No. 2, 141–206.

COMMITTEE ON FOOD HABITS. *The Problem of Changing Food Habits, 1943: Report of the Committee on Food Habits, 1941–43.* (National Research Council Bull. 108.) Washington, D.C.

Dance and Trance in Bali (film, 2 reels, sound). Produced by GREGORY BATESON and MARGARET MEAD in series entitled "Films on Character Formation in Different Cultures." Institute for Intercultural Studies. Distributed by New York University Film Library, New York 3.

DAVIS, CLARA M. 1935. "Self-selection of Food by Children," *American Journal of Nursing,* XXXV, No. 5, 403–10.

DOLLARD, JOHN. 1937. *Caste and Class in a Southern Town.* New Haven: Yale University Press.

FRANK, LAWRENCE K. 1948. *Society as the Patient.* New Brunswick: Rutgers University Press.

Karba's First Years (film, 2 reels, sound). Produced by GREGORY BATESON and MARGARET MEAD in series entitled "Films on Character Formation in Different Cultures." Institute for Intercultural Studies. Distributed by New York University Film Library, New York 3.

KELIHER, ALICE V. 1938. *Life and Growth.* New York and London: D. Appleton Co.

MEAD, MAGARET. 1928. *Coming of Age in Samoa.* New York: William Morrow & Sons.

———. 1942. "The Comparative Study of Culture and the Purposive Cultivation of Democratic Values." In *Science, Philosophy, and Religion: Second Symposium,* ed. LYMAN BRYSON and LOUIS FINKELSTEIN, pp. 56–69. New York: Conference on Science, Philosophy, and Religion.

———. 1947. "The Concept of Culture and the Psychosomatic Approach," *Psychiatry,* X, No. 1, 57–76.

———. 1949a. "The International Preparatory Commission of the London Conference on Mental Hygiene," *Mental Health,* XXXIII, No. 1, 9–16.

——. 1949*b*. *Male and Female*. New York: William Morrow.& Sons.

——. 1950. "The Comparative Study of Cultures and the Purposive Culti- vation of Democratic Values, 1941–1949." In *Prespectives on a Troubled Decade: Science, Philosophy, and Religion, 1939–1949: Tenth Sym- posium,* ed. LYMAN BRYSON, LOUIS FINKELSTEIN, and R. M. MACIVER, pp. 87–108. New York: Harper & Bros.

——. 1951. "A Natural History Approach to Soviet Character," *Natural History,* LX, No. 7, 296–303, 336.

——. 1952. "Some Relationships between Social Anthropology and Psy- chiatry." In *Dynamic Psychiatry,* ed. FRANZ ALEXANDER and HELEN ROSS, pp. 401–48. Chicago: University of Chicago Press.

——. 1954*a*. *Cultural Discontinuities and Personality Transformation* (Kurt Lewin Memorial Lecture, 1954), *Journal of Social Issues,* suppl. ser. (In press.)

——. 1954*b*. "Manus Re-studied: An Interim Report," *Transactions of the New York Academy of Sciences,* XVI, No. 8, 426–32.

——. 1954*c*. "Some Theoretical Considerations on the Problems of Mother- Child Separation," *American Journal of Orthopsychiatry,* XXIV, No. 3, 471–83.

——. 1955. *The Cross Cultural Approach to the Study of Personality,* ed. E. MCCARY. (Houston Lectures.) New York: Dryden Press. (In press.)

MEAD, MARGARET, CHAPPLE, ELIOT D., and BROWN, G. GORDON. 1949. "Report of the Committee on Ethics," *Human Organization,* VIII, No. 2, 20–21.

SODDY, KENNETH (ed.). *Mental Health and Infant Development,* Vol. II. London: Routledge. (In press.)

THRASHER, FREDERIC M. 1936. *The Gang.* Chicago: University of Chicago Press.

WILKINS, LAWSON, and RICHTER, CURT P. 1940. "A Great Craving for Salt by a Child with Cortico-adrenal Insufficiency," *Journal of the American Medical Association,* CXIV, No. 10, 866–68.

WOLFENSTEIN, MARTHA. 1946. *The Impact of a Children's Story on Mothers and Children.* ("Monographs of the Society for Research in Child De- velopment," Vol. XI, Ser. 42.) Washington, D.C.: National Research Council.

ZACHRY, CAROLINE B. 1940. *Emotions and Conduct in Adolescence.* New York and London: D. Appleton–Century Co.